with MyMarketingLab®

- **Reporting Dashboard**—View, analyze, and report learning outcomes clearly and easily, and get the information you need to keep your students on track throughout the course with the new Reporting Dashboard. Available via the MyLab Gradebook and fully mobile-ready, the Reporting Dashboard presents student performance data at the class, section, and program levels in an accessible, visual manner.

- **Quizzes and Tests**—Pre-built quizzes and tests allow you to quiz students without having to grade the assignments yourself.

- **Writing Space**—Better writers make great learners who perform better in their courses. Designed to help you develop and assess concept mastery and critical thinking, the Writing Space offers a single place to create, track, and grade writing assignments, provide resources, and exchange meaningful, personalized feedback with students, quickly and easily.

Thanks to auto-graded, assisted-graded, and create-your-own assignments, you decide your level of involvement in evaluating students' work. The auto-graded option allows you to assign writing in large classes without having to grade essays by hand. And because of integration with Turnitin®, Writing Space can check students' work for improper citation or plagiarism.

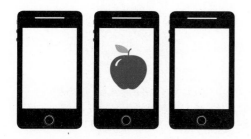

- **Learning Catalytics™**—Is an interactive, student response tool that uses students' smartphones, tablets, or laptops to engage them in more sophisticated tasks and thinking. Now included with MyLab with eText, Learning Catalytics enables you to generate classroom discussion, guide your lecture, and promote peer-to-peer learning with real-time analytics. Instructors, you can:
  - Pose a variety of open-ended questions that help your students develop critical thinking skills
  - Monitor responses to find out where students are struggling
  - Use real-time data to adjust your instructional strategy and try other ways of engaging your students during class
  - Manage student interactions by automatically grouping students for discussion, teamwork, and peer-to-peer learning

Integrated Advertising, Promotion, and Marketing Communications

Integrated Advertising, Promotion, and Marketing Communications

Eighth Edition

Kenneth E. Clow
University of Louisiana at Monroe

Donald Baack
Pittsburg State University

Pearson

New York, NY

Vice President, Business Publishing: Donna Battista

Director of Portfolio Management: Stephanie Wall

Portfolio Manager: Emily Tamburri

Editorial Assistant: Eric Santucci

Vice President, Product Marketing: Roxanne McCarley

Director of Strategic Marketing: Brad Parkins

Strategic Marketing Manager: Deborah Strickland

Product Marketer: Becky Brown

Field Marketing Manager: Lenny Ann Kucenski

Product Marketing Assistant: Jessica Quazza

Vice President, Production and Digital Studio, Arts and Business: Etain O'Dea

Director of Production, Business: Jeff Holcomb

Managing Producer, Business: Ashley Santora

Content Producer: Lauren Russell

Operations Specialist: Carol Melville

Creative Director: Blair Brown

Manager, Learning Tools: Brian Surette

Content Developer, Learning Tools: Lindsey Sloan

Managing Producer, Digital Studio, Arts and Business: Diane Lombardo

Digital Studio Producer: Monique Lawrence

Digital Studio Producer: Alana Coles

Full-Service Project Management, Composition, and Design: SPi Global

Cover Art: HelenStock/Shutterstock

Printer/Binder: LSC Communications Owensville

Cover Printer: Phoenix Color Hagerstown

CIP data on file with the Library of Congress

2 17

ISBN 10:   0-13-448413-4

ISBN 13: 978-0-13-448413-6

To my sons Dallas, Wes, Tim, and Roy, who provided encouragement, and especially to my wife, Susan, whose sacrifice and love made this textbook possible.

Kenneth E. Clow

I would like to dedicate my efforts and contributions to this edition to my wife Pam.

Donald Baack

Brief Contents

Part One ▶ **THE IMC FOUNDATION** 2

1 Integrated Marketing Communications 2
2 Brand Management 22
3 Buyer Behaviors 54
4 The IMC Planning Process 90

Part Two ▶ **IMC ADVERTISING TOOLS** 122

5 Advertising Campaign Management 122
6 Advertising Design 154
7 Traditional Media Channels 188

Part Three ▶ **DIGITAL AND ALTERNATIVE MARKETING** 222

8 Digital Marketing 222
9 Social Media 254
10 Alternative Marketing 280

Part Four ▶ **IMC PROMOTIONAL TOOLS** 308

11 Database and Direct Response Marketing and Personal Selling 308
12 Sales Promotions 338
13 Public Relations and Sponsorship Programs 366

Part Five ▶ **IMC ETHICS, REGULATION, AND EVALUATION** 394

14 Regulations and Ethical Concerns 394
15 Evaluating an Integrated Marketing Program 420

Contents

PREFACE xvii

Part One

THE IMC FOUNDATION 2

1 INTEGRATED MARKETING COMMUNICATIONS 2

The Nature of Communication 3

Integrated Marketing Communications 5
    An Integrated Marketing Communications Plan 6

Emerging Trends in Marketing Communications 7
    Emphasis on Accountability and Measurable Results 7
    Integration of Digital Media 8
    Integration of Media Platforms 8
    Changes in Channel Power 9
    Increases in Global Competition 10
    Increases in Brand Parity 11
    Emphasis on Customer Engagement 11
    The Role of Integrated Marketing Communications 12

IMC Components and the Design of this Text 12
    IMC Foundation 13
    Advertising 13
    Digital and Alternative 14
    Selling Components 14
    Integration 14

International Implications 15

2 BRAND MANAGEMENT 22

Corporate and Brand Image 23
    Components of Brand Image 24
    The Role of Brand Image—Consumer Perspective 25
    The Role of Brand Image—Company Perspective 27

Brand Names and Brand Types 28
    Family Brands 30
    Brand Extensions 30
    Flanker Brands 30
    Co-Branding 31

Brand Logos 32

Identifying the Desired Brand Image 34
    Creating the Right Brand Image 34
    Rejuvenating a Brand's Image 35
    Changing a Brand's Image 36

Developing and Building Powerful Brands 37
    Brand Loyalty 39
    Brand Equity 40
    Measuring Brand Equity 41

Private Brands 42
    Advantages to Retailers 43
    Responses from Manufacturers 44

Packaging 44
    Labels 45
    Ethical Issues in Brand Management 46

International Implications 47

3 BUYER BEHAVIORS 54

Information Searches and the Consumer Purchasing Process 55
    Internal Search 56
    External Search 56
    Consumer Attitudes 59
    Consumer Values 61
    Cognitive Mapping 62

Evaluation of Alternatives 65
    The Evoked Set Method 66
    The Multiattribute Approach 67
    Affect Referral 68

Trends in the Consumer Buying Environment   69
Age Complexity   69
Gender Complexity   70
Active, Busy Lifestyles   71
Diverse Lifestyles   71
Communication Revolution   71
Experience Pursuits   72
Health Emphasis   72

Business-to-Business Buyer Behaviors and Influences   73
Organizational Influences   74
Individual Factors   74

Types of Business-to-Business Sales   77

The Business-to-Business Buying Process   79
Identification of Needs   79
Establishment of Specifications   79
Identification of Vendors   80
Vendor Evaluation   80
Vendor Selection   80
Negotiation of Terms   80
Postpurchase Evaluation   80

Dual Channel Marketing   81
Spin-Off Sales   81
Marketing Decisions   82

International Implications   83

4 THE IMC PLANNING PROCESS   90

Communications Research   92

Market Segmentation by Consumer Groups   93
Segments Based on Demographics   94
Psychographics   99
Segments Based on Generations   100
Segmentation by Geographic Area   101
Geodemographic Segmentation   101
Benefit Segmentation   102
Usage Segmentation   102

Business-to-Business Market Segmentation   103
Segmentation by Industry   104
Segmentation by Size   104
Segmentation by Geographic Location   104
Segmentation by Product Usage   105
Segmentation by Customer Value   105

Product Positioning   105
Approaches to Positioning   106
Other Elements of Positioning   108

Marketing Communications Objectives   108

Types of Budgets   109
Percentage of Sales   109
Meet the Competition   109
"What We Can Afford"   110
Objective and Task   110

Payout Planning   110
Quantitative Models   110
Communications Schedules   111

IMC Components   112
International Implications   112

Integrated Campaigns in Action   114

Part Two

IMC ADVERTISING TOOLS   122

5 ADVERTISING CAMPAIGN MANAGEMENT   122

Advertising Theory   124
Hierarchy of Effects   124
Means–End Theory   126
Verbal and Visual Images   127

The Impact of Advertising Expenditures   129
Threshold Effects   130
Diminishing Returns   131
Carryover Effects   131
Wear-Out Effects   131
Decay Effects   131

In-House Versus External Advertising Agencies   132
Budget Allocation Considerations   133
Crowdsourcing   134

Choosing an Agency 135
Goal Setting 135
Selection Criteria 135
Creative Pitch 137
Agency Selection 138

Roles of Advertising Personnel 138
Account Executives 138
Creatives 138
Traffic Managers 138
Account Planners 139

Advertising Campaign Parameters 139
Advertising Goals 139
Media Selection 140
Taglines 142
Consistency 142
Positioning 143
Campaign Duration 143

The Creative Brief 143
The Objective 144
The Target Audience 144
The Message Theme 144
The Support 145
The Constraints 145

International Implications 146

6 ADVERTISING DESIGN 154

Message Strategies 156
Cognitive Message Strategies 157
Affective Message Strategies 159
Conative Message Strategy 160

Types of Advertising Appeals 161
Fear Appeals 162
Humor Appeals 163
Sex Appeals 164
Music Appeals 168
Rational Appeals 169
Emotional Appeals 169
Scarcity Appeals 171

Executional Frameworks 171
Animation Executions 171
Slice-of-Life Executions 172
Storytelling Executions 172
Testimonial Executions 173
Authoritative Executions 173

Demonstration Executions 174
Fantasy Executions 174
Informative Executions 174

Sources and Spokespersons 175
Celebrity Spokespersons 175
CEO Spokespersons 177
Experts 177
Typical Persons 177
Source Characteristics 177
Matching Source Types and Characteristics 180
International Implications 181

7 TRADITIONAL MEDIA CHANNELS 188

The Media Strategy 189

Media Planning 190
Media Planners 190
Media Buyers 191
Small versus Large Markets 192

Advertising Terminology 192
Frequency 192
Opportunities to See 192
Gross Rating Points 193
Cost 193
Ratings and Cost per Rating Point 194
Continuity 195
Impressions 195

Achieving Advertising Objectives 195
The Three-Exposure Hypothesis 196
Recency Theory 196
Effective Reach and Frequency 196
Brand Recognition 197
Brand Recall 198

Media Selection 198
Television 198
Radio 205
Out-of-Home Advertising 206
Print Media 208
Magazines 208
Newspapers 210

Media Mix 211

Media Selection in Business-to-Business Markets 212
International Implications 214

Integrated Campaigns in Action 215

9 SOCIAL MEDIA 254

Social Networks 256

Social Media Sites 256
- Facebook 256
- Instagram 257
- Twitter 259
- Pinterest 260
- YouTube 260

Social Media Marketing 262

Social Media Marketing Strategies 265
- Building a Social Media Presence 266
- Content Seeding 266
- Real-Time Marketing 267
- Video Marketing 268
- Influencer Marketing 269
- Interactive Blogs 270
- Consumer-Generated Reviews 271
- Viral Marketing 272
- Following Brands on Social Media 273

International Implications 274

Part Three

DIGITAL AND ALTERNATIVE MARKETING 222

8 DIGITAL MARKETING 222

Digital Marketing 223

Web 4.0 224

E-Commerce 225

Mobile Marketing 230

Digital Strategies 232
- Interactive Marketing 232
- Content Marketing and Native Advertising 233
- Location-Based Advertising 235
- Remarketing 237
- Behavioral Targeting 238
- Blogs and Newsletters 239
- Email Marketing 240

Web Advertising 242
- Banner Advertising 242
- Impact of Online Advertising 243
- Offline Advertising 244

Search Engine Optimization (SEO) 244

International Implications 246
- Shipping Issues 246
- Communication Issues 246
- Technology Issues 247

10 ALTERNATIVE MARKETING 280

Alternative Marketing Programs 281
- Buzz Marketing 282
- Consumers Who Like a Brand 282
- Sponsored Consumers 282
- Company Employees 284
- Buzz Marketing Stages 284
- Buzz Marketing Preconditions 285
- Stealth Marketing 285
- Guerrilla Marketing 286
- Lifestyle Marketing 288
- Experiential Marketing 288

Product Placements and Branded Entertainment 289
- Product Placements 289
- Branded Entertainment 290
- Achieving Success 291

Alternative Media Venues 292
- Video Game Advertising 292
- Cinema Advertising 294
- Other Alternative Media 294

In-Store Marketing 295
- In-Store Marketing Tactics 295
- Point-of-Purchase Marketing 296
- Designing Effective Point-of-Purchase Displays 297
- Measuring Point-of-Purchase Effectiveness 298

Brand Communities 298

International Implications 300

Integrated Campaigns in Action 300

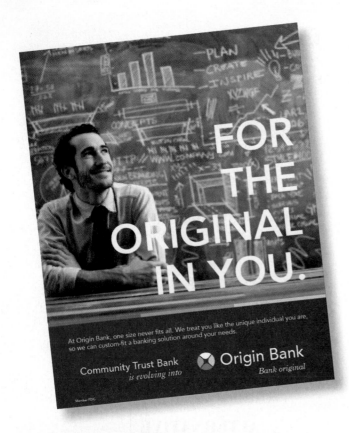

Personalized Communications   316
Customized Content   317
In-Bound Telemarketing   317
Trawling   317

Database-Driven Marketing Programs   318
Permission Marketing   318
Frequency Programs   320
Customer Relationship Management   322

Direct Response Marketing   323
Direct Mail   324
Catalogs   325
Mass Media   325
Internet and Email   326
Direct Sales   326
Telemarketing   326

Personal Selling   327
Generating Leads   327
Qualifying Prospects   328
Knowledge Acquisition   329
The Sales Presentation   329
Handling Objections   330
Closing the Sale   330
Follow-Up   331

International Implications   331

Part Four

IMC PROMOTIONAL TOOLS 308

11 DATABASE AND DIRECT RESPONSE MARKETING AND PERSONAL SELLING 308

Database Marketing   309
Building a Data Warehouse   311
Email, Mobile, and Internet Data   311
Purchase and Communication Histories   311
Personal Preference Profiles   312
Customer Information Companies   312
Geocoding   312
Database Coding and Analysis   313
Lifetime Value Analysis   313
Customer Clusters   314
Location Data Tracking   314
Data Mining   315

Database-Driven Marketing Communications   315
Identification Codes   316

12 SALES PROMOTIONS 338

Consumer Promotions vs. Trade Promotions   339

Consumer Promotions   340
Coupons   340
Coupon Distribution   340
Types of Coupons   341
Disadvantages of Coupons   342
Premiums   342
Types of Premiums   343
Keys to Successful Premium Programs   343
Contests and Sweepstakes   344
Contests   345
Sweepstakes   345
Perceived Value   345
The Internet and Social Media   346
Goals of Contests and Sweepstakes   346
Refunds and Rebates   346
Sampling   347
Sample Distribution   347
Benefits of Sampling   348
Successful Sampling Programs   348
Bonus Packs   348
Types of Bonus Packs   348
Keys to Successful Bonus Packs   349

Price-Offs   349
Benefits of Price-Offs   349
Problems with Price-Offs   350
Overlays and Tie-Ins   350

Planning for Consumer Promotions   351

Trade Promotions   353
Trade Allowances   353
Trade Contests   355
Trade Incentives   356
Trade Shows   357

Concerns with Trade Promotions   359

International Implications   359

13   PUBLIC RELATIONS AND SPONSORSHIP PROGRAMS   366

Public Relations   368
Internal versus External Public Relations   368
Public Relations Tools   369

Public Relations Functions   369
Identifying Stakeholders   370
Internal Stakeholders   370
External Stakeholders   371
Assessing Corporate Reputation   371
Corporate Social Responsibility   372

Creating Positive Image-Building Activities   373
Cause-Related Marketing   373
Green Marketing and Pro-Environmental Activities   375

Preventing or Reducing Image Damage   377
Proactive Prevention Strategies   377
Reactive Damage-Control Strategies   378

Sponsorships   380
Forms of Sponsorships   380
Sponsorship Objectives   382

Event Marketing   382
Selecting Sponsorships and Events   383
Determining Objectives   383
Matching the Audience to the Company's Target Market   383
Promoting the Event   383
Advertising at the Event   384
Tracking Results   384
Cross-Promotions   384

International Implications   385

Integrated Campaigns in Action   386

Part Five

IMC ETHICS, REGULATION, AND EVALUATION   394

14   REGULATIONS AND ETHICAL CONCERNS   394

Marketing Communications Regulations   396
Governmental Regulatory Agencies   396
The Federal Trade Commission   397
Unfair and Deceptive Marketing Practices   397

Deception versus Puffery   397
Substantiation of Marketing Claims   398
How Investigations Begin   400
Consent Orders   400

FTC Settlements   400
Administrative Complaints   400
Courts and Legal Channels   401

Corrective Advertising   402

Trade Regulation Rulings   402

Industry Oversight of Marketing Practices   402

Council of Better Business Bureaus   403

IMC and Ethics   405

Ethics and Advertising   405

Perpetuating Stereotypes   406

Advertising Unsafe Products   406

Offensive Advertisements   407

Advertising to Children   407

Marketing and Ethics   407

Brand Infringement   408

Marketing of Professional Services   408

Gifts and Bribery in Business-to-Business Marketing Programs   409

Spam and Cookies   409

Ambush Marketing   410

Stealth Marketing   411

Responding to Ethical Challenges   412

Ethics Programs   412

Ethics Training Programs   412

Codes of Ethics   413

Ethics Consulting Systems   413

International Implications   414

15   EVALUATING AN INTEGRATED MARKETING PROGRAM   420

Evaluation Metrics   422

Matching Methods with IMC Objectives   423

Message Evaluations   424

Advertising Tracking Research   425

Copytesting   426

Emotional Reaction Tests   428

Cognitive Neuroscience   430

Evaluation Criteria   431

Online Evaluation Metrics   433

Behavioral Evaluations   436

Test Markets   439

Purchase Simulation Tests   440

International Implications   441

ENDNOTES   447

NAME INDEX   463

SUBJECT INDEX   473

CREDITS   485

Preface

Advertising, promotions, and communications remain integral components of marketing. For marketing majors, understanding how companies effectively communicate and interact with customers and potential customers creates the foundation they need to develop effective marketing skills. This will help our readers succeed in their marketing careers.

If your students are not marketing majors, consider all of the marketing communications around them. Any company or organization they work for will be involved in marketing its products or services. Knowing how marketing communications are developed constitutes valuable knowledge. It helps them recognize the methods used by the people in the marketing departments where they will work and provides them with better information to function as consumers.

We continue to refine *Integrated Advertising, Promotion, and Marketing Communications,* in part, to help students understand the importance of integrating all marketing communications (IMC) and how they are produced and transmitted. When the first edition was written, most marketing communication textbooks focused primarily on advertising. As your students know from their everyday experiences and the courses they have taken in college, marketing communications incorporates much more. It includes promotions, such as coupons, price discounts, and contests. Marketing has expanded to extensive use of social media, internet blogs, customer product reviews, messages delivered to mobile phones, and other programs, such as buzz marketing and stealth marketing. These venues create vital links to effectively reach consumers. These should be carefully integrated into one clear message and voice for customers to hear and see.

We prepared this textbook and the additional materials in ways that will best help your students to understand integrated marketing communications. Students need opportunities to apply concepts to real-life situations. This helps them clearly understand and retain the ideas. As a result, we have composed a variety of end-of-chapter materials designed to help them practice using the concepts. These materials now include an ongoing blog, integrated campaigns in action, integrated learning exercises, discussion and critical-thinking exercises, creative exercises, blog exercises, and updated cases.

What's New in the Eighth Edition?

The eighth edition of *Integrated Advertising, Promotion, and Marketing Communications* offers several new features. The most exciting may be the addition more blog posts devoted to supporting this textbook for both professors and students. The blog may be found at: blogclowbaack.net and is incorporated into the text in end-of-chapter exercises. These exercises feature links to news articles, YouTube videos, social media networks and other web sites presenting interesting and engaging marketing communications ideas and tactics.

- **Increased emphasis on social media.** One of the most rapidly evolving aspects of advertising and promotion has been the increased usage of social media. This edition expands coverage in that area. The emphasis is on the ways companies currently use social media for marketing purposes and how it is integrated with other communication strategies.

- **Updating of digital media chapter.** Digital media and especially mobile devices have changed the ways companies market products. The digital media chapter has been updated with information about the most current industry practices. The section on mobile marketing has been expanded to coincide with a shift of marketing dollars to those activities.

- **New opening vignettes and cases.** Many of the chapter opening vignettes and cases are new to this edition. These materials keep the book updated and current.

- **New advertisements.** Throughout the text, a significant number of new advertisements have been added. These resulted from interactions with advertising agencies by the authors. These new advertisements keep the content as fresh and up-to-date as possible.

- **Updated examples.** New examples of marketing communications principles have been incorporated to provide relevant information about companies. New discussion and critical thinking exercises have been provided to help students understand and apply the materials presented in each chapter.

- **Active blog.** The authors continue to maintain a blog at blogclowbaack.net. The authors post weekly news articles, videos, and items of interest to individuals using this text. The goal of the blog is to provide information about current events that relate to the book. Textbook adopters can use these blog entries to enhance classroom presentations or as assignments for individual students or even small groups.

Integrated Learning Package

We have created several devices that are designed to help students learn the materials in this text. Advertising and marketing communications are interesting and enjoyable subjects, and these materials have been developed to make learning interactive and fun!

- **Lead-in vignettes.** Each chapter begins with a short vignette related to the topic to be presented. The majority of the vignettes revolve around success stories in companies and about products most students will recognize, such as Oreo cookies and Lean Cuisine. In this edition, new vignettes have been introduced, including stories about Nescafe, Sephora, and McDonald's All-Day Breakfast program. These accompany vignettes featured in the seventh edition regarding Wholly Guacamole, Zehnder Communications, Huggies Pull-ups and Interstate Batteries. The vignettes introduce your students to the concepts presented throughout the chapter.

- **International marketing issues.** Some of you have traveled to other countries. Most of you interact with students from around the globe. This book features international concerns that match the presented materials. Also, a section called "International Implications" is found at the end of every chapter.

- **Critical-thinking exercises and discussion questions.** The end-of-chapter materials include a variety of exercises designed to help your students comprehend and apply the chapter concepts. These exercises are designed to challenge students' thinking and encourage them to dig deeper. The best way to know that your students have truly learned a concept or theory is when they can apply it to a different situation. These critical-thinking and discussion exercises require them to apply knowledge to a wide array of marketing situations.

- **Integrated learning exercises.** At the end of each chapter, a set of questions guides students to the Internet to access information that ties into the subject matter covered. These exercises provide students an opportunity to look up various companies and organizations to see how they utilize the concepts presented in the chapter.

- **Blog exercises.** This edition offers a set of exercises from the authors' blog. These exercises can be fun for students to do and can be used for individual assignments or group assignments. Some are ideal for classroom instruction or to gain the interests of students at the beginning of class.

- **Creative Corner exercises.** Most students enjoy the opportunity to use their creative abilities. As a result, we feature a new exercise called the "Creative Corner," which asks students to design advertisements and other marketing-related materials. The exercises are designed to help students realize that they are more creative than they might think. Ken Clow has taught students who said they had zero creative ability. Yet these same students were able to produce ads that won ADDY awards in student competitions sponsored by the American Advertising Federation (AAF). If you are not familiar with the AAF student competition, go the organization's web site at **www.aaf.org**. Entering the annual competition is exciting, and participating looks great on a student's resume.

- **Cases.** At the conclusion of each chapter, two cases are provided. These were written to help students learn by providing plausible scenarios that require thought about- and review of chapter materials. The short cases should help students conceptually understand chapter components and the larger, more general marketing issues.

- **Integrated Campaigns in Action.** One unique new feature in this textbook is the addition of media based assignments for the Integrated Campaigns in Action, a series of presentations about actual marketing programs, as created and designed by professional agencies. The Integrated Campaigns in Action features are noted at the end of each section and in the instructor's Power-Point materials. To access and submit the media-based assignments associated with the Integrated Campaigns in Action, go to MediaShare for Business at mymktlab.com. Additional Integrated Campaigns in Action can be found at the authors' blog, clowbaack.net.

Instructor Resources

At the Instructor Resource Center, www.pearsonhighered.com, instructors can easily register to gain access to a variety of instructor resources available with this text in downloadable format. If assistance is needed, our dedicated technical support team is ready to help with the media supplements that accompany this text. Visit http://support.pearson.com/getsupport for answers to frequently asked questions and toll-free user support phone numbers.

The following supplements are available with this text:

- **Instructor's Resource Manual**
- **Test Bank**
- **TestGen® Computerized Test Bank**
- **PowerPoint Presentation**

Acknowledgments

We would like to thank the following individuals who assisted in the development of the previous editions through their careful and thoughtful reviews:

John Bennett, *Univeristy of Missouri–Columbia*
Donna Falgiatore, *St. Joseph's University*
Larry Goldstein, *Iona College*
Joni Jackson, *Robert Morris University*
Laurel Schirr, *VA Polytech Institute/State University*
Allen Smith, *Florida Atlantic University*
Debbie Campbell, *Temple University*
Rick Morris, *University of North Texas*
Steve Edwards, *Southern Methodist University*

We are grateful to these reviewers for the fifth edition:

Joni Jackson, *Robert Morris University*
Rick Morris, *University of North Texas*
Charles Larson, *Northern Illinois University*
Charlie Schwepker, *University of Central Missouri*
John Bennett, *University of Missouri*
Prema Nakra, *Marist College*
Linden Dalecki, *Pittsburg State University*
Kathleen Havey, *University of Maryland*
Bryan Johnson, *Pennsylvania State University*
Debbie Campbell, *Temple University*

We are grateful to these reviewers for portions of the fourth edition:

John Bennett, *University of Missouri–Columbia*
MaryEllen Campbell, *University of Montana, Missoula*
Donna Falgiatore, *St. Joseph's University*
Deanna Mulholland, *Iowa Western Community College*
Jim Munz, *Illinois State University*
Prema Nakra, *Marist College*
Allen Smith, *Florida Atlantic University*
Amanda Walton, *Indiana Business College*

We are grateful to these reviewers for the third edition:

Jeffrey C. Bauer, *University of Cincinnati–Clermont*
MaryElllen Campbell, *University of Montana, Missoula*
Sherry Cook, *Missouri State University*
Catherine Curran, *University of Massachusetts–Dartmouth*
Michael A. Dickerson, *George Mason University*
Donna Falgiatore, *St. Joseph's University*
Charles S. Gulas, *Wright State University*
Diana Haytko, *Missouri State University*
Al Mattison, *University of California–Berkeley*
Deanna Mulholland, *Iowa Western Community College*

Jim Munz, *Illinois State University*
Charlie Schwepker, *University of Central Missouri*
Eugene Secunda, *New York University*
Allen E. Smith, *Florida Atlantic University*
Bonni Stachowiak, *Vanguard University*
Rod Warnick, *University of Massachusetts–Amherst*
Patti Williams, *Wharton Business School*

We are grateful to these reviewers for the second edition:

Craig Andrews, *Marquette University*
Robert W. Armstrong, *University of North Alabama*
Ronald Bauerly, *Western Illinois University*
Mary Ellen Campbell, *University of Montana*
Les Carlson, *Clemson University*
Newell Chiesl, *Indiana State University*
Jerome Christa, *Coastal Carolina University*
John Cragin, *Oklahoma Baptist College*
Charlene Davis, *Trinity University*
Steven Edwards, *Michigan State University*
Everett Fergenson, *Iona College*
James Finch, *University of Wisconsin–La Crosse*
Stefanie Garcia, *University of Central Florida*
Robert J. Gulovsen, *Washington University–Saint Louis*
Thomas Jensen, *University of Arkansas*
Russell W. Jones, *University of Central Oklahoma*
Sreedhar Kavil, *St. John's University*
Franklin Krohn, *SUNY–Buffalo*
Dave Kurtz, *University of Arkansas*
Tom Laughon, *Florida State University*
Monle Lee, *Indiana University–South Bend*
Ron Lennon, *Barry University*
William C. Lesch, *University of North Dakota*
Charles L. Martin, *Wichita State University*
James M. Maskulka, *Lehigh University*
Robert D. Montgomery, *University of Evansville*
Darrel D. Muehling, *Washington State University*
S. Scott Nadler, *University of Alabama*
Ben Oumlil, *University of Dayton*
Esther S. Page-Wood, *Western Michigan University*
Melodie R. Phillips, *Middle Tennessee State University*
Don Roy, *Middle Tennessee State University*
Elise Sautter, *New Mexico State University*
Venkatesh Shankar, *University of Maryland*
Albert J. Taylor, *Austin Peay State University*
Janice E. Taylor, *Miami University*
Robert L. Underwood, *Bradley University*
Jerald Weaver, *SUNY—Brockport*
Robert Welch, *California State University–Long Beach*

We would also like to thank the following people for their contributions to MyMarketingLab:

Kim Norbuta
Todd Korol, *Monroe Community College*
Mahmood Kahn, *Virginia Tech*
Barbara Sue Faries, *West Valley College*

Although there were many individuals who assisted us with advertising programs, we want to thank a few who were particularly helpful. We appreciate the owners and employees of Zehnder Communications, Choice Marketing, and Origin Bank for providing a large number of advertisements. We especially want to thank Jeff Zehnder from Zehnder Communications as well as Karen Plott and Dave Woods from Choice Marketing for their assistance. Stan Richards, Mary Price, Dave Snell, Elena Petukhova, and Carrie Dyer from The Richards Group; Bill Breedlove and Elena Baca from Pink Jacket Creative; Charlie Brim from Interstate Batteries; Lee McGuire from Skyjacker were very generous with their time. Thanks to W. Peter Cornish, former senior vice president for the J. Walter Thompson company and current professor at the University of South Carolina for his inputs and advice. Also, thanks to Julie Boyles for her accuracy review of this edition's test bank.

On a personal note, we wish to thank many individuals at our publisher, Pearson Education, including Leah Johnson, who signed us for the first edition of the book. Thank you to Emily Tamburri, Lauren Russell, and Stephanie Wall for their work on this edition plus Mark Gaffney, Jennifer Collins, Jackie Martin, and Ashley Santora for helping with previous editions. We appreciate Meredith Gertz and Debbie Ryan at SPi Global for guiding the editing and production processes. Finally, we would like to thank the entire Pearson production group.

Kenneth Clow would like to thank the University of Louisiana at Monroe for providing a positive environment to work on this text. He especially appreciates the school chair, Dr. Henry Cole, and the Dean, Dr. Ron Berry, for their understanding of the time involved in working with a textbook and their willingness to offer support. He is thankful to his sons Dallas, Wes, Tim, and Roy, who always provided encouragement and support.

Donald Baack would like to acknowledge Mimi Morrison and Paula Palmer for their continued assistance in all his work at Pittsburg State University.

We would like to especially recognize our wives, Susan Clow and Pam Baack, for being patient and supportive during those times when we were swamped by the work involved in completing this edition. They have been enthusiastic and understanding throughout this entire journey.

Integrated Advertising, Promotion, and Marketing Communications

Part 1

THE IMC FOUNDATION

Chapter 1 Integrated Marketing Communications

Chapter Objectives

After reading this chapter, you should be able to answer the following questions:

1.1 How does communication take place?

1.2 What is an integrated marketing communications program?

1.3 Which trends are affecting marketing communications?

1.4 What are the components of an integrated marketing communications program?

1.5 What is meant by *GIMC?*

Overview

Advertising and marketing face a rapidly shifting landscape. The decline in traditional media viewership combined with a rise in internet and social media usage has created a new order. The variety of available media means that effective advertising and marketing promotions require more than just one well-made commercial. Advertising and marketing venues range from simple stand-alone billboard advertisements to complex, multilingual global websites. As a result, the number of ways to reach potential customers continually increases while alternative methods expand and become increasingly popular.

In the face of these cluttered conditions, firms continue to seek to be heard. Marketing experts know that a company's communications should speak with a clear voice. Customers must understand the essence of a business along with the benefits of its goods and services. The vast number of advertising and promotional outlets combined with a multitude of companies bombarding potential customers with messages makes the task challenging. In response, some advertisers and companies have moved to the innovative approaches featured in this chapter.

LEAN CUISINE

How do you convince consumers that the same product should be viewed in a different way? This challenge faced marketers at Lean Cuisine as consumer thinking processes evolved over time. The response began with an effort to create effective communication.

The marketing team realized that the term "diet" was fading in usage and popularity. In response, Lean Cuisine brand manager Chris Flora noted, "We didn't really have a brand soul. For us to really thrive in this marketplace we wanted to find that brand soul." Flora suggested that "we want to really connect with our consumers."

The process involved a multi-faceted approach that included new product developments, new marketing messages, and even cooperation with other companies. Nestle, ConAgra, Kellogg and General Mills jointly launched a three-year, $30 million image campaign entitled "Frozen. How Fresh Stays Fresh." The goal was to convince consumers, many of whom had begun to strongly prefer fresh food over frozen, that the latter was equally tasty and healthy. Consequently, the campaigned portrayed the freezing process as "nature's pause button." New product offerings were developed, including sweet and spicy Korean style beef, Vermont white cheddar mac and cheese, pomegranate chicken, and other options labeled as "marketplace meals," "craveables," "comfort," and "favorites".

Most important, however, was the effort to instill new attitudes regarding Lean Cuisine in consumers. Consequently, a social media campaign entitled "WeighThis" launched, seeking to shift feelings about the relative importance of a person's weight as compared to other aspects of life. Advertisements designed to develop more emotional bonds with products followed, including a "Feel Your Phenomenal" campaign.

Product labels statements also changed, highlighting consumer trends toward favoring organic foods, high protein content, gluten-free, and No GMO product features. The company's website noted that products are "freshly made, simply frozen," a statement designed to emphasize the message sent out by the entire industry.

Every element of this new approach sought to generate a change in consumer perceptions of a longstanding product with "lean" in the brand name, noting that in FDA standards the word "lean" means food items cannot contain more than 10 grams of fat per serving. Time will tell if such an approach will succeed in an ever-changing and fickle consumer environment.[1]

The Lean Cuisine program highlights many of the themes present in this chapter, including how to use the communications process to reach consumers and break through the advertising clutter. It illustrates the importance of integrating all communications and that company leaders must understand current advertising and promotions trends in order to succeed.

The Nature of Communication

Communication involves transmitting, receiving, and processing information. As a person, group, or organization sends an idea or message, communication occurs when the receiver (another person or group) comprehends the information. The communication model shown in Figure 1.1 displays the pathway a message takes from one person to another or others.[2]

Communication constitutes the essence of any advertising or marketing program. Consider a person planning to dine at a quick-serve chicken restaurant. In the communications model (Figure 1.1), the **senders** include the chains KFC, Chick-fil-A,

▶ **FIGURE 1.1**
The Communication Process

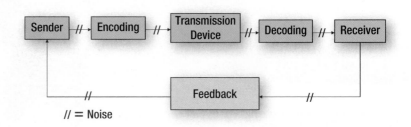

// = Noise

Popeye's, Church's Chicken, Bojangles, and Raising Cain's Chicken Fingers. These companies company tries to capture the customer's attention. Most of these firms hire advertising agencies, although some utilize in-house teams.

Encoding is forming verbal and nonverbal cues. In marketing, the person in charge of designing an advertisement transforms an idea into an attention-getting message. A commercial consists of cues placed in various media, such as television, magazines, and billboards. The message may also be encoded on the firm's website and social media page.

Messages travel to audiences through various **transmission devices**. Marketing communications move through various channels or media. The channel may be a television station carrying an advertisement, a Sunday paper with a coupon placed inside, a website, or a Facebook page.

▼ Decoding occurs when a consumer sees this advertisement and understands JD Bank is a viable option for a home loan.

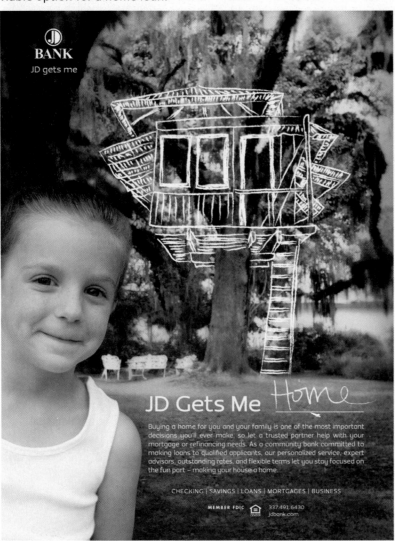

Decoding occurs when the message reaches one or more of the receiver's senses. Consumers both hear and see television ads. Other consumers handle (touch) and read (see) a coupon offer. An individual can even smell a message. A well-placed perfume sample might entice a buyer to purchase the magazine containing the sample and the perfume being advertised. Hungry people tend to pay closer attention to advertisements and other information about food.

Quality marketing communication takes place when customers (the **receivers**) decode or understand the message as it was intended by the sender. In the JD Bank advertisement shown on this page, effective marketing communications depend on receivers encountering the right message and responding in the desired fashion, such as by obtaining a home loan or refinancing a home mortgage.

Chick-fil-A's approach to social media provides an example of a successful communication strategy that integrates the web with both online and offline advertising to build customer loyalty.[3] Engaging consumers constitutes the primary goal for Chick-fil-A. According to John Keehler, director of interactive strategy at ClickHere, "One of the mistakes we've seen is brands would gather a lot of friends, but wouldn't get people to interact with them." With Chick-fil-A, people interact through its various social media platforms including Facebook, Twitter, Instagram, Tumblr, and YouTube. When a new store opens, marketers make the announcement on various social media outlets, which allows fans to participate in grand-opening festivities.

- Talking on the phone during a commercial on television
- Driving while listening to the radio
- Looking at a sexy model in a magazine ad and ignoring the message and brand
- Scanning a newspaper for articles to read
- Talking to a passenger as the car passes billboards
- Scrolling past internet ads without looking at them
- Becoming annoyed by ads appearing on a social media site
- Ignoring tweets on Twitter because they are not relevant
- Being offended by the message on a flyer for a local business

◀ **FIGURE 1.2**
Examples of Communication Noise

Social media messages can be combined with offline advertising and promotions. Chick-fil-A holds a "Cow Appreciation Day" each July that encourages customers to dress as cows and post their photos on Facebook and Instagram and videos on YouTube. Television and billboard advertising features cows urging people to "Eat Mor Chikin." Using the same tagline and theme on all channels transmits the same message to consumers A stronger brand presence becomes the result.

In the communication process, **feedback** takes the form of the receiver's response to the sender. In marketing communications, feedback includes purchases, inquiries, complaints, questions, store visits, blogs, and website hits.

Noise consists of anything that distorts or disrupts a message, including marketing communications. It occurs during any stage in the communication process. **Clutter** remains the most common form of noise affecting marketing communications. Figure 1.2 provides examples of noise that affects advertising messages.

The marketing professionals involved in the communication process pay attention to each aspect of the communications model to ensure that every audience encounters a consistent message. They make sure the message cuts through noise and clutter. Common objectives marketing teams seek to achieve include an increase in market share, sales, and brand loyalty. Once again, note that communicating with consumers and other businesses requires more than creating attractive advertisements. An effective program integrates all marketing activities. The upcoming section describes the nature of integrated marketing communications.

▲ A Chick-fil-A contest winner.

Integrated Marketing Communications

The communications model provides the foundation for advertising and marketing programs. **Integrated marketing communications (IMC)** is of the coordination and integration of all marketing communications tools, avenues, and sources in a company into a seamless program designed to maximize the impact on customers and other stakeholders. The program covers all of a firm's business-to-business, market channel, customer-focused, and internally-directed communications.[4]

Before further examining an IMC program, consider the traditional framework of marketing promotions. The **marketing mix** — price, product, distribution, and promotions —represents the starting point. For years, one view was that promotional activities included advertising, sales promotions, and personal selling activities. This approach has expanded to incorporate digital marketing, social media, and alternative methods of communication.

objective 1.2
What is an integrated marketing communications program?

▶ **FIGURE 1.3**
Components of Promotion

It also includes activities such as database marketing, direct response marketing, personal selling tactics, sponsorships, and public relations programs (see Figure 1.3).

A complete IMC plan combines the elements of the marketing mix: products, prices, distribution methods, and promotions. While this textbook primarily deals with the promotions component, note that, in order to present a unified message, the other elements of the marketing mix should be blended into the program.

An Integrated Marketing Communications Plan

A strategic marketing plan forms the basis for integrated marketing communications. The plan coordinates the components of the marketing mix in order to achieve harmony in the messages and promotions relayed to customers and others. Figure 1.4 lists the steps required to complete a marketing plan.

A *current situational analysis* involves examination of the firm's ongoing market situation. Next, marketers conduct a *SWOT analysis* by studying the factors in the organization's internal and external environments. SWOT identifies internal company strengths and weaknesses along with the marketing opportunities and threats present in the external environment.

Defining primary *marketing objectives* establishes targets such as higher sales, an increase in market share, a new competitive position, or desired customer actions, such as visiting the store and making purchases. Marketing objectives are paired with key target markets. Understanding both helps company leaders prepare an effective integrated marketing communications program.

Based on the marketing objectives and target market, the team develops *marketing strategies*. These strategies apply to the ingredients in the marketing mix and include all positioning, differentiation, and branding strategies. *Marketing tactics* guide the

- Current situational analysis
- SWOT analysis
- Marketing objectives
- Target market

- Marketing strategies
- Marketing tactics
- Implementation
- Evaluation of performance

▶ **FIGURE 1.4**
Steps of a Marketing Plan

◀ Matching marketing objectives with the key target market is an important step in developing the "Visit South Walton (Florida)" campaign.

day-by-day activities necessary to support marketing strategies. The final two steps in the marketing plan consist of stating how to *implement* the plan and specifying methods to *evaluate performance*.

The steps of the strategic marketing plan help pull together all company activities into one consistent effort. They provide guidance to company leaders and marketing experts as they coordinate the firm's overall communications package.

Emerging Trends in Marketing Communications

Many forces impact marketing communications. Financial pressures have caused the company leaders who hire advertising agencies to conclude that they cannot pay unlimited dollars for marketing programs. Competition, both domestic and global, forces managers to examine their communications plans to ensure maximum effectiveness. The internet and emerging social media trends influence marketing messages and means of communicating with consumers and businesses. Figure 1.5 highlights the current trends affecting marketing communications.

objective 1.3
Which trends are affecting marketing communications?

Emphasis on Accountability and Measurable Results

Company leaders expect advertising agencies to produce tangible outcomes. They spend promotional dollars carefully. Any coupon promotion, contest, social media program, or advertising campaign should yield measurable gains in sales, market share, brand awareness, customer loyalty, or other observable results to be considered successful.

The increasing emphasis on accountability and measurable results has been driven by chief executive officers (CEOs), chief financial

- Emphasis on accountability and measurable results
- Explosion of the digital arena
- Integration of media platforms
- Shift in channel power
- Increase in global competition
- Increase in brand parity
- Emphasis on customer engagement

▲ **FIGURE 1.5**
Trends Affecting Marketing Communications

▲ This app for Gulf Coast Seafood illustrates the use of digital media.

officers (CFOs), and chief marketing officers (CMOs). According to Martyn Straw, chief strategy officer of the advertising agency BBDO Worldwide, corporate executives and business owners are less willing to "funnel cash into TV commercials and glossy ads" that keep increasing in cost while appearing to achieve less and less.

Many companies have replaced 30-second television spots with digital, social and alternative communication advertisements. Marketing messages can be tied to special events in which names, profiles, and addresses of prospective customers are collected and tracked. Straw suggests that marketing should not be viewed as an expense, but rather as an investment in which promotional dollars generate sales and profits.[5]

Integration of Digital Media

Internet-based marketing communications include individual web advertisements along with interactive websites, blogs, and social media networks. Smartphones, tablets, and text-messaging systems have created a new landscape and nearly a new language. Ingenious digital marketing techniques seek to create experiences with a brand rather than mere purchases with little or no emotional attachment. The advertisement for a smartphone app shown on this page was created for Gulf Coast Seafood. It offers a recipe along with a GPS function that assists consumers in locating the nearest Gulf Coast Seafood.

Many companies have cut traditional media expenditures, moving the dollars to digital media. Procter & Gamble (P&G), AT&T, Johnson & Johnson, Kraft Foods, and Toyota are some of the organizations that have reduced company television advertising budgets while expanding funds for digital and social media. Campbell's Soup doubled digital spending to 40 percent of the total media budget.[6] A General Motors executive noted, "Some 70 percent of consumers who shop for a new car or truck do web research."[7] The same holds true for other products.

Social media and the internet provide consumers with access to a wealth of information about companies, products, and brands. Individuals communicate with each other, sending favorable or unfavorable ratings and information. Messages travel almost instantaneously. Digital marketing has evolved into a mandatory ingredient rather than an option for companies. Marketers seek to engage all current and prospective customers with the brand in order to achieve success.

When P&G introduced its Star Wars limited edition of CoverGirl, the company utilized Snapchat and geo-targeted advertising to drive in-store sales. With Snapchat, P&G set up geofilters around its 868 Ulta stores throughout the United States. As individuals posted photos or videos to Snapchat within the designated boundaries around the Ulta stores, a branded overlay, or filter, was placed at the top of the post. Anyone who viewed the photo or video would also see the Covergirl Star Wars cosmetic line and the location of the a nearby Ulta store. This digital approach allowed P&G to focus on consumers who were near Ulta stores and most likely to be interested in the Star Wars CoverGirl cosmetics.[8]

Integration of Media Platforms

Today's consumers spend an average of five hours and 16 minutes in front of a screen that does not involve television. When combined with television (which consumers watch for an additional four hours and 31 minutes per day), the total becomes more than 10 hours per day examining some kind of screen, whether it is a computer, tablet, mobile phone, or television.[9] Understanding the ways consumers include multiple devices into their daily lives is important to marketers as they devise methods to reach them. Recent research by Flamingo Research and Ipsos OTX identified four venues in which consumers interact across multiple media formats (see Figure 1.6).[10]

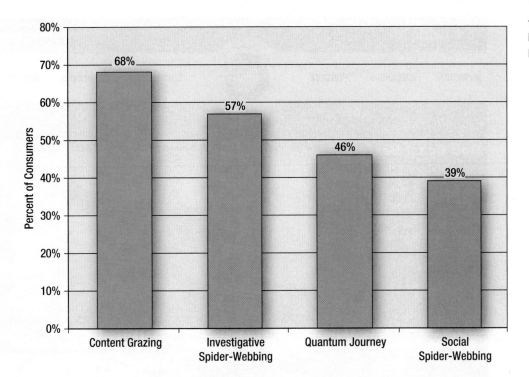

Content grazing involves looking at two or more screens simultaneously to access content that is not related. For instance, someone watching TV and texting a friend at the same time is grazing. *Investigative spider-webbing* occurs when a consumer pursues or investigates specific content across multiple platforms, such as a person watching a football game and accessing stats for various players on a PC or mobile phone. *Quantum journey* focuses on completing a specific task, such as when a consumer looks for a Chinese restaurant using a PC to locate one in the area, then obtains consumer reviews of the units close by on a smartphone, and finally employs a map app to locate the restaurant or to place an order. The fourth pathway, *social spider-webbing*, takes place when consumers share content or information across multiple devices. Posting pictures on Facebook from a laptop and then texting friends to go check them out is an example.

To reach consumers, marketers recognize that today's consumers use multiple devices in several ways. An individual television ad or banner ad will likely go unnoticed. Advertisers try to find ways to engage consumers with a brand through portals such as tablets and mobile phones. That same ad or message delivered across all of the platforms in various formats increases the chances it will be heard and assimilated by consumers.

Changes in Channel Power

A marketing channel consists of a producer or manufacturer vending goods to various wholesalers or middlemen, who, in turn, sell items to retailers who offer the items to consumers. Recent technological developments have altered the levels of power held by members of the channel.

Retailers seek to maintain channel power by controlling shelf space and purchase data that allows them to determine which products and brands are placed on store shelves. Through checkout scanners, retailers know which products and brands are selling. Many retailers share the data with suppliers and require them to ensure that store shelves remain well stocked. The size and power of mega-retailers mean manufacturers and suppliers have no choice but to follow their dictates.

At the same time, the growth of internet along with other methods of communication has shifted some channel power to consumers.[11] Consumers obtain information about goods and services and purchase them using the internet. Internet-driven sales have risen at a tremendous rate. According to Forrester Research, U.S. online retail purchases have grown from $262 billion in 2013 to $370 billion in 2017.[12]

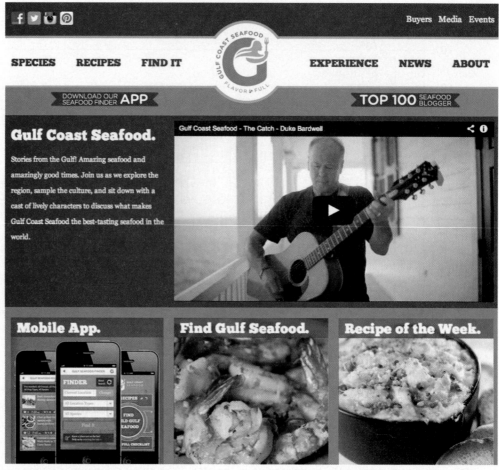

▲ In designing Gulf Coast Seafood's website, marketers for the brand understand that consumers integrate various media platforms and desire an experience with the brand.

Consumer relationships with brands have transformed. Individuals wield tremendous power. Social media allows dissatisfied customers to instantly vent about bad experiences to enormous audiences, where little forgiveness of mistakes takes place. Fifty-seven percent of consumers say they will not buy a particular brand after one negative experience and 40 percent are likely to tell others not to purchase that brand.[13] Previously held positive feelings about a company are quickly forgotten.

The same principles apply to business-to-business purchasing activities. Buyers who shop on behalf of organizations and other company members seeking business-to-business products also are quick to use social media to complain about brands that did not deliver. Consequently, a similar shift in channel power has taken place in the business-to-business sector.

Fortunately, the environment is not completely negative. Approximately 50 percent of consumers share positive experiences with a brand. Consumers often seek the opinions of friends and relatives concerning products. As a result, about 70 percent of consumers say friends and families are a primary source of information regarding various brands.[14]

Understanding these shifts in channel power has become essential. Marketers know they cannot rely solely on mass media advertising. They must incorporate social media and engage consumers with their brands.

Increases in Global Competition

Advances in information technology and communication mean competition no longer takes place with just the company down the street —it may be from a firm 10,000 miles away. Consumers desire high quality along with low prices. The company that delivers the best value of quality and price makes the sale, often regardless of location. Advancements in delivery systems make it possible for purchases to arrive in a matter of days from anywhere in the world.

Doritos' marketing team recognized that new communication technologies and social media have made the world smaller. Consumers travel and communicate with each other. As a result, Doritos launched its first global campaign by updating packaging and the company's logo to give a consistent look across 37 countries. Before this global effort, Doritos offered 25 different package designs and utilized a number of different marketing approaches in various countries. The global campaign, called "For the Bold," included digital and TV spots in the United States, Mexico, England, Canada, Spain, and Turkey as well as digital and social media initiatives. The global campaign provided a venue to connect fans worldwide, a consistent storyline, and the same look and feel for the Doritos brand across multiple countries. Today, Doritos remains the largest tortilla/corn chip brand in the world with a 39-percent market share.[15]

▲ Advances in information and communication technologies have created global competition for goods and services.

Increases in Brand Parity

Many currently available products offer nearly identical benefits. When consumers believe that various brands provide the same set of attributes, **brand parity** results. When it occurs, shoppers select from a group of brands rather than one specific brand.[16] Brand parity means quality becomes less of a concern because consumers perceive only minor differences between brands. Consequently, other criteria —such as price, availability, or a specific promotional deal — impact purchase decisions. The net effect becomes a steady decline in brand loyalty.[17] When consumers do not have a specific brand they believe is significantly superior, they more readily switch brands. In response, marketers try to convince consumers that their company's brand is not the same; that it remains superior or different in some meaningful way.

Emphasis on Customer Engagement

The expanding number of available brands perceived to be roughly equivalent requires an additional response. To build loyalty, marketers seek to engage customers with the brand at every **contact point**; that is, any place where customers interact with or acquire additional information about a firm. Customer engagement programs often utilize digital and social media and have become part of the total integrated marketing approach.

An effective contact establishes two-way communication. Engagement can be built by offering incentives and reasons for the consumer to interact with a company. For customers to take advantage of these initiatives, however, they must develop emotional commitments to the brand and experience feelings of confidence, integrity, pride, and passion toward it.[18] The brand, in turn, must deliver on promises and provide reasons for consumers to continue to interact with the company.

▲ Nonprofits such as the Red Cross must seek to engage donors to ensure sufficient funds are available when disasters strike.

- Unifies strategy and message across channels
- Streamlines timing
- Connects with multiple audiences
- Creates meaningful insights
- Maximizes impact

▲ **FIGURE 1.7**
Five Reasons Why Integrated
Marketing Works

The Role of Integrated Marketing Communications

The trends described in this section have forced a shift in the mindsets of marketing executives. They realize that integrating all marketing communication efforts, including the digital and social media components, is vital to success. Zehnder Communications, an advertising agency that created a number of ads in this textbook, posted five reasons on the company's blog why integrated marketing works and why it is essential (see Figure 1.7). According to Zehnder, "integrated marketing combines multiple types of outreach tactics to most effectively reach a brand's key audiences at every phase of the customer journey."[19]

Effective integrated marketing communications ensures a brand's target audiences hear the same message across all traditional and new media channels. Each piece of a campaign should be driven by a single strategy that guides the creative development process. An integrated approach times the release of individual campaign components in a manner that maximizes a customer's journey from awareness to purchase. Most brands seek to reach multiple audiences. An integrated approach connects brands with each audience, simultaneously or sequentially.

Integrated marketing communications produce meaningful insights across multiple channels. The marketing team measures the impact of the individual components of a campaign and the various channels that are featured, although these elements should be analyzed within the context of the entire campaign. This allows a brand manager to identify the channels that work best and the components that resonate with the target audience. These insights maximize the impact of a promotional effort.

IMC Components and the Design of this Text

objective 1.4

What are the components of an integrated marketing communications program?

Figure 1.8 presents an overview of the IMC approach featured in this textbook. As shown, the foundation of an IMC program consists of a careful review of the company's image, the buyers to be served, and the markets in which the buyers are located. Advertising

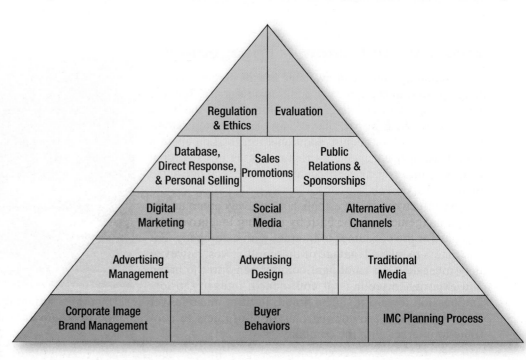

▶ **FIGURE 1.8**
Overview of Integrated
Marketing Communications

programs are built on this foundation, as are the other elements of the promotional mix. The integration tools located at the peak of the pyramid help the company's marketing team make certain all of the elements of the plan are consistent and effective.

IMC Foundation

The first section of this text builds the foundation for an IMC program. Chapter 2 examines the elements of corporate image and brand management. Strengthening the firm's image and brand answers the question, "Who are we, and what message are we trying to send?" Branding includes the development of packages and labels that speak with the same voice as other marketing messages.

Chapter 3 describes buyer behaviors. The steps of the consumer purchasing process explain how individuals make choices. Marketers identify the motives leading to purchases and factors affecting those decisions. Then, the IMC program can be designed to influence consumer thinking. The chapter also examines business-to-business (B2B) buyer behaviors. Discovering viable business-to-business marketing opportunities by reaching purchasing managers and other decision makers in the target business often plays a vital role in overall company success.

Chapter 4 explains the IMC planning program. This includes identifying all target markets, most notably consumer and business-to-business market segments. Then quality communications objectives can be set. The plan becomes complete when communications budgets have been developed and all appropriate media have been identified.

Advertising

Advertising issues are described in the second section of this text. Chapter 5 describes advertising campaign management and addresses the major advertising activities, including the selection of an advertising agency. Campaign management identifies the general direction the company will take. Chapter 5 also explains various advertising theories along with the principles of advertising effectiveness. Advertising theories form the background used to design advertisements.

Chapter 6 begins with an analysis of the ingredients involved in creating effective message strategies. Then, various advertising appeals can be used, including those oriented toward fear, humor, sex, music, and rational methods. Next, the chapter discusses the types of executional frameworks used in advertising. Executional frameworks provide the means to construct the actual commercial or advertisement. Finally, the chapter examines the employment of sources or spokespersons as part of an advertising program.

The traditional media channels, including television, radio, outdoor, magazines, and newspapers, are described in Chapter 7, along with the advantages and disadvantages of each one. The chapter explains the roles provided by media planners and media buyers.

▲ Advertising is an important integrated marketing component for Interstate Batteries.

Digital and Alternative

The third section of this book contains information about digital and alternative methods of reaching potential customers. Chapter 8 examines digital marketing efforts designed to integrate e-commerce programs with recent trends in interactive marketing. Online advertising approaches are presented. Many online activities begin with a search. As a result, concepts regarding search engine optimization (SEO) are discussed in the chapter. Due to the rise in smartphone use, the chapter explores new trends in mobile advertising.

Social media has exploded in usage in recent years and is the topic of Chapter 9. While Facebook remains the leading social media platform, others have created an impact on both consumer and business markets. The chapter examines current trends in social media and how businesses can use these venues to encourage brand engagement.

Many communication channels are available beyond the traditional networks, the internet, and social media. Chapter 10, entitled "Alternative Marketing," describes methods such as buzz marketing, guerrilla marketing, product placements, branded entertainment, and lifestyle marketing. The chapter also explains brand communities.

Selling Components

The next level of the IMC pyramid adds database and direct response marketing programs, personal selling, trade promotions, consumer promotions, public relations efforts, and sponsorship programs. Each of these efforts helps to stimulate sales. When marketing managers carefully design all of the steps taken up to this point, the firm can integrate these activities. Messages presented in the advertising campaign can be reinforced through a variety of communication promotions.

Chapter 11 explains database programs, direct response marketing efforts, and personal selling tactics. The chapter first describes effective data collection and analysis. Then, the information gained can be used to develop data-driven marketing programs, including permission marketing, frequency programs, and customer relationship management (CRM) systems as well as personal selling activities. Personal selling involves contacts with retail customers and other businesses.

Chapter 12, entitled "Sales Promotions," describes consumer and trade promotions. Trade promotions include trade incentives, cooperative advertising, slotting fees, and other promotions and discounts that help the manufacturer or channel member to push the product through the distribution channel. Consumer promotions are directed at end users and include coupons, contests, premiums, refunds, rebates, free samples, and price-off offers.

Chapter 13 explores public relations programs that connect with consumers in positive ways. This involves emphasizing positive events and dealing with negative publicity. The marketing team utilizes public relations efforts to help a sponsorship program achieve the greatest impact.

▼ Companies often utilize the expertise of marketing research firms such as ReRez to evaluate IMC programs.

Integration

The final level of an IMC program adds the integration tools needed to make sure the company effectively serves all customers. Chapter 14 begins with a presentation of the many legal and regulatory issues that are part of the advertising and promotions environment. The chapter discusses several ethical issues that emerge in marketing communications.

Finally, Chapter 15 explains the evaluation of integrated marketing communications (IMC) programs. Evaluations can begin prior to any promotional campaign and continue during the campaign to post-campaign evaluations. These evaluations generate valuable information to alter campaigns before they

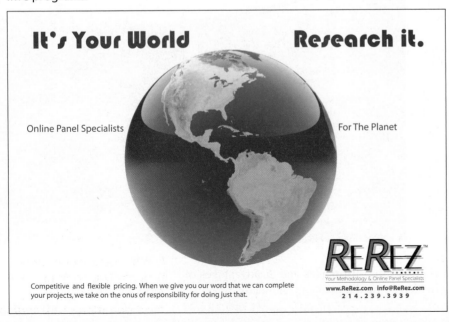

It's Your World   Research it.

Online Panel Specialists   For The Planet

Competitive and flexible pricing. When we give you our word that we can complete your projects, we take on the onus of responsibility for doing just that.

ReRez

Your Methodology & Online Panel Specialists

www.ReRez.com   info@ReRez.com
2 1 4 . 2 3 9 . 3 9 3 9

are commercially introduced, as well as provide input to modify programs that have already run. A promotions evaluation process holds everything together and drives the entire IMC process. Fully integrated marketing requires a well-defined linkage between planning and evaluation processes.

International Implications

The same trends that exist among advertising agencies in the United States occur in the international arena. Instead of IMC, international programs are called *GIMC*, or *globally integrated marketing communications* programs.[20] The goal remains the same: to coordinate marketing efforts across all platforms. The challenges become greater due to larger national and cultural differences in target markets.

Marketers can employ two different strategies for global companies. **Standardization**, in which a company features a uniform product and message across countries, is one option. The approach involves generating economies of scale in production while creating a global product using a more universal promotional theme. The language may be different, but the basic marketing message stays the same.

The second approach, **adaptation**, results in the creation of products and marketing messages designed for and adapted to individual countries. The manner in which a company markets a product in Mexico differs from the methods used in Italy, India, or Australia.

The standardization method may be easier to apply; however, GIMC principles can and should be used with either adaptation or standardization.[21] To reduce costs, careful coordination of marketing efforts should occur across countries. Even when a firm uses the adaptation strategy, marketers from various countries learn from each other. Synergies take place between countries and regions. More important, learning can occur.

Recently, Adrian Hallmark, global brand director of Jaguar, commented that "for too many luxury consumers, there is awareness of the Jaguar brand, but not consideration and modern relevance." To restore its iconic status, Jaguar's marketing group launched a multinational ad campaign created by Spark 44, a London ad agency. The campaign debuted on websites **JaguarUSA.com**, Facebook, and YouTube with a 45-second version of a 30-second TV ad. Jaguar then introduced print, digital, and outdoor advertising in the United States, Austria, Spain, France, Germany, Italy, Russia, Korea, Japan, Australia, and South Africa. The campaign included an 18-city road show in the United States to encourage prospective buyers to try the new Jaguar. The ads were adapted to individual markets in each country using the central theme of the campaign "How alive are you?" which was featured in every print, digital, outdoor, television, and video ad.[22]

objective **1.5**
What is meant by *GIMC?*

◀ In developing global communication campaigns, company leaders must choose the best approach, standardization or adaptation.

Summary

Communication consists of transmitting, receiving, and processing information. It represents a two-way street in which a sender establishes a connection with a receiver. Effective communication forms the basis for a solid and successful marketing program. The components of the communication process include the sender, an encoding process, the transmission device, the decoding process, and the receiver. Noise is anything that distorts or disrupts the flow of information from the sender to the receiver.

In the marketing arena, senders are companies seeking to transmit ideas to consumers, employees, other companies, retail outlets, and others. Encoding devices provide the means of transmitting information and include advertisements, public relations efforts, press releases, sales activities, promotions, and a wide variety of additional verbal and nonverbal cues sent to receivers. Transmission devices include the media and spokespersons that carry the message. Decoding occurs when the receivers (customers or retailers) encounter the message. Noise takes many forms in marketing, most notably the clutter of an abundance of messages in every available channel.

Integrated marketing communications (IMC) takes advantage of the effective management of the communication channels. Within the marketing mix of products, prices, distribution systems, and promotions, firms that speak with one clear voice are able to coordinate and integrate all marketing tools.

The fields of advertising, promotions, and marketing communications have experienced several new trends. Marketing departments and advertising agencies, as well as individual account managers, brand managers, and creatives, encounter strong pressures. They are held accountable for expenditures of marketing communications dollars. Company leaders expect tangible results from promotional campaigns and marketing programs.

IMC plans are vital to achieving success. The explosion of digital media, new information technologies, and social media strongly influences IMC programs. Marketing professionals seek to find ways to integrate all media platforms together to present a consistent message.

Channel power has shifted in many ways. Company leaders adjust in order to maintain a strong market standing, and IMC programs can assist in this effort. New levels of global competition drive marketers to better understand customers and be certain that those end users hear a clear and consistent message from the firm.

As consumers develop a stronger sense of brand parity, wherein consumers perceive no real differences in product or service quality, marketers seek to create situations in which a company or brand develops a distinct advantage. This may be difficult because consumers collect and integrate information about products from a wide variety of sources, including the internet and social media. Quality IMC programs help maintain the strong voice a company needs to ensure customers hear its message through an emphasis on customer engagement in all marketing activities.

When a firm conducts business internationally, a GIMC, or globally integrated marketing communications system, can be of great value. By developing one strong theme and then adapting it to individual countries, the firm conveys a message that integrates international operations into a more coherent marketing package.

This textbook explains several issues involved in establishing an effective IMC program. The importance of business-to-business marketing efforts is noted because many firms market items as much to other companies as they do to consumers. Successful development of an IMC program helps firms remain profitable and vibrant, even when the complexities of the marketplace make these goals more difficult to attain.

Key Terms

communication Transmitting, receiving, and processing information

senders The person(s) attempting to deliver a message or idea

encoding The verbal (words, sounds) and nonverbal (gestures, facial expressions, posture) cues that the sender utilizes in dispatching a message

transmission devices All of the items that carry a message from the sender to the receiver

decoding What occurs when the receiver employs any of his or her senses (hearing, seeing, feeling) in an attempt to capture a message

receivers The intended audience for a message

feedback The information the sender obtains from the receiver regarding the receiver's perception or interpretation of a message

noise Anything that distorts or disrupts a message

clutter What exists when consumers are exposed to hundreds of marketing messages per day, and most are tuned out

integrated marketing communications (IMC) The coordination and integration of all marketing communications tools, avenues, and sources in a company into a seamless program designed to maximize the impact on customers and other stakeholders

marketing mix The elements of a marketing program, including products, prices, places (the distribution system), and promotions

brand parity What occurs when there is the perception that most goods and services are essentially the same

contact point Any place where customers interact with or acquire additional information about a firm

standardization A program in which a firm features uniform products and market offerings across countries with the goal of generating economies of scale in production while using the same promotional theme

adaptation What takes place when products and marketing messages are designed for and adapted to individual countries

---

MyMarketingLab

To complete the problems with the ⭐ in your MyLab, go to the end-of-chapter Discussion Questions.

Review Questions

1-1. Define communication. How does it play a crucial role in marketing and business?

1-2. What are the parts of an individual communications model?

1-3. Who are the typical senders in marketing communications? Who are the receivers?

1-4. Name the transmission devices, both human and non-human, that carry marketing messages.

1-5. Define clutter. Name some of the forms of clutter in marketing communications.

1-6. Define integrated marketing communications (IMC).

1-7. What are the four parts of the marketing mix?

1-8. What steps are required to write a marketing plan?

1-9. What trends were given to explain the growth in importance of IMC plans in this chapter?

1-10. How has the use of digital media impacted marketing communications?

1-11. Identify and describe four ways consumers can interact with multiple media formats.

1-12. What is channel power? How has it changed in the past few decades?

1-13. What is brand parity? How is it related to successful marketing efforts?

1-14. Identify the role of integrated marketing in relation to new marketing trends.

1-15. What is a contact point? How do marketers link contact points to customer engagement?

1-16. What are the components of an integrated marketing communications program, as outlined in this textbook?

1-17. What is a GIMC? Why is it important for multinational firms?

1-18. What is the difference between standardization and adaptation in GIMC programs?

Critical Thinking Exercises

DISCUSSION QUESTIONS

1-19. The Lean Cuisine effort to shift consumer perceptions of frozen products included a multi-faceted approach. Access the firm's website and evaluate the marketing messages presented. Do they convince you to reconsider your views of various products? Is the effort working, or do you still perceive Lean Cuisine to just be "diet" food? Explain your answer.

⭐ **1-20.** The marketing director for Tempur-Pedic mattresses is assigned the task of emphasizing the mattress's superior sleep quality in the company's next integrated marketing communications program. Discuss the problems the director might encounter in each step of the communication process since the campaign will emphasize something consumers cannot see or observe. Explain how noise or clutter interferes with the communication process.

1-21. What do you typically do during commercials on television? What percentage of the time do you watch commercials? What makes you watch? Ask these same questions of five other people. What types of activities do people engage in during commercials?

⭐ **1-22.** Explain the four ways consumers interact across multiple media formats. Which best describes you? Explain why.

⭐ **1-23.** The use of social media has grown during the last decade. Discuss your personal use of social media. Which social media platforms do you use? Why did you select those particular ones? How do you use social media?

⭐ **1-24.** Explain how advances in information technology and communication have increased global competition for goods and services. How has the increased global competition, in turn, impacted brand parity, the need for customer engagement, and changes in channel power? Be specific by identifying examples to illustrate your thoughts.

1-25. Brand parity has become a major issue for companies. Identify three product categories in which the brand you purchase is not very important. Why is the brand not important? Identify three product categories in which the brand is important. What brand or brands do you typically purchase in each category? Why?

1-26. The marketing director for a manufacturer of automobile tires has been asked to integrate the company's global marketing program. Should the director use a standardization or adaptation approach? How could the company be certain that its marketing program will effectively be integrated among the different countries in which it sells tires?

Integrated Learning Exercises

1-27. Examine the advertisement for JD Bank in the section entitled "The Nature of Communication." Explain each of the steps in the communication process (Figure 1.1) in terms of the JD Bank print ad. Go to the authors' website at **clowbaack.net/video/ads.html**. Watch the ad for JD Bank entitled "JD Gets Me." Explain each of the steps in the communication model in relation to this television ad.

1-28. Access the website of Chick-fil-A at **www.chickfila .com**. Access the websites of Chick-fil-A's competitors: KFC (**www.kfc.com**), Popeye's (**www.popeyes. com**), Church's Chicken (**www.churchschicken.com**), and Bojangles (**www.bojangles.com**). Identify the social media used by each brand. Compare and contrast the information available and the design of each company's website. Which website did you like the best? Why? Which one did you like the least? Why?

1-29. Pick one of the brands listed. Access the brand's website. Identify the social media listed on the brand's website, then access each of the social media pages. Go to YouTube and locate a TV ad of the brand. Discuss how well the website, social media sites, and ad you located on YouTube are integrated. (Provide the URLs for the website, social media sites, and TV ad).

    a. *JD Bank (***www.jdbank.com***)*

    b. *Red Lobster (***redlobster.com***)*

    c. *Salvation Army (***www.salvationarmy.org***)*

    d. *Visit South Walton* **www.visitsouthwalton.com***)*

1-30. Information is one key to developing a successful integrated marketing communications program. Access each of the following websites. Describe the type of information and news available on each site. How would this information help in developing an integrated marketing campaign?

    a. *Adweek (***www.adweek.com***)*

    b. *Interbrand (***www.interbrand.com***)*

    c. *Media Industry Today (***media.einnews.com/***)*

    d. *Branding Asia (***www.brandingasia.com***)*

Blog Exercises

Access the authors' blog for this textbook at the URLs provided to complete these exercises. Answer the questions posed on the blog.

1-31. American Eagle, **http://blogclowbaack.net/2015/ 12/03/american-eagle-chapter-1**

1-32. Chick-fil-A, **blogclowbaack.net/2014/04/24/ chick-fil-a-chapter-1**

1-33. Integrated marketing, **blogclowbaack.net/2014/04/24/ imc-chapter-1**

Student Project

CREATIVE CORNER

Executives at Red Robin Gourmet Burgers have decided to open a restaurant near your campus. You have been chosen as a marketing intern to help establish this restaurant. Examine the company's website at **www.redrobin.com**. Read the "About Us" section of the website in order to fully understand the Red Robin brand. When you have a good understanding of Red Robin, prepare a newspaper ad for your student newspaper about a grand opening near your campus. Next, examine each of the company's social media platforms listed on the Red Robin website. Write a report that discusses each of the social media used by Red Robin and how effective each would be in reaching students at your college. Cite specific examples from the company's social media pages using screen shots.

CASE 1 ▶ MIKE'S OLD-TIME ICE CREAM AND CHOCOLATE SHOP

Mike Swann was excited to open his new business venture in the springtime. Mike's Old-Time Ice Cream and Chocolate Shop was established to take advantage of several opportunities and reach multiple audiences, all in one location. In the summertime, ice cream should sell best. In the winter and spring, chocolate products may be given as Christmas, Valentine's, Easter, and Mother's Day presents. Mike also decided to sell fast food throughout the year, including hamburgers, hot dogs, grilled cheese sandwiches, pretzels, fries, and other items.

To make his store stand out, Mike chose to locate on the outskirts of town, where parking would be readily available and the store would be surrounded by a more natural environment including a nearby forest. Then, he was able to obtain a passenger car and caboose from a now-defunct railroad company that could be set up as a place to enjoy ice cream in a unique seating arrangement in addition to the regular tables inside the shop. Outside of the rail cars, Mike placed a swing set and other items for children.

The biggest challenge Mike faced was getting the word out. He contacted a local advertising and promotions agency to help him get started. The first question the account executive asked was, "Well, what is going to make your store stand out?"

Mike responded, "Several things. First, I am re-opening a company that served this area for years, called "Stevenson's Ice Cream." I plan to generate publicity letting everyone know that we will be selling the same kind of great-tasting ice cream that used to be offered by that company. Second, I have a partnership with a local chocolatier that is on the far side of town. We'll be selling their products in our store. And third, we are appealing to that old-fashioned, old-time relaxation that people enjoy in the summer. Families should love that."

Next the executive asked, "Who are your major competitors?"

Mike answered, "For ice cream I suppose it is Baskin Robbins and Dairy Queen. For chocolate, it's probably Nestlé and Hershey's. But we are set up in such a unique way we should be able to attract people differently."

The executive and Mike agreed that the company's launch was a key time to communicate this difference. They also believed the target audience would be pretty large, including families with children, grandparents with grandkids, and other people looking to enjoy high quality chocolate and ice cream in a unique atmosphere, possibly after enjoying a quick meal. The executive pointed out that getting people to visit for the first time would be one factor but that generating return business throughout the year was the real key to long term success. It was time to get started.

▲ Mike's biggest challenge was getting word out about his "Old-Time Ice Cream and Chocolate Shop."

1-34. Mike's store will be a local business that competes with large national companies. What communication challenges does that present? What opportunities does it offer?

1-35. Which of the emerging trends in marketing communications can Mike use to promote his new business? Explain how it can be used.

1-36. What should be the first message that Mike should try to communicate to all potential customers? Should he emphasize price, value, or some other element of his business?

1-37. Will Mike be able to use social media in his marketing communications efforts? If so, how? If not, why not?

CASE 2 ▶ WAKE UP CALL FOR 8:00

Any longstanding product runs the risk of becoming stale in the eyes of consumers. Eight O'Clock Coffee's marketing team recently decided that the company's brand and promotion program needed rejuvenation. The net result was an entire "refresh" marketing effort.[23]

Eight O'Clock Coffee has been available to consumers since 1859. To combat recent sluggish sales, company leaders began with a renovation of the product itself, creating new flavors such as Dark Chocolate Cherry, Cinnamon Bun, and others. The company complemented the new items with updated packaging that was slimmer and featured a bright red color.

To launch these innovations, the marketing program began with a redesigned website highlighting a major event. The campaign included a social-media driven sweepstakes that was incorporated into Fashion Week in New York. Participants in the fashion show were offered red bags. The program featured the theme "The Red Bag Collection in Support of Dress for Success," which added a cause-related tie-in to the refresh rollout. Individuals involved in the fashion event were encouraged to "Spot the Red Bag" in order to win prizes. They accessed the company through the hash tag "#SpottheRedBag" to post photos of their discoveries. The company posted photos of red bags on its Facebook page.

Beyond the social media and fashion show elements, the company added more traditional advertising during the Emmy awards on television. The tagline "Put Coffee First" punctuated these messages. Company leaders extended the campaign to other programs in many of the company's major markets.

These marketing efforts for Eight O'Clock Coffee stress the value of a multifaceted approach to enticing, exciting, and engaging customers and potential customers. Use of new methods, such as social media, combined with more traditional marketing

▲ Eight O'Clock Coffee's marketing team understood that it must engage consumers with the brand to obtain long-term loyalty.

programs (sweepstakes, television advertising) signals the wave of the future for integrated marketing communications.

1-38. What coffee brands would constitute Eight O'Clock Coffee's primary competition?

1-39. Would you characterize coffee consumption as a situation in which brand parity exists? Why or why not?

1-40. Examine the emerging trends in marketing communications presented in the chapter? Which trends can Eight O'Clock Coffee use to their advantage? Explain how.

1-41. Evaluate the value of using social media for this type of marketing communications effort. Is it necessary or helpful? Why or why not?

MyMarketingLab

Go to the Assignments section of your MyLab to complete these writing exercises.

1-42. Reebok's tagline is now "Be More Human." Examine Reebok's website (**www.Reebok.com**). Define each of the components of the communication process (see Figure 1.1). Then explain each component as it relates to the Reebok tagline and website.

1-43. Find each of the following companies on the internet. For each company, discuss how effective its website is in communicating an overall message. Also, discuss how well the marketing team integrates the material on the website. How well does the website integrate the company's advertising with other marketing communications?

   a. Revlon (**www.revlon.com**)

   b. J.B. Hunt (**www.jbhunt.com**)

   c. Interstate Batteries (**www.interstatebatteries.com**)

Chapter 2 Brand Management

Chapter Objectives

After reading this chapter, you should be able to answer the following questions:

2.1 How does a brand's image affect consumers, other businesses, and the company itself?

2.2 What are the different types of brands and brand names?

2.3 What are the characteristics of effective logos?

2.4 What elements are involved in identifying, creating, rejuvenating, or changing a brand's image?

2.5 How are brands developed, built, and sustained in order to build brand equity and fend off perceptions of brand parity?

2.6 What current trends affect private brands?

2.7 How can packaging and labels support an IMC program domestically and in foreign settings?

2.8 How are brands managed in international markets?

MyMarketingLab™

⭐ **Improve Your Grade!**

More than 10 million students improved their results using the Pearson MyLabs. Visit **mymktlab.com** for simulations, tutorials, and end-of-chapter problems.

Overview

A **brand** is the word, term, or phrase featured as the name of a product, product line, or company. Managing an organization's brand image constitutes a critical element in the successful development of an integrated marketing communications plan. A corporation's **brand image** reflects the feelings consumers and businesses have about the overall organization as well as its individual products or product lines. Advertising, consumer promotions, trade promotions, personal selling, the company's website, and other marketing activities all affect consumer perceptions. A strong brand creates major advantages for any good or service. Conversely, when the image of an organization or one of its brands becomes tarnished, sales revenues and profits can plummet. Rebuilding or revitalizing the brand's image then becomes difficult.

The marketing team seeks to understand the firm's overall brand image and the strengths of individual brands in order to make solid connections with consumers and business-to-business customers. A strong integrated marketing communications (IMC) foundation combines an analysis of the firm's image and brands with assessments of consumer and business buyer behaviors. Marketers then prepare consistent messages designed to reach any individual that might purchase a firm's products. At times, such a process involves rejuvenating or adjusting the image a brand conveys.

Brand Image Overhaul

The brand name Domino's Pizza has been around for many decades. Over that time, the company has experienced growth, success, problems, and efforts to improve the organization's image. During the past decade, company leaders created new tracking systems designed to keep customers informed as their orders are received, baked, and delivered. Soon after, new pizza products were developed to cater to more sophisticated tastes, with the company even insisting that customers could not add or delete ingredients from several of the Artisan line of products.[1]

Unfortunately, even these changes did not completely deliver the boost in sales and profits the company leaders wanted to achieve. Recently, a major new effort took place. The marketing team identified a trend in which more customers were picking up pizza rather than having it delivered. In response, some stores added big screen TVs, improved seating for those waiting to pick up orders, and established places where people could watch their pizza or carry-out items being put together. The approach somewhat resembles what occurs in a Subway store.

To accentuate these new methods of operation, the company's name was also changed, from Domino's Pizza to simply Domino's. As Russell Weiner, the company's chief marketing officer noted, "So much of our menu is beyond pizza right now, that we feel like we're more than just a pizza place." Sandwiches and other menu items had been added over time, giving credence to his claim. Along with the revised name came a simplified logo, which removed the name but maintained the original red, white, and blue domino.[2]

As is true with any marketing effort, the brand name change and product line alterations were carefully orchestrated with the firm's integrated marketing communications program, including advertising accompanied by social media messages. The coming years will yield evidence as to whether this course of action achieves success.

The first part of this chapter notes the activities involved in managing a corporation's brand image, including its name and logo. The second part addresses ways to develop and promote the various forms of brand names. Brand equity and brand parity are described. Finally, packages and labels, which should be included in any marketing communications program, are assessed. Ethical and international considerations are noted.

Corporate and Brand Image

A corporate or brand image expresses what the company stands for as well as how it is known in the marketplace. Whether it is the "good hands" of Allstate Insurance or the "good neighbors" at State Farm Insurance, creating a specific impression in the minds of clients and customers should be the goal of image management. Insurance companies often accomplish this by stressing helpfulness, safety, and security as elements of a strong image.

Consumer beliefs about a firm are more important than how company officials perceive the image. Corporate brand names such as Bank of America, Toyota, Kraft Heinz, and BP (British Petroleum) create impressions in the minds of clients and customers. Although the actual version of the image varies from consumer to consumer or for each business-to-business buyer, the combined views of all publics determine the overall brand image, which can be positive or negative.

The same holds true for individual brands. Some companies, such as Kraft Heinz, sell several brands. The corporate name Kraft Heinz projects an image and identity along with

objective 2.1

How does a brand's image affect consumers, other businesses, and the company itself?

▲ This ad effectively enhances the image of the Kraft Singles brand.

the individual brands the company offers, including Oscar Mayer, Maxwell House, Planters, and Velveeta. Other companies only feature one brand for the entire organization, which means the corporation's and brand image coincide. Therefore, with regard to the various concepts presented in this chapter, the ideas can refer to various brands sold by a company, such as Kraft Heinz, or to an overall corporate brand, such as State Farm, Allstate, or Walmart.

Components of Brand Image

Brand images contain invisible and intangible elements (see Figure 2.1). Consumers encounter these elements as they interact with a company or brand. A recent study of the restaurant industry indicated that the quality of a company's goods and services ranked as the most important component of brand image. The willingness of a firm to stand behind its goods and services when something went wrong was second. Third were perceptions of how the firm dealt with customers by being pleasant, helpful, or professional.[3]

Negative publicity can stain or injure consumer perceptions of a corporation's or brand's image. Examples include the damage to reputations of financial institutions, such as Bank of America when it faced charges of misleading investors, Toyota following quality control problems, and Domino's after poor customer evaluations of its pizza in 2010.[4] Each organization undertook efforts to restore a more positive image.

An image consists of a unique set of features. The corporate brand image of an automobile manufacturer such as Porsche, Mazda, Toyota, Ford, or General Motors is based on: evaluations of its vehicles; whether the company is foreign or domestic; customer views of each company's advertisements; and reactions to the local dealership. A corporation's image often includes consumer assessments of company employees. In fact, the mechanic repairing a vehicle at a local Chevrolet dealership garage might become the dominant factor that shapes a customer's perception of General Motors.

In the past, Walmart faced criticisms regarding employee discontent, conditions at foreign factories, and bribery allegations in other countries. To boost the image of the brand, Walmart's marketing team launched a multimillion dollar "American

Tangible elements	Intangible elements
• Goods or services sold	• Corporate personnel
• Retail outlets where the product is sold	– Ideals
• Advertising	– Beliefs
• Marketing communications	– Conduct
• Name and logo	• Environment policies
• Package and labels	• Corporate culture
• Employees	• Country location
	• Media reports

▶ **FIGURE 2.1**
Elements of Brand Image

◀ A mechanic at a local Chevrolet dealer can impact the image a customer has of General Motors and the Chevrolet brand.

Success Story" campaign. The national campaign featured customers, store employees, and truck drivers sharing personal stories and warm feelings about Walmart.[5] The campaign sought to show the public another side of the company by featuring positive aspects of Walmart.

A strong brand image also provides tangible and intangible benefits. Organizational leaders devote considerable amounts of time and energy to building and maintaining a positive brand image. Client companies expect advertising agencies to help design marketing programs that take advantage of the benefits of a strong brand image. Both customers and organizations benefit from a well-known firm with an established reputation.

The Role of Brand Image—Consumer Perspective

From a consumer's perspective (or business customer's perspective), brand image serves several functions, including those displayed in Figure 2.2. A well-known brand offers customers positive assurance about what to expect. A can of Coke or Pepsi purchased in Santa Cruz, California, tastes like one purchased in Liverpool, England, or Kuala Lumpur, Malaysia. Products ordered online from Bed Bath & Beyond are the same as those purchased in retail stores in California or New Jersey.

Positive assurance generates value when customers purchase goods or services with which they have little experience. Consider families on vacation. A family visiting Brazil might normally not stay at the Holiday Inn, but the familiar name makes it a lower-risk option. Consumers often believe that purchasing from a familiar corporation will be a

- Provides confidence regarding purchase decisions
- Gives assurance about the purchase when the buyer has little or no previous experience
- Reduces search time in a purchase decision
- Provides psychological reinforcement and social acceptance of the purchase

◀ **FIGURE 2.2**
Brand Image: Benefits to Consumers

▲ This advertisement for Del Frisco's Grille illustrates it is the ideal location for social interactions with friends.

"safer" option than buying something from an unknown company. Taking a room at an unfamiliar hotel feels riskier than staying at one with a recognizable name.

Purchasing from a familiar firm reduces search time and saves effort. An individual or company loyal to Ford spends fewer hours searching for a new car than someone without such loyalty. The same may be true when buying low-cost items such as groceries or office products.

Purchasing from a highly recognized company often provides psychological reinforcement and social acceptance. Psychological reinforcement comes from concluding that a wise choice was made and the confidence that the good or service will perform well. Social acceptance comes from believing that other individuals including family and friends who purchased the same brand are likely to accept the choice.

Interbrand produces a yearly list of the top 100 best brands. The list does not include companies offering portfolios of products and brands, such as Procter & Gamble. Also, privately-held companies, including VISA and those that operate under different names in different countries, such as Walmart, are not considered. The list only notes corporations that provide products under one name. Using these criteria, Interbrand ranked Apple as the top global corporate brand, followed by Google and Coca-Cola.[6] Figure 2.3 provides a list of the top 10 brands along with the value of each.

The Role of Brand Image—Company Perspective

From the viewpoint of the firm, a highly reputable image generates benefits, as noted in Figure 2.4. A quality image provides the basis for the development of new goods and services. The introduction of a product becomes easier when potential customers recognize the brand name and image. Long-term patrons are willing to try new items and transfer trust in and beliefs about the brand to those products. A *brand alliance*, in which two companies use brand strength to develop and co-market a new product featuring both names (such as Old Spice and Head & Shoulders) has recently begun to emerge.

Many customers believe they "get what they pay for." Consumers often associate better quality with a higher price. A strong brand image allows a company to charge more for goods and services, which can lead to improved markup margins and profits.

▲ Social acceptance can become one benefit of purchasing a well-known brand.

Rank	Company	Brand Value (Billions)
1	Apple	$170.3
2	Google	$120.3
3	Coca-Cola	$78.4
4	Microsoft	$67.7
5	IBM	$65.1
6	Toyota	$49.1
7	Samsung	$45.3
8	General Electric	$42.3
9	McDonald's	$39.8
10	Amazon	$38.0

◀ **FIGURE 2.3**
Top 10 Best Global Brands

▶ **FIGURE 2.4**

Brand Image: Benefits to Companies

- Extension of positive customer feelings to new products
- Ability to charge a higher price or fee
- Consumer loyalty leading to more frequent purchases
- Positive word-of-mouth endorsements
- Higher level of channel power
- Ability to attract quality employees
- More favorable ratings by financial observers and analysts

▲ Interstate Batteries has accrued positive benefits from a strong brand name.

Firms with well-developed brand images enjoy more loyal customers, which leads them to purchase products more frequently. Loyal customers are less inclined to make substitute purchases when other companies offer discounts, sales, and similar enticements.

Heightened levels of customer loyalty often lead to positive word-of-mouth endorsements. Favorable comments generate additional sales and attract new customers. Consumers and business buyers have more faith in personal references than other forms of advertising or promotion.

Positive customer attitudes create stronger loyalty to the brand, which then provide greater channel power. Retailers stock the brands customers view favorably and seek brands that pull people into stores. A product or brand with a high positive image retains control and channel power when marketing items to retailers.

Attracting quality employees can be another advantage of a dominant brand image. Potential workers become willing to apply for jobs at companies with solid reputations, thereby reducing recruiting and selection costs. Southwest Airlines holds the image of a great place to work, which assists in recruiting. A high-quality work force normally experiences lower turnover rates.

A strong reputation often leads to favorable ratings by Wall Street analysts and other financial institutions, which help a company raise capital when needed. Legislators and governmental agencies tend to act more sympathetically toward companies with strong and positive reputations. Lawmakers may be less inclined to pursue actions that might hurt the business. Members of regulatory agencies will be less likely to believe rumors of wrongdoing.

Brand Names and Brand Types

objective 2.2

What are the different types of brands and brand names?

A brand name provides the overall banner for operations. David Placek, president and founder of Lexicon, Inc., said, "The brand name is really the cornerstone of a company's relationship with its customers. It sets an attitude and tone and is the first step toward a personality."[7] Brand names can be placed into four categories based on their actual, implied, or visionary meaning (see Figure 2.5).[8]

Overt names include American Airlines, Maxwell House Coffee, and BMW Motorcycles USA. *Implied names* include FedEx and Home Depot. *Conceptual names*, such as Google, Twitter, and Krispy Kreme, take a different approach. The name "Google" evokes a vision of a place where an endless number of items can be found, and "Krispy

◀ **FIGURE 2.5**
Categories of Brand Names

- **Overt names.** Reveal what a company does.
- **Implied names.** Contain recognizable words or word parts that convey what a company does.
- **Conceptual names.** Capture the essence of what a company offers.
- **Iconoclastic names.** Represent something unique, different, and memorable.

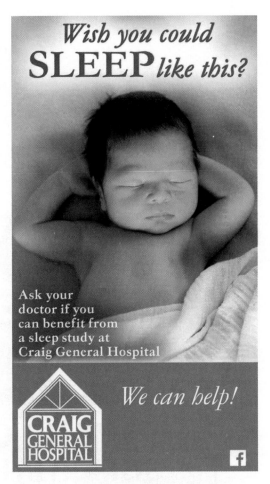

Kreme" suggests confectionaries filled with tasty crème. Samsung, Nabisco, and Reebok are examples of *iconoclastic names*.

Marketing the first two categories (overt and implied) should be easier because consumers more readily recall the name, which implies the type of good or service offered. The other two categories (conceptual and iconoclastic) necessitate greater efforts to ensure that consumers connect the name with the product offered. Figure 2.6 provides backgrounds for some well-known brand names.

Developing a brand name can generate a great deal of excitement and interest in a company. For example, approximately 1,000 Kraft Heinz employees from around the world submitted more than 1,700 names for a new high-growth snack business spun off by Kraft Heinz. The conceptual name that was chosen, Mondelez, combines "monde" the Latin word for "world" with "delez," a new word that conveys "delicious." The name fit well with the company's purpose, which is to make today delicious.[9]

Brand names develop histories. They have personalities. A current trend in branding involves creating a human persona or personality for the brand. Key human traits that brands espouse include customer empathy, talking and acting like people, and empowering individuals. The copy in the Maxwell House coffee ad on the next page contains a play on the words "stay grounded" by referring to both the coffee grounds and the human characteristic of being grounded.

The powerful impact branding has on purchase behaviors means that marketers should make branding decisions thoughtfully. Figure 2.7 identifies several types of brands.

▲ Craig General Hospital is an overt name because it reveals what the organization does.

- Google—name started as a joke about the way search engines search for information. The word googol is one followed by 100 zeros.
- Lego—combination of Danish phrase "leg godt" which means "play well" and Latin word lego which means "I put together."
- Reebok—alternative spelling of "rhebok" which is an African antelope.
- Skype—original name was "sky-peer-to-peer," which was changed to "skyper" then to "skype."
- Verizon—combination of Latin word "veritas" which means "truth" and horizon.
- Volkswagen—created by Adolph Hitler as a car for the masses that could transport 2 adults and 3 children at speeds up to 62 mph. Name means "people's car."
- Yahoo—word from Jonathan Swift's book Gulliver's Travels, which represented a repulsive, filthy creature that resembled Neanderthal man. Yahoo! founders, Jerry Yang and David Filo considered themselves to be yahoos.

◀ **FIGURE 2.6**
Origins of Some Unique Brand Names

▶ **FIGURE 2.7**
Types of Brands

- **Family brands.** A group of related products sold under one name.
- **Brand extension.** The use of an established brand name on products or services not related to the core brand.
- **Flanker brand.** The development of a new brand sold in the same category as another product.
- **Co-branding.** The offering of two or more brands in a single marketing offer.
- **Ingredient branding.** The placement of one brand within another brand.
- **Cooperative branding.** The joint venture of two or more brands into a new product or service.
- **Complementary branding.** The marketing of two brands together for co-consumption.
- **Private brands.** Proprietary brands marketed by an organization and sold within the organization's outlets.

▼ This advertisement for Maxwell House coffee features a play on words to convey the human characteristic of staying grounded.

Family Brands

Many brands produce family trees. A **family brand** means a company offers a series or group of products under one brand name. The Campbell's brand applies to lines of soups and other vegetable products. Consumers seeing the Campbell's brand expect a certain level of quality in existing products and any product line addition or modification, such as Healthy Choice soups. These transfer associations occur as long as the new product remains within the same product category. When the additional products are not related to the brand's core merchandise, the transfer of loyalty does not occur as easily.

Brand Extensions

A **brand extension** involves the use of an established brand name on new goods or services. The extension might not be related to the core brand. Nike has been successful in extending its brand name to a line of clothing. Black & Decker effectively extended its brand name to new types of power tools, but was not as successful in extending the brand to small kitchen appliances.

Flanker Brands

As an alternative to brand extensions, a **flanker brand** is the development of a new brand by a company in a good or service category in which it currently has a brand offering. Procter & Gamble's primary laundry detergents are Cheer and Tide. Over the years, P&G introduced a number of additional brands, such as Era, Dreft, and Gain (see Figure 2.8). P&G's

Body Wash & Soap	Laundry & Fabric Care	Hair Care
• Ivory	• Bounce	• Aussie
• Olay	• Cheer	• Head & Shoulders
• Old Spice	• Downy	• Herbal Essences
• Safeguard	• Dreft	• Pantene
• Secret	• Era	
	• Febreze Air Fresheners	
	• Gain	
	• Tide	

◀ **FIGURE 2.8**
Select Brands Sold by
Proctor & Gamble

marketing team creates flanker brands to appeal to target markets a brand does not reach. This helps the company offer a more complete line of products and reach a higher percentage of customers. It also establishes barriers to entry for competing firms.

A flanker brand may be introduced when company leaders conclude that vending the product under the current brand name might adversely affect the overall marketing program. Several years ago, Hallmark's marketers created the flanker brand Shoebox Greetings to sell cards in discount stores as well as Hallmark outlets. At first, the Hallmark brand was only sold in retail stores carrying the Hallmark name. The marketing team discovered that although Shoebox Greeting cards are lower priced, they allow Hallmark to attract a larger percentage of the market, even in its own stores.

Firms such as Nestlé that operate in low-end or middle markets may use flanker brands to compete in high-end markets. The Nestlé brands San Pellegrino and Perrier are more mainstream; however, the company did not have a premium brand to compete with Smartwater, Fiji, and Evian until the introduction of Resource. Women who are trendier, earn higher incomes, and are around age 35 were the target market. The ad campaign promoted Resource by noting that it provides more than hydration. The new premium brand featured total "electrolytenment," and was packaged in bottles that were 50 percent recycled plastic content.[10]

Flanker brands are used in international expansion. Procter & Gamble sells Ariel laundry detergent in Argentina, Brazil, Chile, Mexico, Peru, and Venezuela, but not in the United States. Offering different brands for specific markets helps a firm to operate in international markets.

Co-Branding

Co-branding, or **alliance branding**, is the combination or alliance of two brands and can take three forms: ingredient branding, cooperative branding, and complementary branding (see Figure 2.9). **Ingredient branding** involves the placement of one brand within another brand, such as Intel microprocessors in Dell computers or Nestlé chocolate in Pillsbury brownie mix. **Cooperative branding** is a joint venture in which two or more brands are placed in a new good or service, such as when Citibank combines American Airlines and VISA into a credit card. **Complementary branding** is the marketing of two brands together to encourage co-consumption or co-purchases, such as Velveeta cheese marketed with Rotel Tomatoes and Diced Green Chilies.

Co-branding succeeds when it builds brand equity in both brands. Wholly Guacamole formed brand alliances with several brands including Sonic, Disney, Schlotzksy's, and Jennie-O. According to Tracy Altman of Wholly Guacamole, the advertising and

◀ **FIGURE 2.9**
Forms of Co-Branding

▲ Wholly Guacamole developed a brand alliance with Sonic.

marketing budgets of many brands are stretched extremely thin and at the same time greater results are expected. One way to maximize advertising dollars is to develop alliances with other brands.[11]

Co-branding involves some risk. If the relationship fails to do well in the marketplace, both brands may be hurt. When one brand suffers, it can impact the sales of the other. For instance, a few years ago rumors surfaced that aspartame might contribute to certain types of cancer. Both NutraSweet and Equal contain aspartame. Sales of products such as Diet Coke that featured the co-brand NutraSweet on product labels began to slip. To reverse this trend, Diet Coke and other products containing aspartame went on the offensive to convince consumers the product was safe.

While risk cannot be eliminated, alliances between highly compatible brands of goods and services generally will be less precarious. Ingredient and cooperative branding tend to be less risky than complementary branding because both companies have more at stake and devote greater resources to ensure success.

For small companies and brands that are not as well known, co-branding can be an effective strategy. Finding a well-known brand willing to create an alliance with a lesser-known product may be difficult. When such an alliance forms, the co-brand relationship often builds brand equity for the lesser-known brand more than the established brand.

Brand Logos

objective 2.3

What are the characteristics of effective logos?

A **brand logo** is the symbol used to identify a brand. It should be designed to accentuate the brand name. A logo contributes an additional aspect to a brand's image. Organizations have spent millions of dollars selecting, meshing, and promoting brand names and logos. A strong name featuring a well-designed logo helps consumers remember brands and company messages. Consumers can reduce search time when they look for product names identified by effective logos. Quality logos and brand names should pass the four tests identified in Figure 2.10.[12]

Logos assist in-store shopping. The mind processes visuals faster than words. A logo may be more quickly recognized by shoppers. Logo recognition can occur at two levels. First, a consumer might remember seeing the logo in the past. An image stored in the consumer's memory will be jogged when it is seen at the store. Second, a familiar logo may remind the shopper of the brand or corporate name. This reminder can elicit positive (or negative) feelings regarding the branded item.

Successful logos elicit shared meanings among consumers, a process known as **stimulus codability**. Logos with high stimulus codability evoke consensual meanings within a culture or subculture. Consumers readily recognize logos with high degrees of codability, such as those used by Apple, McDonald's, and Pepsi. Companies that have logos with lower degrees of codability often spend more money on advertising. At first, Nike spent a considerable amount of dollars making the "Swoosh" more recognizable,

▶ **FIGURE 2.10**
Four Tests of Quality Logos and Names

- Recognizable
- Familiar
- Elicits a consensual meaning among those in the firm's target market
- Evokes positive feelings

because at first the logo by itself did not conjure any specific image of Nike. Now, almost everyone recognizes the Nike Swoosh. The brand name does not even have to be present.

Some companies modify logos as market conditions change. Others maintain the same logo for decades with only minor changes. John Deere holds a long-lasting logo, which was designed in 1876 and is still used. Figure 2.11 identifies some of the oldest logos and when they were created.

Creating quality logos can be challenging. Logos that pass the test of time are even more difficult. Logos are a reflection of a brand. Consequently, a cheap, poorly designed logo might suggest an inferior brand to consumers. Quality logos require careful thought, planning, and the expertise of designers who understand the principles behind creating or changing one into a version that will be effective. Figure 2.12 lists tips for creating or changing logos.

A logo does not have to be complex and contain every element of the brand's meaning. Simple logos can be valuable.[13] The Nike Swoosh and McDonald's arches are simple but powerful logos. A logo should complement the brand name and not overpower it, the product's packaging, or the product itself. Effective logos are media transferrable; they can be used in all media formats, from print ads to broadcast ads to the internet and social media. The best logos transcend cultures and can be featured around the world.

Changing logos has risks. Organizations cannot always predict consumer reactions, especially now with social media. American Airlines discovered this the hard way when the company tweeted via social media the message that its new logo on the tail of its planes reflected the spirit of America & innovative, progressive, and open to the world." The public saw it differently. One Twitter quote said, ". . . a new paint job [does not] make up for crappy service [and] operating model deficiencies." The new logo design's impact was best summarized by the words of Massimo Vignelli when he said, "It seems to me that there was no need for American Airlines to undertake such a change. . . . but many people do not understand the difference between design and styling, and believe in a change for the sake of change.[14]

Logo changes for IHOP and StubHub received the opposite reaction. The new logo for IHOP deleted the blue and red background framing and cast the O and P of IHOP into a smiley face designed to reflect IHOP's Twitter-savvy persona. According to Kirk

▲ When Community Trust Bank changed the company's name to Origin Bank, it required a new logo.

Company/Brand	Year Company Founded	Year Logo First used
John Deere	1837	1876
Coca-Cola	1886	1886
Johnson & Johnson	1886	1886
Union Pacific Railroad	1862	1888
Prudential Life Insurance	1875	1896
Campbell's Soup	1869	1898
General Electric	1892	1900
Goodyear	1898	1901
Sherwin-Williams	1866	1905
DuPont	1802	1907

◀ **FIGURE 2.11**
Some of the Oldest Logos

- The logo is a reflection of the brand
- Creating logos requires knowledge and expertise
- Use professional designers
- Make the logo simple
- Make the logo media transferrable

◀ **FIGURE 2.12**
Tips for Creating or Changing Logos

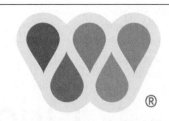

THE WATER INSTITUTE OF THE GULF

▲ This logo for The Water Institute of the Gulf was created by advertising agency Zehnder Communications.

Thompson, Vice-President of Marketing, the new logo design reflected the essence of IHOP, delivering world-famous pancakes that make customers smile and offers great memories shared with family and friends.[15]

StubHub's marketing team decided to redesign the company's logo in order to help redefine its identity. The new version removed the two tickets from the exclamation point and outlined the brand name with a dark blue border. Changing the company's mission into providing customers with a whole-event experience rather than just being a ticket re-seller was the goal. In addition to finding tickets, consumers can use the site to find information about where to eat and park, which modes of transportation would work best, and even what the weather is likely to be. Changing the logo represented an essential component of StubHub's business evolution.[16]

Changing logos can be expensive. Vice president of Pepsi, Frank Cooper, noted that a change was needed in the Pepsi logo to move the brand out of traditional mass marketing to convey a more dynamic and alive brand that is engaged with consumers. The new logo took five months to create and cost more than $1 million. Additional costs were incurred when the company placed the new logo on delivery trucks, vending machines, stadium signage, and point-of-purchase materials.[17]

Identifying the Desired Brand Image

objective 2.4

What elements are involved in identifying, creating, rejuvenating, or changing a brand's image?

When creating a program to promote a desired brand image, the marketing team first evaluates its current image. Marketers study the brand's image in order to identify its strengths and weaknesses. This helps to compare the current image with competitors. The marketing team also tries to discover how those outside of a company view the brand.

Once a team understands how various groups view the brand, decisions can be made regarding ways to correct misperceptions and/or build on the image that customers currently hold. Marketers then tailor future communications to promote the target image. These messages are sent to every constituency, including customers, suppliers, and employees.

At one time Nokia was the market leader in the mobile phone industry. Recently, after years of declining sales and a lower market share, the company became more of an underdog and was forced to act more like a challenger. As the market leader, the company sought to defend its share. The new goal of Nokia, according to CMO Tuula Rytilä, was to reignite the brand by bringing meaning, relevancy, and emotion to it. The messages were created to resonate with customers in the United States, and also those in Europe, China, and India.[18]

Creating the Right Brand Image

The right image sends a clear message about the unique nature of an organization and its products. A strong image accurately portrays what the firm sells, even in large corporations that offer multiple brands. As an example, the top management team at Kraft Heinz developed the phrase "Make today delicious" in an effort to unite the corporation and its various brands by focusing its employees in a more cohesive direction.[19]

In a business-to-business operation, creating the right image can be challenging. Scott Equipment sells new and used construction, agricultural, and industrial equipment. The company was founded in 1939 and grew to 25 locations in five different states. Scott's management team and marketing director Jamie Salter faced a difficult circumstance in which each location took care of its own marketing and advertising, which had the effect of creating 25 different brand images. Recognizing the need to create a consistent image among all of its outlets, Scott Equipment hired the New Orleans-based Peter Mayer advertising agency. The agency worked to unify communications, promoting one common brand image while at the same time allowing each location some flexibility in portraying that image. As shown in the advertisement on the next page, the Peter Mayer agency helped develop the tagline "Heavy-Duty Commitment" as an integral part of Scott's brand image. The key message to business buyers was that Scott was committed to providing quality "heavy-duty" equipment and support to its customers.[20]

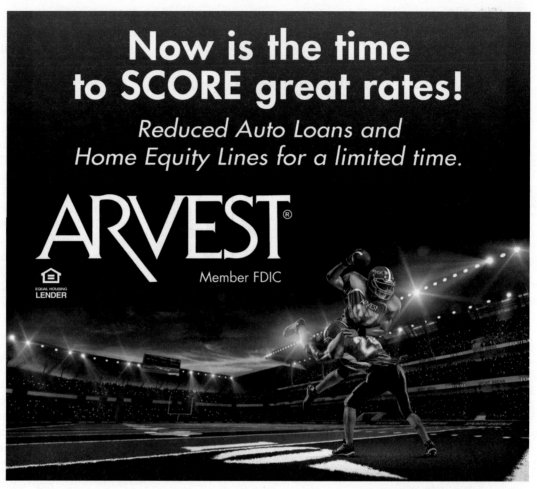

▲ Creating the right brand image for Arvest bank begins with identifying its current image.

Rejuvenating a Brand's Image

Rejuvenating an image helps a firm sell new products and can attract new customers. At the same time, reinforcing previous aspects of an image enables the company to retain loyal patrons and those who are comfortable with the original version. Quality image reengineering programs require companies to remain consistent with a previous image while at the same time incorporating new elements to expand the firm's target audience.

Successful rejuvenation includes attention to four key areas (see Figure 2.13).[21] First, former customers need to rediscover the brand. For these individuals, brand involvement evokes nostalgia. For other consumers, usually in the younger age groups, the brand represents a totally new experience. Connecting the nostalgic and new consumer groups requires attention to some timeless value such as authenticity, simplicity, or a compelling brand story or heritage. When making this connection, the message should stay true to what originally made the brand great. Then the brand can be contemporized. Successful rejuvenation involves building a brand community through social

- Help former customers rediscover the brand
- Offer timeless consumer value
- Stay true to original, but contemporize
- Build a community

◀ **FIGURE 2.13**
Keys to Successful Image Rejuvenation

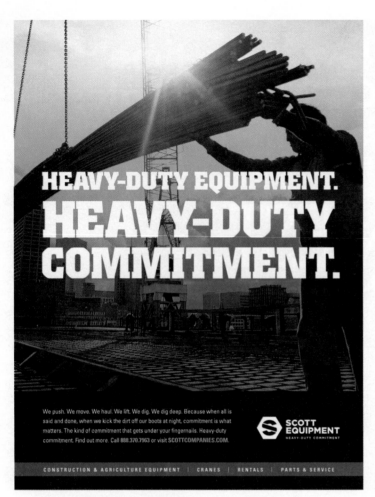

▲ The goal of Scott Equipment's rebranding campaign was to present a consistent image to its customers across all 25 locations.

media, mobile technologies, and interactive marketing techniques. Energizing brand advocates and influencers to spread the word about the "new and improved" version of the brand becomes the goal.

L'eggs represents a once highly-visible brand that recently achieved rejuvenation. Twenty years ago, the slogan "Nothing beats a great pair of L'eggs" was well known, as was the jingle that went with it. When the fashion industry changed and fewer females wore hosiery, L'eggs brand name and market share almost vanished. Angela Hawkins of Hanes Brands (corporate owner of L'eggs), said, "We wanted to move on, contemporize, and modernize [the L'eggs brand]. We needed to speak to a new generation, [but] we wanted to stay true to our brand positioning and personality, which is fun and kind of flirty." In addition to a new website, L'eggs developed a strong presence in social media and developed a new slogan "You're in luck. You're in L'eggs." L'eggs also used television and print advertising to reach its target market, women ages 18 to 34.[22]

Changing a Brand's Image

Completely changing the image people hold regarding a company or a brand is extremely difficult. Attempting to change an image becomes necessary when target markets have begun to shrink or disappear or when the brand's image no longer matches industry trends and consumer expectations. At that point, company leaders consider what they wish to change, why, and how they intend to accomplish it.

Several years ago, the retailer Target faced a unique situation when the companied tried to buy advertising space in *Vogue* magazine. Target was told "no." Tom Novak, president of Target's advertising agency (Peterson Milla Hooks), said the company received a letter from *Vogue* stating "We don't want your money because including a brand like Target would diminish the quality of our advertising." As a result,

▶ Target developed an aggressive advertising campaign designed to alter its brand image.

Target and its advertising agency realized that the company had an image of being a "dowdy Midwestern discounter." The Peterson Milla Hooks agency faced the challenge of designing an advertising and communications program that would change that image for media outlets such as *Vogue* as well as current and new customers.

Target attacked its image problem on two fronts. First, company leaders changed the product mix by including designer labels, such as a collection from the Italian fashion house Missoni. Second, Target's advertising agency created a campaign entitled "Signs of the Times" designed to elevate the Target brand rather than sell merchandise. Marketers positioned Target as a place where consumers could purchase high-end designer lamps, clothes, and other merchandise for less. The Peterson Milla Hooks agency created the now famous red and white bull's-eye image that consumers recognize as Target's logo. The efforts changed the image of Target among consumers as well as with media outlets. In a recent issue, Target placed a 20-page insert as well as an advertisement on the back cover of *Vogue*.[23]

At times, changing an image requires trying to influence views of the product or service category. The two advertisements for Maxwell House coffee in this section were created by the mcgarrybowen agency. The campaign seeks to persuade consumers that gourmet coffee is available at grocery stores and not just from coffee shops.

Developing and Building Powerful Brands

Developing a strong brand begins with discovering why consumers buy a brand and why they rebuy the brand. When assessing a brand, marketing professionals ask questions such as:

- Where does your brand stand now?
- What are your objectives?
- What are you doing to build your brand and business?

▲ These Maxwell House coffee advertisements seek to change consumer perceptions by suggesting that they can purchase and enjoy gourmet coffee at home.

objective 2.5

How are brands developed, built, and sustained in order to build brand equity and fend off perceptions of brand parity?

- What are your brand's strengths? Weaknesses?
- Which opportunities should be pursued first? Where are the pitfalls?[24]

The answers to these inquiries assist the company's marketing team or its agency in developing a plan that cultivates a stronger brand position.

A primary feature that keeps a brand strong occurs when it contains something **salient** to customers, which can come from several sources. A product or brand that provides benefits consumers consider important and of higher quality than other brands enjoys salience. The view that the brand represents a good value also creates this advantage. The brand may be deemed superior to others because its image leads to customer loyalty based on such salient properties.[25]

Powerful brands result from careful planning. Figure 2.14 identifies the ingredients required to build powerful brands including Google, IBM, Apple, Microsoft, Coca-Cola, and McDonald's. As shown, strong brands require substantial investments. These expenditures create the communications needed to effectively portray the brand to consumers and businesses.

▼ Skyjacker built a high level of brand equity through domination in the vehicle suspension market.

Branding begins with awareness, which may be achieved by featuring the brand name prominently in repeated advertisements and other marketing messages. Repetition captures the buyer's attention. It increases the odds that a brand and the accompanying message will be stored in a consumer's long-term memory and recalled later during a purchase process.

Brands should be authentic or unique in some manner. The brand name should be associated with the product's most prominent characteristic that makes it stand out from competitors. Many consumers connect Crest with "cavity prevention." Coca-Cola seeks to associate its name with a product that is "refreshing." For BMW, it is "performance driving," and for 3M it is "innovation." Marketers seek to identify the "one thing" the brand stands for, that consumers recognize, and that will be salient to them. When these factors are present, more powerful brand recognition occurs. In the marketplace for automotive suspension systems, the Skyjacker brand is well-known to consumers, distributors, and automobile manufacturers.

Business and retail customers trust powerful brands. **Trust** is the customer's belief in the efficacy and reliability of the brand. It can be established over time through personal experiences. Trust results from the product performing consistently and fulfilling a promise, its authenticity, and its uniqueness. For decades, Tide has consistently kept its pledge to consumers. To sustain that trust, the

- Invest in the brand
- Create awareness
- Offer authenticity uniqueness
- Build trust
- Deliver an experience
- Offer value
- Utilize social media
- Utilize mobile
- Act responsibly

◀ **FIGURE 2.14**
Building Powerful Brands

marketing team at Tide continues to pay attention to the brand's image. Recent advertisements note how well Tide cleans clothes, using themes such as "Tide knows fabrics best," "Dirt can't hide from Tide," "If it's got to be clean, it's got to be Tide," and "Style is an option. Clean is not." To make sure consumers see and hear the message, Tide employs traditional mass media advertising; alternative media, including YouTube and Facebook; signs known as *wild postings* in urban locations; and sponsorship of events in South Beach, Florida, and other resort areas. The company enhances its brand image by delivering cleaning products to victims in disaster areas, such as those affected by tornadoes and hurricanes.[26]

Powerful brands focus on providing an experience that can be customized and personalized. The iPhone, with more than 100,000 apps, allows users to customize the phone to fit their personalities. The brand becomes a central part of their lives. When delivered effectively, the experience creates a strong emotional bond between the consumer and the brand. The Apple, Nike, Harley Davidson, and Jeep brands enjoy strong communities of followers.

Retailers can develop similar experiences. Tom Novak of Peterson Milla Hooks, the advertising agency for Target, states "A lot of retailers focus on the transaction, but we really believe that an emotional connection trumps selling. Because you like Target, you feel better buying your toothpaste there even though you could buy it at Walmart.[27]

"Value" has become a buzz word in marketing. Consumers and businesses look for brands that offer the best value, which is a balance between quality and price. Currently, only seven percent of consumers focus entirely on price while discarding quality considerations. Even fewer individuals focus on quality without any price considerations.

Building powerful brands includes the effective use of social media. It should be authentic and in tune with the brand. Merely creating a Facebook page or posting videos to YouTube does not suffice. An effective social media strategy engages consumers and enriches their experiences with the brand.

Building brands incorporates the creative use of mobile advertising. Marketers for more powerful brands have discovered ways to use mobile to enhance the customer's experience through personalization and customization of content. Mobile advertising offers companies the opportunity to interact with customers anywhere at any time; however, the interaction should enhance the customer's experience and not be an intrusion. A text or an ad every time the user turns on her phone will quickly alienate even a brand loyal customer.

The final ingredient of a powerful brand results when the company acts ethically. Consumers want to purchase brands from companies that understand the importance of not harming the earth or people. Also, using sweat shops to produce products alienates customers. In essence, consumers tend to prefer brands sold by socially responsible companies.

▲ Gulf Coast Seafood crated an effective app as part of its mobile advertising campaign.

Brand Loyalty

Brand loyalty constitutes the ultimate objective of building powerful brands. Consumers express loyalty when they purchase only one brand. They consider no other choice, regardless of price differences. Figure 2.15 identifies some of the major brands of vehicles and

▶ FIGURE 2.15
Top Vehicle Models and
Brand Imagery

Model	Percent Loyal	Imagery
Ford F-150	45%	Functional, reliable, leader
Honda Civic	40%	Sensible, safe, smart
Toyota Camry	49%	Economical, reliable, conservative
Honda Accord	44%	Reliable, safe, honest
Honda CR-V	44%	Sensible, economical, reliable
Chevrolet Silverado 1500	62%	Safe, honest, functional
Toyota Corolla	42%	Reliable, safe, functional
Ford Escape	54%	Technological, sporty, powerful
Ram 1500	46%	Powerful, sporty, bold

the percent of customers who recently purchased the brand that would be considered brand loyal. The percentage of loyal customers ranged from 40 for the Honda Civic to 62 for the Chevrolet Silverado 1500. The imagery connected with each vehicle also plays a role. For instance, the Ford F-150 was viewed as functional, reliable, and the leader in small trucks. On the other hand, the Ram 1500 was perceived as powerful, sporty, and bold.[28]

The Brand Keys Customer Loyalty Engagement Index (CLEI) suggests that emotion and value are the core drivers of brand loyalty, rather than rational thought based on product attributes. Loyalty results from the consumer's experience with the brand and emotional connection she has with it. In essence, loyalty represents what a brand stands for or means to the consumer on an emotional level.[29]

The degree to which the brand has established a unique or authentic proposition determines the value of the brand. Value depends heavily on the "delight factor," or the degree to which the brand exceeds basic expectations by delivering benefits or an emotional connection that enhances a consumer's day-to-day life. Using the Customer Loyalty Engagement Index, Brand Keys identified the top performing brands in 54 different product categories. Figure 2.16 identifies some of the top brands in select categories.

Brand Equity

Many companies encounter the brand parity problem, which takes place when consumers conclude that few tangible distinctions exist between competing brands in mature markets. Customers see only minor product differences and, in many product categories, even minor variations are difficult to identify.

In contrast, **brand equity** represents a set of characteristics that are unique to a brand. Equity helps to fight the brand parity problem. The perception of brand equity means that

Category	Top Brand	CLeI emotional engagement
Athletic Footwear	Skechers	86%
Bank	JP Morgan Chase	79%
Car Insurance	State Farm	82%
Casual Dining	Applebee's	82%
Cosmetics	Clinique	93%
Gasoline	Shell	80%
Major League Sports	NFL	86%
Pizza	Domino's	84%
Quick Service Restaurant	Subway	95%
Soft Drinks (Diet)	Diet Coke	89%

▶ FIGURE 2.16
Top Brands Based on Brand Keys
Customer Loyalty Engagement
Index (CLEI)

consumers view a good or service's brand name as different, better, and one that can be trusted. In business-to-business markets, brand equity influences selections in the buying decision-making process. Products with strong brand equity are often chosen over products with low brand equity or brands that employees in other firms know less about. The same scenario occurs in international markets. Brand equity opens doors to foreign firms, brokers, and retailers and provides privileges that products with low brand equity cannot obtain.

Brand equity dissuades consumers from looking for cheaper products, special deals, or other incentives. It prevents erosion of a product's market share, even when a proliferation of brands is coupled to promotional maneuvers by competitors.

Measuring Brand Equity

Assessing brand equity can be difficult. To do so, marketing experts apply brand metrics to measure which measure the return on branding investments. According to Millward Brown Optimor, a strong brand constitutes one of the most valuable assets a company holds and accounts for about one-third of shareholder value.[30]

There are no concrete, scientific, or quantitative methods available to measure brand equity, which remains an abstract concept. Consequently, marketers have developed four methods to measure it (see Figure 2.17). Arguments can be made for each. The personal preference of the company's CEO or the one that yields the highest value for a particular brand often dictates method selection.

Brand equity based on *financial value* estimates the future cash flows of a brand based on its unique strength and characteristics, which will then be discounted to determine a net present value. With the *stock market* approach, the financial value of the company is determined through stock valuation. Then, an estimate of the portion of the value allocated to brand equity & not physical assets can be made.

The third approach, *revenue premium*, compares a branded product to the same product without a brand name. To calculate a brand's revenue premium, the revenue generated by a particular brand will be compared to a private label brand. The difference is the revenue premium, or value of that brand, and would equate to the accrued brand equity.

The final method, *consumer value*, attempts to assess the value of a brand based on input from consumers. Typical measures include familiarity, quality, purchase considerations, customer satisfaction, and willingness to seek out the brand. The difficulty

▲ Kraft Singles enjoy a high level of brand equity, which produces brand loyalty.

- Financial value
- Stock market value
- Revenue premium
- Consumer value

▲ **FIGURE 2.17**
Methods of Measuring Brand Equity

▲ Origin Bank can evaluate its brand equity by measuring consumer value of the brand.

objective 2.6

What current trends affect private brands?

with this approach is that all of the measures are based on consumer attitudes. No concrete financial or accounting numbers are calculated.[31]

The CLEI index from Brand Keys described in the "Brand Loyalty" section of this chapter offers one example of the consumer value approach. Another is the "Most Beloved Brands" produced by APCO Worldwide from a survey of 70,000 consumers. The study measured eight emotional feelings consumers have toward a brand: understanding, approachability, relevance, admiration, curiosity, identification, empowerment, and pride.[32] Figure 2.18 displays the top 10 most beloved brands using this methodology.

Private Brands

Private brands, private labels, and store brands are proprietary brands marketed by an organization and are normally distributed exclusively within the organization's outlets. Private brands have experienced a rollercoaster ride in terms of popularity and sales. To some individuals, private brands carry the connotation of a lower price and inferior quality. Historically, the primary audiences for private labels were price-sensitive individuals and low-income families. This is no longer the case. Retailers invest significant dollars to develop private brands, which account for approximately 18 percent of total retail sales in the United States.[33]

Many consumers report that they cannot tell the difference in quality between national brands and private brands. In a Nielsen survey of consumers, two-thirds said private brands are equivalent to national brands. Another survey suggested that only 19 percent of consumers believe national brands are worth paying more money for.[34] These changes, as well as others that have occurred in the private-brand arena, are summarized in Figure 2.19.[35]

Rank	Company	Emotional Index
1	Disney	74.7
2	Yahoo!	74.3
3	Google	74.2
4	Sony	74.1
5	Nestle	73.3
6	Auchan	72.9
7	Netflix	72.8
8	Whole Foods	72.7
9	Apple	72.7
10	Lowe's	72.5

▶ **FIGURE 2.18**
Top 10 Most Loved Brands

Advantages to Retailers

Although private labels tend to be priced between five and 20 percent lower than national brands, they generate higher gross margins than national brands because middlemen are not used. Higher margins enable retailers to earn larger profits on private brands or, alternatively, to reduce the prices of the private brands to make them more attractive to price-sensitive consumers. Retailers that maintain the higher markup on private labels have the opportunity to use some of the margin for advertising and promotions of the brands.

One emerging trend in retailing indicates that loyalty to retail stores has been growing while loyalty to individual brands has been on the decline. Rather than going to outlets selling specific brands, many shoppers visit specific stores and buy from the brands offered by those stores. The increase in loyalty to retailers has caused several stores to expand the number of private-brand products offered. Doing so requires the retailer to develop private brands that are congruent with consumer images of the company.[36]

▲ Private labels are often displayed in retail store windows and made to look as attractive as manufacturers' brands.

Savvy retailers recognize the value of private labels and how they can be used to differentiate the store from competing retailers and from national brands. These stores promote these labels as distinctive brands aimed toward specific market segments. Retailers can emphasize meeting consumer needs with a quality product rather than simply focusing on price.

JC Penney has been successfully utilizing private branding in apparel lines. The company offers more than 30 private labels, accounting for more than 40 percent of sales.[37] Liz Sweeney of JC Penney stated, "We are dedicated to creating and managing winning private brands that develop customer loyalty. This means managing and marketing our key private brands as true brands versus labels.[38]

Emerging trends in the use of private labels include retailers spending marketing dollars on improving labels, on designing noticeable in-store displays, and on packaging. Retailers without large national ad budgets rely more on displays and attractive packaging. A drab, cheap package does not convey the message that the private brand represents the equivalent or better alternative to a national brand. Many consumers blur the distinction between private labels and national brands. Unless a customer is familiar with the store's private brand labels, the individual might believe he is purchasing a national brand.[39]

Some retailers go one step further by designing the advertising of private brands apart from the store's regular advertising program. Recently, Sears launched a series of advertisements featuring its Kenmore and Craftsman brands. Sears was only mentioned in the context of being the place to purchase Kenmore and Craftsman products. Kmart employed a similar approach for its private labels including Bongo, Jaclyn Smith, and Joe Boxer. The company promoted these private brands separately in order to establish the

- Improved quality
- Perceived as a value purchase
- Higher loyalty toward retail outlets and lower loyalty toward specific brands

- Used to differentiate retail outlets
- Increased advertising of private brands
- Increased quality of in-store displays and packaging of private brands

◀ **FIGURE 2.19**
Changes in Private Brands

▲ The Sears private label, Kenmore, is now advertised as a national brand.

names as bona fide brands, competing head-to-head with national brands and to distance them from the retail parent.

Responses from Manufacturers

Manufacturers respond to the inroads made by private labels in various ways. Figure 2.20 lists some tactics.[40] A manufacturer can focus on a few core brands rather than split advertising dollars among a large number of brands. Core brands are advertised heavily, which helps the manufacturer maintain its brand name and reinforces the idea that consumers are making the right decision when they purchase the manufacturer's national brand. Creating bonds with consumers both before and after purchases will be the goal.

Manufacturers may attempt to reduce the impact of private labels on sales by expanding product offerings. Aggressively introducing new products and new versions of current products may help a manufacturer maintain the loyalty of its current customers while being seen as an innovator. To further combat the impact of private brands, manufacturers can focus on in-store selling to emphasize core brands. Also, alternative methods of marketing, such as brand communities and social networks, might increase loyalty to a brand rather than a private label.

Packaging

objective 2.7

How can packaging and labels support an IMC program domestically and in foreign settings?

A product's package represents the final opportunity to make an impression on a consumer. Packaging constitutes a marketing activity as much as television advertising and social media. Marketing surveys reveal that only 31 percent of purchases are planned prior

▶ **FIGURE 2.20**

Tactics Used by Manufacturers to Combat Private Labels

- Focus on core brands
- Increase advertising
- Introduce new products

- Focus on in-store selling and packaging
- Use alternative methods of marketing

to reaching a retail outlet. This means 69 percent of consumers make purchase decisions while in the store. Other research indicates that when an individual walks within 10 to 15 feet of a product, the item has as little as three seconds to catch the person's attention.[41]

Figure 2.21 displays the primary purposes of packaging. Currently, packages and labels are viewed as a key part of a company's integrated marketing communications program. It makes little sense to spend millions of dollars on advertising only to lose the sale in the store because of a lackluster, unattractive, or dull package.

Consumers often make retail purchase decisions based on familiarity with a brand or product at a specific store. Consequently, a unique and attractive package that captures the buyer's attention increases the chances the product will be purchased, sometimes as an impulse buy. In the grocery market, customers prefer fast, convenient, portable, and fresh foods. Someone who encounters an inferior package will be more likely to switch to another brand.[42]

▲ Packaging represents the final opportunity to make an impression on consumers.

Not long ago, the marketing team at Alcoa Rigid Packaging watched people as they purchased groceries and stocked refrigerators. The team noticed that the standard 3-by-4-can (12-pack) beverage box was too large for the refrigerator, and consumers would only take out a few cans at a time to cool. It seemed logical that if more cans were cold, consumers might drink more. This observation led to the design of a box that was easier and more convenient to use, the longer and slimmer 6-by-2-can self-dispensing box. The new design fits into the refrigerator door or on a shelf. As an individual takes out a can, a new one automatically slides down. The innovation improved sales for both Alcoa and soft-drink manufacturers, who embraced the new package.[43]

Labels

Labels on packages serve several functions. First, they must meet legal requirements. This includes identifying the product contained in the package and any other specific information about content, such as nutritional information on foods. The Food and Drug Administration (FDA) regulates food labels in the United States. Many companies print warranties and guarantees on product labels.

The label represents another marketing opportunity. It can make the difference in whether an individual purchases a particular item. Simple, yet powerful, changes can be made to influence purchasing behaviors. For Honest Tea, it was a matter of the label for the peach tea showing the peach cut open rather than a whole peach. The same approach

- Protect product
- Provide for ease of shipping and handling
- Provide for easy placement on shelves
- Prevent or reduce theft
- Prevent tampering (drugs and food)
- Meet consumer needs for speed, convenience, and portability
- Communicate marketing message

◀ **FIGURE 2.21**
Primary Purposes of Packaging

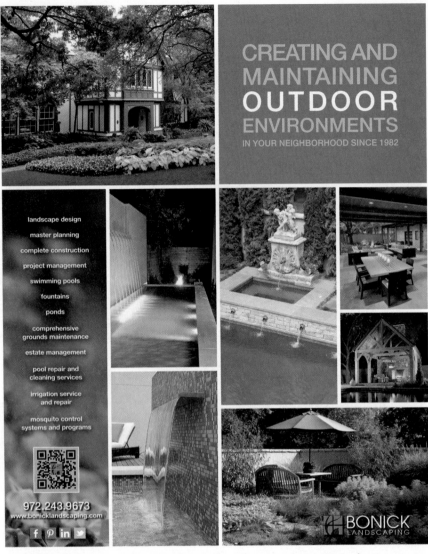

CREATING AND MAINTAINING **OUTDOOR** ENVIRONMENTS

IN YOUR NEIGHBORHOOD SINCE 1982

landscape design

master planning

complete construction

project management

swimming pools

fountains

ponds

comprehensive grounds maintenance

estate management

pool repair and cleaning services

irrigation service and repair

mosquito control systems and programs

972.243.9673

www.bonicklandscaping.com

BONICK LANDSCAPING

▲ This advertisement for Bonick Landscaping contains a QR code consumers can access for more information.

was applied to pomegranate tea; a picture of a cut pomegranate instead of a whole one was featured on the label.[44]

A typical label contains the company's logo and the brand name. Labels may reveal special offers and other tie-ins, such as a box of cereal with a toy inside. Labels often carry terms designed to build consumer interest and confidence. The words "gourmet," "natural," "premium," "adult formula," and "industrial strength" make a product appear to be a better buy. A company's image, brand, logo, and theme extend to the design of the package and label, which grants the marketing team the opportunity to make the sale when the consumer is in the store making a purchasing decision.

The placement of QR codes for consumers to access with mobile devices represents a recent trend in labeling. Consumers use the codes to access product information as well as videos or instructions about how to use the product. While in a retail store, consumers can access via the QR code information about the product to see if it fits their needs. The information helps assure customers that they are purchasing the kind of product, size, or style that satisfies their desires.

QR codes can be linked to Facebook, Pinterest, and Instagram sites. Marketers hope the consumer will "like" the brand on Facebook and follow it on Twitter or other social media sites. Realizing the power of word-of-mouth and peer-to-peer recommendations, the goal becomes to have consumers help spread the word about the brand.

Ethical Issues in Brand Management

A variety of ethical issues are associated with brand management. For years, the most common problem, *brand infringement*, occurred when a company created a brand name that closely resembled a popular or successful brand, such as Korrs beer. In that case, the courts deemed the brand an intentional infringement on the Coors brand, and the name was abandoned. Another brand-infringing company that was forced by the courts to give up its name was Victor's Secret.

Brand infringement becomes more complex when a brand is so well-established that it may be considered a generic term, such as a Kleenex tissue or a Xerox copy. Band-Aid encountered the problem in the 1970s, forcing the marketing team to make sure the product was identified as "Band-Aid Brand Strips" rather than simply "band aids," to prevent the competition from using the name. The most vulnerable new brand names might be Google and Twitter because the names have entered everyday conversation, as in "I googled myself" or "I tweeted you."

According to many sources, *cyber squatting*, or *domain squatting*, constitute another form of unethical behavior. The practice involves buying domain names (e.g., **barnesandnoble.bus, kohls.com, labronjames.net**, etc.) that are valuable to specific people or businesses in the hopes of making a profit by reselling the name. Any new company trying to build a presence in the online marketplace might find itself stifled by domain squatters. Names matter. Cyber squatters take advantage of that to make profits at someone else's expense.

International Implications

In international markets, product development, branding, and maintaining an image are more complex. As noted previously, firms can employ either an *adaptation* strategy or a *standardization* strategy in promotional programs. These two approaches apply to the products as well as to brand names. With standardization, the same brand name and product are sold in all countries. With adaptation, the brand and/or the actual product may be different in each country or region. This can mean a product may be viewed as a local brand. Mr. Clean uses the adaptation brand approach for some products. Items are sold under the names of Mr. Proper and Maestro Limpio as well as other names in various countries.

Using a standardized global brand reduces costs. Instead of advertising each local brand with a separate communication strategy, one standardized message can be sent. Standardized global brands also allow for the transference of best practices from one country to another. Further, purchasing a standardized global brand may be viewed as a better choice than buying a local brand. The global brand might have a higher perceived quality. The consumer's self-concept of being cosmopolitan, sophisticated, and modern can be enhanced when buying a global brand. As the world continues to shrink through advances in telecommunications, consumers are becoming increasingly similar, displaying comparable consumer characteristics and purchase behaviors. This may lead to greater use of standardized global brands.

Recently, Banana Republic moved to a global brand-management structure across its 700 stores worldwide. The goal was to establish a single brand voice and consistent brand experience worldwide. The challenge was to create a brand voice that resonated with long-time customers as well as new customers. In analyzing Banana Republic's customer base, Catherine Sadler (chief marketing officer) was "struck by the common customer profile that I see in all of our stores around the world." She described this customer as fashion aware and tech-savvy.[45]

A common global integrated marketing communications (GIMC) strategy is to "think globally, but act locally." This approach applies to branding. Developing global brands might be the ultimate goal; however, the marketing team still considers each local market's unique features and should be sensitive to supporting and developing local brands. The success of a global brand largely depends on the brand's ability to adapt to local needs and tastes or, as Eileen Campbell, CEO of Millward Brown Group, noted, "Cultural relevance is important." For example, the "Real Beauty" campaign developed by Ogilvy and Mather for Unilever's Dove featured images of women in underwear in Western countries, but was modified to reveal a face behind a woman's veil for the Middle East.[46]

Packaging and labeling issues are complex for global firms. The label must meet legal requirements of the country in which the product is sold. An attractive label can be an attention-getting device that draws the consumer to the product. Labels remain vitally important in the United States as well as in Asian countries where purchases, in part, are driven by the appeal of the label.[47] At the same time, some culturally-sensitive items,

▼ A market in Hong Kong.

such as lingerie and other personal products, carry labels that basically disguise or hide the contents. Packages must also be able to withstand the rigors of long-distance shipping, meet any legal restrictions, and be as cost-effective as possible.

Summary

An effective integrated marketing communications program emphasizes a strong and positive brand image. A brand's image consists of the feelings consumers and business-to-business customers have toward the organization and each individual brand. Brands carry both tangible and intangible elements.

A brand name provides an overall banner. The logo accompanying the name presents the symbol used to identify the brand, helping to convey the overall image. Brands are names given to goods or services or groups of complementary products. Effective brands create an advantage, especially in mature markets containing fewer products or where service differences exist. Strong brands convey the most compelling benefits of the product, elicit proper consumer emotions, and help create loyalty.

Various versions of brands include family brands, flanker brands, and co-brands. In each, marketers build brand equity through domination or the recognition that the brand has one key advantage or characteristic.

Creating an effective image requires understanding of how various consumers and organizations view the firm before seeking to build or enhance an image. Rejuvenating an image involves reminding customers of their previous conceptions of the company while at the same time expanding into a closely related area of concern. A strongly established image becomes difficult, if not impossible, to change.

Private brands and private labels have grown in usage. Consumers view many private brands as having quality equal to or close to that of manufacturer brand names; however, they still expect price advantages in private label products.

Company leaders remain aware of legal and ethical brand challenges. Brand infringement remains both a domestic and international problem. The phenomenon of brands becoming generic may also affect a new generation of products and services.

International marketers utilize both standardization and adaptation tactics with regard to brands and products. Packages and labels must meet the legal and cultural needs of individual countries.

Key Terms

brand The word, term, or phrase featured as the name of a product, product line, or company

brand image The feelings consumers and businesses have about the overall organization as well as its individual products or product lines

family brand A strategy in which a company offers a series or group of products under one brand name

brand extension The use of an established brand name on goods or services not related to the core brand

flanker brand The development of a new brand by a company in a good or service category in which it currently has a brand offering

co-branding / alliance branding The marketing or alliance of two or more brands in a single marketing effort

ingredient branding A form of co-branding in which one brand is placed within another brand

cooperative branding A form of co-branding in which two firms create a joint venture of two or more brands into a new good or service

complementary branding A form of co-branding in which the marketing of two brands together encourages co-consumption or co-purchases

brand logo The symbol used to identify a brand, helping to convey the overall brand image

stimulus codability Feelings attached to items that evoke consensually held meanings within a culture or subculture

salient A situation in which consumers are aware of the brand, have it in their consideration sets (things they consider when making purchases), regard the product and brand as a good value, buy it or use it on a regular basis, and recommend it to others

trust A customer's belief in the efficacy and reliability of a brand

brand equity The perception that a good or service with a given brand name is different, better, and can be trusted

brand metrics Measures of returns on brand investments

private brands (also known as *private labels* and *store brands*) Proprietary brands marketed by an organization and normally distributed exclusively within the organization's outlets

MyMarketingLab

To complete the problems with the ⭐ in your MyLab, go to the end-of-chapter Discussion Questions.

Review Questions

2-1. Describe the concept of brand image. What are the tangible aspects of a brand image? What are the intangible aspects?

2-2. How does a brand image help customers? How does it help the specific company?

2-3. Describe the use of brand extension and flanker brand strategies.

2-4. Identify and describe three types of co-brands or alliance branding.

2-5. What is a brand logo? What are the characteristics of an effective logo?

2-6. What is meant by the term "stimulus codability?"

⭐**2-7.** How will company leaders know when they have created the desired brand image?

2-8. What four areas require attention when seeking to rejuvenate a firm's brand image?

2-9. What are the characteristics of a strong and effective brand name?

2-10. Explain the role of trust in creating a strong brand.

2-11. What is the difference between brand equity and brand parity?

2-12. What methods can be used to measure brand equity?

⭐**2-13.** How has private branding, or private labeling, changed in the past decade?

2-14. What role does a product's package play in the marketing program?

2-15. How can a label support an IMC program or advertising campaign?

2-16. What ethical issues are associated with brand management?

2-17. How do the concepts of standardization and adaptation apply to branding strategies?

Critical Thinking Exercises

DISCUSSION QUESTIONS

⭐**2-18.** Ashley Drake just purchased a small clothing boutique two blocks from your campus. The current name of the store is College Fashions. She feels she needs a new name that projects an image of offering trendy, hip fashions to your college's students. What name would you suggest? Discuss your brand name in terms of which category it fits and the four tests of quality names. To succeed, Ashley knows she needs to retain the store's current customers as well as gain new ones. Outline a plan to rejuvenate the company's brand image using the keys to image rejuvenation identified in Figure 2.5.

2-19. Henry and Becky Thompson plan to open a new floral and gift shop in Orlando, Florida. They want to project a trendy, upscale, and fashionable image. They are trying to decide on a name and a logo. What should be the name of the company? What kind of logo should be developed?

2-20. Brand image affects purchase decisions. Identify two brands you consider to hold a positive image, and explain why. Identify two brands that you believe should either change or rejuvenate their brand images,

and explain why. How can the change or rejuvenation be accomplished for each brand?

⭐**2-21.** Identify a brand that you have recently purchased that is not well-known, but you like. Using the concepts presented in the "Building Powerful Brands" section of this chapter, discuss how the brand you identified can be built into a powerful brand. Be specific.

2-22. Identify five different brands for which you have a high level of brand loyalty. Describe your level of loyalty and discuss why you are loyal. Explain how brand equity impacts your loyalty for each brand.

⭐**2-23.** Pick a private label that you have recently purchased. What is your evaluation of the private brand quality compared to national brands? The chapter discussed a number of changes in private label branding that has occurred (see Figure 2.19). Discuss each of these changes in relation to the private brand you picked.

2-24. Look through your cupboard and locate three packages that you believe are effective. Describe why they are effective. Choose three labels that are effective at capturing attention. What are the attention-getting aspects of each label?

Integrated Learning Exercises

2-25. Websites constitute an essential element of a brand's image. Access the websites of the following brands to get a feel for the image each brand tries to project.

Locate on YouTube an advertisement for each brand (supply the URL in your response). Is the image projected on the website consistent with the YouTube advertisement and the image portrayed in the other advertisements for the brand?

   a. *Sonic (*www.sonicdrivein.com*)*

   b. *Skechers (*www.skechers.com*)*

   c. *Clinique (*www.clinique.com*)*

   d. *Maxwell House Coffee (*www.maxwellhouse coffee.com*)*

2-26. A leading consulting firm that has been a leader in extending marketing knowledge and in the area of brand development is the Boston Consulting Group. Other companies that have actively been involved in brand development include Lexicon Branding and Corporate Branding. Access each firm's website. Describe the services provided by each firm.

   a. *Boston Consulting Group (*www.bcg.com*)*

   b. *Lexicon Branding, Inc. (*www.lexicon-branding.com*)*

   c. *Tenet Partners (*www.tenetpartners.com*)*

   d. *Brand Keys (*www.brandkeys.com*)*

2-27. Brand extension and flanker branding are common strategies for large corporations. Access the following websites. Identify the various brand extension strategies and flanker brands used by each company.

   a. *Procter & Gamble (*www.pg.com*)*

   b. *VF Corporation (*www.vfc.com*)*

   c. *General Mills (*www.generalmills.com*)*

2-28. Private labels provide a significant source of revenue for many retail stores and manufacturers. The Private Label Manufacturers' Association promotes manufacturers that produce private labels. Visit the organization's website at **www.plma.com**. Access each item on the menu. Summarize the information provided for each item.

2-29. Conduct an internet search for brand logos. Identify five logos that you think are well designed. Screen-capture the logos and explain what you think makes each logo effective. Identify five logos that you think are poorly designed. Screen-capture them and explain why you think they are ineffective.

2-30. Go to the authors' website at **clowbaack.net/video/ads.html**. Watch a television ad for each of the medical institutions: DuPage Medical Group, Terrebonne General Medical Center, and St. Francis Medical Center. For each of the TV ads, identify the primary message of the ad and the image conveyed by the TV ad. Be specific in describing each medical facility's image. If you had to choose among the three for medical services, which would you choose? Why?

2-31. Go to the authors' website at **clowbaack.net/video/ads.html**. Watch a television ad for each of the financial banking institutions: JD Bank, Ouachita Independent Bank, Progressive Bank, and Centric Federal Credit Union. For each of the TV ads, identify the primary message of the ad and the image conveyed by the ad. Be specific in describing each financial institution's image. If you had to choose among the four for banking services, which would you choose? Why?

Blog Exercises

Access the authors' blog for this text at the URLs provided to complete these exercises. Answer the questions posed on the blog.

2-32. Kenmore, Craftsman, and Diehard: **blogclowbaack.net/2014/05/07/private-brands-sears-chapter-2/**

2-33. Target: **blogclowbaack.net/2014/05/07/target-chapter-2/**

2-34. Branding: **blogclowbaack.net/2014/05/07/branding-chapter-2/**

Student Project

CREATIVE CORNER

The brand name and logo constitute critical elements a marketing manager considers when introducing a new product. Pick one of the products from the following list. Assume you are the product manager and your company has introduced a new brand within the product category. Your first task is to choose a brand name. Using the internet, identify three key competitors and make a case for how the brand name you select will help the item stand out in the marketplace. Once you have created your brand name, create a logo that will fit well with the brand name and will be distinctive on your product or the product's packaging.

PRODUCTS

   a. A new brand of skis for recreational boating

   b. A new line of eyeglasses

   c. A new chocolate candy bar

   d. A new line of jeans

   e. A new energy drink

   f. A new perfume or cologne

CASE 1 ▸ PRODUCT NAMES

Product names take many forms. One set of product name is called *descriptive of use*. Examples include Mop & Glo floor cleaner, Shake 'n Bake cooking additives, and Easy-Off Oven Cleaner. Another category, called *descriptive of contents*, invokes the nature of the item, such as Tums (for the tummy) and Gas X (for, well, you know). Wholly Guacamole constitutes such a name. A third type, *action-oriented*, means the product name implies some type of movement or action; Febreze suggests breeze moving through a stuffy room. Breathe Right Strips combine elements of product use, product content, and action.

In many instances, a strong brand name can inspire new approaches to naming specific products. One recent example took place with the development and launch of two new forms of vitamins. The Centrum brand enjoys a strong reputation in that industry. Most notably, the company's Centrum Silver line for older consumers has achieved a strong market share.

▴ Centrum Silver has achieved a strong market share among older consumers.

At the same time, other segments remain inviting targets. For example, the Flintstones line reaches younger consumers. One a Day targets active males and females among other more specific consumer groups. Both products are marketed by the Bayer Group. Flintstones vitamins for kids are chewable and easier to swallow. One a Day delivers multivitamins designed to help active adults remain healthy.

The Centrum brand (owned by Pfizer) combines the two elements (adult-oriented, chewable) in order to create two new products. VitaMints were launched using traditional television and radio advertising as well as additional venues such as Twitter and Facebook (which offered free samples). A second product, Centrum MultiGummies, received the same treatment.

Competition for vitamins comes from the herbal industry, where Nature's Own and other companies sell specific items along with multivitamin products. In addition, other food products, most notably the cereal Total, markets that advantage of providing "100% of the Daily Value of at least 11 vitamins and minerals." Campbell's V8 juice concentrates on Vitamins A and C.

Seeking to create interest in a new product line in a cluttered market is always difficult. The marketing team at Centrum believes that the combination of an innovative product and an effective marketing communications program can help the company achieve a greater market share and customer loyalty.

2-35. What type of product name is VitaMints? MultiGummies? Do you think such names will succeed? Why or why not?

2-36. Should the Centrum brand be emphasized in marketing VitaMints, or should the product name stand alone in the promotional program? Defend your answer.

2-37. Do you think marketing messages for VitaMints and Centrum MultiGummies should focus on the products themselves or make comparisons with other vitamin products, such as One a Day?

2-38. Design an advertising campaign for VitaMints or Centrum MultiGummies that will follow the introductory launch stage. Identify the product features and brand characteristics that should be emphasized to create brand equity and customer loyalty over time.

CASE 2 ▸ BRAND ALLIANCES AND BRAND RESURRECTIONS

In the past few years, two trends have emerged in the world of brand management: creating brand alliances and developing brand rejuvenations. Both approaches seek to take advantage of the strength of a brand or set of brands by tapping into positive consumer perceptions of them.

Brand alliances involve the co-branding of two powerful product names in the marketing of either an existing or a new product.

Examples may be found in a wide range of brand areas. The first approach, marketing existing brands, includes tie-ins between existing products with various forms of entertainment. For instance, the television program *Hawaii 5-0* features Chevrolet vehicles both in the program and during advertising breaks, both online and in traditional television channel systems. The show's primary characters drive the Chevrolet Camaro (after several seasons in which the

▲ Glad marketed the Glad Odor Shield System trash bags featuring the Febreze brand.

Chevrolet Cruz was used), while other cast members motor around in Chevrolet trucks. The program actively promotes the relationship between the stories and the vehicles.

In a similar fashion, the *Fast and Furious* movies created tie-ins with Dodge. Firestone developed commercials co-marketing the company's products with the *Turbo* movie. The 2013 Superman movie *Man of Steel* involved co-marketing with Hardees' and Carl's Jr. Many films also promote toy action figures along with the main characters, such as the popular Buzz Lightyear from the *Toy Story* series.

A second form of brand alliance includes two strong brands promoted as part of a new product. In the past few years, Old

Spice has combined with Head and Shoulders to create a line of shampoos; Scope and Crest developed the DualBlast tooth and breath cleaning systems; TidyCat and Glade created the Breeze Litter System; Tide and Downey offered the Tide Touch of Downy line, Act Kids featured products carrying the faces of Scooby-Doo and SpongeBob SquarePants on its labels, and Glad has marketed the Glad Odor Shield System (trash bags) featuring the Febreze brand.

Another marketing approach involves resurrecting a brand that appeared in the past with a twist: The new product is upscale and trendy. Automobile manufacturer Dodge re-released the Dodge Dart, only the new car is sporty and up-tempo. Ford has reissued a line of cars with the Taurus brand. Nissan now offers the Datsun brand in some international markets.

The goal of a brand resurrection appears to be to take advantage of some consumer familiarity with the name while promoting an entirely new product experience. In some ways, such an approach mirrors a brand launch while in others it represents an entirely different type of marketing experience.[48] One key is the degree of consumer familiarity with the resurrected brand.

Brand alliances and brand resurrections share the objective of making the best use of limited marketing dollars. Both attempt to build on the strength of brands consumers remember. In general, these new approaches represent innovative methods for seeking to take advantage of brand equity.

2-39. Provide an analysis of the brand alliances mentioned in this story. What factors shape your perceptions of the brands involved?

2-40. In each of the brand alliances, which of the two co-brands do you believe is the more powerful name? What causes you to hold that perception?

2-41. Can you think of any potential disadvantages of brand alliances? Explain your answer.

2-42. Do you recall the names Datsun, Dodge Dart, or Taurus? What perceptions do you have of those brands? Ask your parents what they think of those brand names. Are their answers different from yours?

2-43. Describe what you believe are potential advantages and disadvantages of brand resurrections.

MyMarketingLab

Go to the Assignments section of your MyLab to complete these writing exercises.

2-44. Explain the difference between brand parity and brand equity. How does brand equity impact brand loyalty. Look through the list of top brands shown in Figure 2.16. Identify what you believe is the top brand in five of the categories that are listed. Explain why you believe the brands you identified are the best for that particular category.

2-45. Look up each of the following brands on the internet. Discuss the image conveyed by each brand's website. Describe the four tests of quality logos and brand names presented in the chapter. How well do each of the brands meet these tests? Identify the ingredients necessary to build powerful brands present in the chapter. Evaluate each brand along these dimensions.

  a. Canyon Beachwear (**www.canyonbeachwear.com**)

  b. Applebee's (**www.applebees.com**)

Chapter 3 Buyer Behaviors

Chapter Objectives

After reading this chapter, you should be able to answer the following questions:

3.1 Which elements are involved in internal and external information searches by consumers, as part of the purchasing process?

3.2 What three models explain how individuals evaluate purchasing alternatives?

3.3 What trends are affecting the consumer buying environment?

3.4 How do the roles played by various members of the buying center and the factors that influence them impact business purchases?

3.5 What types of business-to-business sales are made?

3.6 What are the steps of the business-to-business buying process?

3.7 How does dual channel marketing expand a company's customer base and its sales?

3.8 How can a company overcome international differences when adapting to buying processes?

Overview

Enticing people to buy goods and services continues to be a primary goal of many integrated marketing communications programs. Understanding how buyers make purchase decisions helps the marketing team achieve this goal. Two types of buyer behaviors—consumer buyer behaviors and business-to-business buyer behaviors—attention in this chapter. Utilizing the steps consumers and businesses follow when making purchase decisions assists the marketing team in creating quality communications.

This chapter first examines consumer purchasing processes. Two stages of the process are the keys to marketing communications. In the *information search* stage, the customer reviews previous memories and experiences looking for acceptable ways to meet a need by buying a product. During the *evaluation of alternatives* stage, the individual compares various purchasing possibilities. An effective IMC program targets potential buyers involved in these activities. This chapter provides a review of the traditional factors affecting consumers, along with discussion of the newer trends present in the consumer buying environment.

How do you convince nearly one billion people to change their daily routines? Essentially, that is the task facing Nescafé in mainland China. In rural areas of the country, consumers drink about five cups of coffee per year. In contrast, for consumers in urban centers and in neighboring Hong Kong, the number of daily and annual coffee purchases is much higher. In fact, Starbucks has been able to grow and attract new consumers in many major cities in China.

Nescafé instant coffee has been China's market leader for nearly two decades. Instant coffee has traditionally been the more favored product, although fresh coffee sales have risen much more quickly in the past few years. To help increase sales of Nescafé, the company's marketing team decided that new technologies presented the greatest opportunities.

E-commerce through the Alibaba web site and social media offered the best chances to reach the most ideal target market—urban white collar employees in their 20s. The primary venue for social media, the Weibo microblogging service, was chosen for a new campaign. Focusing on a holiday known as White Valentine's Day, in which women would give gifts to men in return for presents received from them on traditional Valentine's Day, the message centered on "the natural fragrance of Nescafé Gold." Online discussions and a contest designed to generate interest were created by the Ogilvy Public Relations agency for Nescafé.[1]

In a country dominated by tea consumption, creating a new mindset in which coffee would be selected more often by younger consumers represents a major challenge but also a great opportunity. The entire consumer buying decision-making process would need to be influenced in order to achieve long term success.

The second part of this chapter examines business-to-business buyer behaviors. First, a review of the five major roles played in the buying center takes place. Next, the types of purchases companies make are presented, along with the steps involved in the purchasing process. Finally, dual channel marketing, which involves selling the same product to both consumers and business buyers, is discussed. Effective IMC programs identify potential customers from both markets in order to increase sales and maintain a strong presence in the marketplace.

Information Searches and the Consumer Purchasing Process

Finding ways to influence the consumer purchasing process constitutes a vital marketing communications activity. Figure 3.1 models the consumer buying decision-making process. The first step occurs when the consumer experiences a need or want. A problem or gap exists between an individual's current state and desired state. The need can be physical, such as hunger or thirst. It might be social, such as when a consumer visits a friend's apartment and sees his new HDTV and wants one as a result. Needs may be psychological in nature, including the desire for love or protection from fear.

Marketing communications can also trigger consumer needs. The advertisement for Skyjacker suspensions on the next page may act as a catalyst for an individual to want a lift kit for his vehicle. Once this occurs, consumers enter the next phase of the process, information search, which is one of the two stages most directly related to integrated marketing communications, the other being the evaluation of alternatives stage.

objective 3.1
Which elements are involved in internal and external information searches by consumers, as part of the purchasing process?

▶ **FIGURE 3.1**
Consumer Decision-Making
Process

```
Problem
Recognition
        →
    Information
    Search
            →
        Evaluation
        of
        Alternatives
                →
            Purchase
            Decision
                    →
                Postpurchase
                Evaluation
```

▼ This advertisement for Skyjacker might trigger a search for additional information about truck suspension lift kits.

Discovering how customers seek out product information and then the manner in which they evaluate the information are keys to creating effective marketing messages.

As shown in Figure 3.1, once a need emerges the consumer begins an internal search, mentally recalling products that might satisfy it. Often, the individual remembers how the need was previously met. If a particular brand was chosen and a positive experience followed, the consumer becomes likely to repeat the purchase decision, and the information search ends. When a previous purchase did not work out, or the consumer wishes to try something else, a more complete internal search may commence.

Internal Search

During an internal search, the consumer thinks about the brands she will consider. This group may not contain every brand the consumer has experienced, because she eliminates brands associated with negative experiences. Brands she knows little about are also eliminated. In other words, the consumer quickly reduces the number of potential brands.

Making sure a company's brand becomes part of the consumer's set of potential purchase alternatives in an internal search constitutes a key marketing communications objective. A product with a high level of brand awareness or brand equity will likely be included in the consumer's set of alternatives. The Kraft Singles advertisement on the next page features appealing visuals coupled with compelling copy to persuade consumers it should be the first and only choice when it comes to sliced cheese. Kraft wants to be viewed as the solution when the internal search process occurs.

External Search

Following an internal search, the consumer makes a mental decision regarding an external search. When the customer has sufficient internal information, he moves to the next step of the decision-making process: evaluating the alternatives. A consumer who remains uncertain about the right brand to purchase undertakes an external search.

Individuals gather external information from a variety of sources, including friends, relatives, experts, books, magazines, newspapers, advertisements, in-store displays, salespeople, the internet, and social media. The amount of time a consumer spends on an external search depends on three factors: ability, motivation, and costs versus benefits (see Figure 3.2).[2]

Ability to Search The extent to which an information search will be undertaken is partially determined by the ability to search. Ability consists of a person's educational level combined with the specific knowledge he has about a product and the various brands in a specific category. Educated individuals are more inclined to spend time searching for information. They are often more willing to visit stores or search online prior to making decisions. Consumers possessing extensive knowledge about individual brands and product categories are better able to conduct more involved external searches. For instance, someone who knows a great deal about digital cameras has a more sophisticated ability to examine information about them than someone who knows little about the technology. In addition, a person with more comprehensive knowledge of a product area often collects additional information, even when she is not in the market for the product.[3]

In terms of the amount of time an individual devotes to the external search process, an unusual phenomenon occurs. Although extensive product category knowledge means an individual has greater ability to search for external information, the consumer will normally spend less time on the external search process due to the extensive knowledge he already possesses.

Consumers at the other end of the spectrum also spend less time in the external search process—but for the opposite reason. They do not have knowledge about the product category and do not know what type of information to ask for or what type of information would be useful, which means they lack the ability to search for information. Individuals in the middle, who have some knowledge of a product category but require additional information in

▲ A Kraft Singles advertisement designed to convince consumers that the Kraft brand should be the first choice when selecting cheese to make a "new kind of burger".

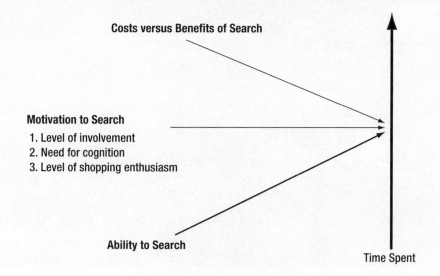

◀ **FIGURE 3.2**
Factors Affecting the Amount of Time a Consumer Spends Conducting an External Search

order to make intelligent decisions, typically spend the most time searching for external information.

Level of Motivation   The degree to which an external search takes place further depends on the customer's level of motivation. The greater the motivation, the more time spent on an external search. Motivation is determined by the consumer's:

- Level of involvement
- Need for cognition
- Level of shopping enthusiasm

Individuals experience greater motivation to search for information when involvement levels are high. **Involvement** summarizes the extent to which a stimulus or task is relevant to a consumer's existing needs, wants, or values. When a consumer deems a product to be important, it becomes more likely she will engage in an external search. The amount of involvement will be determined by factors such as the *cost* of the product and its *importance*. The higher the price, the more time an individual spends searching for information.

The same holds true for importance. Choosing clothes might not be a crucial decision for some males, which suggests such purchases typically carry low involvement. Picking a tuxedo for the high school prom, however, may spur greater involvement and a higher level of information search due to the social ramifications of dressing poorly at such an important event. The higher level of involvement emerges from the addition of a new element—a major occasion in the person's life.

The **need for cognition** personality characteristic identifies individuals who engage in and enjoy mental activities. Mental exercises have a positive impact on the information search process. People with high needs for cognition gather more information and search more thoroughly. The search also depends on a person's **enthusiasm for shopping**. Customers who enjoy shopping undertake more in-depth searches for goods and services.[4]

Costs Versus Benefits   Two final factors that influence an information search are the perceived costs versus the perceived benefits of the search. Higher perceived benefits increase the inclination to search.

▶ A utility tractor is a high involvement purchase that would trigger an external search process.

The ability to reduce purchase risk becomes a benefit that many consumers seek while examining external information. Additional information lowers the chances of making a mistake in the purchase selection. The cost of the search consists of several items:

- The actual cost of the good or service
- The subjective costs associated with the search, including time spent and anxiety experienced while making a decision
- The opportunity cost of foregoing other activities to search for information (for example, going shopping instead of playing golf or watching a movie)

▲ Enthusiasm for shopping has an impact on the amount of time spent on an external search.

Higher perceived subjective costs associated with collecting external information decrease the likelihood that the consumer will conduct a search.[5]

Consumers normally consider three factors that make up an external search (ability, motivation, costs versus benefits) simultaneously. When the perceived cost of a search is low, and the perceived benefit is high, a consumer has a higher motivation to search for information. A consumer with a minimal amount of product knowledge and a low level of education will be less likely to undertake an external search, because the consumer lacks the ability to identify the right information.

From a marketing communications perspective, the search process represents an important time to reach the consumer. The consumer's objective during an external search will be to acquire information leading to a better, more informed decision. The marketing team provides information that leads consumers to the company's products. One ideal time to attempt to influence the decision-making process will be when the consumer has not yet made up his mind. Marketing experts utilize three models of the information search process: attitudes, values, and cognitive mapping.

Consumer Attitudes

Effective marketing communications influence consumer attitudes. An **attitude** is the mental position taken toward a topic, a person, or an event that influences the holder's feelings, perceptions, learning processes, and subsequent behaviors.[6] Attitudes drive purchase decisions. A consumer holding a positive attitude toward a brand becomes more likely to buy it. Someone who enjoys an advertisement will also be more inclined to purchase the product.

Attitudes consist of three components: affective, cognitive, and conative.[7] First, the *affective* component contains the feelings or emotions a person has about the object, topic, or idea. The *cognitive* component refers to a person's mental images, understanding, and interpretations of the person, object, or issue. The *conative* component holds an individual's intentions, actions, or behavior. These components may occur in various sequences. One common sequence of events that takes place in attitude formation is:

Cognitive → Affective → Conative

Most of the time, a person first develops an understanding about an idea or object. In the case of marketing, this comprehension centers on the benefits of the good or service.

▲ This advertisement for Centric Credit Union is designed to influence a person's beliefs (cognitive component of attitude) about the financial institution's fees and rates.

▼ What emotions does this advertisement for the Craig General Hospital elicit?

Thoughts about the product emerge from watching or reading advertisements. Other thoughts may result from exposure to information from other sources, such as the internet, social media, or a friend's referral. Eventually, these ideas become beliefs the consumer holds about a particular product. A consumer who sees the Centric Federal Credit Union advertisement shown on this page might notice the emphasis on fewer fees and better rates for banking.

The affective part of the attitude carries the general feeling or emotion a person attaches to the idea. In the case of goods and services, the product, its name, and other features can all generate emotions. Consider your emotional reactions to the following goods and services:

- Cough medicine
- Diapers
- Motorcycles
- Children's toys made in China
- *Sports Illustrated*'s annual swimsuit issue
- Condoms

Some emotions or attitudes about particular goods and services remain relatively benign. Others are more strongly held. Cough medicine does not typically evoke an emotional response; however, the swimsuit issue or condoms may generate stronger reactions.

What emotions and thoughts do you associate with the Craig General Hospital advertisement shown on this page? The images in the ad and the headline "Bringing the best in healthcare home" attempts to instill emotional feelings toward the local hospital.

Decision and action tendencies constitute the conative parts of attitudes. Therefore, when a person feels strongly about the quality of healthcare, Craig General Hospital may be selected. However, attitudes are not always strongly held. Some people might feel favorably about a topic, such as green marketing, but this does not necessarily change their purchasing behaviors.

Attitudes develop in other ways. An alternative process is:

$$\text{Affective} \rightarrow \text{Conative} \rightarrow \text{Cognitive}$$

Advertisements and other marketing communications can first appeal to the emotions or feelings held by consumers in order to move them to like the product and make a purchase (the conative component). Cognitive understanding of the product comes after the purchase. A woman viewing an ad for Platinum Motorcars may be draw to the idea of being "pampered" by renting a luxury automobile. Emotionally, she has a desire to rent the car and takes action. Cognitive reasoning about renting the luxury car follows the emotional experience.

Some attitudes result from a third combination of the components, as follows:

$$\text{Conative} \rightarrow \text{Cognitive} \rightarrow \text{Affective}$$

Purchases that require little thought, have a low price, or do not demand a great deal of emotional involvement might follow this path. For instance, while shopping for groceries, a customer may notice a new brand of cookies. The person may have never seen the brand or flavor before, but decides to give them a try. As the consumer eats the cookies, he develops a greater understanding of their taste, texture, and other qualities. Finally, he reads the package to learn more about contents, including how many calories were present. He then develops feelings toward the cookies that affect future cookie purchases.

No matter which path a consumer takes to develop attitudes, each component will be present to some extent. Some attitudes are relatively trivial (for example, "I like ping-pong, even though I hardly ever get to play"). Others are staunchly held, such as "I hate cigarette smoke!" Both are associated with feelings toward things, including products in the marketplace.

Consumer Values

Attitudes reflect an individual's personal values. **Values** are strongly held beliefs about various topics or concepts. Values frame attitudes and lead to the judgments that guide personal actions. Values tend to endure. They normally form during childhood, although they can change as a person ages and experiences life.

Figure 3.3 identifies some common personal values. People hold them to differing degrees. Factors that affect a person's values include the individual's personality, temperament, environment, and one's culture. By appealing to these values, marketers try to convince prospective customers that the company's products align with what they view as important.

In terms of consumer decision-making processes, both attitudes and values carry influence. A good or service tied to a relatively universal value, such as patriotism, helps the firm take advantage of the linkage and present the product in a positive manner. In a survey of 4,500 consumers, Brand Keys found that Jeep was regarded as the most patriotic brand followed by Hershey's, Coca-Cola, Levi-Strauss, and Disney. According to Brand Keys, patriotism remains an emotionally-engaged and ingrained value that can become part of a brand's equity. Figure 3.4 lists the top 10 most patriotic brands.[8]

Some People cannot wait for you to get home.

Do you need any other reason to work safely?

Safety Poster 1002   318.388.9300   www.scottcompanies.com
Committed to the safety of our employees.

SCOTT EQUIPMENT
HEAVY-DUTY COMMITMENT

▲ An advertisement for Scott Equipment focusing on the personal value of security.

Cognitive Mapping

The manner in which individuals store information further affects decisions, because it impacts recall. Knowing how people store, retrieve, and evaluate information assists the company's marketing team in developing advertisements and marketing communications. Understanding how various thought processes and memories work constitutes the first step.

Cognitive maps simulate the knowledge structures and memories embedded in an individual's mind.[9] These structures contain a person's assumptions, beliefs, interpretation of facts, feelings, and attitudes about the world. Such thought processes interpret new information and determine responses to fresh information or a novel situation. Figure 3.5 depicts a simplified hypothetical cognitive map of an individual thinking about a Ruby Tuesday restaurant.

Based on the cognitive structures illustrated, when this customer considers Ruby Tuesday, she connects images of it with similar restaurants that provide dine-in services. The consumer may believe that Ruby Tuesday offers excellent food, but that the service is slow. Next, when the customer thinks about slow service, her thoughts turn to Mel's Diner. When she considers excellent service, she recalls Applebee's.

- Comfortable life
- Equality
- Excitement
- Freedom
- Fun, exciting life
- Happiness
- Inner peace
- Mature love
- Personal accomplishment

- Pleasure
- Salvation
- Security
- Self-fulfillment
- Self-respect
- Sense of belonging
- Social acceptance
- Wisdom

▶ **FIGURE 3.3**
Personal Values

Rank	Company	Patriotic Emotional Engagement Score
1	Jeep	98%
2	Hershey	97%
3	Coca-Cola	97%
4	Levi-Strauss	95%
5	Walt Disney	95%
6	Colgate	94%
7	Zippo	93%
8	Wrigley's	92%
9	Ralph Lauren	91%
10	Kodak	90%

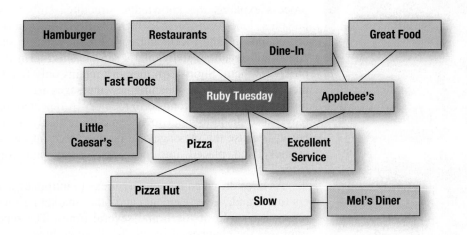

◀ **FIGURE 3.5**
A Hypothetical Cognitive Map
for Ruby Tuesday

Cognitive Linkages Cognitive structures contain many linkages and they exist on several levels. For instance, one level of cognition may be the map shown in Figure 3.5. At another level, a cognitive map becomes more spatial and conjures images of the actual physical location of Ruby Tuesday and the surrounding businesses. A third cognitive level related to Ruby Tuesday may be the person's recall of the interior of the restaurant along with other linkages that occur at that level. The consumer may have thoughts about Ruby Tuesday that focus on employees, including a relationship she had with a friend who was a server. Therefore, cognitive processing occurs on several levels using highly complex mechanisms.

Processing New Information In terms of cognitive mapping, when a consumer receives information or sees an advertisement, it can be processed in two primary ways. New information that remains consistent with current information tends to strengthen an existing linkage. A different response occurs when a message has no current linkages. The customer creates a new linkage between the new information and brand.

When the marketing team at Esurance observed individuals engaged in an online purchasing process, the marketers discovered that when potential customers arrived at the end of the process they were not pushing the purchase button. Thus, conversions (sales) were not occurring. Additional research indicated that consumers felt uneasy or unsure about the company, primarily because no linkages for the Esurance brand existed in the minds

▲ This advertisement tries to create a linkage between the Wholly Guacamole brand and the Sonic brand.

of many potential customers. This was true especially for the older, multicar, higher-income individuals that Esurance was trying to reach.

As a result, company leaders had a choice: They could spend millions of dollars on establishing a brand name and linkages in the cognitive maps of consumers or partner with an established brand that was already present in peoples' cognitive maps. The dilemma was solved when Allstate purchased Esurance. The company could then focus on current linkages consumers had with Allstate insurance through a campaign with the tagline "insurance for the modern world." Allstate gave the Esurance brand instant linkages to credibility, trustworthiness, and value.[10] It was no longer necessary to develop an entirely new cognitive map.

Retaining Information Hearing something once may not cause it usually does not cause it to be retained in a person's long-term memory, due to differences between short-term recall and long-term memories. The cognitive mapping process explains the knowledge structures embedded in a person's long-term memory. Ordinarily, information will be retained in short-term memory for only a few seconds. As stimuli reach an individual's senses, short-term memory processes them. Short-term memory retains only five to nine pieces of information, meaning new messages are either soon forgotten or added to long-term memory. A repeated message may cause an individual to become more likely to remember it, because the message will be processed into long-term memory and placed into previously developed cognitive maps.

As a result, when a company seeks to introduce consumers to a brand, advertisements and other marketing messages repeat the name of the brand several times. The repetition improves the chances of recall. To illustrate how this works, consider what happens when a person gives a phone number to a friend. To help remember it, the individual repeats the number several times.

New Concepts Another way a consumer processes information is to link the message to a new concept. For example, if a consumer sees an advertisement from Ruby Tuesday emphasizing that it has great food, but has never thought about the restaurant in terms of quality food, that linkage does not currently exist. If the advertisement persuades the consumer, she might construct a linkage between Ruby Tuesday and good food without even traveling to the restaurant. If she does not believe the message, she will ignore or forget the information, and no new linkage results. A third possibility is that the consumer recalls the advertisement at a later time and decides to try Ruby Tuesday. If the food is great, then the link becomes established. If it is not, the consumer continues thinking that Ruby Tuesday does not offer good food.

Marketing Messages It terms of a marketing perspective, strengthening linkages that already exist should be easier. Adding or modifying linkages is more difficult (see Figure 3.6). Regardless of how marketers present information, repetition remains important due to the limitations of short-term memory. Consumers experience hundreds of marketing messages daily. They only process a few of those messages into long-term memories.

Cognitive mapping and persuasion techniques designed to change attitudes or tap into strongly held values represent two key ingredients of any IMC program. When the marketing team understands the needs and attitudes of the target market, messages can be structured to meet them. A message should capture the consumer's attention by exposing him to concepts that travel effectively through a core mental processing channel or peripheral channels, either through logic or alluring emotional appeals.

Creatives attempt to design ads that reach the linkages consumers have already made between a product and other key ideas. For instance, for a long time, a linkage existed between Cadillac and quality, as witnessed by the advertising and promotional phrase "This product is the *Cadillac* . . . [of all products in the market]." Common linkages exist between products and ideas, such as quality, value, low cost, expense, fun, sex, danger, practicality, exoticness, and others. Carefully planned marketing campaigns identify linkages that entice the consumer to buy a brand and to believe in or be loyal to that brand in the future. This advantage remains as the consumer considers various purchasing alternatives.

▲ This advertisement seeks to create linkages between "Your City, Your News" and *The Times-Picayune* and NOLA.com.

Evaluation of Alternatives

Evaluating alternatives is the third step in the consumer buying decision-making process (see Figure 3.7). Three models portray the nature of the evaluation process: the evoked set approach, the multiattribute approach, and affect referral. Understanding how consumers evaluate choices enables the firm's marketing team to develop more effective materials.

objective 3.2

What three models explain how individuals evaluate purchasing alternatives?

The Evoked Set Method

A person's **evoked set** consists of the brands the individual considers in a purchasing situation. An evoked set might be reviewed during both the information search and evaluation

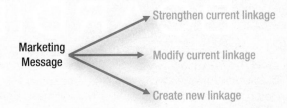

Marketing Message → Strengthen current linkage

Modify current linkage

Create new linkage

◀ **FIGURE 3.6**

The Role of Marketing Messages in Cognitive Mapping

▶ **FIGURE 3.7**
Methods of Evaluating
Alternatives

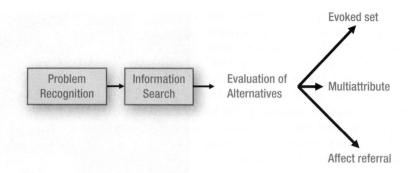

stages of the buying decision-making process. Two additional brand sets become part of the evaluation of purchase alternatives: the inept set and the inert set. The **inept set** contains the brands that are part of a person's memory that are *not considered* because they elicit negative feelings. These negative sentiments are normally caused by a bad experience with a vendor or particular brand. They can also originate from negative statements by a friend, seeing an advertisement that the potential customer did not like, or comments made in social media outlets about poor products and services and/or corporate misconduct.

The **inert set** holds the brands that the consumer is aware of, but the individual has neither negative nor positive feelings about them. Using the terms from cognitive mapping, these brands have not been entered into any map, or they only have weak linkages to other ideas. The lack of knowledge about these brands usually eliminates them as alternatives. In other words, in most purchase situations a consumer only considers brands in her evoked set.

Placing a brand name in the evoked sets of consumers may be the primary goal of a marketing message. Doing so requires promoting the brand name and that brand's primary benefit extensively and consistently using multiple venues. The consumer should see the brand name frequently in as many locations as possible. Then, to make

▶ This advertisement for Visit South Walton seeks to make the area part of a consumer's evoked set as she considers vacation spots.

sure the name becomes part of an evoked set, the concepts described related to cognitive mapping can be employed. By tying the brand to its primary benefit, the marketing team seeks to embed the brand's name in the consumer's long-term memory. The message establishes or reinforces linkages between the benefit and the brand name. When a consumer evaluates alternatives using his evoked set and the company's brand becomes the part of the set being considered, the advertisement succeeds.

The Multiattribute Approach

The multiattribute approach may be useful for understanding high-involvement purchases. Consumers often examine sets of product attributes across an array of brands. The multiattribute model suggests that a consumer's attitude toward a brand is determined by:[11]

▲ The multiattribute model can be used in the purchase of high-involvement products, such as furniture.

- The brand's performance on product or brand attributes
- The importance of each attribute to the consumer

The higher a brand rates on attributes that are important to the consumer, the more likely it becomes the brand that will be purchased. Figure 3.8 notes various products, along with some of the characteristics that affect their selection. Each has potentially a lesser or greater value to individual consumers.

From an integrated communication standpoint, providing consumers with information about a brand's performance on criteria they are likely use becomes the key. This can be achieved on a brand's website, where consumers often gather information about high-involvement decisions. Brochures and print ads can also be prepared; thereby placing them into the hands of consumers just as they desire information.

In advertising, a creative often features a product with multiple benefits by designing a series of messages. Advertisements highlight price, style, service contracts, software, memory, storage, or other product features. Only one or two of the benefits should be presented in a message. Otherwise, the advertisement becomes overloaded. Consumers who see commercials featuring one or two benefits learn about a brand's

Product	Characteristics				
Computer	Price	Style	Service contract	Software	Memory storage
Telephone	Price	Style	Speed dial	Caller ID	Cordless feature
Car	Price	Style	Safety	Room	Other features
T-bone steak	Price	Age	Fat content	Degree cooked	Seasonings
Sunglasses	Price	Style	UV protection	Durability	Prescription lenses
Sofa	Price	Style	Foldout bed	Stain resistance	Color
Credit card	Interest rate	Fees	Billing cycle	Access to ATM	Credit limit

Consider each item. Which characteristic is most important to you personally? Least important?

◀ **FIGURE 3.8**

Product Attributes That May be Important in a Multiattribute Approach

MADE FOR
the
Family

A limited-time offer
you can't refuse!

CHICKEN CACCIATORE PIZZA

The Old-World flavor of diced chicken simmered in fresh vegetables and spices, blended with
mozzarella cheese, marinara and pizza sauce on fresh-made dough.

▲ Loyal patrons of SteviB's
Pizza Buffet may use the affect
referral method in evaluating
pizza restaurants.

characteristics. Over time, consumers obtain sufficient information to evaluate the product.

Affect Referral

The concept of **affect referral** suggests that consumers choose brands they like the best or the ones with which they have emotional connections. The individual does not evaluate brands or think about product attributes. Instead, the consumer buys the brand he likes the best or the one that incites positive feelings. Toothpaste, chewing gum, soft drinks, and candy are some of the products consumers normally select in this way. These purchases typically have low levels of involvement. They also tend to be frequently purchased products.

The affect referral model may apply to the use of artificial sweeteners, such as Splenda, Equal, and Sweet'N Low. Previously, many consumers gave little thought to brand selection when choosing sweeteners. Several years ago, negative publicity about the health impact of some products may have changed those perceptions. As a result, the Truvia marketing team modified its advertising to focus on consumer education. The messages suggest the brand as being a "natural sweetener" for consumers, who have a choice. Those with concerns about health and wellness might then switch to Truvia. In essence, a new affect referral model in which Truvia represents the first and best choice may be cultivated.[12]

The affect referral model explains three things. First, this approach saves mental energy. Making a quick choice will be easier than going through the process of evaluating every alternative. Some purchases do not deserve much effort, and the affect referral model applies to those situations.

Second, a multiattribute approach might have been used previously when making a purchase. The person already spent a great deal of time considering various product attributes, deciding which are most critical, and reaching a decision. Going through the process again would be "reinventing the wheel." A teenager buying jeans may have already spent considerable time evaluating styles, prices, colors, durability levels, and "fit" of various brands. After making the purchase, the teen continues to purchase the same brand as long as the experience remains positive. The affect referral model explains this buying behavior. Making a repurchase based on positive feelings becomes simple and convenient.

Third, at times consumers develop emotional bonds with brands. In terms of the purchase decision, an emotional bond with a product can be the strongest and most salient factor in the decision.[13] It can be more important than any other attribute or product benefit. Successful brands establish emotional bonds with consumers. A bond generates brand loyalty, enhances brand equity, and reduces brand parity. Consequently, consumers do not evaluate alternatives because of their bond with the brand. Harley-Davidson enjoys such a bond with many of its customers. These individuals hold strong feelings toward the company and do not even consider other alternatives. The Jeep and Apple brands have also obtained emotional brand followers. Affect referral explains this phenomenon.

Trends in the Consumer Buying Environment

Studying the steps consumers take while making purchasing decisions helps to create effective marketing communications. The environment in which consumers make purchases continually changes and evolves. Several trends in the consumer buying environment affect purchasing patterns (see Figure 3.9).

▲ Customers often use affective referral when purchasing clothes.

objective 3.3
What trends are affecting the consumer buying environment?

Age Complexity

Technology affects the ways children grow up. They are bombarded with advertisements, video games, television shows, movies, and a myriad of other images. Most become fashion-conscious as preteens. Many social observers believe children "grow up" at a much earlier age.

At the other end of the spectrum, some adults refuse to grow old. They wear fashions that resemble those worn by college students. They drive sports cars or convertibles. Many middle-aged adults apparently do not want to age, acting like younger people and buying products normally purchased by them. This trend challenges marketers to try to create messages that reflect these behaviors but do not offend or confuse more traditional middle-aged people.

- Age complexity
- Gender complexity
- Active, busy lifestyles
- Diverse lifestyles
- Communication revolution
- Experience pursuits
- Health emphasis

▲ **FIGURE 3.9**
Trends Affecting Consumer Buying Behaviors

Gender Complexity

Gender complexity refers to the manner in which the traditional roles, lifestyles, and interests of men and women have become blurred. Many women attend college, delay marriage, and wait to start families. Some choose to focus on moving up the corporate ladder instead of other options.

Men have become more likely to play active roles in parenting, help with household chores, and do more of the shopping. Since 1985, a shift in the number of men who are the primary household shopper has occurred. Almost one-third of men are now the principal shopper. Males spend 38 percent of all grocery dollars.[14] The percentage of men who take care of household cleaning is almost as high, 31 percent. According to Alexandra Smith, editor of Mintel Inspire, "The next generation of men is coming of age in an era when gender roles are less rigidly defined and men are set to become only more domestic."[15]

▶ This advertisement for Kraft Fresh Taste provides "endless inspiration" for individuals with active, busy lifestyles.

Active, Busy Lifestyles

Active lifestyles impact consumer behaviors.[16] Economic conditions and global competition have led many individuals to work longer hours in order to protect their jobs as corporations are forced to downsize. In one survey, 47 percent of respondents stated that they would prefer additional free time over more money. Further, many people concentrate less on material possessions and more on experiences with friends and family.

Time pressures also account for increases in sales of convenience items, such as microwave ovens, drive-through dry-cleaning establishments, and one-stop shopping outlets (most notably superstores). Services such as housecleaning and lawn care continue to escalate. People on the go use smartphones and social media sites to stay in touch with others and make sure they do not miss any messages during busy days.

Diverse Lifestyles

The percentage of young people who follow the traditional path of growing of age, marrying, and having children continues to decline. Instead, a wide diversity exists in the paths individuals take into adulthood, along with the living arrangements they create during that time. More college students have moved home to live with parents. Others live with roommates of mixed genders and ethnicities. Many delay marriage until later in life or choose to remain single or live with a partner.

Divorce and remarriage alter many family units. Remarried divorcees represent about 10 percent of the population. Divorcees tend to develop a new outlook on life. Members of this group, called *second chancers*, are usually between the ages of 40 and 59 and often have higher household incomes. Second chancers are more content with life than average adults. They tend to be happy with their new families but also have a different life focus. Second chancers spend less time trying to please others and more time seeking fuller, more enriching lives for themselves and their children or spouses. Although the home and family continue to be a major emphasis, entertainment and vacation services also appeal to this group.[17]

The number of openly lesbian, gay, bisexual, and transgender (LGBT) people has grown to approximately five to 10 percent of the population. These consumers tend to favor products and companies featuring gay themes in advertisements and support causes that are important to them. Wes Combs, President of Witeck-Combs Communication, notes that "LGBT consumers express an unmistakable and stronger sense of brand loyalty to companies that support their communities." Digital ads may be especially effective with this group, because they have a higher than average ownership of smartphones.[18]

Communication Revolution

Advances in telecommunications, primarily social media and smartphones, influence consumers all over the world and alter the ways citizens communicate with each other, with brands, and with companies. Many people communicate with one another through Facebook or Twitter rather than in person or by telephone. Someone in Florida can chat with a friend in Alaska or in Japan instantaneously. Smartphones allow these individuals to take the internet with them,

▼ Second chancers and families who want to invest in their home's kitchen are the target for this ad for Poggenpohl.

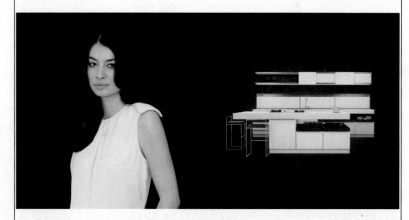

Hide and Reveal

+MODO

We don't just look at kitchens, we live and feel them. Our **+MODO** introduces sensuous emotions to the world of the kitchen through the interplay of open and closed elements. Place your favourite objects in stimulating open spaces. Hide and reveal as the mood takes you. The kitchen is now a platform for a journey of constant creation and discovery.

poggenpohl.com

Poggenpohl Kitchen Studio
1804 Hi Line Drive
Dallas
214-572-9190
www.dallas.poggenpohl.com
info@dallas.poggenpohl.com

which means they do not have to phone someone to visit. Instead, they send text messages or access the internet and correspond using email, Skype, or social media platforms.

Emerging technologies have altered the ways brands and firms are influenced by word-of-mouth communication. An individual who has a bad experience with a brand is not limited to telling just a few friends and family members. A dissatisfied consumer can use social media and Twitter and instantly be "heard" by thousands of people within hours, or even minutes. This type of negative word-of-mouth can be devastating.

Fortunately, these same technologies can be used to engage consumers and stimulate positive endorsements. Many companies monitor social media. Marketers listen to what consumers say and respond to them. Social media offers pathways to engage in two-way communications with consumers, at a point of purchase in a retail store, in their homes, or at their places of business.

Experience Pursuits

Some people handle the stress of a hectic, busy lifestyle through occasional indulgences or pleasure binges, such as expensive dinners out and smaller luxury purchases. Pleasure pursuits include getaway weekends in resorts, short cruises, or visit to beaches such as South Walton in Florida (see the ad is this section). These self-rewarding activities help the consumer feel that all the work and effort is "worth it." Instead of buying "things," people purchase "experiences," which vary from visiting theme parks, enjoying virtual reality playrooms, going to casinos, and taking exotic vacations.

Recognizing that consumers often prefer experiences over things, companies provide customers with moments to remember rather than more items to put in their homes. Ritz-Carlton presented the theme "Let us stay with you" in a recent campaign to emphasize the memories of staying in a Ritz-Carlton luxury property rather than the usual campaign requesting consumers to "Please stay with us." Orient-Express Hotels created a similar campaign featuring the theme "Embark on a journey like no other." The ad emphasized a positive and memorable consumer experience.[19]

Health Emphasis

The U.S. population continues to age, leading to two trends: a blossoming interest in health and in maintaining a youthful appearance. Many consumers try to develop a balanced lifestyle with an emphasis on nutrition, exercise, and staying active.[20]

Recently, Reebok launched a global marketing campaign called "Live with Fire" that reflected the holistic benefits of exercise. The messages featured ordinary people rather than millionaire celebrities and athletes. Instead of focusing on the solitary battles individuals face when exercising, the commercials showed communities and groups of people exercising together. TV spots highlighted a running club doing sprints, a Latin Dance class, two women on an early morning walk, two men racing each other to the top of a stadium, and a yoga class. Reebok also developed, Reebok developed print, digital, and out-of-home campaign components. Marketers created Reebok Fitness apps for Apple and Android phones that featured workouts for walking, running, dance, yoga, and training. The campaign encouraged individuals to transform their lives through fitness programs and community support.[21]

▼ This advertisement for Visit South Walton focuses on the current trend of people wanting "experiences" rather than purchasing things.

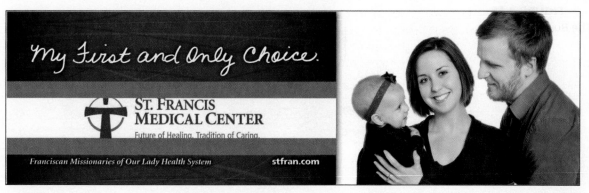

▲ With the emphasis on health, St. Francis Medical Center promotes itself as the first and only choice for medical care.

- Monitor consumer environment for changes
- Create goods and services that are compatible with the changes
- Design marketing messages that reflect the changes

◀ **FIGURE 3.10**
Marketing Responses to Changing Trends in the Consumer Buying Environment

Purchasing healthier foods with less sodium or a lower sugar content are additional ways to pursue healthy lifestyles. At the same time, consumers do not want to sacrifice convenience. Busy lifestyles mean consumers are less willing to cook from scratch. They prefer prepared foods that can be assembled easily and cooked quickly. Products that combine health attributes with convenience sell well.

In sum, these new trends in the consumer buying environment create several challenges for marketing experts, as shown in Figure 3.10. Company leaders monitor changes so their organizations are not surprised by them; rather, their companies can create goods and services that match changing values. Then, marketing messages can reflect and build on the values people express. Incorporating new trends into the marketing program may be undertaken while at the same time being careful not to alienate any current customers who might not like those trends.

Business-to-Business Buyer Behaviors and Influences

In business-to-business purchases, *people* still make the decisions. At the same time, when selling to a business organization, the marketing team knows that normally several individuals will be involved. Further, corporate policies create restrictions and decision rules that affect purchasing activities. Factors such as costs, quality, and profit considerations also influence the final choice.

The **buying center** consists of the group of individuals making a purchase decision on behalf of a business. This complicates buying decisions. The buying center contains five different purchasing roles shown in Figure 3.11. The roles are:

- **Users**—Members of the organization who actually use the good or service
- **Buyers**—Individuals given the formal responsibility of making the purchase
- **Influencers**—Individuals, such as engineers, who shape purchasing decisions by providing the information or criteria utilized in evaluating alternatives

objective 3.4

How do the roles played by various members of the buying center and the factors that influence them impact business purchases?

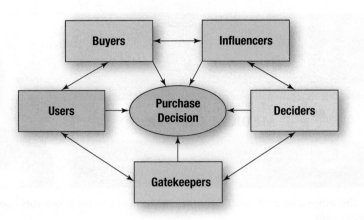

▶ **FIGURE 3.11**
The Buying Center

- **Deciders**—Individuals who authorize the purchase decisions
- **Gatekeepers**—Individuals who control the flow of information to members of the buying center

These roles often overlap. Also, several individuals can occupy the same role in a buying center, especially for large or critical purchases. A variety of members of the organization may serve as influencers, because the roles usually are not fixed and formal.

Every organization engages in a unique purchasing process. The process also varies within an organization from one purchase decision to the next. Salespeople calling on a business seek to locate members of the buying center and understand their roles in the process. When these roles change from one purchase situation to another, the marketing and selling task becomes more complicated.[22]

A series of organizational and individual factors influence the behaviors of members in the buying center.[23] These influences change the manner in which decisions are made and affect the eventual outcomes or alternatives chosen.

Organizational Influences

Several organizational factors influence ways employees make purchasing decisions. The factors include the company's goals and its operating environment (recession, growth period, lawsuits pending, and so on). Decisions are further constrained by the organization's finances, capital assets, market position, the quality of its human resources, and the country in which the firm operates.

Studies of organizational decision making indicate that employees tend to adopt *heuristics*, which are decision rules designed to reduce the number of viable options to a smaller, manageable set. Company goals, rules, budgets, and other organizational factors create heuristics. One frequently used decision rule, *satisficing*, means that when an acceptable alternative has been identified, it is taken and the search ends. Rather than spending a great deal of time looking for an optimal solution, decision makers tend to favor expedience.[24]

Individual Factors

At least seven factors affect each member of the business buying center (see Figure 3.12).[25] Each has an impact on how the individual interacts with other members of the center.

Personality   Numerous personality facets exist. A decisive person makes purchase decisions in a different manner from someone who vacillates. Confidence, extroversion, shyness, and other personality traits influence how a person performs the various buying-center roles. An aggressive person takes charge and makes quick

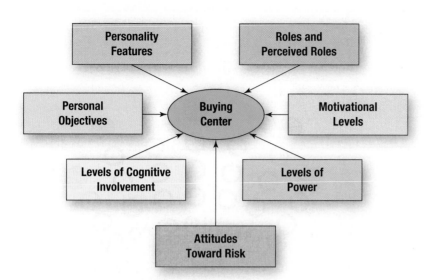

decisions. An extrovert tends to become more involved in the buying process than a more introverted individual. The extrovert spends more time talking while the introvert spends more time listening. The introvert might be too timid with salespeople and other members of the buying center and consequently does not ask important questions.

Roles   An individual's age, heredity, ethnicity, gender, cultural memberships, and patterns of social interaction influence the roles the person plays. Roles are socially constructed, which means people define how they intend to play roles as part of a negotiation process with others. A person's perception of how her role fits into the buying center process and the overall organization influences the manner in which she becomes involved in a purchasing process.

A buying center member who views his role as merely giving approval to decisions made by the boss (the decider) does not actively participate. Members who believe their inputs are valued and are being solicited become more active. One person might think providing information constitutes her role. Another might perceive his role as being the person who synthesizes information provided by vendors and then relays the information to the buying center to save time. Roles and perceptions of roles are crucial factors that determine how members of the buying center engage in the decision.

Motivation   A person's degree of motivation largely depends on the match between the individual's goals and the organization's objectives. A factory foreman with a personal goal of becoming the vice president of operations will be more likely to become involved in the purchasing decisions that affect his performance and that of his department. A purchasing agent who has been charged by the CEO to reduce expenses seeks to ensure that cost-cutting selections are made. The need for recognition motivates many individuals. For someone with a strong recognition need, the goal of making successful purchasing decisions will be to ensure that others recognize the effort, because the person believes a link exists between recognition and promotions or pay raises.

Level of Power   A person derives her level of power in the buying process from the role in the buying center, her official position in the organization, and the impact of the purchase decision on a specific job. When a particular purchase decision directly affects an employee, she may try to gain more power through the buying process. For instance, a factory foreman will have greater power within the buying center in the purchase of raw materials, whereas the maintenance foreman has more power in the purchase of

▶ This advertisement for Gaedeke Group illustrates the importance of personality in the decision for a firm's office location.

▼ Buying Center decisions are affected by both organizational and individual factors.

maintenance supplies. In these situations, each strives to influence the decision that affects her area and job performance.

Risk Oftentimes, vendors are chosen because buyers believe the choice poses the lowest risk. Risk avoidance leads buyers to stay with current vendors rather than switching. In marketing to businesses, reducing risk remains a priority, especially when signing large contracts or when a purchase might affect company profits. People believe that taking risks, especially when a failure occurs, affects performance appraisals, promotions, and other outcomes.

Levels of Cognitive Involvement Both consumer and business buying behaviors are influenced by levels of cognitive involvement. Individuals with higher levels of cognitive capacity seek more information prior to making decisions. They ask more questions when interacting with a salesperson. They spend more time deliberating prior to making decisions. Clearly-stated message arguments help persuade both consumers and business buyers with higher cognitive levels.

Personal Objectives Motivational forces, personality types, perceptions of risk, and the other individual factors shape personal objectives. These objectives can lead buyers to make purchases that help them politically in the organization, even when they are not the best choice. For example, if someone knows his boss is friends with a vendor, the buyer might choose that vendor even when others offer higher quality, lower prices, or both. Personal objectives in buying decisions can be tied to obtaining promotions, making rivals look bad, "brown-nosing" a boss, or the genuine desire to help the organization succeed.

In sum, a buying center consists of a complex set of relationships. Members can serve different roles and may play more than one role. Understanding these dynamics helps when marketing to businesses. The marketing team identifies who will make the decision, how the decision will be made, and any forces or factors that might affect the decision-making process. Examining the organizational and individual influences makes it possible to design a communications program that reaches the key people at the right time.

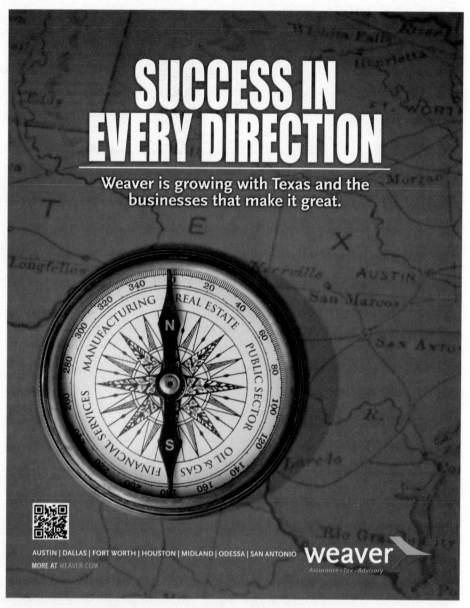

A business-to-business ad for Weaver designed to reduce risk by offering assurance, tax, and advisory services.

Types of Business-to-Business Sales

Business buyers make different types of purchasing decisions. The marketing team adapts to the type of decision being made. The three categories of buying activities include a straight rebuy, a modified rebuy, and a new task (see Figure 3.13).[26]

A **straight rebuy** occurs when the firm has previously chosen a vendor and places a reorder. This routine process normally involves only one or a few members of the buying center. Often the purchasing agent (buyer) and the users of the product are the only ones aware of a rebuy order. The user's role in this purchase situation will be to ask the buyer to replenish the supply. The buyer then contacts the supplier and places the order. Little or no evaluation of alternatives or information takes place. These purchases often take place electronically.

objective 3.5

What types of business-to-business sales are made?

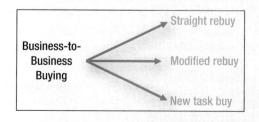

◀ FIGURE 3.13
Types of Business-to-Business Buying Situations

▶ **FIGURE 3.14**

Reasons to Make a
Modified Rebuy

- Dissatisfaction with current vendor
- A different vendor makes an attractive offer
- End of contractual arrangement with current vendor
- Individuals involved in decision process have no or little experience with the product

When making a **modified rebuy**, the buying team considers and evaluates alternatives. As identified in Figure 3.14, a modified rebuy purchase can be made for four different reasons. First, when a company's buyers are *dissatisfied with the current vendor*, they look for new options. A greater level of dissatisfaction creates a strong enticement to examine new possibilities. Second, if a new company offers what is perceived by a member of the buying center to be a *better buy*, the purchase decision may be revisited.

A third type of modified rebuy occurs at the *end of a contractual agreement*. Many organizations, as dictated by corporate policy, must ask for bids each time a contract is written. This situation often occurs when governmental and nonprofit organizations make purchases. The final reason for a modified rebuy is that the people in the company assigned to make the purchase might have only *limited or infrequent experience with the good or service*. When a company purchases delivery trucks, the typical time between decisions may be five to seven years. This creates a modified rebuy situation, because many factors change over that amount of time. Prices, product features, and vendors (truck dealerships) change rapidly. Also, in most cases, the composition of the buying group will be different. Some may have never been part of the decision to purchase delivery vehicles.

In **new task** purchasing situations, the company considers a good or service for the first time or it has been a long time since the last purchase. Further, the product involved is one with which organizational members have no or extremely little experience. This type of purchase normally requires input from a number of buying center members. A considerable amount of time will be spent gathering information and evaluating vendors. In many cases, purchasers ask vendors to assist in identifying the required specifications.

▶ This advertisement
for ReRez seeks to
influence members of a
buying center who are
evaluating a marketing
research firm.

The Business-to-Business Buying Process

The steps involved in the business-to-business buying process are similar to those made by individual consumers. In new task purchasing situations, members of the buying center tend to go through each of the seven steps as part of the buying decision-making process. In modified rebuy or straight rebuy situations, one or more of the steps may be eliminated.[27] Figure 3.15 compares the consumer buying process to the business-to-business buying process.

objective 3.6
What are the steps of the business-to-business buying process?

Identification of Needs

Just as consumers identify needs (hunger, protection, social interaction), businesses also make purchases based on needs ranging from raw materials to professional services. The manner in which managers determine business needs may be different.

Derived demand, which creates many business needs, is based on, linked to, or generated by the production and sale of some other good or service.[28] The demand for steel used in automobile frames results from the number of cars and trucks sold each year. When the demand for vehicles goes down during a recession or economic downturn, the demand for steel also declines. Steel manufacturers find it difficult to stimulate demand because of the nature of derived demand. Purchases of raw materials used in the production of goods and services—such as steel, aluminum, concrete, plastic, petroleum products (e.g., jet fuel for airlines), construction materials, and others—are impacted by derived demand. It also exists for services. Most of the demand for mortgages depends on housing sales.

Once a need has been recognized, the order will be placed with the current vendor in a straight rebuy situation. When the purchase constitutes a modified rebuy or new task, members of the buying center move to the next step.

Establishment of Specifications

In a new task purchase, the most complete specifications are spelled out. Many times, various vendors assist the buyer in developing clear specifications. In modified rebuy situations, managers examine specifications to ensure they are current and meet the company's needs. While they occasionally change, normally most are minor alterations.

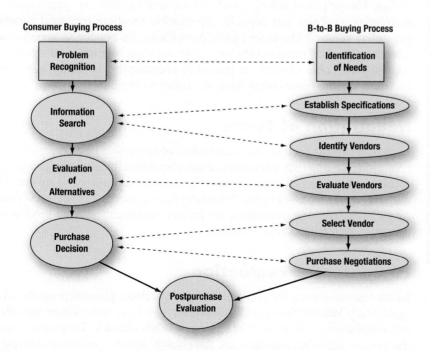

◀ **FIGURE 3.15**
A Comparison of the Business-to-Business Buying Process to the Consumer Buying Process

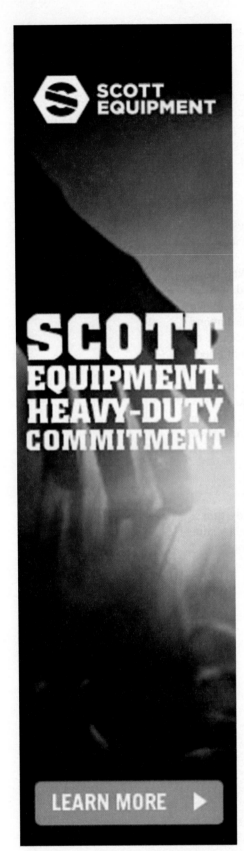

This banner ad encourages firms looking to purchase heavy equipment to consider Scott Equipment as a vendor.

Identification of Vendors

Once specifications have been identified, potential vendors are located and asked to submit bids. In most business situations, written, formal bids are required. A vendor's ability to write a clear proposal often determines whether that company's bid will succeed. Effective proposals spell out prices, quality levels, payment terms, support services, and other conditions requested by the company.

Vendor Evaluation

Evaluations of vendors normally occur at two levels. The first, an *initial screening* of proposals, narrows the field of vendors down to three to five competitors. The number of people from the buying center involved in the initial screening depends on the dollar value of the bid and whether the product is critical to the firm's operation. As dollar values increase and the product becomes more critical, the number of individuals from the buying center involved also rises. Managers often delegate minor choices to a single individual.

The second level of evaluation occurs as the firm undertakes a *vendor audit*. An audit becomes especially important when members of the company work to develop a long-term relationship with a supplier. Vendors that are the primary sources for critical components or raw materials recognize that long-term connections benefit both the vendor and the purchasing firm, because they save time and build trust. Members of the audit team often include an engineer, someone from operations, a quality-control specialist, and members of the purchasing department. An audit serves several purposes, including an evaluation of each potential supplier's ability to meet demand, provide the level of quality needed, and deliver the product on time.

Vendors are people, as are members of the buying center. Attitudes, values, first impressions, and opinions influence evaluations made about vendors. All messages, including bids and proposals, should be designed to create favorable impressions.

Vendor Selection

Once company officials have studied the vendors and the bids have been considered, the final choice can be made. In the decision-making process, members of the buying center experience the individual and organizational pressures presented earlier. The selection criteria used include quality, delivery, performance history, warranties, facilities and capacity, geographic location, technical capability, and per-dollar value.[29] The team rarely deems a single vendor as superior across all selection criteria. Consequently, the marketing team for each vendor emphasizes the company's specific strengths as part of its presentation. In reality, however, politics and other similar forces often have an impact on the final decision.

Negotiation of Terms

In most purchasing situations, negotiation of terms will be a formality because the conditions have already been worked out. Occasionally, however, changes are made at this point in a contract or purchase. These tend to be minor and are normally negotiated by the purchasing agent. When the final agreement is set, goods are shipped or services provided. Assuming no further complications, the buying process is complete until the next cycle begins.

Postpurchase Evaluation

In the business-to-business arena, the postpurchase phase represents a marketing opportunity. Vendors that provide high-quality products, make follow-up calls and offer additional services often move into a straight rebuy situation. They avoid going through the process again because they are the chosen vendor—unless something changes.

Even for products purchased occasionally, the firm that gives attention to the postpurchase component of the selling process gains an edge the next time the client company makes a purchase.

Dual Channel Marketing

Firms sell virtually the same goods or services to both consumers and businesses in **dual channel marketing**.[30] The approach fits several situations. The most common scenario occurs when a product sold in business markets is then adapted to consumer markets. New products often have high start-up costs, including R&D expenditures, market research, and other tasks. Businesses tend to be less price-sensitive than retail consumers, which make it logical to approach them first.

As sales grow, economies of scale emerge. Larger purchases of raw materials combined with more standardized methods of production make it possible to enter consumer markets. Products including digital cameras, calculators, computers, fax machines, and mobile phones were first sold to businesses and then later to consumers.

To make the move to the retail arena possible, prices must be lower and products need to be user-friendly. For example, consumers often have their photos put on a CD rather than obtaining prints. The imaging technology developed by Kodak and Intel was first sold to various businesses and now is offered to retail customers. By forming an alliance with Intel, Kodak brought the cost down and developed the economies of scale necessary for consumer markets.

objective 3.7

How does dual channel marketing expand a company's customer base and its sales?

Spin-Off Sales

Another type of dual channel marketing—spin-off sales—occurs when individuals who buy a particular brand at work enjoy positive experiences and, as a result, purchase the same brand for personal use. This situation often takes place with computers and software. Favorable feelings about more expensive items can also result in spin-off sales. A salesperson who drives a company-owned Lincoln for work might like it so well that she purchases one for personal use. Holiday Inn's marketing team discovered that many of its private stays come from business-related spin-offs. Approximately 30 percent of Holiday Inn's business customers also stay with the chain on private vacations.[31]

◀ Digital cameras first sold to businesses because of the high cost, but are now owned by most consumers.

- Use different communication messages
- Create different brands
- Use multiple or different channels

▲ **FIGURE 3.16**
Dual Channel
Marketing Strategies

Marketing Decisions

In dual channel marketing, a primary decision will be made about how to represent the product in each channel. The firm can either emphasize similarities between the two markets or focus on differences. Figure 3.16 identifies three approaches companies use in dual channel marketing.

In some instances, the product's attributes are the same, but the value or benefit of each attribute differs. Messages focus on the benefits individual segments derive from the product. Mobile phones marketed to businesses stress area coverage and service options. For consumers, mobile phone marketing messages center on the fashionable design of the product, ease of use, or price.

To avoid confusing individuals who might see both messages from the same producer, companies may apply dual branding. For instance, when Black & Decker launched a professional line of power tools, the DeWalt brand name was chosen. This avoided confusion with the Black & Decker name.

In most cases, business customers and consumers seek the same basic benefits from products. In these situations, a single approach for both markets will be used. Tactics include:

- Integrating communications messages
- Selling the same brand in both markets
- Scanning both markets for dual marketing opportunities

In addition to creating economies of scale, integrating consumer markets offers another advantage: the potential to create the synergies that arise from increased brand identity and equity. An image developed in the consumer market can be used to enter a business market, or vice versa. Featuring one brand makes it easier to develop awareness and recall.. For instance, a business customer who uses a company-owned American Express card may obtain another card from the company for personal consumption.

Scanning both types of customers for new opportunities is part of dual channel marketing. For example, the firm Intuit, which sells Quicken software, discovered that individuals who use Quicken at home were willing to buy a similar version for their small businesses. Capitalizing on this advantage, Quicken added features including payroll and inventory control to its business software package while maintaining the easy-to-use format. By identifying a business application for a consumer product, Quicken captured 70 percent of the small-business accounting software market.[32]

Dual channel marketing can create a major competitive advantage as products are sold in both markets. A complete IMC planning process includes the evaluation of potential business market segments as well

▲ Quicken discovered a dual channel opportunity for its accounting software.

as consumer market segments. Firms that integrate messages across these markets take major steps toward reaching every potential customer.

International Implications

Selling to consumers and businesses requires the marketing team to understand cultural differences related to products, messages, and selling techniques. Individual buyers and members of companies from other countries exhibit cultural differences as they consider purchasing alternatives. Consequently, a *cultural assimilator* will be a valuable member of the marketing team in international projects.

Understanding the nuances of the purchasing process for transactions that take place in foreign countries can be helpful. For example, at domestic U.S. trade shows, actual purchases are normally not finalized. Instead, information is collected and transferred between the buyer and the seller. At international trade shows, however, sales are often completed. Higher-ranking members of the purchasing company attend the shows and want to complete transactions. Knowing these kinds of differences helps a company succeed in international trade.

Building a powerful brand represents an important activity in any IMC program. A strong brand means the product becomes part of the consumer's initial set of brands to consider when making a purchase. A powerful brand crosses national boundaries and becomes part of an effective globally integrated marketing communications program. Successful global brands are built over time. It takes a combination of high-quality products and effective marketing communications to reach that point.

In business-to-business marketing, a visible global brand presence is equally crucial. The existence of multiple vendors, increasing perceptions of brand parity, and growing use of the internet make it impossible for a company to succeed using only price differentiation. To combat such situations, a strong brand is a necessity in the global environment. Brand equity increases the chances of being selected. As Robert Duboff writes, "It is no longer sufficient to be a great company; *you must be a great brand*."[33]

objective 3.8
How can a company overcome international differences when adapting to buying processes?

Summary

Buyer behaviors are part of the purchasing process in both consumer markets and business-to-business transactions. An effective IMC program accounts for the ways in which goods and services are purchased in both markets. The consumer buying decision-making process consists of five steps. For the purposes of creating effective marketing communications, the information search stage and the evaluation of alternatives stage are the two most important.

After recognizing a want or need, a consumer searches for information both internally and externally. Marketing messages attempt to place the product or service in the consumer's evoked set of viable prospects. Three factors that influence search behaviors include involvement, needs for cognition, and enthusiasm for shopping. Customers consider the benefits and costs of searches and make decisions regarding how extensively they will seek information. Evoked sets, attitudes, values, and cognitive maps explain how individuals evaluate various purchasing choices.

Marketers face an evolving buying decision-making environment. Cultural values and attitudes, time pressures, and busy lifestyles influence what people buy, how they buy,

and the manner in which they can be enticed to buy. Many consumers try to escape through indulgences and pleasure binges, by finding excitement or fantasy, and by planning to meet social needs. An aging baby boom population concentrates more on lasting values and on health issues. Social media has affected the ways in which consumers communicate with one another. Marketing experts can address these needs and lead customers to purchases based on them.

By understanding business buyer behaviors, the marketing team constructs a more complete and integrated marketing communications program. Business purchases are driven by members of the buying center. These members include users, buyers, influencers, deciders, and gatekeepers. Members of the buying center are influenced by both organizational and individual factors that affect various marketing decisions.

Business-to-business sales take three forms. A straight rebuy occurs when the firm has previously chosen a vendor and intends to place a reorder. A modified rebuy occurs when the purchasing group is willing to consider and evaluate new alternatives. A new task purchase takes place when a company buys a good or service for the first time, and the product involved is one with which organizational members have no experience.

The business-to-business buying process is similar to the consumer purchase decision-making process. A more formal purchasing process includes formal specifications, bids from potential vendors, and a contract finalizing the purchasing agreement.

Dual channel marketing means that the firm sells virtually the same goods or services to both consumers and businesses. The challenge to the marketing team is to create strong and consistent marketing messages to every potential buyer, accounting for how buyer behaviors are present in purchasing processes.

Key Terms

involvement The extent to which a stimulus or task is relevant to a consumer's existing needs, wants, or values

need for cognition A personality characteristic of an individual who engages in and enjoys mental activities.

enthusiasm for shopping Customers who like to shop will undertake a more in-depth search for details about goods and services

attitude A mental position taken toward a topic, person, or event that influences the holder's feelings, perceptions, learning processes, and subsequent behaviors

values Strongly held beliefs about various topics or concepts

cognitive maps Simulations of the knowledge structures embedded in an individual's mind

evoked set The set of brands a consumer considers during the information search and evaluation processes

inept set The part of a memory set that consists of the brands held in a person's memory but are *not considered* because they elicit negative feelings

inert set The part of a memory set that consists of the brands the consumer has awareness of but has neither negative nor positive feelings about

affect referral A purchasing decision model in which the consumer chooses the brand for which he or she has the strongest liking or feelings

buying center The group of individuals who make a purchase decision on behalf of a business

straight rebuy A repurchase from a supplier during which no alternatives are considered

modified rebuy A situation in which the company's buying center considers and evaluates new purchasing alternatives

new task A purchase in which the company buys a good or service for the first time or the product involved is one with which organizational members have no experience

derived demand Demand based on, linked to, or generated by the production and sale of some other good or service

dual channel marketing Marketing virtually the same goods or services to both consumers and businesses

---

MyMarketingLab

To complete the problems with the ★ in your MyLab, go to the end-of-chapter Discussion Questions.

Review Questions

3-1. What are the five steps of the consumer buying decision-making process? Which two steps are the most important with regard to developing quality integrated marketing communications?

3-2. Describe the natures of an internal search and an external search in a purchasing decision.

3-3. Define attitude. What are the three main components of attitude, and how are they related to purchasing decisions?

3-4. How do values differ from attitudes? Name some personal values related to purchasing decisions.

3-5. Explain what a cognitive map models.

3-6. What is an evoked set? Why are evoked sets, inept sets, and inert sets important to the marketing department?

3-7. What are the key features of the multiattribute approach to evaluating purchasing alternatives?

3-8. What is meant by affect referral? When is a person likely to rely on such a cognitive approach to evaluating purchasing alternatives?

3-9. What new trends in the consumer buying environment affect consumer purchasing decisions?

3-10. Name and describe the five roles played in a buying center.

3-11. What organizational and individual factors affect members of the business buying center?

3-12. Describe the three main forms of business-to-business sales.

3-13. Name the steps in the business-to-business buying process.

3-14. Describe dual channel marketing and explain why it is important to a company's well-being.

Critical Thinking Exercises

DISCUSSION QUESTIONS

3-15. Compulsive buying and/or shopping takes place when a person becomes obsessed with making purchases, many of which are unnecessary or impractical. For college students and other individuals with compulsive buying behaviors, a primary influence is the family. Often one or both parents are compulsive shoppers. Families that display other forms of dysfunctional behaviors—such as alcoholism, bulimia, extreme nervousness, or depression—tend to produce children who are more inclined to exhibit compulsive shopping behaviors. Why do dysfunctional behaviors among parents produce compulsive shopping behavior among children? Another component of compulsive buying behaviors is self-esteem. Again, self-esteem is partly inherited, but it also develops in the home environment. How would self-esteem be related to compulsive shopping behaviors? What influences other than family might contribute to compulsive shopping behaviors? If an individual has a tendency to be a compulsive shopper, what can (or should) be done?

★3-16. Examine the consumer decision-making process that is illustrated in Figure 3.1. Think of a recent high-involvement purchase you made that involved every step in the process. Discuss each of the steps, especially the information search and evaluation of alternatives.

3-17. Think about the ways you purchase products and consider a recent purchase that involved an external search. Discuss your ability to search, the need for cognition, your personal level of shopping enthusiasm, and the perceived costs versus the perceived benefits of the search. How much time did you spend in the external search, and what was the outcome?

★3-18. Study the list of personal values presented in Figure 3.3. Identify the five most important to you. Rank them from first to last. Beside each value, identify at least one product you have purchased to satisfy those values. Explain how that good or service satisfied that value.

★3-19. Review the three methods of evaluating alternatives. Briefly explain each method. For each of the following product categories, which method of evaluation would you use for your next purchase? Explain why.

   a. *Meal with your significant other at a dine-in restaurant*

   b. *Auto service repair for your vehicle*

   c. *Pair of jeans*

   d. *Resort location for spring or winter break*

★3-20. Pick two of the product categories below. Identify brands in your evoked set, inept set, and inert set for that product category. Explain the rationale for the placement of each of the brands.

   a. *Quick service restaurants*

   b. *Retail clothing stores*

   c. *Grocery stores*

   d. *Computers*

3-21. Review the trends in the consumer buying environment presented in this chapter. For each trend, discuss the level of impact it has on your purchase behavior. Cite an example of a good or service you have recently purchased as a result of that trend.

3-22. A buying center member for a shoe manufacturer tries to purchase soles for shoes from outside vendors. Study the individual and organizational factors that affect buying center members. Discuss the effect of each factor on the roles of members in the shoe company's buying center. How does the factory foreman's role differ from that of the purchasing agent? How do these roles differ from the company president's role?

3-23. A purchasing agent for a clothing manufacturer is in the process of selecting vendors to supply the materials to produce about 30 percent of its clothes. The clothing manufacturer employs about 300 people. As the audit nears completion, what factors are most important to the purchasing agent?

3-24. Identify four brands you have used in a work environment that you also have purchased in your personal life. Discuss the dual channel marketing approach each of the brands use. Discuss the process that occurred in purchasing the product for personal use and the influence that using the brand in the work environment had on the purchase, or the reverse if you used it personally first.

Integrated Learning Exercises

3-25. Consumers and businesses conduct external searches when they lack sufficient internal knowledge to make a wise decision. Assume you have $150,000 to $200,000 to spend on a sailboat. Locate four websites that sell sailboats. Select one in your price range. Discuss the external search process you used to arrive at a decision. Relate this process to the concepts of external search, consumer attitudes, and consumer values presented in this chapter. Which method of evaluation did you use? Explain why.

3-26. Almost everyone has an opinion about tattoos. Some attitudes are positive whereas others are negative. Few are neutral. Go to **www.tattoos.com** and examine the material there. Did this information modify your attitude toward tattoos? What factors on the website influenced your attitude? Find at least one additional website of a company that offers tattoos. Provide the URL for the site and discuss the components of the website in terms of which components of attitude it is trying to influence: cognitive, affective, or conative.

3-27. Go to the authors' website at **clowbaack.net/video/ads.html**. Choose one of the television ads. Which component of an attitude is the primary focus of the ad? Justify your answer. Which consumer value is being emphasized? Justify your answer. For the evaluation of alternatives, which method of evaluation would be used by most consumers? Explain why. Which one of the trends in the consumer buying environment identified in the text does the ad target? Explain why. (Be sure to identify which ad you watched in your response.)

3-28. Go to the authors' website at **clowbaack.net/video/ads.html**. Watch the two advertisements for NOLA, The Times-Picayune. For each ad identify the component of attitude that you think is the primary focus and the personal value being emphasized. Justify your choice.

Who do you think is the target audience for these two ads? Explain why. Which of the two ads did you like the best? Why? Were the ads effective? Why or why not?

3-29. Review the trends in the consumer buying environment. Examine each of the following websites. Which trend or trends does each website seem to utilize on its website? Use screen shots to justify your thoughts.
   a. *Chipotle Mexican Grill* (**chipotle.com**)
   b. *Visit South Walton* (**www.visitsouthwalton.com**)
   c. *Ralph Lauren* (**www.ralphlauren.com**)
   d. *Scott + Cooner* (**scottcooner.com**)

3-30. Examine the following websites. What kind of information is provided? Which component of an attitude is the site designed to influence: cognitive, affective, or conative? Explain why.
   a. *Kenneth Cole* (**www.kennethcole.com**)
   b. *Starbucks* (**www.starbucks.com**)
   c. *Cadillac* (**www.cadillac.com**)
   d. *IKEA* (**www.ikea.com**)

3-31. A member of the buying center has been asked to gather information about possible shipping companies for international shipments. Visit the following websites. What companies have the most appealing websites? Beyond online materials, what additional information do they need to supply to the buying center in order to win the contract?
   a. *ABC India Limited* (**www.abcindia.com**)
   b. *SR International Logistics, Inc.* (**www.srinternational.com**)
   c. *Allison Shipping International* (**www.allisonshipping.com**)
   d. *Shipping International* (**www.shippinginternational.com**)

Blog Exercises

Access the authors' blog for this textbook at the URLs provided to complete these exercises. Answer the questions posed on the blog.

3-32. Jeep: **blogclowbaack.net/2014/05/07/jeep-chapter-3/**

3-33. Olive Garden: **blogclowbaack.net/2014/05/07/olive-garden-chapter-3/**

3-34. Consumer behavior, buying process: **blogclowbaack.net/2014/05/07/consumer-behavior-chapter-3/**

Student Project

CREATIVE CORNER

A local travel agency decides to advertise in the student newspaper on your campus to promote spring break packages. The company hires you to perform the creative work. The marketing department is not sure which type of advertising approach to use. The agency knows that attitude consists of three parts: cognitive, affective, and conative. They also know that an advertisement can appeal to any one of the attitude components. The agency's management team is not sure which component to use. Consequently, they have asked you to design three advertisements, with one designed to appeal to the cognitive component of attitude, the second to the affective component, and the third to the conative component. After you have finished designing the ads, discuss the pros and cons of each and make a recommendation to the travel agency about which one to use. The ads should be for a 5-day spring break vacation on the beach in Fort Lauderdale, Florida.

CASE 1 ▶ CHOOSING A LIFE INSURANCE POLICY

John Mulvaney just reached an important milestone in his life—birth of his first child. After seven years as a DINK (dual income-no kids) family, he and his wife Sandy decided it was time add a new member. At that point the couple had solid health insurance plans and policies protecting their home and automobiles. Life insurance was another matter.

As a novice, John had no idea about the types of policies that were available. He contacted his insurance agent, who represents a variety of insurance companies, and asked for a summary. The agent mentioned three potential forms of life insurance, each offered by a separate company that specialized in a specific type.

Company A's primary product, term life insurance, has the advantage of being the lowest annual cost option. John would be able to specify the policy's death benefit amount, which typically would be enough to care for his spouse and child (and vice versa for Sandy) for an extended period of time. A term policy covers a stated period of time (often 10 years) and then expires. All premiums go to the insurance company. The low cost often means a higher death benefit can be purchased at a lower price, especially for a healthy younger person. When a term policy is renewed, the premium amount rises for the same amount of coverage because the person is now older and has a higher potential of dying. At the same time, the individual's level of income may have also risen, making the renewal price easier to manage.

Company B's best policy, whole life insurance, features much higher fixed annual premiums, but works in a different manner. A cash value accrues as payments are made, and the value of the policy (a type of regular savings) grows over time, often collecting interest on the cash value. The policy also specifies a death benefit. At the end of the policy's specified time (often 40 years or more), the death benefit amount can continue to grow until the policy is redeemed. Many financial analysts argue that the higher costs and low rate of return (the interest rate paid on the case value) make whole life insurance a less viable investment. Others suggest it is a form of "forced" savings that benefits the policy holder over time. The amount of coverage (death benefit) remains the same over the life of the policy. For more coverage, a second policy or a term policy would need to be purchased.

Company C specializes in universal life insurance, which is a flexible form of permanent life insurance. It features the low cost of term life insurance combined with a savings element which is invested to provide a cash value buildup. John and Sandy would be able to review and change their death benefit amounts, the savings element, and their premiums over time. Also, universal life insurance allows the policyholder to use the interest from his or her accumulated savings to help pay premiums.

▲ John and Sandy discuss life insurance options as they prepare a meal.

John and Sandy had many things to consider as they made choices. First, they would need to decide on the amount of the death benefit for each of them, considering their present incomes, expected future incomes (based on promotions and pay raises), and whether they would have a second child. They also needed to think about how much money they could currently afford to spend on policies. And finally, the reputations of the three companies involved would deserve consideration. "I never realized this would be so complicated," John lamented. Sandy agreed.

3-35. Identify the need (or needs) that would begin the consumer buying decision making process in this case.

3-36. How would the elements involved in an external search affect John and Sandy as they explore their purchase options? Discuss in terms of:
   a. ability to search
   b. level of motivation
   c. costs versus benefits

3-37. Explain how John and Sandy could evaluate their options using each of the following concepts and models:
   a. attitudes and values
   b. cognitive mapping
   c. multiattribute

3-38. What types of marketing messages should each of the three life insurance companies design to reach consumers such as John and Sandy, for either the information search, evaluation of alternatives, or both stages of the buying decision-making process?

CASE 2 ▶ THE CHOICE

The Planter's Insurance Company's home office operations are located in Kansas City, Missouri. The agency provides health insurance packages to other businesses. The company's reputation has been built on professional service delivered at competitive prices. Currently, the agency's contract with its office supply company is about to expire. Planter's Insurance purchases paper and other materials and leases copiers and printers on a 3-year cycle. There are five members of the buying center: Martin Garza, Suzette Simon, Jason Talley, Paul Johnson, and Rose Knotts.

Martin Garza serves as the purchasing agent for the company. He is actively seeking to be promoted into a vice presidential role in the area of support staff. Martin's outgoing personality has made him friends and rivals. His approach to managing the purchasing function has been to save the company money whenever possible, believing this approach will help when the next promotion decision will be made. Martin is willing to use political tactics to achieve his personal and organizational goals.

Suzette Simon manages the copy center. She believes taking the offer from the lowest bidder is normally not a wise choice. When reviewing the bids, Suzette noticed that the lowest offer came from a company that had been retained previously. The company did a poor job, its service was inadequate, and its copiers regularly broke down. Suzette has a strong personality and does not back down in a disagreement, even with higher-ranking and male employees.

Jason Talley, the vice president of finance, is the highest-ranking member of the buying center. He will make the final decision because of his position. Jason is an introvert who listens, seldom takes a stand, and tries to get the group to make a unanimous decision. If not, he normally goes with the lowest risk solution—which, in this case, would be the current vendor.

Paul Johnson manages the IT department, which maintains the computers and printers. He wants to exclude printers from the contract and purchase them instead of leasing, which he believes will save the company money. He sees this purchasing decision as a chance to demonstrate his power. He dislikes Martin Garza and believes Garza has secret motives in pursuing the low-cost bidder.

Rose Knotts is the administrative assistant to the president. She is the lowest-ranking member of the buying center. Rose sees her role as providing information and keeping peace. She is reluctant to voice an opinion and almost always defers to Jason Talley, the vice president of finance.

Planter's Insurance has received four bids for the contract. Basic information about each is as follows:

Company 1: Is the current vendor, and has bid $123,000 for the copier and printer lease contract. Suzette says the company delivers "acceptable" quality but is often slow to respond when a repair is needed.

Company 2: Has an excellent reputation for quality service. The company's salesperson is a friend of Suzette

▲ A buying center meets to discuss coper and printer bids.

Simon. She argues that his company will save Planter's Insurance money in the long run due to fewer instances of down time and the best quality equipment. The bid was $139,000 for the copier and lease contract.

Company 3: Is new to Kansas City. No one in the buying center has knowledge about the company. Its bid was $115,000 with the notation that repairs are made within 24 hours and a repair person is on duty at all times, including overnight.

Company 4: Is the company that Suzette noted was of poor quality. The company's bid was $114,000, making it the low offer. Paul Johnson believes that Martin Garza revealed the bid of Company 3 to this company so that it could make an offer that was lower.

Jason Talley opens the final meeting of the buying center team. He asks each member to name the company they think should receive the bid. The opinions are as follows:

- Martin Garza: Company 4
- Suzette Simon: Company 2
- Paul Johnson: Company 3
- Rose Knotts: Company 1

Jason favors Company 3, for two reasons. First, he respects the opinion of Paul Johnson. Second, he thinks the 24-hour service feature makes the company stand out.

Questions

3-39. Discuss the reasoning behind each person's choice based on the information provided and the individual factors outlined in this chapter.

3-40. Identify the factors that favor each vendor and the factors that are the vendor's weaknesses.

3-41. How should Jason make the final choice, given there is such a great divergence in opinion?

3-42. What should Jason say to the members of the buying center whose favorite companies are not chosen?

MyMarketingLab

Go to the Assignments section of your MyLab to complete these writing exercises.

3-43. Describe each of the trends in the consumer behavior environment. Discuss the impact that each trend has on clothing purchases, especially current fashions.

3-44. Identify and define the factors that affect the amount of time consumers spend in conducting an external search. Suppose you wanted to purchase a boat (sailboat, powerboat, or fishing boat). Discuss each of the factors that would affect your external search process in the purchase of the boat. Explain why.

Buzz Marketing

Communications

Social Media

Advertising

Promotions

Digital

Branding

Mobile Marketing

Chapter 4 # The IMC Planning Process

Chapter Objectives

After reading this chapter, you should be able to answer the following questions:

4.1 What makes marketing research critical to the IMC planning process?

4.2 What categories are used to identify consumer target markets or market segments?

4.3 What categories are used to identify business-to-business market segments?

4.4 How do the various approaches to positioning influence the IMC planning process?

4.5 How do the marketing communications objectives interact with the other elements of an IMC planning process?

4.6 How are communications budgets established?

4.7 What elements are considered in developing an IMC program?

Overview

An integrated marketing communications planning process requires careful oversight by the company's marketing personnel and any agency the firm employs. They make decisions with regard to matching products to marketing messages and communications tactics. Successful marketing efforts occur when the company's marketing team identifies every opportunity to make quality contacts with current customers and potential new customers. An example of this type of work may be found in the case of an approach taken by McDonald's.

IMC PLANNING AND MCBREAKFAST

I n 2015, the marketing team and and other McDonald's executives decided to take a decisive step in the attempt to bolster sales and encourage traffic. The longstanding McDonald's breakfast menu was to be offered throughout the day. Customers of all ages who love breakfast would no longer be limited to mornings when craving an Egg McMuffin or other staples, such as eggs, sausage, and hash browns.

The launch of this new tactic included a dramatic rollout of traditional advertising produced by several agencies, along with digital elements including GIFs, Snapchat filters and a Twitter relay. Each promoted a special All Day Breakfast event. It also included partnering with the Threadless organization to allow consumers to create t-shirts, bags, and other merchandise with All Day Breakfast themes. Planning for such a major undertaking reflects many of the key elements of IMC planning.

The first unique challenge was that the McDonald's brand and its breakfast line were already well-known. Slumping sales hinted that a major objective would be to generate new excitement and customer engagement while encouraging traffic and repeat business. McDonald's U.S. Chief Marketing Officer Deborah Wahl referred to the program as "the people's launch," She added, "It shows the breadth of what we're working on here and the fact that we think there are a lot of people who are going to engage on everything."

The company established a considerable budget for the rollout and marketing program. As might have been expected, several other chains created responses seeking to reduce the impact of the McDonald's campaign. For instance, White Castle began a similar program that took place just nine days before the McDonald's All Day rollout. As a result, a strong messaging program aimed at focusing customers on McDonald's event was in order.

Next, to create a sustained effort, the company committed to a year-long program designed to reinforce the main message – that breakfast wasn't just for mornings anymore, at least at McDonald's.[1] Early returns indicated customer interest in and positive responses to the new approach.[2]

This chapter describes the nature of the IMC planning process. As illustrated in Figure 4.1, it begins with communications research. This helps the marketing team identify potential target markets and positioning strategies that match the brand. Next,

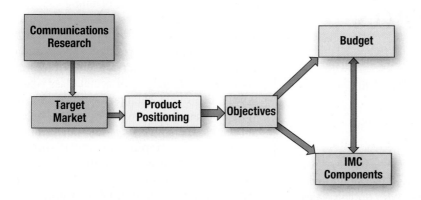

◀ **FIGURE 4.1**
The IMC Planning Process

objective 4.1

What makes marketing research critical to the IMC planning process?

▼ Through product-specific research, it was determined that trust is an important consideration in the selection of a financial institution.

communications objectives are specified. Finally, the team designs a budget to achieve the communications objectives with the IMC components in mind. International considerations are also taken into account.

Communications Research

The communications planning process begins with research. Those individuals involved in designing a communications campaign must thoroughly understand the product being sold and the consumers (or businesses) who are potential buyers.

More than just basic product attributes influence purchase decisions. Many customers consider the benefits a product provides. Individuals purchasing makeup, cologne, perfume, and other beauty products may not be concerned about the specific ingredients but care a great deal about how the items will make them look or smell. Consequently, communications research should go beyond identifying demographic profiles or target markets. Key insights regarding how, when, and why products are used emerge from effective research. Three primary research approaches are product-specific research, consumer-oriented research, and target-market research.

Product-specific research involves identifying key product characteristics that become selling points. For example, the marketing team might try to discover the most desirable app features for a cell phone. The team might find that consumers use certain apps when they are bored and passing time, whereas others provide specific functional information, such as the location of a restaurant. One feature or the other becomes the focal point of a commercial or marketing message.

To be effective, product-specific research goes beyond discovering attributes or characteristics. It includes an understanding of the product's benefits. A smartphone offers several. It provides a means of communicating with other people through the phone feature or through social media. It can be used to access product information through a QR code at a retail store. It delivers entertainment through watching TV shows or consumer-posted videos. While understanding the features of a smartphone will be important, finding the types of benefits customers derive from those features becomes even more critical to effective communications planning.

Consumer-oriented research assists marketers in identifying the context of a product's use. An *anthropological* approach involves direct observations of consumers using the good or service. Other research may feature a *sociological* analysis of social class issues, trends, and family life cycle changes. A third consumer-oriented approach analyzes *psychological* motives for product purchases, such as feeling sexy, powerful, or intelligent.

Before developing an advertising campaign for Scotts Miracle-Grow lawn fertilizer, The Richards Group engaged in consumer-oriented research. The Richards team interviewed 4,000 consumers and gained the

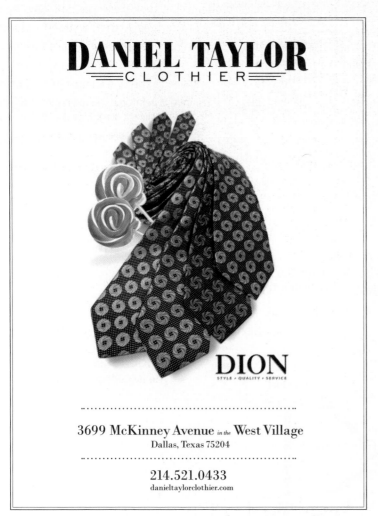

▲ Consumer-oriented research can be used by Daniel Taylor Clothier to better understand individuals who purchase ties.

valuable insight that "people would change their behaviors if an expert spoke to them about lawn care." The investigation revealed that many people reported that usually someone in the neighborhood is "knowledgeable about lawn care." Using this information, The Richards Group's advertising team created the spokesperson "Scottish." His name is a mnemonic play on the Scotts brand. Early evaluations of the campaign indicate that it resonated well with consumers.[3]

Target-market research identifies those who will be the recipient of a communications campaign. For instance, product-oriented research may determine that one benefit of joining a fitness center can be improved heart health. Consumer-oriented research might indicate that the elderly and those who have developed some type of heart trouble would be the most likely to want this particular benefit. Thus, target-market research looks at the best market for a particular benefit of a good or service.

Sometimes a company's marketing team becomes so close to products and customers that they do not see these issues. Consequently, agencies often seek out more information from clients. One common approach used by agencies to understand a client's customers is a **focus group**, which consists of consumers who talk about a particular topic, product, or brand in front of a moderator or panel who tracks consumer comments and ideas. The insights gained become crucial elements in the IMC planning process.

Market Segmentation by Consumer Groups

▲ This Philadelphia Cream Cheese advertisement is targeted to the market segment that loves chocolate.

Communications research identifies the target markets a company seeks to serve. Target markets exist in two areas: consumer markets and business-to-business markets, which are also known as market segments. A **market segment** consists of a set of businesses or group of individual consumers with distinct characteristics. For a market segment to be viable, it should pass the following tests:

- The individuals or businesses within the market segment should be similar in nature, with the same needs, attitudes, interests, and opinions. Persons or businesses within the segment are *homogenous*.
- The market segment differs from the population as a whole. Segments are distinct from other segments and from the general population.
- The market segment must be large enough to be financially viable to target with a separate marketing campaign.
- The market segment must be reachable through some type of media or marketing communications method.

objective **4.2**

What categories are used to identify consumer target markets or market segments?

Market researchers spend considerable resources and time working to discover viable market segments. The **market segmentation** process consists of identifying the specific consumer and business groups that are the most likely to purchase the brand based on their needs, attitudes, and interests.

Consumers, or end users, represent one primary target market for a firm's offerings. Effective IMC programs identify sets of consumers who are potential buyers. Figure 4.2 lists the most common consumer market segmentation approaches.

▶ **FIGURE 4.2**

Methods of Segmenting
Consumer Markets

- Demographics
- Psychographics
- Generations
- Geographic
- Geodemographics
- Benefits
- Usage

Segments Based on Demographics

One primary method of segmentation employs **demographics**, or various population characteristics. Typical demographic variables include gender, age, education, income, and ethnicity. Companies create goods and services to meet the needs of individual demographic segments.

Gender   Men and women purchase different products, buy similar products with different features (e.g., deodorants), desire products for dissimilar reasons (laptops, televisions), and buy the same products after being influenced by different kinds of appeals through different media. For example, both genders use deodorant.

Degree deodorant was introduced as a unisex brand in 1990. In 2005, the company divided the product into two forms, Degree Men and Degree Women, featuring different advertising approaches. Ads for Degree Women emphasized that the deodorant left no marks on clothing and that it would hold up as she worked and socialized. For men, the focus was more on physical feats such as riding mountain bikes or snowboarding. Both brands were placed under one agency that designed a new campaign, a shared strategy, and a new tagline. The ads featured famous athletes, both male and female, training in something other than their primary sport. The voiceover promises "Degree won't let you down" with the tagline is "Do More." The message suggests that Degree, whether for men or women, provides the same benefit and works in all situations that create sweat.[4]

Other products focus on a specific gender. One recent study suggested that women control 66 percent, or $12 trillion, of the world's annual consumer spending. Women influence or make purchases in product categories traditionally controlled by men.[5] For instance, in the United States:

- 96 percent of women are involved in purchasing high-priced electronics.
- 90 percent of women deal with financial advisors.
- 80 percent of women buy and sell stocks.
- 70 percent of women are their household's primary "accountant."

Some companies that have done well in response include Olay and Paige Premium. Olay advertises skin care products for females and tells women that the company wants to help them enjoy beautiful skin. Paige Premium encourages women to love their bodies and places a card in each pair of denim jeans that reads "I want you to love your body. Feel comfortable in your skin. Feel comfortable in your jeans. Thanks for believing in our product."[6]

Other marketing programs target men. Researchers indicates that men are shopping more, whether for their own clothes or for groceries. To reach males shoppers, marketers work to understand how males differ from females. Males tend to focus on product performance. Men enjoy activities that they can do well and dislike things they cannot. They do not like browsing and instead prefer looking for specific information. **Amazon.com** meets both of these needs by helping men purchase books and music online. Consumer lists, reviews, and suggestions provide the concise information males desire in order to feel confident about their purchases. Men favor products reflecting status that demonstrate "I have good taste." As a result, males tend to purchase well-known brand names and look for other indicators of quality.[7]

◀ An advertisement for Origin Bank segmented by gender.

Gender offers the opportunity to match a product with a large category of individuals. Careful thought should be given as to whether it should be aimed at only one sex, because gender roles have evolved over the past half-century.

Age   Marketing programs often concentrate on persons of a certain age, most notably children, teens, young adults, middle-age adults, and senior citizens. Age can be combined with another demographic, such as gender. Consequently, older women may be primary targets for specific types of vitamins and medical products, including those combatting osteoporosis. Young working women with children are more likely to notice advertisements for conveniences, including ready-made foods and snacks, and automotive oil

When my child is ill, if I need a blood test or a prescription filled— St. Francis Community Health Center is my first and only choice.

Our team of healthcare professionals are here for you—including physicians, registered x-ray techs, cardiac rehab nurses, nutritionists, therapists, pharmacists, nurse practitioners to nurses and more!

ST. FRANCIS
COMMUNITY HEALTH CENTER
Franciscan Missionaries of Our Lady Health System

Future of Healing. Tradition of Caring.

920 Oliver Road, Monroe • (318) 966-6200
stfran.com

▲ A St. Francis advertisement targeted to females making health care provider decisions.

and lube facilities. The advertisement for JD Bank on the next page highlights retirement and investment services and targets senior men.

Small children constitute an attractive, if somewhat controversial market. A Campaign for Commercial-Free Childhood study revealed that by six months of age babies form mental images of brand logos and mascots. Other research indicates by the time children are three years old they recognize as many as 100 brand images. Reaching babies has become easier now more than ever before, primarily because of technology and parental use of technology. A Joan Ganz Cooney Center study indicates that 80 percent of children age five and under use the internet weekly and 60 percent of children three and younger watch online videos. One in four parents allows children to interact with a mobile phone or iPad by the age of two.[8]

Despite criticisms from parental and other watchdog groups, advertising to children (even babies) generates large revenues. If brand loyalty can be obtained at a young age, a company might retain a customer for a lifetime.

Tweens represent an additional age-based market segment. Figure 4.3 presents some interesting information about tweens. As shown, tweens influence household purchases. They are online and have already started making purchases using the internet.[9]

The marketing push to reach young consumers continues through the teen years. At the same time, recent research suggests that marketers may need to modify the methods they use to reach this target group. Teens have switched a substantial amount of shopping from specialty and department stores to online. Value may be more important than brand names. The digital world takes up more of their time and has become the primary source of product and brand information. For this group, Facebook has declined in popularity while the use of Twitter, Instagram, and other social media venues has risen.[10]

Income A family's income level income and educational attainment are often closely related. Members of lower-income homes, often with less education, primarily purchase *necessities* such as food, clothing, and housing needs; however, members of these households also buy cell phones, automobiles, and other, more costly, products. As income and educational attainment increase, household members purchase from a greater selection of expensive items. These products, or *sundry* items, include vacations, more expensive automobiles, more fashionable clothes, and meals at higher-end restaurants. The items are purchased occasionally by those who can afford them, but not on a routine basis. At the extreme, the wealthy purchase *luxury* products, such as yachts and private planes.

Some companies use income segmentation to help create products and advertisements. One demographic group that receives attention is the "exhausted affluent." Individuals in this group generate household incomes from $100,000 to $150,000. They are affluent but identify with the working class. They bridge the gap between "the haves" and "the have nots."

In furniture, they desire style and quality rather than something overly fancy. In landscaping, they want designs that make their homes unique and stylish, but at the same time functional.[11] The advertisement by Bonick Landscaping on the next page focuses on this unique market segment.

Ethnicity The United States is becoming increasingly diverse. Ethnic minorities represent $2.5 trillion in buying power. This growth represents both an opportunity and a threat: an opportunity for companies able to adapt their messages to other cultures and heritages, and a threat to those that cannot. Seventy percent of ethnic minorities state that ethnicity constitutes a significant part of their personal identities. Ethnic marketing succeeds in some, but not all, product categories. Sixty-two percent of African Americans want health and beauty products marketed specifically to them; 53 percent of Hispanics said ethnicity is important for consumer packaged goods, entertainment, and clothing; and 50 percent of Asians stated that ethnicity was important for entertainment services.[12]

Chrysler Group LLC created a campaign that targeted Hispanics using television, radio, print, newspaper, and digital media ads in the top 15 Hispanic markets. The campaign spots were not trans-created or translated from English ads. Instead they were produced for the Hispanic audience, although the ads were in Spanish and English. Large pick-up trucks are historically one of the best-selling vehicles among Latinos. As a result, the campaign focused on the Ram 1500 and Ram 2500. The creative focused on unscripted, real-life testimonies from Hispanic truck owners talking about the values that are essential to them and how the Ram truck is an extension of their lives. The campaign

▲ This advertisement for JD Bank includes both gender and age segmentation.

◀ **FIGURE 4.3**
Influence of Tweens

Influence/Opinion	Percent
Want instant gratification	56%
Want customized product	59%
Want what others have	41%
Sometimes visit online stores	31%
Shop online	28%
Influence on household purchases	
Movies	55%
Food	29%
Personal care products	26%
Family vacation destination	27%
Technology	23%

▶ This advertisement for Bonick Landscaping targets the "exhausted affluent" market segment.

DESIGN CREATE SUSTAIN

GREAT DESIGN IS ONLY AS GOOD AS ITS EXECUTION AND SUSTAINABILITY

Bonick Landscaping's impeccable designs speak for themselves, but being recognized within our industry as a leader in tackling complex build-out challenges to exacting standards is what makes us different. In fact, Bonick is a top choice among DFW's premier landscape architects to execute *their* designs. Our standards for excellence permeate everything we do, from design and build-out to maintaining and growing your landscape design investment once it is complete. For more information, call 972.243.9673 today.

bonicklandscaping.com

theme "A Todo Con Todo," which translates as "To everything, with everything," captured the consumer mindset and "true essence" of the Ram truck for the Hispanic target market.[13]

Similar approaches were used by Kraft's marketing team in developing ads for Kraft Mac & Cheese as well as by the advertising group for Domino's pizza. Rather than focus on the product, both brands focused on people. Kraft sent the message that eating an American food (Mac & Cheese) does not make a Latino less Latino. A graphic popup states, "Mantente 100%," which means "Stay 100% [Latino]." The Domino's spots featured Mauricio Arroyave, who was born in Colombia and now owns ten franchises. The commercials told his story and that of other Hispanic employees. Both approaches were well-received in the Hispanic segment.[14]

In recent years, the ways marketing professionals approach ethnic marketing have changed. Rather than separate campaigns for each ethnic group, agencies take a more holistic approach that incorporates insights into various ethnic groups in order to create more universally-appealing messages.

Psychographics

Demographics are relatively easy to identify. They do not, however, fully explain why people buy particular products or specific brands or the type of appeal that works to reach them. To assist in the marketing effort while building on demographic information, psychographic profiles have been developed. **Psychographics** emerge from patterns of responses that reveal a person's activities, interests, and opinions (AIO). The measures can be combined with demographic information to supply marketers with a more complete understanding of the target market.[15]

▲ Hispanics are a viable ethnic group for market segmentation.

Strategic Business Insights provides a popular classification of lifestyles using psychographic segmentation. The VALS (Values and Lifestyles) typology categorizes respondents into eight different groups based on resources and on the extent to which they are action-oriented.[16] The VALS typology includes the following segments:

- **Innovators**—Successful, sophisticated, and receptive to new technologies. Their purchases reflect cultivated tastes for upscale products.
- **Thinkers**—Educated, conservative, practical consumers who value knowledge and responsibility. They look for durability, functionality, and value.
- **Achievers**—Goal-oriented, conservative consumers committed to career and family. They favor established prestige products that demonstrate success to peers.

▼ An advertisement for Visit South Walton (Florida) targeted to the "Experiencers" VALS group.

- **Experiencers**—Young, enthusiastic, and impulsive consumers who seek variety and excitement and spend substantially on fashion, entertainment, and socializing.
- **Believers**—Conservative, conventional consumers who focus on tradition, family, religion, and community. They prefer established brands and favor American-made products.
- **Strivers**—Trendy, fun-loving consumers who are concerned about others' opinions and approval. They demonstrate to peers their ability to buy.
- **Makers**—Self-sufficient consumers who have the skill and energy to carry out projects, respect authority, and are unimpressed by material possessions.
- **Survivors**—Concerned with safety and security, focused on meeting needs rather than fulfilling desires. They are brand loyal and purchase discounted products.

This type of information helps marketers design more effective communications. For instance, reaching strivers requires advertisements that convey fun and trendy products. Ads for believers focus on traditional and patriotic values.

Revel, the $2.4 billion resort casino in Atlantic City, developed an advertising campaign aimed at the VALS experiencer group. The target market was defined as "leisure and lifestyle consumers among the 47 million people age 21 and over who live within a 5-hour drive of Atlantic City." The emphasis of the campaign was not on gambling, but on "elevationism," which suggests, "when you go to Revel, you experience something you've never experienced before" —you feel elevated as a result of it. The TV, radio, print, and digital ads focused on presenting an elevated experience and featured the resorts, concerts, cabanas, beaches, and bonfires—of the amenities except gambling. The campaign and resort was built "on the belief that the more fun we have, the more fun we have!"[17]

Segments Based on Generations

Marketing efforts can target generational cohorts, because the approach does not require the use of psychographic information but does possess the richness of psychographics. Marketing to generational cohorts relies on the common experiences and events that create bonds between people who are about the same age.

Generational segmentation proponents suggest that people experience significant events during late adolescence or early adulthood. These events create an impact on social values, attitudes, and preferences based on shared experiences. This may lead to common preferences for music, foods, and other products. A cohort group may respond favorably to the same type of marketing appeal. Figure 4.4 identifies six generational cohorts along with basic characteristics.

The millennial generation garners the most advertising dollars. While some common characteristics are present, a research study by Turn identified four distinct segments of millennials (see Figure 4.5). The largest segment contains struggling aspirationals (57%) who are healthy, fit, and concerned about the environment. Financial constraints lead this millennial segment to look for bargains, sales, and promotions, yet as the name implies, they aspire to high quality products and experiences. In contrast, the successful homeowners (18%) have the highest incomes among millennials and own their homes. The active affluents (17%) love the outdoors, leisure travel, and most are new parents. The most traditional group is the comfortable TV watchers (8%). As the name implies, the lives of this millennial segment center on their televisions, but not always high-definition sets in living rooms. They are as just likely to watch on a tablet, mobile phone, or computer.[18]

Name of Segment	Year of Birth	Characteristics
Millennials	1978–2002	Spend money on clothes, automobiles, college, televisions, and stereos. Ninety percent live at home or in a dorm or rent an apartment.
Generation X	1965–1977	Focus on family and children. Spend on food, housing, transportation, and personal services.
Younger Boomers	1954–1964	Focus on home and family. Spend on home mortgage, pets, toys, playground equipment, and large recreational items.
Older Boomers	1952–1953	Spend on upgrading homes, ensuring education and independence of their children, and luxury items, such as boats.
Seniors	Up to 1951	Most have fixed incomes. Spend heavily on health care and related medical items.

▶ **FIGURE 4.4**
Characteristics of Generation Segments

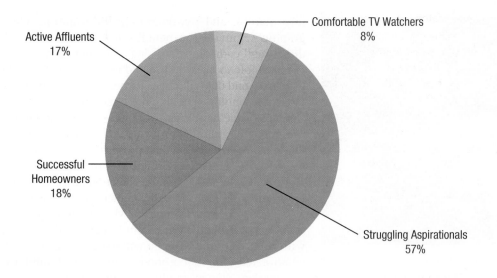

Despite these differences, many millennials are passionate about brands that support causes and the environment. Engagement and interaction brands through social media are important. They want to be active participants with brands, not just passive customers. Being different is acceptable. These individuals tend to be more accepting of persons from every race, social class, and sexual orientation than those from any other generation. This characteristic transfers to brands. Brands can also be different but should incorporate the multiculturalism present in society.[19]

Only a small number of millennials own their homes. Consequently, grilling brands such as Weber, Char-Broil and Lynx have changed tactics to reach this segment. Rather than television advertising, these brands utilize digital display ads, social media, mobile advertising, and video advertising. Products have also been modified. Millennials want grills that are portable, that can be taken to parks, camping, or other social events, such as tailgating at a football game. Char-Broil and Lynx Grills have created a mobile app that enables users to monitor temperatures on their grills and provides suggestions for cooking various types of meats and other foods.[20]

Segmentation by Geographic Area

Marketing appeals made to people in a geographic area or region is **geo-targeting**. Retailers often seek to limit marketing communications programs to the specific areas where primary customers live in order to maximize the impact of advertising dollars. Increased ownership of smartphones with built-in GPS devices allows marketers to expand geo-targeting programs. For instance, during a snow storm along the East Coast, consumers in that area received Home Depot ads related to snow removal while other areas of the country were sent ads related to fall lawn care or other relevant topics. With geo-targeting, digital advertisements can be aimed to specific regions with messages that fit consumers, the region, and specific events.

Geodemographic Segmentation

Geodemographic segmentation identifies potential customers by combining demographic information, geographic

▼ A promoted post on Pinterest by Visit South Walton targeting the millennial generation.

There's always something exciting happening in our 16 beach neighborhoods! Ready to see what's on the South Walton horizon?

✈ 40   ♥ 83   💬 1

Promoted by
📍 South Walton

▲ Restaurants can use geo-targeting to reach individuals that are near.

information, and psychographic information. Geodemographic segmentation benefits national firms conducting direct-mail campaigns or using sampling promotions. Mailing a sample to every household in a geographic area can be expensive and unproductive. Through geodemographics, only those households matching the target market profile receive samples or messages. For instance, colleges and universities use geodemographics to locate ZIP codes of communities that match particular student profiles.

PRIZM (Potential Rating Index by Zip Marketing), specializes in geodemographics. The company identified 66 different market segments in the United States, and categorized every U.S. ZIP code. The PRIZM methodology is based on the concept that ZIP codes identify neighborhoods of people with relatively uniform characteristics. Consumers tend to be attracted to neighborhoods consisting of similar people. Recognizing that more than one market segment might live within a ZIP code, however, PRIZM identifies the top market segments within each ZIP code.[21]

A PRIZM-coded map of downtown Jackson, Mississippi, identifies two primary clusters. The predominant one is "Southside City" residents. The cluster contains mainly young and elderly African Americans employed in low-paying blue-collar jobs. They tend to have lower levels of formal education, rent apartments, and read sports and fashion magazines. The second cluster within downtown Jackson holds the "Towns and Gowns" neighborhoods. Inhabitants of these neighborhoods also rent apartments, but they tend to be college graduates with better-paying white-collar jobs. This group likes to ski, reads beauty and fitness magazines, and frequently uses ATM cards.[22]

Benefit Segmentation

Benefit segmentation focuses on advantages consumers receive from a product rather than characteristics of consumers themselves. Marketers combine demographic and psychographic information with benefit information in order to identify viable segments.

Benefit segmentation appears in the fitness market. Regular exercisers belong in one of three benefit segments. The first group, "Winners," do whatever it takes to stay physically fit. This segment tends to be younger, upwardly mobile, and career-oriented. The second group, "Dieters," exercise to maintain their weight and enhance physical appearance. This group is comprised of females over the age of 35. They are primarily interested in reliable wellness programs offered by hospitals and weight-control nutritionists. The third group, "Self-Improvers," exercise to feel better and to control medical costs.[23] Recognizing that individuals exercise for different reasons provides excellent material for designing marketing programs.

Usage Segmentation

The final type of consumer segmentation examines groups based on usage or purchases, including the company's best customers or heavy users, average users, casual or light users, and nonusers. Marketers provide the highest level of service to the best customers while promoting the company to the other two usage groups in an attempt to move them up to the next usage group.

Marketing teams identify heavy users through internal databases. Bar-code scanners, point-of-sale systems, and data from credit, debit, and in-house transaction cards provide marketers a wealth of customer information. Many companies experience a situation in which 10 to 30 percent of a company's customers generate 70 to 90 percent of total sales. Instead of using firms such as PRIZM to create customer clusters, marketers develop customer clusters from in-house databases. They place customers in clusters based on common attitudes, lifestyles, and past purchase behaviors. This technique offers a business the following advantages:[24]

1. A meaningful classification scheme to cluster customers based on a firm's various levels of users.

2. The ability to reduce large volumes of customer data down to a few concise, usable clusters.

3. The ability to assign a cluster code number to each customer in the database. Each number is based on the customer's actual purchases and other characteristics (e.g., address, amount spent, spending potential, demographics, etc.).

4. The capacity to measure the growth and migration of customers over time and from one cluster to another, which allows for the evaluation of marketing programs.

5. The ability to develop different marketing programs for each cluster that matches the characteristic of the clusters.

▲ The fitness industry is often segmented based on the benefit each segment seeks from exercise.

Instead of heavy users, Dairy Queen developed a campaign aimed at light users who visited only once a month and saw the brand as merely an ice cream stand. The company's marketers developed the tagline "Fan food, not fast food" to encourage individuals to visit Dairy Queen instead of a competing fast-food restaurant. The campaign sought to bump once-per-month visitors to two or three visits per month. The messages featured ice cream as the bonus to great food.[25]

Occasionally, a marketing team creates a communications program for nonusers. For instance, a Carnival Cruise Lines campaign targeted the 76 percent of Americans who had never taken a cruise. A dozen humorous ads were prepared featuring the theme of "land versus sea." Scenes compared disastrous land vacations to peaceful and calm moments on the cruise ship. Along with the humorous scenes, the ads pointed out the prices were competitive with the costs of land vacations, seeking to dispel the belief that cruises are expensive. Passengers were shown in roomy cabins and relaxing on deck to change the perception that cruise rooms are small and cramped as well as that schedules were too structured to just relax and enjoy some private time.[26]

▲ Carnival Cruise Line created a campaign targeting the 76 percent of Americans who have never taken a cruise.

Business-to-Business Market Segmentation

Another set of target markets comes from identifying business-to-business segments (see Figure 4.6). Business segmentation efforts group similar organizations into meaningful clusters in order to create marketing messages specifically for them and to provide them with better service.

objective 4.3

What categories are used to identify business-to-business market segments?

- Industry (NAICS code)
- Size of business
- Geographic location
- Product usage
- Customer value

▲ **FIGURE 4.6**
Methods of Segmenting
Business-to-Business Markets

Segmentation by Industry

When segmenting by industry, many marketers use the NAICS (North American Industry Classification System) coding system. NAICS helps the marketing team examine specific industries, such as construction (23) or wholesale trade (42). There are also segments within specific categories. For example, NAICS codes health care and social assistance services as 62. A manufacturer of health-related products may find four segments, based on these subsections:

621	Ambulatory Health Care Services
622	Hospitals
623	Nursing and Residential Care Facilities
624	Social Assistance

The segments can be broken down into smaller subcomponents. For example, Ambulatory Health Care Services includes physicians, dentists, chiropractors, and optometrists.

The NAICS system divides the economy into 20 broad sectors using a six digit code. The code allows for stratification of industries and provides flexibility in creating classifications. The federal government records corporate information and data using the NAICS, making it a useful system for identifying market segments.

Segmentation by Size

Some market segments are identified based on a company's sales volume or number of employees. Large firms with 100,000 employees experience needs that differ from mid-size firms and smaller companies employing 100 or fewer individuals. Marketing approaches vary based on the size of a target prospect. For instance, for a large prospect firm, a selling company may utilize the outside sales staff to make sales calls. For mid-size corporate prospects, outside sales people make contact after a company shows initial interest through digital and telephone inquiries. For smaller firms, email and surface mail may be combined with inbound telemarketing. A salesperson would not make a sales call on the customer, because the revenue generated would be too small to warrant the expense.

Segmentation by Geographic Location

Identifying market segments by geographic location can be a successful tactic. This approach benefits businesses with customers concentrated in geographic pockets, such as the Silicon Valley area of California. It works for other firms as well.

When the Applied Microbiology firm developed a new antimicrobial agent, the goal was to introduce the product to dairy farmers. The traditional agricultural marketing and distribution channel required a budget for a national launch that was estimated to be $3 million. Such a traditional marketing plan involved national advertising in agriculture magazines plus recruiting sales agents and brokers to announce the product.

Instead, Applied Microbiology used geodemographics. The marketing team identified areas with dairy herds consisting of 1,000 or more cows per ranch. These farmers were contacted for two reasons. First, large dairy farmers who adopted the product would purchase greater quantities. Second, the company's leaders believed the larger farmers were the opinion leaders who could influence smaller farmers, thereby causing them to adopt the product as well.

The marketing team sent several separate direct-response pieces offering discounts for and samples of Applied Microbiology's new product to larger farms. After sales began to rise, the marketers asked farmers for testimonials. They incorporated most powerful testimonials into new direct-marketing pieces. One brochure contained three testimonials and validation of the product by Cornell University. After a dairy farmer adopted the product, the company sent direct-marketing pieces to farmers in the surrounding area. The method yielded excellent sales figures and reduced marketing costs to one-third of the traditional approach. Using geodemographics, marketing costs were $1 million rather than the proposed $3 million, and sales increased substantially.[27]

Segmentation by Product Usage

Business markets may be segmented based how companies use the good or service. Some services such as finance (not financial), transportation, and shipping offer a variety of uses to individual businesses. For example, many times companies require protection services. The Reynolds Protection advertisement featured in this section identifies services for three different situations: hostile meetings, workplace threats, and employee terminations. The company also delivers protection services in other circumstances. By segmenting the market based on the specific type needed, Reynolds is able to prepare marketing materials for various clients.

▲ Applied Microbiology used geographic targeting to reach dairy farmers.

Segmentation by Customer Value

One final method of business segmentation examines the value associated with each customer. Business-to-business firms are more likely to use this approach than consumer-oriented businesses due to the availability of in-depth data about each customer. A more precise value can be assigned to every individual business through sales records and other sources of data and information, placing them into low-, medium-, and high-value groups.

   In summary, marketers identify consumer and business-to-business segments in many ways. When choosing market segments to approach, the marketing team looks for groups that best match the company's goods and services as well as the firm's overall message. Marketers structure messages to meet the needs of the various segments and aligned them with the company's positioning strategy.

Product Positioning

Each target market or market segment will be selected, in part, because the company, product, or brand position matches the segment. **Product positioning** summarizes the perception in the consumer's mind of the nature of a company or brand and its products relative to competitors. Positioning perceptions include variables such as the quality of products, the price, methods of distribution, packaging, image, and other factors. Typically, two elements stand out—customer evaluations of the brand and the brand's standing relative to the competition.

   Consumers ultimately determine the position a brand holds. Marketing programs help position a brand effectively. Marketing communications either reinforce what consumers already believe about a brand or try to shift consumer views. The first outcome will be easier to accomplish. It also facilitates selection of target markets. When attempting to reposition a brand, the marketing team considers whether the new position continues to match existing market segments.

   Positioning enables companies such as Procter & Gamble, VF Corporation, Sara Lee Corporation, and Campbell's Soups to prevent cannibalism among various brands within a product category. For instance, Campbell's produces five different types of V8 juice. Each one targets a different market segment. Celestial Seasonings offers several types of tea, each one designed for a different set of consumers.

objective 4.4
How do the various approaches to positioning influence the IMC planning process?

▶ **FIGURE 4.7**
Product Positioning Approaches

- Attributes
- Competitors
- Use or application
- Price-quality relationship

- Product user
- Product class
- Cultural symbol

Approaches to Positioning

Effective positioning can be achieved in seven different ways (see Figure 4.7). Although companies might try two or three approaches, such efforts generally only manage to confuse customers. Normally, staying with one approach achieves the best results.

Product Attributes Any product trait or characteristic that sets a brand apart from other brands may be considered an attribute. Advertising for Dove Men+Care emphasized this concept by noting that the deodorant line contains moisturizers, which led to the tagline "Tough on sweat, not on skin." The Chickme advertisement shown on this page features hummus that comes in seven different flavor combinations.

Competitors Using competitors to establish position can be accomplished by contrasting the company's product against others. For years, Avis ran advertisements comparing itself to Hertz. Avis admitted it was not number one, but turned that position into an advantage because Avis was willing to "try harder" for business. Chevrolet developed a series of ads comparing its vehicles to Ford, Toyota, and other brands.

Flavors to Savor

Jalapeño Cilantro

Roasted Garlic

Roasted Red Pepper

Spicy Avocado   Original

7 Flavor Combinations.
All Organic.
All Non-GMO.
All Gluten Free.
What's stopping you? Try them all today.
www.chickmehummus.com

Chickme Hummus

▲ This advertisement for Chickme hummus features a product attribute positioning approach.

Use or Application Positioning that involves creating a memorable set of uses for a product emphasizes the use or application approach. Arm & Hammer employed this approach for many years, seeking to convince consumers to use baking soda in other ways, such as a deodorizer in the refrigerator. Arm & Hammer is also a co-brand in toothpaste, creating another use for the product and enhancing its position. Tide employed this method with its revolutionary Tide Pods. The pods took the guess-work out of how much detergent to use. Consumers simply toss one into the washing machine.

Price-Quality Relationship Businesses that offer products at the extremes of the price range may position by price-quality relationships. At the high end, quality becomes the emphasis. At the low end, price or value is emphasized. Hallmark cards cost more but are for those who "only want to send the very best." Other firms seek to be a "low-price

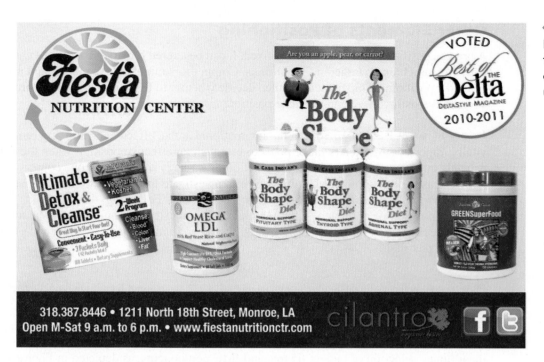

◀ This advertisement for Fiesta Nutrition Center focuses on health conscious consumers using a product user positioning approach.

leader," with no corresponding statement about quality. Instead of focusing solely on low prices, Wal-Mart's tagline "Save Money, Live Better" highlights the importance of price and how it can improve the customer's quality of life.

Product User   Another positioning strategy can distinguish the brand or product by specifying who might use it. GoDaddy has shifted its approach in an effort to reach small-business owners. For these users, GoDaddy focuses on its products and services and seeks to create the image of being a helpmate. Lean Cuisine shifted its focus from a diet brand focused on individuals who wanted to lose weight to a healthy lifestyle brand that emphasizes individuals seeking healthier, trendier foods that allowed them to maintain an active lifestyle.[28]

Product Class   Position may be based on product class. In the beverage category, soft drinks compete with energy drinks and others, such as breakfast drinks. Recently, Denny's marketers repositioned company facilities as diners instead of family restaurants. Focus groups did not consider Denny's a family restaurant. According to Frances Allen, chief marketing officer for Denny's, "People think of the brand as a diner, with great comfort food at a great price, and they feel that incredible warmth and connection to the servers. There's a soul to a diner that is very authentic, very warm, and very accepting."[29]

Occasionally, a company creates a new brand in a product class designed to stress superiority; such was the case with Swiffer. The Swiffer Sweeper provides an alternative to traditional floor-mopping, sweeping floors with brooms, and dusting with feather dusters. Marketers identified the "Quick Clean" category and positioned Swiffer as the best brand within that category.

Cultural Symbol   Positioning a product as a cultural symbol will be difficult. When the company successfully achieves such a position, it can gain a strong competitive advantage. For many years, Chevrolet enjoyed such status. General Motors advertised Chevrolet with the theme of being as American as baseball and apple pie. A slight variation was recently utilized in a campaign for the Chevrolet Silverado pickup. The messages focused on American patriotism and values such as independence and commitment. The campaign launched during baseball's All-Star game.

Other Elements of Positioning

A brand's position is never completely fixed. It can be altered if market conditions change over time or a brand's target market shrinks. Competitors might enter a market and usurp a brand's position. Company leaders then decide whether to fight for the position through strong advertising or seek an alternate position.

International Positioning   In the international arena, effective positioning remains vitally important. Marketers make plans to establish an effective position when the firm expands into new countries. Often the positioning strategy presented in one country will not work as well in another. Marketing experts investigate the competition as well as the consumers or businesses that are potential customers. Following this analysis, they choose a positioning approach. Although the positioning strategy might need to be modified for each country, the company's overall theme and brand image should stay as consistent as possible.

Marketing Communications Objectives

objective 4.5

How do the marketing communications objectives interact with the other elements of an IMC planning process?

An effective IMC planning process requires quality communications objectives. These objectives tie the organization's context, target markets, and positioning approaches to the ultimate selection of budget figures and IMC components, as depicted in Figure 4.1. Further, communications objectives guide account executives and advertising creatives in designing the actual advertising messages.

Communications objectives are derived from overall marketing objectives. These objectives tend to be general because they are for the entire company. Some examples include:

- Sales volume
- Market share
- Profits
- Return on investment

In contrast, a communications plan might emphasize a specific communications objective. Figure 4.8 identifies some common objectives. A large firm may establish different objectives for each brand within a product portfolio. Oftentimes, a communications plan for an individual brand emphasizes a single objective.

Some advertising message programs accomplish more than one communications objective. This occurs when marketers identify logical combinations of communications objectives. For example, the same advertisement could develop brand awareness and enhance a brand's image. Increasing sales can be accomplished through price changes, contests, or coupons. Matching the objective to the medium and the message remains the key.

Many marketing professionals believe that benchmarks provide helpful tools. A **benchmark measure** establishes a starting point to be compared with the degree of change following a promotional campaign. In other words, the benchmark constitutes a baseline to be used in assessing future outcomes.

• Develop brand awareness	• Build customer traffic
• Increase category demand	• Enhance firm image
• Change customer beliefs or attitudes	• Increase market share
• Enhance purchase actions	• Increase sales
• Encourage repeat purchases	• Reinforce purchase decisions

▶ **FIGURE 4.8**
Communication Objectives

◀ Benchmark measures can provide Ouachita Independent Bank's marketing team with an indication of the success of this advertising campaign.

When market research revealed that a dry cleaning company's name was only known by 20 percent of the community's population and that the company held a three percent share of the city's total market, a benchmark was present. In response, the firm's communications objective for the next advertising cycle became to increase awareness to 30 percent and market share to five percent. Then a campaign featuring advertisements, coupons, and discounts for certain days of the week (Tuesday specials) and to senior citizens was designed by establishing a budget that matched these IMC components. If the company achieved the desired target, it would indicate a level of success based on the previously specified benchmarks.

Types of Budgets

Marketers prepare communications budgets in a number of ways. Figure 4.9 provides a list of the methods.[30]

Percentage of Sales

In a **percentage-of-sales budget**, allocations are derived from either sales from the previous year or anticipated sales for the next year. This method offers simplicity in preparing the budget.

The approach also encounters problems. First, it tends to change in the opposite direction of what might typically be needed; that is, when sales go up, so does the communications budget. When sales weaken, the communications budget also declines. In most cases, when sales fall the communications budget should be increased to help reverse the trend. Further, during growth periods, the communications budget may not need to be increased. The method also experiences the disadvantage of failing to allocate money for special needs or to combat competitive pressures. Therefore, many marketing experts believe the disadvantages of the percentage of sales method tend to outweigh its advantages.

Meet the Competition

A **meet-the-competition budget** seeks to prevent loss of market share. Companies raise or lower expenditures to match amounts spent by the competition. This format may be found in highly competitive markets in which intense rivalries exist between competitors.

The potential drawback to meet-the-competition budgeting is that marketing dollars might not be spent efficiently. Matching the competition's spending does not guarantee success. Market share can still be lost. Rather than *how much* is spent, *how well* money has been allocated and *how effectively* the marketing campaign retains customers and market share should be the key.

objective 4.6

How are communications budgets established?

- Percentage of sales
- Meet the competition
- "What we can afford"
- Objective and task
- Payout planning
- Quantitative models

▲ **FIGURE 4.9**
Methods of Determining Marketing Communications Budgets

▶ **FIGURE 4.10**
Ad Spending and Market Share
of Top Credit Card Companies

Rank	Credit Card	Market Share	Ad Spending (millions)
1	American Express	25.1%	$336
2	JP Morgan Chase	19.4%	$200
3	Bank of America	10.7%	$139
4	Citibank	8.3%	$214
5	Capital One	6.7%	$317
6	Discover	4.4%	$132

Expenditures for advertising in the credit card industry have grown dramatically in the last decade and now exceed $2.4 trillion per year. Each company encounters pressures to increase its advertising budget to match the competition, because the level of brand recognition often corresponds with the level of spending. Market share, however, may not be affected quite as much, because exposure to and recognition of a credit card brand do not always equate to purchases. It takes time. Figure displays the level of spending of the top six credit card companies and the market share for each.[31]

"What We Can Afford"

A **"what we can afford" budget** sets the marketing allotment after all of the company's other budgets have been established or while determining other budgets. Company leaders allocate money based on what they feel can be spent. Use of this method suggests that management may not recognize the benefits of marketing communications. Instead, company leaders view marketing expenditures as non-revenue-generating activities. Newer and smaller companies with limited finances often employ the "what we can afford" approach.

Objective and Task

To prepare an **objective-and-task budget**, marketers identify the communications objectives to pursue and then calculates the cost of accomplishing each objective. The communications budget becomes the cumulative sum of the estimated costs for all objectives.

Many marketing experts believe that the objective-and-task method represents the best budgeting approach because it relates dollar costs to achieving specific objectives; however, a large company, such as Procter & Gamble, may find it difficult to apply. With hundreds of products on the market, producing a budget based on objectives for each brand and product category would be time consuming. Despite these challenges, about 50 percent of major firms use some form of the objective-and-task method.[32]

Payout Planning

With a **payout-planning budget**, management establishes a ratio of advertising to sales or market share. This method normally allocates greater amounts in early years to yield payouts in later years.[33] Allocating larger amounts at the beginning of a product introduction helps build brand awareness and brand equity. As the brand becomes accepted and sales build, a lower percentage of advertising dollars will be required in order to maintain a target growth.

Quantitative Models

In some instances, computer simulations can be developed to model the relationship between advertising or promotional expenditures with sales and profits. These models are far from perfect. They do offer the advantage of accounting for the type of industry and product in the model. In most cases, quantitative models are limited to larger organizations with strong computer and statistics departments.

Therefore, as the marketing team constructs a budget, they first examine the assumptions that drive the process. The newness of the product, the economy, and any other complicating factors should be reviewed when attempting to tie budgeting expenditures to marketing and communications objectives. A budget becomes finalized when the company marketing team specifies how funds will be spent on each of the major communications tools.

Communications Schedules

After establishing the total amount of dollars to be allocated to marketing communications, the next step is to choose the proper schedule approach to reach the communications goal. Marketers emphasize one of three basic tactics to allocate communication funds:

- Pulsating schedule
- Flighting schedule
- Continuous schedule

A **pulsating schedule** involves continuous advertising and communications during the year with bursts of higher intensity at specific times (more ads in more media). Companies can also select a **flighting schedule** or approach, whereby communications are presented only during peak times and not at all during other times of the year.

Firms often advertise more during peak seasons such as Christmas, seeking to send messages during the times when customers are most inclined to buy, or when they are *on the hot spot.* Weight Watchers, Diet Centers, and others advertise heavily during the first weeks of January. Many New Year's resolutions include going on a diet.

Marketing communications during slow sales seasons focuses on "drumming up business" when people do not regularly buy. In retail sales, slow seasons occur during January and February. Some companies advertise more during these months to sell merchandise left over from the Christmas season and to encourage customers to shop. Manufacturers also realize that many retailers are not advertising and hope that the ads will capture greater attention as a result.

Many marketing experts believe spending in level amounts keeps the brand repetitively in front of consumers, which is a **continuous campaign schedule**. Consumers purchase durable goods, such as dishwashers and refrigerators, on an "as needed" basis. A family ordinarily buys a new dishwasher only when the old one breaks down or when they build or remodel a home. Level advertising increases the odds that the buyer will see an advertisement or remember the name (Kenmore, Whirlpool, or General Electric) at the right time.

Matching the pacing of communications with the message, the media, and the nature of the product should be the objective. Some media make it easier to advertise for longer periods of time. Contracts for billboards are normally for a month or a year. They can be rotated throughout a town or city to present a continuing message. At the same time, budgetary constraints can influence the strategies and tactics deployed in any advertising or communications program.

◀ A pulsating advertising schedule might be used to promote dark chocolate Philadelphia Cream Cheese with a burst during the Christmas season.

IMC Components

objective 4.7
What elements are considered in developing an IMC program?

As has been noted, marketing communications consists of much more than traditional advertising. In fact, advertising expenditures may not make up the major portion of a marketing communications budget. In terms of dollars spent, media advertising normally accounts for about 41 percent of a marketing communications budget. Trade promotions receive about 28 percent and consumer promotions average about 28 percent of overall marketing expenditures (see Figure 4.11).[34] These percentages vary considerably from industry to industry. Consumer product manufacturers spend more on trade promotions directed toward retailers. Service companies tend to favor media advertising.

Budgets also vary the type of product. For transportation services, the average expenditure on media advertising as a percentage of sales is 24.6 percent, whereas for office furniture, expenditures on media advertising represent only 0.1 percent of sales. Figure 4.12 provides the ad spending as a percent of sales for various industries.[35]

Selecting IMC components and media takes place in conjunction with preparation of the budget. Figure 4.13 highlights the ways marketers allocate global advertising dollars among various media. Television ranks first, primarily because of the high cost of advertising time. Although digital expenditures represent only 4.3 percent of total global ad spending, they are the fastest-growing component.[36]

Choosing the best IMC components remains a challenge. A company's marketing personnel often work with its external agencies to analyze the firm's target audience, communications objectives, and budget to determine the optimal media mix.

International Implications

Globally integrated marketing communications (GIMC) programs are vital for international firms. Each message should fit a country's language and culture. Brand names, marketing ideas, and advertising campaigns designed for one country do not always translate correctly to another. Consequently, understanding the international market becomes essential. Figure 4.14 highlights the ingredients of successful GIMC plans.

Marketing campaigns do not necessarily require a unique program for each country and every cultural group within a country. Marketers try to make sure the company's products and marketing messages will be *understood in the region*. When needed, the message can be tailored to an individual area. The goal is to *create a borderless marketing plan* that uses the same basic marketing approach for all of a company's markets. This grants each subsidiary the freedom to determine how to implement that marketing plan; in essence, to *think globally but act locally*. It also presents the opportunity to maintain a theme while targeting the message to a given region.

Another key to a successful GIMC is developing *local partnerships*. Local partners can be marketing research firms or advertising firms that are familiar with the local

▶ **FIGURE 4.11**
Breakdown of Marketing Communications Expenditures

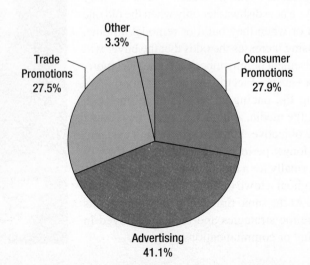

Other
3.3%

Trade Promotions
27.5%

Consumer Promotions
27.9%

Advertising
41.1%

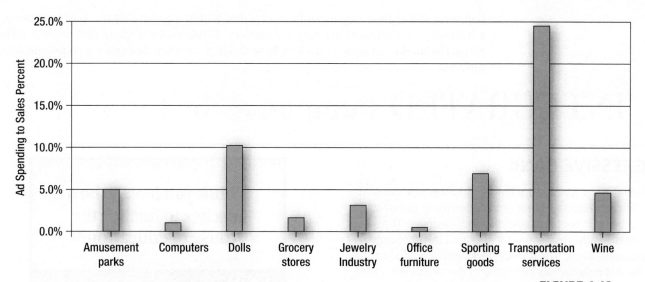

▲ **FIGURE 4.12**
Ad Spending as Percent of Sales for Select Industries

language and culture. *Communication segmentation* means creating a communications package that effectively reaches all possible target markets in another country. Many times, both consumer and business-to-business segments are present. A well-designed *market communications analysis* begins with the marketing team identifying strengths and weaknesses of local competitors and places in which opportunities exist. They also develop an understanding of how the firm is perceived in the international marketplace.

Finally, *solid communications objectives* should be established. Linguistics represents one major hurdle. Translating an English advertisement into another language requires expertise, because exact word translations often do not exist. For example, the slogan of Ruth's Steak House, "We sell sizzle as well as steaks," could not be translated into Spanish, because there is no equivalent word for "sizzle." Therefore, the translator found a Spanish idiom conveying a similar meaning in order to solve the problem.

The IMC planning process becomes more complicated in international settings; however, it constitutes a crucial element in creating an effective GIMC. Marketers take into account language, culture, norms, beliefs, and local laws. Literal translation of a

◀ **FIGURE 4.13**
Global Ad Spending by Media

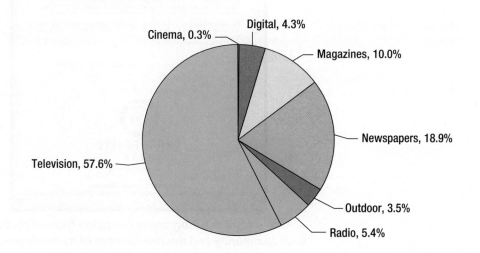

◀ **FIGURE 4.14**
Successful Global Integrated Marketing Tactics

- Understand the international market
- Create a borderless marketing plan
- Think globally but act locally
- Local partnerships

- Communication segmentation strategies
- Market communications analysis
- Solid communications objectives

commercial's tagline might not be acceptable within a given culture. Laws concerning advertising and promotions vary by country. Cultures view ideas and objects differently. The marketing team considers these differences when designing a communications program.

))) INTEGRATED Campaigns in Action

PROGRESSIVE BANK

Banks operate in a competitive market. Making one standout can be difficult, especially through an advertising campaign. For a local bank, it becomes even more challenging. The French Creative advertising agency accepted this challenge with Progressive Bank. The agency developed a unique campaign that not only highlighted some of the bank's strengths but also brought a human touch into the campaign to make the bank more personal.

▲ One part of the Progressive campaign focused on the local community and the involvement of its employees.

MyMarketingLab

To submit media-based assignments for the Integrated Campaigns in Action, go to MediaShare for Business at **mymktlab.com** ⭐.

Summary

A marketing communications planning program will often be based on information derived from communications research. Product-specific, consumer-oriented, and target market research assist marketers in understanding the ways in which products are viewed and purchased. When the analysis is complete, target markets may be selected in conjunction with product-positioning tactics.

Market segmentation identifies sets of business or consumer groups with distinct characteristics. Segments must be clearly different, large enough to support a marketing campaign, and reachable through some type of media. Consumer groups that can be segmented include those identified by demographics, including gender, age, income, and ethnicity. Markets can also be identified using psychographic, generational, and geographic delineations. Geodemographic segmentation combines demographic, psychographic, and geographic information together. Other ways to categorize consumers are by the benefits they receive from goods or services and by the ways they use products.

Business-to-business segmentation can be accomplished by targeting business customers by industry, business type,
the size of the company, geographic location, usage, and customer-value calculations. Marketing managers specify the company's consumer and business market segments. All other promotions opportunity analysis processes are tied to the identification of key customers.

Product positioning represents the perceptions in consumer minds of the nature of a company and its products relative to the competition. Positioning may be based on product attributes, competitors, product uses or applications, the price–quality relationship, product class, or through the association with a cultural symbol.

Marketing objectives lead to the development of communications objectives that are matched to the product, target market, and product positioning. These objectives form the basis for developing communications budgets and selecting IMC components for actual marketing campaigns.

Globally integrated marketing communications efforts are guided by the IMC planning process. National differences, cultural concerns, language issues, and other challenges must be viewed in light of the target markets an individual company intends to serve.

Key Terms

product-specific research A form of communications research that seeks to identify key product characteristics that become selling points

consumer-oriented research A form of communications research that seeks to discover the context of a product's use through anthropological, sociological, or psychological analysis

target-market research A form of communications research that identifies the recipients of a planned communications campaign

focus group A set of consumers who talk about a particular topic, product, or brand in front of a moderator or panel who tracks consumer comments and ideas.

market segment A set of businesses or group of individual customers with distinct characteristics

market segmentation Identifying specific groups (target markets) based on needs, attitudes, and interests

demographics Population characteristics such as gender, age, educational levels, income, and ethnicity

psychographics Patterns of responses that reveal a person's activities, interests, and opinions (AIO)

geo-targeting Marketing appeals made to people in a geographic area or region

product positioning The perception in the consumer's mind of the nature of a company and its products relative to the competition

benchmark measures Starting points that are studied in relation to the degree of change following a promotional campaign

percentage-of-sales budget A form of communications budgeting in which budgeting is based on sales from the previous year or anticipated sales for the next year

meet-the-competition budget A communications budget in which expenditures are raised or lowered to match the competition

"what we can afford" budget A communications budget that is set after all of the company's other budgets have been determined or while the other budgets are set;

communications money is allocated based on what company leaders feels they can afford to spend

objective-and-task budget A communications budget in which management first lists all of the communications objectives to pursue during the year and then calculates the cost of accomplishing those objectives

payout-planning budget A budgeting method that establishes a ratio of advertising to sales or market share

pulsating schedule An advertising program that is continuous throughout the year with bursts of higher intensity at specific times

flighting schedule An advertising schedule in which communications are present only at peak times during the year

continuous campaign schedule An advertising schedule that involves level amounts of spending and messages throughout the year

---

MyMarketingLab

To complete the problems with the ⭐ in your MyLab, go to the end-of-chapter Discussion Questions.

Review Questions

4-1. What three forms of market research are used to develop marketing communications?

4-2. What functions are performed by focus groups?

4-3. Define market segment and market segmentation.

4-4. Define demographics. How are they used to segment consumer markets?

4-5. How can firms take advantage of target markets by gender?

4-6. How do firms use age to identify market segments?

4-7. What role does ethnicity play in identifying market segments?

4-8. What problems are associated with markets segmented according to geographic areas?

4-9. What are geodemographics? How can they be successfully used to define market segments?

4-10. Describe usage segmentation and benefit segmentation.

4-11. What are the common business-to-business market segments?

4-12. Describe the NAICS approach to business market segmentation.

4-13. Describe a usage segmentation approach in a business to-business setting.

4-14. Describe a segmentation approach based on company size.

4-15. Define product positioning and identify the types of positioning approaches that can be used in the IMC planning process.

4-16. What is a benchmark measure?

4-17. What common marketing communications objectives do firms establish?

4-18. Describe the methods that can be used to establish a communications budget.

4-19. Describe the three types of advertising schedules that may be used during the course of a year.

4-20. Which IMC components are more likely to be used in business-to-business marketing communications programs, as compared to consumer markets?

Critical Thinking Exercises

DISCUSSION QUESTIONS

⭐**4-21.** Assume you are a marketing intern for Lululemon and have been asked to conduct some communications research around the brand's leggings. Identify the three types of communications research and describe how you could use each to gather information that can be used in marketing Lululemon's leggings.

⭐**4-22.** Daniel Taylor Clothier has experienced a decline in sales of men's ties. Company marketers believe they should focus advertising efforts on the market segment most likely to purchase ties. Examine the segmentation variables identified in Figure 4.2. If you were responsible for the segmentation strategy for Daniel Taylor Clothier's, which segmentation variables would you use? Justify your answer.

⭐**4-23.** Make a list of five consumer goods or services that are segmented on the basis of gender but sold to both genders. Are there any differences in the product or service attributes? Are there differences in how they are marketed? What are those differences? Do you think using a different marketing approach has worked?

4-24. Make a list of five consumer goods or services that are segmented on the basis of age. Are there actual differences in the product or service attributes? Are there differences in how they are marketed? What are those differences? Do you think using a different marketing approach has worked?

4-25. Examine the list of demographic segmentation variables. For each demographic variable listed in the text, identify two products that are marketed to a specific demographic segment. Identify the specific demographic segment and explain why the product is aimed at that particular market segment. Identify one brand that has been especially successful at reaching a specific demographic segment.

⭐**4-26.** Examine the VALS psychographic groups presented in the chapter. For each of the following goods or services, identify the VALS segment that would be the best to target. Justify your choice. Describe an advertisement or marketing communication that could be used for the VALS segment you identified for each product.

    a. Seafood restaurant

    b. Home accounting software

    c. Optometrist or eye-care clinic

    d. Florida resort

    e. Home furniture

4-27. Millennials are an attractive generation for marketers. Examine the millennial segments described in the chapter. Which segment do you belong to? Identify a friend or relative that would fit into each of the other millennial segments. Explain why you would put them into that particular millennial segment.

⭐**4-28.** Usage segmentation targets heavy users, average users, light users or nonusers. Describe campaigns for each of the usage segments for a tanning salon. In your discussion, identify the best communications objective for each of the campaigns and the product positioning strategy that you would use for each segment. Justify your decisions.

4-29. For each of the product-positioning strategies discussed in this chapter, identify two brands that feature the strategy and explain how the strategy is used to successfully market the brand.

Integrated Learning Exercises

4-30. Use a search engine to locate five companies on the internet that sell swimwear. For each company, discuss the types of products sold and the types of promotional appeals used. Review each website. Describe the segmentation strategy you think the company is using and the specific market segments being targeted. For each company, which product-positioning strategy is being used? Justify your choice.

4-31. A brand's product positioning strategy should be an integral part of the company's advertising and marketing strategy, including its website. Examine the following websites and identify the product-positioning strategy you think is being used. Explain your answer.

    a. Polaris (**www.polaris.com**)

    b. Edgewater Beach & Golf Resort (**www.edge waterbeachresort.com**)

    c. Celestial Seasonings (**www.celestialseasonings .com**)

    d. Sony (**www.sony.com**)

    e. Stetson cologne (**www.stetsoncologne.com**)

4-32. VALS psychographic segmentation can be a valuable tool for marketers as they prepare their marketing materials. Access VALS through the Strategic Business Insights (SBI) website at **www.strategic businessinsights.com/vals** and examine the characteristics of each of the groups. Then take the test to determine which group you belong to. How can VALS help marketers develop advertising messages?

4-33. A current trend for many companies is the development of marketing messages for specific demographic, ethnic, or lifestyle groups. This allows for a more targeted message than is possible for the mass audience. Go to the following websites. What types of marketing messages are on each site? How could the information on these websites be used to develop integrated marketing communications plans?

    a. Parents (**www.pbs.org**)

    b. Women (**womensenews.org**)

    c. African Americans (**www.targetmarketnews.com**)

    d. Gays and lesbians (**www.gaycenter.org**)

4-34. For the following firms, examine the company's website to determine what segmentation strategy is being used. Describe the intended target market for the website. What communications objective(s) do you think the company is trying to accomplish? What product-positioning strategy is being used? Explain your responses.

    a. Sara Lee Desserts (**saraleedesserts.com**)

    b. Skeeter boats (**www.skeeterboats.com**)

    c. Reynolds Protection (**reynoldsprotection.com**)

4-35. Go to the authors' website at **clowbaack.net/video/ads.html**. Watch one of the television ads for DuPage Medical Group, one of the television ads for Terrebonne General Medical Center, and one of the ads for St. Francis Medical Center. Identify which three ads you watched. For each ad describe who you think is being targeted using the methods of consumer segmentation described in the chapter. Define each of the approaches to product positioning described in the chapter. For each of the three TV ads you picked, decide which positioning approach is being used. Justify your answer.

4-36. Go to the authors' website at **clowbaack.net/video/ads.html**. Watch one of the television ads for Ouachita Independent Bank, one of the television ads for Progressive Bank, and one of the ads for Centric Federal Credit Union. Identify which three ads you watched. For each ad describe who you think is being targeted using the methods of consumer segmentation described in the chapter. Define each of the approaches to product positioning described in the chapter. For each of the three TV ads you picked, decide which positioning approach is being used. Justify your answer.

Blog Exercises

Access the authors' blog for this textbook at the URLs provided to complete these exercises. Answer the questions posed on the blog.

4-37. Motel 6: **blogclowbaack.net/2014/05/05/motel-6-chapter-4/**

4-38. Carnival Cruise Line: **blogclowbaack.net/2014/05/05/carnival-cruise-line-chapter-4/**

4-39. Segmentation and positioning: **blogclowbaack.net/2014/05/05/segmentation-and-positioning-chapter-4/**

Student Project

CREATIVE CORNER

A number of companies and advertising agencies use the VALS typology to create marketing materials. Your task is to design two advertisements for Yamaha boats. Pick one of the following pairs of VALS segments and design an advertisement promoting Yamaha for each segment. When you are finished, write a paragraph explaining how the ads you created will appeal to their respective VALS segment and how the two ads are different. Before you begin work on the ads, go to the Strategic Business Insights (SBI) website at **www.strategicbusinessinsights.com/vals** to obtain more information about the two segments you will be targeting with your ads.

    Pair 1: Innovators and Survivors

    Pair 2: Thinkers and Makers

    Pair 3: Believers and Achievers

    Pair 4: Strivers and Experiencers

CASE 1 ▶ THE JAPANESE STEAKHOUSE EXPERIENCE

Hiroaki Rocky Aoki founded the first Benihana restaurant in New York in 1964. His innovative approach to dining featured an authentic Japanese farmhouse interior. Food preparation took place in front of customers on steel cooking grills. Chefs were taught to be entertaining, engaging employees with fascinating knife skills and a flair for the dramatic, including the use of fire as part of the show. A famous restaurant critic at the time, Clementine Paddleford wrote a raving, positive review in a local newspaper and the business grew dramatically as a result. Soon after, a second location was added in New York.

By 1972, six Benihana locations were opened across the United States. Currently more than 70 restaurants are active, with franchising possibilities offered to others. The chain has expanded to include locations in other countries as well and has acquired three other restaurant chains, HARU, RA Sushi, and Rudy's Restaurant Group.

The success of the original Benihana concept can be explained in part by the unique dining experience the company was first to offer. Groups of up to eight individuals are combined in each serving area, which means smaller sets, such as couples, often share the food preparation activities with other guests. Benihana currently holds the title of the longest running dinner show in the world.[37]

Not surprisingly, a series of entrepreneurs has jumped on the bandwagon and created similar dining programs. Some have developed chains of restaurants while others offer single locations in various cities in the United States.

The concept of combining food preparation, dining, and entertainment is not limited to Japanese steakhouse-type organizations. A series of restaurants features singing waiters. Missouri-based Lambert's Café sells "throwed rolls" that the servers literally toss at patrons. To achieve success, one key appears to be creating a logical combination of the entertainment program with the food to be served.

At the same time, other elements deserve attention, including the colors chosen for the restaurant's décor. For example, the Logo Company states that green suggests something "natural, organic, youth, nurturing, (and) instructional" among other attributes. Green fits with medicine, science, government, and ecology, but maybe not food (think mold). Orange generates cheerfulness, red creates excitement, gold conjures images of warmth, and blue suggests dependability and strength.[38]

▲ Benihana offers diners a unique dining experience.

Colors combine with music, furniture, server outfits, and many other ingredients in order to construct a total dining experience. Then, marketing communications can be added to the mix. Focus groups and other forms of research help the marketing team discover if all of the elements work together. Eventually, a company name, logo, and advertising program can be designed to entice patrons to try something new and different.

4-40. Which consumer market segments best match with Benihana?

4-41. Explain the positioning approach used by Benihana.

4-42. If you were assigned to create a competitor restaurant that prepared and served Japanese-style hibachi meals, which colors would you choose for the restaurant? What type of music should be played? What other features should be key parts of the interior of the restaurant? How would you differentiate the restaurant from Benihana and other similar chains?

4-43. For the same competitor restaurant, assume that it has only one location, in Seattle, Washington. Design an advertising campaign and identify the types of media that would reach your target market and create the right positioning.

4-44. The color red holds special meaning in Asian culture as a symbol of celebration. Consequently, red is featured in much of Benihana's marketing materials. Which colors would match other restaurant types, such as fried chicken, fast food hamburgers, or pizza parlors? Would your answer be different if the food were to be sold in other countries? Why or why not?

CASE 2 ▶ PHASE 2 FITNESS CENTER

Allen Goldschmidt loves exercise and fitness. At age 42 he survived a cardiac scare in which doctors first believed a heart attack had taken place. Even though subsequent tests determined such was not the case, Allen was told that being overweight and in poor physical condition might at some point lead to an actual episode. In response, he moved from a sedentary lifestyle to an activity-based approach to keeping trim and healthy.

After several months of developing his own program with the help of a fitness trainer, an opportunity arose. Allen was able to purchase a fitness center from an individual who was moving out of town and wanted to sell as much of the business intact as possible.

Allen and his trainer created a system that they named Phase 2. Their idea was that Phase 1 was an under-represented aspect of staying healthy: diet and lifestyle. They designed a program that encouraged members and visitors to eat right (low sugar, low salt, low fat, low calorie) but also to sleep in regular cycles and take steps to avoid the effects of stress, which can lead to other bad habits, such as alcohol abuse.

Phase 2 would be the fitness aspect. The center would provide both individual training and group activities including Zumba and other exercise programs. Customers could create individually tailored programs for special events, such as marathon training or getting into a smaller sized dress or suit for a class reunion. Group activities would stress socialization and having fun as parts of getting fit.

The building Allen purchased contained a walking track, a swimming pool, and a wide variety of exercise equipment including free weights, weight training machines, treadmills, and more specific devices such as Stairmasters. A dining area was added to serve snacks and light meals, but also to provide a location for cooking classes to be taught by experts in quality nutrition.

Allen was aware of the competition in his area. A Gold's Gym operated in the same city, as did a Curves, which focused on attracting women to a 30-minute workout program. He believed his combination of Phase 1 and Phase 2 would make it possible to stand out from the competition. He hired a local advertising and

▲ Females participating in a Zumba class at Phase 2 Fitness Center.

promotions company to help him find the right mix of people to become regular clients.

4-45. Explain each of the types of research presented in the chapter in terms of the Phase 2 Fitness Center. Which would you recommend? Why?

4-46. Discuss the potential consumer market segments that Phase 2 Fitness Center could serve using the information on consumer segmentation. Which segment or segments would you recommend? Why?

4-47. Are there any business-to-business segmentation opportunities present? Why or why not?

4-48. What positioning approach would be most valuable to Phase 2 Fitness Center? Defend your answer.

4-49. Explain the most viable marketing communications objectives for the opening of the Phase 2 Fitness Center. Then note how those objectives might change over time.

MyMarketingLab

Go to the Assignments section of your MyLab to complete these writing exercises.

4-50. A dog breeder recognizes the need for segmenting her advertising and marketing. Discuss the merits of each of the methods of segmentation presented in the text (see Figure 4.2). Based on your discussion of each method, which would you recommend? Why? Define in your own words each of the product positioning strategies. Based on your segmentation decision, which positioning strategy would you use? Why?

4-51. Use a search engine to locate three companies on the internet that sell activewear. For each website, discuss the types of clothing sold and the types of promotional appeals used. For each website identify the market segmentation strategy you believe is being used and the product positioning strategy that is being used. Justify your choice.

Part 2

IMC ADVERTISING TOOLS

Chapter 5

Advertising Campaign Management

Chapter Objectives

After reading this chapter, you should be able to answer the following questions:

5.1 Why is an understanding of advertising theories important in the advertising management process?

5.2 What is the relationship of advertising expenditures to advertising effectiveness?

5.3 When should a company employ an external advertising agency rather than completing the work in-house?

5.4 How do companies choose advertising agencies?

5.5 What are the primary job functions within an advertising agency?

5.6 What are the advertising campaign parameters that should be considered?

5.7 How does a creative brief facilitate effective advertising?

5.8 What are the implications of advertising management in the global arena?

Overview

The average person encounters about 600 advertisements per day, delivered by a variety of media. Television and radio have long been advertising staples, along with newspapers, magazines, and billboards. More recently, internet advertisements, social networks, and mobile phone apps offer additional venues to contact and interact with customers.

Today's marketers face the challenge of developing advertisements that can be viewed in multiple mediums and at the same time break through the highly cluttered world in which people are increasingly adept at simply tuning ads out. **Advertising campaign management** is the process of preparing and integrating a specific advertising program in conjunction with the overall IMC message. One advertising agency that has achieved success in advertising campaign management is Zehnder Communications. Several of the agency's ads are featured in this textbook.

ZEHNDER COMMUNICATIONS

Zehnder Communications provides a variety of services, including strategic planning, creative, web and application development, media, public relations, and social media. The company also delivers research and analytics services to clients. As stated on the company's website, "We have a unique situation at Zehnder in that we are a full-service agency that continually challenges traditional thinking."

Zehnder's client list includes Visit South Walton (Florida), Visit Baton Rouge, Burger King, Origins Bank, Gulf Seafood Marketing Coalition, NOLA.com/The Times Picayune, along with others. The firm specializes in the Advocacy, Attractions/Entertainment, Automotive, Energy Services, Financial Services, Food and Beverage, Healthcare, Hospitality/Tourism, and Insurance industries.

Zehnder states, "As experts, it's not enough that we remain well versed in new media trends. We owe it to our clients to remain at the forefront of innovation, dedicated to developing new ways to reach the consumer. That's what it all comes down to—connecting with your audience through all available means. Innovation and

▲ Lobby of Zehnder Communications.

campaign integration mean nothing unless you can make that connection which changes perception and ultimately behavior."

The company has been recognized as a "best place to work" in the area for more than 12 years in a row. Founder Jeffrey Zehnder developed an innovation he labels the VAN ("Vacation as Needed") system. The program allows employees to take time off when they feel it is appropriate, so long as it does not interfere with or slow down the activities of other employees. The sense of freedom and empowerment that results helps build morale over time.

Zehnder Communications provides a quality example of the nature of advertising in today's complicated marketplace. This section of the textbook describes the role advertising plays in an integrated marketing communications program. Figure 5.1 portrays the overall IMC approach. The three chapters in this section focus on developing an effective integrated advertising program. This chapter explains advertising management, which lays the groundwork for the total advertising campaign program. Chapter 6 reviews advertising design issues including the message strategy, appeals, executions, and the use of spokespersons. Chapter 7 presents traditional media that can be used for advertising. While the use of social media and digital media continue to grow, traditional media remain vital for the advertising of most brands.

Advertising management consists of several important activities. First, those involved choose an advertising theory or approach as a guide. Next, company leaders develop guidelines that help everyone

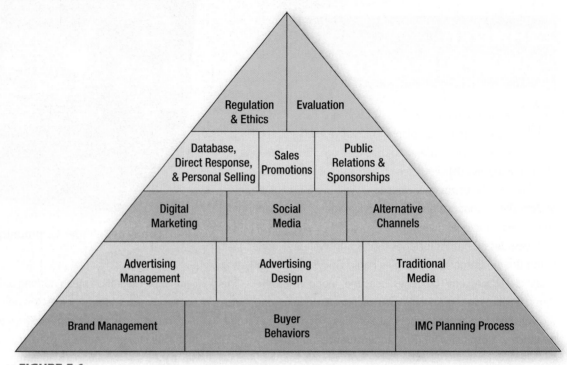

▲ **FIGURE 5.1**

Overview of Integrated Marketing Communications

understand the relationship of advertising to eventual success. Then, the company's management team decides whether to complete advertising work as an in-house activity or in conjunction with an advertising agency. Next, they generate advertising parameters to help control the process. A creative brief will then be prepared to direct the actual design of the advertising campaign. The conclusion of this chapter examines the international implications of these activities.

Advertising Theory

objective 5.1

Why is an understanding of advertising theories important in the advertising management process?

In developing an advertising campaign, two theoretical approaches help provide a solid foundation. The hierarchy of effects model and a means–end chain assist in developing effective campaigns. Advertisers also consider the mix of visual and verbal elements within an advertisement.

Hierarchy of Effects

The **hierarchy of effects model** helps to clarify the objectives of an advertising campaign. The model outlines six steps a consumer or a business buyer moves through when making a purchase:

1. Awareness
2. Knowledge
3. Liking
4. Preference
5. Conviction
6. The actual purchase

These steps are sequential. The model suggests that a consumer spends a period of time at each one before moving to the next. Thus, before a person develops a liking for a product, she must first know about it. Once the individual has the knowledge and develops liking for the product, the advertiser tries to influence the consumer to favor a particular brand or company.

The hierarchy of effects approach enjoys the benefit of allowing marketers to identify common steps consumers and businesses take when making purchases. Building brand loyalty requires all six steps. A customer cannot be loyal to a brand without first being aware of it. The customer typically will not develop loyalty to a brand without sufficient knowledge. Then, the person must like the brand and build a strong preference for it. Finally, the customer experiences the conviction that the particular brand is superior to the others. The components of the hierarchy of effects approach highlight the responses that advertising or marketing communications should stimulate in both consumers and business-to-business customers.

▲ When making high-involvement purchases, such as with a 35 mm digital camera, consumers will typically go through all six hierarchy of effects steps.

The hierarchy of effects model features similarities with theories regarding attitudes and attitudinal change, including the concepts of cognitive, affective, and conative elements. As presented in Chapter 3, the cognitive component refers to the person's mental images, understanding, and interpretations of the person, object, or issue. The affective component contains the feelings or emotions a person has about the object, topic, or idea. The conative component consists of the individual's intentions, actions, or behavior. The most common sequence that takes place when an attitude forms is:

▼ This introductory price may spur a consumer to make a purchase without going through the first five steps of the hierarchy of effects model.

Cognitive → Affective → Conative

The sequence parallels the six-step hierarchy of effects process. As a general guideline, cognitive-oriented ads work best for achieving brand awareness and brand knowledge. Affective-oriented advertisements are better at inspiring liking, preference, and conviction. Conative ads are normally best suited to facilitating product purchases or other buyer actions.

Although the hierarchy of effects approach may help a creative understand how a consumer reaches a purchase decision, recent literature questions some of the theory's assumptions. For one, these six steps might not always constitute the route a consumer takes. A person may make a purchase (such as an impulse buy) and then later develop knowledge, liking, preference, and conviction. Also, a shopper could purchase products with little or no preference involved, because a coupon, discount, or purchase incentive caused him to choose one brand instead of another. The introductory price of $3.59 in the newspaper ad shown here for Chickme

Flavors to Savor

7 Different Flavors to Choose From:

* Original
* Jalapeño Cilantro
* Roasted Garlic
* Spicy Avocado
* Roasted Red Pepper
* Kalamata Olive
* Spinach & Artichoke

www.chickmehummus.com

Introductory Price

$3.59

Chickme Hummus

▶ **FIGURE 5.2**
Personal Values

- Comfortable life
- Equality
- Excitement
- Freedom
- Fun, exciting life
- Happiness

- Inner peace
- Mature love
- Personal accomplishment
- Pleasure
- Salvation

- Security
- Self-fulfillment
- Self-respect
- Sense of belonging
- Social acceptance
- Wisdom

▶ **FIGURE 5.3**
Means-End Chain for Milk

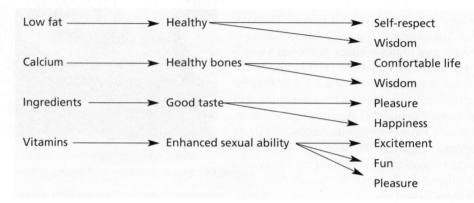

▼ A milk advertisement based on the means-end chain.

We both need *Calcium*

DRINK MILK

may spur a consumer to purchase the product with no prior brand knowledge or preference. At other times, the individual might not even remember the name of the brand purchased previously. This may be the case with commodity products, such as sugar or flour, or some clothing purchases, such as socks and shirts. Even with these criticisms, however, the framework remains a popular approach to the development of advertising messages and campaigns.

Means–End Theory

The second theoretical approach available to creatives, a **means–end chain**, suggests that an advertisement should contain a message, or *means*, that leads the consumer to a desired end state. These *end* states are personal values (see Figure 5.2). A means–end chain should start a process in which viewing the advertising message leads the consumer to believe that using the product will help achieve a personal value.

Means–end theory forms the basis of the **Means–End Conceptualization of Components for Advertising Strategy (MECCAS)** model.[1] The MECCAS model explains ways to move consumers from product attributes to personal values by highlighting the product's benefits. Advertisers link the attributes of the product to specific benefits consumers derive. These benefits, in turn, lead to the attainment of a personal value. Using the elements in Figure 5.3, the product attribute of calcium found in milk connects to the benefit of healthy bones. The personal value the consumer obtains from healthy bones may be feeling wise for using the product, or a comfortable life. The milk ad shown in this section highlights the use of this means–end chain.

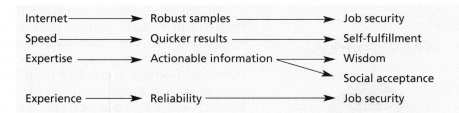

The MECCAS approach applies to business-to-business advertisements. Members of the buying center may be influenced by personal values, organizational values, and corporate goals. Consider the advertisement for ReRez shown in this section and the means–end chain provided in Figure 5.4. Each attribute in the ad leads to benefits business customers can obtain. Although not explicitly stated, the personal values of members of the buying center choosing ReRez might include job security for making good decisions, self-fulfillment, wisdom, and social acceptance by other members of the buying group that believe ReRez offers quality marketing research.

Verbal and Visual Images

Most major forms of advertising contain visual and verbal or written elements. A visual ad places the greatest emphasis on a picture or the optical element of the presentation. A verbal or written ad places more emphasis on the copy. Visual and verbal elements work together to create an advertisement that meets the desired stage of the hierarchy of effects model or the attribute-benefit-personal value chosen from a means–chain.

Visual images often lead to more favorable attitudes toward the advertisement and the brand. Visuals tend to be more easily remembered than verbal copy. They are stored in the brain as both pictures and words. This dual-coding process makes it easier for people to recall the message. Further, verbal messages tend be stored in the left side of the brain only; images are usually stored in both the left and right sides of the brain. The advertisement for OIB Reward Plus in this section illustrates the power of visual imagery. Created by the Newcomer, Morris and Young advertising agency, the visual image of the child immediately garners attention and is more likely to be remembered than an ad that only features copy.

Visual images range from concrete and realistic to highly abstract. A concrete visual displays something recognizable as a person, place, or thing. In an abstract image, the subject becomes more difficult to recognize. Concrete pictures instill a higher level of recall than abstract images because they allow the image to be stored in the brain with both visual and verbal elements. Viewers process an advertisement with a picture of spaghetti as both a picture and as a verbal representation. Ads with concrete images also tend to lead to more favorable attitudes than those without pictures or abstract images.[2]

Radio advertisers often seek to create visual images for the audience. Pepsi produced a radio commercial in which listeners could hear a can being opened, the soft drink being poured, and the sizzle of the carbonation—an excellent example of creating a visual image. If consumers visualize a picture in their imaginations, the effect may be greater than actually viewing a visual. A visual image requires less brain activity than using one's imagination. The secret is getting the person to think beyond the advertisement and picture the scene being simulated.

Visual Esperanto   Advertisers often use visual imagery in international marketing. Global advertising agencies try to create *visual Esperanto*, the universal language that makes global advertising possible for any good or service. *Visual Esperanto* advertising recognizes that visual images are more powerful than verbal descriptions and transcends cultural differences.[3]

▲ A ReRez business-to-business advertisement for marketing research that illustrates the use of the means-end chain.

▲ An advertisement for OIB (Ouchita Independent Bank) with a strong visual image.

To illustrate the power of a visual image compared to a verbal account, think of the word "exotic." To some, exotic means a white beach in Hawaii with young people in sexy swimsuits. To others, it may be a small cabin in the snow-capped mountains of Switzerland. To others still, exotic may be a close-up of a tribal village in Africa. The word "exotic" varies in meaning. At the same time, a picture of a couple sitting close together viewing the ocean has practically the same significance across all cultures, because the image conveys a similar emotional experience of love and a personal relationship with another.

Finding the appropriate image constitutes the most important challenge in creating *visual Esperanto*. The creative looks for one that will convey the intended meaning or message. Brand identity can be emphasized using visuals rather than words. The creative uses words to help support the visual image. For example, the creative may decide that a boy and his father at a sports event illustrate the priceless treasure of a shared family moment. In Mexico, the setting could be a soccer match instead of a baseball game in the United States. The specific copy (the words) can then be adapted. Identifying an image that transcends cultures represents the most difficult part of inspiring *visual Esperanto*. Once a universal image has been found, creatives in each country represented take the image and modify it to appeal to the local target audience.

▶ While the meaning of "exotic" may vary across cultures, the visual created in this photo can transcend cultures through *visual Esperanto*.

Business-to-Business   In the past, creatives who designed business-to-business advertisements relied on verbal or written elements rather than visuals. The basis of this approach was the the belief that many business people make decisions in a rational, cognitive manner. In recent years, more business ads incorporate strong visual elements to heighten the emotional aspects of purchases.

In summary, the two theoretical models, along with ideas regarding visual and verbal messages, provide useful ideas for the advertising creative. Each suggests key concepts to be followed in developing a campaign. The endpoint will be reached when the viewer remembers the product, thinks favorably about it, and looks for that brand.

The Impact of Advertising Expenditures

In developing advertising campaigns, there may be unrealistic assumptions concerning the relationship of advertising budgets to effectiveness. For instance, a manager may believe that a direct relationship exists between expenditures on advertising communications and subsequent sales revenues. One common concept was that a 10-percent increase in advertising would lead to a two-percent increase in sales. Unfortunately, recent studies indicate that the increase might be closer to one percent, although the actual amount varies widely.[4] Figure 5.5 displays a more realistic conceptualization of the relationship between marketing expenditures and advertising. The factors present in the relationship include:

objective 5.2

What is the relationship of advertising expenditures to advertising effectiveness?

- The communications goal
- Threshold effects
- Diminishing returns
- Carryover effects
- Wear-out effects
- Decay effects

An unrealistic assumption about the relationship between promotional expenditures and sales

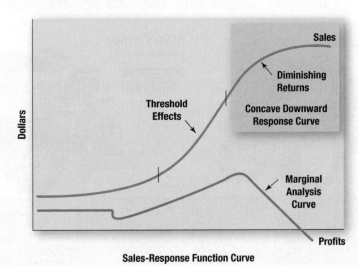

Sales-Response Function Curve

◀ **FIGURE 5.5**

Relationships between Advertising and Marketing Expenditures and Sales and Profit Margins

▲ An advertisement for Visit South Walton designed to move individuals from awareness to actually visiting South Walton.

Communications goals differ depending on the stage in the buying process. The hierarchy of effects model suggests that prior to making a purchase, a consumer goes through the stages of awareness, knowledge, liking, preference, and conviction. The communications objective and stage in the hierarchy of effects model influence the advertising goal, budget, and message to be sent. For example, the early advertising campaign for South Walton, Florida was to create awareness of the beaches and amenities offered. Over time, advertising shifted to building brand preference. Thus, the entire campaign began at one place (awareness) and ended at another (encouraging action). It would not be logical to expect that early marketing expenditures would create a high sales yield when the primary objective was to create awareness.

Threshold Effects

As shown in Figure 5.5, the early effects of advertising may be minimal. The same holds true for every communications expenditure. At first, few behavioral responses occur, especially when companies rely on advertising by itself. Then, over time, a consumer who has been repeatedly exposed to a company's message will recall the brand and eventually becomes willing to make an inquiry or purchase.[5] Coupons, free samples, and other marketing tactics can also help a good or service reach the threshold point sooner. **Threshold effects** occur at the point in which the advertising program begins to have a significant impact on consumer responses.

In some circumstances threshold effects may be relatively easy to achieve. For instance, a new good or service may be so innovative that consumers become quickly aware of its advantages and become willing to buy the item immediately. Such was the case with the

▶ By offering a $50 appreciation bonus, Cub Cadet hopes to reach the threshold point sooner.

first iPhone. Also, when a company with a strong, established brand name introduces a product, the threshold point will be reached more quickly.

Diminishing Returns

Eventually, almost all campaigns reach a point of saturation where further expenditures have a minimal impact. The S-shaped curve displayed in Figure 5.5 displays a *sales-response function curve* and diminishing returns from additional advertising expenditures. **Diminishing returns** are part of the *concave downward function*, in which incremental increases in expenditures in advertising result in smaller and smaller increases in sales. A *marginal analysis* reveals that further advertising and promotional expenditures adversely affect profits, because sales increases are less than what the company spends on the additional marketing or advertising.

Carryover Effects

Consumers purchase many products only when they need them, such as washing machines and refrigerators. Promotions for these products should be designed to create brand recall, which occurs when the consumer has been exposed to the company's message for so long that, when the time comes to buy, the individual remembers the brand name. This indicates the presence of **carryover effects**. In other words, when a washing machine breaks down and requires a replacement, remembering the Maytag brand will be the company's goal. Consequently, if the consumer remembers Maytag's products, the advertisements have effectively carried over. The same concept applies to medical facilities, such as St. Francis Medical Center shown on this page, which appeals to people for times when they need medical services.

Wear-Out Effects

An additional complication to an advertising campaign may emerge. At a certain point, an advertisement or particular campaign simply becomes "old" or "boring." Consumers tend to ignore the advertisement or tune it out.[6] Some consumers may develop negative attitudes toward the brand if they become annoyed at the marketing communication and believe the advertisement should be discontinued. This indicates **wear-out effects**.

Research regarding advertising campaigns over the last 50 years indicates that about half of all campaigns last too long and experience wear-out effects. On the other hand, the same research suggests that the long-term effect of advertising remains twice as high as the short-term effect. As a result, marketers try to continue a campaign long enough to capture that long-term effect but not so long that wear-out sets in.[7] Discovering the balance between wear-out and long-term impact remains challenging.

Decay Effects

When a company stops advertising, consumers often begin to forget the message, which indicates **decay effects** (see Figure 5.6). In some instances, a dramatic degree of decay takes place. In others, the carryover effects are strong enough that some time elapses

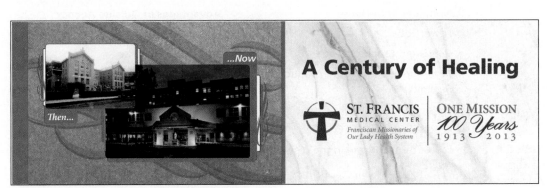

◄ The concept of carryover effects applies to this advertisement for St. Francis Medical Center.

▶ **FIGURE 5.6**
A Decay Effects Model

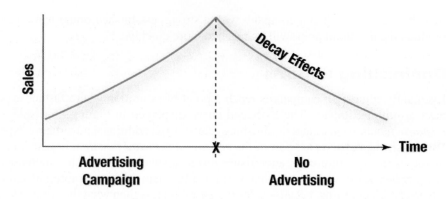

before the brand drops out of the consumer's mind. The presence of decay effects means that companies should continue to engage in some form of marketing communications to keep the brand in people's thoughts.

In-House Versus External Advertising Agencies

objective 5.3

When should a company employ an external advertising agency rather than completing the work in-house?

When beginning an advertising program, deciding whether to use an in-house advertising group or an external advertising agency constitutes the first issue. Figure 5.7 compares the advantages of an in-house facility to an outside agency.

With tightening marketing budgets, more companies use in-house advertising resources. Recently, Apple significantly expanded its in-house department from 300 to more than 500 employees. An Association of National Advertisers study revealed that 58 percent of the association's members currently utilize in-house advertising resources, compared to 42 percent five years ago.[8]

In-house advertising creates several advantages. First, marketing managers may believe the approach lowers costs and retains better control of the message, which can be aligned with the brand and other company communications. The CEO can work closely with the marketing team to make sure this occurs. Consequently, members of the marketing department may conclude they have a better understanding of the firm's products and mission and more quickly produce advertisements. An in-house program will be more consistent, due to a lower turnover rate in the creative team.

While companies may take advantage of in-house resources, many also outsource specific functions, such as writing, filming, recording, and editing advertisements. Most utilize media companies to plan and purchase media time (on television and radio) and space (in magazines, in newspapers, and on billboards). Many employ external agencies to handle social media activities.

Advantages of In-House	Advantages of Outside Agency
• Lower costs	• Reduce costs
• Consistent brand message	• Greater expertise
• Better understanding of product and mission	• Outsider's perspective
• Faster ad production	• Access to top talent
• Works closer with CEO	
• Lower turnover rate in the creative team	

▶ **FIGURE 5.7**
Advantages of In-House versus External Agencies

An outside agency often costs less when compared to less efficient in-house facilities. This occurs when in-house employees spend more time on campaigns and ad designs than would an agency. The agency provides greater expertise and may have access to top talent in the industry. Advertising agencies offer an outside perspective not influenced by internal corporate politics and personal biases. Many agency professionals better understand consumers and trends because they work with a number of clients over an array of products. Knowledge gained from one product can often be transferred to other, even unrelated products.

Advertising agencies provide a variety of options. All sizes and types of agencies exist. At one end of the spectrum, highly specialized, boutique agencies offer one specific service (for example, making television ads) or serve one type of client. G+G Advertising of Albuquerque, New Mexico, specializes in advertising to Native Americans—a market of an estimated 10 million people.[9]

At the other end of the spectrum, full-service agencies such as mcgarry-bowen, Zehnder Communications, and The Richards Group deliver every type of advertising and promotional activity. These companies offer advice and assistance in working with other components of the IMC program, including consumer and trade promotions, direct-marketing programs, digital programs, and social media (see Figure 5.8).

Some agencies provide specialized services. *Media service companies* negotiate and purchase media packages (called *media buys*) for companies. *Direct-marketing agencies* handle every aspect of a direct-marketing campaign through telephone orders (800 numbers), internet programs, and direct mail. Some companies focus on *consumer promotions, trade promotions*, or both. A new group of agencies specializes in developing *digital services*. Boxcar Creative designs *interactive websites* and widgets that can be used on multiple sites. Other companies offer *social media services* to reach consumers and businesses through a wide array of social media techniques. *Public relations* firms provide experts to help companies and brands develop positive public images, as well as damage control responses when negative publicity arises.

▲ Skyjacker performs all advertising functions in-house.

Budget Allocation Considerations

The size of the account affects the selection of an in-house team versus an external advertising agency. A small account may not be attractive to an advertising agency, because it generates lower revenues. If the agency charges a higher fee to compensate, it becomes too costly for the small firm. Smaller accounts can create other challenges. Less money can be spent on media time and space purchases because the company spends the majority of the advertising budget on production of the advertisement.

One rule of thumb marketers consider, the 75–15–10 breakdown, suggests that 75 percent of the money to be spent on advertising should be used to purchase media time or space, 15 percent to the agency for the creative work, and 10 percent for the actual production of ads. In contrast, for smaller accounts, the breakdown may be 50–30–20. Only 50 percent of expenditures are for media purchases; the other 50 percent of the funds goes to the creative and production work.

- Advice about how to develop target markets
- Specialized services for business markets
- Suggestions about how to project a strong company image and theme
- Assistance in selecting company logos and slogans
- Preparation of advertisements
- Planning and purchasing media time and space

◀ **FIGURE 5.8**

Common Services Provided by Full-Service Agencies

▲ Crowdsourcing of creative work involves fans and can generate considerable buzz for a brand.

Unless the majority of the company's advertising budget can be used to pay for media purchases, it may be wise either to perform the work in-house or to develop contracts with smaller specialty firms to prepare various aspects of an advertising campaign.

Crowdsourcing

Crowdsourcing involves outsourcing the creative aspect of an advertisement or campaign to the public. It offers an alternative to creating commercials in-house or hiring an external advertising agency. Crowdsourcing can create a viral buzz as users view advertisements online, recommend or send favorites to friends, and post links.

Doritos used crowdsourcing to create Super Bowl ads over a 10-year span. Many of the ads have been selected as some of the best of the Super Bowl. Although it may seem that crowdsourcing would be a cheaper method, in reality the total cost stays about the same as hiring a professional agency. The costs of running the crowdsourcing campaign as a contest, paying prize money, creating the microsite to host the contest, and producing the commercial, combined with the time spent by Doritos and the agency in choosing from the thousands of entries, are nearly equal to what would have been spent on an agency. Crowdsourcing, however, yields the advantage of involving fans and generating the buzz that surrounds the contest for the consumer-generated advertisement.[10]

Harley-Davidson employs an extreme approach to crowdsourcing. The company obtains all creative work through crowdsourcing, with agencies only responsible for producing the ads. According to Harley-Davidson CMO Mark-Hans Richer, "We made a decision to turn over the major creative to owners because we have a passionate customer base who wants to engage with us." The creative work comes through Facebook. Harley-Davidson has about 3 million Facebook fans. About 8,000 signed up to be part of the Fan Machine, the creative forum for Harley. The Fan Machine group reviews advertising briefs, submits ideas, and votes on ideas from members. While the company offers some branded products, according to Richer, "it's really about the spirit and creativity and passion of the brand than the financial reward." A recent project received 300 idea submissions, with 20,000 votes for the best ideas. "What really shocked me was how good the ideas actually were. There were a lot of surprising insights. It's like a focus group and creative wrapped into one," he said.

Recent research regarding consumer-generated advertising reveals several trends. First, consumer-generated advertising works best when targeted to current customers and customers who have high levels of brand loyalty. Consumers with lower levels of loyalty are more skeptical of the ad and the campaign. Second, sharing background information about the ad creator increases the persuasiveness of the consumer-generated ad by establishing credibility and showing similarities between the ad creator and consumers. The social media and public relations components of crowdsourcing constitute important ingredients in successfully using this approach to advertising. Consequently, while consumer-generated ads may be effective at generating customer retention, they are less successful for increasing a customer base.[11]

Critics of crowdsourcing argue that while the approach may lead to innovative and eye-catching advertisements, no consistent message or theme results over time. The commercials may or may not reinforce the brand's major selling points or elements. Stan Richards of The Richards Group suggests that without a strategic approach, key components of the overall communications effort can be lost.

Choosing an Agency

Choosing an agency begins with the development of quality selection criteria. The choice of an agency represents a key component of the advertising management process for many companies. Figure 5.9 lists the steps involved in selecting an agency.

objective 5.4

How do companies choose advertising agencies?

Goal Setting

Prior to making any contact with an advertising agency, company leaders identify and prioritize corporate goals. The targets provide a sense of direction and prevent personal biases from affecting selection decisions. Goals guide marketers by providing a clear idea of what the company wishes to accomplish. They also help the marketing team as they make requests for campaign proposals.

Campbell Soup Co. recently issued a request for proposals that would consolidate four of the company's iconic brands – Prego, Pace, SpaghettiOs and Ready Meals. Campbell wanted an agency that could combine creative, content, digital and social efforts for all four brands. According to Megan Haney, senior manager-communication for Campbell's, the company wanted an agency that would "drive better efficiencies, better thinking, and more collaboration with us as a partner." By determining the goal in advance, Campbell's marketing team was able to select the best agency.[12]

Selection Criteria

Firms with experience often set selection criteria in advance in order to reduce any biases that might affect decisions. Emotions and other feelings can lead to poor choices. Figure 5.10 identifies some of the major issues to be considered during the process. The list can be especially useful during the initial screening, when the field narrows to the top five (or fewer) agencies.

Agency Size As noted earlier, a company marketer should consider the size of the agency versus the size of her firm. A good rule of thumb to follow is that the account should be large

1. Set goals.
2. Select process and criteria.
3. Screen initial list of applicants.
4. Request client references.
5. Reduce list to two or three viable agencies.
6. Request creative pitch.

◀ **FIGURE 5.9**
Steps in Selecting an Advertising Agency

- Size of the agency
- Relevant experience of the agency
- Conflicts of interest
- Creative reputation and capabilities
- Production capabilities
- Media purchasing capabilities
- Other services available
- Client retention rates
- Personal chemistry

◀ **FIGURE 5.10**
Evaluation Criteria in Choosing an Advertising Agency

GET FED. We're always coming up with new ways to prepare food. We've got boiled, broiled, blackened and fried. The only thing we have more of than the ways we prepare food is the number of places we have to eat food. It's one of the things that make us who we are.

VISIT OUR MOBILE SITE

Visit Baton Rouge.com
800 LA ROUGE

▲ Visit Baton Rouge is just one of the accounts being handled by Zehnder Communications.

enough for the agency so that it is important to the agency but small enough that, if lost, the agency would not be badly affected.

Relevant Experience When an agency has experience in a given industry, the agency's employees are better able to understand the client firm, its customers, and the structure of the marketing channel. At the same time, the client company makes sure the agency does not have any *conflicts of interest*. An advertising firm hired by one manufacturer of automobile tires would experience a conflict of interest if another tire manufacturer attempted to hire the agency.

An advertising agency might have relevant experience without representing a competitor. Such experience is gained when an agency works for a similar company operating in a different industry. For example, when an agency has a manufacturer of automobile batteries as a client, the experience will be relevant to selling automobile tires.

The agency should have experience with the business-to-business program, so that retailers, wholesalers, and any other channel parties are considered in the marketing and advertising of the product. A number of advertisements in this textbook were created by The Richards Group. In addition to the Orkin advertisements in this section, The Richard's Group's clients include Motel 6, Home Depot, Sub-Zero, and Bridgestone. Note that the list does not include competing firms within the same industry.

Creative Reputation and Capabilities One method used to assess an agency's creativity is asking for a list of awards the company has received. Although awards do not always translate into creating effective advertisements, in most cases a positive relationship exists between winning awards and writing effective ads. Most creative awards are given by peers. As a result, they represent effective indicators of what others think of the agency's creative efforts.

Production and Media-Purchasing Capabilities Agency capabilities should be examined when production and media-purchasing services are desired. A firm that needs an agency to produce a television commercial and also buy media time should check on these activities as part of the initial screening process. Many agencies either employ subsidiary companies to perform the media work or subcontract it to a media firm. The advertising agency does not necessarily need to make media buys, but it should have the capacity to make sure they are made to fit with the ads being designed.

Other Criteria The final three selection criteria—*other services available, client retention rates*, and *personal chemistry*—are utilized during the final steps of selection. These criteria help make the final determination in the selection process.

Creative Pitch

When the company reduces the list to two or three finalists, the selection team asks each for a creative pitch. The advertising agencies chosen to compete provide a formal presentation that addresses a specific problem, situation, or set of questions—a process also called a *shootout*. The presentations reveal how each agency would deal with specific issues that might arise during preparation of a campaign. The process helps a client company choose the agency that best understands the issues at stake and offers a comprehensive approach to solving the problem or issue. Recently, Arby's reached a point at which advertising had lost its impact. The brand had been through various taglines, ad agencies, logos, and nothing had worked. The creative pitch requested of agencies under review was how each would solve these issues and the $150,000 loss in sales per restaurant over the previous four years. The winning agency, Fallon, suggested the restaurant chain break away from happy people running around eating a sandwich to a focus on the meats Arby's serves. The new campaign drew a younger client to Arby's. Prior to the new campaign, only 35 percent of its customers were under 35. Today, 50 percent are under 35.[13]

▲ During a creative pitch, an agency presents ideas on the problem or campaign posted by the potential client.

Preparing a pitch takes time and creates expenses for advertising agencies; therefore, they only want to prepare pitches that have a decent chance of acceptance. When an agency spends time preparing a presentation only to find out later that the company had no desire to switch agencies, but were told by upper management to solicit pitches, it becomes frustrating.[14] A company seeking to retain an advertising agency should provide sufficient time for the competing finalists to prepare the pitch. Pink Jacket Creative's Bill Breedlove reports, "I would prefer at least 30 days to prepare a pitch. Even 45 to 60 days would be wonderful sometimes, and for some companies."

Recently, Oscar Mayer, a brand under the Kraft Heinz umbrella, sought ways to unify its portfolio of products and contemporize its image. The mcgarrybowen agency demonstrated how Oscar Mayer could contemporize the brand and build emotional ties with customers. The agency's ideas were fresh, contemporary, and had the emotional spark the organization desired.[15]

Successful creative pitches result from hard work and thorough planning. Figure 5.11 highlights some of the "do's" and "don'ts" for advertising agencies in making pitches.

- Do listen. Allow the client to talk.
- Do your preparation. Know the client and its business.
- Do make a good first impression. Dress up, not down.
- Do a convincing job of presenting. Believe in what you are presenting.
- Don't assume all clients are the same. Each has a unique need.
- Don't try to solve the entire problem in the pitch.
- Don't be critical of the product or the competition.
- Don't overpromise. It will come back to haunt you.
- Don't spend a lot of time pitching credentials and references.

◀ **FIGURE 5.11**
Pitching Do's and Don'ts

Agency Selection

During the presentation phase, company marketers meet with agency creatives, media buyers, account executives, and other people who will work on the account. *Chemistry* between employees of the two different firms becomes critical. The client company's leaders should be convinced that they will work well together. Chemistry can break or make the final decision.[16]

After completing the selection process, the agency and the company will work together to prepare the advertising campaign. Those who did not win the account are also notified, in order to maintain more positive relations with them over time. The account executive, account planner, and advertising creative all play key roles in this process.

Roles of Advertising Personnel

objective 5.5

What are the primary job functions within an advertising agency?

Advertising agency employees perform a wide variety of roles. In small agencies, an individual may carry out multiple roles. In a large agency, multiple individuals will be employed in the various departments and perform similar functions. The primary roles within the agency consist of the account executives, creatives, traffic managers, and account planners.

Account Executives

The account executive acts as the go-between for the advertising agency and the client company. In some agencies, the executive will be actively involved in soliciting the account, finalizing details of the contract, and working with personnel within the agency to make sure the advertisements meet the client's specifications. In other agencies, especially larger firms, account executives do not solicit accounts, but rather manage the relationship and work that the agency performs for the brand. The account executive often helps the company define the theme of the overall IMC program and how advertising fits into the brand's marketing strategy.

▼ Account executives work with creatives, traffic managers, and account planners in developing advertising campaigns for clients.

Creatives

Creatives develop and design advertisements. They are either members of advertising agencies or freelancers. Some smaller agencies provide only creative advertising services without becoming involved in other marketing programs and activities. Creatives may appear to hold the "glamour" jobs in agencies, because they get to actually create ads and marketing materials. At the same time, creatives work long hours and face enormous pressures to design effective advertisements that produce tangible results.

Traffic Managers

The traffic manager works closely with the advertising agency's account executive, creatives, and production staff. The individual's responsibilities include scheduling the various aspects of the agency's work to make sure it is completed on time. During production, the traffic manager assumes the responsibility of making sure props, actors,

and other items needed have been ordered and are in place at the time of the filming or recording.

Account Planners

The account planner provides the voice and serves as the advocate for the consumer within the advertising agency. Planners make sure the creative team understands the consumer (or business). Account planners interact with the account executive and the client to understand the target audience of the ad campaign. They then work to make sure the messages reach the right customers.

The account planner assists in developing long-term communication strategies and provides direction for individual advertising campaigns. In small agencies, an account executive may perform the role. Larger firms employ separate individuals and/ or departments to conduct the account planning role.

Advertising Campaign Parameters

Producing effective advertising campaigns requires the joint efforts of the account executive, creative, account planner, and media planner. Working independently might produce some award-winning ads, but often does not achieve the client's objectives. Advertising agencies seek to produce campaigns that stand out among the competing messages. Creating effective campaigns requires attention to the advertising campaign parameters listed in Figure 5.12.

▲ The account planner represents the consumer's viewpoint so that a creative can design effective advertisements, such as this one for Maxwell House coffee.

Advertising Goals

Advertising goals are derived from the firm's overall communication objectives that were presented in Chapter 4. Figure 5.13 identifies the most common advertising goals. These should be consistent with the marketing communications objectives and other components of the integrated marketing communications plan.

Build Brand Awareness   A strong global brand often constitutes a key advertising goal, especially for larger companies. Building a brand's image begins with developing brand awareness. *Brand awareness* means the consumers recognize and remember a particular brand or company name as they consider purchasing options. Advertising offers an excellent venue to increase brand awareness.

Successful brands possess two characteristics: the top of mind and the consumer's top choice. When consumers are asked to identify brands that quickly come to mind from a product category, one or two particular brands are nearly always mentioned. These names are the **top of mind** brands. For example, when asked to identify fast-food hamburger restaurants, McDonald's and Burger King almost always head the list. The same may be true for Nike and Reebok for athletic shoes in the United States, as well as in many other countries.

The term **top choice** suggests what the term implies: A top choice brand is the first or second pick when a consumer reviews her evoked set of possible purchasing alternatives.

objective 5.6

What are the advertising campaign parameters that should be considered?

- Advertising goals
- Media selection
- Tagline
- Consistency
- Positioning
- Campaign duration

▲ **FIGURE 5.12**
Advertising Campaign Parameters

- To build brand awareness
- To inform
- To persuade
- To support other marketing efforts
- To encourage action

▲ **FIGURE 5.13**
Advertising Goals

Many products become top of mind or top choice due to brand equity. Advertising can strengthen brand equity.

Provide Information   Advertising achieves other goals, such as providing information to both consumers and business buyers. Typical information for consumers includes a retailer's store hours, business location, or sometimes more detailed product specifications. Information may make the purchasing process appear to be simple and convenient, which can entice customers to travel to the store to finalize a purchase.

Persuasion   When an ad convinces consumers of a brand's superiority, persuasion has taken place. Changing consumer attitudes and convincing them to consider a new purchasing choice can be challenging. Advertisers utilize several persuasion methods. One involves showing consumers the negative consequences of failing to buy a particular brand. Alternatively, an advertising campaign can highlight the superior attributes or benefits of a brand.

Supporting Marketing Efforts   Advertising often supports other marketing functions. Manufacturers use advertising to accompany trade and consumer promotions, such as theme packaging or combination offers. Contests such as the McDonald's Monopoly game require additional advertising to be effective.

Retailers also advertise to support marketing programs. Any type of special sale (white sale, buy-one-get-one-free, pre-Christmas sale) requires effective advertising to attract customers. Manufacturers and retail outlets both run advertisements in conjunction with coupons or other special offers. The advertisement in this section for Wholly Guacamole features a brand alliance with Disney along with a coupon on any Wholly product, plus a rebate for Disney's *The Lion King* movie.

Encouraging Action   Many firms set behavioral goals for advertising programs. A television commercial encouraging viewers to take action by dialing a toll-free number to make a quick purchase serves as an example. Everything from ShamWow to Snuggies has been sold using action tactics. Infomercials and home shopping network programs rely heavily on immediate consumer purchasing responses.

▲ This advertisement supports a brand alliance between Wholly Guacamole and Disney.

Action-oriented advertising takes place in the business-to-business sector. Generating leads becomes the primary goal. Many business advertisements provide web addresses or telephone numbers so that buyers can request more information or make a purchase.

The five advertising goals of building image, providing information, being persuasive, supporting other marketing efforts, and encouraging action are not separate from each other. They work together in key ways. For instance, awareness and information are part of persuasion. The key is to emphasize one goal without forgetting the others.

Media Selection

Selecting the appropriate media requires an understanding of the media usage habits of the target market and then matching that information with the profile of each medium's audience. Volkswagen positioned the Tiguan crossover as a fun vehicle aimed at young, active individuals who love the outdoors. Although the campaign featured television commercials, the more unusual component of the campaign was the outdoor segment. The theme "people want an SUV that parks well with others" was featured in a series of outdoor ads placed at bike racks and trail heads at 150 national parks and resorts. Brian Martin, CEO of Brand Connections Active Outdoor, which placed the ads, noted that more than 30 million impressions were made with hikers, bikers, and other outdoor lovers.[17]

The marketing team identifies the media the target market favors. Teenagers surf the web and watch television. Only a small percentage reads newspapers and news magazines. Various market segments exhibit differences in when and how they view various media. Older African Americans watch television programs in patterns that differ from those of older Caucasians. Males watch more sports programs than females, and so forth.

In business-to-business markets, identifying the trade journals or business publications that various members of the buying center most likely read assists in the development of a print advertising campaign. Engineers, who tend to be the influencers, often have different media viewing habits than vice presidents, who may be the deciders.

Although media buys are guided by the advertising agency and the client company, media companies typically make the purchases. A trend toward involving media companies at an earlier stage in the campaign process has evolved in recent years. Previously, most media companies were contacted after a campaign became ready or was nearly complete, with the specific task of purchasing media space or time. Companies including Procter & Gamble, Johnson & Johnson, Clorox, Kimberly-Clark, Verizon, and HP enlist media companies as strategic partners as they develop advertising and marketing campaigns.[18] Agencies invite media companies to participate in the strategy development stage because many have quality insights regarding the target audience. They are able to provide valuable information to the creative staff about how to best reach the client's target market, employing the primary media that target consumers favor.

In some cases, media companies actually create commercials. Joe Kuester, senior brand manager for Kimberly-Clark, stated, "It doesn't matter to us where the idea comes from or who champions that idea." That statement was in response to Kimberly-Clark's media company, Mindshare Entertainment, creating a series of webisodes involving Whoopi Goldberg for its Poise brand. Another media company, MEC Entertainment, worked with its client Ikea to produce a campaign for A&E called "Fix this Kitchen." This trend to involve media companies in all facets of advertising campaign development is quickly gaining momentum.[19]

▲ Selecting the right media ensures that the consumers who are the most likely to use Progressive Bank for trust and wealth management will see this advertisement.

- American Express—"Don't leave home without it."
- Avis—"We try harder."
- Bounty—"The quicker picker-upper."
- Capital One—"What's in your wallet?"
- CNN—"The most trusted name in news"
- Energizer—"It keeps going, and going, and going."
- Hallmark—"When you care enough to send the best."
- John Deere—"Nothing runs like a Deer."
- Maxwell House—"Good to the last drop."
- Nokia—"Connecting people"
- Office Depot—"Taking care of business."
- Target—"Expect more. Pay less."
- UPS—"What can Brown do for you?"
- Wal-Mart—"Save money. Live better."

◀ **FIGURE 5.14**
Taglines Used by Various Brands

Taglines

The key phrase in an advertisement, the **tagline**, should be something memorable that identifies the uniqueness of a brand or conveys some type of special meaning. "Just Do It" has been Nike's tagline for many years. Figure 5.14 identifies other well-known taglines.

Taglines provide consistency across various advertising platforms. Consumers often remember taglines and identify them with specific brands. A catchy tagline identifies a brand and then stays with it over successive campaigns. In order to bring freshness to a campaign, company marketers may tweak or modify a tagline every few years. With shorter attention spans, taglines have been shrinking from short sentences to just two or three words. L'Oreal Paris has used the shortened tagline "Because I'm Worth It" for more than 40 years. Other taglines that have been shortened include BMW's "ultimate driving machine," Lucozade's (British energy drink) "Yes" and Wal-Mart's "Save money, live better."

In other instances, a completely new version may be developed. To make the Oscar Mayer brand more contemporary, the company's marketing personnel and its agency, mcgarrybowen, created a new tagline. Oscar Mayer was known for trust, nostalgia, heritage, jingles, bologna, hot dogs, and kids. The image needed to be freshened, made more contemporary, and designed to reach adults as well as kids. The Oscar Mayer marketing team wanted to take the brand to a place that was energetic, culturally relevant, and that captured the spirit of everyday food making people feel good. Real joy, real moments, real friendship, real emotion, and real people were at the forefront. The idea was that Oscar Mayer is "good mood food." One Oscar Mayer ad conveys the good mood feeling that resulted from marketing brainstorming sessions and music collaborations and led to the campaign tagline "It doesn't get better than this."[20]

▼ This advertisement for JD Bank, combined with the one on the next page, uses variability theory concepts to create consistency within the campaign.

Consistency

Repeatedly seeing a specific visual image, headline, copy, or tagline helps to embed a brand into a person's long-term memory. Visual consistency becomes especially important because most customers spend very little time viewing an advertisement. In most cases, an individual gives just a casual glance at a print advertisement or cursory attention to a television commercial. Visual consistency leads the viewer and moves the message from short-term to long-term memory. Consistent logos, taglines, headlines, and campaigns aid in this process.

Repetition helps increase consumer ad recall as well as brand recall. While mere repetition of the same ad may accomplish this goal, varying the ad appears to have better results. Some advertisers emphasize the principles present in **variability theory**,[21] which suggests that variable encoding occurs when a consumer sees the same advertisement in different environments. These varied environments increase recall and effectiveness by encoding the message into the brain through various methods. Creatives can generate the effect by varying the situational context of a particular ad. For example, Capital One campaigns use various settings to convey the same basic message, "What's in your wallet?"

Changing the context of the ad increases recall and offers an effective method for overcoming competitive ad interference.[22]

Selecting two media to convey a message generally can be more effective than repeating an advertisement in the same medium. An advertisement placed in more than one venue reduces competing ad interference. In other words, a message presented on television and in magazines works better than one that appears only on television. Consumers seeing an advertisement in a different medium are more likely to recall the ad than when it appears in only one.

Whether across different media or modifications of ads within the same media, consistency constitutes the key to effectiveness. It reduces wear-out effects and maintains interest in the advertising campaign. Consistency aids in providing carryover effects when the consumer is in the purchasing stage.

Positioning

Maintaining consistent product positioning throughout a product's life makes it more likely that a consumer will place the product in a cognitive map. When the firm emphasizes quality in every advertisement, it becomes easier to tie the product into the consumer's cognitive map than if the firm stresses quality in one ad, price in another, and convenience in a third campaign. Inconsistency in positioning makes the brand and company more difficult to remember. Consistent positioning avoids ambiguity; the message stays clear and understandable.

Campaign Duration

The length or duration of a campaign should be identified. Using the same advertisement for an appropriate period of time allows the message to embed in the consumer's long-term memory. It should be changed before it becomes stale and viewers lose interest; however, changing ads too frequently impedes retention. Creating new campaigns also increases costs.

Typical campaigns last about six months; however, exceptions do occur. Some run for years. The criterion that typically determines when it is time to change a campaign is the wear-out effect. When consumers ignore ads and it no longer is producing results, it becomes time to launch a new campaign. One method used by advertisers to lengthen advertising campaigns and delay wear-out effects is to create multiple versions of ads within the campaign, as was the case in the JD Bank ads that used variability theory.

The Creative Brief

When an advertising agency prepares a document to guide in the production of an advertising campaign or for a specific commercial, the document is a *creative strategy* or **creative brief**. Although various forms exist, the basic components of a standard creative brief are displayed

objective **5.7**
How does a creative brief facilitate effective advertising?

- The objective
- The target audience
- The message theme
- The support
- The constraints

▲ **FIGURE 5.15**
The Creative Brief

in Figure 5.15. A quality creative brief, when prepared properly, saves the agency considerable time and effort and results in a stronger advertising campaign for the client.

Ineffective communications between agencies and clients sometimes occurs when those involved do not properly prepare a brief. A survey of senior executives of advertising agencies indicated major problems with creative briefs, and most agencies voiced some level of frustration. The most common problem cited was a lack of focus. Fifty-three percent of the executives said the briefs were complete but lacked focus, and 27 percent said they were both incomplete and inconsistent. Only 20 percent said they were complete and focused most of the time. Not one, zero percent, said they were complete and focused all of the time.[23]

The Objective

A creative brief identifies the objective of the advertising campaign, such as those noted previously. The creative staff reviews the main objective (or goal) before designing specific ads or the advertising campaign. The objectives guide the advertising design and the choice of execution. For instance, for an increased brand awareness goal, the name of the product will be prominently displayed in the advertisement or repeated several times in a television ad. Building brand image normally results in the actual product being more prominently displayed in the ad.

▼ An advertisement targeted to human resource individuals within businesses.

The Target Audience

The creatives need an understanding of the target audience. An advertisement designed to persuade a business to inquire about new computer software differs from one directed to consumers by the same company. The business advertisement focuses on the type of industry and a specific member of the buying center. The more detail available regarding the target audience, the easier it becomes for a creative to design an effective advertisement. The LUBA Worker's Comp ad shown here targets individuals who work in human resource departments within companies.

Overly general target market profiles do not help. Rather than specifying "males, ages 20 to 35," more specific information will be needed, such as "males, ages 20 to 35, college-educated, and professionals." Other information, including hobbies, interests, opinions, and lifestyles, make it possible to more precisely develop an advertisement. A campaign directed to active, outdoor enthusiasts differs from one designed for individuals who pursue video games, watch movies, and surf the web.

The Message Theme

The message theme presents an outline of key idea(s) that the advertising program conveys. The message theme not represents the benefit or promise the advertiser emphasizes to reach consumers or businesses. The promise, or unique selling point, describes the major benefit the good or service offers customers. A message theme for an automobile might emphasize toward luxury, safety, fun, fuel efficiency, or driving excitement. A message theme for a hotel could focus on luxury, price, or unusual features, such as a hotel in Paris, France, noting the ease of access to all of the nearby tourist attractions. The message theme matches the medium selected, the target market, and the primary IMC message.[24]

Message themes can be oriented toward either rational or emotional processes. A "left-brain" advertisement oriented toward the logical, rational side informs individuals using numbers, letters, words, and concepts. Left-brain advertising features a logical, factual, rational appeal. A number of rational attributes (size, price, special features) influence the decision to buy a car. At the same time, many consumers purchase cars for emotional reasons. The right side of the brain processes abstract ideas, images, and feelings. An automobile may be chosen for its color, sportiness, or other, less-rational reasons.

Most advertising targets either the right brain or the left brain. Advertising can also be effective by balancing the two sides. Rational, economic beings have difficulty defending the purchase of an expensive sports car such as a Porsche. Many product purchases are based on how a person feels about the good or service, combined with rational information.[25]

The Support

Support should be provided as the fourth component of the creative brief. **Support** takes the form of facts that substantiate the message theme. When Aveeno products won "Best of Beauty" awards from *Allure* magazine, its "Best of Beauty" seal was placed on the company's products. Company advertising mentioned the award to support Aveeno's claims of superiority.

In this section, the advertisement for St. Francis Medical Center shows three Best Regional Hospital awards by *US News* and two Best Employers awards. This type of support indicates to patients the high quality of care they will receive from St. Francis.

▲ An advertisement for St. Francis Medical Center showing the awards the institution has received.

The Constraints

Constraints apply to every legal and mandatory restriction placed on advertisements. Constraints spell out legal protections for trademarks, logos, and copy registrations. They also specify all disclaimers about warranties, offers, and claims. For warranties, a disclaimer details the conditions under which they will be honored. Tire warranties, for example, often state that they apply under normal driving conditions with routine maintenance. A person cannot ignore tire balancing and rotation and expect to get free new tires when the old ones quickly wear out.

Disclaimer warranties notify consumers of potential hazards associated with products. Tobacco advertisements contain statements and images regarding the dangers of smoking and chewing tobacco. Disclaimers about marketing offers specify the terms of financing agreements as well as when bonuses or discounts apply. Claims identify the exact nature of the statement made in the advertisement. This includes nutritional claims as well as statements about serving sizes and other information describing the product.

After these components have been completed, the creative brief is ready. From this point forward, the message and the media match, and actual advertisements can be produced. Effective creative briefs take the overall IMC message and tailor it to a specific advertising campaign. This, in turn, gives the company a better chance of reaching customers with messages that return measurable results and help guarantee success. Recent research suggests that campaigns designed in two months or less have the greatest likelihood of being "highly effective." Those that take longer tend not to be as effective. At the same time, marketers try to move forward without rushing. A campaign designed in two weeks or less is also likely to be ineffective.[26]

International Implications

objective 5.8

What are the implications of advertising management in the global arena?

Advertising management involves major expenditures overseas. The top 100 global advertisers spend an average of 62 percent of advertising budgets outside the United States. Figure 5.16 compares the non-U.S. advertising budget to non-U.S. sales revenue for six major corporations. As shown, Coca-Cola spends 83.5 percent of company advertising dollars outside the United States, where 74.9 percent of its total revenues are generated. Colgate-Palmolive spends 85.6 percent of its advertising dollars on non-U.S. ads and generates 76.7 percent of its revenues outside the United States. Data for Ford, Mattel, McDonald's, and Procter & Gamble are also provided.[27]

Two differences emerge when considering advertising management in an international perspective. The first is in regard to the process itself. The second concerns preparing international advertising campaigns.

The general processes used to prepare advertising campaigns remain fairly uniform. Some of the most important differences are in the areas of availability of qualified advertising agencies and the manner in which agencies are selected. For example, in many Asian cultures, the beginning of a face-to-face meeting includes a gift exchange. Further, business cards have differing uses and meanings across cultures. In some countries, cards are only presented to highly trusted allies. In others, they are freely passed out. The marketing team carefully studies the nuances of business meetings, including the use of formal titles, eye contact, who speaks first, and other variables, before beginning a relationship with an advertising agency in another country.

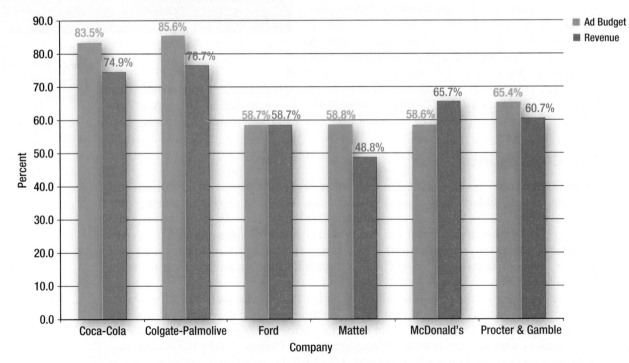

▲ **FIGURE 5.16**

Non-U.S. Ad Budgets and Sales Revenue Comparisons for Major Brands.

Agencies in other countries might not follow typical procedures such as a shootout or the preparation of a creative brief. Forms of preplanning research may also vary. In some countries, it is not possible to conduct the same types of research as in the United States and other Western cultures.

Advertising campaigns designed for an international audience require an understanding of the various languages and cultures that might be involved. In Europe, French, Spanish, Portuguese, Italian, and other languages need translation and back-translation of advertising themes and messages to make certain the idea can be clearly presented in various countries. Media selection processes may also require adjustment; some countries have state-run television networks and others place restrictions on what can be shown in an advertisement.

Summary

This chapter reviews the advertising campaign management process. Effective advertising occurs when the firm has a well-defined mission statement and targets its energies in the direction of creating goods or services to meet the needs of a target market.

Quality advertising begins with an understanding of various advertising theories that explain consumer purchasing processes. The hierarchy of effects model and a means–end analysis or MECCAS model can be combined with an analysis of the visual and verbal elements needed to create an effective method to provide marketers with quality guidelines for creating marketing messages. *Visual Esperanto* is a universal language that makes global advertising possible.

Advertisers should also understand the impact of advertising expenditures. The relationships between marketing expenditures and eventual success can be modeled using threshold effects, diminishing returns, carryover effects, wear-out effects, and decay effects.

Advertising management continues with the decision to employ an in-house department to develop advertisements or to retain an external advertising agency. When choosing an external agency, the company's leaders establish clear steps to lead to the selection of the optimal agency. The steps include spelling out and prioritizing organizational goals, establishing quality selection criteria, screening firms based on those criteria, requesting references from firms that are finalists, requesting creative pitches, making on-site visits to get to know those in the agencies, and offering and finalizing a contract.

Common selection criteria used in selecting agencies include the size of the agency matching the size of the company, relevant experience, no conflicts of interest, production capabilities, quality creative capabilities, suitable media-purchasing skills, other services as needed, client retention rates, and a good chemistry between those in the company and those in the agency.

Within the advertising agency, the account manager performs the functions of soliciting accounts, finalizing contracts, and selecting creatives to prepare campaigns. Account executives are go-betweens who mediate between the agency and the client company and aid client organizations in refining IMC messages and programs. Traffic managers help to schedule various aspects of the agency's work. Account planners serve as the voice and advocate for the consumer within the advertising agency.

Creating effective advertising campaigns requires attention to various parameters. Advertising goals are derived from the firm's overall communication objectives and include building brand awareness, providing information, generating persuasion, supporting other marketing efforts, and encouraging action. Then media selection can commence. Quality taglines express something memorable and unique about the brand or convey a special meaning. Consistency assists in recall of the advertisement. Variability theory suggests that variable encoding can help build strong campaigns. Advertisers also pay attention to quality positioning and seek to understand the best duration for the campaign.

Creatives who prepare advertisements are guided by the creative brief, which spells out the objective of the promotional campaign, the target audience, the message theme, the support, and the constraints. The message theme presents an outline of the key idea(s) that the program seeks to convey. The constraints include logos, warranties, disclaimers, or legal statements that are part of various advertisements. These processes are carried out by domestic U.S. agencies as well as by advertisers around the world.

Key Terms

advertising campaign management The process of preparing and integrating a company's advertising efforts with the overall IMC message

hierarchy of effects model A method advertisers use to help clarify the objectives of an advertising campaign

means–end chain A conceptual model that shows how a message, or means, can lead consumers to a desired end state

Means–End Conceptualization of Components for Advertising Strategy (MECCAS) A model that explains ways to move consumers from product attributes to personal values by highlighting the product's benefits

visual Esperanto A form of universal language that makes advertising possible for any good or service

threshold effects What occurs when an advertising program begins to have a significant impact on consumer responses

diminishing returns A point at which a promotional campaign has saturated the market and further advertising and promotional expenditures adversely affect profits

carryover effects An instance in which an individual becomes ready to buy a product and remembers a key company due to the effectiveness of its marketing program

wear-out effects An instance in which consumers ignore or even develop negative attitudes toward a brand because the campaign has become "old" or "boring"

decay effects What occurs when a company stops advertising and consumers begin to forget the message

crowdsourcing The process of outsourcing the creative aspect of an advertisement to the public

top of mind The brands that quickly come to mind when consumers are asked to identify brands from a product category

top choice The first or second pick when a consumer reviews his or her evoked set of possible purchasing alternatives

tagline A key, memorable phrase in an advertisement that conveys a special meaning

variability theory A theory that suggests variable encoding will be more effective as consumers view advertisements in differing environments

creative brief A document that guides in the production of an advertising campaign or a specific commercial

support The facts that substantiate the unique selling point of a creative brief

constraints The company, legal, and mandatory restrictions placed on advertisements, which include legal protection for trademarks, logos, and copyright registrations

---

MyMarketingLab

To complete the problems with the ⭐ in your MyLab, go to the end-of-chapter Discussion Questions.

Review Questions

5-1. Define advertising campaign management.

5-2. What are the six stages of the hierarchy of effects model? Do they always occur in that order? Why or why not?

⭐ **5-3.** How are the three components of attitudes related to the hierarchy of effects model?

5-4. In a means–end chain, what are the means? The ends? How do they affect advertising design?

⭐ **5-5.** Why are visual elements in advertisement important? What is the relationship between visual and verbal elements? Can there be one without the other?

5-6. What is *visual Esperanto*?

5-7. What are threshold effects? Diminishing returns? Carryover effects?

5-8. What are the differences between wear-out effects and decay effects?

5-9. What factors influence the decision of whether to use an in-house advertising group or an external advertising agency?

5-10. Besides advertising agencies, what other types of organizations play roles in the communications process?

5-11. What is crowdsourcing? What are its advantages and disadvantages?

5-12. What steps should be taken in selecting an advertising agency?

5-13. What evaluation criteria should be used in selecting an advertising agency?

5-14. What is a creative pitch?

5-15. Describe the various roles within an advertising agency.

5-16. What advertising campaign parameters were described in this chapter?

5-17. Describe the terms *top of mind brand* and *top choice*.

5-18. What is a tagline, and what role does a tagline play in an advertisement?

5-19. Explain how variability theory can be used to create consistency in an advertising campaign.

5-20. What elements are included in a creative brief?

Critical Thinking Exercises

DISCUSSION QUESTIONS

⭐**5-21.** Select two of the print ads in this chapter. Identify the part of the hierarchy of effects model the advertisement targets. Explain why. In terms of attitude formation, which sequence is being used? Justify your answer. Discuss the relationship of the visual and verbal elements in the ad. Which is prominent?

5-22. Choose one of the following brands. Develop a means–ends chain similar to the two that are shown in this chapter.

   a. St. Francis Medical Center

   b. JD Bank

   c. Orkin Pest Control

   d. Maxwell House Coffee

⭐**5-23.** Explain means-end theory and why it is important in advertising design. Pick two ads in this textbook, other than the milk and ReRez ones used to explain means-end theory. Identify the attribute(s) featured in the two ads and the benefits derived from those attributes. Construct a means-end chain for one of the ads. (Be sure to provide the page number of the two ads you selected).

5-24. Think about recent advertisements you have seen or watched. Explain each of the concepts listed below, then give an example of an advertisement you believe illustrates the concept. Explain why you believe the ad fits the category.

   • Threshold effects
   • Diminishing returns
   • Carryover effects
   • Wear-out effects
   • *Visual Esperanto*

5-25. Look through the ads in this chapter. Which ad do you like the best? Why? Which ad is the least appealing? Why? Discuss the relationship between the visual and verbal elements. Locate one ad you believe displays the characteristic of *visual Esperanto*. Explain why.

5-26. Review the responsibilities of each of the jobs under "Roles of Advertising Personnel." Which one most appeals to you? Why? Which is least appealing? Why?

⭐**5-27.** Identify and briefly describe the five advertising goals presented in the chapter. Examine each advertisement in this chapter and identify the primary advertising goal you believe is being used for the ad. Justify your choice.

5-28. Choose one of the following products. Use the information in this chapter to prepare a creative brief. You can pick a brand from within the product category.

   a. Energy drink

   b. Frozen apple juice

   c. Fast-food restaurant

   d. Coffee

   e. Pest control

Integrated Learning Exercises

5-29. Making the decision to use an external advertising agency as opposed to an in-house program for advertising or some other aspect of the advertising function can be difficult. Access the American Association of Advertising Agencies website at **www.aaaa.org**. What type of information is available at this website? How would it benefit companies looking for an advertising agency? Explain your answer. How would it benefit advertising agencies? Explain your answer.

5-30. A number of agencies assist business organizations with integrated marketing communications programs. Whereas some firms try to provide a wide array of services, others are more specialized. Access the following association websites. What type of information is available on each site? How would the information provided be useful in building an IMC program?

   a. International Social Marketing Association (**www.i-socialmarketing.org**)

   b. Brand Activation Association (**www.bbalink.org**)

   c. Outdoor Advertising Association of America (**www.oaaa.org**)

   d. Direct Marketing Association (**www.the-dma.org**)

   e. Digital Marketing Association (**www.digital marketingassoc.com**)

5-31. Part of an advertising management program includes understanding the media usage habits of consumers and their attitudes toward various media. An excellent source of information in Canada is the Media Smarts Program at **www.mediasmarts.ca**. Review the types of information available at the website. Examine the news articles. What type of information is available at this website, and how could it be used in developing an advertising campaign?

⭐**5-32.** Many advertisers direct ads toward the right side of the brain and develop advertisements based entirely on emotions, images, and pictures. Companies often advertise auto parts and tools with a scantily-clad woman to attract the attention of men. The woman has nothing to do with the product itself, but gains attention. The rationale for using a sexy woman is that if consumers like her, they will like the product and then purchase that brand. Effective advertisements integrate elements from both the left side of the brain as well as the right. They contain elements that appeal to emotions but also have rational arguments. A laundry detergent can be advertised as offering the rational benefit of getting clothes cleaner but also contain the emotional promise that your mother-in-law will think of you more favorably. For each of the following websites, discuss the balance of left-brain versus right-brain advertising appeal.

   a. Pier 1 Imports (**www.pier1.com**)

   b. Pig O' My Heart Potbellies (**www.potbellypigs.com**)

   c. Popeyes Louisiana Kitchen (**www.popeyes.com**)

   d. Backcountry.com (**www.backcountry.com**)

5-33. You have been asked to select an advertising agency to handle an account for Red Lobster, a national restaurant chain. Your advertising budget is $30 million. Study the websites of the following advertising agencies. Follow the selection steps outlined in the chapter. Narrow the list down to two agencies and justify your decision. Then choose between the two agencies and justify your choice.

   a. The Richards Group (**www.richards.com**)

   b. Leo Burnett (**www.leoburnett.com**)

   c. Slingshot (**www.slingshot.com**)

   d. mcgarrybowen (**www.mcgarrybowen.com**)

   e. Zehnder Communications (**www.z-comm.com**)

⭐5-34. A marketing manager has been placed in charge of a new chain of sporting goods stores to be introduced into the market. The company's corporate headquarters are in Atlanta, and the firm's management team has already decided to use a local advertising agency. The primary objective in choosing an agency is that the firm must have the capability to develop a strong brand name. Type "advertising agencies in Atlanta" into a search engine. Identify an initial list of six ad agencies. Follow the steps outlined in the chapter to narrow the list to two agencies. (Please provide the URLs for all six agencies.) Discuss the steps you used in choosing the two agencies and why you selected them. Then describe a project for the agencies to prepare as part of an oral and written presentation (shootout) to the company's marketing team.

5-35. Go to the authors' website for this textbook at **clowbaack.net/video/ads.html** and watch the TV ad for JD Bank. Examine the two JD Bank ads featured in the chapter section "Advertising Campaign Parameters." Discuss how well the TV ad matches the print ads. What do you think is the primary goal of the TV and print ads? Discuss the concept of consistency, variability theory, and positioning as it relates to the TV ad and two print ads.

Blog Exercises

Access the authors' blog for this textbook at the URLs provided to complete these exercises. Answer the questions that are posed on the blog.

5-36. Oreo Cookies: **blogclowbaack.net/2014/05/07/oreo-cookies-chapter-5**

5-37. John Deere: **blogclowbaack.net/2014/05/07/john-deere-chapter-4**

5-38. Advertising Agencies: **blogclowbaack.net/2014/05/07/advertising-agencies-chapter-5**

Student Project

CREATIVE CORNER

Use the following creative brief for this exercise.

Product:	Porsche
Objective:	To change consumer views that the Porsche can't be driven every day.
Target Audience:	30- to 55-year-old consumers, slightly more male, college educated, with annual incomes of approximately $100,000. Psychographically, the targeted market is a group known as *individualists*. They tend not to buy mainstream products. In automobile selection, they place greater emphasis on design elements, distinctiveness, and utility. Social status is important.
Background Information:	Market research found that potential customers balked at the idea of buying a car just to sit around. When asked what kept them from driving the car every day, they said, "I don't feel comfortable driving in city traffic. It doesn't have the technology that I need to manage my everyday life. It doesn't have space for passengers."
Message Theme:	The Porsche can be driven every day for normal activities. It does not have to sit in the garage and be driven only on weekends. It has the newest technology and can comfortably carry passengers.
Constraints:	All ads must contain the Porsche logo.

5-39. As an account executive for an advertising agency, discuss the creative brief in terms of the completeness of the information provided and whether the objective is realistic. What additional information should Porsche provide before a creative can begin working on the account?

5-40. The media planner for the Porsche account suggests a media plan consisting of cable television, print advertising, internet ads, and network advertising on *Family*

Guy, *CSI*, *Monday Night Football*, *Big Bang Theory*, and *American Idol*. Evaluate this media plan in light of the creative brief's objectives. Can these shows reach the target audience? What information does a creative and the account executive want from the media planner before starting work on actual commercials?

5-41. Using the information provided in the creative brief, prepare a magazine advertisement. Which magazines might match the target audience? Why?

CASE 1 ▸ JAKE'S TROPHY SHOP

Jake Brown was about to begin an exciting new phase in his business. His original retail outlet, Jake's Trophy Shop, located in the east-central part of Kansas City, Missouri, had reached its peak. It was time to expand to a second location, which would be on the south side of town close to the Kansas border (Overland Park and other nearby suburbs), where a great deal of population growth had taken place. Along with new residential neighborhoods in that part of the city, many larger companies had opened offices in that area.

The marketplace for trophies includes several types of customers. One large group includes the many children's sports programs in the community, from little league baseball, to soccer, basketball, football, tennis, gymnastics, swimming, and others. The buyers for trophies for this age group include sports leagues such as those provided by the YMCA, individual team sponsors, and occasionally parents and/or team coaches.

A second market contains trophies for adults participating in various activities, such as bowling leagues and other recreational sports. Once again, league officials, team sponsors, and individual venues including bowling alleys and tennis court providers purchased trophies for winners of various events.

Business-to-business opportunities also created sales. Jake's target marketing includes individual companies seeking to buy "thank you" plaques for those retiring or commemorating long-standing years of service, along with trophies for some events, such as sales contests winners. This market includes plaques for local citizens and business awards provided by city government leaders, Chambers of Commerce, The United Way, and others. The Kansas City Royals also presented plaques to various individuals for their accomplishments, support of the city, and support of the team itself through activities as diverse as singing the National Anthem at games and throwing out the first pitch before a game starts.

Recently, Jake had launched another product line—essentially, "gag" trophies for parties and other occasions. For example, plaques for people turning 40 or 50 years old, individually-designed items with punch lines aimed at various personal foibles as well as accomplishments, and some items poking fun at people for individual characteristics were added to his store. Jake had been disappointed by the advertising campaign efforts that were part of the launch of this line of products, and sales were slow as a result.

Jake had several important decisions to make. He would need to choose target markets to reach along with product lines

▲ Trophies can be marketed to both retail and business customers.

to emphasize. He wanted to encourage not only the first visit but also return business. There was sufficient competition in the area to make a choice between competitors based on price or quality. He believed his edge was offering fast service, high quality, and reasonable prices. The new location had been chosen and would open in two months. It was time to get started promoting this new store.

5-42. Explain how the hierarchy of effects model would apply to the four main trophy-buying groups.

5-43. Would threshold effects, diminishing returns, and wear-out effects apply to Jake's upcoming advertising program? Explain why or why not.

5-44. Should Jake utilize a local advertising agency or do as much of the work as he could by himself? Defend your response.

5-45. Would the concepts of top of mind and top choice apply to advertising for the second location of Jake's Trophy Shop? If so, how? If not, why not?

5-46. Design two creative briefs. The first should seek the goal of enticing customers in the south end of town to visit the new store, seeking especially to reach business-to-business buyers. The second should emphasize the "gag" gift line of trophies for both stores in order to increase sales following the launch of the second store.

CASE 2 CLASSIC CRYSTAL

Every day, most people in developed countries use a glass or cup as part of their routines. Glassware is sold in a variety of stores, from large discount retailers such as Wal-Mart and Target to small specialty stores. Customers purchasing glassware range from individuals seeking the simplest, most economical versions, to brides making choices at various registries, to bars, restaurants, and hotels requiring vessels to hold drinks of all types.

Glasses can be made from plastic, actual glass, crystal, and other elements. Designs can be nonexistent to exotic. Some glasses are round; others square or in more unusual shapes. Some are dishwasher safe and even designed for heavy-duty use. Arcoroc sells "drinkware" in conjunction with flatware and silverware, giving various businesses, such as restaurants, the option of purchasing an entire dinner setting that meshes together. In its marketing materials, Arcoroc stresses the durability of its products. Heavy-duty glassware can also be found in some Army surplus stores.

Other glassware forms are dainty and can only be hand washed or should at least be handled with a great deal of care. Novica offers hand-blown drinkware that the company describes as "our artisan-crafted treasures." Two popular products include "Amber Feast," with a light amber tint, and "Night Sky," which is a dark, cobalt blue.

Glassware is often designed to match the fluid it will hold and the setting it will serve. Wine glasses tend to have stems and seek to enhance the aroma of the drink. Some are created to generate "snob appeal." Beer mugs tend to be sturdy and feature handles. Milk glasses for children are short, round, and stout. Dinner glasses assume a variety of forms.

Advertising campaign management for glass manufacturers would feature all of the elements described in this chapter. Advertising theories would help explain how a product is chosen and why. Advertising expenditures should be managed to achieve the highest levels of effectiveness. The manufacturer will decide on an in-house or agency-based approach to marketing. When an agency is chosen, the campaign parameters will be outlined and a creative brief should be developed to guide the advertising process.

5-47. Using the internet, identify a glassware brand and/or manufacturer that interests you. Based on the information provided for the brand, choose a particular type of glassware. Explain why you chose this particular brand. In your explanation, include the brand's website address and a screenshot of its main page.

5-48. Develop a means–end chain that explains the purchasing process for the brand's specific products.

▲ Drinkware comes in a variety of shapes and sizes.

5-49. Using the internet, identify five advertising agencies in your area. Evaluate each advertising agency in terms of its ability to handle an advertising campaign for your company. Choose one of the five to handle your account and explain why it was chosen. (Include each agency's URL in your response).

5-50. Develop a creative brief for an advertising campaign that you believe would best fit your glassware company.

5-51. Design a print ad that fits the creative brief you developed.

MyMarketingLab

Go to the Assignments section of your MyLab to complete these writing exercises.

5-52. Explain in your own words the three primary advertising concepts presented in this chapter: hierarchy of effects, means-end theory, and relationship of verbal and visual elements. Examine the two JD Bank ads shown in the "Advertising Campaign Parameters" section of the chapter. Discuss each of the concepts as it relates to the JD Bank ads.

5-53. You have been asked to select an advertising agency to handle an account for Red Lobster, a national restaurant chain. Your advertising budget is $30 million. Study the websites of the following advertising agencies. Follow the selection steps outlined in the chapter. Narrow the list down to two agencies and justify your decision. Then choose between the two agencies and justify your choice.

  a. The Richards Group (**www.richards.com**)

  b. Leo Burnett (**www.leoburnett.com**)

  c. DDB (**www.ddb.com**)

  d. Lucas Design & Advertising (**www.aladv.com**)

  e. mcgarrybowen (**www.mcgarrybowen.com**)

  f. Zehnder Communications (**www.z-comm.com**)

Chapter 6 Advertising Design

Chapter Objectives

After reading this chapter, you should be able to answer the following questions:

6.1 How are message strategies used in designing effective advertisements?

6.2 What are the seven main types of advertising appeals?

6.3 What role does the executional framework play in advertising design?

6.4 How are sources and spokespersons decisions related to advertising design?

MyMarketingLab™

⭐ **Improve Your Grade!**

More than 10 million students improved their results using the Pearson MyLabs. Visit **mymktlab.com** for simulations, tutorials, and end-of-chapter problems.

Overview

Which recent advertising message made the biggest impression on you? Was it funny, sexy, or emotional? Did it appear during the Super Bowl? In an *Adweek* Media and Harris Interactive survey, a majority of consumers (55 percent) stated that advertisements were somewhat or very interesting. Only 13 percent replied that ads were not interesting at all. When making purchase decisions, six percent of the respondents reported that advertisements were "very influential" and 29 percent viewed them as "somewhat influential." Contrary to popular belief, advertising does influence younger consumers. Nearly half of 18- to 34-year-olds in the survey indicated that they were influenced by advertising, compared to 37 percent for 35- to 44-year-olds and 28 percent for consumers age 45 and older.[1]

This poll emphasizes the importance of designing a compelling and influential advertising campaign. Doing so can be a challenging element of an integrated marketing communications program. A successful advertising campaign results when people do more than merely enjoy what they see; it also changes their behaviors and attitudes. At the least, viewers should remember the good or service. One advertising agency with a strong track record of success in advertising design is mcgarrybowen.

MCGARRYBOWEN

In 2002, three partners came together to form a new competitor in the advertising and communications world, the mcgarrybowen agency. John P. McGarry, Jr., Gordon Bowen, and Stewart Owen designed a company that would be both "gracious" and "tenacious." Instead of one distinct style with a predetermined media solution, the agency delivers a strategic approach focused on the client's business and brand.

▲ Planning is critical to good creative design.

◀ Brainstorming sessions are used to generate ideas for a brand's story.

◀ Before designing ads, creatives discuss the strategy, appeal and execution that will be used.

The agency's impressive client list includes Chevron, Canon, Disney, J. P. Morgan, Kraft Heinz, Marriott, Oscar Mayer, Pfizer, Sharp, *The Wall Street Journal*, and Verizon. Specific products advertised and marketed through mcgarrybowen include 7UP, Advil, Miracle Whip, Snapple, and Viagra. Not long ago, the firm recaptured the Reebok account while adding new clients, including Sears, Burger King, United Airlines, and Bud Light. *Advertising Age* named mcgarrybowen Agency of the Year in 2009, #2 on its A-List in 2010, and Agency of the Year in 2011.

The mcgarrybowen agency's full service approach covers nearly every marketing and communications activity. Among them, advertising, brand strategies, digital messages, mobile, social networks, data analytics, direct marketing, sponsorships, entertainment marketing, media planning, and multicultural marketing are featured. Company leaders emphasize collaboration. The net result is a motivated and inspired work force that delivers high-quality, creative solutions to clients.

A creative at mcgarrybowen noted, "We pride ourselves on storytelling. The foundations of those stories come out as a product truth." Another employee noted, "Our account planning has more fluidity. Planning becomes most crucial when strategy is the first chapter of the story. The premise of our brand strategy is how we are going to connect the brand story on a human level." In essence, storytelling involves "getting to a single insight that interprets the brand and makes a personal connection."

Chapter 5 described the overall advertising management program, such as the approach used by mcgarrybowen. As noted, account executives lead advertising agencies by working with creatives, media planners, and media buyers. This chapter turns the focus to message design. The work will be completed by the agency's staff based on the creative brief that was prepared by the client in conjunction with the account executive.

The first three topics in this chapter are message strategies, appeals, and executional frameworks. These elements of advertising design are similar to what takes place when developing a movie or television program. The message strategy resembles what the actor says says—the verbal message. The appeal represents the manner in which a message is conveyed; through a serious tone, laughter, or sexual cues. The executional framework is comparable to the plot or story of the movie in which the action takes place.

The chapter's final topic is sources or spokespersons. These individuals present the message verbally and visually through the various media used in the advertising program. Agencies and companies carefully consider who will become the "face" of the company and its products.

Message Strategies

objective 6.1

How are message strategies used in designing effective advertisements?

The message theme outlines the key idea in an advertising campaign and becomes the central part of the creative brief described in Chapter 5. The message theme helps the advertising team derive a **message strategy**— the primary tactic or approach used to deliver the message theme. The three broad categories of message strategies include cognitive, affective, and conative approaches.[2] The categories represent the components of attitudes, as noted in the previous chapter. Figure 6.1 identifies the various forms or approaches from each category.

- Cognitive
  - Generic
  - Unique selling proposition
  - Hyperbole
  - Comparative
- Affective
  - Resonance
  - Emotional
- Conative

▶ **FIGURE 6.1**
Message Strategies

Cognitive Message Strategies

A **cognitive message strategy** presents rational arguments or pieces of information to consumers. The ideas require cognitive processing. The advertising message describes the product's attributes or the benefits customers can obtain by purchasing the product.[3]

A cognitive message strategy advertisement influences the person's beliefs and/or knowledge structure by suggesting one of a variety of potential product benefits. Foods may be described as healthy, pleasant tasting, or low calorie. Marketers can depict a tool as durable, convenient, or handy to use. The five major forms of cognitive strategies are generic messages, preemptive messages, unique selling propositions, hyperbole, and comparative advertisements.

Generic Messages   An advertisement that directly promotes the product's attributes or benefits without any claim of superiority transmits a **generic message**, which works best for a brand leader or one that dominates an industry. A generic message makes the brand synonymous with the product category. Several years ago, Campbell's declared that "Soup is good food" without claiming superiority. The company leads the industry. When most consumers think of soup, they think of Campbell's, which sells 69 percent of all cans sold annually.[4] Nintendo employs a similar approach. The company dominates the game-console category with a 47 percent market share.[5] In the business-to-business arena, Intel features the generic message strategy "Intel inside" because the company controls 80 percent of the microchip market.[6]

Generic message strategies help stimulate brand awareness. The advertiser may try to develop a cognitive linkage between a specific brand name and a product category, such as Skechers and sporty footwear. The advertisement might contain little information about the product's attributes. Instead, it attempts to place the brand in a person's cognitive memory and cognitive map.

Preemptive Messages   A claim of superiority based on a product's specific attribute or benefit with the intent of preventing the competition from making the same or a similar statement is a **preemptive message**. Crest toothpaste's reputation as "the cavity fighter" preempts other companies from making similar claims, although all toothpastes fight cavities. An effective preemptive strategy occurs when the company states the advantage first. Competitors saying the same thing become viewed as "me too" brands or copycats.

Unique Selling Proposition   An explicit, testable claim of uniqueness or superiority that can be supported or substantiated in some manner is a **unique selling proposition**. In the advertisement for P&S Surgical Hospital shown here, the company claims to have the best smaller-sized hospital. Substantiation of these claims comes through being rated #1 in Louisiana by CareChex and receiving a 5-star rating by HealthGrades.

▲ An advertisement for Community Trust Bank featuring a cognitive message strategy stating that checks can be deposited anytime and anywhere.

▲ An advertisement for P&S Surgical Hospital featuring a unique selling proposition message strategy P&S.

▲ This advertisement for Karns Quality Foods includes a hyperbole message strategy.

Hyperbole   An *untestable* claim based on some attribute or benefit is **hyperbole**. If ABC states that it has America's favorite dramas, the claim is hyperbole. It does not require substantiation, which makes this cognitive strategy quite popular. Hyperbole often employs puffery terms, including *best* or *greatest,* such as in the ad for Karns Foods shown in this section.

Comparative Advertising   The final cognitive message strategy, a **comparative advertisement**, allows an advertiser to directly or indirectly compare a product to the competition based on some attribute or benefit. The advertisement may mention the competitor by name or present a make-believe competitor with a name such as "Brand X."

Comparative ads often capture the consumer's attention. When comparisons are made, both brand awareness and message awareness increase. Consumers tend to remember more of what was said about a brand than when a non-comparative format presents the same information.

Low believability and negative consumer attitudes constitute the potential downside of comparative ads. Many consumers think comparative ads are less believable. They view the sponsoring brand's information as exaggerated and may conclude that the advertisement misstates information about the comparison brand to make the sponsor brand appear superior. This in turn leads to negative consumer attitudes toward the brand using the comparative approach.

Another danger with comparative ads arises when consumers experience negative attitudes toward the advertisement, which can then transfer to the advertiser's product. This becomes more likely when a brand runs a *negative comparative ad* about the competition's product. Research suggests that negative comparative ads typically result in lower believability of the advertising claim and may result in less favorable attitudes toward the brand.[7] In psychology, the concept of *spontaneous trait transference* posits that when a comparative advertisement criticizes the competition's brand based on a particular attribute, it may lead viewers to also attribute the deficiency to the promoted brand. The transference becomes more likely when the consumer purchases the comparative brand, not the advertised brand.[8]

Negative ads can succeed. One negative comparative campaign that achieved the desired outcome was the "Scroogled" campaign by Microsoft's search engine, Bing. It presented negative information about Google, such as invasive ads in Gmail, sharing data with app developers, and exploiting private data to maximize Google's advertising profits. Most of the ads did not mention Bing until the end, when the voiceover states, "For honest results, try Bing." Effectiveness research indicated that 53 percent of viewers said they would look at Bing after viewing the ads.[9]

Company leaders carefully choose an appropriate comparison firm and use caution when using negative comparisons. The comparison brand must be considered to be viable competing brand. Comparisons consisting of hype and opinion with no substantial differences are less likely to succeed. Misleading comparisons might cause the Federal Trade Commission (FTC) to investigate. The majority of complaints filed with the FTC are concerned with potentially misleading comparison advertisements.

Comparing a brand with a low market share to the market leader works well, because viewers concentrate more carefully on the advertisement's content and message. Such was the case in a recent campaign for the Kindle Fire, which was compared to the iPad. The commercials argued that the Kindle Fire included superior quality product attributes at a lower price. Comparing a high-market share brand with another high-market share brand may not be as effective. In these cases, a better strategy may be to simply make the comparison without naming the competitor.

The five cognitive message strategies are based on rational logic. Advertisers can design messages that lead consumers to pay attention to the ad and take the time to cognitively process the information. In terms of attitudes, the sequence of *cognitive* → *affective* → *conative* represents the rational approach. The cognitive message strategy first presents consumers with rational information about a good, service, or company and then leads them to develop positive feelings about the same brand or company.

Affective Message Strategies

Advertisements trying to evoke feelings or emotions and match those feelings with the good, service, or company feature **affective message strategies**. These messages attempt to enhance the likeability of the product, recall of the appeal, or comprehension of the advertisement. Affective strategies should elicit emotions that lead the consumer to act, preferably by buying the product and subsequently by affecting the consumer's reasoning process.

Resonance   Connecting a brand with a consumer's experiences in order to develop stronger ties between the product and the consumer is affective resonance advertising. Playing music from the 1980s takes Echo Boomers back to that time. Any strongly held memory or emotional attachment becomes a candidate for resonance advertising.

Subaru's advertising team designed a resonance approach for an online marketing effort attempting to tap into a person's nostalgia for his first car. The program included an animation generator at a microsite called **FirstCarStory.com** where consumers could recreate the look and feel of their first cars. The program's technology transferred words into custom images. Alan Bethke, director of marketing communications at Subaru, noted, "The First Car Story campaign provides a creative outlet for reliving those unique, funny, unforgettable experiences anyone who had a first car can relate to."[10]

A new form of resonance advertising, **comfort marketing**, gained traction when marketers looked for ways to encourage consumers to purchase branded rather than generic products. The approach reassures consumers looking for value that a branded product stands the test of time. Comfort marketing involves bringing back vintage

◀ This advertisement for visit South Walton (Florida) presents an affective message strategy through the headline "Make Connections."

If you could hold onto any moment in time,

which?

pheel the moment the moment

PHILADELPHIA REGULAR

▲ This advertisement for Philadelphia Cream Cheese uses an emotional message strategy through the image and tagline "pheel the moment."

characters, themes, and jingles from the past to evoke fond memories when times were better. To ensure the brand does not look old-fashioned, most refresh the mascot, music, taglines, and other aspects of the ad to the twenty-first century. Brands that have employed this approach include StarKist, Alka-Seltzer, Bacardi, Doritos, Dr. Pepper, Pepsi-Cola, and Planters. Robert Furniss-Roe of Bacardi North America said, "People, particularly in this environment, are looking for substance and authenticity."[11]

Emotional   An **emotional affective** approach attempts to elicit powerful feelings that help lead to product recall and choice. Many emotions can be connected to products, including trust, reliability, friendship, happiness, security, glamour, luxury, serenity, pleasure, romance, and passion. Companies incorporate emotional appeals into both consumer-oriented and business-to-business advertisements. Members of the buying center in a business are human. They make purchasing decisions based on more than simple rational thought processes. Emotions and feelings also affect choices. When an advertisement presents a product's benefits in an emotional framework, it will normally be more effective, even in business-to-business ads.[12]

Many creatives believe affective strategies build stronger brands. Affective advertisements guide consumers to like the brand, develop positive feelings toward it, and eventually purchase the item. Cognitive beliefs then follow. This approach relies on the attitude development sequence of *affective → conative → cognitive*. For some products, affective advertisements succeed because few real tangible differences among brands actually exist. The St. Francis Medical Center advertisement in this section utilizes an affective strategy by depicting a warm mother/daughter relationship.

Conative Message Strategy

Conative message strategies seek to lead directly to consumer responses. They can support other promotional efforts, such as coupon redemption programs, cash-back rebates, or encourage consumers to access a website. Advertisements seeking to

▶ An advertisement for St. Francis Medical Center featuring an emotional message strategy.

My first and only choice.

✝ ST. FRANCIS MEDICAL CENTER
Future of Healing. Tradition of Caring.

Franciscan Missionaries of Our Lady Health System   stfran.com

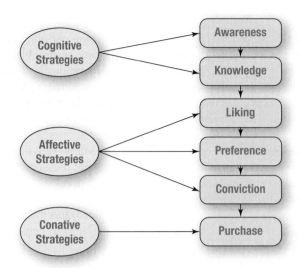

◀ **FIGURE 6.2**
The Hierarchy of Effects Model
and Message Strategies

▼ This Skyjacker ad uses a conative message strategy by offering consumers a cash rebate with a purchase.

persuade viewers to call a toll-free number to purchase DVDs or other merchandise have the goal of eliciting behaviors. Conative ads typically encourage quick action by stating that the item cannot be purchased in stores and will be available for only a limited time.

With conative advertising, cognitive knowledge of the brand or affective liking of the product often come later (after the actual purchase) or during product usage. For instance, a point-of-purchase display can be designed (sometimes through advertising tie-ins) to cause people to make *impulse buys*. Making the sale constitutes the goal, with cognitive knowledge and affective feelings forming as the product is used. The attitude sequence for conative message strategies becomes *conative → cognitive → affective*.

Cognitive, affective, and conative strategies can be matched with the hierarchy of effects approach, which, suggests that consumers pass through a set of stages, from awareness to knowledge, liking, preference, conviction, and, finally, to the purchase. As shown in Figure 6.2, each message strategy highlights a different stage of the hierarchy of effects model.

Choosing the right message strategy remains a key ingredient in creating a successful advertising program. To be effective, the message strategy should match the message to the appeal and executional framework. These should mesh with the media to be utilized. The creative and the account executive remain in constant contact throughout the process to be certain all of these advertising ingredients remain consistent.

Types of Advertising Appeals

Through the years, advertisers have employed numerous advertising approaches. Of these, seven **advertising appeals** have achieved the most success. Normally, one or a combination of these types of appeals appears in an advertisement (see Figure 6.3).

The type of appeal chosen will be based on a review of the creative brief, the objective of the campaign, the means–end chain to be conveyed, and the message strategy. Advertisers consider a number of factors, including the product being sold, the target market of the campaign, and the personal preferences of the advertising agency and client.

objective 6.2

What are the seven main types of advertising appeals?

- Fear
- Humor
- Sex
- Music
- Rationality
- Emotions
- Scarcity

▲ **FIGURE 6.3**
Types of Appeals

Fear Appeals

Advertisements featuring fear appeals are commonplace. Some car companies, such as Subaru, have focused on the consequences of not having a safe automobile in a crash or accident, as featured in the "They Lived" campaign, in which various individuals dealing with a badly wrecked car note that those inside the auto survived the accident. Shampoo and mouthwash ads invoke fears of dandruff and bad breath, which can make a person a social outcast. Advertisements feature fear more often than most realize.

Advertisers employ fear appeals because they work. Fear increases viewer interest in an advertisement and can enhance the ad's persuasiveness. Many individuals remember commercials with fear appeals better than they do warm, upbeat messages.[13] Consumers pay greater attention to ads using fear and are more likely to process the information conveyed, which makes it possible to accomplish an advertisement's main objective.

The *behavioral response model* displayed in Figure 6.4 illustrates the ways fear works in advertising.[14] As shown in the figure, various incidents can lead to negative or positive consequences, which then affect future behaviors.

Severity and Vulnerability   When developing fear advertisements, the creative includes as many aspects of the behavioral response model as possible. A business-to-business advertiser offering internet services tries to focus on the **severity** of downtime if a company's internet server goes down or is hacked. Another ad describes the firm's **vulnerability** by showing the probability that a company's server will crash or can be hacked into and have its customer data stolen. The ReRez advertisement for marketing research services shown on the next page features a picture of a man hanging to illustrate the danger of poor marketing research. The advertisement attempts to cause business leaders to believe low-quality decisions would result from inadequate research. ReRez can help them identify these potential problems before they turn into disasters.

Rewards to Response Efficacy   As an example of the behavioral response model, consider a young smoker who sees an ad for the Nicoderm CQ patches, which help a person quit. The man considers three things in evaluating the advertisement and making a decision to purchase Nicoderm CQ.

Intrinsic and extrinsic rewards constitute the first factor. Intrinsic rewards come from gaining social acceptance by quitting and feeling healthier. Extrinsic rewards may include savings on the cost of cigarettes as compared to the price for Nicoderm CQ.

The smoker then considers the second factor, *response costs*. When smoking leads to peer acceptance it becomes rewarding, which means there is a lower incentive to quit,

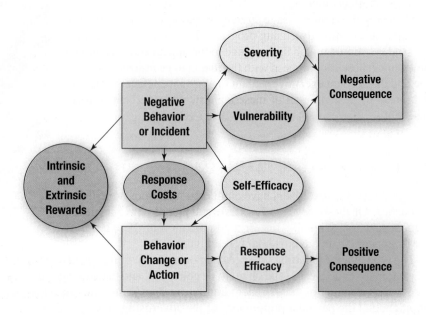

▶ **FIGURE 6.4**
The Behavioral Response Model

◀ This business-to-business advertisement for ReRez features a fear appeal.

because smoking creates intrinsic value, making quitting more difficult. A man who quits smoking becomes more likely to gain weight and lose the friends who continue to smoke. The higher the perceived costs, the less likely the decision to quit smoking becomes.

Self-efficacy, the third factor, summarizes the man's confidence in his ability to stop smoking. Many individuals have tried and failed. Thus, they have little hope that Nicoderm CQ works. The smoker who believes Nicoderm CQ can truly help him quit will be more likely to make a purchase.

The combination of intrinsic and extrinsic rewards, response costs, and the degree of self-efficacy contribute to the smoker's *response efficacy*. The decision to purchase Nicoderm CQ with the idea of stopping smoking will be based on the conclusion that doing so leads to net positive consequences. The person concludes he will fit in with family and friends, feel better, improve his health, and believes that he is capable of quitting smoking.

Appeal Strength   The strength of the appeal constitutes another key factor when using a fear approach. Most advertisers believe a moderate level of fear will be the most effective. A low level of fear may not be noticed and may not be convincing in terms of severity or vulnerability. An advertisement containing a strong fear level also backfires when the message generates feelings of anxiety. This leads the viewer to avoid watching the commercial by changing the channel or muting the sound.[15] Consequently, a fear appeal should be powerful enough to capture a viewer's attention and to influence her thinking but not so scary that she avoids watching the advertisement.

Humor Appeals

Clutter presents a significant problem in every advertising medium. Capturing a viewer's attention continues to be difficult. Even after grabbing the audience's attention, keeping it can be challenging. Humor has proven to be one of the best techniques for cutting through clutter, by getting attention and maintaining it. Consumers, as a whole, enjoy advertisements that make them laugh. A funny message offers intrusive value and attracts attention.[16]

▲ Marketers use humor in advertising because people like to laugh.

Humor appears in about 30 percent of television and radio advertisements.[17] Humorous ads often win awards and tend to be favorites among consumers. In a *USA Today* consumer survey of the most likeable advertising campaigns, humor was a key ingredient.[18]

Humorous ads succeed for three reasons. Humor causes consumers to watch, laugh, and, most important, remember. In recall tests, consumers most often mention humorous ads. The best results occur when the humor connects directly with the product's benefits. The advertisement should link the product's features with the advantage to customers and personal values in a means–end chain.

Advertising research indicates that humor elevates people's moods. Happy consumers often associate a good mood with the advertiser's products. In essence, humor helps fix the brand in the consumer's cognitive structure with links to positive feelings. Figure 6.5 summarizes the primary reasons for using humor.

Although a funny advertisement captures the viewer's attention, cuts through clutter, and enhances recall, it can go wrong. A Snickers commercial that appeared in a recent Super Bowl featured two mechanics eating from opposite ends of the same candy bar until they accidentally ended up kissing. The two men responded in disgust by ripping out their own chest hairs. The outcry from some groups was loud enough that it was immediately pulled.[19]

Advertisers avoid allowing the humor to overpower the message. Humor fails when consumers remember the joke but not the product or brand. In other words, the advertisement is so funny that the audience forgets or does not catch the brand's name.

Using humor in global campaigns can create difficulties. Humor rooted in one culture may not transfer to another. Further, not all audiences experience a humorous ad in the same way. To avoid these potential problems, the humor in an advertisement should focus on a component of the means–end chain. The humor can relate to a product's attributes, a customer benefit, or the personal value obtained from the product. The most effective ads are those in which the humor incorporates all three elements.

Sex Appeals

Advertisers use sexual appeals to break through clutter. Advertisements in the United States and other countries contain more visual sexual themes than ever. Nudity and other sexual approaches are common. Sexual themes in ads, however, do not always work. Sex

▶ **FIGURE 6.5**
Reasons for Using Humor in Ads

- Captures attention.
- Holds attention.
- Often wins creative awards.
- High recall scores.
- Consumers enjoy ads that make them laugh.
- Evaluated by consumers as likeable ads.

no longer has shock value. Today's teens grow up in societies immersed in it. One more sexually-oriented ad captures little attention. Currently, many advertisers prefer subtle sexual cues, suggestions, and innuendos.[20] Figure 6.6 lists the ways marketers employ sexuality in advertisements.

Subliminal Approach   Placing sexual cues or icons in advertisements in an attempt to affect a viewer's subconscious is the subliminal approach. In an odd paradox, consumers may not truly notice some subliminal messages, which means they did not create any effects. People already pay little attention to ads. A subliminal cue that registers only in the viewer's subconscious will not be effective. If it worked, there would be no need for stronger sexual content in advertising.

Sensuality   Some women respond more favorably to a sensual suggestion than an overtly sexual approach. An alluring glance across a crowded room can draw attention to a product. Many view sensuality as being more sophisticated, because it relies on the imagination. Images of romance and love may be more enticing than raw sexuality.

Sexual Suggestiveness   A suggestive advertisement hints that sex is about to take place. Recently, Pine-Sol included suggestiveness to advertise a household cleaner. Several television ads feature shirtless, muscular men mopping the floor while a woman watches or fantasizes. Diane Amos, who has been featured in Pine-Sol ads for the last 16 years and appears in this new series of ads featuring men, says, "We would all like our husbands to mop. It can be fun, it can be sexy, and women like it clean."[21]

Nudity or Partial Nudity   Products that contain sexual connotations or elements, such as clothing, perfume, and cologne, may feature a degree of nudity. Some ads are designed to solicit a sexual response. Others are not. In 1987, underwear companies were first allowed to use live models in television advertisements. The first commercials were modest and informational, emphasizing the design or materials used in the undergarment. The first Playtex bra commercials with live models drew strong criticism from organizations such as the American Family Association. Currently, advertisements for undergarments go much further and involve superstars, such as actress Jennifer Love Hewitt, who appeared in television and print ads for the Hanes All-Over Comfort Bra and the Perfect Panty. The campaign included an online element with footage from the photo shoots, a "bad bra toss" game, and a blog about bad bra moments.[22]

Overt Sexuality   Advertisements for sexually-oriented products featuring overt approaches will normally be deemed acceptable. Overt sexuality becomes more controversial when applied to other types of products. After Procter & Gamble launched a television campaign for Dentyne, some eyebrows were raised. The commercial showed two teens in a living room. The girl pops a piece of Dentyne Fire bubble gum into her mouth and then rips off her blouse and jumps on her boyfriend. At first, the parents stare in shock. Then, the mom tries a piece of Dentyne Fire and promptly jumps on the dad. The controversy centered on whether the ad promoted

- Subliminal techniques
- Sensuality
- Sexual suggestiveness
- Nudity or partial nudity
- Overt sexuality

▲ **FIGURE 6.6**
Sexuality Approaches Used in Advertising

▼ A milk advertisement using a sex appeal.

Is milk part of your daily routine?

Soft drinks and energy drinks did not create this body. It was milk, exercise, and basketball with the big boys.

Milk has the calcium my body needs for healthy bones. That same milk reduces my chances of developing bone problems, the osteoporosis my mom now lives with daily. Watching her suffer is my motivation to stay fit.

▲ Live models are now featured in lingerie ads using a sex appeal.

teenage sexuality by suggesting that parents should openly display sexual feelings and desires.[23]

Decorative Models One common sexual tactic involves placing **decorative models** into advertisements. These individuals adorn products as sexual or attractive stimuli. They serve no other purpose than to attract attention. In the past, commercials for automobiles, tools, and beer often used female models dressed in bikinis standing by the products. Marketers conducted a number of studies in order to determine the effectiveness of decorative models. Figure 6.7 provides some basic conclusions regarding this tactic.[24]

Effectiveness of Sex Appeals Numerous studies have examined the effectiveness of sexual appeals and nudity in advertising. Almost all conclude that sex and nudity increase attention. At the same time, brand recall tends to be lower than advertisements with other types of appeals. It appears that although people watch the advertisement, the sexual theme distracts them from noticing the brand name.[25]

Observers often rate sexually-oriented advertisements as more intriguing. Both males and females rate highly controversial sexual ads as being more interesting. The paradox, however, is that although they are more interesting, they fail to increase the transmission of information. Respondents are less likely to remember any more about the message.[26]

Commercials featuring overt sexual stimuli or containing nudity produce higher levels of physiological arousal responses. These arousal responses have been linked to the formation of both affective and cognitive responses. If the viewer is male and the sexual stimulus is female, such as a nude female in an ad for cologne, then the viewer tends to develop a strong feeling (affective) toward the ad based on the arousal response his body experiences. Female viewers of male nudity in an advertisement often experience the same type of response, although the arousal response may not be as strong. The cognitive response depends on whether the viewer sees the advertisement as pleasant or offensive. When the viewer likes the ad, it results in a positive impression of the brand. When the viewer thinks the ad exhibits poor taste, negative feelings and beliefs about the brand often emerge.[27]

▶ **FIGURE 6.7**
Factors to Consider before Using Decorative Models

- The presence of female (or male) decorative models improves ad recognition, but not brand recognition.

- The presence of a decorative model influences emotional and objective evaluations of the product among both male and female audiences.

- Attractive models produce a higher level of attention to ads than do less attractive models.

- The presence of an attractive model produces higher purchase intentions when the product is sexually relevant than if it is not sexually relevant.

Societal Trends When an advertising team determines the level of sex appeal to feature in an advertisement, they consider society's views and prevalent levels of acceptance.[28] Just as economies go through cycles, attitudes toward sex in advertising experience acceptance fluctuations.

The use of and approval of sexual themes in advertising had swung to a high level of tolerance in the early part of the 2000s, until the Super Bowl of 2004. The public reaction to Janet Jackson's breast-baring halftime show sent ripples all the way to Madison Avenue. Shortly afterward, Victoria's Secret dropped its TV lingerie fashion show. Abercrombie & Fitch killed the company's quarterly catalog, which had been strongly criticized for featuring models in sexually suggestive poses. Anheuser-Busch dropped some of its risqué ads.[29]

The pendulum has begun swinging back toward greater acceptance of sexually-oriented ads, but it has not reached the pre-2004 level yet. A recent Calvin Klein ad featuring actress Eva Mendes in the nude in a provocative pose for its Secret Obsession fragrance was rejected by the major networks in the United States but accepted by television stations in Europe. A less controversial version was created for the United States, although it was not shown until after 9:00 p.m.[30]

Criticisms of Sex Appeals One common criticism of sexually based advertising is that it perpetuates dissatisfaction with one's body. Often, thin females adorn print and television advertisements. The prevailing idea seems to be "the thinner the better." As advertising models have gotten thinner, body dissatisfaction and eating disorders among women have risen. Research indicates that many women feel unhappy about their own bodies and believe they are too fat after viewing advertisements featuring thin models. Dove's recent "Campaign for Real Beauty"

▲ Sexually-oriented images in advertisements stimulate physiological responses in both males and females.

included a series of advertisements and social media posts highlighting this criticism. The 2016 *Sports Illustrated* swimsuit edition featured the first-ever plus-sized model on one cover, indicating a change in attitudes. Still, ads featuring thin models are more likely to convince women to purchase a product.[31]

With men, the reverse is true. Many men worry they are not muscular enough and are too thin or too fat to buy the item. It does not make any difference whether the male views a male model or a female model in advertisements.[32]

Recently, a new criticism has gained attention. The idea that advertising objectifies women in many circumstances has caused some marketing professionals to respond. The Badger & Winters agency, led by advertising executive Madonna Badger, uses four criteria to determine whether an ad objectifies women: First, does the woman have a choice or voice in this situation? If not, she becomes more of a prop than something truly necessary to the message. Second, is she reduced to just a sexually provocative body part? Third, is the image manipulated to the extent that the look is not humanly achievable? This approach has become a common tactic used by advertisers. And fourth, would you be comfortable to see your sister, best friend, or yourself in this image? Badger & Winters' website and social media program states that "In 2016, Badger & Winters made a commitment to never

▲ One of the criticisms of sex appeals in advertising is that it perpetuates dissatisfaction with one's body.

objectify women in our work." The agency has sent out a two-minute video called #WomenNotObjects. As Madonna Badger states, "We can do a lot better."[33]

Music Appeals

Music often adds an important ingredient to an advertisement. A musical theme connects with emotions, memories, and other experiences. Music is intrusive; it gains the attention of someone who previously was not listening to or watching a program. It may provide the stimulus that ties a particular musical arrangement, jingle, or song to a certain brand. As soon as the tune begins, consumers recognize the brand being advertised because they have been conditioned to tie the product to the music.

Music gains attention and often increases the retention of information when it becomes intertwined with the product. Even when a consumer does not recall the ad message argument, music can lead to a better recall of an advertisement's visual and emotional aspects. Music can increase the persuasiveness of an argument. Subjects who compared ads with music to identical ads without music almost always rated those with music higher in terms of persuasiveness.[34] Several decisions are made when selecting music for commercials, including the following:

● What role will music play in the ad?
● Will a familiar song be used, or will something original be created?
● What emotional pitch should the music reach?
● How does the music fit with the message of the ad?

Music plays a variety of roles in advertisements. Sometimes music will be incidental. In others, it is the primary theme. An important decision involves selecting a familiar tune as opposed to creating original music. Writing a jingle or music specifically for the advertisement occurs more often and has become the current trend. Background or mood-inducing music is usually instrumental, and advertisers often pay musicians to write music that matches the scenes in the ad. A number of advertising agencies have formed in-house recording labels for the sole purpose of writing jingles, songs, and music for ads.[35]

In the early 2000s, using a well-known song in an advertisement was common. A popular, well-known song creates certain advantages. One primary benefit is that consumers already have developed an affinity for the song. Brand awareness, brand equity, and brand loyalty become easier to encourage when consumers are familiar with the tune. This occurs when consumers transfer an emotional affinity for the song to the brand. Some companies purchase an existing song and adapt the ad's verbiage to the music.[36] Using popular songs may be expensive. The price for the rights to a popular song can be in the range of six to seven figures.[37] The internet company Excite paid $7 million for the rights to Jimi Hendrix's song "Are You Experienced," and Microsoft paid about $12 million for the Rolling Stones' "Start Me Up."[38]

An alternative method of developing music has emerged, primarily because of the internet. Greater cooperation now exists between musicians and marketers. Some musicians view advertisements as a way to get their songs heard. Marketers see an opportunity to tie a new, exciting song to a product.

When a commercial only plays part of a song, many firms place entire tunes on company websites or on YouTube, where individuals can download them. Occasionally, a song written for a commercial reaches Billboard's Top 100 list. Jason Wade, a singer in the band Lifehouse, had never written a song for a commercial before. After viewing a copy of the 60-second commercial for Allstate Insurance produced by Leo Burnett Agency, Wade wrote a song entitled "From Where You Are." The commercial promoted Allstate's safe-driving program for teenagers. After the commercial aired, the song was made available on iTunes. Within two weeks, sales were high enough for the song to reach number 40 on Billboard's charts.[39]

Rational Appeals

A rational appeal follows the hierarchy of effects stages of awareness, knowledge, liking, preference, conviction, and purchase. A creative designs the advertisement for one of the six steps. An ad oriented to the knowledge stage transmits basic product information. In the preference stage, the message shifts to presenting logical reasons that favor the brand, such as the superior gas mileage of an automobile. A rational advertisement should lead to a stronger conviction about a product's benefits, so that the consumer eventually makes the purchase.

Rational appeals rely on consumers actively processing the information presented in the advertisement. The consumer must pay attention to the commercial, comprehend the message, and compare the information to knowledge embedded in a cognitive map. Messages consistent with the current concepts in a person's cognitive map strengthen key linkages. New messages help the individual form cognitive beliefs about the brand and establish a new linkage from her current map to the new brand. As a result, print media and the internet offer the best outlets for rational appeals. Television and radio commercials are short, which makes it harder for viewers to process message arguments.

Marketers feature rational appeals in many business-to-business advertising campaigns. A business customer who sees a Kinko's advertisement about videoconferencing services already may have the company in his cognitive structure. The customer may have used Kinko's in the past but was not aware that the company offers videoconferencing. When Kinko's has been established in this person's cognitive map, creating a new linkage to entice the customer to try its videoconferencing services becomes easier.

In general, rational appeals succeed when potential customers have high levels of involvement and willingly pay attention to an advertisement. Message arguments, product information, and benefits should be placed in the copy. A rational appeal works best when individuals have a particular interest in the product or brand. Otherwise, people tend to ignore them.

Emotional Appeals

Emotional appeals are based on three ideas (see Figure 6.8). First, consumers ignore most advertisements. Second, rational appeals go unnoticed except for consumers in the market for a particular product at the time it is advertised. Third, and most important, emotional advertising can capture a viewer's attention and create an emotional attachment between the consumer and the brand.

▲ Music can be an integral part of a broadcast advertisement.

▲ This advertisement for Crowe Horwath features a rational appeal targeting the construction industry.

- Consumers ignore most ads.
- Rational appeals generally go unnoticed.
- Emotional appeals can capture attention and foster an attachment.

▲ **FIGURE 6.8**
Reasons for Using Emotional Appeals

Most creatives view emotional advertising as the key to brand loyalty. Creatives want customers to experience bonds with the brand. Visual cues in advertisements are often key components of emotional appeals. The visual elements in the ad for Colorado shown in this section help contribute to a feeling or mood of serenity. Although individuals develop perceptions of brands based largely on visual and peripheral stimuli, this does not happen instantly. With repetition, perceptions and attitudinal changes emerge. Figure 6.9 displays some of the more common emotions presented in advertisements.

Godiva employed an emotional appeal in its latest advertising campaign entitled "the golden moment." Created by Lipman Agency, the campaign focused on giving, sharing, or eating Godiva chocolates. Laurie Len Kotcher, Chief Marketing Officer and Senior Vice President for Global Brand Development of Godiva Chocolatier, said, "When you give the gold box, receive the gold box, eating something from the gold box, there is something special about that moment."[40]

Many consumer product ads feature emotional appeals and the approach has begun to appear more frequently in business-to-business settings. In the past, only five to ten percent of all business-to-business ads featured emotional appeals. The figure has risen to nearly 25 percent. A magazine advertisement created by NKH&W Advertising Agency for a product to treat racehorses switched from a rational appeal to an emotional appeal. The target market was veterinarians. In the past, an advertisement would have opened with such ad copy as "For swelling in joints use . . ." The emotional ad shows the horse thinking, "I will prove them wrong. I will run again. I will mend my spirits."[41]

Television remains one of the best medium to present emotional appeals, because it offers advertisers intrusion value and incorporates sound and sight. Ad models can be real people. Facial expressions convey emotions and attitudes. Consumers learn about a particular brand and develop attitudes based on these experiences. Television ads also are more vivid, lifelike, and often create dynamic situations that pull viewers in. Music can be incorporated to make the commercial more dramatic. Peripheral cues constitute important components of emotional appeals. The cues, such as music and background visuals, help capture and hold the viewer's attention.

Emotions are often tied with humor, fear, music, and other appeals to make a compelling case for a product. The same ad can influence a consumer both emotionally and rationally. The creative selects

CARING HANDS NEVER CUT CORNERS

You can tell when something's done right, by someone who knows what they're doing. DuPage Medical Group is owned and led by our board-certified physicians. We understand that each decision affects the important care we provide your family. There's no room for short cuts, because your well-being is always our top priority.

Schedule an appointment today:
1.888.MY.DMG.DR (888.693.6437).

DuPage Medical Group
WE CARE FOR YOU
DuPageMedicalGroup.com

▲ This advertisement for DuPage Medical Group features visual elements that create the emotional appeal of serenity and peace.

▶ **FIGURE 6.9**
Emotions Featured in Advertising

- Trust
- Reliability
- Friendship
- Happiness
- Security
- Glamour-luxury

- Serenity
- Anger
- Protecting loved ones
- Romance
- Passion

- Family bonds
  - with parents
  - with siblings
  - with children
  - with extended family members

the most appropriate emotional appeal for the product and company.

Scarcity Appeals

Scarcity appeals urge consumers to buy a product because of a limitation. It can be that a limited number of the item is available or that the product will be sold for only a short period of time. When consumers believe only a finite supply of a product exists, the perceived value of the product might increase. For the Olympics, General Mills introduced USA Olympic Crunch cereal and Betty Crocker Team USA desserts for a limited time.[42] McDonald's, Wendy's, and Burger King offer sandwiches (McRib, Hot N' Spicy Chicken, 2 for $5 Whoppers) for limited time periods throughout the year. The scarcity concept applies to musical compilations, encouraging consumers to buy a CD because of its restricted availability. By making sure it is not available in retail stores, marketers increase its scarcity value. Notice in the advertisement for Wholly Guacamole shown in this section that the company's guacamole is only free on one day, March 20, and only at Schlotzsky's.

Executional Frameworks

An **executional framework** or **execution** signifies the manner in which an ad appeal will be presented and a message strategy conveyed. Figure 6.10 displays the various frameworks. Each will be matched with the type of appeal and message strategy as part of the overall advertising design process.

Animation Executions

Animation has become an increasingly popular executional framework, and its use has risen dramatically. The growing sophistication of computer graphics programs makes new and exciting animation technologies available. Successful animated films such as *Shrek* and *Frozen* continue to generate interest in animation advertising, which can be featured in television spots, on the internet, and in movie trailers. Single shots of animated characters, such as *Dora the Explorer*, are placed in print ads.

The *rotoscoping* process facilitates digitally painting or sketching figures into live sequences, which makes it possible

- Animation
- Slice-of-life
- Storytelling
- Testimonial
- Authoritative
- Demonstration
- Fantasy
- Informative

▲ **FIGURE 6.10**
Executional Frameworks

▲ This advertisement for DuPage Medical Group utilizes an emotional appeal.

▲ This advertisement features a scarcity appeal because Wholly Guacamole is free at Schlotzsky's only on March 20.

objective **6.3**

What role does the executional framework play in advertising design?

to present both live actors and animated characters in the same frame.[43] The creative can also merge or modify various live scenes. With this technology creatives are able to do just about anything they desire, but at a price. Rotoscoping is an expensive digital process. In the future, as costs decline advertising agencies will undoubtedly increase usage of this process.

For years, marketing professionals rarely used animation in business-to-business advertisements. Many marketers viewed it negatively, believing animation appealed to children but not to businesspeople. These opinions have changed. Business ads shown on television now take advantage of high-quality graphics to illustrate a product's uses with animation.

Slice-of-Life Executions

In slice-of-life commercials, advertisers provide solutions to the everyday problems consumers or businesses face. Proctor & Gamble made this format famous during the early days of television advertising in the 1950s. Slice-of-life commercials depict common experiences, especially the problems people encounter, and introduce the brand to solve the problem. The most common slice-of-life format contains four components: encounter, problem, interaction, and solution (see Figure 6.11). In some ads, the actors portray the dilemma or problem and solve the problem themselves. In others, a voiceover explains the benefits or solution to the problem that the good, service, or company provides.

Business-to-business advertisements often utilize the slice-of-life method because it allows the advertiser to highlight the ways a brand meets business needs. A typical business-to-business ad begins with a routine problem, such as a sales manager making a presentation to the board of directors. Then, a projector being used does not have a clear picture. The ad offers the solution: a projector from Sony. The presentation resumes with great clarity, and the board of directors accepts the customer's bid for the account. As with all slice-of-life commercials, a disaster has been avoided and a happy ending results instead.

Storytelling Executions

Storytelling does not include an encounter where a brand solves a problem faced by a consumer or business, as in the slice-of-life approach. Instead, a storytelling execution resembles a 30-second movie with a plot or story in which the brand is more at the periphery rather than at the center of the ad. A "hard-sell" approach directly presents a brand's benefits or features. The storytelling format allows the viewer to draw his own conclusions about the product. In a recent ad for Subaru, the commercial depicts a loving dad handing his daughter the car keys for the first time. He still sees her as his little girl, but now she is a teenager. The Subaru brand does not appear in the ad until the end. The story focuses on a little girl growing up and the dad trusting his beloved daughter with a Subaru. Many of the Super Bowl ads now feature the storytelling approach. Budweiser

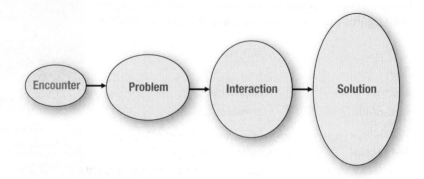

▶ **FIGURE 6.11**

Components of a
Slice-of-Life Execution

developed ads showing a small calf and colt growing up together and developing a strong bond. Another Budweiser ad features a dog that keeps returning to a farm because he has a relationship with one of the Clydesdales.

Testimonial Executions

Advertisers have achieved success with a testimonial type of execution for many years, especially in the business-to-business and service sectors. A customer relating a positive experience with a brand offers a testimonial. In the business-to-business advertisements, testimonials from current customers add credibility to the claims. Most buyers believe what others say about a company more than they believe what a company says about itself. Testimonials generate greater credibility than self-proclamations.

Testimonials are an effective method for promoting services. Services are intangible; they cannot be seen or touched and consumers cannot examine them before making decisions. A testimony from a current customer relays a succinct description of the benefits or attributes of the service. Choosing a dentist, an attorney, or an automobile repair shop often leads customers to ask friends, relatives, or coworkers. A testimonial advertisement simulates this type of word-of-mouth recommendation.

Testimonials can enhance company credibility. Endorsers and famous individuals do not always have high levels of credibility, because consumers know they are being paid for their endorsements. The same holds true for paid actors who look like everyday consumers. The most believable testimonies come from everyday people, actual customers. Retailer Stein Mart featured actual customers talking about their favorite merchandise in a recent TV campaign. Marketers recruited customers through the company's Facebook page. The TV spots encouraged customers to create videos about their favorite merchandise at Stein Mart and upload them to the website. The goals were to reach a younger target market, women between 35 and 55, and to create an online community of avid customers who found something they love at Stein Mart.[44]

I Can Smile Again

Six months ago it looked bleak. I wasn't sure if my business was going to make it. No one knew us. Our website was a disaster. That has changed. My business has picked up thanks to the new website designed by Clow Creations. Now I can smile. Now I can put food on the table for my family. Thank you Clow Creations. I could not have done it without you.

-Dennis. Rooker, DJ Rooker Construction

▲ An advertisement featuring a testimony execution.

Authoritative Executions

Advertisers use the authoritative execution to convince viewers of a brand's superiority. *Expert authority* constitutes one form. The ads employ a physician, dentist, engineer, or chemist, who describes the particular brand's advantages compared to other brands. Firms also feature less-recognized experts, such as automobile mechanics, professional house painters, and aerobics instructors. These individuals talk about the attributes or benefits of the product that make the brand superior.

Many authoritative advertisements include scientific or survey evidence. Independent organizations, such as the American Medical Association, undertake a variety of product studies. Quoting the results generates greater credibility. Survey results may be less credible. Stating that four out of five dentists recommend a particular toothbrush or toothpaste may not be effective, because consumers do not have details about how the survey was conducted or even how many dentists were surveyed (five or 500). In contrast, an American Medical Association statement that an aspirin a day reduces the risk of a second heart attack will be highly credible. Bayer can take advantage of the finding by including the information in the company's ads. The same holds true when *Consumer Reports* ranks a particular brand as the best.

The authoritative approach assumes consumers and business decision makers rely on cognitive processes when making purchase decisions, that they will pay attention to an ad, and that they will carefully think about the information conveyed. The approach works well in print ads, because buyers take the time to read the claim or findings presented in the advertisement.

Demonstration Executions

A demonstration execution displays how a product works. It provides an effective way to communicate the product's benefits to viewers. Recent advertisements for Swiffer demonstrated the product's multiple uses by cleaning a television screen, a wooden floor, a saxophone, and light fixtures. Consumers were shown how to use the product while at the same time hearing about its advantages.

Business-to-business ads often present demonstrations. These allow a business to illustrate how a product meets the specific needs of another business. For example, Gold-Touch, Inc. can demonstrate the InstaGold Flash System, which deposits a bright and uniform gold surface finish on products, such as jewelry, through a nonelectrical current process of immersion plating. Such demonstrations can be presented via television ads or video ads on the internet.

▼ This airport takeover for Visit South Walton uses a fantasy approach for an escape to the beach.

Fantasy Executions

Fantasy executions lift the audience beyond the real world to a make-believe experience. Some are realistic. Others might be completely irrational. Viewers often can recall the most irrational and illogical ads. Fantasies can deal with anything from a dream vacation spot or cruise ships to a juicy hamburger or an enticing DiGiorno pizza.

Common fantasy themes include sex, love, or romance. Some marketing experts believe sex and nudity in advertising have lost their impact. Instead, advertisers feature a softer, more subtle presentation. Fantasy fits with target audiences that have a preference for a tamer presentation. Instead of raw sexuality, fantasy takes them into a world of romantic make-believe.

The perfume and cologne industries often employ fantasy executions. In the past, a common theme was that splashing on the cologne caused women to flock to a man. For women, the reverse was suggested. Although used extensively, these ads were not particularly effective because people did not believe them. Currently, perfume advertisers tend to portray the product as enhancing a couple's love life or making a man or woman feel more sensuous.

Informative Executions

Informative advertisements speak to the audience in a straightforward manner. Agencies prepare them extensively for radio commercials, where only verbal communication takes place. Informative ads are less common in television and print, because consumers tend to ignore them. With so many ads bombarding the consumer, it takes more than the presentation of information to capture someone's attention. The Philadelphia Cream Cheese ad shown in this section has an excellent chance of being noticed for two reasons: it utilizes an eye-catching image, and it provides a recipe with instructions on how to prepare the cheesecake bars.

Consumers who are highly involved in a particular product category pay attention to an informational ad. Business buyers in the process of gathering information for either a new buy or a modified rebuy will notice an informative commercial. When a business does not need a particular product, buying center members often pay less attention to the advertisement. Thus, informative ads tend to work best in high-involvement situations.

Correct placement of an informative advertisement is vital. An informative advertisement about a restaurant placed on a radio station just before noon will be listened to more carefully than one that runs at 3:00 p.m. An informative ad for a diet product in an issue of *Glamour* that includes an article about weight control or exercise will be noticed more than if it is placed in the fashion section of the magazine. An informative business ad featuring a new piece of industrial equipment works well next to an article about the capital costs of equipment.

Beyond these executional frameworks, the creative selects the other ingredients, including music, copy, color, motion, light, and the size of a print ad. Almost any of these executions can be used within the format of one of the various appeals and message strategies. A slice-of-life can depict a fear appeal and cognitive message strategy. Informative ads may be humorous, as can animations. Testimonials or demonstrations are rational or emotional, and can deploy any of the three message strategies. As the advertising campaign comes together, one element remains: finding the face or voice for the product.

▲ An advertisement for Philadelphia Cream Cheese using an informative execution.

Sources and Spokespersons

When creating a commercial or ad, the final issue facing the creative, the company, and the account executive will be the choice of the **source** or **spokesperson**, who delivers an advertising message visually and/or verbally. Selection of this individual often constitutes a critical choice. Consider, for example, the impact of the spokesperson Flo in Progressive Insurance ads, or The Most Interesting Man in the World in commercials for Dos Equis beer. Both have greatly enhanced the visibility of the products they represent. Figure 6.12 identifies four types of sources and spokespersons.

Celebrity Spokespersons

Of the four types, celebrity spokespersons are the most common, even though their appearances in ads have waned. The research firm Millward Brown noted that only around six percent of advertisements feature celebrity endorsements.[45] The high cost of celebrity endorsements may be the cause of the decline. Many celebrities demand millions of dollars and ask for multiyear deals. Others may sign on for only one campaign. It cost the high-end fashion label Louis Vuitton $10 million for actress Angelina Jolie's appearance in a single advertising campaign.[46]

An advertiser employs a celebrity endorser when the person's stamp of approval enhances the brand's equity. Celebrities can also help create emotional bonds with brands. Transferring the bond that exists between the celebrity and the audience to the product being endorsed is the objective. A bond transfer will often be more profound for younger consumers. A MediaEDGE survey revealed that 30 percent of 18- to 34-year-olds would try a brand promoted by a celebrity. The survey also indicated that younger people are

objective 6.4
How are sources and spokespersons decisions related to advertising design?

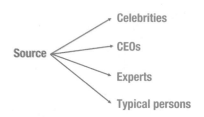

▲ **FIGURE 6.12**
Types of Sources and Spokespersons

50 percent more likely than older consumers to recommend a celebrity-endorsed product to others. Older consumers are less likely to be influenced by celebrity endorsements. Fewer than 14 percent reported that they would try a celebrity-endorsed product. Still, many advertisers believe that celebrity endorsements improve brand awareness and help define the brand's personality.[47]

Agencies feature celebrities to help establish a brand "personality." The objective is to tie the brand's characteristics to those of the spokesperson, such as in ads for **Priceline.com** featuring actor William Shatner and his daughter. A brand personality emerges after the brand has been established. The celebrity helps to define the brand more clearly.

A new trend emerging with athletes is the promotion of new brands or startup companies. LeBron James terminated his relationship with McDonald's to serve as the brand ambassador for the upstart chain Blaze Pizza. Prominent athletes such as James can use their popularity on social media to shape the personality of new companies and encourage trial purchases. James owns 10% of Blaze Pizza, which may make his endorsement more believable. Consumers report that while his endorsement of McDonald's may be suspect, James eating pizza is more believable.[48]

Additional Celebrity Endorsements Three additional variations of celebrity endorsements include celebrity voiceovers, dead person endorsements, and social media endorsements. Celebrities provide *voiceovers* for television and radio ads without being shown or identified. Agencies use a voiceover because the celebrity provides a quality voice to the advertisement, even when individuals listening to the ad do not recognize the voice. Celebrities can take a script and bring it to life. One negative of voiceovers is that they can be a distraction to the consumer if they become focused on identifying the speaker rather than hearing the content of the ad.

A *dead person endorsement* occurs when a sponsor uses an image or past video or film featuring an actor or personality who has passed away. Dead person endorsements are somewhat controversial but are becoming common. Bob Marley, Marilyn Monroe, John Wayne, John Lennon, Elvis Presley, and many others have appeared in ads and

▶ Interstate Batteries features NASCAR driver Kyle Busch in some of its advertising.

have even become spokespersons for products after dying. The Paul Harvey voiceover for the "So God made a farmer" Dodge Ram truck campaign was deemed highly successful in 2014.

The newest form of endorsement may be found on *social media*. Firms now pay celebrities to send promotional tweets. Most of the tweets are not cheap, costing between $200 and $10,000 per message. Snoop Dog was recently paid to tweet about the Toyota Sienna, which he called a "swagger wagon." Kathy Ireland has been hired by Therapedic International to endorse the company's mattresses through social media and Twitter.[49]

CEO Spokespersons

Instead of celebrities, advertisers can employ a CEO as the spokesperson or source. Michael Dell has appeared as the spokesperson for Dell. A highly visible and personable CEO can become a major asset for the firm and its products. Many local companies succeed, in part, because their owners are out front in small-market television commercials. They then begin to take on the status of local celebrities.

Experts

Expert sources include physicians, lawyers, accountants, and financial planners. These experts are not celebrities or CEOs. Experts provide backing for testimonials, serve as authoritative figures, demonstrate products, and enhance the credibility of informative advertisements.

Typical Persons

Typical persons are one of two types. The first includes paid actors or models that portray or resemble everyday people. The second is actual, typical, everyday people. Wal-Mart has featured store employees in freestanding insert advertisements. Agencies also create "man-on-the-street" types of advertisements. For example, Pert shampoo recently prepared ads showing an individual asking people if they would like to have their hair washed. Dr. Scholl's interviews people about foot problems that might be resolved with cushioned shoe inserts.

Use of real people sources has increased. One reason may be the overuse of celebrities. Many experts believe consumers have become bored by celebrity endorsers and that the positive impact will be less than in the past. One study conducted in Great Britain indicated that 55 percent of the consumers surveyed reported that a famous face was not enough to hold their attention.[50]

Source Characteristics

In evaluating sources, most account executives and companies consider several characteristics. The effectiveness of an advertising campaign that utilizes a spokesperson depends on the degree to which the person has one or more of the characteristics listed in Figure 6.13.

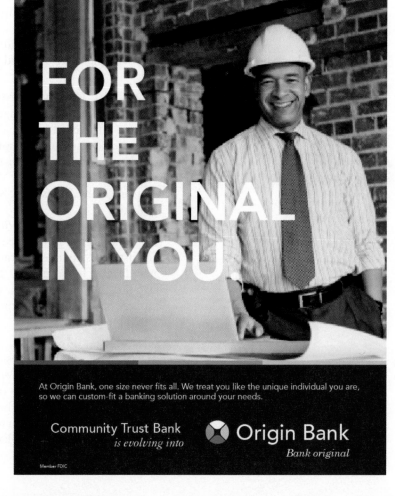

▼ An advertisement for Origin Bank using a typical person.

▶ **FIGURE 6.13**
Characteristics of Effective
Spokespersons

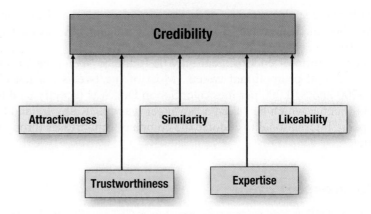

Credibility   The composite of attractiveness, similarity, likeability, trustworthiness, and expertise creates credibility, which in turn affects the receiver's acceptance of the spokesperson and message.[51] People believe credible sources. Most sources do not score highly on all five attributes, yet they need to score highly on multiple characteristics to be viewed as credible. Celebrities may be the most likely to possess at least an element of all characteristics. A CEO, expert, or typical person usually lacks one or more characteristics.

Attractiveness   Two forms of attractiveness are physical and personality characteristics. Physical attractiveness contributes an important asset for an endorser. Advertisements with physically attractive spokespersons fare better than advertisements with less attractive people, for both male and female audiences. The attractiveness of the spokesperson's personality will also be important to many consumers, because it helps viewers form emotional bonds with the spokesperson. When the spokesperson exhibits a sour personality, even if physically beautiful, consumers become less likely to develop an emotional bond with the individual and the product.

Similarity   Closely related to attractiveness is similarity. Consumers are more inclined to be influenced by a message delivered by a similar person. A "stay-at-home" mom may be more influenced by an advertisement that starts out with a woman saying, "Since I made the decision to stay home and care for my family full-time . . . ." Similarity leads the viewer to identify with the spokesperson. Dove recently launched a series of ads featuring male athletes, but the focus was on them and their families, not sports. Magic Johnson, Drew Brees, and Shaquille O'Neal talked about being "comfortable in their own skin."

At other times, *identification* comes from the belief that the source has similar beliefs, attitudes, preferences, or behaviors, or faces the same or a similar situation as the customer. Female fans are able to identify with female jockey Anna Roberts as the "new face of horse racing" because many females have enjoyed horseback riding and have dreamed of winning a famous horse race. Identification was also gained because most jockeys are males. Anna Roberts immediately gained similarity and identification with female fans.

Likeability   Attractiveness and similarity are closely linked to likability. Consumers respond positively to spokespersons they like. Viewers often like an actor or the character played by the actor in a movie. La-Z-Boy signed a multiyear agreement with Brook Shields to serve as its celebrity spokesperson. The campaign targeted females ages 35 to 64 who report a high degree of likeability for her.[52] Terry Bradshaw remains one the most well-known and well-liked retired athletes and hosts of football telecasts. Choosing him as a spokesperson for Community Trust Bank was easy, because he is also one of the bank's customers.

Trustworthiness A celebrity may be likeable or attractive but may not be viewed as trustworthy. Trustworthiness represents the degree of confidence or the level of acceptance consumers place in the spokesperson's message. A trustworthy spokesperson helps consumers believe the message. A connection exists between likeability and trustworthiness. People who are liked tend to be trusted while people who are disliked are not. Bill Cosby's ranking according to The Marketing Arm, which ranks celebrities using online polls, dropped from number 3 to number 2,746 because of the allegations against him. The research company has 3,000 celebrities in its database. The two most trusted celebrities are Betty White and Tom Hanks.[53]

Expertise Spokespersons exhibiting higher levels of expertise become more believable. Kyle Bush and Jeff Gordon are experts when advertising automobile products and lubricants. Some view Willie Robertson, star of reality TV show *Duck Dynasty*, as an expert for off-road vehicles.

Often when a commercial requires expertise, the advertising agency opts for the CEO or a trained or educated expert in the field. American Express features Maria Barraza, a small-business owner and designer, to promote its Small Business Services. Expertise can be valuable in persuasive advertisements designed to change opinions or attitudes. Spokespersons with high levels of expertise are more capable of persuading an audience than someone with zero or low expertise.[54]

▼ Terry Bradshaw's high degree of likeability makes him an excellent choice to be the spokesperson for Community Trust Bank.

With Skyjacker®, the places you can go are endless. Don't be limited to concrete. Blaze your own trail. With Skyjacker®, you can make your own roads while others conform. Skyjacker® picks up where the pavement ends. We offer leveling kits, sport lifts and suspension kits from mild to extreme. You better hang on.

"I've spent my life in the swamps of Louisiana. Skyjacker helps me look at ruts in my rearview mirror." – Willie Robertson star of Duck Dynasty

▲ Willie Robertson, star of reality TV show *Duck Dynasty*, has expertise in truck suspensions and lift kits.

Matching Source Types and Characteristics

The account executive, agency, and corporate sponsor, individually or jointly, choose the type of spokesperson. They can choose a celebrity, CEO, expert, or typical person, and the specific individual should have the key source characteristics.

In terms of trustworthiness, believability, persuasiveness, and likeability, celebrities tend to score well. These virtues increase when the match between the product and celebrity consists of a logical and proper fit. Phil Mickelson endorsing golf merchandise offers a good fit. Some celebrities have become almost as famous for their advertising appearances as for an acting or athletic career. Danica Patrick has signed endorsement contracts with Honda, Secret, Boost Mobile, Pepsi, and Go Daddy, possibly gaining as much notoriety from endorsements as she has from competing in races.[55]

Two dangers exist when using celebrities. First, any negative publicity about a celebrity caused by inappropriate conduct may damage credibility, such as the allegations against Bill Cosby. A second danger of using celebrities occurs when they endorse too many products. Advertising research indicates that when a celebrity endorses multiple products, it tends to reduce likeability as well as consumer attitudes toward the brand.[56]

A CEO or other prominent corporate official may or may not possess the characteristics of attractiveness and likeability. CEOs should, however, appear to be trustworthy, have expertise, and maintain a degree of credibility. A CEO is not a professional actor or model. It might be difficult for the CEO to come across well in a commercial.

First and foremost, experts should be credible. The advertising agency seeks an attractive, likeable, and trustworthy expert. Experts are helpful in promoting health care products and other high-involvement types of products. Recent research indicates that experts are more believable than celebrities for high-technology products. As a result, the use of an expert reduces a consumer's level of perceived risk in purchasing the brand, which means they are the most helpful when consumers or businesses perceive high levels of risk involved in a purchase.[57]

Advertisements featuring typical persons can be difficult to prepare, especially when they employ real persons. Typical person sources do not have the name recognition of celebrities. Consequently, advertisers often include multiple sources in an advertisement to build credibility. Increasing the number of sources makes the ad more effective. Hearing three people talk about a good dentist will be more believable than hearing it from only one person. By using multiple sources, viewers are motivated to pay attention and process its arguments.[58]

Real person ads present a double-edged sword. On the one hand, trustworthiness, similarity, and credibility rise for a bald or overweight source or someone with other physical imperfections. This can be especially valuable when the bald person promotes a hair replacement program or the overweight source talks about a diet program. On the other hand, attractiveness and likeability may be lower.

In general, the advertising agency looks for the source or spokesperson with the characteristics the advertisement requires. Likeability is important when creating a humorous appeal. In a rational or informational ad, expertise and credibility are crucial, especially in business-to-business ads. In each case, trying to include as many of the characteristics as possible when retaining a spokesperson will be the goal.

International Implications

Many of the international implications of advertising design have been described in this chapter. Message strategies, advertising appeals, and executions should be adapted to cultural differences. As a small example, fear of body odor often sells products in the United States. In other cultures, body odor does not carry the same meaning. Another example is when marketers adjust sexual appeals to fit the laws and customs of a region. Advertisers seek to understand these differences before designing advertising messages. For instance, a combination of humor and sex would not be advisable in a commercial designed for a French audience. The French culture, while quite comfortable with overt sexuality and nudity, does not find sex to be funny.

Care should also be given to language and translation. For example, Sega discovered that its product's name is slang for "masturbation" in Italian, after a major advertising campaign had started. Marketers make great efforts to avoid such mistakes. Musical tastes vary, as do perceptions of rationality and scarcity. Emotions may be stronger in some cultures, whereas in others people are much more reserved.

An international company or a firm seeking to expand into additional countries should adapt and adjust the message strategy, appeal, and execution in order to create effective advertisements. Sources and spokespersons may have differing levels of success, depending on the culture of the country involved. Finally, finding universal themes, such as *visual Esperanto*, may be of great help to the international advertising creative.

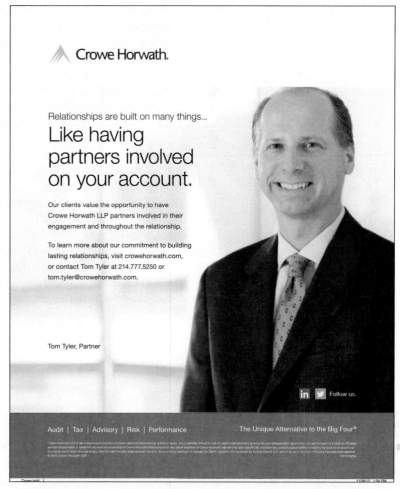

▲ Showing Tom Tyler, a partner in the firm, presents the source characteristics of trustworthiness, expertise, and credibility.

Summary

A message strategy represents the primary tactic or approach used to deliver an advertisement's message theme. Three categories of message strategies include cognitive, affective, and conative approaches. Cognitive message strategies present rational arguments or pieces of information to consumers. Cognitive approaches include generic messages, preemptive messages, unique selling propositions, hyperbole, and comparative advertisements. Affective message strategies seek to evoke feelings or emotions that match those feelings with a good or service. Affective approaches include resonance advertising, comfort marketing, and emotional methods. Conative message strategies seek to lead directly to a consumer response. Marketing teams match the strategy with the message theme.

Advertising creatives form advertising messages using one or more of the seven major appeals: fear, humor, sex (through sensual, suggestive, nudity-based, or overt formats), music, rationality, emotions, or scarcity. Logical combinations of these appeals for various messages can be utilized.

Executional frameworks constitute the manner in which an advertising appeal will be presented and the message strategy will be conveyed. Executions include animation, slice-of-life, storytelling, testimonial, authoritative, demonstration, fantasy-based, and informative approaches.

Sources or spokespersons present the advertising message visually and/or verbally. Celebrities, CEOs, experts, and typical persons can serve as sources. Advertisers seek to enhance the quality of the message by relying on the credibility, attractiveness, similarity, likeability, trustworthiness, and expertise of the spokesperson.

The process of designing ads for international markets is similar to that for domestic ads. The major difference is careful consideration of local attitudes and customs, with due care given to the language, slang, and symbols of the area.

Key Terms

message strategy The primary tactic or approach used to deliver a message theme

cognitive message strategy A strategy used to present rational arguments or pieces of information to consumers

generic message An advertisement that directly promotes a product's attributes or benefits without any claim of superiority

preemptive message An advertising claim of superiority based on a product's specific attribute or benefit with the intent of preventing the competition from making the same or a similar statement

unique selling proposition An explicit, testable claim of uniqueness or superiority in an advertisement

hyperbole An untestable advertising claim based on some attribute or benefit

comparative advertisement A direct or indirect advertising comparison with a competitor based on some product attribute or benefit

affective message strategies Advertisements trying to evoke feelings or emotions and match those feelings with the good, service, or company

comfort marketing A form of resonance advertising designed to encourage consumers to purchase a branded

product rather than generic versions because the branded product has stood the test of time

emotional affective approach An advertising method that attempts to elicit powerful emotions that will lead to product recall and choice

conative message strategy An advertising approach designed to lead directly to a consumer response

advertising appeals Advertising approaches to reaching consumers with ads that feature an element of fear, humor, sex, music, rationality, emotions, or scarcity

severity The part of the fear behavioral response model that leads the individual to consider how strong certain negative consequences of an action will be

vulnerability The part of the fear behavioral response model that leads the individual to consider the odds of being affected by the negative consequences of an action

decorative models Individuals in advertisements whose primary purpose is to adorn the product as a sexual or attractive stimulus without serving a functional role

source or spokesperson The individual who delivers an advertising message visually and/or verbally

MyMarketingLab

To complete the problems with the ⭐ in your MyLab, go to the end-of-chapter Discussion Questions.

Review Questions

6-1. What is a message strategy?

6-2. Describe a cognitive message strategy and identify the five major forms advertisers can use.

6-3. What is spontaneous trait transference in comparison advertising?

6-4. Describe an affective message strategy and identify the primary forms it can take in an advertisement.

6-5. What is comfort marketing?

6-6. What is the attitude sequence present in a conative message strategy advertisement?

6-7. What are the seven most common types of advertising appeals?

6-8. What are the advantages and disadvantages of fear appeals in advertising?

6-9. When does humor work in an ad? What pitfalls should companies avoid in using humorous appeals?

6-10. What types of sexual appeals can advertisers use?

6-11. When are sexual appeals most likely to succeed? To fail?

6-12. Name the different ways music can play a role in an advertisement. Explain how each role should match individual appeals, media, and other elements in the design of the ad.

6-13. Compare the advantages and disadvantages of rational appeals compared to emotional appeals.

6-14. What types of executional frameworks can be used when developing an advertisement?

6-15. Describe how each of the executional frameworks can be used in ad development.

6-16. What four types of sources or spokespersons can be used by advertisers?

6-17. What are the most desirable characteristics of a source or spokesperson?

Critical Thinking Exercises

DISCUSSION QUESTIONS

⭐**6-18.** Describe the characteristics of each of the message strategies presented in this chapter. Select ten ads in this chapter not found in the "Message Strategy" section. Identify the message strategy used. Provide a rationale for your choice.

6-19. Studies involving comparative advertisements versus noncomparative ads produced the following findings. Discuss why you think each statement is true. Try to think of comparative ads you have seen that substantiate these claims.

    a. Message awareness was higher for comparative ads than for noncomparative ads if the brands are already established brands.

    b. Brand recall was higher for comparative ads than for noncomparative ads.

    c. Comparative ads were viewed as less believable than noncomparative ads.

    d. Attitudes toward comparative ads were more negative than toward noncomparative ads.

6-20. Describe the unique characteristics of each of the appeals presented in this chapter. Choose ten ads in this chapter not found in the "Appeals" section. Identify the appeal being used. Provide a rationale for your choice.

⭐**6-21.** Examine the print ad for the Snoring Center featured in the "Animations" section of this chapter. Explain in your own words all of the elements of the behavioral response model in Figure 6.4. Then explain each element of the behavioral response model in terms of the Snoring Center advertisement. Some of the elements will require thinking beyond what is visually present in the ad itself.

6-22. Locate five television commercials on YouTube or find five print advertisements on the internet that use sex appeals. Identify which of the four ways sexuality was used. Evaluate each ad in terms of the appropriateness and effectiveness of the sex appeal. Provide a copy of the print ad or the URL to the TV ad on YouTube.

6-23. Identify an advertisement that uses each of the following executional frameworks. Evaluate the advertisement in terms of how well it is executed. Also, did the appeal and message strategy fit well with the execution? Was the ad memorable? What made it memorable?

    a. Animation

    b. Slice-of-life

    c. Testimonial

    d. Authoritative

    e. Demonstration

    f. Fantasy

    g. Informative

    h. Storytelling

6-24. Describe the characteristics of each of the executional frameworks presented in this chapter. Pick ten ads in this chapter not found in the "Executional Frameworks" section. Identify the execution being used. Provide a rationale for your choice.

6-25. Find a copy of a business journal such as *Business Week* or *Fortune* or a trade journal. Also locate a copy of a consumer journal such as *Glamour*, *Time*, *Sports Illustrated*, or a specialty magazine. Look through an entire issue. What differences between the advertisements in the business journal and consumer journal are readily noticeable? For each of the concepts listed below, discuss specific differences you noted between the two types of magazines. Explain why the differences exist.

    a. Message strategies

    b. Appeals

    c. Executional frameworks

    d. Sources and spokespersons

6-26. Select five ads in this chapter that you like. Identify the message strategy, the appeal, and the execution that is being used. Provide a rationale for your choices. For each ad, give it a grade of A, B, C. or D based on its overall design. Explain the reason for your grade.

6-27. A manager from a resort in Florida wants to develop an advertisement highlighting scuba diving lessons. The target market will be college students. Identify the best combination of message strategy, appeal, and execution. Justify your choice. What message strategy, appeal, and execution would you use if the target market was families with children? Justify your choice. Choose one of the target markets. Design a print ad using the design combination you selected.

⭐**6-28.** Define each of the characteristics of effective spokespersons shown in Figure 6.13. Name three influential spokespersons. For each one, discuss the five characteristics used to evaluate spokespersons and their overall level of credibility. Next, make a list of three individuals who are poor spokespersons. Discuss each of the five evaluation characteristics for each of these individuals. What differences exist between an effective and a poor spokesperson?

Integrated Learning Exercises

⭐**6-29.** Describe the unique characteristics cognitive, affective, and conative message strategies presented in this chapter. Go to YouTube and find one example of each type of message strategy. Identify the subgroup, such as generic, hyperbole, or resonance. Provide a rationale for your choice. For each of the three ads you chose, identify the appeal and execution used. Explain your reasoning. Provide the URLs for the three ads.

6-30. Current as well as past Super Bowl ads are available at **www.superbowl-ads.com**. Access the site and compare Super Bowl ads over the last several years. What types of message strategies were used? What types of appeals were used? What types of executions were used? Who and what types of endorsers or spokespersons were used? Compare and contrast these four elements of ads over the last three years of Super Bowl ads.

6-31. Most advertising agencies provide examples of advertisements on company websites. The goal is to display the agency's creative abilities to potential clients. Using a search engine, locate three different advertising agencies. Locate samples of their work. Compare the ads produced by your three agencies in terms of message strategies, appeals, executions, and spokespersons. What similarities do you see? What differences do you see? Which agency, in your opinion, is the most creative? Why?

⭐**6-32.** Describe in your own words the unique characteristics of each of the appeals presented in this chapter. Locate four ads on YouTube that illustrate different types of appeals. Explain the appeal that is being used in each ad. Provide a rationale for your choice. For each of the four ads you chose, identify the message strategy and execution used. Explain your reasoning. Provide the URLs for the four ads.

6-33. Describe in your own words the characteristics of each of the executional frameworks presented in this chapter. Locate four ads on YouTube that illustrate different types of executions. Explain the execution that is being used in each ad. Provide a rationale for your choice. For each of the four ads you chose, identify the message strategy and appeal used. Explain your reasoning. Provide the URLs for the four ads.

6-34. Visit the following websites. Identify the primary message strategy, appeal, and execution used. Evaluate the quality of the website based on message strategy, appeal, and execution. Do the sites utilize a spokesperson? If so, who is it and which type is he or she? Evaluate the spokesperson in terms of the components of credibility.

    a. Johnson & Johnson (**www.jnj.com**)

    b. Hyundai Motors, USA (**www.hyundaiusa.com**)

    c. Skechers (**www.skechers.com**)

    d. Bijan Fragrances (**www.bijan.com**)

6-35. Visit the following websites. Identify the primary message strategy, appeal, and execution used. Evaluate the quality of the website based on message strategy, appeal, and execution. Do the sites utilize a spokesperson? If so, who is it and which type is he or she? Evaluate the spokesperson in terms of the components of credibility.

a. Visit South Walton (**www.visitsouthwalton.com**)

b. Jockey International (**www.jockey.com**)

c. ReRez (**www.rerez.com**)

d. DuPage Medical Group (**www.dupagemedical-group.com**)

6-36. Study the print advertisement for DuPage Medical Group used in this chapter as an illustration of an emotional ad. Go to the authors' website at **www.clowbaack.net/video/ads.html** and watch the television ad for DuPage Medical Group entitled "No More Rushing." Notice its similarity to the print ad. What type of message strategy and execution was used in the TV ad? What type of spokesperson was used? Discuss each of the characteristics of effective spokespersons as it relates to the TV ad.

6-37. List the four types of spokespersons presented in the chapter. For each type identify a major advantage and a major disadvantage. Locate an example of each type of spokesperson on YouTube. For each ad and

spokesperson used, discuss the characteristics of effective spokespersons highlighted in Figure 6.13. Provide the URLs for the four ads.

6-38. Go the authors' website at **clowbaack.net/video/ads.html**. Pick one of the TV ads for DuPage Medical Group. Identify the message strategy used in the TV ad. Justify your choice. Identify the type of appeal being used. Justify your choice. Identify the type of execution used. Justify your choice. What type of spokesperson was used? Justify your choice. Be sure to provide the URL in your response and identify the ad you chose.

6-39. Go the authors' website at **clowbaack.net/video/ads.html**. Pick one of the TV ads for one of the financial institutions. Identify the message strategy used in the TV ad. Justify your choice. Identify the type of appeal being used. Justify your choice. Identify the type of execution used. Justify your choice. What type of spokesperson was used? Justify your choice. Be sure to provide the URL in your response and identify the ad you chose.

Blog Exercises

Access the authors' blog for this textbook at the URLs provided to complete these exercises. Answer the questions that are posed on the blog.

6-40. Television ads, set 1 **blogclowbaack.net/2014/05/08/television-ads-set-1-chapter-6/**

6-41. Television ads, set 2 **blogclowbaack.net/2014/05/08/television-ads-set-2-chapter-6/**

6-42. Television ads, set 3 **blogclowbaack.net/2014/05/08/television-ads-set-3-chapter-6/**

6-43. Television ads, set 4 **blogclowbaack.net/2014/05/08/television-ads-set-4-chapter-6/**

Student Project

CREATIVE CORNER

It is time to apply your creativity to a television advertisement. Borrow a smartphone or camcorder and develop a 30- or 45-second television spot for one of the following products, using the suggested appeal. Before designing the ad, decide on the message strategy and execution you will use. Justify your decision. If you do not have access to a smartphone or camcorder, then develop a magazine print advertisement.

a. Denim skirt, sex appeal

b. Tennis racket, humor appeal

c. Ice cream, emotional appeal

d. Vitamins, fear appeal

e. Golf club, rational appeal

f. Spring break trip package, scarcity appeal

g. Restaurant, emotional appeal

 CASE 1 FELICITY'S FINE FORMALWEAR

Certain occasions require special clothing. Felicity's Fine Formalwear provides tuxedos and other dress-up essentials for men along with wedding and prom dresses for women. The store, which is located in a major metropolitan area, has been in business for nearly a decade.

Formal attire experiences several key seasons. First, the late spring is when teenagers rent prom dresses and tuxedos. Early summer, especially June, is the time when rentals for weddings reach their peak. A third season takes place in the months of December and January, when many social occasions surrounding Christmas and other winter festivals take place. Often the customers for these events are older than high school or college age.

Recently, Felicity noticed a drop in tux rentals and prom dress purchases. A new competitor in town might explain the loss of some of this business. In the past Felicity used one major tactic to entice high schoolers to her store: She would offer a free tux rental to a few males in each high school if they would, in exchange, wear a different tux to class every day for one week, usually about four weeks before the dance. She would do the same for females and prom dresses. This in-person approach worked well for many years but seemed to be losing its punch.

After a great deal of thought, Felicity decided it was time to engage in two new tactics. First, she developed a relationship with the primary limousine service in the city. Many high school prom-goers would rent a car for that night. Offering a tie-in between the automobile and prom attire seemed like a logical and enticing approach for both rental companies. Second, it was time to engage in advertising directed at the high school crowd and their parents. Some ads would appear on television, especially evening news programs that Mom and Dad would be more likely to watch; others would be streamed online to reach the students themselves.

The primary goal of these ad campaigns was to reach prom attendees and their parents. The secondary goal was to entice those who would attend other events, including weddings and formal Christmas galas to recall Felicity's Fine Formalwear when the time was right. Felicity also hoped to build long-term loyalty and return business.

6-44. If Felicity's Fine Formalwear used television advertising, what message strategy, appeal, and execution would you recommend? Why? Briefly describe the television ad you envision.

▲ The wedding season is a primary target for Felicity's Fine Formalwear.

6-45. Would the television ad designed for parents on the nightly news be different than one designed to stream online for students? Why or why not?

6-46. Suppose Felicity decided to create a flyer to be placed on cars at the local high school. Decide which message strategy, appeal, and execution you would use. Explain why you chose this particular combination. Now design the flyer for Felicity. You can make up contact information such as phone number, address, and website URL.

6-47. What type of spokesperson should be used in ads for Felicity's Fine Formalwear? Would the person change for each of the three target markets (prom-goers, wedding participants, winter gala attendees)? Defend your answer.

CASE 2 BLACK-EYED MARKETING

If Black Eyed Peas band member will.i.am weren't in music, "He'd be the best ad executive on Madison Avenue," says Randy Phillips, president and CEO of the concert promoter AEG Live. "I've never seen anyone more astute at dealing with sponsors' and companies' needs and understanding their brands." The Black Eyed Peas have been able to move beyond their status as a high-energy band into the world of corporate sponsorship without missing a beat.

Marketers love the Black Eyed Peas for the diverse ethnicity of the band's members, writes the *Wall Street Journal.* The band's corporate backers include Coors, Levi's, Honda, Apple, Verizon, and Pepsi. The advertisement featuring the group's song "Hey Mama" and dancing silhouettes that was used to help launch Apple's iTunes store gained almost iconic status.

What makes this group of musicians such an effective set of spokespeople? Part of the appeal is the group's global fan base and the Peas' fetching party anthems, with powerful dance beats, crazy special effects, and repetitive hooks that are integrated into

numerous party mixes. As one critic noted, the band achieves the nearly impossible—making both kids and their parents feel cool at the same time.

Beyond the glitz and glitter of the shows, the group gives careful thought to its marketing. Oftentimes, will.i.am pitches concepts to corporate sponsors himself, using "decks" that sum up the Peas' package, frequently in PowerPoint form. He reports, "I consider us a brand. A brand always has stylized decks, from colors to fonts. Here's our demographic. Here's the reach. Here's the potential. Here's how the consumer will benefit from the collaboration."

There was a time when rock and roll was nearly synonymous with rebellion. Bands with corporate ties would be viewed as sellouts. For some companies, such a move would seem too risky, especially if the band's fans felt betrayed. Over the years, music has become less threatening, as Baby Boomers near retirement age.

The economics of music have also changed. Downloading and pirating CDs is commonplace. Bands can no longer count on record sales to make money. Many younger bands now look for other sources of income and publicity. The Peas were among the fastest learners of the industry's new math. Even now, however, the band hears complaints that they are merely shills. "You have to take the criticism, and sometimes it hurts a lot," says band member Stacy Ferguson, who is also known as Fergie.

Currently, many top-name musicians and groups have corporate sponsors. Cooperative advertisements promote the brand, the band, and often a tour. The Rolling Stones began the movement when the group's "Tattoo You" tour was sponsored by Jovan Musk cologne. Even groups that at first resolutely avoided corporate tie-ins, such as U2, have changed. U2 developed a relationship with Apple that included commercials featuring the song "Vertigo." The band helped with BlackBerry commercials and had a sponsored tour with the brand.

The Black Eyed Peas continues to expand its corporate connections. A concert in Times Square that promoted Samsung's new line of 3-D televisions led to a meeting with *Avatar* director James Cameron, who agreed to direct a feature film about the Peas. The 3-D film incorporates concerts, travel footage, and narrative themes about technology, dreams, and the brain.

According to will.i.am, all corporate partnerships are equally important. The band lends its music at relatively small charges in exchange for exposure. "It wasn't about the check," says former manager Seth Friedman.

The efforts have paid off. The Black Eyed Peas have performed at an NFL season-kickoff show, New Year's Eve in Times Square, the Grammys, a Victoria's Secret fashion show, and the season opener for *The Oprah Winfrey Show*, for which they summoned a flash mob of synchronized dancers to downtown Chicago. As will.i.am puts it, "I get the credit from the brands. They know. I used to work with the marketing people and the agencies, now I work with the CEOs of these companies."

6-48. Discuss each of the source characteristics in terms of the Black Eyed Peas serving as a spokesperson for a product. Would it make a difference as to what type of product the Black Eyed Peas were endorsing? Explain.

6-49. What types of brands or products are best suited to endorsements by the Black Eyed Peas? By rock bands in general? What about country music artists? What about hip-hop artists?

▲ The Black Eyed Peas use marketing to enhance the band's image and presence.

6-50. If you were going to design a television advertisement for a concert for the Black Eyed Peas, who would be your target market? What message strategy, appeal, and executional framework would you use? Why? Describe your concept of an effective television ad.

6-51. Suppose the Black Eyed Peas were contracted to perform at your university. Design a print ad for your local student newspaper. Discuss the message strategy, appeal, and execution you used and why you used it.

MyMarketingLab

Go to the Assignments section of your MyLab to complete these writing exercises.

6-52. Define each of the message strategies that can be used in advertising and match each to the appropriate step in the hierarchy of effects model and attitude formation sequence (such as cognitive → affective → conative). Suppose a local pizza restaurant near your campus wanted to develop print ads for your school newspaper. For each message strategy, describe the content that would be in that print ad.

6-53. Hardee's and Carl's Jr. recently used a television commercial featuring a schoolteacher dancing on top of her desk while a room full of guys performed a rap song entitled "I Like Flat Buns." The song seemed appropriate because the ad was for the Patty Melt on a flat bun. Instead, the ad received considerable flack because the sexy blonde schoolteacher was wearing a short, tight skirt. Teachers' associations complained that it was inappropriate because it was a "sexually exploitive assault" on teachers, students, and schools. Which type of sex appeal is being used? Discuss the appropriateness of this ad in terms of the concepts presented in the chapter in the "Sex Appeals" section. What makes it effective? What makes it ineffective?

Chapter 7 # Traditional Media Channels

Chapter Objectives

After reading this chapter, you should be able to answer the following questions:

7.1 What is a media strategy?

7.2 What elements and individuals are involved in media planning?

7.3 How do the terms used to describe advertising help the marketing team design effective campaigns?

7.4 What are some of the primary advertising objectives?

7.5 What are the advantages and disadvantages associated with each traditional advertising medium?

7.6 How can the marketing team use the media mix to increase advertising effectiveness?

7.7 What are the key issues associated with media selection for business-to-business markets?

7.8 What issues are associated with media selection in international markets?

Overview

If a tree falls in the forest and no one is present, does it make a sound? This philosophical question has been posed for many years and even recently appeared in a Geico Insurance commercial. Unfortunately, in the world of advertising, far too many "trees" fall as unheard and unseen advertisements. Successful marketing involves identifying target markets and finding the media to reach the members of those markets. Once the advertising team identifies the best media, creatives can design clever, memorable, exciting, and persuasive advertisements. When an advertising campaign succeeds, it may not only reach customers in traditional ways (television, magazines, radio), but in the new world of digital media it will be passed along and shared via the internet and in other ways.

Traditional media continue to play an important role in developing a fully integrated marketing program. This chapter explains the various traditional media channels. It begins with an analysis of the media strategy and media planning processes. Next, common advertising terms are explained followed by an examination of advertising objectives. These processes lead to media choices and selection. Messages can be targeted to specific consumers, businesses, and customers in other countries.

Advertising agencies design a campaign within the framework of the overall integrated marketing communications program. Client companies depend on effective advertisements to attract customers and entice them into purchasing various goods and services. This helps build the firm's image and creates a larger customer base. Advertising media selection remains an important element in the process.

Recently, Oreo cookies celebrated their 100th birthday. In honor of the event, the Virginia-based Martin Agency created the Wonderfilled Oreos campaign. Using animation, the campaign was driven by the theme, "Celebrate the Kid Inside." Television commercials served as the anchor. They were combined with print advertising promoting Oreo-themed events across the country, supported by a strong social media presence.

A special music piece was performed by the group Chitty Bang to pull the events together, called the "Wonderfilled Anthem." *Adweek* magazine labeled the music a "branded pop song cover." Sam Thielman from *Adweek* noted, "The loose-limbed Adventure Time-y animation seems to be getting a lot of traction with viewers on YouTube. At least one commenter proclaimed the original version 'the only YouTube ad that I'll sit through."[1]

The musical television campaign included commercials suggesting that eating Oreos makes bad things good, such as a vampire wanting milk to go with the cookies rather than stalking another victim. Another ad implies that Oreos would cause a shark to make friends with baby seals and squid. Oreo's advertising team then adapted the commercials to individual markets in other countries, creating an entertaining international campaign that gained significant traction in the world of social media.[2]

The Media Strategy

A **media strategy** involves analyzing and choosing media for an advertising and marketing campaign. The average consumer examines only nine of the more than 200 consumer magazines on the market. A radio listener usually tunes in to only three of the stations available in an area. Television viewers on average watch fewer than eight of the stations available via cable or satellite. Network prime-time ratings have declined by more than 30 percent over the last decade. Most consumers under the age of 40 now do not have cable or satellite TV. Consequently, choosing the optimal media to speak to potential customers creates challenges.

To make the account executive and media buyer's jobs more difficult, prices for advertising time and space have risen. Client budgets for advertising have not gone up as quickly, even as stronger demands for results and accountability emerged. The marketing team faces difficulties in locating cost-effective media outlets. After developing a media strategy, other aspects of media selection can proceed.

objective 7.1
What is a media strategy?

Media Planning

objective **7.2**

What elements and individuals are involved in media planning?

Media planning commences with a target market analysis. It involves understanding the processes customers use in making purchases and what influences their final decisions. One method of addressing media planning starts with a study of the media choices that members of a specific, defined target market might make at different times during the course of a day (see Figure 7.1).

Details of the type shown in Figure 7.1 become valuable when developing a media strategy. Information about the listening and viewing patterns of a designated target audience helps the marketing team design the most effective messages and select the best times and places for the ads to appear. No two media plans are alike. The components of a media plan include the elements identified in Figure 7.2.

A marketing analysis provides a comprehensive review of the marketing program. It includes a statement about current sales, current market share, and prime prospects to be solicited (by demographics, lifestyle, geographic location, or product usage). These elements reflect a compatible pricing strategy based on the product, its benefits and distinguishing characteristics, and an analysis of the competitive environment.

An advertising analysis states the primary advertising strategy and budget to be used to achieve advertising objectives. The media strategy spells out the media to be used and the creative considerations. The media schedule notes when ads will appear in individual vehicles. The justification and summary outlines the measures of goal achievement. It also explains the rationale for each media choice.[3]

Several individuals take part in media planning. In addition to account executives, account planners, and creatives, most agencies utilize media planners and media buyers. In smaller agencies, the media planner and media buyer may be the same person. In larger companies, they are usually different individuals. Some agencies employ media firms to handle media planning and buying or hire a subsidiary agency.

▼ Understanding consumer media choices is important for newspapers, such as *The Times-Picayune* of New Orleans.

Media Planners

The **media planner** formulates a program stating where and when to place ads. Media planners work closely with creatives, account executives, account planners, agencies, and media buyers. The creative should know which media will be used to help design effective messages. Creatives construct television ads in different ways than for radio or newspaper.

Media planners provide valuable services and are in high demand. The issue of accountability for advertising results combined with the need to create a return on investment on marketing dollars has led the media buying side of an agency to hold greater power.

Media planning influences the strategic approach. Marketing experts at companies such as Procter & Gamble and Unilever consider media planning to be at the heart of a communications strategy. In both companies, setting brand priorities and objectives constitutes the first step.[4] The task media buyers in this environment undertake, according to Carl Fremont of the media services company Digitas, is "to integrate marketing messages across a range of media, and sometimes this involves working with several agencies to accomplish the client's goals."[5]

- A favorite wake-up radio station or one listened to during the commute to work
- A favorite morning news show or newspaper
- Trade or business journals examined while at work
- A radio station played during office hours at work

- Favorite computer sites accessed during work
- Favorite magazines read during the evening hours
- Favorite television shows watched during the evening hours
- Internet sites accessed during leisure time
- Shopping, dining, and entertainment venues frequented

- Marketing analysis
- Advertising analysis
- Media strategy
- Media schedule
- Justification and summary

▲ **FIGURE 7.2**
Components of a Media Plan

The media planner conducts research to match the product with the market and media. If JD Bank's executives decide to run a print campaign directed at farmers who need loans for tractors or other farming equipment, the media planner researches the best media to reach them. The media planner matches the target market with the venues farmers would most likely view.

The media planner gathers information about various media. This includes newspaper and magazine circulation rates along with the characteristics of the people who read them. The audience for a television show may be different from those of a radio station or a magazine. Quality research improves the chances of selecting the appropriate media.

▼ The media planner will locate the best medium for this JD Bank advertisement.

Media Buyers

After the media are selected, the **media buyer** purchases the space and negotiates rates, times, and schedules for the ads. Media buyers keep in contact with media sales representatives. They know a great deal about rates and schedules. Media buyers watch for special deals and tie-ins between media outlets (for example, radio with television or magazines with the same owner).

Placement in a television show or magazine continues to be an important consideration, both in terms of price and effectiveness. The Pink Jacket Creative advertising agency recently purchased magazine space for The Snoring Center consisting of the outer sides of adjacent pages containing an article. The slender ads on the edges of the two pages bracketed the article. As individuals read the story, they first noticed the ad on the left side of the article and the second half on the right side as they held the magazine open. The cost of the ad space was lower and it turned out to be more effective in conveying the two-part message.

A **spot ad** is a one-time placement of a commercial in a medium. Agencies negotiate rates individually based on the number of times the ads appear. Spot television prices fluctuate by as much as 45 percent for the same time slot. Radio time slot prices vary by as much as 42 percent and national print ads by as much as 24 percent.[6] Negotiation skills affect media purchase outcomes.

Small versus Large Markets

Some research indicates that little connection exists between the size of an advertising firm and the prices it can negotiate. Differences in media costs are based on the time of the actual purchase (closer to the day the ad is to run) rather than the size of the agency.[7] A media plan costing one firm $10 million can cost another $12 million, because the first firm made the purchase at a different time than the second. Other major factors in cost differences are knowledge of the marketplace and the ability to negotiate package deals.

Karen Plott, CEO of Choice Marketing, notes that smaller agencies may enjoy certain advantages in media planning and buying in local markets. First, the local agency will be more in tune with conditions and changes in the area. For example, when a popular radio disc jockey changes affiliation to a new station, his/her audience often follows, and the local agency knows how this might affect advertising purchases. The same holds true when a well-known television anchor moves. The local agency will often be better able to adapt to such changes. Second, many of Plott's customers report that they receive closer attention and more responsive service. She notes, "Our customers often comment they wish they had come to us sooner, rather than relying on the 'big boys'."

The quality of media choices, creativity, financial stewardship, the agency's culture and track record, and the relationship between the agency and the medium's sales representative lead to differences in the effectiveness of various advertising campaigns. The quality of the media selections made combined with the advertisement's content determines levels of success.

Advertising Terminology

objective 7.3

How do the terms used to describe advertising help the marketing team design effective campaigns?

Advertising has its own unique set of terms and measures (see Figure 7.3). **Reach** represents the number of people, households, or businesses in a target audience exposed to a media vehicle or message schedule at least once during a given time period, which normally consists of four weeks. In other words, how many targeted buyers did the ad reach at least once during a four-week period?

Frequency

The average number of times an individual, household, or business within a particular target market is exposed to a particular advertisement within a specified time period—again, usually four weeks—constitutes **frequency**. It specifies how many times the person encountered the ad during a campaign. A regular viewer will see the same ad shown daily on *Wheel of Fortune* more frequently than the ad shown once on *CSI*, even though the *CSI* program has a greater reach.

Opportunities to See

In media planning, instead of frequency, buyers use **opportunities to see (OTS)** or the cumulative exposures achieved in a given time period. When a company places two ads on a weekly television show, eight OTS (four shows × two ads per show) occur during a four-week period. OTS does not measure how many times consumers actually see an ad, but how many opportunities they have to see it.

- Reach
- Frequency
- Opportunities to see (OTS)
- Gross rating points (GRP)
- Cost per thousand (CPM)
- Cost per rating point (CPRP)
- Ratings
- Continuity
- Gross impressions

▶ **FIGURE 7.3**
Advertising terminology

Gross Rating Points

Gross rating points (GRPs) measure the impact or intensity of a media plan. Advertisers calculate gross rating points by multiplying a vehicle's rating by the OTS, or number of insertions of an advertisement. GRPs provide the advertiser with a better idea of the odds that members of the target audience actually viewed the commercial. By increasing the OTS or frequency, the chances of a television viewer seeing an advertisement rises. An advertisement featured in each weekly issue of *People* during a four-week period is more likely to be seen than one appearing in a monthly periodical.

Cost

To evaluate how cost-effective one medium or ad placement is compared to another, the **cost per thousand (CPM)** figure can be calculated. CPM identifies the dollar cost of reaching 1,000 members of a media vehicle's audience. Marketers calculate CPM using the following formula:

$$\text{CPM} = (\text{Cost of media buy}/\text{Total audience}) \times 1,000$$

Figure 7.4 displays hypothetical cost and readership information for a campaign for a 35mm digital camera. The first three columns of the figure provide the name of the magazine, the cost of a four-color full-page advertisement, and the magazine's paid and verified circulation. The fourth column contains a measure of the CPM of each magazine. The CPM for *Better Homes and Gardens* is $66.21 and has a circulation of 7.6 million. *Sports Illustrated* has a smaller circulation, 3.2 million, but the CPM is $122.69. In terms of cost per thousand readers, *Reader's Digest* offers the best buy, at $26.04 per thousand.

▲ Opportunities to see measures the number of times consumers have an opportunity to see this advertisement for Philadelphia Cream Cheese.

Publication	4C Base Rate	Total Paid & Verified Circulation	CPM	Target Market (20 Million)			
				Percent of Readers Fit Target Market	Number of Readers Fit Target Market	Rating (Reach)	Cost per Rating Point (CPRP)
Better Homes and Gardens	$506.380	7,648,600	$66.21	13.51%	1,033,000	5.2	$97,381
Glamour	$219,190	2,320,325	$94.47	24.65%	572,000	2.9	$76,640
Good Housekeeping	$387,055	4,652,904	$83.19	10.81%	503,000	2.5	$153,899
National Geographic	$225,455	4,495,931	$50.15	26.96%	1,212,000	6.1	$37,204
Reader's Digest	$185,300	7,114,955	$26.04	18.62%	1,325,000	6.6	$27,970
Southern Living	$198,800	2,855,973	$69.61	10.57%	302,000	1.5	$131,656
Sports Illustrated	$392,800	3,201,524	$122.69	16.77%	537,000	2.7	$146,294
Time	$320,100	3,376,226	$94.81	18.60%	628,000	3.1	$101,943

▲ **FIGURE 7.4**

Hypothetical Media Information for a 35 mm Digital Camera

Ratings and Cost per Rating Point

Consider the target market's profile when a company seeks to advertise a 35mm digital camera. The number of readers that fit the target market's profile becomes the key goal. **Ratings** measure the percentage of a firm's target market exposed to a television show or the number of readers of a print medium. In order to compare media, a measure called the **cost per rating point (CPRP)** may be used. The cost per rating point formula that measures the relative efficiency of a media vehicle relative to a firm's target market is:

$$\text{CPRP} = \text{Cost of media buy} / \text{Vehicle's rating}$$

Assume there are 20 million potential buyers of 35mm digital cameras. Figure 7.4 shows the rating for *Better Homes and Gardens* is 5.2, which means that 5.2 percent of the defined target market for 35mm digital cameras read *Better Homes and Gardens*. Backing up a step, 13.51 percent, or 1.033 million, of *Better Homes and Gardens'* readership fits the target profile for the 35mm digital camera. The 5.2 rating is then obtained by dividing the 1.033 million *Better Homes and Gardens* readers that fit the target profile by the 20 million total for the target market. The CPRP for *Better Homes and Gardens* becomes $97,381. It specifies the average cost for each rating point, or of each 1 percent of the firm's target audience (35mm digital camera buyers) that can be reached through an advertisement in *Better Homes and Gardens*. Not all readers of a magazine are part of the firm's target market. The CPRP more accurately measures an advertising campaign's efficiency than does CPM. Notice that the CPRP is the lowest for *National Geographic* and *Reader's Digest*. It is the highest for *Good Housekeeping*.

CPRP provides a relative measure of reach exposure in terms of cost. It costs $37,204 to reach 1 percent, or 200,000, of the 20 million in this firm's target market using *National Geographic*. It costs $146,294 to reach 1 percent, or 200,000, using *Sports Illustrated*. To reach 1 percent, or 200,000, using *Reader's Digest* costs only $27,970. *Reader's Digest* is the most efficient, which raises the question, "Why wouldn't a media planner just do all of the advertising in that magazine?" The answer lies in *Reader's Digest*'s rating. Advertising in only that magazine reaches just 6.6 percent (or 1,325,000) of the target audience; 93.4 percent of the target market does not read *Reader's Digest* and would not see the ad. Another magazine or media outlet is needed to reach them. This explains why diversity in media is essential to reach a large portion of a firm's target market.

An alternative method of determining whether an ad has reached the target market efficiently is a **weighted (or demographic) CPM** value, which can be calculated as:

$$\text{Weighted CPM} = \frac{\text{Advertisement cost} \times 1,000}{\text{Actual audience reached}}$$

Referring to Figure 7.5, the cost of an advertisement in *Good Housekeeping* is $387,055. Although it has a circulation of 4,652,904, only 503,000 of the readers fit the target profile for the 35mm digital camera. Using the formula for weighted CPM, the

▼ **FIGURE 7.5**
Calculating Weighted (or Demographic) CPM

Publication	4C Base Rate	Total Paid & Verified Circulation	CPM	Target Market (20 Million)		
				Percent of Readers Fit Target Market	Number of Readers Fit Target Market	Weighted (Demographic) CPM
Better Homes and Gardens	$506,380	7,648,600	$66.21	13.51%	1,033,000	$490.20
Glamour	$219,190	2,320,325	$94.47	24.65%	572,000	$383.20
Good Housekeeping	$387,055	4,652,904	$83.19	10.81%	503,000	$769.49
National Geographic	$225,455	4,495,931	$50.15	26.96%	1,212,000	$186.02
Reader's Digest	$185,300	7,114,955	$26.04	18.62%	1,325,000	$139.85
Southern Living	$198,800	2,855,973	$69.61	10.5%	302,000	$658.28
Sports Illustrated	$392,800	3,201,524	$122.69	16.77%	537,000	$731.47

cost to reach 1,000 readers of *Good Housekeeping* that fit the target profile is $769.49. As with CPRP, marketers can compare the various magazines to determine which offer the best buy in terms of reaching the target demographic. The difference in the numbers is that CPRP measures the cost of reaching 1 percent of the target market, whereas the weighted CPM measures the cost of reaching 1,000 members of the target market.

Continuity

The exposure pattern or schedule used during a campaign signifies its **continuity**. The three types of patterns are continuous, pulsating, and discontinuous. A *continuous campaign* uses media time in a steady stream. Home construction companies such as Buford Hawthorne would use a continuous schedule, because individuals making decisions to build homes do not follow any consistent time frame for when they will be ready to buy. Consequently, media buyers would look for ad space in specific magazines for a period of one to two years. By using different ads and rotating them, readers will not get bored, because they will see more than one advertisement for the same product.

A retailer such as JCPenney might feature a *pulsating schedule* by placing ads in various media throughout the entire year, but then increasing the number of advertisements in small, short bursts around holidays, including Christmas, Easter, Memorial Day, Mother's Day, Father's Day, Labor Day, and Thanksgiving. Pulsating advertising should reach consumers when they are most likely to make purchases or buy special merchandise, such as during the holidays. A Barnes & Noble advertisement just prior to Christmas can encourage consumers to purchase gift cards.

A *flighting* (or *discontinuous*) *campaign* schedule, in which advertisements run at only certain times of the year, differs from the first two approaches. It would be more likely to be used by a ski resort that runs ads during the fall and winter seasons but none during the spring and summer. A lawn service or lawn mower repair service would likely use a flighting schedule.

▲ In terms of continuity, a continuous schedule is a logical choice for home construction firm Buford Hawthorne.

Impressions

The final advertising term is impressions. The number of **gross impressions** represents the total exposures of the audience to an advertisement. It does not account for the percentage of the total audience that sees the advertisement. Figure 7.5 indicates that *National Geographic*'s total circulation is approximately 4.5 million. If six insertions were placed in *National Geographic*, multiplying the insertions by the readership would yield approximately 27 million impressions.

Achieving Advertising Objectives

Advertisers consider the number of times a person will be exposed to an advertisement before it creates an impact. Most agree that a single exposure will not be sufficient. The actual number inspires a great deal of debate. Some argue it takes three. Others say as many as 10 or more.

objective 7.4
What are some of the primary advertising objectives?

From Cassina - Mex Cube sofa and island by Piero Lissoni and LC3 chair by Le Corbusier, Pierre Jeanneret and Charlotte Perriand

YOUR EX DESERVED THAT PAIR OF COLONIAL SIDE TABLES.

Dallas 214.748.9838   Austin 512.480.0436   scottcooner.com

▲ Based on recency theory, a person looking for home furnishings would be more likely to notice this advertisement.

The Three-Exposure Hypothesis

Most media planners believe an advertisement requires a minimum of three exposures for an advertisement to be effective. The three-exposure hypothesis, as developed by Herbert Krugman, suggests that an advertisement can make an impact on an audience regardless of individual needs or wants.[8] Further, the **intrusion value** of an advertisement represents the ability of a medium or an advertisement to capture the attention of a viewer without her voluntary effort. This reasoning concludes that it takes at least three exposures to capture a viewer's attention.

Recency Theory

Currently, many advertisers believe that clutter has diminished the viability of the three-exposure hypothesis. **Recency theory** notes that a consumer exhibits selective attention and focuses on personal needs and wants as he considers advertisements.[9] When a consumer pays attention to messages that might meet his needs or wants, the closer an exposure to a commercial is to the purchase decision, the more powerful the ad becomes. Further, when a consumer contemplates a future purchase of the product being advertised, the consumer becomes more likely to notice and react favorably toward an ad. A member of a buying center from a business in the market for a new copier more readily notices copier advertisements. Someone who is not in the market for a copier ignores the same ad. The same holds true in consumer markets: An individual desiring a new pair of jeans notices clothing ads, especially ones that feature jeans.

Recency theory proposes that *one ad exposure* may actually be enough to affect a person or business that needs the product being promoted. Additional exposures may not be necessary. Therefore, companies should advertise almost continually to ensure an advertisement reaches a buyer when she thinks about making a purchase.

The advertising approach that matches recency theory would be to spread the message around using a variety of media, each type providing limited exposure per week or time period. In the case of selling supplemental health insurance to the elderly, magazines such as *Senior Living*, television spots on local news and weather programs, and newspaper ads can quickly reach the target audience in a cost-effective manner. This method, which maximizes reach, accomplishes more than increasing frequency.

In the business-to-business arena, recency theory suggests that advertisements should appear in a number of outlets and over a longer period of time rather than running a series of ads in one trade journal. Many times, buying centers consist of several members, each with differing responsibilities. Making sure each one sees an advertisement would mean placing ads in every journal that might be read by buying center members. To facilitate the purchasing process for a company seeking to acquire an audio-conferencing system, the media buyer purchases space in trade journals, human resource journals, sales journals, and business journals. This increases the odds that the message will reach buying center members. One exposure might be enough for each, because the member actively looks for information and is ready to make a decision.

Effective Reach and Frequency

Seeking to discover the minimum number of exposures needed to be effective may be based on two concepts: effective frequency and effective reach. **Effective reach** identifies the *percentage of an audience* that must be exposed to a particular message to achieve a specific objective. **Effective frequency** refers to the *number of times* a target audience

◀ Effective reach and effective frequency are important considerations in reaching the target market for Office Furniture.

must be exposed to a message to achieve a particular objective. The effective frequency concept implies that a minimum number of exposures will be needed.

Effective frequency and effective reach provide crucial guidelines. Too few exposures means the advertiser might fail to attain its intended objectives. In contrast, too many exposures waste resources. Discovering the optimal reach and frequency mix to accomplish the intended objectives without experiencing diminishing returns from extra ads should be the goal. The optimal mix for an objective dealing with brand recognition will be different than when brand recall serves as the objective.

Other elements enhance effective frequency and effective reach. They include the size and placement of an advertisement. A small magazine advertisement does not create the same impact as a larger ad. If a firm uses 15-second television ads, effective frequency may require six exposures. In comparison, a longer 45-second spot may require only four exposures to be remembered. In television advertising, a spot in the middle of an ad sequence usually has less of an impact than the ads shown at the beginning and end of the series.

The number of different media used in a campaign also influences effectiveness. In general, a campaign featuring ads in two types of media, such as television and magazines, generates greater effective reach than a campaign in only one medium, such as magazines only.

In recent years, some media companies have designed computer models to optimize reach and frequency, including Nielsen SAVE and Adware. These programs are based on probability theory, which helps a marketing team effectively allocate advertising dollars. The interaction between an attention-getting television commercial and a magazine ad with copy explaining the product's features may create a more potent synergistic effect than either ad would generate by itself.

Brand Recognition

Brand recognition requires an emphasis on the visual presentation of the product and/or logo. Strengthening or creating links between the brand and other nodes of information that exist in the person's knowledge structure will be the goal. Rather than leading the individual to recall the brand name from memory, the advertiser wants the person to recognize the brand name and logo at the retail store or in the advertisement. Media that are effective at maximizing reach include television, billboards, magazines, the internet, and direct mail.[10]

▶ Billboards offer an excellent medium for achieving brand recognition objectives for Ouachita Independent Bank.

▶ **FIGURE 7.6**
Brand Recognition Versus Brand Recall

Objective	Brand Recognition	Brand Recall
Goal	Create or strengthen mental linkages	Place brand in evoked set
Method	Increase reach	Increase frequency (repetition)
Best media	Television	Television
	Billboards	Radio
	Magazines	Newspapers
	Internet	Internet
	Direct mail	

Brand Recall

To increase brand recall, frequency becomes more important than reach. Repetition helps embed a brand in the consumer's cognitive memory. Repetition makes it more likely that a particular brand will come to mind. When a 30-second commercial repeats the name of a restaurant seven times, it becomes easier to remember than when it is stated only once or twice. In terms of media selection, television, radio, newspapers, and the internet offer the potential for higher frequency.[11] Figure 7.6 compares brand recall with brand recognition.

Once the media buyer, media planner, account executive, and company leaders agree to basic objectives of the advertising campaign, they select the actual media, seeking to identify logical media combinations. The next section examines traditional advertising media.

Media Selection

objective 7.5

What are the advantages and disadvantages associated with each traditional advertising medium?

Effectively mixing advertising media remains a vital element in the design of a quality advertising campaign. To do so, marketing professionals consider the advantages and disadvantages of each individual medium.

Television

Some experts believe the internet is slowly killing traditional television. Individuals 18 to 24 years old, who are highly mobile with smartphones and tablets, exhibit the greatest decline in traditional TV viewing. Many have never subscribed to cable or satellite TV. Even the heavy television viewers, consumers 50 and older, now consume more digital media. By 2020, traditional television is expected to decline to 30 percent of all media consumption while digital media will constitute 56 percent of media consumption. If it

▶ This banner advertisement for "Visit Baton Rouge" should help increase brand recall.

were not for live sports, television viewing would decline even more. Long-term deals with the major sports and college sports will keep advertising dollars flowing to television.[12]

While the power of television has declined, for many brands and companies it remains a viable advertising option. At the same time, advertisers should be aware that television viewing has changed. It often occurs on a tablet or laptop computer rather than a regular television screen. Figure 7.7 lists the pros and cons of television advertising.

Advantages of Television Advertising   Television provides the most extensive coverage and the greatest reach. A single advertisement can reach millions. Television offers a low cost per contact, which justifies spending as much as $4 million for a 30-second spot on the Super Bowl, where a vast audience of more than 110 million households and nearly one billion people worldwide may watch. The cost per person reached by the commercial is low.

Television provides intrusion value. Commercials featuring a catchy musical tune, sexy content, or humor can quickly capture a viewer's attention. Television offers opportunities to be creative in designing advertisements. Visual images and sounds can be incorporated in a commercial. Advertisers are able to demonstrate products and services on television in a manner not possible in print or using radio advertisements. Segmentation may be achieved by targeting specialty shows and networks such as *The Food Channel* or *ESPN*.

Disadvantages of Television Advertising   Clutter continues to be the primary problem for television advertising. Many programs include 31 commercials per hour and take as long as 19 minutes to run. Four- and five-minute commercial breaks are common.[13] As a result, many viewers switch channels during commercial breaks. Often, low recall exists, especially for commercials placed in the middle of an advertising segment. Messages at the beginning or near the end of the break have better chances to be recalled. Also, ads near the beginning of a television show or during the last commercial break have a higher recall, because individuals want to catch the start of the show and make sure they see the last part of a show for its climax or conclusion.

Some viewers cope with clutter by using a DVR, recording favorite programs and watching them later. Advertisers fear the DVR users will skip over the commercials. Recent research indicates, however, that fewer than half fast-forward through commercials. Also, the majority watches the television show the same day it is recorded, and 75 percent have viewed it by the end of the next day. This means that time-sensitive ads are seen close to when they first were run. Consequently, the fear that DVRs cause viewers to skip commercials may be unjustified.[14]

Television airtime is expensive, as are the costs of producing ads. The average cost of production for a 30-second national ad is $358,000. Production fees account for the largest portion of the cost, an average of $236,000. Other costs include director fees ($23,000), fees for editing and finishing the ad ($45,000), and creative/labor fees and music ($34,000).[15]

Ratings   To gain a sense of how well an advertisement fared in terms of reaching an audience, a given program's rating can be calculated. The typical ratings formula is:

$$\text{Rating} = \frac{\text{Number of households tuned to a program}}{\text{Total number of households in a market}}$$

Advantages	Disadvantages
• High reach	• High level of clutter
• High frequency potential	• Low recall due to clutter
• Low cost per contact	• Channel surfing during ads
• High intrusion value	• DVRs skipping ads
• Quality creative opportunities	• Short amount of copy
• Segmentation through cable	• High cost per ad

◀ **FIGURE 7.7**
Television Advertising

▶ A storyboard illustrating a television commercial for Interstate Batteries.

In the United States, approximately 109.7 million households own television sets. To calculate the rating for a particular *Sunday Night Football*, if the number of households tuned to the game was 17.8 million, the rating would be:

$$\text{Rating} = \frac{17,800,000}{109,700,000} = 16.2$$

Next, if the advertiser was interested in the percentage of households that actually were watching television at that hour, the program's share could be calculated. Assuming 71 million of the 109.7 million households had a television turned on during the time *Sunday Night Football* aired, the share would be:

$$\text{Share} = \frac{\text{Number of households tuned to } Sunday \, Night \, Football}{\text{Number of households with a television turned on}} = \frac{17,800,000}{71,000,000} = 25$$

A 16.2 rating would mean that 16.2 percent of all televisions in the United States were tuned to *Sunday Night Football*. A 25 share means 25 percent of the households with a television actually turned on were watching the game. Ratings do not guarantee viewers saw the commercial. Ratings and shares only indicate how well the television program fared.

▼ A storyboard illustrating a TV ad for DuPage Medical Group.

C3 Ratings Some advertisers have adopted a new system—the commercial C3 rating—which calculates a rating for the actual commercial time slot rather than the television program. It computes a commercial's rating plus any viewing of the commercial three days after the original ad ran. Many firms now use the C3 rating to determine national television advertising rates. Marketers calculate the C3 rating by computing the average rating of all commercials within a particular pod or commercial segment. Various advertisers have criticized the system, claiming that not all ads within a pod receive equal exposure. For instance, the first position in a pod generates 28 percent higher awareness than ads in the middle of the commercial sequence.

American Idol	$467,617
Sunday Night Football	$415,000
Glee	$272,694
Family Guy	$259,289
The Simpsons	$253,170
House	$226,180
Grey's Anatomy	$222,113
The Office	$213,617
Desperate Housewives	$210,064

Thus, the position of a particular ad in the commercial break and the length of the pod have no impact on the rates being charged.[16]

◀ Local and regional television provide excellent options for Terrebonne General Medical Center.

AC Nielsen intends to expand the C3 rating system to correct this problem. Called "On Demand C3" the new system will produce a rating for each commercial. It will include the show's live telecast viewing along with the three-day post viewing period via DVRs. Some CEOs have pushed for a C7 rating, instead of a C3. They believe measuring viewership over seven days more accurately reflects consumer viewing habits.[17]

Figure 7.8 provides the costs of 30-second ads using the C3 system. The higher a show's rating over time, the more that can be charged. The highest average costs are for *Sunday Night Football* at $623,425 and *The Walking Dead* at $413,695.[18]

Ratings Providers   ACNielsen is the primary organization that calculates and reports ratings and shares. The company provides information regarding shares of stations in local markets known as *designated marketing areas* (DMAs). Data-gathering techniques used by ACNielsen include diaries written by viewers who report what they watched, audience meters that record what is being shown automatically, and people meters that track the viewing habits of individual members of families. Nielsen augments TV ratings with information about viewing from tables and smartphones, because the number of individuals using these alternative screens to watch television programming continues to grow, especially among younger consumers.

These numbers can be further refined to help advertisers understand whether an advertisement reached a target market. Within rating and share categories, viewers can be subdivided by certain demographics, such as age, income, gender, educational level, and race or ethnic heritage. Organizations that prepare this information include Nielsen Media Research; Starch INRA; Hooper, Inc.; Mediamark Research, Inc.; Burke Marketing Research; and Simmons Market Research Bureau. Psychographic information can be then be added, such as whether outdoor enthusiasts watch certain programs. This gives the advertiser a sense of whether the program provides the best audience for an advertisement or campaign.

Local and Regional Television Advertising   For local and regional companies, spot TV may be the best television advertising option. In many cases, national brands supplement national commercials with spot TV purchases in select markets. Media planners use this approach primarily due to the high cost of national ad time and because 75 to 80 percent of prime-time slots are sold out during the spring, shortly after they go on the market. By selecting local early news, late news, and local prime access, a media planner generates higher GRP at a lower cost than national ad time yields.

Denver pizza operation Anthony's Pizza & Pasta switched from 90 percent out-of-home billboard advertising to 90 percent television. The company used a concentrated flighting schedule during the first and fourth quarters to build awareness and drive traffic to the restaurants. Spots were run in Denver on all of the national broadcast networks and 14 cable channels including ESPN, Comedy Central, Cartoon Network, Food Network, and AMC. The spots featured the key message/tagline "authentic, New York-style pizza." Five spots focused on the crafting of the pizza, and six spots utilized humor. During the six months when no ads were run, the company used social media, especially Facebook, to maintain contact with customers.[19]

Dynamic Advertising   Television networks, cable, and satellite TV companies have introduced a new technology that helps advertisers zero in on specific target markets. **Dynamic advertising** allows a company such as DirecTV to obtain consumer information from marketing research firms and combine it with the company's data to send targeted ads to its subscribers that meet specific criteria and live in targeted areas. It can be Spanish-speaking consumers, individuals who want to lose weight, or early adopters of

▼ Through dynamic advertising and retargeting individuals can receive an ad for Visit South Walton on their mobile phones after seeing an advertisement on TV.

technology. Toyota used dynamic advertising to target ads to DirecTV customers who were identified as tech-savvy early adopters who live in San Francisco, Los Angeles, and San Diego. No other DirecTV subscribers saw the ads.[20]

Another version of dynamic advertising involves sending follow-up ads to a person's mobile phone after viewing the ad on TV. Millennial Media's new technology can insert follow-up video ads into webpages or apps being viewed by individuals who have already watched the ad on television. This process is called **retargeting** because the follow-up message targets individuals who have already viewed the ad on television. Retargeting provides additional opportunities to re-engage consumers and to transmit sequential messaging. An alternative to retargeting is to send a digital ad to the smartphone after an individual has viewed a competitor's advertisement on television. These strategies seek to tie a person's mobile phone to a cable or satellite TV account, which Millennial Media and other companies can now do.[21]

Social Media and Television The rise of social media and the internet has led some advertisers to become concerned that television provides less of an impact. While many consumers watch less TV as they spend more time online, for others the opposite takes place. Social media, mobile, and the internet can be used to enrich television viewing experiences and actually drive consumers to watch more programs. Individuals who spend considerable time with social media tend to watch more TV, although some of it may be on tablets and other portable devices. Adam Rossow of iModerate notes that these individuals "love the social interaction and frequently add shows to their viewing lineup due to social chatter. They spend more time on social networks and more hours watching television." A Deloitte Research study revealed that 75 percent of consumers multitask while watching TV—42 percent are online, 29 percent are talking on phones, and 26 percent are sending text messages.[22] Research by Nielsen's SocialGuide service suggests that the heaviest Twitter activity occurs during television shows, not during commercial breaks.[23]

The interaction between social media and television viewing caused the marketing team for Bluefin Labs to examine online buzz about brands and television shows. People who commented online about Wal-Mart also tweeted or commented about television shows *America's SuperNanny*, *Dallas Cowboys Cheerleaders*, *Wife Swap*, *Cell Block 6: Female Lockup*, and *America's Most Wanted*. In contrast, social media comments about Target were tied to online comments and tweets about *Top Secret Recipe*, *My Yard Goes Disney*, *HGTV'd*, *Fashion Hunters*, and *Free Agents*.[24]

▼ SteviB's can use social media to engage fans with the brand during the football kickoff sweepstakes.

As people spend greater amounts of time on social media, the amount of online buzz about television shows also rises. By monitoring this type of online chatter, advertising professionals and their clients can gain better perspectives regarding the television shows that provide the best matches for placing ads.

YouTube and Television　Many companies and advertising agencies post television commercials on YouTube. Some of the ads are placed on the site simultaneously with the TV launch (called *in-stream*) while others are submitted to YouTube prior to the national launch (called *pre-roll*). For the Super Bowl, part of the ad, a teaser, may appear on YouTube prior to the game, or the entire ad may be posted.

Google and Ipsos research indicates that YouTube pre-roll of TV ads as well as in-streaming of TV ads result in higher recall. Individuals who watched the commercial on YouTube and on TV had a 200 percent higher recall than individuals who saw the ad only on TV. Those who saw the ad online on YouTube only had a 150 percent higher recall. More than 3 billion consumers watch videos on YouTube daily.[25]

Super Bowl Advertising　The Super Bowl offers the biggest television advertising event of the year. Many of the 110 million viewers tune in to see new ads as much as to watch the game. Recent research indicated that 39 percent of the viewers stated the new commercials were their favorite part of the game, and 73 percent consider Super Bowl advertisements to be entertainment. These findings reinforce the statement by Paul Chibe, vice president of marketing at Anheuser-Busch, that, "the Super Bowl is a huge brand-building opportunity."[26]

In the past, companies kept ads under wraps until the moment they appeared during the game. The rise of social media changed this approach. Many Super Bowl commercials first show up on YouTube, Facebook, the company's website, or on the agency's site prior to the game. As noted, pre-roll teaser ads entice viewers to watch the entire commercial during the game. Pre-rolling ads generates excitement and allows viewers to see, share, and discuss the ads before, during, and after the game. Many companies and agencies now spend as much time developing a marketing plan for the pre-roll as they do for the actual Super Bowl commercial. Further, another new approach involves the release of extended versions of advertisement with more content or additional information about the ad spot on the website.

One pre-roll teaser ad for Volkswagen released to YouTube three weeks prior to the Super Bowl was viewed 11 million times. Then, marketers uploaded an extended version of the sequel to YouTube the week prior to the Super Bowl, which resulted in over 1.3 million views. A Super Bowl commercial for the Chevrolet Camaro went online 17 days before the Super Bowl. Brian Sharpless, chief executive of HomeAway, stated that, "Because social media can build buzz for Super Bowl commercials before, during, and after the game, if you don't take advantage of all that, you're not getting the most bang for your buck."[27]

Super Bowl advertising generates nearly immediate feedback. A number of companies run various types of ad meters during the game and monitor social media buzz to determine the best ads and those that missed the mark. By the next morning, a number of websites and newspapers such as *USA Today* will publish a list of Super Bowl ad winners and losers.

▼ The Super Bowl has become a showcase for advertisers.

Radio

Despite CDs, iPods, audio books, and other types of audio devices, the majority of Americans, approximately 80 percent, still listen to the radio daily.[28] While radio may not seem as glamorous as television, it remains an effective advertising medium (see Figure 7.9). A well-placed, clever commercial delivers a one-on-one message (announcer to driver in a car stuck in traffic). Many smaller local companies rely heavily on radio advertising. Most radio ads are produced locally and with small budgets.

Advantages of Radio Advertising Quality radio advertisements cause the listener to remember the message by creating powerful images to visualize and by employing repetition. These actions move the information from the consumer's short-term to long-term memory. Sound effects and lively tunes assist in the process. Through repetition a person hears an advertisement often enough to generate recall.

▲ Radio enjoys the advantage of intimacy with the local DJ.

A radio station reaches definable target markets based on its format, such as talk radio, lite mix, oldies, or country. A firm can advertise on a specific type of station across the country. Radio advertisers examine the rating and share of a program as well as the estimated number of people listening. Arbitron calculates these numbers for local stations. Radio's All-Dimension Audience Research (RADAR) reports ratings for national radio networks.

Radio creates intimacy. Listeners often feel personally close to DJs and radio personalities. The attachment grows over time. Listening to the same individual becomes more personal and intimate, especially if the listener has a conversation with the DJ during a contest or when requesting a song. The bond or intimacy level gives the radio personality a higher level of credibility and an edge to goods and services the radio celebrity endorses.

Beachbody, a fitness brand based in Santa Monica, California, used radio as the prime medium to promote its P90X, a home exercise system that promised total body improvements within 90 days. Robinson Radio from Virginia developed and managed the radio campaign. Robinson realized the best approach was to deploy "radio's secret weapon," the DJs, who used the product, documented their successes, and then described their progress on the air. The DJs also posted photos on the company's website, created chat rooms for listeners, and asked listeners to share their success stories. Early in the campaign, it became clear that the micro website had become the key component of the radio campaign,

Advantages	Disadvantages
• Recall promoted	• Short exposure time
• Narrower target markets	• Low attention
• Ad music can match audience	• Difficult to reach national audiences
• High segmentation potential	• Target duplication with several stations using the same format
• Flexibility in making ads	• Information overload
• Modify ad to local conditions	
• Intimacy with DJs	
• Mobile – listen anywhere	
• Creative opportunities with sound and music	

◀ **FIGURE 7.9**
Radio Advertising

▲ Radio can be important component of an integrated advertising campaign.

because it allowed communications between the listeners, customers of the product, and the DJs. Another advantage of emphasizing radio was the ease and low cost of making changes as the campaign progressed. The campaign enjoyed significant success in California. Beachbody expanded the campaign nationally within a few months.[29]

Radio advertising offers a low-cost option for local firms. Ads can be placed at ideal times and adapted to local conditions. For business-to-business advertisers, radio provides the opportunity to reach businesses during working hours. Many employees listen to the radio on the job. An important key to radio as with other traditional media is to integrate it with other advertising venues.

Disadvantages of Radio Advertising

Short exposure time creates one problem for radio. Most commercials last 15 or 30 seconds. Listeners involved in other activities, such as driving or working on a computer, may not pay attention. Further, people often use radio as a background to drown out other distractions, especially at work.

It can be difficult for national advertisers to cover large areas with radio advertisements. To place a national advertisement requires contacting several companies. Few large radio conglomerates means contacts must be made with multiple stations. Negotiating rates with individual stations based on volume may be difficult. Local businesses can often negotiate better rates than national advertisers because of the local company's relationships with the radio stations.

The four main national radio networks in the United States are Westwood One, ABC, CBS, and Unistar. These are joined by a few other strong networks, such as ESPN Radio and CNN. Nationally syndicated programs such as those on the Fox radio network offer some opportunities to national advertisers.

In large metropolitan areas, duplication presents another problem. Several stations may try to reach the same target market. Chicago has several rock stations. Advertising on each one may not be financially feasible, yet reaching everyone in that target market might not be possible unless all rock stations are included.

Out-of-Home Advertising

Billboards along major roads continue to be the most common form of out-of-home (OOH) advertising; however, there are others. Outdoor advertising includes signs on cabs, buses, park benches, and fences of sports arenas. A blimp flying above a major sporting event constitutes another form of out-of-home advertising.

In the past, many company leaders did not consider outdoor advertising to be part of the planning process for an integrated marketing communications program or developing a media plan; however, that has changed. Advances in technology have dramatically improved OOH advertising. Global positioning systems, wireless communications, and digital display technology have transformed outdoor advertising. LED technology creates animated videos in locations such as Times Square in New York and the Strip in Las Vegas. It can present static messages and visuals that change electronically. Consequently, annual

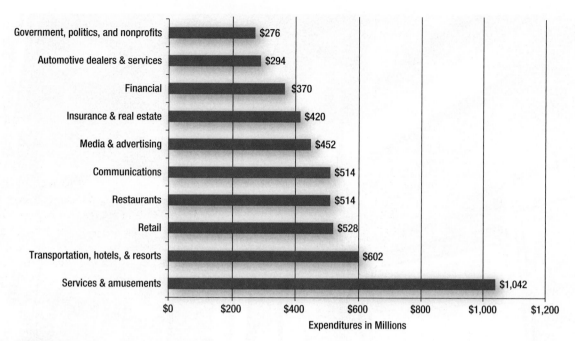

▲ FIGURE 7.10
Expenditures on Out-of-Home Advertising

expenditures on outdoor advertisements have grown to more than $5.5 billion. Figure 7.10 provides a breakdown of outdoor spending by categories.

Zehnder Communications recently created a unique out-of-home advertising campaign for Visit South Walton that utilized billboards, airport ground passenger delivery vehicles in cities such as Dallas, and the Chicago train. The airport and train advertisements were designed to capture people's attention as they traveled in order to get them thinking about possible vacation destinations. The images displayed in the airport and train ads matched digital ads that appeared on Amazon and Pandora. Similar images were also placed in print and television ads.

Advantages of Out-of-Home Advertising
Out-of-home advertising offers long life. For local firms, billboards and other out-of-home advertisements provide quality exposures, because the messages will primarily be seen by residents. Out-of-home provides a low-cost medium in terms of cost per impression. It features a broad reach and a high level of frequency when advertisers purchase multiple billboards or venues. Every person traveling past a billboard or who sees a moving message counts as an exposure. Many out-of-home companies feature rotation packages in which an ad travels to different locations throughout an area during the course of the year, thereby increasing its reach. Digital boards and signs deliver higher resolution graphics as well as capabilities of changing messages on demand or on a routine schedule. Figure 7.11 lists the advantages and disadvantages of out-of-home ads.

Disadvantages of Out-of-Home Advertising
Short exposure time remains the major drawback of out-of-home advertising. Drivers must pay attention to the traffic as they go by a billboard. As a result, advertisers keep messages short. Pedestrians often get only a quick look at an advertisement placed on a vehicle. Most either ignore outdoor ads or give them just a casual glance. Ironically, in large cities along major arteries billboard costs have increased. The reason: traffic jams. People stuck in slow-moving traffic spend more time looking at billboards. Purchasing locations where traffic stops for signals or at stop signs creates additional options.

▲ These ads for Visit South Walton inside a Chicago train were part of an integrated out-of-home campaign created by Zehnder Communications.

Print Media

Printed outlets continue to be an important component of traditional media. A growing number of print magazines and newspapers have developed digital versions to be viewed on computers, tablets, and smartphones. In some cases, the digital format will be identical to the print version. In others, the site includes additional or different content. Just as websites became essential for businesses, print media companies now develop digital components to compete effectively. This chapter covers traditional print media. The next chapter describes the digital component.

Magazines

For many advertisers, magazines represent a secondary choice in media buying. Recent research indicates, however, that magazines often deliver a quality option. An Affinity

Advantages	Disadvantages
• Select key geographic areas	• Short exposure time
• Accessible for local ads	• Brief messages
• Low cost per impression	• Little segmentation possible
• Broad reach	• Clutter
• High frequency on major commuter routes	
• Large visuals possible	
• Digital capabilities	

▶ **FIGURE 7.11**
Out-of-Home Advertising

Research study suggests that half of readers take action, such as accessing a website, after seeing an ad in a magazine. Others develop a stronger positive attitude toward the advertised brand. Several studies conclude that magazines drive purchase intentions and boost the effectiveness of other media.[30] Figure 7.12 identifies some potential advantages and disadvantages of magazines.

Advantages of Magazine Advertising Use of magazines facilitates high levels of market segmentation by topic area. Even within certain market segments, such as automobiles, a number of magazines exist. High audience interest constitutes another advantage. An individual who subscribes to *Modern Bride* has an attraction to weddings. People reading magazines tend to view and pay attention to advertisements related to their needs and wants. Often, readers linger over an ad for longer periods of time because they read magazines in waiting situations, such as in a doctor's office, or during leisure time. The high level of interest, segmentation, and differentiation, when combined with high-quality color, are ideal for products with well-defined target markets.

Trade and business journals remain the primary choice for business-to-business marketers. Businesses target advertisements to buying center members. The ad's copy can deliver a greater level of detail about products. Interested readers take more time to study the information provided. Ads often contain toll-free telephone numbers and website addresses so that interested parties can obtain further details.

Magazines have long lives that reach beyond an immediate issue. An avid magazine reader may examine a particular issue several times and spend a considerable amount of time with each issue. Advertisers know the reader will be exposed to the ad more than once and might be more likely to pay attention. Other individuals may also review the magazine. In the business-to-business sector, several individuals or members of the buying center may pass around a trade journal. As long as the magazine lasts, the advertisement stays available for viewing.

In addition to the standard sniff-patches that can be placed in magazines for perfume and cologne, advertisers can add QR codes or special mobile apps. DirecTV partnered with

▲ Print advertising is a valuable IMC component for LUBA Workers' Comp.

Advantages	Disadvantages
• High market segmentation	• Declining readership
• Targeted audience by magazine	• Clutter
• Direct-response techniques	• Long lead time
• High color quality	• Little flexibility
• Long-life	• High cost
• Read during leisure—longer attention to ads	
• Availability of special features	

◀ **FIGURE 7.12**
Magazine Advertising

THE CHEF'S COMPLEMENT

GE Café™ appliances give builders and remodelers a unique opportunity to attract homeowners who love to live in the kitchen. With inspired aesthetics and impressive power that mimics great restaurants, GE Café helps you create kitchens that aspiring and seasoned cooks would give anything to own.

Factory Builder Stores	Capital Distributing	Ferguson Enterprises	Builder Sales & Service
512 E Dallas Road #500	2910 N Stemmons Fwy.	All Locations DFW	2201 E Loop 820 South
Grapevine, TX 76051	Dallas, TX 75247		Fort Worth, TX 76112
817-410-8868	214-638-2681		817-457-7900

For additional information, check online at www.geappliances.com

▲ Magazines offer an excellent medium for GE Café to reach its target audience.

Sports Illustrated to create a free Android and IOS app for *SI*'s annual swimsuit edition. Individuals who downloaded the app to their smartphones could hold the phone over the swimsuit models in the *SI* magazine and watch videos of the model's picture shoot. The magazine had 19 embedded videos, each approximately 30 seconds in length.[31]

Disadvantages of Magazine Advertising

Although the overall readership of magazines has declined, the trend is not as dramatic for "influential Americans." Individuals with incomes of $100,000 or more read an average of 15.3 publications, and individuals with incomes over $250,000 read an average of 23.8.[32] Still, magazine advertisements require a great deal of lead time and are expensive to prepare. They may be less viable for more general consumption products such as basic necessities.

In general, magazines deliver an effective advertising medium. In both consumer and business markets, it appears that magazines, used in conjunction with other media, enhance the effectiveness of an advertising campaign.

Newspapers

USA Today has become a popular staple for many newspaper readers. At the same time, news reporting has changed. Many local papers no longer exist and conglomerates, such as Gannett, own most major city newspapers. Still, daily readership continues in some market segments for the print version while the online versions continue to grow in popularity.

For many smaller local firms, newspaper ads, billboards, and local radio programs provide the most viable advertising options. Newspapers are distributed daily, weekly, or in partial form as the advertising supplements found in the front sections of grocery stores and retail outlets. The online versions have also become viable options for local businesses.

Advantages of Newspaper Advertising

As Figure 7.13 notes, many retailers rely on newspaper because it offers geographic selectivity (local market access). Promoting sales, retail hours, and store locations is easier. Short lead time permits retailers to quickly change ads and promotions. Such flexibility presents the advantage of allowing advertisers the ability to keep ads current, and ads can be modified to meet competitive offers or to focus on recent events.

Newspapers retain high credibility levels. Most readers rely on newspapers for factual information. A recent survey of shoppers revealed that newspapers were the most trusted source of information for purchase decisions.[33] Newspaper readers hold high interest levels in the articles as well as advertisements. Greater audience interest permits advertisers to include more copy detail in ads. Newspaper readers take more time to read copy unless an advertiser jams too much information into a small space.

Recognizing a match between newspaper readers and its customer base, Starbucks launched a unique newspaper campaign designed by the agency Wieden + Kennedy of

Portland, Oregon. Starbucks invited coffee drinkers to stop at a local Starbucks for a free cup of coffee on March 15. Four-page full-color ads were placed in daily newspapers of 11 major markets, including New York, Los Angeles, Chicago, Boston, and Dallas. The ads were placed in the newspapers the week before the giveaway and again the day before. Then, on the day of the giveaway, Starbucks hired street vendors to pass out free copies of the newspapers containing the Starbucks ad. The newspapers were banded with the distinctive Starbucks' coffee cup sleeve. The campaign cost $545,000, but resulted in a half-million customers going into a Starbucks store. Lines wrapped around the block in some locations. Starbucks estimated the newspaper campaign resulted in 12 million impressions.[34]

Disadvantages of Newspaper Advertising   Newspapers cannot be easily targeted to specific market segments, although sports pages carry sports ads, entertainment pages contain movie and restaurant ads, and so forth. Newspapers have short lives. Once read, a newspaper will be cast aside, recycled, or destroyed. If a reader does not see an advertisement during the first pass through a newspaper, it may go unnoticed. Readers rarely pick up papers a second time. When they do, it is to continue reading, not to reread or rescan a section that has already been viewed.

Newspaper readers continue to age. Younger consumers obtain news either through the internet or from television; few read a print newspaper. The average age of those who read printed papers is 51 compared to 44 for those who read the digital version. Digital readers are younger, better educated, and are often more affluent than the print readers.[35]

Media Mix

Marketers recognize that selecting the proper blend of traditional media outlets for advertisements will be crucial. As they prepare campaigns, advertisers make decisions regarding the appropriate mix of media. Media planners and media buyers provide information regarding the most effective type of mix for a particular advertising campaign. Figure 7.14 displays the media mix in the United States for Coca-Cola. Total U.S. spending for advertising by Coca-Cola was $752 million; 63.4 percent went to television advertising. Coca-Cola spent far less on the other media.[36]

Recent Millward Brown and ACNielsen studies highlight the benefits of combining media.[37] The Millward Brown report indicates that ad awareness became strongest when consumers were exposed to an advertisement on television and in a magazine. Ad awareness was considerably lower for only those who read the magazine ad and even less for those who only saw the television commercial.

The **media multiplier effect** suggests that the combined impact of using two or more media will be stronger than using either medium alone. A recent integrated campaign for Ouachita Independent Bank featured a multiple media approach that included television, radio, newspapers, the internet, and out-of-home. Similar images and copy

objective 7.6
How can the marketing team use the media mix to increase advertising effectiveness?

Advantages	Disadvantages
• Geographic selectivity	• Poor buying procedures
• High flexibility	• Short life span
• High credibility	• Clutter
• Strong audience interest	• Poor quality reproduction
• Longer copy	• Internet competition
• Cumulative volume discounts	• Aging readership
• Coupons and special-response features	

◀ **FIGURE 7.13**
Newspaper Advertising

▲ Newspapers remain an excellent medium for local businesses to advertise, such as Fiesta Nutrition Center.

objective 7.7

What are the key issues associated with media selection for business-to-business markets?

unified the campaign to create a stronger brand impression and improve brand recognition.

The media multiplier effect is equally useful for business-to-business advertisers. An American Business Media study indicated that 89 percent of the business respondents believed that an integrated marketing approach raised their awareness of a company or brand. Seeing advertisements in more than one medium moved the company or brand name to become top-of-mind. It also resulted in more businesses making purchases.[38] Finding effective combinations of media is the key to utilizing the media multiplier effect. Figure 7.15 displays the process for choosing the best media for a particular advertising message. Media experts decide which go best together for individual target markets, goods and services, and advertising messages.

Media Selection in Business-to-Business Markets

Fewer differences between consumer ads and business-to-business ads exist, especially on television, outdoor, and the internet. In the past, business-to-business advertisements were easy to spot, because the content was aimed at another company. Marketers seldom used television, outdoor, or the internet. Now companies spend more than half of all business advertising dollars on nonbusiness venues.[39]

Several explanations have been offered regarding the shift to nonbusiness media. First, business decision-makers also consume goods and services. The same psychological techniques used to influence and gain consumer attention can be used for business decision-makers.

Second, reaching business decision makers at work can be challenging. Gatekeepers (secretaries, voice mail systems, etc.) often prevent the flow of information to users,

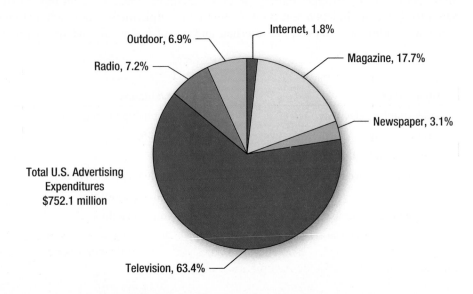

▶ **FIGURE 7.14**
US Advertising Expenditures by Medium for Coca-Cola

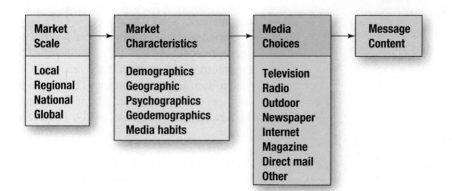

▲ This billboard for Ouachita Independent Bank was just one component of an integrated media campaign.

◄ **FIGURE 7.15**
Developing Logical Combinations of Media

influencers, and decision-makers. The problem becomes worse in straight rebuy situations in which orders are routinely placed with the current vendor. Any company other than the chosen vendor finds it tough to reach buying center members. Consequently, some business-to-business vendors try to find them at home, in the car, or in some other nonbusiness setting.

Third, clutter among the traditional business media makes it more challenging to get a company noticed. Business advertisers recognize that a strong brand name can be a major factor in making a sale. Taking lessons from major giants such as Nike, Kraft Heinz, and Procter & Gamble, business marketers seek to develop strong brands because the name helps a company gain the attention of members of the buying center.

In the past, many business ads were fairly dull. Currently, business ads are more likely to resemble those aimed at consumers. Ads feature creative appeals and the use of music, humor, sex, and fear. The boldest business ads sometimes include nudity or other more risqué materials.

Figure 7.16 identifies the ways business-to-business advertising expenditures are divided among the various media. In the past, business publications accounted for most of the expenditures, often half of the dollars. Business publications now represent about one-fourth of the more than $14 billion spent annually on business-to-business advertising. As more dollars shift to nonbusiness types of media, the amount being spent on television, newspapers, and consumer magazines has steadily increased.[40]

Although the use of business publications has decreased, trade journals still present an excellent opportunity to contact members of the buying center whom salespeople cannot reach. Gatekeepers do not prevent trade journals from being sent to members of the buying center. An advertisement has the best chance of success when a firm makes a modified rebuy and the buying center is in the information search stage.

▲ In business-to-business advertising, print remains an important medium for companies such as ReRez.

objective **7.8**

What issues are associated with media selection in international markets?

In addition to trade journals, business-to-business advertisers use business publications such as *BusinessWeek*. These publications have highly selective audiences and the ads have longer life spans in print. Business decision makers and members of the buying center spend more working time examining print media than any other medium.

International Implications

Understanding media viewing habits in international markets constitutes an important part of a successful advertising program. In Japan, television provides a major advertising tool; in other countries, it is not as prevalent. In Europe, an effective way to reach consumers involves print media, such as magazines and newspapers.

For several years, reports have surfaced that teenagers are watching less TV and spending more time on the internet. A Forrester Research study contradicted that notion, at least in Europe. Thousands of teenagers in Europe were surveyed about their media usage.[41] The general conclusions of the Forrester study are that:

- European teens spend more time watching TV than they do with any other medium, averaging 10.3 hours per week.
- Average personal time on the internet is 9.1 hours per week.
- Europeans ages 10 to 17 spend less time on the internet than individuals 18 and older.
- Only 41 percent of European teens visit social networks at least once a week.
- Teenagers like to multitask—watching TV while texting friends or playing video games while listening to music or TV.

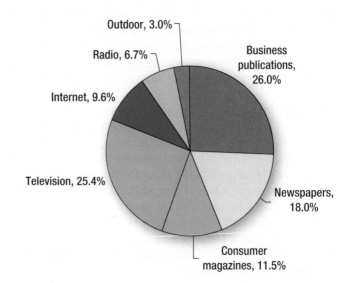

▶ **FIGURE 7.16**
Business-to-Business Advertising
Expenditures

- Younger European teens love video games, playing twice as much as individuals 18 and older.
- Most teenagers do not read the paper. They get news from TV or the internet.

Although a large number of media buying agencies operate throughout the world, nearly three-quarters of all media buying is conducted by only six large global agencies or their holding agencies. The largest global media company, the WPP Group, holds 22 percent of the market share.[42] To combat these large media networks, a global media consortium has formed. The consortium consists of a number of smaller independent agencies and offers services in Europe, North America, the Russian Federation, and Asia. Central offices are located in New York and London to serve business clients and to pitch for regional and national accounts.[43]

Large global media agencies have faced some criticism in recent years from marketing managers. They complain about the inability to provide effective media buys throughout all the countries where the clients operate. Although a few agencies do cover the world, it is difficult to be strong in every country in which an agency has a presence. The global agency may not be the best option in every country. For this reason, local media agencies and the consortium of independent agencies believe they have a better opportunity to increase their market shares.

In general, the tactics used to develop advertising campaigns and choose appropriate media in the United States apply to other countries throughout the world. What differs is the nature of the target markets, consumer media preferences, and the processes used to buy media. Company representatives carefully attend to cultural norms to make sure the buying process does not offend the cultural and religious attitudes in any given region. Agency employees seek to fully understand the target market as a company purchases advertising time or space and prepares advertising campaigns.

))) INTEGRATED Campaigns in Action

ST. FRANCIS MEDICAL CENTER

Newcomer, Morris, and Young advertising agency was retained to develop a marketing campaign for St. Francis Medical Center. The medical facility has three locations and a rich history of providing medical care in the area. From dialog with the client and agency staff, the tagline "My first and only choice" was born. To present this idea, the agency recruited patients that had experienced the excellent care provided by St. Francis.

◀ An advertisement designed as part of the "My first and only choice" campaign.

Summary

In traditional advertising, the roles of media planners and media buyers have grown in importance. Bob Brennan, chief operating officer of Chicago-based Leo Burnett Starcom USA, stated that in the past "Ninety-five percent of your success was great creative and 5 percent was great media. Now it's much closer to 50–50."[44]

A media strategy is the process of analyzing and choosing media for an advertising and promotions campaign. Media planners and buyers complete much of this work. The media planner formulates a program stating where and when to place advertisements. Media planners work closely with creatives and account executives. Media buyers purchase the space, and they negotiate rates, times, and schedules for the ads.

The goals of reach, frequency, opportunity to see, gross rating points, effective rating points, cost, continuity, and gross impressions drive the media selection process. Reach identifies the number of people, households, or businesses in a target audience exposed to a media vehicle or message schedule at least once during a given time period. Frequency represents the average number of times an individual, household, or business within a particular target market is exposed to a particular advertisement within a specified time period. Gross rating points (GRPs) measure the impact or intensity of a media plan. Cost per thousand (CPM) is one method of finding the cost of the campaign by assessing the dollar cost of reaching 1,000 members of the media vehicle's audience. Cost per rating point (CPRP), a second cost measure, assesses the efficiency of a media vehicle relative to a firm's target market. Ratings measure the percentage of a firm's target market exposed to a show on television or an article in a print medium. Continuity sets the schedule or pattern of advertisement placements within an advertising campaign period. Gross impressions are the number of total exposures of the audience to an advertisement.

The three-exposure hypothesis suggests that a consumer must be exposed to an ad at least three times before it has the desired impact; other experts believe even more exposures are necessary. In contrast, recency theory suggests that ads truly reach only those wanting or needing a product and that the carryover effects of advertising diminish rapidly. It is necessary, therefore, to advertise on a continuous basis to ensure that the message is noticed by consumers as they make purchase decisions. Effective frequency identifies the number of times a target audience must be exposed to a message to achieve a particular objective. Effective reach is the percentage of an audience that must be exposed to a particular message to achieve a specific objective.

In seeking advertising goals, marketing experts, account executives, and others assess the relative advantages and disadvantages of each individual advertising medium. Thus, television, radio, out-of-home, magazines, and newspapers should all be considered as potential ingredients in a campaign. Other new media can be used to complement and supplement traditional media outlets. Logical combinations of media should be chosen.

In business-to-business settings, companies can combine consumer media outlets with trade journals and other venues, such as trade shows conventions, to attempt to reach members of the buying center. In many cases, enticing ads using consumer appeals such as sex, fear, and humor have replaced dry, dull, boring ads with an abundance of copy.

International advertising media selection is different in some ways from that which takes place in the United States, because media buying processes differ as do media preferences of locals in various countries. At the same time, the process of media selection is quite similar. Marketing experts choose media they believe will be the most effective.

Key Terms

media strategy The process of analyzing and choosing media for an advertising and promotions campaign

media planner The individual who formulates the media program stating where and when to place advertisements

media buyer The person who buys the media space and negotiates rates, times, and schedules for the ads

spot ad A one-time placement of a commercial on a local television station

reach The number of people, households, or businesses in a target audience exposed to a media vehicle or message schedule at least once during a given time period

frequency The average number of times an individual, household, or business within a particular target market is exposed to a particular advertisement within a specified time period

opportunities to see (OTS) The cumulative exposures to an advertisement achieved in a given time period

gross rating points (GRPs) A measure of the impact or intensity of a media plan

cost per thousand (CPM) The dollar cost of reaching 1,000 members of the media vehicle's audience

ratings A measure of the percentage of a firm's target market exposed to a show on television or an article in a print medium

cost per rating point (CPRP) A measure of the efficiency of a media vehicle relative to a firm's target market

weighted (or demographic) CPM A measure used to calculate whether an advertisement reached the target market effectively

continuity The schedule or pattern of advertisement placements within an advertising campaign period

gross impressions The number of total exposures of the audience to an advertisement

intrusion value The ability of media or an advertisement to intrude upon a viewer without his or her voluntary attention

recency theory A theory suggesting that consumer attention is selective and focuses on individual needs and wants and therefore has selective attention to advertisements

effective reach The percentage of an audience that must be exposed to a particular message to achieve a specific objective

effective frequency The number of times a target audience must be exposed to a message to achieve a particular objective

dynamic advertising A research method that allows a company to obtain consumer information from marketing research firms and combine it with the company's data to send target ads to consumers

retargeting Sending a follow-up message to individuals who have already viewed an advertisement or accessed a website

media multiplier effect The combined impact of using two or more media is stronger than using either medium alone

---

MyMarketingLab

To complete the problems with the ⭐ in your MyLab, go to the end-of-chapter Discussion Questions.

Review Questions

7-1. What is a media strategy? How does it relate to the creative brief and the overall IMC program?

7-2. What does a media planner do?

7-3. Describe the role of media buyer in an advertising program.

7-4. What is reach? Give examples of reach in various advertising media.

7-5. What is frequency? How can an advertiser increase frequency in a campaign?

7-6. What are gross rating points? What do they measure?

7-7. What is the difference between CPM and CPRP? What costs do they measure?

7-8. What is continuity?

7-9. Describe the three-exposure hypothesis.

7-10. How does recency theory differ from the three-exposure hypothesis?

7-11. What is effective frequency? Effective reach?

7-12. What are the major advantages and disadvantages of television advertising?

7-13. What are the major advantages and disadvantages of radio advertising?

7-14. What are the major advantages and disadvantages of out-of-home advertising?

7-15. What are the major advantages and disadvantages of magazine advertising?

7-16. What are the major advantages and disadvantages of newspaper advertising?

7-17. Is the strong intrusion value of television an advantage? Why or why not?

7-18. What special challenges does media selection present for businesses? What roles do gatekeepers play in creating those challenges?

⭐ **7-19.** What special challenges does media selection present for international advertising campaigns? What differences and similarities exist with U.S. media selection processes?

Critical Thinking Exercises

DISCUSSION QUESTIONS

7-20. To be effective, multiple media should be chosen and integrated carefully. Individuals exposed to advertisements in combinations of media selected from television, radio, magazines, newspapers, and outdoor are more inclined to process the information than when a message appears in only a solitary medium. For each of the media, what is the probability of you being exposed to an advertisement? The percentages should add up to 100 percent. Which media are most effective in reaching you? Explain why.

7-21. Billboard advertising in Times Square has become so popular that space has already been sold for the next 10 years. Coca-Cola, General Motors, Toshiba, Prudential, NBC, Budweiser, and *The New York Times* pay rates in excess of $100,000 per month to hold these spaces. Why would companies pay so much for outdoor advertising? What are the advantages and disadvantages of purchasing billboards at Times Square?

⭐ **7-22.** The Super Bowl is the most-watched program on television. Many tune in just to watch the ads. Discuss the concepts of effective reach, effective frequency, ratings, gross rating points, brand recognition, brand recall, and opportunities to see as it relates to Super Bowl advertising. What are the advantages for a brand to advertise on television during the Super Bowl? What are the disadvantages?

⭐ **7-23.** Xerox offers a color printer that sells for $1,200. The goal is to market it to business buyers. What media mix would you suggest for a $5 million advertising campaign? Justify your answer.

7-24. Complete the following table by calculating the missing values. Based on the values you calculated, identify two magazines and two television shows for advertising sports equipment. Support your answer with specific data from the table.

7-25. Use the internet or phone directory to identify all of the radio stations in your area. What type of format does each have (for example, talk, country, hip hop, easy-listening, or rock)? Is radio a good advertising

medium to reach college students at your university? Why or why not? Which of the radio stations on your list would be the most effective in reaching college students?

7-26. As you drive to school (or home) make a list of all of the billboards and outdoor advertising you see. Which are the most effective? Why? Which are the least effective? Why? How effective are billboards at reaching you with an advertising message?

7-27. Pick three different magazines on a wide range of topics. For each, describe the types of ads and the number of ads in the issue. Did you see any business-to-business ads? What similarities did you see in the ads across the three magazines? What differences did you notice? Which would be most effective at reaching people in your demographic?

⭐ **7-28.** Explain the concepts of recency theory and three-exposure hypothesis in your own words. Discuss an example of an advertisement that was a catalyst to a purchase you made. How many times did you see the ad before you made the purchase? How did the ad impact your action to make the purchase? Think of an ad you recently saw or heard that made no impact on your purchase behavior. Explain why in the context of recency theory.

⭐ **7-29.** Define brand recognition and brand recall. Explain the difference between the two concepts? Suppose a home furniture store wants to increase its brand recognition. Explain the process and media that should be used. Instead of brand recognition, suppose the furniture store wanted to increase brand recall. How would the media and message be different? Be specific.

Publication	4C Base Rate or 30-second Ad	Circulation or Audience	CPM	Target Market (30 million)				
				Percent of Readers Fit Target Market	Number of Readers Fit Target Market	Rating (reach)	Cost per Rating Point (CPRP)	Weighted (Demographic) CPM
Magazines								
Allure	$165,554	1,080,000		12.2%				
Ebony	$81,167	1,170,000		16.1%				
Men's Health	$215,850	1,900,000		22.7%				
Road & Track	$119,421	720,000		28.4%				
Sports Illustrated	$412,500	3,170,000		7.8%				
Television shows								
NCIS	$180,264	19,700,000		6.3%				
2 Broke Girls	$175,506	9,000,000		4.2%				
Big Bang Theory	$316,912	20,000,000		10.8%				
Criminal Minds	$119,052	10,400,000		12.5%				
Modern Family	$281,961	9,100,000		17.8%				

Integrated Learning Exercises

7-30. Go to internet and do a search for "Nielsen TV ratings." What were the top 10 television shows last week? What other information is available at the website about the top TV shows?

7-31. Access Nielsen's top ten list at **www.nielsen.com/us/en/top10s.html**. Identify the categories listed on the webpage. Examine each of the lists and identify any brands or media that you have accessed or purchased.

7-32. In Canada, a valuable source of information is BBM (Bureau of Broadcast Measurement). Access this website at **www.bbm.ca**. What type of information is available on the site? What media does the BBM cover? How can it be used to develop a media plan for Canada?

7-33. A trade organization for magazines is the Magazine Publishers of America. Access the association's website at **www.magazine.org**. What type of information is available? How could it be used by a company wanting to advertise in magazines?

7-34. Two websites important for radio advertising are the Radio Advertising Bureau at and the top 100 radio sites at **www.100topradiosites.com**. Access both sites. What information is available on each site? Discuss how the information can be used to develop an advertising plan using radio.

7-35. A major company for outdoor advertising is Lamar Advertising Company. Access its website at **www.lamar.com**. Access the outdoor advertising component of the company and locate the rates for your area or another area of interest to you. What type of outdoor advertising is available? What other products does

Lamar offer? What services does Lamar offer? Write a short report on what types of advertising Lamar can provide for a company.

7-36. An excellent source of information for business advertisers is at *Entrepreneur*. Access the advertising section of *Entrepreneur* at **www.entrepreneur.com/advertising**. What type of information is available at this website? How can it be used by a small business? Pick an article from the page that is of interest to you. Report on the article. Provide the URL in your report.

7-37. The Newspaper Association of America is a trade association for newspaper. Access the website at **www.naa.org**. What type of information is available? How could this information be used by your local newspaper to increase business?

7-38. Go to the authors' website at **www.clowbaack.net/video/ads.html** and watch the two television ads for NOLA *The Times-Picayune*, which is the New Orleans newspaper. Which TV ad did you like the best? Why? Why would a newspaper, such as *The Times-Picayune*, need to advertise on television?

7-39. Go to the authors' website at **www.clowbaack.net/video/ads.html** and watch the TV ad for JD Bank. Locate the print ad in the "Media Planning" section of the chapter. Explain the concepts of media multiplier effect and recency theory as it relates to the TV and print ads. Would the media plan for the TV ad and print ad be different? Why or why not? Could JD Bank use dynamic advertising and retargeting with the TV ad? Explain how they could use it, or why they couldn't use it.

Blog Exercises

Access the authors' blog for this textbook at the URLs provided to complete these exercises. Answer the questions that are posed on the blog.

7-40. Duracell Batteries **blogclowbaack.net/2014/05/08/duracell-chapter-7/**

7-41. Geico Insurance **blogclowbaack.net/2014/05/08/geico-chapter-7/**

7-42. Media **blogclowbaack.net/2014/05/08/media-chapter-7/**

Student Project

CREATIVE CORNER

Horse racing has struggled to maintain attendance at some race tracks. The majority of serious fans of horse racing are older, white males. One challenge in drawing new fans to horse racing is to help them understand this complex sport. Recognizing which horse won a race is easy; however, after that it becomes very complex and difficult to grasp horse racing stats. A steep learning curve that requires thoughtful

and complex analysis is needed. Many potential fans do not want to invest the time or energy to learn. According to Tim Capps, a professor at the University of Louisville College of Business, horse racing "has been run more for itself than for its fans. One thing racing has to do is make participation in our sport easier for fans, because the fan has not come first in our industry." He adds, "People don't want to go to school. They want to be entertained."

While all agree there is a need to attract new fans, wide disagreement exists regarding the type of fan it should be. Do you market to the individuals who are already going to the track, or do you go after new individuals? Do you go after young people, or middle-age individuals, or work harder to reach baby boomers? Which gender—male or female—do you seek?

First, choose the target audience for an advertising campaign. Defend your choice. Second, select the media that would be most appropriate. Third, design a magazine ad for the target market chosen. Fourth, develop a billboard or outdoor ad to accompany the magazine ad.

CASE 1 ▸ CINDY'S AUTO BODY REPAIR SHOP

After a car wreck, most drivers would probably believe that an auto body shop would be run by a man. Cindy Kleis wants to defy this stereotype by running her own dent and body repair operation. Her company is set to open in 3 months. It will offer services ranging from touch-up painting to minor and major repairs from crashes.

Cindy learned the trade from her father, who worked as an employee for a repair company for more than 30 years. He recently retired, and his former employer closed his shop. This left an opening for a new firm. After purchasing a highly visible location on a major street in the city, Cindy contacted a local advertising and marketing agency. She set aside $15,000 for the marketing of her launch.

The agency specializes in small business advertising and promotion. The question becomes how to reach the highest number of potential customers and the message that should be sent when making contact with them. Cindy believed that her primary advantage would be a set of skilled and experienced repair experts, with a combined 40 years of previous work. All three individuals were friends of her father and had been taught by him.

One question which would need to be resolved centered on whether the advertising should emphasize or de-emphasize the fact that the shop was owned and run by a woman. Cindy believed it was a true advantage. She noted that many women take charge when a family car is damaged, and that they might enjoy dealing with a female manager.

Media selection constitutes another major decision. Cindy knows she needs to entice people to make the first visit, which could be months or even years down the road. She needs to place her company's name in their minds so that when the time comes they will visit her location.

The city in which the company is located has about 150,000 residents. When combined with the county, about 300,000 potential customers are present. The new company will have 3 major competitors in the city.

▲ Cindy Kleis faced a daunting task in deciding the best marketing approach to use for her body repair shop.

7-43. Discuss the pros and cons for Cindy's Auto Body Repair Shop of each of the media presented in this chapter. If you were the media planner assigned to this account, which of the media would you recommend, and why?

7-44. Describe the roles that reach, frequency, effective reach, and effective frequency should play in the campaign designed to acquaint customers with this new business.

7-45. Which theory best applies to Cindy's situation, recency theory or the three-exposure hypothesis? Explain your answer.

7-46. Create an effective media mix and describe the campaign you would create for the grand opening and subsequent months for Cindy's Auto Body Repair Shop.

7-47. Create the ad for Cindy's Auto Body Repair Shop that will be placed in the local newspaper.

CASE 2 ▸ RUNNING FREE

Dog owners constitute a large target market. Most members share something in common: the desire to let the pet run free and unfettered. If other friendly dogs are nearby and want to play—all the better. The Running Free Dog Park was created to meet this need for owners in the greater Atlanta area.

Out-of-home advertising can be the critical component of an IMC program and, in some cases, the primary medium. To help launch the new venture, a local advertising agency created a feeling of expectancy and mystery with a "Running Free Dog Park" campaign.

The first billboard displayed a dog tied up with a leash; however, it was only a partial picture. The unfinished nature of the image helps capture interest. Next, the same dog is shown with an unfastened leash and the word "running" appears beneath the pet. In the final billboard, the dog appears unfetters, the leash is gone, and the message "Running Free Dog Park" appears. The billboard displays the services offered, the website address of the park, and the location of the park. In addition to billboards, street kiosks and bus wraps were used to get the message out.

The early results of the campaign were positive. Many dog owners became aware of the new park. What followed represented common challenges in marketing communications: sustaining initial interest, moving consumers to action, and building repeat business.

In this next phase, dog owners needed to be encouraged to try the facility. They should be led to believe that the price of entry was a value. Then, over time, they can be enticed to make return visits and to offer word-of-mouth referrals to other pet owners. Only if these objectives can be attained will the initial success of the Running Free campaign become validated.

7-48. Define the marketing goals for the second phase of the Running Free Dog Park promotional efforts.

7-49. How would the three-exposure hypothesis or recency theory apply to this advertising program in its initial stages? What about the second campaign after consumers are aware of the dog park?

7-50. Which traditional advertising media should the marketing team use for the second campaign? Discuss the pros and cons of each in terms of the Running Free Dog Park campaign and the desire to stimulate trial usage.

▲ A dog park can be marketed as a place for pets to run free.

7-51. How could social media and nontraditional media be used to supplement a traditional media campaign in this circumstance?

7-52. Design a newspaper ad and an out-of-home ad that will be placed at Little League baseball parks in the area. Explain why having these two ads in different media is better than having two ads within the same media.

MyMarketingLab

Go to the Assignments section of your MyLab to complete these writing exercises.

7-53. The Super Bowl is the most watched program on television. Many tune in just to watch the ads. Discuss the concepts of brand recognition versus brand recall for the Super Bowl. Which is more appropriate? Why?

7-54. Identify the primary advantage of each of the media discussed in the chapter (television, radio, out-of-home, magazines, and newspapers). Explain why you think it is the primary advantage. For each medium, identify the primary disadvantage. Explain why. Consider an advertising campaign for a 35mm camera targeted towards individuals your age, your gender, and your ethnicity. If the company is limited to only two media, which two should it be? Explain why.

Buzz Marketing
Communications
Social Media
Advertising
Promotions
Digital
Branding
Mobile Marketing

Part 3

DIGITAL AND ALTERNATIVE MARKETING

Chapter 8 Digital Marketing

Chapter Objectives

After reading this chapter, you should be able to answer the following questions:

8.1 What is digital marketing?

8.2 How has the transition to Web 4.0 affected the field of marketing communications?

8.3 How can e-commerce programs and incentives build a stronger customer base and overcome consumer concerns at the same time?

8.4 How do mobile marketing systems enhance digital marketing programs?

8.5 What digital strategies do marketing professionals employ?

8.6 What types of web advertising can companies use to reach consumers?

8.7 What is a search engine optimization strategy?

8.8 How can companies successfully conduct digital marketing programs in international markets?

Overview

Developing quality advertising and communications programs has become increasingly complex. The previous section of this textbook reviewed the essential ingredients of a marketing communications program: the traditional media programs working in combination with other elements of the promotions mix. Thus, a television–radio–magazine campaign would incorporate coupons, discounts, personal selling techniques, sponsorships, and other ingredients to create a strong, coherent message.

Today's marketers and advertising professionals recognize that these efforts, while necessary, do not constitute a complete program. This section explains the additional elements needed to fully reach a target market and all potential customers (see Figure 8.1). The activities to be added include the digital marketing programs detailed in this chapter; social media messages, which are the subject of Chapter 9; and the additional alternative marketing channels described in Chapter 10.

CHOICE MARKETING

Local advertising and marketing agencies continue to play important roles in representing small businesses. Choice Marketing, which began operations in 2000, serves Joplin, Missouri and the surrounding area known as the "Four States" (Missouri, Kansas, Oklahoma, and Arkansas). Founder and CEO Karen Plott began the business working out of her spare bedroom. The firm now operates in a spacious location on a busy street in the city.

Choice Marketing provides numerous services, including graphic design, media research and buying, traditional media advertising and public relations assistance, branding efforts, custom promotional items, and other services. Both Plott and her Digital Media Manager, Dave Woods, note the growing importance of digital and social media marketing.

"Mobile marketing is exploding," Woods commented. "You can't really separate mobile marketing from 'traditional' e-commerce," he said, "because 80% of folks are using mobile devices when they are away from home and work and more standard e-commerce sites in their offices for their jobs and at home when they shop online."

Choice Marketing provides assistance for a variety of activities described in this chapter. These efforts include interactive and behavioral marketing, remarketing, blogs, newsletters, email and content marketing, along with native advertising. The company also facilitates search engine optimization programs as well as the social media component noted in Chapter 9.

Woods notes the importance of two emerging trends. He points out the value of "second and third screen" viewing, whereby a customer engages in one activity (watching television) and engages with other technologies such as a smart phone,

▲ Dave Woods and Karen Plott direct the efforts of Choice Marketing to respond to new trends in digital, alternative, and social media marketing.

laptop, or tablet at the same time. The individual notices a product or advertisement and quickly engages in additional research about it, leaving the first screen running.

The second trend involves a new form of marketing. "We have been involved in B-to-C (business-to-consumer) and B-to-B (business-to-business) programs, but now our companies can take advantage of C-to-C (customer-to-customer)." Woods noted. "Friends of friends now see advertisements that people pass along by texting, tweeting, or in some other way. This really adds to the impact of an ad."

Newer technologies create challenges for agencies such as Choice Marketing. Ad design must be adapted to every size screen so that each fits comfortably on the device. At times this involves adjusting a message to as many as 19 sizes. Woods emphasizes the importance of a "good media mix." He adds, "We have to demonstrate measureable results." The many successes enjoyed by Choice Marketing provide evidence that this company, and others of similar size, can succeed in these new aspects of marketing and advertising.

Digital Marketing

The internet has changed the ways individuals communicate and how the world conducts business. It presents an open environment. A buyer can locate numerous sellers offering practically the same merchandise at comparable prices and with similar offers at any time. The internet offers more than a method to conduct business transactions: It serves as a communication highway.

This chapter presents the various digital marketing concepts. The first section examines the evolution to Web 4.0. Next, e-commerce programs, including the incentives used to attract customers as well as consumer concerns with internet shopping, are presented. Then, the use of smartphones also leads to an examination of mobile marketing techniques. Digital strategies designed to maximize a company's reach are described. Web advertising programs also receive attention along with search engine optimization (SEO) techniques. Finally, international implications of these activities are drawn.

Digital marketing combines all of the components of e-commerce, internet marketing, and mobile marketing. It includes anything with a digital footprint. Today's consumers and businesses rely on the internet to research products, make comparisons, read comments by other

objective 8.1
What is digital marketing?

223

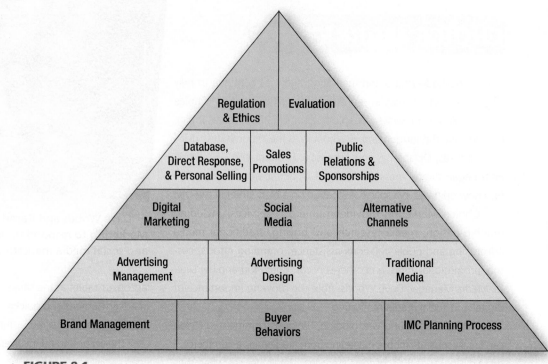

▲ **FIGURE 8.1**

Overview of Integrated Marketing Communications

consumers, interact with other consumers and businesses, and make product purchases. One such company that helps create effective digital marketing programs is Choice Marketing.

Web 4.0

objective 8.2

How has the transition to Web 4.0 affected the field of marketing communications?

One recent study revealed that many companies have slashed traditional media marketing budgets and moved the funds to online communications. Many marketing experts believe that online searches, email, social media conversations, digital ads, and mobile marketing will soon constitute a significant portion of marketing expenditures. The transition from Web 1.0 to Web 4.0 changed the ways consumers communicate and interact (see Figure 8.2).

In the 1990s, the internet (Web 1.0) was typified by static content provided by a site's creator. Businesses and institutions included little consumer involvement on websites. These commercially-and technically-based organizations created sites that were crude, simple, and designed to accomplish one specific function.

As Web 2.0 dawned, content became more socially-based and audience-oriented. Social networking sites such as Facebook and MySpace emerged. People wrote blogs. E-commerce expanded and consumers began purchasing products online. Sites became more appealing and customer-focused as competition drove web designers to create customer-friendly experiences.

Integration, online metrics, and real-time instant communications characterized Web 3.0. As marketers realized the wealth of online metrics available and the ability to track browser behavior on the web, content on sites became metric-driven. Individuals searching on a site for hiking supplies found that the next time they logged onto the site, hiking-related supplies would be prominently promoted on the main page. With online metrics came integration of the web with every aspect of a company's marketing program, both online and offline. The things consumers viewed online matched what they encountered offline.

Web 4.0 contains the key characteristics of customer engagement, cloud operations, and web participation. Companies cannot just sell products to individuals and then allow customers to post reviews. Engagement constitutes the primary business model for Web 4.0. Successful marketing programs utilize the web to connect with customers through

◀ **FIGURE 8.2**
Primary Characteristics of Web
1.0 to 4.0

- Web 1.0
  - Static content provided by creator
  - Dominated by institutions and businesses
  - Commercially and technically based
- Web 2.0
  - Content is socially based and audience generated
- Web 3.0
  - Content driven by online metrics
  - Integration of content and communications
  - Instant real-time communications
- Web 4.0
  - Customer engagement
  - Cloud operating systems
  - Web participation a necessity

various venues such as social media, blogs, and Twitter. Smartphones and tablets grant consumers access to thousands of apps and the ability to operate using the cloud. People can access brands anywhere, at any time. Consequently, websites must function on all platforms from desktop computers to tablets to mobile phones.

E-Commerce

E-commerce focuses on selling goods and services over the internet. Many types of e-commerce businesses exist, ranging from click-only operations that vend entirely online to bricks-and-clicks that supplement physical store operations with an online presence. E-commerce involves both businesses selling to consumers (B-to-C) and businesses selling to other businesses (B-to-B). Mega-retailers such as Wal-Mart as well as mom-and-pop operations offering merchandise from home engage in e-commerce. Online sales account for approximately 7.5 percent of all retail activity and this percentage continues to grow at a faster rate than brick-and-mortar retail sales.[1] Figure 8.3 identifies some common characteristics of successful e-commerce operations.

objective 8.3
How can e-commerce programs and incentives build a stronger customer base and overcome consumer concerns at the same time?

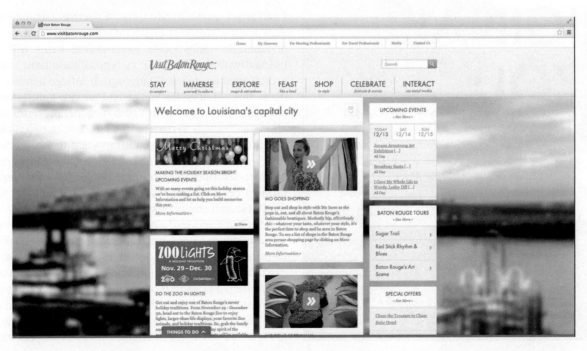

◀ This Visit Baton Rouge website encourages interaction and engagement with site visitors.

▶ **FIGURE 8.3**
Characteristics of Successful
E-Commerce Sites

- Search-optimized design
- Customer-centric design
- Mobile-optimized design
- Consistent customer experience
- Channel integration
- Brand engagement
- Shopping cart abandonment strategies
- E-commerce incentives
- Offline marketing integration

Search-Optimized Design A Pew Research Center survey noted that 80 percent of Americans have researched a product online before making a purchase.[2] Some searches resulted in online purchases, but many occurred in retail stores. Regardless of the final purchase location, e-commerce sites should be designed to optimize search results. Few consumers go directly to a retail website. Instead, most type the product into a search engine. The design of the e-commerce page influences where the website appears on a **search engine results page (SERP)**.

A web search crawler normally first looks at the title tag of a webpage when examining options. While not readily visible to consumers visiting a webpage, the **title tag** presents a short line of meta-copy, which is extremely important to search engines. Every page of an e-commerce site should provide a different title tag. The title tag must accurately describe the content of the page in terminology that a consumer might use during a web search. Placing the name of the business in the title tag is not necessary because doing so detracts from the tag, which contains only a limited number of characters. Consequently, the retailer Cabela's might feature the title tag "men's waterproof hiking boots" on its title page. Using descriptive words such as these enhances search results. More details regarding how search engines work along with the process of search engine optimization (SEO) are presented later in this chapter.

Customer-centric design Effective e-commerce sites feature customer-centric designs which allow individuals to easily locate merchandise. Items will be indexed with terms customers typically use rather than professional or technical language. If a large number of items are sold, then the site should provide a drill-down search function that features customer-friendly terms and allows individuals to find items within one or two clicks.

Product descriptions are important to both a customer-centric design and to search engines. Powerful product descriptions encourage people to buy. Unique product descriptions result in better locations on the SERP (search engine results page).

Search engines do not like thin copy nor do they value duplicate copy. Google has been known to penalize websites with duplicate content. E-commerce designers can fall into the trap of duplicating content when a company offers a large number of items. The web designer may be tempted to copy the product description for multiple versions of a product with only minimal changes. Google and other search engine providers suspect such

▼ The design of Origin Bank's website will influence where it appears on the SERP.

FOR THE ORIGINAL IN YOU.

At Origin Bank, one size never fits all. We treat you like the unique individual you are, so we can custom-fit a banking solution around your needs.

Community Trust Bank *is evolving into* ◈ Origin Bank *Bank original*

Member FDIC

duplicate content seeks to fool the search engine and subsequently penalizes the site with a poorer search rank. While it takes considerably more time, writing unique descriptions for each product enhances search results and, in the long run, customer conversions.

Pictures garner attention more effectively than words. Therefore, increasing the sizes of product pictures on e-commerce sites improves conversion rates. This is especially important for mobile devices. Using more, not less, white space around products enhances the image. Including a zoom function that allows shoppers to enlarge all or certain components of a product also generates conversions.[3]

Many e-commerce website designers believe that placing a greater number of products on a page means that individuals will be more likely to find something of interest. Research indicates the opposite. Reducing the number of options actually increases purchases. Too many choices create information overload. Consequently the consumer quits because she cannot decide. Limiting product options to 4 to 6 produces more conversions than offering 15 versions.[4]

Mobile-Optimized Design   Websites designed for a desktop computer will not load properly on a mobile device or tablet. Most sites have moved to an **adaptive design**, which automatically adjusts content to the screen size of the device being used to access the webpage. Criteo research revealed that adaptive design for mobile optimization increased interaction and conversions. The average conversion rate for mobile-optimized sites was 3.4 percent compared to 1.6 percent for non-optimized sites.[5] Doubling the number of conversion (purchases) justifies the cost of the mobile-optimization design.

Mobile-optimized design produces two other advantages. First, consumers make approximately 50 percent of all online purchase from mobile devices. This percentage is likely to continue to rise, because mobile shoppers tend to be younger consumers. Second, Moovweb research indicates that websites lacking mobile-optimized designs ranked lower in Google's search pages. More conversions, more people purchasing products via a mobile device, and higher SERP rankings all verify the importance of using adaptive design to optimize e-commerce pages for all types of devices, including mobile.[6]

Consistent Customer Experiences   Consumers will expect consistent, positive experiences when they access websites, whether from a desktop computer, tablet, or mobile device. They have nearly a zero tolerance for poor website performance. Poor experiences translate into dissatisfaction and lost sales, as evidenced by a number of studies:[7]

- Wal-Mart experienced a sharp decline in its conversion rate when the company's website load time increased from one second to four seconds.
- Amazon discovered that for every 100-millisecond decline in site load time, revenue increased one percent.
- Research by Torbit revealed that as load time increased, so did the bounce rate (individuals leaving the site without exploring other pages).
- Of consumers who were dissatisfied with a website's performance, 40 percent were unlikely to ever visit the site again and 25 percent were less likely to purchase the brand.

These studies highlight the importance of a positive, consistent customer experience and the impact of load-time of pages, especially the front page, on visitor actions.

▲ Creating customer-centric designs that work on tablets as well as desktop computers and mobile devices is important for financial institutions.

▲ Terrebonne General Medical Center offers a mobile-optimized website.

▼ Channel integration is an important feature of Skyjacker's website.

Channel Integration Channel integration is essential when the business sells through additional channels beyond the web. A company that offers a printed catalog or has a retail store should match the printed catalog with its web catalog. Victoria's Secret features a "catalog quick order" system which enables customers to enter the product number from the print catalog and then go straight to checkout. The program saves considerable time in trying to find and buy a product on the web.[8] The Skyjacker website shown in this section features an extensive line of products. The company's marketers integrated the site with channel partners to ensure customers can find the right part, whether on Skyjacker's website or from a local parts store.

Sears Holdings developed the online shopping experience "Shop Your Way" that assists customers by letting them shop in the manner they feel most comfortable. The customer can access **Sears.com**, **Kmart.com**, **LandsEnd.com**, **TheGreatIndoors.com**, or the new mobile application site **Sears2Go**. Each gives the person the ability to select a product from any retail operation in the manner desired.[9]

Brand Engagement E-commerce sites create opportunities for brand engagement and customer interaction. Blogs, feedback applications, and customer reviews provide ways for e-commerce sites to encourage customers to interact with the website. Facebook and Twitter permit customers to "like" a brand and become fans. Involvement in social causes that involve customers enhances brand engagement.

Many company leaders remain hesitant about adding reviews and feedback options to websites due to the potential for negative comments; however, customer reviews represent an emerging trend in the Web 4.0 environment. These venues present opportunities for active interactions with customers and generate more honest relationships. They encourage customers to become brand advocates and provide a company with insights into customer thoughts and lifestyles.[10] Review and feedback pages also generate confidence for new customers visiting the site. Some e-commerce sites include "tell a friend" functions encouraging positive word-of-mouth recommendations.

Personalization and customization play key roles in brand enhancement. Personalization welcomes individuals by name as they access sites. After an individual registers, cookies deposited on the visitor's computer recall the person's name and browsing records each time the individual accesses the site. The browsing and purchase records help customize the page to fit the person's history. Software suggests additional items based on basket purchases of other customers. For example, when someone buys a romance mystery novel, the next time she returns to the site, it suggests additional titles based on what other customers have purchased.

Most customers enjoy the convenience customization provides. Shoppers do not want to take time to sift through details. They favor the sites that remember them and the merchandise they prefer. Customization features also include the ability to:

- Locate the nearest retail store on a website or via mobile phone.
- Print coupons or other promotions from the website or use a mobile phone to access discounts at the retail store.
- Access information on the website or via a mobile phone that notes that an item is in stock prior to a purchase.[11]

Shopping Cart Abandonment

Some online retailers experience high percentages of customers abandoning shopping carts prior to checkout. The reasons vary, but the most common include hidden charges, difficulty in checking out, and sites that require customers to register in order to pay. Greg Hintz of Yahoo! Shopping offers these suggestions to keep customers from abandoning a shopping cart:

- Show any additional costs, such as shipping and handling, up front, so there are no surprises when the customer reaches checkout.
- Make checkout easy, and allow customers to make purchases without registering a user name and password.
- Make it easy for customers to enter discount codes from coupons, gift certificates, and other promotions.
- Provide safe checkout procedures customers believe can be trusted.[12]

▲ Wholly Guacamole encourages individuals to engage with the brand through Twitter, Facebook, Pinterest, YouTube, Google+, and Instagram.

E-Commerce Incentives

Any lure or attraction that brings people to a website is **cyberbait**. The most common forms include financial incentives, convenience incentives, and value-added incentives (see Figure 8.4).

Financial incentives help persuade individuals and businesses to make first-time purchases and encourage them to return. The incentives take the forms of a reduced price, free shipping, or an e-coupon. A recent BizRate Research survey concluded that free shipping remains the most popular online promotion.[13] Financial incentives require two ingredients. First, they should be meaningful to individuals visiting the site. Second, they should be changed periodically to entice new visitors to buy and to encourage repeat purchases by current visitors.

Making the shopping process easier creates a convenience incentive that encourages customers to visit a website. Instead of traveling to a retail store, customers place orders in their offices, at home, or while traveling by using a smartphone or app. The order can be made at any time, day or night, and the merchandise can be shipped directly to the customer. The convenience and speed of purchasing merchandise online drives many consumers to e-retailers.

Value-added incentives lead consumers to change purchasing habits over the long term (see Figure 8.5). They often make the difference between an ordinary and an exemplary

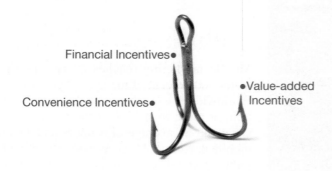

Financial Incentives•

Convenience Incentives•

•Value-added Incentives

◀ **FIGURE 8.4**
Common Forms of Cyberbait

◀ **FIGURE 8.5**
Value-Added Incentives

- Customized shopping
- Unique product-information
- Mobile apps
- Social media engagement
- Exclusive shopping
- Tutorials, usage tips and repair instructions

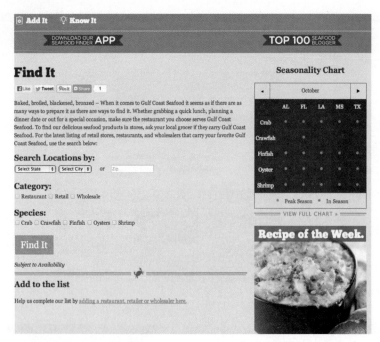

▲ The Gulf Coast Seafood website offers a number of value-added incentives.

▼ This advertisement for Visit South Walton encourages individuals to visit the website for additional information.

site. Added value may come from customized shopping, whereby the software system recognizes patterns in a customer's purchasing behaviors and makes offers matched to past purchasing behaviors or search patterns. The Gulf Coast Seafood website shown in this section offers information about species of fish, a seasonality chart, the recipe of the week, and the top 100 seafood bloggers. It incorporates engagement tools including Facebook, Twitter, and Pinterest. Visitors can download the seafood finder app and search for locations. These features add significant value to the website.

Exclusive shopping provides a value-added incentive many customers appreciate. A before-launch peek at new fashions, new products, and future product changes are some of the exclusive shopping opportunities offered to a website's best customers. Being considered an exclusive customer builds loyalty and engages the individual with the website. Often this exclusive customer becomes a brand advocate on her social media page.

Tutorials, usage tips, and repair instructions establish additional value-added incentives. The key to value-added incentives is providing something that a customer values. If he shares it with friends, it becomes even more valuable.

Combining incentives is the best strategy for luring customers back to a website. Cyberbait may include a discount or special price on a pair of jeans (financial-based incentive) and at the same time offer the freedom to place an order at 3:00 a.m. (convenience-based incentive). The same site might feature a game or offer a weekly fashion tip on some topic (value-added incentive). This combination entices consumers and businesses to return. E-shoppers find it easy to surf the internet and search competing sites. When they do, brand names and specific websites are not as important. Consumers need reasons to regularly return to sites.

Offline Marketing Integration   E-commerce encounters global competitors. Without any type of offline advertising or marketing, attracting and keeping customers becomes difficult. Offline marketing efforts should be integrated with the e-commerce site. Information provided in a magazine ad, television ad, or through social media should match the information presented on the website. Ideally, every piece of marketing collateral includes the firm's web URL.

Mobile Marketing

Mobile marketing reaches every type of device. Approximately 60 percent of the U.S. population owns a smartphone. Worldwide, the number of smartphones users exceeds 2.16 billion, or more than 25% of the world's population. Individuals spend an average of 3 hours and 18 minutes per day on mobile devices.[14] Most access the internet from a smartphone rather than a desktop or laptop computer, especially younger individuals.

Mobile devices help individuals communicate with each other and link them to social networks, thereby allowing users to post comments, pictures, and videos while reading the thoughts of others. People check in, tweet, and update their status at any time and anywhere. They download deals from companies, read reviews, check prices, and share information. A mobile device facilitates comparison shopping and viewing product information. Consumers check store hours, obtain directions to a business, and compare prices. These activities take place anywhere, including inside the retailer's store.

As shown in Figure 8.6, mobile differs from other media in ways that result in both opportunities and challenges for marketers. A mobile device is personal, and, as such, tends to be used by a single individual, which feature provides companies the opportunity to build loyalty and engage consumers with the brand. At the same time, it runs the risk of quickly alienating consumers when they feel the marketing approach has become too intrusive. Mobile devices incorporate tracking features through a GPS, beacon, or NFC (near field communication) technologies designed to pinpoint a person's geographic location. This information can be more valuable in determining a person's behavior than demographic information as it opens the way for highly targeted marketing tactics.

Mobile features a unique form of two-way communication that differs from text messaging, social media, and the internet. Brands and individuals engage in conversations and interact in several ways. These take place at any time and in any location. The quality of such conversations may be enhanced using camera/video technology and voice recognition.

Mobile users share photos and videos rather than relying only on text. Finding meaningful ways to incorporate photos and visuals into the brand experience becomes the marketing challenge. As society turns more visually-based rather than text-based, this aspect of communication grows in prominence.

Voice recognition adds another key advantage to mobile devices. Individuals do not have to type a reply or send a video. They can simply talk into their phones. Then apps, programs, and conversations take place through voice recognition.

Mobile devices contain numerous sensors, which provide new options. Galaxy phones hold nine sensors that track temperature, humidity, barometric pressure, and human gesturing through movement of the phone. These sensors compile information regarding how, when, and where devices are used, along with the context.

Mobile apps fall into two primary categories. First, some apps are designed to engage consumers with the brand. Second, apps can be designed to streamline the business use or the purchasing process. Starbuck's loyalty app serves as an example of the first category. The app entices consumers to engage with the brand.

Uber developed an app that streamlines the buying process. It transmits the location of the Uber vehicle, an image of the vehicle and driver, and enables voice or video interactions. The app makes purchasing easy and convenient. It takes one or two taps on the app to book a reliable ride within minutes. The driver knows where the person will be going and whether the payment will be cashless.

Globally, people download 32 billion apps to smartphones each year. Advertisers pay $2.9 billion for in-app advertising and brand app development while consumers spend $26.1 billion buying apps. In the early years of mobile apps, brand leaders rushed to develop apps with little regard for how consumers would use them or even if people wanted such a product. Most failed. Brand managers began to realize that getting people to download an app does not present the primary challenge. Rather,

objective 8.4

How do mobile marketing systems enhance digital marketing programs?

▲ Mobile devices enable brands such as Chila Orchata to interact with consumers through social media, such as Facebook.

- Personal
- Geo-location
- Two-way communication
- Camera/video technology
- Voice recognition
- Phone sensors

▲ **FIGURE 8.6**

Ways Mobile Differs from Other Media

Origin Bank
APP ICON

BUSINESS   PERSONAL

ADRENALINE 2015

▲ An example of an app developed by Origin Bank for its customers.

providing a positive experience when the consumer uses the app will be the key. AppDynamics research indicates that 70 percent of consumers say that the performance of an app influences their perceptions of the brand along with their levels of satisfaction, loyalty, and the amount of money they become willing to spend on a brand.[15]

QR codes, watermarks, and 2D barcodes direct consumers with smartphones to websites. These frequently appear in magazines and other print advertisements. The codes are especially popular in magazines that focus on home, family, beauty, health, travel, and fashion. The QR code placed in the Philadelphia Cream Cheese advertisement in this section offers recipes to shoppers.

Engaging customers constitutes the primary purpose of action codes in magazines. A Nellymoser study revealed that the greatest usage was for viewing videos (35 percent). These videos may provide a behind-the-scenes look, product demonstrations, a how-to video, or entertainment. Action codes help the marketing team collect data and build opt-in lists for permission marketing. Figure 8.7 displays other uses for action codes.[16]

Digital Strategies

objective 8.5

What digital strategies do marketing professionals employ?

The movement from desktop computers to laptops, tablets, and smartphones has led marketers to adapt to multiscreen formats. Advances in technology create new digital marketing opportunities along with pressures to develop campaigns that can be viewed from any type of screen. Figure 8.8 identifies the primary digital marketing strategies brands feature.

Interactive Marketing

The development of marketing programs to create interplay between consumers and businesses, or **interactive marketing**, assists two-way communication and customer involvement. Interactive marketing emphasizes two primary activities. First, it helps marketers target individuals, specifically potential and current customers, with personalized information. Second, it engages the consumer with the company and product. The consumer becomes an active rather than passive participant in the marketing exchange.

▶ **FIGURE 8.7**
Marketing Uses for Action Codes

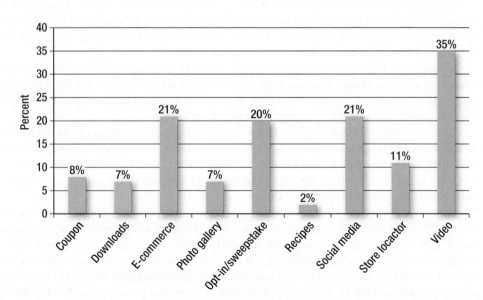

Category	Percent
Coupon	8%
Downloads	7%
E-commerce	21%
Photo gallery	7%
Opt-in/sweepstake	20%
Recipes	2%
Social media	21%
Store locator	11%
Video	35%

- Interactive marketing
- Content and native marketing
- Location-based advertising
- Remarketing

- Behavioral targeting
- Blogs and newsletters
- E-mail marketing

The internet is an ideal medium for interactive marketing due to the ability to track browser activities and translate the information into instant reactions. Software such as the Relationship Optimizer and Prime Response by NCR provides a powerful data analysis technique to personalize marketing messages. The NCR software analyzes customer interactions such as click-stream data traffic—any type of customer interaction with the firm—and combines it with demographic information from external or internal databases. As the data are processed, the software launches complex interactive and personalized marketing materials in real time.

A company that specializes in interactive marketing, MediaBrix, obtains data from each individual's browsing activities and mobile app usage. Coca-Cola, BMW, Taco Bell, and CoverGirl use MediaBrix to target customers at just the right moment. For instance, minutes after the St. Louis Cardinals win a baseball game, a targeted message can be sent to fans congratulating them on the win and then offering 50 cents off of the next purchase at Taco Bell. The message can be sent via a banner ad on a desktop or through a mobile app. If the Cardinals lose, no message is sent. CoverGirl employs MediaBrix to deliver "congratulatory" video ads when an individual finishes a workout based on the mobile app input data. The success of MediaBrix comes from tying an advertising message to a specific event.[17]

While interactive marketing messages can be sent to desktop and laptop computers, they achieve greater success on mobile devices, because targeted messages are more likely to be seen during or immediately after the specific event. Desktop and laptop interactive marketing rely more on asynchronous interactions.

▼ Arvest Bank can use interactive marketing to reach potential customers who are in the process of buying a home.

Content Marketing and Native Advertising

The tendency of consumers to ignore traditional advertising and digital advertising has led several companies to turn to content marketing and native advertising. **Content marketing**, or *branded content*, consists of providing useful information and product-use solutions to potential customers on a brand's website or microsite. *Sponsored content marketing* is the same as *branded content*, but a third party hosts the information. The brand does not own or operate the site.

Native advertising is also hosted on a third-party site. It appears to look like an article that provides useful information to solve a problem, but the solution depends on purchasing a particular brand of a product or service. Unfortunately, articles and websites

	Content Marketing		Native Advertising
	Branded Content	**Sponsored Content**	
Location	Brand's website or microsite	Third-party site	Third-party site
Goals	Provide information	Provide information	Generate sales
	Increase brand awareness	Increase brand awareness	Increase brand awareness
	Improve search results	Increase social engagement	Increase social engagement
Tone	Educational	Educational	Solve problem through brand
	Solve a problem	Authentic, expert tone	purchase
Audience	Brand's customers and prospects	Sponsor's audience	Third-party's audience

▲ **FIGURE 8.9**
Content Marketing and Native Advertising

about content marketing and native advertising often use these terms interchangeably when there are distinct differences, which are highlighted in Figure 8.9.

Marcus Sheridan, owner of River Pools and Spas, used a blog and videos that provide an example of branded content (marketing). These activities were hosted on his website. He turned to this approach when orders for in-ground fiberglass pools at River Pools and Spas declined from an average of six per month to barely two. Four customers who had made deposits during the winter requested their money back after changing their minds. Sheridan was spending $250,000 per year on radio, television, and pay-per-click web advertising. He reduced the budget to $25,000 and focused on providing

▼ Marcus Sheridan saved his pool and spa business by using content marketing in his blog and videos.

useful information through blog posts and videos. He answered questions about costs from potential customers.[18] The approach saved his business.

Content marketing does not attempt self-promotion or trickery to generate sales. Instead, it focuses on providing authentic content. Marcus Sheridan shared truthful information, good and bad, about fiberglass pools. Customers appreciated his honesty and responded through interactive dialogue and purchases.

While providing information that solves consumer problems will be the primary goal of branded content, secondary objectives should be to increase brand awareness and improve search results. The tone of branded content should be educational with no sales lingo. Authenticity is vital to effective branded content.

When a pool supply company, such as Dalton Pool Supplies, hosts Sheridan's blog or posts his articles on Dalton's website, it becomes sponsored content. Typically Sheridan pays a fee for being included on the Dalton website. Dalton's marketing team sees it as a way to improve customer service. Dalton's goal for including the Sheridan blog will be to provide information while building brand awareness and social engagement with individuals sharing the information on social media sites. Sheridan's willingness to post his articles on the Dalton site results from the belief that doing so will expand his target audience to include all of Dalton's customers and site visitors. Again, the information needs to be authentic, educational, and provide solutions to problems individuals face. It should not be sales gimmickry. The only identification on the articles will be a "sponsored by River Pools and Spas" at the beginning, end, or along the margins of the information.

Another example of sponsored content may be found on a YouTube video showing how to create perfect curls. It includes references to the Remington curling iron brand embedded in the video. Spectrum Brands, which owns Remington, pays bloggers to create stories, articles, and videos for the web. An article and video entitled "Get the Right Swimsuit for Your Body" featured references to Remington that were also embedded in the content. The goal was for the article and video to be shared through social media venues such as Twitter and YouTube.[19] The information is hosted on bloggers' websites, not Remington's, which makes it an illustration of sponsored content.

Native advertising is paid advertising. Doheny manufactures swimming pool chemicals. In a native advertising program, someone from Doheny prepares an article about various types of pool algae. The article describes which Doheny products to use and how to use them. To gain maximum exposure, Doheny seeks to place the article in landscaping, outdoor, and pool type magazines in the spring and early summer. The magazines can be print or digital. To someone reading the print magazine or the digital version, the native advertisement looks like one of the articles; however, the only solutions mentioned for pool algae are for Doheny products.

An alternative for Doheny would be to prepare a video showing the various types of algae and then indicating how Doheny products kill the algae and help to maintain an algae-free pool. Doheny could pay websites to post this video. The company could also pay for the video to be posted on social media pages, such as Facebook, Twitter, Google+, or Instagram. Generating sales by showing how a particular brand solves various problems would be the goal.

Location-Based Advertising

Mobile phones enable marketers to create location-based mobile advertising campaigns, often called geo-targeting. **Geo-targeting** involves reaching customers where they are located by contacting their mobile communication devices. Geo-targeting represents a unique and attractive feature of mobile marketing. By downloading an app, a fast-food restaurant can identify a person's location, show him how far he is from the nearest outlet, and then provide walking or driving directions to that unit.

Many smartphone owners have check-in services at Foursquare, Gowalla, Facebook Places, and Twitter geolocation. Starbuck's, McDonald's, Chipotle, and Burger King provide the largest number of restaurant check-ins. When someone checks in, software

▲ A mobile sponsored Instagram post by Visit South Walton.

instantly sends a special promotion and information about the nearest locations. Marketing experts believe this location-based marketing approach will continue to grow. Businesses harness the ability to drive consumers to retail outlets near where they are located, which can be an effective method of engaging consumers with a brand on a one-to-one basis.

Applebee's restaurant employs location-based targeting. The brand's mobile banner ad reads "See You at Applebee's." When the consumer taps on the mobile ad, the content asks if it can access the person's current location through the phone's GPS. If the person responds "yes," she is taken to a mobile landing page that provides the nearest Applebee's location (with a map), menu items, and specials. Through the app, consumers may purchase gift cards and receive them from Facebook, Twitter, or other social media venues. A click-to-call button will dial the Applebee's with just a tap.

According to Shuli Lowy, marketing director at Ping Mobile, "Mobile is no longer an option for restaurants." A Nielsen study revealed that 95 percent of smartphone users conduct restaurant searches on their mobile devices and 90 percent of those convert within a day. Sixty-four percent convert within an hour.[20]

Other brands also feature geo-targeting. Nissan, Procter & Gamble, Pepsi, Macy's, Kenneth Cole, and Timberland have conducted successful geo-targeted campaigns. Swirl is a mobile app used by retailers such as Timberland. Shoppers who agree to download the Swirl app and let it track their locations are notified of a 20 percent discount on merchandise. The app provides a consumer with a store's location and the individual has one hour to take advantage of the special. A clock within the app begins the time countdown. According to the VP of retail and digital commerce at Timberland, "Because it's opt-in . . . you're receptive to it." According to Shadrin, 75 percent of recipients checked out the special offer, and 35 percent redeemed the discount.[21]

Figure 8.10 displays the forms of location-based advertising and the approximate percentage quantity of each.[22] Targeting by demographic marketing areas (DMAs) is the most common approach. Everyone within the DMA that has granted permission receives the targeted message. Geo-fencing reaches consumers near a specific retail location. Usually, the location will be coupled with third-party demographic data or retail transactional data to determine audience clusters within a geographic area around the store. Timberland used this approach. Only consumers who fit the cluster profile receive the targeted message.

Restaurants including McDonald's and Applebee's use geo-aware advertising targeting real-time locations to deliver advertising messages based on the person's proximity to a unit's location. For other companies, audience-data targeting incorporates audience behaviors and characteristics to reach individuals. The person's location determines the exact brand and nature of the ad to be sent.

Creating successful geo-targeting campaigns requires two actions. First, consumers should be in control of the engagement. They opt-in for the app. Second, the brand should provide a discount or something of value to consumers. Campaigns that follow these principles routinely yield engagement and performance measures that are higher than any other type of digital advertising.

▶ **FIGURE 8.10**
Location-Based Advertising

- Targeting by DMAs (designated marketing areas), 30%
- Geo-fencing, 27%
- Audience-data targeting, 24%
- Geo-aware advertising, 14%
- City or zip code, 5%

Remarketing

Digital technology makes it possible to send ads to individuals that have visited a brand's website or accessed the brand's app. These individuals have displayed an interest in the brand. Consequently, conversion rates using remarketing are considerably higher than general banner or search ads. The remarketing ads appear the next time an individual accesses the internet or uses a mobile device. It can be just minutes, or hours, or the next day. Immediacy is an important feature of remarketing as well as targeting individuals who have already shown some level of interest.

Remarketing re-engages individuals who have visited a site but did not make purchases. A consumer who visits the Ujena website and looks at various swimsuits but does not put anything in the shopping basket will be an ideal recipient. The remarketing ad can be sent to the individual's computer or mobile device that was used to access the website. It would show the swimsuits she looked at during her visit to Ujena. If there is no response, then additional ads could offer other swimwear or products.

For a potential customer who places items in the shopping basket but does not make the final purchase, remarketing becomes valuable, especially when the person did not provide an email address or register at the website. In that instance, the items placed in the shopping cart will be shown in the remarketing ad. The customer already displayed interest in the items, but left for some reason. Leaving may have resulted from getting a phone call, being interrupted by work or children, or just wanting to think more about

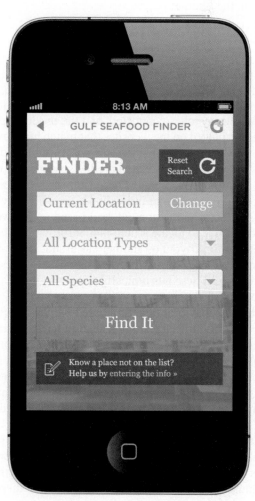

▲ This app for Gulf Seafood uses geo-targeting.

▲ This Gulf Seafood app utilizes location-based technology to locate nearby seafood sources with a click-to-call option.

the purchase. Sending remarketing ads featuring items she selected might nudge her to complete the transaction.

Transmitting the same ad to everyone who visits a website does not work. Instead, remarketing ads should be customized to the products, or similar products, that were viewed on a website or those placed in a shopping basket or on a wish list. Financial incentives or other forms of cyberbait can be offered to entice the person to revisit the site and make a purchase. Remarketing ads leads to high conversion rates because visitors to a site have already indicated interest. The ads often succeed more than any other form of digital marketing as they reduce acquisition costs for new customers.

Behavioral Targeting

Marketers for some brands can target the individuals who are most likely to purchase the item in ways other than merely placing ads on websites. **Behavioral targeting** utilizes web data to identify potential customers. The difference between behavioral targeting and remarketing is with remarketing ads are sent to individuals from a brand whose website was visited. With behavioral targeting, ads are sent to individuals based on browsing behavior rather than visiting a specific website. Behavioral targeting occurs in three different ways. It can be based on

- Pages a person visits on the internet
- Keyword searches or content read
- Past visitors to a site

▲ A female who looks at swimsuits on the Ujena website would be an ideal candidate for remarketing.

The most common form of behavioral targeting involves tracking a person's movements on the internet. Cookies placed on the individual's computer track the data points as he moves from site to site. They record the types of sites visited, the information read, the searches conducted, and the products purchased. Based on this information, ads will be placed on the websites that match his browsing history. If he has visited a number of websites about fishing, the screen will display advertisements for fishing supplies, boats, or other fishing-related products. Marketers can place a coupon or other form of cyberbait on the ad to encourage the consumer to click on it.

The second form of behavioral targeting examines an individual's search behavior. It identifies keywords typed into search engines and the content read based on keyword searches. If an individual has used a search engine to locate articles and information about new cars, she then may see an advertisement for Toyota or another car brand. If she has been reading about SUVs, then the ad may actually be for an SUV rather than a sedan or other type of vehicle. These ads typically appear on the search engine being used.

▼ Behavioral targeting can be used to target fishing-related digital advertisements to individuals have visited fishing-related websites.

The final form is behavioral targeting based on past visitors. Amazon uses this method to suggest books and movies that may interest a person shopping on the company's website. When someone places a book or movie in a shopping basket or on a wish list, it triggers the behavioral marketing program. An ad will be generated suggesting that others who purchased a certain book have also purchased these titles. Several suggestions are made based on combinations of purchases of other customers.

Behavioral targeting takes place in seconds without a person even realizing it has occurred. Algorithms can be written to trigger these ads as the page loads. The brand being advertised may rotate or change based on the bidding process for display advertising.

Blogs and Newsletters

Blogs are online musings that cover a wide range of topics. Some permit visitors to post comments; others do not. Company-sponsored blogs can emulate word-of-mouth communication and engage customers with a brand. Fashion retailers entice customers to visit the company's blog to enjoy postings on new styles, upcoming designers, and fashion *faux pas*. In the past, customers may have relied on magazines such as *Vogue* for fashion news. Company blogs allow them to obtain information quicker, and, more important, interactively. This makes it possible for the marketing team to engage with customers and establishes a two-way communication channel.

A company-sponsored blog provides a number of potential benefits; however, analysts stress the importance of identifying a specific reason for the blog before launching it. The goal may be to make the company more open (Dell), to humanize the organization (Microsoft), or to show a fun and happy company (Southwest Airlines).[23] When Coca-Cola acquired 40 percent of Honest Tea, many customers became unhappy about the move and voiced opinions on the Honest Tea blog. Seth Goldman, CEO of Honest Tea, answered each one. While some customers still did not like the idea, "The blog at least helps people see how we think about it," Goldman said.[24]

Company managers carefully respond to negative customer comments. About 20 percent of the blog's readership consists of employees. Marriott employees monitor the comment section. No comment will be posted until it has been approved. The company does not remove comments simply because they are negative. Only those not germane to the discussion or blog are taken down. Those remaining are left up and addressed by Bill Marriott, which provides credibility to the blog through his willingness to listen to negative feedback.

For small businesses, blogs provide a relatively inexpensive way to communicate with customers. Robb Duncan began a blog for his Georgetown gelato shop, Dolcezza. When a second store was opened in Bethesda, Maryland, he announced an ice cream giveaway on opening night through the blog. More than 1,000 individuals showed up.[25]

The Thrillist (**thrillist.com**) and UrbanDaddy (**urbandaddy.com**) websites take advantage of the power that newsletters provide. Companies send newsletters via email to approximately 1.1 million subscribers. Most subscribers are college graduates with median incomes of $88,000. The UrbanDaddy newsletter emphasizes an exclusive and luxurious approach, advising men about where to shop and how to fit in. The Thrillist newsletter features a fun and relaxed tone. Both sites organize free, heavily sponsored events for newsletter subscribers. The newsletter engages the subscribers with the websites.[26]

Blogs and newsletters follow the same principles as those pertaining to content marketing. They provide useful information and present solutions to consumer problems. Authentic messages offering something individuals want to share receive more positive attention. Marketers integrate them with the brand's web content, search strategy, and social media outreach.

Effective blogs and newsletters are consistently updated. For blogs, this normally involves entries three times per week. For newsletters, publication frequency depends on the industry, content, target audience, and purpose of the newsletter. At a minimum, marketers should add new materials once each month. A lower frequency sends the message that the company does not have anything interesting or new to provide. It also conveys the hidden message of, "We are doing this only to get your business, to increase sales."

▲ Blogs and newsletters can be used effectively by fashion retailers to engage customers with the store.

Email Marketing

Email can be a vital part of a company's digital marketing strategy. To achieve success, companies integrate email marketing programs with other channels. It cannot simply be a program where marketers purchase addresses and send mass emails to individuals on the list. Most people resent spam, and response rates are extremely low, in addition to damaging the brand's reputation.

Response rates increase when an email message resembles the information presented on the company's website and in its advertisements and direct mail messages. When Data Inc. introduced new project management software, the marketing team integrated email with its webinar, direct mail, social media, and telemarketing programs. The webinar explained how the new software tool worked. Direct mail, telemarketing, and email were used to reach 600 influential decision makers. For emails that were returned undeliverable, Data, Inc. used LinkedIn to locate the contact's correct information. The email-integrated approach resulted in a three percent response rate.[27]

In designing email campaigns, marketers try make them mobile-friendly, because 68 percent of all emails are now opened on a mobile device.[28] Segmentation of email lists is essential and greatly improves open rates and click-through rates. With a segmented list, marketers can set up automated campaigns, called drip campaigns, that transmit emails with specific content at specified times. Figure 8.11 identifies some common as well as newer, trendy email tactics.

Web analytics are used to develop behavior-targeted email campaigns. Emails will be based on the browsing history of an individual on a particular website or over multiple sites that were visited. The email highlights products and brands based on the previous website visits. Demographics help segment the mailing list, although they will not be as effective as the other email segmentation approaches.

Email campaigns may be directed at consumers who abandon shopping carts without making purchases. The IT department identifies individuals who abandon shopping baskets. Sending an email to them offering free shipping, a discount if they complete the order; or a simple reminder that they have items in their shopping basket can lead to greater sales. Converting these individuals to customers can be lucrative. Targeted emails experience a conversion rate five to ten times higher than mass emails sent to the firm's customers. In addition, revenues from these follow-up emails are three to nine times higher than other approaches.[29]

- Behavior targeting
  - Browsing history
  - Demographics
  - Abandoned shopping carts
  - Past-purchases
- Dynamic web cropping
- Event targeting
- Weather targeting
- Geo-targeting

▲ **FIGURE 8.11**
Email Marketing Tactics

▼ Target emails can be used to contact individuals who abandon shopping carts without making a purchase.

Companies set up drip campaigns for customers who have made purchases. Scheduled messages can be sent 30 days, 60 days, or 90 days after a purchase. The content of the emails should match previously purchased products and brands. Offering complimentary products might spur another visit. An individual that purchased a 35mm camera can be sent an email 30 days after the purchase that highlights related products, such as special lenses, tripods, and carrying cases. The company may encourage the individual to submit her photos to one a social media sites , such as Instagram or Pinterest.

Digital technology allows for email campaigns featuring dynamic web content. With this process, marketers include a live snippet of content from a website in the email. The content can be changed each time the person opens the email. It may be to present a sale, special graphics, unique photos, or new merchandise.

Marketers send event-targeting emails to those who might attend a specific occasion. For hunters, it could be based on opening of various seasons, such as deer season for bow-and-arrow enthusiasts and then later for those who use guns. For fashion, it could be based on the arrival of new fashions, or the change of seasons from winter clothes to spring, for instance. The event and the manner in which the email will be segmented is based on each person's browsing and purchase history.

A newer email tactic involves weather-targeting. With GPS and location indicators on mobile phones, companies tie the weather to an automated drip campaign. For instance, Starbucks could send an email to individuals who live in the Northeast during snowstorms. People in the West and South would not receive the message. A rainy day in Texas would trigger emails for umbrellas, rain gear, or rain boots. In each case, the content of the email matches the weather event based on the geo-location of the mobile phone.

Individuals can be sent emails based on geo-targeting techniques. For a retail store or service business, a link to a map is included in the email. A tap on the map ties it to the mobile phone's GPS system that then transmits driving or walking instructions. A call-to-action button indicates that a tap will dial the business.

In Figure 8.12 Holly Betts, an email expert with Slingshot, offers several suggestions for developing successful campaigns. It starts with individuals opting-in to the program. She emphasizes being upfront and honest with subscribers. Companies should tell recipients what they can expect, when they can expect it, and then deliver on those promises. As with branded content, emails should offer subscribers something useful that meets their needs or interests.

Marketing professionals make sure all emails are sent from the same source. The subscriber instantly recognizes the source and understands it is an email she gave permission to receive. The messages should be short, neat, and eye-catching. They can include links to all of the brand's social media outlets. Email advertisers should test every campaign and keep records of what worked and what did not. This information makes it possible to build a file of best practices based on previous results.

In summary, mobile devices offer a number of marketing opportunities. These strategies presented are not unique to mobile devices; they can also be used for desktop and laptop computers. The delivery method will be different, but the strategies remain

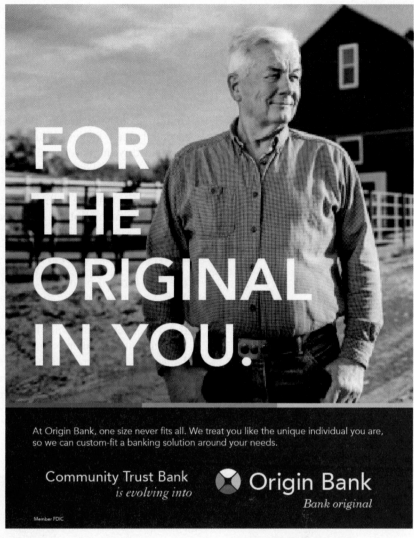

▲ Origin Bank can use digital technology to develop email campaigns directed to individuals who have visited the retailer's website.

- Be upfront, honest with subscribers
- Build list for quality, not quantity
- Give subscribers what they want
- Be familiar to your audience
- Keep e-mails neat and clean
- Be eye-catching
- Integrate social media
- Test, test and test

◀ **FIGURE 8.12**
Developing Successful Email Campaigns

the same. The two unique marketing approaches not feasible with desktop and laptop computers are mobile apps and action codes (such as QR codes, watermarks, and 2D barcodes).

Web Advertising

objective 8.6
What types of web advertising can companies use to reach consumers?

Online advertising presents a highly effective method for reaching today's consumers, especially the younger, affluent, and internet-savvy market. Budgets for online advertising have steadily increased and now exceed $500 billion annually. Online advertising is the fastest-growing medium with annual growth rates exceeding 20 percent. Part of the growth has been fueled by multiscreen advertising, which involves media buys across the various platforms such as the web, mobile, and tablets.[30] Figure 8.13 indicates the percentage of online advertising dollars allocated to each of the primary formats.

Banner Advertising

The first form of online advertising involved the use of a display, or banner, ad. In 1994, AT& T ran one carrying the message "Have you ever clicked your mouse right here? You will." This basic form of advertising generated billions of dollars in advertising revenues. Today, banner ads account for 22.6 percent of online advertising.[31]

Currently, marketers embed banner ads with videos, widget applications, or targeted display ads that increase the chances viewers will see and click the icon. The newest online technology, which has been taken from paid search auction systems, allows advertisers to display a banner ad only to individuals the company chooses. The system is built on a

▶ **FIGURE 8.13**
U.S. Online Ad Spend by Format

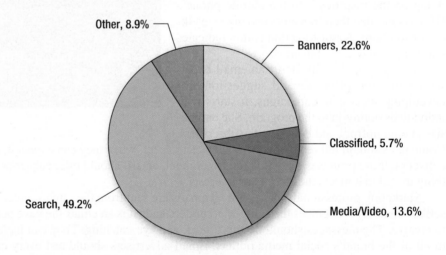

Other, 8.9%
Banners, 22.6%
Classified, 5.7%
Media/Video, 13.6%
Search, 49.2%

▼ A banner ad for Ouachita Independent Bank.

Reward. Reward Plus!

OB OUACHITA INDEPENDENT BANK

NOW MOBILE!

High Interest Checking PLUS Savings!
www.oibank.com
MEMBER FDIC

vast warehouse of user internet data and automated auction advertising exchanges such as Google's Double-Click, Yahoo!'s Right Media ad exchange, and Microsoft's AdECN. Advertisers develop messages for specific audiences.

When a consumer, such as a 20- to 25-year-old female, accesses a website featuring paid search auction technology, in a microsecond the software searches the auction exchange for advertisers that match the profile of the individual who logged onto the page, or that individual's browsing history. Once an advertiser has been located, a banner ad instantly flashes on the computer screen. It may be an advertisement for L'Oréal or Liz Claiborne. If a male with an interest in cross-training logs on, an advertisement for specialized shoes or sports apparel may appear. The automated exchange system grants precise targeting of ads to specific consumers.[32]

Widgets   Mini-applications embedded in a banner ad, or **widgets**, enable a consumer access to some form of dynamic content provided by an external source other than the company where the ad resides. Widgets provide individuals personalized access to web information or functionality from any device connected to the internet.

Boxcar Creative developed a widget application for ConocoPhillips using rich media expandable banners to create interactive polls, fun facts, and a carbon calculator. The poll and the calculator both collected and produced results without the user ever leaving the banner advertisement. When an individual clicked "learn more," she was taken to a microsite landing page with additional content and data collection opportunities.

Location-based widgets can be placed in banner ads. These ads only appear to those individuals who log on to a website in a particular region. The technology can be ideal for retailers, restaurants, and smaller businesses seeking to reach a specific region around a retail outlet.

Impact of Online Advertising

As more dollars shift to online advertising, concerns have arisen about the impact of the ads. Web users, just like television viewers, are becoming immune to advertisements. The percentage of people who respond to banner ads steadily shrinks. The click-through rate on major web destinations has declined to less than one percent. A recent measurement resulted in a response rate of 0.27 percent.[33]

To improve response rates, advertisers have created increasingly complex targeting campaigns that utilize various web metrics. MediaMind survey results indicate that the number of digital ads with two or more third-party tags increased 267 percent over the last two years. These third-party tags track items such as ad interactions, brand impact, and browsing behavior in order to optimize a campaign. Brands that utilize geo-targeting, behavioral targeting, and third-party demographic data tend to have the most tags attached to the ads.[34]

According to comScore Inc., 54 percent of display ads on thousands of websites were not seen. That means almost $6 billion in display advertisements were wasted. Technical issues cause some of the problems, such as the ad appearing below the fold on a screen. The "below the fold" term describes the part a website that is not visible on a computer or smartphone screen that can only be seen by scrolling down. Unless the individual scrolls down the website, the ad will not be viewed. Another technical problem occurs when the ad loads so slowly that the web visitor either switches off the ad or goes to another site. Blocking software also prevents web ads from being visible. An increasing number of consumers have purchased software that blocks all forms of advertising. This is true especially for tech-savvy individuals.[35]

◀ A Scott Equipment banner ad with a call-to-action "Learn More" icon.

The final reason for ads not being seen is fraud, which costs advertisers between $7 billion and $18 billion annually.[36] A significant number of ad impressions that brands pay for are never seen because the impressions are based on fake traffic. Malicious software devices, called bots, are computer programs that simulate real people on the internet. They mimic human activity to generate ad dollars from digital advertisers. With mobile phones, zombie apps infect a mobile phone and run constantly in the background. The mobile phone user has no idea the zombie app is running and currently it cannot be detected by antivirus software. Just like bots, zombie apps create the impression that individuals are engaging with various types of mobile apps. Even if the person turns off his phone, the zombie apps continue to run.

The diminishing impact of online advertising and the high percentage of ads that are never viewed have led many advertisers to bank on new technologies designed to increase response rates and detect fraud. Advertisers also spend more time and dollars in planning integrated campaigns that incorporate digital advertising with social media and traditional advertising.

Offline Advertising

To build a brand's reputation and brand loyalty, online advertising should be integrated with offline branding tactics that reinforce each other to speak with one voice. This process, **brand spiraling**, features traditional media to promote and attract consumers to a website. Marketers design television, radio, newspapers, magazines, and billboards encouraging consumers to visit the firm's website. Marketers seek to maintain a uniform brand presence and advertising message in brand spiraling programs.

▼ Off-line advertising is an important part of building an online presence for brands, such as JD Bank.

A recent study indicates that, after viewing a magazine advertisement, nearly half of the consumers polled said they might go to a website or conduct an online search for the product. More than 40 percent were more inclined to visit a website after seeing a television or newspaper advertisement.[37] Traditional media can be the driving force behind online branding efforts.

Currently, tailor-made websites accompany many direct and email campaigns. These sites are accessed through **personalized URLs**, called **PURLs**, such as the hypothetical **www.kenclow.offer.officedepot.com**. A PURL contains a personalized preloaded web page that contains the customer's personal data, contact information, purchase behavior, and previous interactions with the company. A company such as Ford could display the customer's current vehicle, maintenance record, and other interactions with the company. The PURL creates a one-on-one dialogue with a customer and engages her with the company and provides messages, offers, and incentives tailored to her past data and history.[38]

Search Engine Optimization (SEO)

In terms of online expenditures, marketers spend the greatest amounts for spots on search engines. Funds devoted to search engines constitute nearly 50 percent of online advertising expenditures. About 80 percent of web traffic begins at a search engine.[39] Therefore, making sure that a company's name or brand becomes one of the first ones listed when a person performs a search becomes a key marketing goal. **SEO**, or **search engine optimization**, is the process of increasing the probability of a particular company's website emerging from a search.

Optimization can be achieved in one of three ways. First, a *paid search insertion* comes up when certain products or information are sought. Companies can speed this process by registering with various search engines in order to have the site indexed and by paying a higher placement fee for top positions. The placement of the ad on a search page depends on the price the company pays and the algorithm a search engine uses to determine the advertisement's relevance to a particular search word or phrase. Most search engines now indicate these results with a small "ad" icon by the search results showing it is a paid search result.

Second, a company can increase identification via the *natural* or *organic emergence* of the site. This method involves developing efficient and effective organic results that arise from a natural search process. Each search engine uses a slightly different set of algorithms to identify key phrases that match what was typed into the search box. To be listed first in an organic search requires time and effort. Normally, a new website will probably not emerge at the top of the search results. It takes time for the search engine to locate the site.

Some studies suggest that the impact of organic listings can be impressive. For sites that come up on the first page of a search or within the top ten, web traffic increases nine-fold. For second- and third-page listings, web traffic increases six-fold. In terms of sales, being a top-ten listing has resulted in a 42 percent increase in sales the first month and a 100 percent increase the second month.[40]

The third optimization method, *paid search ads*, includes text boxes or display ads that pop up when a particular word is typed in. A comScore study suggests that search ads have a strong positive impact on brand awareness, perception, and purchase intentions—even

objective 8.7
What is a search engine optimization strategy?

▼ Search engine optimization is a significant component of Visit South Walton's marketing outreach.

BRING A BOOK
BUT WRITE YOUR OWN STORY.

when consumers do not click the paid search ad.[41] The study revealed that for brands in the top search positions:

- The paid search ads generated a 160 percent increase in unaided awareness.
- Consumers were 20 percent more likely to have a positive perception of the brands.
- Consumers were 30 percent more likely to consider purchasing the brand.

Companies spend large amounts on search engine optimization. The typical click-through rate for online advertising remains around 0.2 percent; for search advertising, it is around 5 percent.[42] Although the early results are impressive, marketers should remember that search engine optimization represents a long-term investment. The effects do not occur quickly. Moving to the top ten listings of a search can take months or years. It requires optimizing content, programming, and understanding how search engines work.

Search ads can be effective for local businesses. Barbara Oliver owns a boutique jewelry store in Williamsville, New York. She spent $50 per month in Google search ads targeted to an 80-mile radius of her store. It resulted in more customers than all of her offline advertising. With Google Places local directory, someone typing in the keywords designated by Oliver within an 80-mile radius of Williamsville was likely to see the search ad. Its effectiveness can be enhanced by smartphones and their GPS capabilities as well as Facebook and Foursquare where people sign in with their locations, which means visitors to the Williamsville area may see Oliver's search ad.[43]

International Implications

objective 8.8

How can companies successfully conduct digital marketing programs in international markets?

The ability to reach customers worldwide constitutes one of the major advantages that e-commerce holds over brick-and-mortar retail stores. Some online companies are still forced to turn away international orders because they do not have processes in place to fill them. This means that while the internet makes it possible to sell items in an international marketplace, some companies are not prepared to go global. Obstacles to selling across national boundaries include global shipping problems due to a lack of sufficient structure, communication barriers, and other technological barriers.[44] Also, internet companies must follow local exporting and importing laws.

Shipping Issues

One key to the effective launch of a global e-commerce site is preparing for international shipments. Air transport may be affordable for smaller products; DHL Worldwide Express, FedEx, and UPS offer excellent shipping options. Larger merchandise normally can be shipped by a freight forwarder that finds the best mode of delivery, from ships to trucks to rail. Air transport companies and freight forwarders both offer specialized logistics software and provide the proper documentation and forms to meet importing and exporting regulations in every country served.

Communication Issues

Developing a website that appeals to the audience in each country will be a key task. It includes adding information that someone in another country would require, such as the country code for telephone numbers. It also requires removing or changing colors, words, or images that might offend a particular group of people in another country.

New globalization software has been developed for companies expanding into other countries. One software package translates an English-language website into a large number of foreign languages. Another valuable feature that the software offers is "cultural adaptation," which adjusts a website's terminology, look, and feel to suit local norms. The software also has a feature in which the content developed in one location can easily be deployed to all sites around the world. This provides a more consistent look to the websites, without someone spending time modifying each foreign site. The software makes it easier to prepare a website in the proper native language and conform to local customs.[45]

Technology Issues

The technical side of international e-commerce continues to be challenging. Software compatibility continues to present unresolved technical issues. Ideally, these various technologies will eventually be merged into a single system. Currently, the bandwidth for handling internet traffic varies considerably. Information technology staff members are involved in every step of an internationalization process in order to overcome the potential technical glitches.

A coherent IMC strategy utilizes local input from the various countries involved. The brand on an internet site should stay consistent from one country to the next and present the company's primary marketing message. For IBM, this means hiring local companies in each country to design individual websites and providing the information to be used on each site. To ensure consistency, IBM designs the main marketing messages at its central office, but then local companies translate the messages and add reseller contact and pricing information.

In the future, the growth of international e-commerce will continue to rise. Firms that get in on the ground floor are likely to enjoy a major marketing advantage.

Summary

Digital marketing includes anything with a digital footprint. An effective IMC program incorporates these new elements into the advertising and promotions plan. The transition from Web 1.0 to Web 4.0 changed the ways in which consumers communicate and interact with companies through engagement programs, cloud operations, and web participation.

E-commerce programs continue to grow. Firms seek the best position in search engine postings by utilizing customer-centric designs. Adaptive design systems adjust content to fit all forms of devices and to achieve consistent customer experiences through channel integration. Brand engagement represents a primary objective. To combat shopping cart abandonment, three incentives help people alter buying patterns—financial incentives, greater convenience, and added value. E-commerce programs require offline integration.

Mobile marketing programs take advantage of current technologies, leading to two-way communications with consumers. Digital strategies incorporate multiscreen formats. Interactive marketing is the development of marketing programs that create interplay between customers and businesses. Content marketing can be used to provide useful information and product-use solutions to customers. Native advertising provides useful information that solves a problem by purchasing a company's product or service. Location-based advertising, or geo-targeting, involves reaching customers where they are located by contacting their mobile communication devices. Remarketing re-engages individuals who have visited a site but did not make a purchase, enticing them to reconsider and buy the item. Behavioral targeting utilizes web data to identify the individuals who are most likely to purchase an item. Customer engagement also takes place through the distribution of blogs and newsletters. Blogs, whether company-sponsored or posted by individual internet users, create a new form of word-of-mouth advertising. Email further supplements an integrated program using various tactics.

Online web advertising reaches younger, more internet-savvy consumers. It includes banner advertising and widgets, and its impact continues to grow. Offline advertising can be used to build a brand's reputation and brand loyalty. Brand spiraling may be used to combine the internet program with advertising in traditional media. Tailor-made websites accompany many direct and email campaigns using personalized URLs or PURLs.

Search engine optimization (SEO) is the process of increasing the probability of a particular company's website emerging from a search. Paid search insertions, natural or organic emergence, and paid search ads can help achieve this goal.

International markets may also be served by e-commerce enterprises, especially when cultural differences, shipping problems, and internet capability problems can be solved. Information technology departments play a key role in solving internet problems. Shipping issues and language differences also require attention in this lucrative and growing marketplace.

Key Terms

digital marketing Marketing that incorporates the components of e-commerce, internet marketing, and mobile marketing

e-commerce Selling goods and services on the internet

search engine results page (SERP) The place where a website appears on a search engine

adaptive design A process that adjusts content to the screen size of a device used to access a webpage

cyberbait A type of lure or attraction that brings people to a website

interactive marketing The development of marketing programs that create interplay between consumers and businesses

content marketing (or *branded content*) Providing useful information and product use solutions to potential customers

native advertising Web materials that appear on a hosted website providing useful information that solves a problem in which the solution depends on purchasing a specific product

geo-targeting Advertising designed to reach customers where they are located based on contacting their mobile communication devices

remarketing A program that re-engages individuals who have visited a site but did not make purchases

behavioral targeting Using web data to identify and target individuals most likely to purchase an item

blogs The online musings of an individual or group; the term is derived from "web logs"

widgets Mini-applications embedded in a banner ad that permit a consumer access to some form of dynamic content provided by an external source other than the company where the ad resides

brand spiraling The practice of using traditional media to promote and attract consumers to a website

personalized URLs (PURLs) A personalized web page preloaded with the customer's personal data, contact information, purchase behavior, and previous interactions with the company

search engine optimization (SEO) The process of increasing the probability of a particular company's website emerging from a search

---

MyMarketingLab

To complete the problems with the ⭐ in your MyLab, go to the end-of-chapter Discussion Questions.

Review Questions

8-1. Define digital marketing.

8-2. How has Web 4.0 influenced the field of marketing?

8-3. Describe e-commerce, search-optimized design, and customer-centric design.

8-4. What is cyberbait? What are the three main forms of cyberbait?

8-5. What is adaptive design?

8-6. What is mobile marketing?

8-7. What is interactive marketing?

8-8. Describe content marketing and native advertising.

8-9. What is geo-targeting, or location-based advertising?

8-10. What is remarketing?

8-11. What is behavioral targeting?

8-12. How are blogs and newsletters used in marketing programs?

8-13. Identify and describe the elements of an effective email campaign in marketing.

8-14. What primary forms of online or web advertising are used by marketing teams?

8-15. What is a widget?

8-16. What is brand spiraling?

8-17. What is a personalized URL or PURL?

8-18. What is meant by the term search engine optimization (SEO)? How can it be accomplished?

⭐**8-19.** What challenges must be overcome to establish an international e-commerce operation?

Critical Thinking Exercises

DISCUSSION QUESTIONS

8-20. Examine the characteristics of Web 1.0 to Web 4.0. Discuss how the internet affects your daily life. Interview individuals in each of the following age categories about their use of the internet: 30–39, 40–59, 60+. Relate their conversations to Web 1.0, Web 2.0, Web 3.0, and Web 4.0.

8-21. Examine the value-added incentives listed in Figure 8.5 and described in this chapter. Rank these value-added incentives in terms of your personal online shopping experience. For each incentive, discuss its impact on your shopping behavior and explain why it is important to you or not important.

8-22. Mobile marketing has become an important component of digital marketing campaigns. Assume you are a marketing intern for a local book, comic, and video store. Describe how you could use mobile marketing to drive website visits as well as store visits. Be specific in your ideas.

8-23. Look through the digital marketing strategies identified in Figure 8.7. Discuss each strategy as it relates to your online experience. Which strategies are the most successful at reaching you? Why? Which are the least effective? Why?

8-24. Describe in your own words each of the digital marketing strategies listed in Figure 8.8. Assume you are an intern working in the digital marketing department of a small chain of sporting goods stores in the South. Describe how you could use each of the digital marketing strategies in a digital marketing campaign. Be specific.

8-25. Do you have any apps on your cell phone? If so, describe the apps you have and why you downloaded the app? Is any advertising connected with the app? What are your thoughts about apps that utilize some type of advertising?

8-26. Interview three individuals of different ages about blogs. What percent have read, launched, or participated in blogging on the internet? What was each person's motivation? What is your experience with blogs? If you have never read or contributed to a blog, why not?

8-27. Describe in your own words each of the email marketing tactics presented in Figure 8.11. Assume you are a marketing intern for a small chain of trendy, upscale clothing stores targeted towards professional females, ages 25 to 40. Discuss how you could use each of the email marketing tactics. Be specific in terms of reaching the clothing stores' target audience.

Integrated Learning Exercises

8-28. Best Buy was a late e-commerce entrant, but now has a strong e-commerce component. The key to Best Buy's success, according to Barry Judge, vice president of marketing, is, "We do a lot of one-to-one marketing. We're not overly focused on where the consumers buy." The website carries every product that Best Buy stocks. It offers personalized services, along with convenient pick-up and fair return policies to entice consumers to shop. Consumers can purchase items on the internet and either have them shipped directly to them or pick them up at the closest store. Shoppers can use the internet to see if Best Buy stocks a particular item, to determine what the item costs, and to gather product information. What is the advantage of this strategy? Access the website at **www.bestbuy.com**. Evaluate it in terms of ease of use and product information, and then locate the Best Buy closest to you. Next, access Tiger Direct's website at **www.tigerdirect.com**. Compare it to Best Buy's site. Select a product, such as a big screen television, to compare the two websites.

8-29. Pick one of the following product categories and access the websites of two companies that sell the product. What types of financial incentives are offered on each company's website to encourage you to purchase? What about the other two types of incentives, greater convenience and added value? What evidence do you see for them? Compare and contrast the two companies in terms of incentives offered. Provide the URLs of the two websites and screenshots to illustrate your examples.

   a. Contacts or eyeglasses

   b. Water skis

   c. Camping supplies

   d. Cameras

8-30. Choose two of the following e-commerce sites. Discuss each of the characteristics of successful e-commerce sites listed in Figure 8.3. Compare and contrast the two sites for each of the characteristics and use screenshots to illustrate your evaluations.

   a. Travelocity (**www.travelocity.com**)

   b. Wells Fargo Bank (**www.wellsfargo.com**)

   c. The Knot (**www.theknot.com**)

   d. Bluefly (**www.bluefly.com**)

e. Diesel (**www.diesel.com**)

f. Quiznos (**www.quiznos.com**)

⭐**8-31.** Go to one of your favorite e-commerce sites. If you do not have a favorite, do a search and pick one that looks good to you. Provide the URL of the e-commerce site; then discuss each of the characteristics of a successful e-commerce site listed in Figure 8.3 as it relates to the site you picked. Use screenshots to illustrate your points.

⭐**8-32.** Locate the website of a local lawn service in your area. Provide the URL and a screenshot of the website. In your own words, describe the differences between branded content, sponsored content, and native advertising. Discuss how the lawn service could use branded content. What type of articles should the owner write? Using a search engine, locate two other websites that would be good for sponsored content. Provide the URLs and discuss why you think each of those sites would be good for sponsored content. How could the lawn service use native advertising? Be specific.

8-33. Blogs provide opportunities for individuals and businesses to share information, thoughts, and opinions. Go to **www.blogsearchengine.org**. Type in a topic you are interested in that is related to advertising and marketing communications, such as "advertising to children." Locate three blogs on the topic you chose. Discuss who initiated the blog and the value of the information on the blog. Provide screenshots of your search results page and the landing page of each blog you access.

8-34. Access each of the following search engines. For each one, discuss how it handles paid search advertising when you type in a search term such as "running shoes." Instead of "running shoes" you can type in another search term that interests you. What ads do you see as display ads, text ads and organic search results? Discuss the differences among the four search engines. Which one do you like the best? Why? Be sure to make screenshots of your original search results.

a. Google (**www.google.com**)

b. Yahoo! (**www.yahoo.com**)

c. AOL Search (**search.aol.com**)

d. Bing (**www.bing.com**)

⭐**8-35.** A high percentage of internet traffic begins with someone conducting a search. Compare and contrast the concepts of paid search insertions, organic search results, and paid search ads from the perspective of a consumer wanting to locate websites that provide information and products on camping. Compare and contrast paid search insertions, organic search, and paid search ads from the viewpoint of Coleman, a company that sells camping supplies and equipment.

8-36. Use a search engine to locate three digital advertising agencies. For each agency, describe what type of digital marketing services the agency provides. If you owned a small restaurant chain, which agency would you hire for your digital marketing program? Why? (Provide the URL for each agency in your response as well as pertinent screenshots.)

8-37. Access the internet and locate four banner ads. Copy and paste the banner ads in a Word document. Evaluate each banner ad in terms of design and appeal. Access the landing page of each banner ad by clicking on it. Provide a screenshot of the landing page and discuss each landing page. Of the four banner ads, which yielded the best results in terms of providing useful information on the landing page? Why?

Blog Exercises

Access the authors' blog for this textbook at the URLs provided to complete these exercises. Answer the questions that are posed on the blog.

8-38. Advil **blogclowbaack.net/2014/05/12/advil-chapter-8/**

8-39. Digital Marketing Strategies **blogclowbaack.net/2014/05/12/digital-marketing-strategies-chapter-8/**

8-40. Search Engine Optimization **blogclowbaack.net/2014/05/12/seo-chapter-8/**

Student Project

CREATIVE CORNER

Bluefly's marketing team wants to enhance the company's brand name and internet presence. They have asked you to be an internet advertising consultant. Access the Bluefly website at **www.bluefly.com**. Once you feel comfortable with the company, prepare a banner ad that can be used on the internet. Design a magazine ad that can be used with the banner advertisement. Then, design an email promotion that can be sent to customers who purchased from **Bluefly.com**, but it has been at least 90 days since that purchase.

CASE 1 SKI AND SNOWBOARD SPECIALISTS

Snow skiing and snowboarding remain popular hobbies. More than 10 million people in the United States participate in the activities each year. Ski resorts can be found across the country. The marketplace for equipment continues to grow.

Ski and Snowboard Specialists offers a wide variety of equipment combined with connections to numerous resorts nationwide. Enthusiasts can shop online for skis, poles, snowboards, masks, clothing, and other gear and, at the same time, receive access to information about which areas have the best current conditions combined with discount offers for lodging, lifts, and other accommodations.

Considerable competition exists for both equipment and informational/booking services. Ski and Snowboard Specialists sells products from the major manufacturers of equipment as they compete with local sports equipment stores and the lodges themselves. Travel agencies and other groups offer booking services.

In the midst of this clutter, the marketing team believes the key to future success will rely on continuing engagement with those who have taken advantage of the reasonable prices the company offers for equipment and the convenience provided by the booking side of the business. The company's primary website can be combined with mobile marketing and other new marketing techniques to entice new visitors while building loyalty with returning customers.

To help achieve these overall objectives, the marketing team has established relationships with two professional skiers who serve as instructors at popular resorts. One is located in Colorado and the other in Maine. These individuals and their resorts regularly provide advice about all aspects of the two sports.

Ski and Snowboard Specialists' marketers have recently hired a major national advertising agency to assist in all aspects of the firm's promotional efforts. The goal is to cast a wide net to attract and keep as many new clients as possible.

▲ Ski and Snowboard Specialists offers a wide variety of equipment combined with connections to numerous resorts nationwide.

8-41. What roles might mobile marketing and interactive marketing play in Ski and Snowboard Specialists' efforts?

8-42. How can Ski and Snowboard Specialists offer cyberbait to new customers? To returning customers?

8-43. Explain how the company could take advantage of content marketing and/or native advertising.

8-44. Discuss how location-based advertising could be featured by Ski and Snowboard Specialists.

8-45. Explain how remarketing and behavioral targeting could help increase sales for Ski and Snowboard Specialists.

8-46. Would a blog be useful for Ski and Snowboard Specialists? If so, how? If not, why not?

8-47. Describe the tactics you would use to make the best use of search engine optimization for Ski and Snowboard Specialists.

CASE 2 RUNZA RESTAURANTS

Ethnic foods enjoy a unique place in the dining habits of people around the world. In the United States, one such treat goes by a variety of names and has an unusual heritage. The *runza* (one of the more common names) refers to a sandwich called a *bierock* or *bieroc* in Kansas or a *fleischkuechle* or *kraut priok* in other places. In essence, the sandwich consists of beef, pork, cabbage or sauerkraut, onions, and seasonings loaded into a doughy form of bread.

Various forms of runzas were first devoured in Russia according to some sources; although those are disputed, because others believe the heritage begins in Germany. In either case, family-kept recipes eventually moved to the United States and Canada. Areas in which the sandwich is most popular in the United States include North and South Dakota, Michigan, Wisconsin, Illinois, Oklahoma, and probably most notably in Kansas and Nebraska. In Kansas, the food normally will be served in a round or half-moon shaped bun; in Nebraska, the sandwich tends to be rectangular, even though other versions (square, triangular) are also used.

Perhaps the reason Nebraska may be most associated with the sandwich is that the state features the largest chain of restaurants serving the item: Runza. The chain houses the majority of its outlets in Nebraska (where the first unit was opened), Kansas,

Missouri, Wyoming, Iowa, and Colorado. Currently, the Runza chain has begun opening franchise operations in numerous additional states.

A standard Runza menu includes the "Original Runza," along with a variety of new options using the same basic bun structure. Stores also sell burgers that come from fresh beef, chicken sandwiches, kid's meals, desserts, corn dog "nuggets," and homemade onion rings and crinkle-cut fries. Runza Restaurants feature a distinctive green and yellow logo. The colors appear on all cups, packages, bags, and other elements of the operation.

While Runza Restaurants would probably be considered a form of fast food, the chain differentiates itself from other sandwich and burger chains through the distinctive lead food item. This helps maintain a difference between a Runza location and McDonald's, Burger King, Wendy's, Subway, and Schlotzsky's.

In 1999, the Runza organization celebrated its 50th anniversary with a two-day block party in downtown Lincoln, Nebraska, complete with an appearance by Runza Rex®, the company's dinosaur-like mascot. Soon after, the chain signed a 10-year pact with the University of Nebraska athletic program.

Recently, new items have been added to the menu, including the Spicy Jack, which was chosen by Facebook followers in a contest containing other sandwich entrants. The organization

maintains relationships with Great Books for Great Kids and seeks to maintain a positive image in every community it serves.[46]

8-48. Access Runza Restaurant's website at **www.runza.com**. Describe the content on the site. Examine the characteristics of successful e-commerce sites given in the chapter. Discuss each characteristic as it relates to Runza's website. What is your overall evaluation of the website?

8-49. What types of cyberbaits do you see on the Runza website? Give specific examples of each.

8-50. Explain how the Runza Restaurant could use mobile marketing. Provide details.

8-51. Discuss how location-based advertising could be valuable to an individual Runza Restaurant manager. Which form of geo-targeting would you use? Why?

8-52. Explain how behavioral targeting would be useful to an individual Runza Restaurant manager. Design a behavioral targeting program that could be used by Runza.

8-53. Design a banner ad for Runza Restaurants.

8-54. Examine Runza's website again. Make a list of ten words that could be used for a search engine optimization program. Rank the words in order from what you think would be the best search terms to the least attractive. Justify your list and ranking.

MyMarketingLab

Go to the Assignments section of your MyLab to complete these writing exercises.

8-55. Define each of the email marketing tactics presented in this chapter. Access the website of Calvin Klein (**www.calvinklein. com**). For each email marketing tactic, describe an email marketing campaign that could be used by Calvin Klein. Identify the specific target audience and the manner in which Calvin Klein could use the tactic.

8-56. Blogs provide an opportunity for businesses to share information, thoughts, and opinions. Identify the benefits of a company blog for the business and for its customers. Discuss the ingredients for creating a successful company blog.

Chapter 9 Social Media

Chapter Objectives

After reading this chapter, you should be able to answer the following questions:

9.1 What constitutes a social network?

9.2 What unique characteristics are parts of primary social media websites?

9.3 What is the nature of social media marketing?

9.4 Which social media marketing strategies do companies employ?

9.5 How can marketers use social media strategies in international operations?

Overview

The emergence of social media networks altered the ways individuals interact with families, friends, businesses, and even strangers. The continual growth of social media presents opportunities and challenges to marketing departments from the smallest single family business to major corporations. Instant communication creates the potential to generate buzz and excitement. Marketers can develop more sophisticated interactions with customers. At the same time, negative word of mouth damages a brand across a wide range of customers and the general public. Marketing communications experts understand the need to adapt to this exciting new world. Wholly Guacamole has been able to benefit from the possibilities that social media networks offer.

WHOLLY GUACAMOLE

▲ Guacamole has become a staple for many individuals to use on sandwiches.

The biggest problem with an avocado may be that, as soon as one is cut open, it begins to brown. Wholly Guacamole's founder, Don Bowden, sought to solve this problem. He discovered the process of High Pressure Processing, which he marketed as "fresherized" guacamole. It results in a "100% all natural, fresh tasting product." Pre-made guacamole can be sold in grocery stores and in food markets. It has become a staple for many companies featuring the ingredient in sandwiches and other menu items. Wholly Guacamole's website indicates that, "We always use real Hass avocados and natural ingredients that never include preservatives (except Wholly Salsa Avocado Verde Dip), artificial flavoring or fillers."[1]

Wholly Guacamole's marketing team understands the potential impact of social media. The company successfully leveraged it to create brand awareness, develop a strong brand, and boost sales. While social media played a significant role in several campaigns, the messages were fully integrated with traditional advertising media channels as well as digital components to achieve the greatest impact.

Marketers at Wholly Guacamole increased the power of the company's limited advertising budget by creating alliances with several organizations, including *The Biggest Loser* television program, Sonic Drive-in, Disney, and the Disney movie, *Wimpy Kid*. The marketing and social media efforts designed for the co-brands led to a powerful impact. For instance, the social media component of the alliance with *The Biggest Loser* produced 111,000 Facebook fans; 3,000 Twitter followers; comments from 200+ bloggers; more than 1,350 likes; 2,140 comments; and almost 1.6 million impressions. The connection with *Wimpy Kid* resulted in more than 46 million Facebook impressions leading to 3,700 new Wholly Guacamole fans. The Sonic program generated more than 1,200 tweets and 20 million impressions.

Wholly Guacamole's efforts efforts illustrate the power of social media. The term has multiple meanings. In this chapter, **social media** is defined as any digital tool or venue that allows individuals to socialize on the web.

WIN TICKETS TO THE BIGGEST LOSER® FINALE! CLICK HERE TO LEARN HOW

▲ A digital banner advertisement featuring the tie-in between Wholly Guacamole and the television show *The Biggest Loser.*

A **social network** is a social structure of individuals and/or organizations that are tied together in some manner. **Social media marketing** involves the utilization of social media and/or social networks to market a product, company, or brand.

This chapter first explains the basics of social networks and their relationships with marketing programs. Next, popular websites are briefly described, along with examples of how companies incorporated them into marketing and advertising programs. The third section explains the basics of social media marketing in greater detail. Social media marketing tactics are explored. A brief discussion of the additional issues associated with international social media marketing programs concludes the chapter.

Social Networks

objective 9.1

What constitutes a social network?

- General social networking sites
- Niche social networking sites
  - Business
  - Family and lifestyle
  - Dating
  - Special interests and hobbies
  - Shopping
- Social bookmarking sites

▲ **FIGURE 9.1**
Types of Social Networking Sites

Figure 9.1 identifies several major categories of social networks. Broadly-based **general social networking sites** seek to appeal to all demographics, regardless of gender, age, race, income, or education. General sites provide venues for interpersonal communication. Individuals stay in touch, learn what others in their networks are doing, share events in their lives, and make new friends. Facebook is the most well-known general social networking site.

A **niche social networking site** focuses on an interest, hobby, or demographic group. Some, such as LinkedIn, offer interactions between businesspeople. Dating sites provide an outlet to meet potential mates including target groups on sites such as OurTime, ChristianMingle, and FarmersOnly. Others cater to family or lifestyle interests such as single parents. Special interest and hobby sites vary widely and include sites that focus on a sport, hobby, or other activities. Shopping networks provide venues for individuals to share product reviews and information about brands and products. These are not e-commerce sites but rather provide meeting places that enable individuals to share information with others about products or brands along with comments about their shopping experiences.

Social bookmarking sites allow individuals to share bookmarks of websites. While most people bookmark their favorite sites on computers, social bookmarking sites make these public. They can be organized in many ways and can be accessed at any time by anyone. Individuals provide comments about sites they have bookmarked and encourage comments by others.

Social Media Sites

objective 9.2

What unique characteristics are parts of primary social media websites?

The social media landscape rapidly evolves. Marketers recognize the value of examining the major social media sites and those who use them. Overall, females utilize social media more than males and approximately 42 percent of online consumers contact multiple sites.[2] Facebook, Twitter, Instagram, and Pinterest are the most widely visited sites. For the first time since its inception, more than half of the U.S. population visits Facebook (see Figure 9.2). Instagram and Twitter are a distant second and third in terms of U.S. penetration.[3]

The demographic makeup of each social media network's visitor group differs. Although the social networking sites continually change, marketers find it worthwhile to examine each one in terms of its usefulness to a brand in a social media marketing campaign. A brief review of the most often-visited sites follows.

Facebook

Facebook, the largest social media site, hosts more than 1.2 billion users worldwide. It captures approximately 73 percent of social media advertising dollars, or approximately

▶ **FIGURE 9.2**
Social Media Users

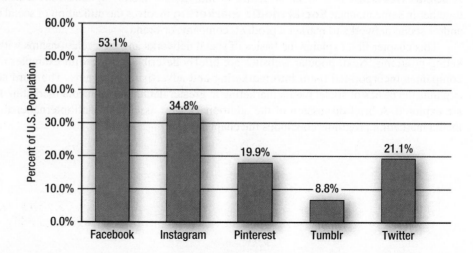

$10 billion.[4] According to *AdWeek*, Facebook's popularity comes from a blend of sheer size, record of publishing useful content, and the extent of consumer interaction available.

In addition to brands advertised on its pages, Facebook recently expanded advertising services to allow marketers to target customers on mobile devices based on an individual's activity outside of the Facebook site. This behavioral targeting tool—called *custom audiences*—allows marketers to gather information from the company's websites and applications, and then uses that data to target individuals when they visit Facebook, whether on a mobile phone, tablet, or desktop computer.[5] Facebook makes it possible to match customer demographics with Facebook characteristics using email addresses, phone numbers, names, gender, and home addresses. This ensures that only those individuals that match a brand's target market will see the Facebook advertising.

▲ Females tend to use social media more than males; African Americans trend toward Twitter and Instagram.

Facebook sells video advertising in an effort to capture advertising dollars. Facebook's marketing team contracts with AC Nielsen, which measures TV ratings, to measure video advertising on the site using gross rating points (GRP) as a metric. This makes it possible for a national advertiser to combine television advertising and Facebook advertising using the same metrics. Facebook's goal is to encourage national brands to supplement TV campaigns with Facebook video ad exposure.[6] This innovation will likely result in a larger share of the digital, social media, and traditional advertising budgets for Facebook.

▼ An advertisement for Wholly Guacamole and Sonic appearing on Facebook.

Although Facebook remains the largest social media network, the number of teen users has declined by more than 25 percent in the last several years. At the same time, the number of older consumers, individuals 55 years old or older, increased 80 percent to 28 million. Part of the reason why teens leave Facebook may be the presence of their parents and grandparents. Many teens prefer the private messaging available on Twitter or Snapchat.

In addition to the changing demographic profile of Facebook users, only a small percentage share details of their lives on a daily basis. Ten percent update their status daily and four percent update it more than once a day. Approximately 15 percent comment on photos once or more a day. Many believe Facebook has peaked in terms of number of users and frequency of use. While this may be true, the site still has more than 1.2 billion worldwide members, which makes it an attractive social network for marketers.[7] According to Brad Kim, vice president of research firm Curebit, compared to Twitter, Facebook generates ten times the number of shares, 20 times the amount of site traffic, and 20 times the number of new customers acquired. According to Kim, the reason for this vast difference in effectiveness is that Twitter tends to be a one-way message service whereas Facebook features two-way communication between friends.[8]

The companies with the most successful Facebook presence, according to *Adweek*, are Starbucks, Coca-Cola, Best Buy, and Microsoft. Starbucks has 3.7 million fans, compared to 3.5 million for Coke.[9] An independent study by WetPaint and the Altimeter Group notes that these companies and others that have high levels of social media activity tend to increase revenues more than companies that lack a social media presence.[10]

Instagram

Instagram, a mobile photo and video social sharing network owned by Facebook, recently enjoyed an explosion in popularity leading to more than 520 million monthly users.

A Facebook post by Chila 'Orchata.

Instagram enthusiasts tend to be young, wealthy, and female. Almost 60 percent visit Instagram daily.

Among the brands with an established Instagram presence, the largest is lingerie retailer Victoria's Secret. with 4 million followers. Of note, Chanel has no official Instagram presence but has attracted 5 million photos using the hashtag #chanel. Other brands with a strong Instagram presence include Ben & Jerry's, Bloomingdale's, Lipton, Macy's, Gucci, and Michael Kors.[11]

Instagram's recent emergence into social media has caused marketers for various brands to explore the best options to use on the site. Currently, the two most popular tactics are contests and crowdsourcing for photos. Bloomingdale's and Lipton held contests on Instagram. In the Bloomingdale's contest, participants submitted selfies with details about a favorite beauty or styling tip. To encourage involvement and social sharing, Bloomingdale's posted the photos on a scoreboard where fans could vote for their favorites. Individuals who submitted photos were encouraged to get their friends to vote for them by sharing the link through Instagram and other social media networks. In Lipton's contest, Instagram users were invited to submit "uplifting moments" via Instagram's image-sharing platform to one of four hashtags.[12]

A closely related trend in retailing involves individuals uploading personal pictures wearing a particular brand of clothing, which provides a consumer-to-consumer recommendation. Katherine Lin uploaded photos of herself with friends at the Coachella music festival on Twitter and Instagram.

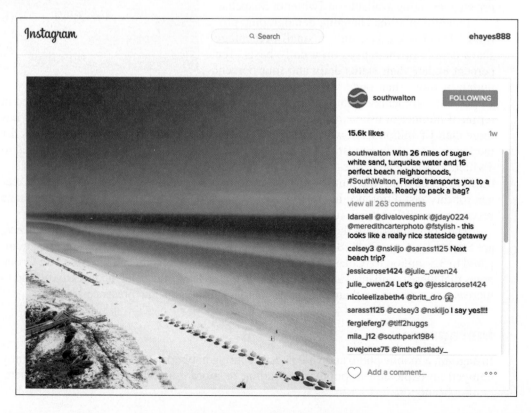

An Instagram post by Visit South Walton.

She wore a Dannijo necklace that was purchased online. Dannijo's marketers saw the photo and posted it on the company's website. Lin was thrilled and instantly shared the posting with friends. Retailers recognize the power of word-of-mouth communications. Some post the photos on company websites while others provide links to the photos. Regardless of the method, featuring consumers wearing the brand's fashions is the objective. The brand's employees can make comments about the photo on Instagram and offer a link to the brand's website. These tactics help consumers connect with the brand and keep them on a website longer. As a result, sales increase.[13]

Instagram contributes to the success of many small businesses, including Bow Truss Coffee Roasters. The Chicago-based roasting facility has twelve coffee shops. Individuals with Bow Truss regularly post images on Instagram. One day a photo shows a mug of steaming coffee from one of the locations. On another day the mug appears on a rock with the ocean as a backdrop. On a third, the site displays the company's new employees and customers. The tactic succeeds because it stays authentic and creative. The images are not photo shopped or altered and are taken and posted by various individuals within the company. Bow Truss now has over 6,000 followers and many posts receive 200 or more red hearts and likes.[14]

▲ A tweet post by Chila 'Orchata.

▼ Starbucks utilized Twitter for a successful campaign entitled "Tweet-a-Coffee".

Twitter

The Twitter microblogging service reaches a wide audience. Twitter's users are more racially diverse than the internet as a whole or Facebook. Minority members constitute approximately 41 percent of the 54 million Twitter users. A large number are Hispanic; however, Twitter's primary strength is among African Americans. About 18 percent of Twitter users are African American, which is almost double that of internet users. Among African Americans ages 18–29, the percentage is closer to 40 percent. For companies targeting minorities, especially African Americans, Twitter provides an effective venue.[15]

Twitter helps marketers identify and reach customers. They can monitor what customers say about a company or brand. Software, such as Tweetscan or Summize, locates a brand or company name mentioned in tweets. Company officials can respond or gather the information for future use or evaluation. This activity generates valuable information regarding customer perceptions of the brand and what people say about it.

JetBlue, Starbucks, Comcast, H&R Block, and Southwest Airlines utilize Twitter. Starbucks launched a Twitter campaign entitled "Tweet-a-Coffee," which enticed individuals to give $5 gift cards to friends by putting the hashtag and the person's Twitter handle in the tweet. Within two months, the campaign generated $180,000 in purchases. In addition to the revenue generated by the program, Starbucks collected 54,000 Twitter IDs along with additional information on the Starbucks account each customer had to set up to utilize the Twitter gift card function.[16]

- Develop a strategy
- Maintain consistent brand voice
- Engage followers
- Focus on relationships
- Respond to customer comments
- Avoid total automation

▲ **FIGURE 9.3**
Tips for Using Twitter

For small local businesses, Twitter delivers an innovative marketing outlet. Three weeks after Curtis Kimball opened his crème pastry cart in San Francisco, he noticed a stranger who had lined up to purchase some of his desserts. When quizzed, the man said he heard about the pastry cart from Twitter. Kimball created a Twitter account and currently has a fan base of 5,400 customers who wait for him to post his store's flavor of the day.[17] Figure 9.3 summarizes the ingredients for a successful Twitter marketing campaign.

To save costs, marketers can automate tweets so that posts are generated on a regular basis; however, followers soon discover that the company does not answer their responses. Although it may be costly, many firms devote employees to monitoring Twitter and replying when appropriate. Not every tweet requires an answer, but if most are ignored, fans will soon realize the brand's Twitter approach is selling rather than engagement.

Pinterest

Pinterest, the bulletin-board style social site on which individuals can post photos and image-based articles about events, special interests, or hobbies, hosts 70 million people. 70 percent are female. Fashion and dining are the two most featured topics on the site, which means retailers and food producers find it to be an attractive outlet.

Land O' Lakes recently offered a promotion on Pinterest entitled "Pin a Meal, Give a Meal." Each time someone pined a meal or recipe from Land O' Lakes the company donated $1 to the Feeding America foundation. Other companies active on Pinterest include Amazon, Wal-Mart, Apple, QVC, Staples, Best Buy, Netflix, and Sears. QVC and Wal-Mart currently have the most followers, but Amazon and Apple have the most pins on user pinboards.[18]

Click-through rates and impressions tend to be high for food and clothing brands on Pinterest, for two reasons. First, Pinterest ads trigger keyword searches and pinning behaviors. This builds a strong connection between the ads that viewers see and the pins consumers encounter, because the Pinterest ad closely matches what the person searches for or pins. Second, the brand's advertisement will be placed side-by-side with organic content. This makes it easy for the Pinterest user to click on the advertisement.

YouTube

The fastest-growing area of social media networking involves posting videos, especially on YouTube. Consumers create their own videos with mobile devices, and, as a result, the number of videos produced grows dramatically every year. The proliferation of videos has led to a new venue for fans to interact with brands. They move from being passive customers to passionate fans who use videos to share thoughts. Figure 9.4 highlights the ways consumers share them on YouTube and Vine.

A large number of consumers maintain YouTube channels where they post their favorite videos. They create some; others are features they like. One type of video that has seen a sharp increase is broadcast ads produced by brands. These may be television ads or digital ads produced for the internet. Passionate fans who see advertisements they like re-post them on their channels for their friends to watch. The vast majority of ads posted by individuals are positive responses to commercials they enjoyed. There are instances in which individuals post ads for some negative reasons. When this occurs, brand managers should quickly react and respond.

▼ A Pinterest post by Visit South Walton highlighting food choices in the area.

A second trend includes video reviews of products. Rather than writing a review and posting it on a blog or a website, consumers create videos in which they talk about the brand and their experiences. Most are made by positive and passionate fans praising a product, although some are negative. In one circumstance, Covergirl had 251 million total viewers of a YouTube message. 249 million responses (99 percent) were consumer-created videos talking about the brand. Similar statistics apply to other brands, such as Oreos, where 92 percent of the responses are fan-created messages and Revlon, with 99 percent consumer-created videos.

Closely tied with consumer video reviews is the re-creation of broadcast ads. Swiffer experienced an explosion of interest in the brand on YouTube. Many of the company's ads have been posted and re-posted by fans, along with a large number of product reviews. Recently, however, people have re-created the Swiffer television ads and posted their own versions. They are shown mopping the floor with a Swiffer mop or dusting with a Swiffer product, just as in the agency-produced ad in which the actor breaks out into a dance. The total number of views for all three types of Swiffer fan-created videos exceeds 10 million, compared to only 225,000 views of the videos produced by Swiffer. Clearly the popularity of fan-produced material outpaces company-produced commercials.[19]

In the past, when consumers wanted to know how to use a product, fix a product, or repair it, they would visit the brand's website or contact technical support. Now, many turn to YouTube. Consumers post how-to videos that exhibit ways to use a particular product and how to fix or repair a particular item. Seeing a demonstration on video makes it easier

- Uploading broadcast ads
- Video reviews of products
- Re-creation of ads
- Creating consumer produced how-to videos
- Capturing real-time events
- Creating branded videos

▲ **FIGURE 9.4**
Trends in Consumer Video Sharing

▼ Individuals will upload to YouTube television ads they like, such as this one for DuPage Medical Group.

▼ Posting ads to YouTube allows businesses to gain additional exposures.

to understand than reading a reference manual or the step-by-step instructions presented on a blog or website.

Built-in video features and still cameras in cell phones let consumers capture events as they occur. Many products become part of the event, either in the video or mentioned by the consumer starring in the video. Occasionally, these go viral. For instance, after Charles Ramsey rescued Amanda Berry, who had been kidnapped by a person in his neighborhood, in his interview about the event he mentioned McDonald's. The Ramsey video resulted in more than 11 million views in less than 24 hours. McDonald's was mentioned more than 6,000 times. Reacting to the buzz, McDonald's marketing team sent a tweet supporting Ramsey and gave him free hamburgers for one year. Such positive buzz only occurs when marketers actively monitor social media and quickly take advantage of real-time events.

One final marketing approach involves creating branded videos. Devin Graham is a 30-year-old filmmaker with the YouTube handle of "devinsupertramp." He creates stunt videos such as the "World's Largest Rope Swing," which had 22 million views; "Human Slingshot Slip and Slide" resulted in 13 million views. Almost 2 million individuals subscriber to his YouTube channel. His popularity drew the interest of several firms. He now makes daredevil-type branded videos through sponsorships by Mountain Dew and Ford.[20]

Social Media Marketing

objective 9.3

What is the nature of social media marketing?

Brand managers develop social media marketing campaigns for many reasons. Figure 9.5 identifies some of the more common.[21] Two frequently reported rationales are to stay engaged with customers and increase brand exposure to potential customers. To do so, most brands appear on multiple social media networks.

On its 30th anniversary, Hooters of America launched a brand overhaul aimed at winning over female customers while maintaining its predominantly male customer base. Social media was an integral part of the brand rejuvenation. Prior to the social media launch, Hooters revamped its menu to include more "female-friendly" items, remodeled many restaurants, and developed a TV and radio advertising campaign. Social media messages were at the heart of the campaign. The company urged Hooters fans to share their experiences on Facebook, Twitter, Instagram, YouTube, and other platforms. Within 30 days of the launch, consumers posted 10,000 photos. During the campaign, Hooters' Instagram account grew to more than 25,000 followers, its Facebook page produced more than 2.5 million likes, and it garnered almost 54,000 Twitter followers. The social media campaign pushed Hooters' ranking in the Nation's Restaurant News Social 200 Index from #56 to #12.[22]

Increase Traffic and Enhance Brand Image   Social media can drive traffic to a brand's website when visitors click on a URL embedded on a site. Marketers utilize social media to entice people to visit retail locations, such as restaurants or car dealerships. In business-to-business programs, social media generates leads to be followed up by members of sales staff, including field salespeople, telemarketers, or the email sales force.

Marketers design social media programs to enhance a brand's image. This approach involves becoming more than just a customer sounding board. It offers a venue for solving problems, gathering useful information, and gaining

▲ Hooters used social media in an effort to win over more female customers.

▶ **FIGURE 9.5**
Reasons for Social Media Marketing

- Engage fans
- Increase brand exposure
- Avenue for customer interaction
- Increase traffic
- Generate leads

- Enhance brand image
- Improve search rankings
- Gather customer intelligence
- Develop loyal fans
- Increase sales

insights. J.D. Power and Associates research revealed that, among the most highly satisfied customers of a brand, 87 percent said their online interactions with the brand positively impacted their perceptions of it and the likelihood of making purchases. Individuals with low satisfaction scores indicated social communications decreased the likelihood of future purchases.[23]

Improve Search Rankings Social media can boost organic search rankings with search engines. Increased rankings occur for two reasons. First, individuals more frequently mention the brand name on social media networks, because most algorithms on search engines examine numbers of mentions. Second, if content or comments made about the brand fit the search terms, then the quality of those interactions increases and various search engines assign greater credibility to the brand.

Customer Intelligence Listening to social chatter, or **social listening**, provides enlightening information to marketing professionals. Comments may be negative or positive, but in most cases visitors render honest opinions. Occasionally, social media buzz creates a situation in which the marketing team should react immediately. For instance, when General Mills launched a television advertisement for Cheerios featuring a family with parents from different races, the ad also ran on YouTube. Some of the social media response was immediate, fierce, and unfortunately racist and negative. Within days, the ad had been viewed more than 1.7 million times. Part of the language and views posted on the comment section of YouTube were not family-friendly, which led officials at General Mills to disable the comment function. Although individuals could not make comments about the ad, it could still be viewed.

Despite the negative reactions present on social media, the management team at General Mills did not back down. Company leaders believed the ad reflected current American society. According to Camille Gibson, vice president of marketing for Cheerios, "There are many kinds of families, and Cheerios celebrates them all. Despite some serious, negative responses online, it's been a very positive response overall."[24] The Cheerios example illustrates one outcome of gathering customer intelligence. Marketing employees seldom have to react as quickly as those at General Mills.

▲ Social media can be used by brands such as Gulf Seafood to drive traffic to its website.

Figure 9.6 displays other functions related to social listening. Marketers can detect potential problems with products or some other aspect of a company before it becomes a larger issue. In monitoring comments on social media, brand managers avoid reacting to a small number of individuals who may not represent the majority of brand users. Typically, those who express a view over social media are passionate about the topic. It can be a bad experience they want others to know about, or it can be a pleasant experience they want to share. Thus, before deciding to alter a product or take action, marketers try to determine whether the view being expressed represents a small subset of its customer base or the views of a larger segment. In the case of Cheerios, General Mills decided those who expressed negative opinions on social media did not represent the majority of the population.

Social listening offers an excellent source of ideas for branded content. Problems consumers face, along with the information they seek, can be presented on branded content pages. By listening, the company appears to be in tune with consumers and seen as striving to meet their needs. New software packages often have bugs that users detect. These problems and how they can be solved can be posted on the software creator's blog or website in advance of the majority of users encountering them.

The Sparks and Honey digital agency monitors social chatter for various brands. In addition to counting brand mentions, the company produces a sentiment score that indicates the level of positive or negative chatter. The agency employs predictive analytics to estimate how quickly a trend might take effect and have an impact on its clients. The firm produces what it calls a "burst quotient." The figure tells a client how quickly or slowly she might need to respond to a trend occurring in society or whether a response will be necessary.

- React to negative feedback
- Detect problems
- Gather topics for branded content
- Predict trends
- Detect patterns or shifts in views
- Identify brand advocates

▲ **FIGURE 9.6**
Functions of Social Listening

▲ Through social listening, the research firm Sparks and Honey discovered younger consumers were open to interracial marriages.

In addition to identifying trends, marketers take advantage of social listening to detect patterns or shifts in views of consumers. In the case of the Cheerios ad featuring parents from different races, Sparks and Honey research discovered that the views expressed on YouTube were from a minority and not those of the overall society. Further, the agency detected younger consumers are more open to mixed race marriages than older consumers. Seeing this pattern and the reaction to the Cheerios ad, Sparks and Honey suggested that another client, Gerber produce a video featuring children and young people talking about biracial couples. Rather than being reactive, the agency recommended a proactive approach.[25]

Social listening patterns assist in identifying customer advocates. According to social media marketing platform EngageSciences, 4.7 percent of a brand's fans generate nearly the entire amount of social buzz. While other companies argue the figure should be 20 percent of a brand's fans, a small percentage of a company's customers create most of the buzz. The vast majority remains silent and seldom says anything. Consequently, this small set of individuals, whether 4.7 percent or slightly more, holds great value to a brand if the group members can be identified. When examining social interactions, brand advocates often exhibit three characteristics:

- Behavioral commitment
- Emotional connection
- Quality communication skills

Advocates often demonstrate behavioral commitment to the brand. They make regular, frequent purchases. A company with customer purchase data in its database can track actual purchase behaviors. Individual customers are identified, and those with emotional connections demonstrate the ties through compliments and praise of the brand. To these consumers, the brand is the best in the world and no other merits consideration. As a result, they are willing to take extraordinary measures to purchase the item. Although advocates exhibit emotional and behavioral commitments, to be useful to marketers they also should exhibit quality communication skills.[26] They need the ability to effectively express their thoughts, feelings, and emotions. When located, brand managers are able to recruit these individuals to be advocates. Their recommendations can be extremely valuable in recruiting other brand loyalists.

Increase Sales and Build Brand Loyalty Developing brand loyalty and increasing sales constitute the ultimate goals of any marketing program, including social media marketing. At the same time, if customers view a social media outreach program as merely a masquerade for selling, they will likely become alienated. Instead, marketers should design social media programs to engage consumers. Increasing sales should be viewed as a by-product of social media marketing.

A recent Coca-Cola study suggests that online buzz, or talk on social media about the brand, did not lead to any measurable impact on sales. This finding surprised many outsiders because Coca-Cola has more than 61 million Facebook fans—a total greater than any other brand.[27] The researchers concluded that what cannot be determined by just counting comments or even looking at sentiments (whether positive or negative) is the impact social media has on brand image and brand loyalty. Further, the researchers asked, "If Coca-Cola was not involved with social media, would the impact be negative

▲ Placing icons for Facebook, Twitter, and YouTube on ads encourages fans of Skyjacker to interact with the brand on social media.

on sales?" For megabrands such as Coca-Cola, social media marketing cannot be considered as an option. Instead, marketers use this valuable new tool to more deeply engage fans.

Although Coca-Cola did not find a positive relationship between sales and social buzz, a McKinsey & Co. study revealed a relationship between sales and negative buzz. One telecom client of McKinsey's suffered a drop in sales of eight percent as a result of negative comments made about the brand on social media.[28]

▲ L'Oreal developed a successful social marketing strategy.

L'Oreal L'Oreal provides an excellent example of successful social media marketing. According to L'Oreal social media chief Rachel Weiss, "The whole point for us with our social strategy is you can touch a customer at any point within the customer's decision journey." Weiss and others at L'Oreal created a three-part strategy designed to maximize the impact of the company's social media efforts.

First, the company employs differing marketing strategies and unique Facebook pages for each country in which products are sold. Georges Edouard-Dias, senior vice president of digital business for L'Oreal, argues that, "This takes us back to the roots of marketing, which is about intuition, intelligence and feeling the market, not about reading or statistics or replicating best practice." In essence, each country is unique and consequently each social media program should be tailored to suit the situation present in each region.

Second, the company seeks to create content that leads to social conversations. As Rachel Weiss says, "Women love to talk about what lipstick they're wearing, what lipstick was Sofia Vergara wearing from the Emmys. Beauty is always part of the social conversation. Women are always interested in what other women are wearing, doing, and beauty tips." To generate conversations, the L'Oreal Facebook page asks questions, provides beauty advice, and seeks to entice customers to share their stories.

Third, social media will work best when customers encounter it before and after purchases. L'Oreal's strategy includes providing "how-to" instructions for consumers in the store prior to any purchase. Then, follow-up and tracking takes place on social media such as YouTube, Facebook, and Twitter.[29] Recently the company launched the premium hair color Casting Creme Gloss in India. To achieve the maximum impact of social media, the marketing team integrated offline sales with a Facebook app that required the user to fill in a unique code found on the pack. The app made it possible for the customer to upload an image with her two best friends to enter a contest to appear in an ad starring Sonam Kapoor. The combination of offline and online promotions led to a 45-percent surge in sales.[30]

Social media efforts may not always be linked directly to sales. Clicking on a link embedded in a site or social media message can still exert a positive influence on other factors, including brand exposure, fan engagement, and enhanced brand image. The quality of fans and their levels of brand engagement remain more important than a company's sales figures or its overall number of Facebook fans or Twitter followers. Social media provides a unique venue for businesses to connect with loyal customers while positively influencing others.

1. Determine social media goals

2. Determine online personality

3. Decide on social media platforms

4. Develop social media strategies

5. Develop an analytical feedback loop

▲ **FIGURE 9.7**
Building a Social Media Presence

Social Media Marketing Strategies

To reap benefits from social media marketing, brand managers try to identify the main motivations behind consumer involvements, which include communication and interaction. Quality brand messages are authentic, responsive, and compelling. Consumers do not want sales pitches. They desire sincere interactions. They prefer genuine responses to contacts. People become most involved when messages feature compelling and interesting content. A methodical approach offers the best opportunity to build an effective presence as marketers plan social media outreach programs (see Figure 9.7).

objective 9.4
Which social media marketing strategies do companies employ?

- Content seeding
- Real-time marketing
- Video marketing
- Influencer marketing
- Interactive blogs
- Consumer-generated reviews
- Viral marketing

▲ **FIGURE 9.8**
Social Media Strategies

Building a Social Media Presence

Setting goals enhances the probability that social media marketing investments will succeed. Building brand advocates requires an approach that differs from one designed to engage consumers with the brand in order to enhance its image. Each brand has a personality, whether intentional or by default. The personality chosen for social media should match the voice used in other venues and marketing communications. The voice can be one of an authority or expert in the brand's industry or it can be in a friendly, lovable, and empathetic tone.

Deciding on the best social media platforms will be a joint decision made by members of the marketing team. The better approach will be to choose only one or two social media platforms and to pay close attention to those outlets. Choosing to be involved with 8 or 10 platforms often results in a, doing a poorer job on each one. Figure 9.8 lists several primary social media strategies.

The evolving state of social media requires an analytical feedback loop. Digital marketing and social media are rich with various metrics. These metrics should be continually analyzed and the results should be reviewed to see if progress toward various goals takes place. If not, then adjustments will be made with the strategies or tactics used in implementation. Chapter 15 covers evaluation programs for marketing campaigns, including social media marketing.

Content Seeding

Farmers, gardeners, and homeowners plant seeds believing they will germinate and grow into living plants that bear fruit or flowers. The same concept applies to social media marketing. **Content seeding** involves offering consumers incentives to share content about a brand. The incentive does not have to be financial, although monetary incentives tend to be the most frequently used. It can be information, uniqueness, novelty, or anything that engages consumers and motivates them to share with others.

Coupons, rebates, contests, and other financial incentives are forms of seeding. Recently, a Chila 'Orchata Facebook post offered individuals the chance to win Chila lip balm by tagging their "weekend sidekick."

Most people like to compete, especially when they think they can win. When Microsoft launched Windows 7, the company invited high school students to submit videos for a computer lab makeover. The "School Pride" campaign invited visitors to vote on the best video submission. To add intrigue and to encourage sharing, Microsoft used a social graph that permitted web visitors to have friends go to the site and vote for the best entry, thereby increasing a school's chances of winning. The contest generated an increase of almost 75 percent in traffic to the website.[31]

Another contest that generated a great deal of social buzz was created for Esurance. Rather than spending $4 million on a Super Bowl ad, the company purchased the first ad slot after the game ended, at a cost of $2.5 million. The ad announced that one lucky viewer would win the difference, about $1.5 million. The winner would be someone who tweeted the hashtag \#EsuranceSave30 within 36 hours of the ad airing. The ad created a tremendous burst of Twitter shares. Leo Burnett, Esurance's agency, reported the following statistics from the campaign:[32]

▼ A Facebook giveaway promoted by Chila 'Orchata.

CHILA 'Orchata with Charlotte Rhoden and 16 others.
Published by Zehnder Communications (?) · Sponsored (demo) ·

Like what you see? Tag your weekend sidekick for a chance to win the both of you a Chila lip balm! You have until Monday morning to enter.

CHILA
LIP BALM
GIVEAWAY

657 Likes 78 Comments 23 Shares

Like   Comment   Share

- 5.4 million tweets were sent with the \#EsuranceSave30 hashtag
- More than 200,000 entries took place within the first minutes of the television ad
- 2.6 billion social impressions on Twitter resulted
- 332,000 views of the Esurance commercial were posted to YouTube
- 261,000 new followers on the official Esurance Twitter account emerged
- A 12-fold spike in visits to the Esurance website occurred within the first hours of the television ad

One value-added incentive marketers incorporate into a seed-sharing program is offering customers something exclusive in order to make them feel special. Sony artist Pitbull generated awareness for a new album prior to its launch through social media. If a person shared a message from Pitbull's website on Facebook or Twitter, it let the individual listen to the CD online before the music went public. If the person got three of his friends to come back to the website, then it unlocked three bonus tracks. The idea of feeling special and offering something unique drove awareness of the album before the launch.[33]

▲ Microsoft used a content seeding contest entitled "School Pride" when it launched Windows 7.

Real-Time Marketing

Real-time marketing existed prior to the 2013 Super Bowl, but a blackout during the game in the New Orleans Superdome created publicity for the approach. Oreo sent a message via Twitter that it is okay to dunk an Oreo cookie "in the dark." The message was placed on an image of an Oreo cookie, set in light, shadow, and darkness. That message became a viral hit and was re-tweeted 15,000 times within the first 14 hours.

Real-time marketing is the creation and execution of an instantaneous marketing message in response to and in conjunction with an occurrence during a live event. The marketers conceived and produced the Oreo tweet in just five minutes. Such a rapid reaction was possible because marketers from Oreo's parent company, Mondelez, and its agency were assembled at a "social media command center" in New York during the game. With creative and technical staff present and in place, the team was quickly able to create a response to the blackout, produce the message, and then send it.[34]

Effective real-time marketing does not occur on the fly without thought. The approach requires upfront strategic planning before a live event. While seeking to display human emotions and reactions to live events, marketers carefully plan actions to ensure they resonate with consumers (or businesses) and remain consistent with the brand's overall brand image and integrated marketing communications program. The tone featured in a real-time marketing message should correlate with messages presented in other company advertisements and social media efforts. Marketing personnel discuss and sometimes even prepare messages and ads to be used for various situations that might occur during a live event. While it may seem the message was a quick reaction, it may have been talked about and designed weeks earlier.

Real-time marketing can be utilized in places other than live sporting events. During a recent snowstorm in the Northeast, Starbucks' marketing department put together a social media plan for Facebook and Twitter that focused on conversations about the anticipated

▲ Brand managers plan real-time marketing scenarios in advance of live events and potential live opportunities.

blizzard. Snow-themed ads appeared on Facebook and Twitter with the focus on an image of a warm cup of java. The Twitter ads appeared when individuals clicked on #blizzard, #snowstorm, and other related hashtags.[35]

McDonald's engages in real-time marketing messages, but at a slower pace. Employees track 2.5 million to 3 million conversations each month listening to what consumers say about McDonald's, other fast food restaurants, and topics relevant to the company's operations. The team watches for trends the company can feature on social media pages. When the company launched its Cheddar Bacon Onion burger, the ads highlighted various attributes of the product; however, the marketing team noticed that the chatter was mostly about the bacon. In response, they quickly changed promotional efforts to focus more on bacon rather than other aspects of the sandwich.[36]

Video Marketing

- Advertising on videos
- Posting of television ads
- Informational videos
- Cause-related videos
- Product reviews
- Vloggers

▲ **FIGURE 9.9**
Video Tactics

Approximately 58 percent of the U.S. population watches digital videos, and 75 percent of internet users view them. Marketing professionals recognize that YouTube and other video sharing platforms present unique opportunities and challenges for social media marketing. Figure 9.9 highlights some of the primary tactics.

Spending on advertising in videos on sites such as YouTube has risen to $4.6 billion annually and currently grows 20 percent to 40 percent per year, a rate much faster than any other form of advertising. Research indicates that consumers are more receptive to online video ads. The average time consumers view online video ads is 21.4 seconds, compared to 13.6 seconds for television. The completion rate for online video ads is 88 percent versus 79 percent for TV. Recall and ad likability are also higher for digital video ads (see Figure 9.10).[37]

Ads embedded in videos can be pre-roll (before the video starts), mid-roll (in the middle of the video content), or post-roll (at the end of the content). Advertisements placed at the end of a video experience better click-through rates, because individuals have

▶ **FIGURE 9.10**
Online Ads versus Television Ads

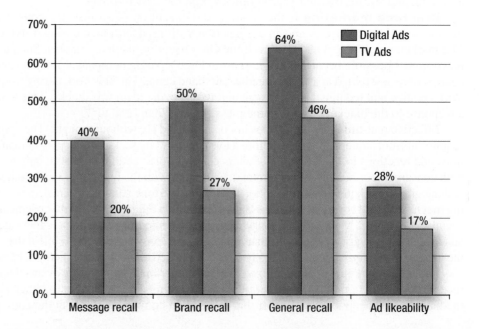

finished watching the video content. Ads at the beginning of the video result in more impressions while those in the middle have the highest completion rate. Therefore, when creating impressions or enhancing recall constitutes the primary goal, advertisers often front-load ads. When the company seeks to increase brand recognition or enhance brand image, then mid-roll ads represent a better option, because viewers tend to watch the entire ad. Post-roll ads best match direct response advertising with some type of call to action.

Many companies maintain YouTube channels in order to share various types of videos. Marketers post ads prepared for television to video websites. Most Super Bowl advertisers post a commercial or a snippet of it on YouTube prior to the game. Often, the digital ad will be viewed by more people than those who see the actual commercial during the Super Bowl. In addition to ads, advertisers post background scenes or videos explaining how the ad was produced. Viewers find these interesting, and the approach often increases engagement with the brand.

Companies produce two other types of videos for online posts. Informational or instructional videos use a strategy similar to a branded content approach. The videos will be designed to provide useful information to consumers and answer questions they may have about the brand. Providing a tutorial on how to use a product, especially a complex item, can be useful. As with branded content, advertisers ensure the videos will be perceived as authentic and useful and not as a sales gimmick.

Another approach involves posting videos with public relations or cause-related marketing messages. Duracell produced a video about firefighters and emergency personnel telling their personal stories. Advil produced a video featuring Melissa Stockwell, who lost her leg in Iraq. John Deere produced a video about a Mexican immigrant who came to the United States with nothing and now owns his own business. This type of video generates goodwill.

Many consumers watch videos as in order to conduct product research. Rather than visiting various websites, **Amazon.com**, or brand sites to obtain reviews, consumers turn to YouTube. An increase in YouTube's popularity as a source of product reviews can be attributed to three causes.[38] First, any product can be reviewed on video, and almost any product a person can think of has been reviewed on YouTube. Second, videos are more engaging because they provide both visual and spoken content. Third, videos represent the best place for early adopters to learn about a new product.

Paying individuals to promote a brand has become a recent strategy in the video arena. These individuals, known as **vloggers**, create videos, post them on video sites such as YouTube or Vine, and seek to build a following. Brand managers for companies such as Unilever pay individuals to create videos that endorse their brands. In the early days, vloggers did not announce that they were being paid; however, recent FTC actions require them to publicly state their relationships with companies. Compensation may not be monetary. Some vloggers receive merchandise along with other perks.

▲ Television advertisements for JD Bank have also been posted on YouTube.

Influencer Marketing

Many times, content sharing is the key goal in of a social marketing program. Consumers often ignore messages posted by individual companies. As a result, many marketing teams seek to locate individuals to share information and other facts about a brand.

▶ Influencer marketing is now a popular social media strategy used by brands to reach consumers.

Influencer marketing involves an individual endorsing a brand on social media sites. Doing so transmits positive word-of-mouth comments from individuals who are seen as thought or opinion leaders within their social circles or as experts within particular fields. A number of agencies now specialize in matching potential influencers with brands seeking to take advantage of this tactic.

The size of an individual's social network does not always correlate with the extent of her influence. An individual can have 20,000 followers, but not be considered an opinion leader within a particular field. The most effective influencers are individuals who lead conversations and shape opinions. Although some celebrities have large followings, they may not be the best choices for influencer marketing campaigns.

Aligning a brand's message with an influencer's motivation will be the key to success. Influencers try to grow networks of followers. One way to achieve such an outcome would be to be viewed as an opinion leader through sharing brand content, especially exclusive or pre-launch content. For instance, for a fashion brand marketers can provide influencers access to new fashions before the public sees them. An influencer may be provided with information on methods of enhancing photographs. She could share methods of creating unique special effects with a Canon or Nikon camera. She might share information about a photo contest hosted by Canon or special online seminars by the company.

To be effective, consumers must consider influencers to be authentic and not as paid spokespersons. Most people are not opposed to an influencer pitching a particular brand as long as it appears to be genuine praise. For instance, Birchbox worked with lifestyle blogger Emily Schuman to promote a makeup box on Instagram. Emily reaches more than 280,000 followers. The Birchbox campaign with Emily yielded more than 18,000 likes and touched more than 50,000 consumers.[39] Most of these consumers were individuals who were not part of Birchbox's fan base and many were not acquainted with the brand's products.

Interactive Blogs

The power of a blog comes from a landscape in which one dissatisfied consumer can now vent to thousands, and in some cases millions, of people. Previously, a bad shopping experience meant that 12 to 15 people would hear about it. Currently, the individual's complaint can be sent to more than just friends and family. A discontented consumer speaks to anyone willing to watch, listen, or read about it. The reverse also occurs. A satisfied customer can rave about a brand and have his comments read by thousands.

Interactive blogs permit visitors to send comments or posts, making them another important component of social media. Chapter 8 covered the basic concept of blogging as primarily a one-way communication device. While effective, blogs that attract followers and encourage active participation become more powerful. Such interactions present a higher level of risk, because the blogging company surrenders some control over content. While employees can squelch and/or delete negative comments, doing so destroys the blog's credibility and damages its reputation. A better approach is for the company's marketing team to face any criticism honestly and humbly and react by seeking a solution to the problem or cause of the dissatisfaction.

Companies feature three different types of interactive blogs (see Figure 9.11). The first occurs when a company or brand creates a blog. Blogs owned and operated by businesses find it difficult to solicit honest interactions with consumers who may be more suspicious. Also, company personnel operating the blog may be more sensitive to negative content and how customers view the organization.

A blog sponsored by a company or brand is the second form. New regulations passed by the Federal Trade Commission require an individual being paid by an organization with merchandise or money, or someone compensated in any other way, to report that information on the blog. While these individuals have freedom to express personal opinions, they will likely have to remain positive about the brand in order to maintain its sponsorship. Site visitors have more freedom to comment as well, but recognizing that a business sponsors the blog's author often will temper their views.

The third type of blog involves individuals who speak about a brand but have no financial connection to it. They truly like the brand. They take pleasure in talking about it and enjoy interacting with others about the brand. When a company has no affiliation with a blog, visitors feel comfortable in making comments and relating their honest opinions. The marketing team finds out what consumers really think about a product or service. They use this type of blog to ask questions and seek opinions, if permission is granted by the blog's author.

- Brand blog
- Individuals sponsored by a brand
- Individual speaking about a brand

▲ **FIGURE 9.11**
Types of Interactive Blogs

▲ Blogs can be a valuable source of information for patients looking for medical care as well as the staff of DuPage Medical Group.

Consumer-Generated Reviews

Word-of-mouth endorsements have changed. Many companies that vend multiple goods or services solicit consumer-generated reviews of those products. **Amazon.com** stands at the forefront of this approach. Each book offered online contains a space where individual customers can write reviews, with words and a one- to five-star rating. The site informs the shopper of the number of reviews, the average star rating, and notes if the reviews are written by anonymous critics or those who provide their real names. A person wishing to place his name on a review must authenticate it by presenting **Amazon.com** with a credit card number. Customers benefit by reading the reviews before making purchases. The system may not be perfect, because an author might use a pseudonym to write a highly favorable review and encourage friends and family members to do the same. At the same time, the author cannot edit or respond to outside reviews.

Best Buy incorporates consumer feedback into online retailing. The company hosts a blog section for consumers to read about and discuss various topics. In each product category, such as cameras, Best Buy provides a discussion forum on a variety of

▶ Consumer-generated reviews are important in tourist decisions for visiting Baton Rouge.

▲ Scott Equipment can provide consumer-generated reviews on its website to help business customers make a decision on which equipment to purchase or lease.

related topics. In a digital camera discussion forum, consumers post photos they have taken with various cameras. Best Buy posts customer reviews of each product, both positive and negative. The reviews may influence the brands consumers consider and eventually purchase. By providing blogs, discussion forums, and consumer reviews, Best Buy offers consumers methods to search for and evaluate products and to make purchase decisions without leaving the company's website.

The growing use of online reviews by consumers has led to an increase in websites devoted to providing them, such as TripAdvisor, Zagat, Edmunds, Yelp, and Foursquare. An online panel study of 3,404 individuals revealed that 75 percent think the information presented on rating sites is generally fair and honest; however, 25 percent still believe the information to be biased or unfair. The larger and more established rating sites, such as TripAdvisor, Zagat, Open Table, Edmunds, Urbanspoon, and Yelp, tend to be the most trusted.[40]

Marketers carefully study customer-generated reviews, because they provide customer evaluations of products and how the item compares to the competition. This information becomes critical when developing marketing plans, product modifications, and service strategies. As the usage of consumer-generated reviews continues to rise, the marketing challenge will be managing this aspect of consumer word-of-mouth endorsements in ways that enhance brand equity and increase sales.

Viral Marketing

Preparing a marketing message to be passed from one consumer to another through digital means, or **viral marketing**, takes the form of an email or a video posted to a personal blog and passed to other blogs or websites such as YouTube. It can evolve into a form of advocacy or word-of-mouth endorsement. The term "viral" derives from the image of a person being "infected" with the marketing message and then spreading it to friends, like a virus. The difference is that the individual voluntarily sends the message to others.

- Focus on the product or business
- Determine why individuals would want to pass along the message
- Offer an incentive
- Make it personal
- Track the results and analyze the data

Viral marketing messages include advertisements, hyperlinked promotions, online newsletters, streaming videos, and games. For instance, about a dozen videos were posted on YouTube of a man claiming to be the "world's fastest nudist." He streaks through various locations in New York City wearing only tennis shoes, tube socks, and a fanny pack positioned strategically in front. The links to the videos were emailed from individual to individual. They were posted on popular blogs such as The Huffington Post and Gawker. One appeared on CNN's *Anderson Cooper 360*. The campaign turned out to be a viral video campaign for **Zappos.com**, an online shoe and apparel store. The viral campaign highlighted that Zappos was selling clothes because additional videos were posted that showed a van screeching up to the "fastest nudist" and several people jumping out wearing Zappos T-shirts. As the van leaves, the video shows the nudist dressed in pants and a shirt.[41]

Figure 9.12 provides suggestions about how to create successful viral campaigns. The viral message should focus on the product or business. In the **Zappos.com** videos, the nudist receives clothes from a Zappos team. The marketing team determines why an individual would want to pass the message along or tell friends about it.

Viral campaigns do not always succeed or yield positive benefits. Most brand managers would be thrilled to have three viral videos within one year, as Kmart did. The first YouTube video that went viral was "Ship My Pants," an advertisement created by Kmart. The video was viewed 20 million times. A short time later, an advertisement posted to YouTube—"Big Gas Savings"—based on a milder naughty double entendre was viewed more than 6 million times. Then "Show Your Joe," a holiday ad that featured men playing "Jingle Bells" with their privates, was viewed more than 15 million times. Despite all three ads going viral and being viewed more than 40 million times in total, sales fell by 2.1 percent.

Research regarding the impact of viral messages suggests that about 61 percent of individuals exposed to a viral message or video expressed favorable opinions about the brand. Purchase intentions increased around five percent but were greater when the viral message was recommended by a friend via social media rather than a company.[42]

Individuals should receive incentives to pass messages along. A message containing entertainment value offers one type of incentive. Others may be financial, such as free merchandise or a discount for messages passed along to friends that lead to purchases, logging onto a website, or registering for an e-newsletter. The incentive should be unique. A personalized message has a greater chance of being passed along.

The many forms of digital marketing mean that viral marketing has lost some of its luster. Some consumers have lower enthusiasm and are less willing to resend messages. Still, the marketing team can take advantage of the ability to track the results of a viral campaign and analyze the results to determine whether such a program will be effective.

Following Brands on Social Media

Figure 9.13 highlights reasons consumers follow brands in social media. Although they vary by social media site, the two top reasons tend to be to keep up with activities of the brand and to learn about the product or service. Typically, individuals do not follow a brand with the goal of making purchases. They have often purchased a brand, enjoy it, and then become a fan or follower. If they are dissatisfied with a brand, they are not likely to

- Keep up with activities
- Learn about products or services
- Sweepstakes or promotion
- Provide feedback
- Join community of fans
- Make purchases
- To complain

▲ **FIGURE 9.13**
Reasons Consumers Follow
Brands

Individuals follow brands, such as Kraft Heinz, on social media because they truly like the brand and use it regularly.

objective **9.5**

How can marketers use social media strategies in international operations?

follow it on social media. They may use social media to register complaints but do not become fans or followers. Understanding why individuals follow brands and why they participate in social media sharing underlines successful social media marketing campaigns.

International Implications

Social media interactions are a worldwide phenomenon. Most Facebook members reside outside the United States. Various social networks have been involved in social movements and political revolutions. They have helped widen the worldwide marketplace for a variety of goods and services while changing the landscape of shopping and purchasing patterns in numerous companies.

Marketing professionals understand that the social network environment creates additional complexities. Among the more notable, language differences, social norms, and technological issues represent three of the greatest challenges to individual companies.

As is the case in any marketing program, language differences complicate the ways in which messages can be constructed and transmitted. In countries where internet systems allow the free flow of messages, a marketing piece designed for viewers in Spain might quickly appear in China or Greece. Consequently, the viewer cannot decipher the intent of the message. Trying to present a consistent theme across languages presents a great deal of difficulty: Language differences enhance the dilemma. One tactic used to combat the problem is an emphasis on *visual Esperanto*, a more universal, emotionally-based approach designed to tap into feelings all citizens experience.

Social norms create a significant test for marketers. Norms regarding sexuality, modes of dress, attitudes toward women and minorities, and other differences become readily noticeable when a tweet or Facebook post is sent across national boundaries. Companies seeking to establish an international presence carefully vet all messages to make sure they do not offend the norms or sensitivities of individuals in countries where the messages or advertisements will be shown.

Technological challenges can be presented by governments or by the nature of a country's infrastructure. Many national governments try to censor various websites from appearing within their boundaries. In other settings, poor internet service creates sporadic access at best. Marketing professionals account for these issues as they design social media programs.

Summary

Social media includes any digital tool or venue that allows individuals to socialize on the web. A social network is a social structure of individuals and/or organizations that are tied together in some manner. Social media marketing is the utilization of social media and/or social networks to market a product, company, or brand.

General social networking sites are broadly designed to appeal to all demographics, regardless of gender, age, race, or education. Niche social networking sites focus on a specific interest, hobby, or demographic group. Common social media sites include Facebook, Instagram, Twitter, Pinterest, and YouTube. Marketing professionals can target all types of sites.

Social media marketing seeks to keep customers engaged with a brand and to increase the brand's exposure. It can drive new traffic through an improve search ranking, and help marketers collect customer intelligence through social listening systems. Successful programs increase sales and build brand loyalty. A quality program identifies customer advocates who exhibit behavioral commitment, emotional connections with the brand, and quality communication skills.

Social media marketing strategies include content seeding, which involves providing incentives for customers to share content about a brand. Effective real-time marketing efforts involve careful planning and preparation in order to provide an instantaneous marketing message in response to a live event. Video marketing takes place pre-roll, mid-roll, and post-roll. Influencer marketing involves an individual marketing a brand through social media. Interactive blogs permit visitors to make comments or posts on the site, including those created by the company, company-sponsored sites, and those prepared by independent fans or advocates. Customer-generated review programs, when correctly managed, provide authenticity and engagement with those who use the systems to gather information about products. Viral marketing helps a company garner interest when a message is sent along via email or a re-post by consumers. Many consumers follow brands on social media, for a variety of reasons.

International challenges in social media include language differences, social norms, and technological complications. Effective marketing teams monitor and respond carefully to these issues.

Key Terms

social media Any digital tool or venue that allows individuals to socialize on the web

social network A social structure of individuals and/or organizations that are tied together in some manner

social media marketing The utilization of social media and/or social networks to market a product, company, or brand

general social networking sites Websites that are broadly based and designed to appeal to all demographics, regardless of gender, age, race, income, or education

niche social networking site A website that focuses on a specific interest, hobby, or demographic group

social bookmarking sites Websites that allow individuals to share bookmarks of websites

social listening A social media marketing strategy that involves listening to social chatter

content seeding A social media marketing strategy that involves providing incentives for consumers to share content about a brand

real-time marketing The creation and execution of an instantaneous marketing message in response to—and in conjunction with—an occurrence during a live event

vloggers Individuals who are paid to promote a brand in the video arena.

influencer marketing A marketing approach that involves an individual endorsing a brand on social media

interactive blogs A marketing strategy in which a blog allows visitors to make comments or posts

viral marketing An advertisement tied to an email or other form of online communication in which one person passes on the advertisement or email to other consumers

MyMarketingLab

To complete the problems with the ⭐ in your MyLab, go to the end-of-chapter Discussion Questions.

Review Questions

9-1. Define social media, a social network, and social media marketing.

9-2. What are the three major forms of social media networks? Describe each.

9-3. What are the most commonly used social media sites?

9-4. How has video posting changed the nature of social media networking?

9-5. What are the major objectives of social media marketing programs?

9-6. What is social listening?

9-7. What three characteristics should consumer advocates demonstrate to be effective spokespersons in social media programs?

9-8. What are the most commonly used social media marketing strategies?

9-9. Describe content seeding.

9-10. Describe real-time marketing.

9-11. What three types of interactive blogs support social media marketing programs?

9-12. Describe viral marketing.

⭐ 9-13. Discuss the reasons why consumers follow brands on social media.

9-14. What issues complicate international social media marketing programs?

Critical Thinking Exercises

DISCUSSION QUESTIONS

9-15. Suppose you were in charge of the social media for your college. Discuss the pros and cons of each of the social media platforms presented in the chapter (Facebook, Instagram, Pinterest, Twitter, and Tumblr). Which two would be the most important? Why? Should the social media be targeted to current students or prospective students? Explain why.

⭐9-16. Compare and contrast the social media sites Facebook, Instagram, Twitter, Pinterest, and YouTube. Discuss ways they are similar and ways they are different. Describe your level of involvement with each of these social media platforms.

9-17. A local pizza chain with nine restaurants has asked for your help in designing a social media strategy. Discuss the pros and cons of each of the primary social media platforms (Facebook, Instagram, Twitter, Pinterest, and YouTube) for the pizza restaurants. Which one do you consider to be the best? Why?

9-18. Describe the current trends of consumer video-sharing. For each trend, discuss your personal experience of sharing, creating, or watching a video. Which trend or trends impact you? Why?

9-19. Why has YouTube gained considerable popularity in recent years? How often do you use YouTube? What types of videos do you watch? Do your friends and relatives access YouTube? If so, how often and why? If not, why not?

9-20. Examine the reasons companies use social media marketing listed in Figure 9.5. Rank the reasons from most effective to least effective based on your personal experience with social media and brands that use it. Discuss your rankings. Explain, with examples, your top three choices.

⭐9-21. Social listening is now being used by most brand managers. Describe the functions of social listening presented in the chapter and discuss the relative importance of each function. How important do you think it is for marketers to listen to social media chatter? Almost all comments on social media are made by a small percentage of consumers. Do you think these comments are representative of most consumers and what they think of a brand? Why or why not? If not, why should brands even pay attention to social chatter? Should Companies make marketing strategy decisions based on social chatter? Why or why not?

9-22. Have you made brand purchases based on comments made on social media? Why or why not? Provide specific details. Have you decided against purchasing a particular brand based on comments on social media? Why or why not? Provide specific details.

9-23. Examine the social media strategies listed in Figure 9.8. Discuss each strategy in terms of your personal experience. Describe whether the strategy impacts your purchases and views of brands. For each strategy, discuss why it does have an impact or why it does not. Provide details to support your thoughts.

⭐9-24. Look at the social media strategies listed in Figure 9.8. Assume you are the marketing manager for a new brand of cosmetics targeted to females between the ages of 18 and 30. Define each strategy, then discuss its appropriateness for a social media marketing campaign for this new brand of cosmetics. If you had money for only two of the strategies, which two would you choose? Why?

9-25. Do you use consumer-generated reviews in making purchase decisions? Why or why not? Are they valuable to consumers?

⭐9-26. Brand managers often become excited when something the company posts on the Internet goes viral and spreads like wildfire among consumers. What factors contribute to a brand's posting going viral? Discuss how the social media strategies listed in Figure 9.8 can contribute to a successful viral marketing attempt or unsuccessful viral marketing. Of the strategies listed in Figure 9.8, which one would have the greatest chance of becoming viral? Why?

Integrated Learning Exercises

9-27. Choose one of the following brands. Go to the company's website and locate the social media links provided. Access each of the social media brand pages and evaluate it in terms of engaging consumers with the brand and how it is integrated with the website. Provide specific information from each social media network that shows how consumers can be engaged. Identify the number of fans, followers, and posts on each site. Provide screenshots of each social media page and website main page.

    a. Wholly Guacamole (**www.eatwholly.com**)

    b. Sonic (**www.sonic.com**)

    c. Starbucks (**www.starbucks.com**)

    d. Coca-Cola (**www.coca-cola.com**)

    e. Lucky Brand (**www.luckybrand.com**)

9-28. Name a brand you really like and for which you have a high level of loyalty. Access the brand's website and the social media pages shown on the brand's website. Discuss the information provided on each social media. Based on the reasons brands use social media shown in Figure 9.5, discuss what you think is the reason for each social media site. Evaluate how successful you think the brand is with social media. Provide screenshots of the social media sites and website to support your thoughts.

9-29. Choose one of the following product categories. Select two prominent brands from that category. Access each brand's website and social media links. Compare and contrast the information provided for each brand and social media. Which brand has the best social media presence? Why? Provide screenshots to illustrate your points.
- a. Sports equipment
- b. Clothing
- c. Restaurants
- d. Beverage

9-30. Examine the reasons brands use social media as shown in Figure 9.5. Pick three of the reasons and identify from your personal experience a brand you believe did well with each. It could be three different brands or one brand for all three. Support your answer with specific information, links to the social media pages, and screenshots illustrating your discussion.

9-31. Figure 9.8 identifies strategies brands can use with social media. Describe each of the strategies in your own words. Find an example of each strategy in social media not described in the textbook. Provide the link and a screenshot, explain why it is an example of the strategy, and give your evaluation of whether the strategy was good or bad, and why.

9-32. Figure 9.9 identifies six video marketing tactics. Go to YouTube and find an example of each strategy. Provide links to your six videos and explain why you think each is a good example of the particular strategy. Evaluate how well the brand or company did with the video marketing strategy.

9-33. Using a blog search engine, locate an example of an interactive blog. Evaluate the blog. Is it effective? Why or why not? Provide a link to the blog and a screenshot.

9-34. Use a search engine to locate an example of a viral marketing campaign. Evaluate the viral marketing. Was it effective? Why or why not? Provide a link to the viral campaign and a screenshot.

9-35. Go to the website of Visit South Walton at **www.visitsouthwalton.com**. What is your impression of the website? Visit each of the social media platforms identified on the Visit South Walton website. Describe the content on each social media site and identify what you think is the primary objective (provide screenshots to support your answer). How well are the social media platforms for Visit South Walton integrated with its website? Be specific.

Blog Exercises

Access the authors' blog for this textbook at the URLs provided to complete these exercises. Answer the questions that are posed on the blog.

9-36. Hooters: **blogclowbaack.net/2014/05/12/hooters-chapter-9/**

9-37. Covergirl: **blogclowbaack.net/2014/05/12/covergirl-chapter-9/**

9-38. Social Media: **blogclowbaack.net/2014/05/12/social-media-chapter-9/**

Student Project

CREATIVE CORNER

Carlos just opened his own hot dog and pastry stand in downtown St. Louis. He believes social media could be used to build awareness of his stand and to build a customer base. Carlos believes having the unique combination of hot dogs and pastries provides him with a combination meal (hot dog, pastry, and drink) that counters what a fast-food restaurant would offer. Develop a social media marketing campaign for Carlos that includes the following elements:

- Objectives (or reasons) for the social media marketing campaign
- Social networking sites he should utilize
- Social media strategies
- Banner ad that Carlos can place on Facebook (design this for him)

In developing the campaign, be sure to provide a rationale to Carlos for your suggestions.

CASE 1 *SHELBY'S STABLES*

Shelby Hernandez is a second-generation U.S. citizen. She grew up around horses and stables. Recently, the owner of a local stable offered to sell Shelby his operation in order to facilitate his retirement. With the help of family members and Small Business Administration loans and grants, she was able to make the purchase.

Shelby's Stables offered four major types of services. First, she rented space to horse owners complete with grooming, stable clean-up and feeding. Horses would be either walked on a regular basis to make sure the animals received sufficient exercise each week or they would be ridden by her or one of her workers, depending on the contract. The fees for housing the horses and taking care of them would contribute greatly to cash flow.

Second, Shelby owned several horses. Horse enthusiasts could take these out for trail rides. Riders ranged from children to senior citizens. Her horses were gentle-natured and patient with inexperienced riders. Shelby offered photo services so that a first-time rider or one celebrating a special occasion, such as a birthday, could capture the moment with a digital image that could be shared with others.

Third, Shelby offered horse-riding lessons to individuals of all ages, although most were teen and preteen females. Shelby loved the opportunity to work with young girls to acquaint them with horses. Most lessons were one-on-one, but she also offered several riding camps through the summer months.

The fourth part of the operation was to service local charities that would provide rides for individuals with disabilities, illnesses, and injuries. Various news stories noted the calming and therapeutic value of horse riding for individuals with developmental problems, those with terminal illnesses, and others facing challenging recoveries from injuries. Shelby charged nominal fees to groups such as the Make-A-Wish Foundation and the local chapter of Wings for Warriors for access to her horses and riding activities, ranging from simple walks within a confined stable area to larger trail rides.

Shelby had the advantage of serving several owners who already kept their horses in her stables, based on contracts with the previous owner. Still, she wanted to expand that part of her company, as she had nearly a dozen unfilled stalls. At the same time, providing rides would generate substantial additional income.

A local marketing professional was willing to assist in the launch of Shelby's business on a *pro bono* basis, due to his interest in the Make-A-Wish Foundation. He advised her about the importance of traditional, digital, and social media marketing efforts. Shelby had set aside $10,000 for marketing to launch her company

▲ How can Shelby take advantage of social media to promote her company?

and would be able to spend an additional $10,000 over the first year of her newly created enterprise.

9-39. Should Shelby's Stables emphasize general social networking sites, niche social networking sites, or both? Explain your answer.

9-40. Which social media sites are best suited to this type of promotional campaign? Why?

9-41. Examine the social media strategies listed in Figure 9.8. For each social media strategy discuss how Shelby could use it for her business. Which would be the best? Why?

9-42. Examine the video marketing approaches listed in Figure 9.9 For each video marketing approach discuss how Shelby could use it with her business. Which would be the most feasible? Why?

9-43. How can the photos taken by Shelby for various patrons be used as a marketing tool for her stables?

CASE 2 *POST-IT: MAKING THE ORDINARY EXTRAORDINARY*

Sooner or later, every business person comes into contact with a Post-it note. These sticky, functional tools have become part of everyday life in homes, offices, and other places. The product remains a steady, profitable staple of the 3-M portfolio. This iconic product has been on the market over 30 years. For many years, the company's marketing strategy appeared to be to sell the Post-it notes by taking what was essentially a functional view of the brand.

▲ Post-it notes have been on the market for over 30 years.

The approach changed a few years ago when a new $10-million marketing campaign was launched. The new approach utilized messages in television commercials, online ads, the company's website, and through social media. The idea was to suggest Post-it notes could be so much more. The campaign emphasized "customization," or the tendency exhibited by younger consumers to want personalized messages from mass media and individualized uses for goods.

With the theme "Go ahead" driving the campaign, customers were encouraged to find new ways to use this longstanding product. Soon "Post-it" wars emerged between local offices, as employees used Post-its to create images and other designs on external windows. Further, the product's flexibility led customers to use it to communicate, collaborate, and to organize their work. In a somewhat surprising turn of events, 3-M's research revealed that many customers felt a strong emotional connection to Post-its.

Post-it hosts an "Idea Headquarters" website that helps people find unique uses for the tool, including becoming more productive and reducing the tendency to procrastinate. Social media posts seek out additional methods for taking advantage of the item's distinctive characteristics.

Television commercials support all other efforts, with messages targeting moms to show ways they use Post-its to organize their days; millennials to be creative in posting the notes to remind themselves about events and to communicate with others (sort of a paper "tweet," according to one observer) as well as to help them remain optimistic; and to a married man who uses a Post-it note to remind himself to "keep the honeymoon going."

Post-it's marketing team faces two trends as the future unfolds. The first involves making the product itself more appealing and amenable to these novel applications. One response has been to increase the number of colors beyond the traditional yellow and more common colors. The second may become a more daunting issue over time. The "generic" problem occurs when a brand becomes so well-accepted that the brand name is used to describe the item, no matter which company sells it. Examples include Band-aids, Xerox copies, and Scotch tape. Don't be surprised if you hear the product referred to as "Post-it brand" in advertisements for the product in the future. Doing so has been the most common response to the generic problem.

Company leaders believed the campaign represented the first time that they had included all forms of (media) creativity under one banner, led by the Grey New York advertising agency. The new approached enticed consumers to take it upon themselves to discover how to use the brand in unconventional ways. In essence, consumers loved it so much that they found new ways to enjoy the product.[43]

9-44. Which social media sites are best suited to this type of promotional campaign? Why?

9-45. How could consumers, fans, and the company take advantage of new video-posting technologies to promote the Post-it brand?

9-46. What were the marketing objectives of the "Go ahead" campaign?

9-47. Would social listening be of value to Post-it's marketing team? If so, how? If not, why not?

9-48. Which social media marketing strategies should Post-it's team use? Provide justification for your response.

MyMarketingLab

Go to the Assignments section of your MyLab to complete these writing exercises.

9-49. Discuss the current trends of consumer video-sharing. Examine reasons brands have become involved in social media marketing. For each of the trends you identify, elaborate on ways brands can use social media marketing to reach video-sharing consumers. Be sure to justify your choices of social media marketing.

9-50. Describe in your own words each of the social media strategies (see Figure 9.8). Suppose you are a marketing intern for a minor league baseball team located in your region. Identify the pros and cons of each of the social media strategies in terms of the minor league baseball team. Pick two of the social media strategies. Describe a social media program the minor league baseball team could use.

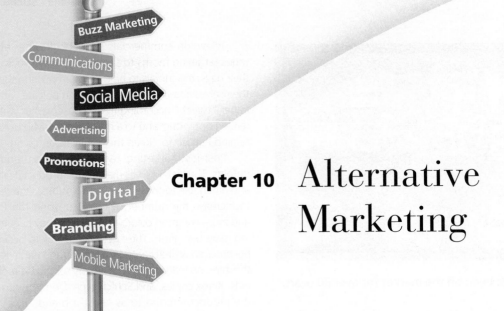

Buzz Marketing
Communications
Social Media
Advertising
Promotions
Digital
Branding
Mobile Marketing

Chapter 10 Alternative Marketing

Chapter Objectives

After reading this chapter, you should be able to answer the following questions:

10.1 How can buzz marketing, guerrilla marketing, lifestyle marketing, and experiential marketing enhance a marketing communications program?

10.2 What methods can be used to effectively employ product placements and branded entertainment?

10.3 Why has the use of alternative media venues, especially video game advertising, grown in marketing communications programs?

10.4 How have in-store marketing and point-of-purchase displays evolved into effective communication and sales tools?

10.5 How can brand communities enhance brand loyalty and devotion?

10.6 What methods are used to adapt alternative marketing programs to international marketing efforts?

Overview

Traditional mass media advertising faces numerous challenges. Although advertisers are not ready to abandon radio, television, magazines, newspapers, and out-of-home programs, they know that many new and valuable media outlets have emerged. As a result, alternative marketing programs and alternative media are on the rise. Marketers spend increasing numbers of dollars finding ways to reach potential customers in new and innovative formats. Successful advertising and promotional programs take advantage of these new alternative approaches, including those targeted to individual segments domestically and consumers in other countries for international firms.

This chapter presents four topics. First, it identifies major alternative marketing programs: buzz marketing, guerrilla marketing, product placements, branded entertainment, and lifestyle marketing. Next, it describes a series of marketing tactics associated with alternative media. Third, in-store marketing

THE PRAIRIE FIRE EXPERIENCE

Many sponsored events take place in local communities that provide opportunities for alternative marketing programs. Wichita, Kansas serves as an example. The community's Prairie Fire Experience offers people of all ages the chance to participate in a variety of events, including an adult 5K runner's race, Sparky's Kids 1-mile race, and a fun run, all as part of the Prairie Fire Marathon Series. Those involved in the full marathon can qualify for the Boston Marathon later in the year. The race is certified by the USATF (U.S.A. Track & Field) association.

Promotions for the event include links to off-race activities that include indoor go-carts, laser tag, mini golf, and rock climbing. Participants can visit several local museums and other attractions. Local restaurants are noted as part of the Top 10 Surprising Food City list compiled by Livability.com. The city of Wichita contains at least 8 major shopping districts.

▲ Wichita's Prairie Fire Experience event is an ideal venue for alternative marketing campaigns.

As a result, many of the programs described in this chapter are possible. The event has special appeal to marketers interested in reaching several audiences, that includes fitness buffs, runners, parents and their children, and those who might like to visit a new city. Marketing programs include traditional advertising combined with alternative marketing methods highlighted in the following pages.[1]

will be examined. Also, brand communities are discussed. The chapter closes with a review of the international implications of these new forms of alternative marketing and alternative media.

Alternative Marketing Programs

Developing alternative marketing programs requires creativity and imagination. Marketers identify new places where a consumer's path intersects with a brand's presence or creates a new intersection point. They then prepare attention-getting marketing messages for those points of contact, which provides the opportunity to supplement mass media and digital advertising with more targeted methods. Figure 10.1 lists common alternative marketing choices. These programs seldom operate independently. A guerrilla marketing campaign might also include buzz and lifestyle marketing components. The same campaign may contain digital components, social media, and traditional advertising.

Alternative marketing relies on buzz, word-of-mouth, and lifestyle messages at times and in places where consumers relax and enjoy hobbies and events. Integrating these

objective 10.1
How can buzz marketing, guerrilla marketing, lifestyle marketing, and experiential marketing enhance a marketing communications program?

◀ **FIGURE 10.1**
Forms of Alternative Marketing

- Buzz marketing
- Guerrilla marketing
- Lifestyle marketing
- Experiential marketing
- Product placement and branded entertainment

Shown: Flying Flames LED candle chandelier.

BRASS FLICKERING FLAME
CHANDELIERS
BELONG TO THOSE
WHO LOVE THEM.

SCOTT + COONER

Dallas 1617 Hi Line Dr. Ste. 100 214.748.9838 Austin 512.480.0436 Visit scottcooner.com

▲ Traditional advertising should be an important component of any alternative marketing campaign.

- Individuals who truly like a brand
- Individuals who are sponsored by a brand
- Company or agency employees

▲ **FIGURE 10.2**
Types of Buzz Marketing Approaches

venues into an integrated marketing program that speaks with a clear voice and message will be the goal.

Buzz Marketing

Buzz marketing has become one of the fastest-growing areas in alternative marketing. Estimated expenditures for these programs total more than $1 billion annually. **Buzz marketing**, or *word-of-mouth marketing*, emphasizes consumers passing along product information. A recommendation by a friend, family member, or acquaintance carries greater credibility than an advertisement. Buzz is more powerful than words spoken by a paid spokesperson or endorser. As shown in Figure 10.2, word-of-mouth endorsements can be supplied by consumers who like a brand and tell others, consumers who like a brand and are sponsored by a company to speak to others, or by company or agency employees who talk about the brand.

Consumers Who Like a Brand

A consumer who genuinely likes a brand and tells others about it presents the ideal marketing situation. Enthusiasts deliver messages in person or through social media. Many musical groups have achieved fame through this type of word-of-mouth support by those who have seen them in bars or as part of a small concert or tour. The ad for Five Star Fitness Center on the next page features Rheagan, who is passionate about exercise and a fan of the company. She shares this enthusiasm with anyone who will listen. Companies often scour social media for individuals who are enthusiastic about its brands and have a significant number of followers.

Sponsored Consumers

Companies sponsor individuals as agents or advocates to introduce new products, share information, and announce special events. This works best when these individuals, or ambassadors, like the brand. A program can involve individuals talking one-on-one to others, or they can host house or block parties to present the product to a group of friends and family.

Brand Ambassadors Customer evangelists, or brand ambassadors, are typically individuals that like the brand they sponsor. The company offers incentives and rewards in exchange for advocacy. Marketers select an ambassador based on his devotion to the brand, level of influence and the size of his social circle. Once recruited, the ambassador delivers messages to her family, friends, reference groups, and work associates. Some are asked to develop grassroots, no- or low-cost marketing events and to promote the brand on the internet through blogs or on social networks. Brand advocates should be upfront and honest about their connections with the company.

On move-in day at the University of North Carolina, students wearing American Eagle Outfitter shirts volunteered to help new students move into dorms. They cheerfully unloaded cars and lugged belongings. They passed out American Eagle coupons, water canisters, and Eagle pens as they helped the students. The helpers were student brand ambassadors. An estimated 10,000 college students work as ambassadors for a variety of companies, including American Eagle, Red Bull, NASCAR, Microsoft, and Hewlett-Packard. In exchange for promoting a particular brand, they receive discounts and/or merchandise.[2]

Marketers use social media used to locate women to become members of the "Disney moms" network. Disney looks for moms that fit the family-friendly theme, use multiple social media platforms with significant online followings, and are actively involved in their local communities offline. The moms are not paid. Instead, they receive incentives such as deep discounts on family trips to Disney World. Each year a group of moms attends the Disney Social Mom Celebration, which is part vacation and part educational. Participants are not told what to post on social media; however, they are required to say something about the event. Last year's celebration produced over 28,000 tweets, 4,900 Instagram photos, and 88 blog posts talking about the event, reviews of various rides, and videos and photos of kids meeting Disney characters.[3]

House or Block Parties Brand ambassadors may host house or block parties. Nestlé Purina spent $50,000 on 1,000 house parties to market a new line of dog food, Chef Michael's Canine Creations. Purina identified childless individuals with household incomes greater than $60,000 who love to pamper their pets. House Party, a firm that matches brands with party hosts, located the homes for Purina. Dianna Burroughs held a party in her Manhattan West Village condo. Fourteen guests and their dogs arrived to sample the filet-mignon-and-potato-flavored kibbles from Chef Michael's Canine Creations. House Party's other clients include Avon, Procter & Gamble, Kraft Heinz, Mattel, Hershey's, and Ford.[4]

BzzAgent offers parties and the ambassador approach for its clients. Suzanne Ermel, a 30-year-old unemployed lawyer, serves as a BzzAgent ambassador for a boxed wine, Black Box. At the grocery store, when she sees a shopper put a box of wine in her shopping cart, Suzanne stops the shopper, declaring "Don't do it! This [Black Box wine] is just a couple of dollars more and you're going to like it a lot more." She adds, "I've pointed Black Box out to random people shopping for wine." She invites friends to her house for a blind tasting party and serves Black Box wine without mentioning the brand name. She then solicits comments from her guests and reveals the name of the wine. The Black Box buzz marketing campaign sought to "increase

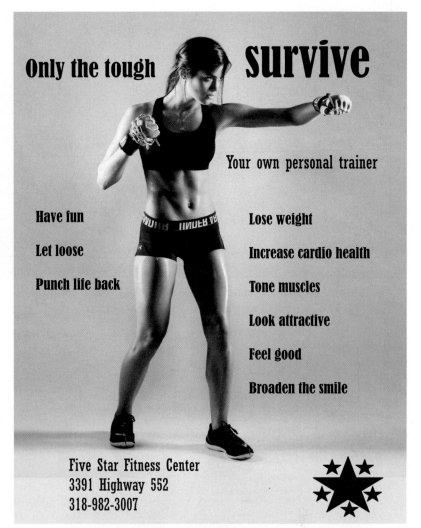

▲ Rheagan generates buzz for Five Star Fitness Center because she is passionate about exercise and the facility.

▼ Many companies employ college students to pitch products as brand ambassadors.

▲ BzzAgent recruits individuals who are influencers among their friends and associates to serve as brand ambassadors.

▼ A current trend is employer branding, which showcases employees raving about the company where they work.

trial, advocacy, and impact sales."[5] The key to these events was that the host was an influencer among his or her friends and associates.

Company Employees

A final group of advocates includes company or agency employees. The company or agency decides whether they should pose as customers or identify themselves as being affiliated with the organization. The Word of Mouth Marketing Association (WOMMA) states that individuals should be upfront and clearly identify themselves as being with the company.

A few years ago, Wal-Mart featured a blog about two ordinary people, Laura and Jim, trekking across the Unites States in an RV and staying in Wal-Mart parking lots. The blog appeared to be written by a couple who were avid customers of Wal-Mart. The blog received attention after *BusinessWeek* exposed Jim as a professional photojournalist employed by Edelman, Wal-Mart's public relations firm. Both Wal-Mart and Edelman received considerable criticism regarding the program due to the lack of transparency.[6]

The Word of Mouth Marketing Association provides guidelines for companies seeking to generate word-of-mouth communications through employees, agency employees, or even sponsors or agents. It encourages:

- Honesty of relationship—be honest about the relationship between consumers, advocates, and marketers.
- Honesty of opinion—be honest in presenting opinions about the brand, both good and bad.
- Honesty of identity—identify honestly who you are.[7]

A new trend, **employer branding** occurs when companies showcase employees discussing what it is like to work for a particular company. In the past, human resource departments used this approach to attract quality employees. Then marketing departments realized that employer branding appealed to customers as well. General Electric, UPS, and Sam Adams have featured employees in advertisements. At first, the ads appeared to be a recruiting tool because the individuals talk about the company and the work environment. At the same time, showing pride and confidence in a company sends a strong brand message to consumers. The approach creates an advantage because these employees truly like the company and their statements appear to be legitimate. Marketers know that what employees say about a company carries considerable weight. Those who like a company where they work share positive thoughts. Consumers seeing the comments will often be favorably impressed.

Buzz Marketing Stages

As Figure 10.3 shows, buzz marketing can be compared to how a virus replicates. The process consists of three stages: inoculation, incubation, and infection.[8] The inoculation stage corresponds to

- Inoculation—the product is introduced
- Incubation—the product is used by a few innovators or trendsetters
- Infection—widespread use of the product occurs

the product being introduced. During incubation, a few innovators or trendsetters try the product. In the infection stage, widespread use of the product occurs.

Only a few companies have been successful deploying buzz marketing during the inoculation stage, or product introduction. In most cases, buzz marketing does not work well at this stage unless the company employs brand agents or brand ambassadors. Otherwise, generating word-of-mouth communication can be virtually impossible. Previous research suggests that true customer-generated buzz occurs after awareness of the product emerges. That awareness typically requires advertising through traditional channels.[9] Now, however, social media provides an alternative method for developing product and brand awareness. Through blogs and social networking, brand managers can generate awareness and buzz, especially when they locate early adopters who are passionate about the brand and are willing to share that enthusiasm within their spheres of influence.

Buzz Marketing Preconditions

Advertising and buzz communication programs from actual customers typically cannot create a successful buzz by themselves unless the preconditions listed in Figure 10.4 are met. The brand must be unique, new, or perform better than current brands. It should stand out and have distinct advantages over competitors. Although not essential, memorable advertising helps to produce buzz. Intriguing, different, and unique advertising captures attention and can inspire talk among people. Getting consumers involved enhances word-of-mouth communications.

Stride Sugarless Gum developed a website to complement the company's traditional advertising. The campaign featured the tagline, "Stride gum lasts a ridiculously long time." The company invited consumers to share what they would like to do for a ridiculously long time and to post photographs of these activities on the Stride microsite developed for Sugarless Gum.[10]

Buzz marketing works for two reasons. First, as noted, people trust someone else's opinion more than paid advertising. Second, consumers like to render their opinions and share thoughts. Many exhibit an innate desire for social interaction and are concerned about the welfare of others. Voicing an opinion can build a person's ego and sense of self-worth, especially when the opinion leads to happiness or satisfaction with a particular product.

Stealth Marketing

Another form of buzz marketing, **stealth marketing**, applies surreptitious practices to introduce a product to individuals while not disclosing or revealing the presenter's true relationship with the brand. Someone posing as a tourist might ask people to take a photo with her camera and then talk to them about the camera. An attractive model ordering a beer or soft drink can tell everyone about how great it tastes. In both instances, the company pays someone to extol the product's benefits.

One stealth marketing ploy that generated national attention, a 6-minute video entitled "Bride Has Massive Hair Wig Out," featured a young bride-to-be who was unhappy with her haircut. In the video, she starts hacking off her hair minutes before the wedding ceremony. Her friends try in vain to stop her. It turned out to be an act. The clever

- Product must be unique, new, or superior
- Brand must stand out
- Advertising should be
  - Memorable
  - Intriguing
  - Different
  - Unique
- Consumer involvement with the brand

▲ **FIGURE 10.4**
Preconditions of Buzz Marketing

▲ After asking someone to take her picture, this individual can talk about the camera as a stealth marketing tactic.

video was produced by an advertising agency for Unilever's Sunsilk Haircare. Millions of viewers believed a real bride and real situation took place. Consequently, they tweeted the "Wig Out" video to thousands. The story appeared on blogs, received coverage on CNN, and became the subject of talk shows before Unilever finally revealed the truth about the stealth marketing campaign.[11]

Stealth marketing thrives in the online world, most notably on social media, due to the ease of creating videos and offering brand endorsements. Most people are not inclined to pass along traditional advertisements and clips. The result has been a rise in stealth approaches as an alternative.

Some argue that stealth marketing represents a shrewd way to reach consumers and generate buzz. At the same time, the Word of Mouth Marketing Association emphasizes the importance of honesty of relationship and honesty of identity. The Federal Trade Commission (FTC) issued an opinion letter supporting the Word of Mouth Marketing Association regarding the full disclosure of any paid individuals in ads. The enticement to create stealth marketing campaigns that generate buzz remains, and the debate over its ethical implications will likely continue.

Guerrilla Marketing

Guerrilla marketing programs obtain instant results using limited resources. Jay Conrad Levinson developed the original concept. Historically, guerrilla marketing offers one of the most successful alternative media marketing programs. Its tactics rely on creativity, quality relationships, and the willingness to try unusual approaches. These programs were originally aimed at small businesses; however, now numerous firms take advantage of guerrilla marketing tactics. Guerrilla marketing emphasizes a combination of media, advertising, public relations, and surprises to reach consumers.

Guerrilla marketing utilizes alternative tactics and venues to focus on finding unique ways of doing things. To be successful, the marketing department must change its thinking process. Discovering "touchpoints" with customers constitutes the first step. Touchpoints include the places where the customers eat, drink, shop, hang out, and sleep. Next, the marketing team identifies unique and memorable ways to reach them at one or more of those places. To do so requires imagination and unorthodox thinking.

Social media and guerrilla marketing tactics were part of the re-launch of Twinkies after Hostess went bankrupt and the product disappeared from store shelves. Brand loyalists passed along the tagline "sweetest comeback in the history of ever" throughout social media. Guerrilla teams, Twinkie the Kid mascot, and food trucks were sent to major markets. The campaign cost $3 million and generated so much demand that the company could barely keep up. Customers purchased 85 million Twinkie cupcakes, with another 100 million ordered by retailers.[12]

Figure 10.5 compares guerrilla marketing to traditional marketing. Guerrilla marketing tends to focus on specific regions or areas. Rather than a national or international campaign, the approach concentrates on personal communication. The objective should be to create excitement that spreads to others by word-of-mouth and social media. Guerrilla marketing involves interacting with consumers, not just sending out a message. Building relationships with customers should be the outcome. By enticing individuals to react, the program enhances the chance that a message will hit home. Advertisements reach consumers where they live, play, and work in noticeable ways. The eventual relationships that evolve help create brand loyalty and positive recommendations to others.

◀ **FIGURE 10.5**
Traditional vs. Guerrilla
Marketing

Traditional Marketing

- Requires money
- Geared to large businesses with big budgets
- Results measured by sales
- Based on experience and guesswork
- Increases production and diversity
- Grows by adding customers
- Obliterates the competition
- Aims messages at large groups
- Uses marketing to generate sales
- "Me Marketing" that looks at "My" company

Guerrilla Marketing

- Requires energy and imagination
- Geared to small businesses and big dreams
- Results measured by profits
- Based on psychology and human behavior
- Grows through existing customers and referrals
- Cooperates with other businesses
- Aims messages at individuals and small groups
- Uses marketing to gain customer consent
- "You Marketing" that looks at how can we help "You"

◀ **FIGURE 10.5**
Traditional vs. Guerrilla
Marketing

Guerrilla marketing requires an aggressive, grassroots approach to marketing. It should produce buzz. When carried out properly, guerrilla marketing becomes a powerful marketing weapon. Figure 10.6 identifies six reasons why companies should use guerrilla marketing tactics.

◀ Guerrilla marketing seeks to connect with consumers to create buzz.

- To find a new way to communicate with consumers
- To interact with consumers
- To make advertising accessible to consumers

- To impact a spot market
- To create buzz
- To build relationships with consumers

◀ **FIGURE 10.6**
Reasons for Using Guerrilla
Marketing

▲ Lifestyle marketing involves reaching consumers during festivals, fairs, and other events.

Lifestyle Marketing

A program that helps companies make contact with consumers in more offbeat and relaxed settings, **lifestyle marketing**, involves identifying marketing methods associated with the hobbies and entertainment venues of a target audience. Lifestyle marketing includes contacting consumers at places such as farmer's markets, bluegrass festivals, citywide garage sales, flea markets, craft shows, stock car races, and other places where large concentrations of individuals convene.

A wide range of consumer lifestyles creates potential target groups, from relatively standard habits to more edgy and extreme behaviors. The energy drink Red Bull and the producers of the energy snack PowerBar gave free samples to people attending sports events, including football and baseball games. The concept was that people who watch sports would be more inclined to try the product. Covergirl offered cosmetics to women attending a fashion show with the idea that those in attendance would be more concerned about personal appearance. Finding a venue where consumers go for relaxation, excitement, socialization, or enjoyment and then matching it with the brand's target market is the focal point of a lifestyle marketing program.

Experiential Marketing

▼ Tracy is passing out samples of a new drink as part of an experiential marketing campaign.

Another alternative marketing form, **experiential marketing**, combines direct marketing, personal selling, and sales promotions into a single consumer experience. It typically involves direct marketing through interactive means such as special events and free samples. Experiential marketing seeks to engage consumers with the brand, rather than merely providing free samples. Bruce Burnett, chief executive of i2i Marketing believes experiential marketing "gives consumers the opportunity to question as well as gain hands-on experience with a brand, allowing them to be more intimate with it, leading to a higher conversion rate."[13]

Cadillac developed a three-part experiential program for current and prospective buyers. All three events were by invitation only. The first part featured a series of 14 golf clinics that paired golf instruction by the David Leadbetter Gold Academy with test drives of the Cadillac. The second element included a culinary tour in 13 different markets paired with the Cadillac SRX model. The third component, a five-track based event, displayed a souped-up V-Series Cadillac sedan in a half-day of high-performance driving and education session led by the Skip Barber Racing School. Invitees participated in three modules: slalom breaking, lane change, and lap driving. GM's head of North American marketing Chris Perry stated that the experiential programs fit the Cadillac brand well because "the Cadillac customer is one who is more entrepreneurial spirited, perhaps more interested in the latest technology, always looking for the new ideas and thinking, more outer directed."[14]

Jack Morton Worldwide created an experiential marketing campaign for Cotton, Inc. aimed at 18- to 34-year-old women. The traveling exhibit presented the songs "The Fabric of Our Lives" and "Dixie" sung by contemporary artists Zooey Deschanel (indie rock), Miranda Lambert (country), and Jazmine Sullivan (R&B). Mall shoppers were able to look into the singers' closets, which were filled with cotton clothes. Shoppers could also record a personal version of "The Fabric of Our Lives." The campaign's budget was $500,000 to $1 million. The exhibit provided mall shoppers with hands-on contact with cotton fabrics.[15]

To increase the probability that a positive experience will occur from an experiential marketing event, companies follow these steps:

Step 1   Choose a clear, concise market segment to target.
Step 2   Identify the right time and place to involve consumers with the brand. Choose opportunities that fit with consumers' lives and when they can engage with the brand emotionally and logically.
Step 3   Make sure the experience reveals clearly the brand's promise and represents the brand well to consumers.

Allowing consumers to enjoy the benefit of a good or service before actually making a purchase gives the program the greatest chance for success.[16]

Product Placements and Branded Entertainment

Most marketers believe getting a product noticed has become increasingly difficult. In response, many firms have increased product placement and branded entertainment expenditures. Each combines the popularity of an entertainment venue with a specific brand.

Product Placements

The planned insertion of a brand or product into a movie, television show, or program, a **product placement** serves the purpose of influencing viewers. Product placements have been a part of motion pictures since the beginning of the industry in the 1890s. Lever Brothers placed the company's soap brand in the early films. In the 1930s, Buick created a 10-picture deal with Warner Brothers for placements. Several tobacco companies paid actors to endorse and use the brands. Television programs, such as the *Colgate Comedy Hour*, were sponsored by brands.

The biggest surge in product placement occurred in 1982 after Reese's Pieces were used to lure E.T. out of hiding as part of the plot of the movie. The placement of the Reese's Pieces spurred a 65 percent increase in sales following the movie's release.[17] With that surge, product placements continued to grow for both brands and TV shows. During a recent month, *American Idol* led all television shows with 208 paid product placements. The top brand in terms of product placement was Coca-Cola.[18] Figure 10.7 displays the top six brands and top six television shows for product placements.

objective 10.2
What methods can be used to effectively employ product placements and branded entertainment?

Top Brands (Total occurrences/month)		Top Shows (total occurrences/month)	
• Coca-Cola	99	• American Idol	208
• AT&T	76	• Celebrity Apprentice	127
• Chevrolet	45	• America's Next Top Model	88
• Ford	39	• Biggest Loser	88
• Apple	32	• Amazing Race	69
• Everlast	32	• Shedding the Wedding	40
• Nike	32	• Dancing with the Stars	38

◀ FIGURE 10.7
Top Television Product Placements

Advertisers believe product placements lead to increased awareness and positive attitudes toward the brand. In a few isolated cases, sales have also increased. In most instances, however, no immediate impact on sales occurs. Research by AC Nielsen reveals the following about product placements:

- Brands placed within "emotionally engaging" television programs were recognized by 43 percent more viewers.
- Brand recognition increased 29 percent for brands placed in highly enjoyed programs.
- Positive brand feelings increased by 85 percent for brands placed in popular programs.[19]

Brand placement features of a low cost per viewer, especially for movies. After a movie has finished its cinema run, it will usually be converted to a DVD format for movie rentals. From there, the movie may be adapted for television viewing on syndicated outlets or one of the premium movie channels. It might also be made available on TV through video-on-demand. This expands a movie's reach beyond the cinema screen to other venues where it may be seen multiple times.

▼ Harley Davidson emphasized product placement in television shows, movies, music, and video games in a recent marketing campaign.

Harley-Davidson hired Davie Brown Entertainment to locate appropriate product placement opportunities in movies, television, music, and video games. For the first time in Harley-Davidson's history, the company relied on product placements as its core marketing strategy. According to Dino Bernacchi, director of advertising and promotions for Harley-Davidson, "We want to use [product placement] to socialize Harley-Davidson motorcycling. . . . Entertainment can sensationalize the excitement and thrill of riding to the point of moving people to check it out." Only three percent of American consumers own a motorcycle, but another 15 to 20 million have the desire to buy one. Harley-Davidson's marketing team believed strategic product placements would encourage those on the edge to go ahead and make purchases.[20]

Branded Entertainment

The integration of entertainment and advertising by embedding brands into the storyline of a movie, television show, or other entertainment medium is **branded entertainment**.[21] In an episode of the CTV drama *The Eleventh Hour*, for example, Nicorette was integrated into a story about a character trying to quit smoking. The movie *Up in the Air* starring George Clooney prominently displayed American Airlines and Hilton Hotels. The movie's plot involves Clooney's character logging ten million miles on American so he can have his name emblazoned on the plane and ride along with American Airlines' chief pilot. Actual American Airlines planes were used in the film. Many of the hotel scenes were filmed at Hilton locations. Integrating the brands into the story made them much more noticeable to the viewing audience.[22]

The use of branded entertainment has increased with the rise of "reality" television shows. The success of branded entertainment in reality shows has led to its use in scripted television shows. Branded entertainment may also be found in novels, plays, songs, and movies.

Achieving Success

Figure 10.8 identifies the major factors that influence the success of brand placements and branded entertainment. The specific medium or media involved will have an impact on effectiveness. Placement clutter has caused some television programs to lose clout because too many brands are shown during the show so no one brand stands out. The same can occur in movies when too many brands are embedded into scenes.

Product placements and branded entertainment work because no "call to action" appears. Instead, increasing brand awareness and generating positive feelings toward the brand are the goals. When a consumer's favorite actor enjoys a particular brand or her favorite show contains a particular brand, it becomes more likely that the individual will transfer those positive feelings to the brand. People between the ages of 15 and 34 are more likely to notice brands placed in a movie or show. Also, individuals in North America and the Asia-Pacific area are more receptive than viewers in Europe. When a consumer sees a brand placement of a product he has purchased, it may reinforce the idea that a wise decision was made, further validating the original purchase choice.[23]

Company Tactics The manner in which marketers place the brand into a movie or show will be important. Brand insertions work best when they seem logical. In other words, the most effective placements are those woven into the program in ways that appear to be natural parts of the story. Brands shown in the background that seem to be artificially inserted will be less effective.

For some companies, product placements in movies make it possible to bypass the legislation and guidance intended to control advertising to children and young adults. A study of the top 25 box office movies revealed that 32 percent were rated for viewing by adolescents and contained prominent brand placements for tobacco products. If these companies had tried to advertise directly to teens, they would have encountered numerous regulations and possibly severe penalties.[24]

Product placement and branded entertainment budgets have been increasing for several reasons. First, a brand's appeal may grow when it appears in a non-advertising context. Second, the perception of what others think about a brand is important to consumers. For many, it can be more significant than how the consumer views the brand. Seeing the brand used in a television show, a movie, or a book makes the brand appear to be acceptable and even desirable. Third, seeing others use the brand provides reassurance for individuals who have already purchased the item.

Fourth, for individuals who place little value in brand names and branded products, having a brand placed in a program provides evidence of the brand's advantages. The evidence may be strong enough for them to consider purchasing the item. In these cases, the brand does not have to directly persuade the consumer of its merits. It does so through the acceptance and use of the product by the actor or as part of the story.

The Media's Perspective For moviemakers and television producers, money represents the primary motivation behind product placements and branded entertainment. In the past, brand mentions were incidental or used by movie producers to create realism in a film. They now generate additional income. Costs for product placement can be as little as $10,000 for a mention or incidental view to as much as $300,000 or more for a primary actor using the brand or incorporating the brand name in a dialogue.

In summary, brand placements present an excellent method to increase share of mind and build brand awareness. Although some believe that certain programs have become saturated with product placements, they continue to be utilized. If clutter becomes too severe, usage will likely decline, but only if the impact on consumer responses and attitudes also decline.

- Media
- Supporting promotional activities
- Consumer attitudes toward placements
- Placement characteristics
- Regulations

▲ **FIGURE 10.8**
Key Factors Influencing the Effectiveness of Product Placement and Branded Entertainment

▼ Seeing brands in television shows and movies can make the brand look more acceptable and desirable.

Alternative Media Venues

objective 10.3

Why has the use of alternative media venues, especially video game advertising, grown in marketing communications programs?

In upper New York, before crossing one of the five bridges operated by the New York State Bridge Authority, a driver pays a toll or presents an EZ-pass. Advertisements now appear on the mechanical arms that come down at the toll booth for a popular tourist attraction called Headless Horseman Hayrides and Haunted Houses. Owner Nancy Jubie reported, "This is so in-your-face advertising, we couldn't pass it up." The cost to place the name of her business on a toll booth arm for 3 months was $18,000.[25] Many companies look for unusual and unlikely places to attract attention. Figure 10.9 identifies some of the alternative forms of media.

Video Game Advertising

Product placements in video games have become common. Products can be part of a stand-alone game purchased at a retail store and played on the computer, or they can be placed in an internet video game. In-game brand placement enjoys all of the advantages of brand placements and branded entertainment. Video game advertising reaches young people who have become more difficult to contact through traditional media. In addition, it has the added feature of interactivity. Advertisers spend approximately $7 billion per year on in-game advertising because it presents an attractive market for the following reasons:

- 75 percent of all U.S. internet users spend at least one hour a month playing online games.
- 27 percent average 30 hours a month playing games.
- The primary game-playing market segment is 16- to 34-year-old males.
- The fastest-growing video game market segment is females.[26]

- Video games
- Cinema
- Subways
- Street and mall kiosks
- Stairs
- Escalators
- Parking lots
- Airlines
- Shopping bags
- Clothes

▲ **FIGURE 10.9**
Examples of Alternative Media

Video game advertising takes several forms (see Figure 10.10). The original and most widespread form of video game advertising involves locating a brand placement in the game. It can take the form of a billboard in a racing game, a Coke vending machine, or a McDonald's restaurant that is permanently integrated into the game. With the cost of producing a game now in the $20 to $30 million range and $1 to $5 million more to launch a game, game producers welcome product placement advertising as a source of revenue.

The number of game-related websites has exploded recently. Instead of placing ads in the game itself, advertisers place ads on these gaming sites. Although the exact number of gaming websites has not been identified, estimates suggest that more than 6,000 exist. Some receive as many as seven million visits per year.[27]

Numerous companies offer video games to be played on branded websites. These branded video games are called **advergames**. Axe, Maxwell House, Holiday Inn, Arby's, Baskin-Robbins, Taco Bell and Suave are a few of the companies offering advergames. Instead of creating a special microsite for these games, advergames are usually placed on

- In-game advertisements
- Rotating in-game advertising
- Interactive ads
- Game-related Websites
- Advergames
- Sponsored downloads
- Mobile game apps

▲ **FIGURE 10.10**
Video Game Advertising

free gaming portals. Blockdot.com research indicates that consumers have positive feelings about brands that sponsor advergames. More specifically, 83 percent of consumers think positively about companies that underwrite them, and 70 percent are more likely to buy products from companies that sponsor the games.[28]

In addition to game-related websites, the social gaming market attracts advertisers. According to Nielsen, gaming has surpassed email as the second most popular online activity just behind social networking. Of the 800 million individuals on Facebook, 53 percent have played games on the site, and 20 percent play them regularly.[29]

Another popular new approach involves mobile gaming that drives traffic into retail outlets. Buffalo Wild Wings, for instance, features a fantasy football game app that requires consumers to play it in the store to be eligible for prizes. Cosi, a newly established sandwich restaurant, requires gamers to visit a store to determine if they are winners. In both instances, the mobile game apps drive customer traffic to retail outlets where they are more likely to purchase food items.[30]

Benefits IGA Worldwide research suggests that the majority of gamers hold positive attitudes about ads placed in video games, if the ads are well done and fit the scene. The study noted that 82 percent of gamers find the games to be just as enjoyable when ads were present. A 44 percent increase in recall of brands resulted from ads presented in games when compared to awareness prior to exposure in the video game. Positive brand attribute associations also increased.[31]

Online video games present advertisers with the luxury of generating quality web metrics. Advertisers can track the length of ad exposure in an online game. In most cases, the marketers are able to tie in demographic information to find out who views the in-game ad, how long they play, and how often. These metrics then make it possible to target ads specifically to the consumer, demographic group, location profile, or type of player.[32]

New Video Game Technology Product placements within a game face the disadvantage of soon becoming overlooked. To combat this problem, Massive, a media company, pioneered a technology that rotates or changes ads in online video games in real time. Advertisers insert new ads and products into the online game each time the person plays it. By changing the ads, the marketing team delivers time-sensitive promotions, and the advertising remains current. Massive can make the advertisement interactive, allowing the player to click on it for additional information. Additional technology measures how much of a billboard or product placement a player sees during the game depending on their in-game actions. Technology can then fine tune the player's surroundings so that the missed ad will reappear later in the game.[33]

Females and Video Games In the past, most marketers believed that mostly teens and young adult males enjoyed video games. Today, IDC Research estimates that females constitute 40 percent of all gamers. One recent estimate suggests that more than 130 million females play video games.

The introduction of new games, such as *Littlest Pet Shop* and *Charm Girls* for girls plus *Your Shape*, *Just Dance*, *Wii Fit Plus*, and *Sports Active* for women, has built demand. Ubisoft's *Imagine* video game series, which sold 14 million copies in 3 years, features games in which girls can play the role of a ballerina or explore female-dominated professions. Courtney Simmons, public relations director for Sony Online Entertainment (SOE), enjoys playing video games with her three children. She argues

▲ The primary game-playing market segment is 16- to 34-year old males.

▼ Approximately 40% of gamers are now female, many starting to play games at a young age.

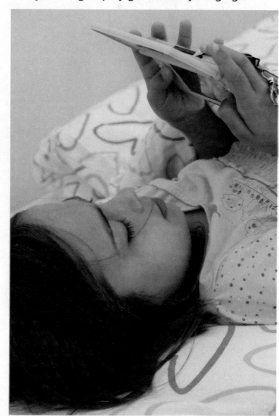

that women are being "gamed down to," because "there is a lack of understanding about how women play." Simmons wants more women making games that females want to play.

From a marketing communications perspective, gaming offers considerable potential. As more females purchase gaming devices and play games tailored to them, sales will increase. Further, the ability to reach girls, young women, and mature women with products placed in the games or advertising messages embedded in them presents a potentially powerful new method to develop brand awareness and brand loyalty in an alternative medium.[34]

▲ More women are needed to design and produce games for the female market.

Cinema Advertising

Prior to a movie showing, theaters present advertisements during pre-feature programming. Some products have direct relationships with the movie; others are totally unrelated. Although clutter exists in the sense that the commercials often run consecutively and will be mingled with new movie previews, they are delivered to what is essentially a "captive" audience waiting for the feature to start.

Cinema advertising rarely appears at the center of an integrated ad campaign, but was the case with HP's launch of the Photosmart Premium printer with TouchSmart Web. According to Tariq Hassan, HP's vice president of marketing, "We had to create more awareness; we had to touch the consumer. The theater was a natural fit." The cinema campaign included a 30-second spot in the pre-feature programming at 17,300 theaters and 2,600 plasma screens in theater lobbies. It also executed an interactive "lobby domination" strategy in 15 theaters in New York, Chicago, San Francisco, San Diego, Miami, and Houston. Theater lobbies were turned into branded events with banners, signage, holographic 3-D kiosks, and large manned booths where the printer was demonstrated. The campaign delivered 50,000 product demonstrations averaging 6 minutes in length and a total of 700,000 lobby impressions.[35]

▼ These floorstands were used to advertise the Coleman Theater.

Other Alternative Media

A number of additional media alternatives are available. Ads appear on subways and other public facilities as local and state governments struggle to balance budgets. Parking lots, stairs, and escalators feature advertising displays. Airlines increase revenues by presenting advertisements on flight-ticket jackets and using in-plane signage. Shopping bags, clothes, and restaurant menus provide additional advertising venues.

The Visit South Walton campaign designed by Zehnder Communications featured alternative media ads in airports. Signage including the one shown in this section was placed strategically throughout the airport. Advertisements were also located on stairs, escalators, moving walkways, floor mats, and on the outside of a parking garage. The goal was to reach travelers within the airport in a number of different locations

◀ A visit South Walton ad placed on an escalator at an airport.

▼ Visit South Walton signage in strategic spots within major airports.

with the hope they would think about South Walton as a future vacation destination. The multiple visual images increased the chances that Visit South Walton would move from just sensory recognition to individual memories and cognitive maps.

A new form of alternative media utilizes facial recognition technology. A digital display in a shopping mall with this technology can recognize a female in her 20s standing in front of it. Ads touting makeup, shoes, fashions, and ice cream then pop up. When a man in his 50s moves in front of the display, a different set of ads appears.

The popularity of nontraditional formats to deliver advertising messages continues to increase. Each time an innovative marketing professional identifies a new venue, a segment of the advertising community jumps on board. These methods make it possible to send messages that either cut through or go around clutter to reach people in moments when they may be more receptive to an advertisement's content.

In-Store Marketing

Consumers make approximately 60 percent of all purchase decisions while in a retail store.[36] Except for point-of-purchase (POP) displays, many marketing departments do not pay much attention to in-store marketing. Funds devoted to it represent a small percentage of advertising and marketing budgets. This may mean that some companies are missing opportunities.

To understand the potential of in-store advertising, consider what factors affect consumers as they purchase clothing. In a survey of about 600 consumers, 52 percent said that in-store signage, displays, or point-of-purchase displays influenced their decisions, far outdistancing print advertising and word-of-mouth communications.[37] Figure 10.11 displays a complete list of these influences.

objective 10.4

How have in-store marketing and point-of-purchase displays evolved into effective communication and sales tools?

In-Store Marketing Tactics

Retailers can engage consumers through signage, end-aisle displays, ceiling banners and overhead mobiles. Use of color, light, and sound are now elements of in-store marketing. Placing and using video screens and television monitors to present messages represents

▶ **FIGURE 10.11**
Types of Advertising that Most
Influenced Clothing Purchases

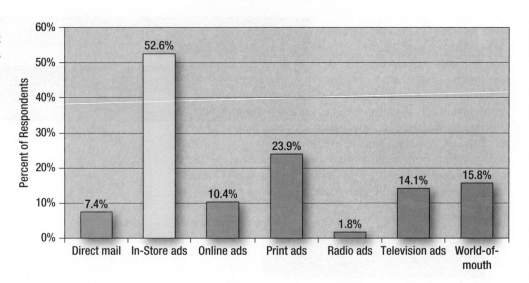

Approximately 60% of all purchase decisions are made in the retail store.

the newest and most expensive in-store marketing tactic. Many static signs have been replaced with high-technology mediums. Also, shopping carts with broken or unreadable static signs may be replaced with video screens. Digital media within the store offer retailers the opportunity to customize messages to fit the store and the aisle where the display is located.[38]

Airplay America produces The Salon Channel, a retail television channel and digital signage network for beauty salons. Programming consists of human interest and lifestyle stories. Beauty shop patrons spend an average of 30 to 45 minutes per salon visit. The Salon Channel provides entertainment, including features about nationally recognized stylists and the latest hairstyles, along with advertisements for products and services, many of which are related to beauty and fashion.[39]

Wal-Mart follows the same path. In the past, Wal-Mart's ads appeared on all in-store televisions. With new technologies, the marketing department distributes ads geared to each department within a store and for specific aisles. Rather than hanging television monitors from the ceiling, flat-screen panel monitors appear at eye level in the aisles, which leads to greater ad recall. Marketers place digital monitors at end-caps and near other displays. These television monitors contain advertising pertinent to the end-cap or the merchandise being displayed. To appreciate the potential impact of this form of in-store advertising, consider each week 68 million viewers watch the combined national television newscasts on ABC, CBS, and NBC. The number of shoppers at Wal-Mart each week tops 127 million. The potential audience for a commercial on the Wal-Mart television system will be nearly twice as large as an advertisement on the three national newscasts.[40] In addition, the Wal-Mart ad reaches consumers as they shop and while they consider purchasing options.

Point-of-Purchase Marketing

Traditionally, one of the most important components of in-store marketing has been **point-of-purchase (POP) displays**, which include any form of special exhibit that advertises merchandise. Retailers locate point-of-purchase displays near cash registers, at the end of an aisle, in a store's entryway, or anywhere they might be noticed.

Point-of-purchase advertising includes displays, signs, and devices used to identify, advertise, or merchandise an outlet, service, or product. POP displays can serve as an important aid to retail selling.

Point-of-purchase displays remain highly effective tools for increasing sales. Coca-Cola reports that only 50 percent of soft drink sales are made from the regular store shelf. The other 50 percent results from product displays in other parts of the store. American Express discovered that 30 percent of purchases charged on the American Express card came from impulse decisions by customers seeing the "American Express Cards Welcome" sign.

Research indicates that an average increase in sales of about nine percent occurs with usage of one POP display. Only about half of POP displays actually impact sales; however, those that increase purchases do so by an average of approximately 20 percent. Consequently, point-of-purchase advertising remains attractive to manufacturers.[41] Currently, manufacturers spend more than $17 billion each year on point-of-purchase advertising materials. Manufacturers place the greatest percentage of POP materials in restaurants, food services, apparel stores, and footwear retailers. The fastest-growing categories include fresh, frozen, or refrigerated foods and professional services.[42]

Many manufacturers view point-of-purchase displays as an attractive way to display a brand more prominently in front of customers. Some retailers hold a different perspective, believing that POP materials should either boost sales for the store or draw customers into the store. Retailers will be less interested in the sales of one particular brand, and instead want to improve overall sales and store profits. Retailers prefer displays that educate consumers and provide information. As a result, they are more inclined to set up displays to match the retailer's marketing objectives.

Designing Effective Point-of-Purchase Displays

Effective POP displays clearly communicate the product's attributes. A quality display incorporates the price and other promotional information. It encourages the customer to stop and look, pick up the product, and examine it. A customer who stops to examine a product on display becomes more inclined to buy the item.

A successful display makes a succinct offer that the customer immediately understands.

▲ Point-of-Purchase displays are often located near cash registers to encourage impulse buys.

▼ Using POP displays that are integrated with Kraft's advertisement for Kraft Parmesan Cheese increases the chances of being noticed by shoppers.

- Integrate the brand's image into the display.
- Integrate the display with current advertising and promotions.
- Make the display dramatic to get attention.
- Keep the color of the display down so the product and signage stand out.

- Make the display versatile so it can be easily adapted by retailers.
- Make the display reusable and easy to assemble.
- Make the display easy to stock.
- Customize the display to fit the retailer's store.

In most cases, a display has a limited time to capture the customer's attention. If it fails, the customer moves on to other merchandise. Colors, designs, merchandise arrangements, and tie-ins with other marketing messages constitute critical elements of effective POP displays.

The best point-of-purchase displays integrate with other marketing messages. Logos and message themes used in advertisements appear on the displays. A Saatchi & Saatchi advertising agency study suggests that consumers make purchase decisions in just four seconds. On average, a consumer only looks at a display or signage for 3–7 seconds.[43] Tying a POP display into current advertising and marketing messages increases the chances it will be noticed. Effective displays present any form of special sales promotion that a company offers. Customers quickly recognize tie-ins with current advertising and promotional themes as they view displays. Figure 10.12 lists some additional pointers for point-of-purchase advertising.

Measuring Point-of-Purchase Effectiveness

Manufacturers and retailers both endeavor to measure the effectiveness of POP displays. Linking the POP display into a point-of-sale (POS) cash register makes it easier to gather results. Codes on the display items enable the POS system to pick them up. Then, individual stores measure sales before and during a point-of-purchase display program by using cash register data. The data also helps the retailer's management team identify the time to withdraw or change a display as sales decline. The technology helps retailers identify the displays that have the largest impact on sales. A retailer might deploy this method to test different types of POP displays in various stores. The most effective displays can then be expanded to a larger number of stores.

From the manufacturer's viewpoint, point-of-sale data helps to improve POP displays. The data may also be used to strengthen partnerships with retailers. These bonds help the manufacturer weather poor POP showings. Retailers are more willing to remain with any manufacturer that tries to develop displays that benefit both parties.

Brand Communities

objective 10.5

How can brand communities enhance brand loyalty and devotion?

The ultimate demonstration of brand loyalty and brand devotion takes the form of **brand communities**. In most cases, a symbolic meaning behind the brand links individuals to the brand community and other owners of the brand. Interactions between the customers and the product lead to a sense of identity and inclusion. A set of shared values and experiences that integrate with feelings about the brand becomes the result.

Brand communities do not form for every product or company. They cannot be created by the company or product; however, a marketing department can facilitate and enhance a community experience. A company with a strong brand community maintains a positive image, has a rich and long tradition, occupies a unique position in the marketplace, and enjoys a group of loyal, dedicated followers.[44] Figure 10.13 highlights some of the reasons that brand communities exist. Most brand communities require some type of face-to-face interactions, although the internet does provide a venue for members to contact each other and to blog about the product.

Jeep, Harley-Davidson, and Apple all enjoy loyal brand communities. In each case, the brand owners come from diverse populations. The highly successful Jeep Jamboree and Camp Jeep events give owners opportunities to share driving experiences, tell stories, and share ideas. Most of the interactions among customers occur during the company-sponsored barbecue. They also take place during roundtable discussions hosted by a Jeep engineer or other Jeep employee.

Many, if not most, of the attendees at a Camp Jeep event have no experience driving a Jeep off-road. Among those who have, some use a "tread lightly" ethos, whereas others have mud-covered vehicles from heavy off-road adventures. First-timers at the camp are often timid and afraid they might not fit in, but soon find they do as repeaters welcome anyone and everyone to the Jeep community. The vehicle provides the common bond that brings individuals together, regardless of demographic and psychographic differences.

Harley-Davidson features a highly successful brand community program. Several years ago, the company's leadership team helped create a unique brand community spirit. An organization called HOG formed around the Harley brand. In return, Harley-Davidson offered benefits, such as information about community gatherings along with special marketing offers for accessories, to HOG members. The benefits are only available to the HOG group, which encourages new Harley-Davidson owners to join the HOG brand community.

Marketers seek to facilitate and enhance the community in which owners can interact. Figure 10.14 provides information on ways a marketing team can assist in creating a brand community.

- Affirmation of the buying decision
- Social identity and bonding
- Swap stories
- Swap advice and provide help to others
- Feedback and new ideas

▲ **FIGURE 10.13**
Reasons Brand Communities Form

▲ The popularity of the reality TV show *Duck Dynasty* has increased enthusiasm for the Skyjacker brand community.

Building a brand community begins with sponsoring events bringing product owners together. As noted, Jeep sponsors the jamborees and a camp. Harley-Davidson sponsors rides, rallies, and local events. These events help create a brand community spirit that leads to bonding between owners. Eventually, this produces a sense of social identity.

Company representatives should become involved in club events. Jeep engineers attend events and mingle with customers. They provide advice and encouragement to any new owner about to take his or her vehicle off-road for the first time. Harley managers, including the CEO, ride Harleys to rallies to talk with owners.

In addition to company-sponsored events, other venues for interaction can be encouraged. The internet offers another place for owners to talk. They can visit through blogs, chat

- Create member benefits to encourage new customers to join a group.
- Provide materials to the group that are not available anywhere else.
- Involve firm representatives in the groups.
- Sponsor special events and regular meetings.
- Promote communications among members of the group.
- Build a strong brand reputation.

◀ **FIGURE 10.14**
Ways to Enhance Brand Community Spirit

rooms, or social network microsites. A company can become involved in these exchange venues. Employees should openly identify themselves. Brand communities enjoy company involvement and want an honest exchange of comments.

While providing venues and means to enhance a brand community spirit, the company continues other advertising and marketing programs. Brand communities normally emerge for brands with strong images. Such images must be maintained. Marketers feature the pride of owning the brand in advertisements, making its uniqueness and position in the marketplace clear.

International Implications

objective 10.6

What methods are used to adapt alternative marketing programs to international marketing efforts?

Alternative marketing can be used to reach minority groups within the United States. An example of buzz marketing occurred when the Clamato company sought to increase brand awareness among U.S. Latinos. The firm gave 2,000 agents a 32-ounce bottle of Clamato and 10 coupons. The agents reached 34,000 potential customers, and positive opinions of the drink rose from 32 to 78 percent.[45]

Alternative marketing methods are also being tried in other countries. Starbucks and Pepsi combined efforts to produce a movie series called *A Sunny Day*. The film follows a girl from the Chinese countryside to the big city, where she discovers love, blogging, Starbucks, and Pepsi. The series was tailored for Shanghai's subway and the 2.2 million who ride it each day. The story was made into a soap opera-style script featuring short daily segments. A website featured story snippets each day for those who missed seeing it on the subway and wanted to know what happened. The Shanghai subway has a network of 4,000 flat-screen monitors that provide train information, clips of soccer highlights, entertainment news, and advertising. Marketers pay to run ads, just like they would on television. *A Sunny Day* was the system's first venture into a short miniseries, with episodes each day for 40 weeks.[46]

Brand communities have emerged in other countries. Jeep employed the brand community concept to build a brand presence in China. The first Jeep was introduced in China in 1983 by American Motors through a joint venture in Beijing; however, recent sales of Jeep have slowed. In response, the first three-day Camp Jeep in China was created. It attracted 700 Jeep owners and 3,000 participants. The event included off-road courses, bungee jumping, a hiking course, wall climbing, a soccer field, and an off-road ATV course. Musical entertainment and time slots for karaoke enthusiasts were provided.[47] The event's purpose was to renew Jeep's strong brand name and to create a strong sense of community among current Jeep owners in China. Through these individuals, Jeep's marketing team hoped to generate word-of-mouth, or buzz, for the Jeep brand, driving new customers to the Jeep brand.

The clutter problems that plague U.S. advertisers are present around the world. The tactics used to overcome it domestically may be adapted to international operations. Firms from other nations can adapt alternative media tactics. International conglomerates will likely respond with new and creative alternative marketing programs.

))) INTEGRATED Campaigns in Action

INTERSTATE BATTERIES

Interstate Batteries employed its internal marketing department to launch a geo-targeted online media plan for company operated Battery Centers that are located in cities throughout the United States. The objectives of the campaign were to:

- Increase awareness of all Interstate Battery Centers
- Drive traffic to all Interstate Battery Centers
- Create awareness of key brand messages

Interstate Batteries used online display advertising to create awareness and provide information about the location of its stores. The campaign was geo-targeted by each store's market zip codes. Consumers who clicked on the ads were taken to a geo-specific landing page that provided information about the closest All Battery Center. The campaign targeted the 25 to 54 age group with the selected zip codes surrounding each of the battery stores.

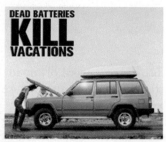

◀ Interstate Batteries launched a geo-targeted online advertising campaign to build awareness and drive traffic to its Battery Centers.

MyMarketingLab

To submit media-based assignments for the Integrated Campaigns in Action, go to MediaShare for Business at **mymktlab.com** ⭐.

Summary

Alternative media enjoys many success stories. The four forms of alternative marketing programs are buzz marketing, stealth marketing, guerrilla marketing, and product placement. Buzz marketing, or word-of-mouth marketing, places the emphasis on consumers passing along information about a brand. The consumers can be those who like a brand, sponsored consumers, or company insiders. Some consider using company insiders to be unethical, which means care should be taken before starting such programs. Employer branding is a program in which companies showcase employees discussing what it is like to work for a particular company.

Stealth marketing uses surreptitious practices to introduce a product to individuals or fails to disclose or reveal the true relationship with the brand. It has also drawn ethical criticism.

Guerrilla marketing programs are designed to obtain instant results with limited resources through creativity, high-quality relationships, and a willingness to try unusual approaches. Lifestyle marketing involves the use of marketing methods associated with the hobbies and entertainment venues of the target audience. Experiential marketing combines direct marketing, field marketing, and sales promotions into a single consumer experience.

Product placements are planned insertions of a brand or product into a movie, television program, or some other media program. Branded entertainment facilitates the integration of entertainment and advertising by embedding brands into the storyline of a movie, television show, or other entertainment medium.

Numerous alternative media venues exist. They include mobile phone advertising, video game advertising and advergames, cinema advertising, airline in-flight advertising, and others. Use of these media has been on the increase.

In-store marketing programs take two forms. Tactics include the use of high-tech video screens and television monitors in new and more visible places. This includes tailoring messages to individual parts of the store. Traditional point-of-purchase advertising continues to be widely utilized. Recently, POP advertising incorporated newer technologies to increase its effectiveness.

Brand communities evolve when consumers feel a great deal of brand loyalty and devotion. They form around events, programs, and exchanges of information. A company with a strong brand and a devoted marketing team can assist in the formation and continuance of brand communities.

Alternative media choices are utilized to reach minority groups in the United States in unique new ways. They are also expanding into international markets. As advertising clutter increases, the use of these media is likely to grow and will likely become cluttered as well.

Key Terms

alternative marketing The use of buzz, word-of-mouth, and lifestyle messages at times when consumers are relaxing and enjoying hobbies and events

buzz marketing An emphasis on consumers passing along information about a product to others; also known as *word-of-mouth marketing*

employer branding A program in which companies showcase employees discussing what it is like to work for a particular company

stealth marketing The use of surreptitious practices to introduce a product to individuals without disclosing or revealing the true relationship with the brand

guerrilla marketing Programs designed to obtain instant results through the use of limited resources by relying on creativity, high-quality relationships, and the willingness to try new approaches

lifestyle marketing Marketing methods associated with the hobbies and entertainment venues of the target audience

experiential marketing A program that combines direct marketing, field marketing, and sales promotions into a single consumer experience

product placement The planned insertion of a brand or product into a movie, television show, or some other media program

branded entertainment The integration of entertainment and advertising by embedding brands into the storyline of a movie, television show, or other entertainment medium

advergames Branded video games

point-of-purchase (POP) displays Any form of in-store special display that advertises merchandise

brand communities A link that forms due to an association between the brand, a consumer, and others who own or purchase the brand

---

MyMarketingLab

To complete the problems with the ⭐ in your MyLab, go to the end-of-chapter Discussion Questions.

Review Questions

10-1. What are the main alternative media programs described in this chapter?

10-2. What is buzz marketing?

10-3. What three types of consumers can pass along buzz marketing messages?

10-4. Why is buzz marketing effective? What preconditions should be met to ensure its effectiveness?

10-5. What is stealth marketing?

10-6. What is guerrilla marketing? How does it differ from traditional marketing?

10-7. What is lifestyle marketing? What types of locations are suited to lifestyle marketing?

10-8. What is experiential marketing?

10-9. What are product placements and branded entertainment? What do they have in common?

10-10. Identify the alternative media venues described in this chapter.

10-11. Describe the forms of video game advertising, including advergames.

10-12. What is in-store marketing? Why is it important?

10-13. What new in-store marketing tactics are being utilized?

10-14. What is point-of-purchase advertising? Why is it important?

10-15. How have new technologies changed some forms of point-of-purchase advertising?

10-16. What is a brand community?

10-17. What should a company's marketing team do to assist in the development and growth of brand communities?

⭐ **10-18.** Is the use of alternative media growing or declining in international markets? Explain why.

Critical Thinking Exercises

DISCUSSION QUESTIONS

10-19. Think about a product category where you have a high knowledge of the various brands. Pick one of the major brands. Discuss the characteristics the brand would want for a brand advocate, ambassador, or evangelist. What type of offers would it take from the company to create a strong brand ambassador? Discuss each of the stages of buzz marketing as it relates to the brand you identified. Which stage is the brand in now? Justify your answer. Discuss each of the preconditions of buzz marketing as it relates to your chosen brand.

⭐**10-20.** Describe in your own words each of the alternative marketing strategies listed in Figure 10.1. Suppose you are a marketing intern at the Five Star Fitness Center. Discuss the pros and cons of each form of alternative marketing for the fitness center. If your budget only allowed one of the alternative marketing approaches, which would you choose? Explain why.

10-21. Consider a recent purchase you made at the recommendation of someone else. Why did you trust that person's recommendation? How important is a recommendation by someone else in your purchase decisions?

10-22. Discuss the difference between buzz marketing and stealth marketing. If you were hired as a marketing manager for a local business, would you support a stealth marketing campaign? Why or why not?

⭐**10-23.** Describe the primary differences between guerrilla marketing and traditional marketing. Imagine being approached by the owner of a small clothing boutique. She has heard about guerrilla marketing and wants to try it. Why should she use guerrilla marketing? What are the pros and cons? What guerrilla marketing techniques would you suggest? Be specific.

10-24. Can you think of a lifestyle marketing program or an experiential marketing campaign that you encountered? What was your reaction? Was the approach effective? Why or why not? What about with other consumers? If you have not experienced lifestyle or experiential marketing, think of a situation and brand where you think it would be effective. Explain why.

10-25. Find a movie or television show that you have already watched and enjoyed. Watch it again, but this time, make a list of all of the product placements in the file. Identify if each was a prominent placement, if

the actor used the brand, or if it was just in the background. When you finish, discuss the product placements that were the most effective and those that were the least effective. What made the placement effective? What made it ineffective?

⭐**10-26.** Explain the difference between product placement and branded entertainment. Do you personally notice product placements in television shows or movies? Why or why not? Identify the factors that make product placement or branded entertainment successful for a brand.

10-27. Do you play video games? If so, approximately how many hours a month do you play games (including online games)? What advertising have you noticed in the games? How effective was the advertising?

⭐**10-28.** Describe in your own words the various types of video game advertising listed in Figure 10.10. Suppose you have a marketing internship with Pizza Hut. Discuss the pros and cons of each method of video game advertising for Pizza Hut. Which method or methods would you recommend for Pizza Hut? Why?

10-29. Look at the graph in Figure 10.11. Rank each of the items in the graph from most effective to least effective for you personally as it relates to purchasing clothes. Justify your ranking.

10-30. Think about point-of-purchase displays. Do they impact your purchases? Why or why not? Describe the most effective point-of-purchase displays for you personally. Why are they effective? Describe the least effective point-of-purchase displays for you personally. Why are they ineffective?

10-31. What brand are you the most passionate about? Does a brand community exist around that brand? Examine the ways a brand can enhance a brand community listed in Figure 10.14. Discuss each one in terms of the brand you mentioned for this question either in terms of what the brand is currently doing or what they should do.

Integrated Learning Exercises

10-32. Type "buzz marketing" into an online search engine. Find two advertising agencies or marketing agencies that offer buzz marketing expertise. What types of buzz marketing services does each provide? Which company do you think offers the best buzz marketing program? Why? Provide the URL of the two agencies as well as screenshots to illustrate your points.

⭐**10-33.** Describe in your own words each of the forms of alternative marketing listed in Figure 10.1. Access the website of Scott + Cooner at **scottcooner.com**. After you have studied the company's website, discuss the pros and cons of each form of alternative marketing listed in Figure 10.1. If Scott + Cooner's budget only

allowed for one of the alternative marketing methods, which would you choose? Why?

10-34. Access **women.igda.org**. What is your opinion of this website? How can it be beneficial to a marketing manager? How can it be beneficial to females who want to pursue video game design? Go to the parent website **www.igda.org**. What types of information are available at this site? Be specific. Provide screenshots to illustrate your answers.

10-35. Access the Word of Mouth Marketing Association website at **womma.org**. What features did you find on the site? What resources are available? What benefits does the site provide to a business? Is there any value for a consumer? Provide screenshots to support your thoughts.

10-36. Type "guerrilla marketing" into an online search engine. Find two agencies that offer guerrilla marketing services. Describe what types of services each offers. Go to an article database and type in "guerrilla marketing." Find two articles about guerrilla marketing that interest you. Summarize the articles. Provide the site for the two articles, the URLs of the two websites, and screenshots to support your answers.

10-37. Explain the difference between lifestyle marketing and experiential marketing. Suppose you have been hired as an intern for a new brand of energy drink. Go to the internet and locate an agency that offers lifestyle marketing. Describe the services the agency could offer for your energy drink. Go back to the internet and locate an agency that provides experiential marketing. Describe the services the agency could offer for your energy drink. Provide the URLs of the two agencies as well as screenshots to illustrate your answers.

10-38. Soap is a digital creative agency that brings brands and consumers together through gaming. Access the agency's website at **www.soapcreative.com**. What information is available on the website? Who are some of the agency's clients? Describe some of the games created by Soap and why they have been successful. Use screenshots to support your response.

10-39. Use an internet search engine to locate two agencies that offer in-store marketing. For each agency discuss the services provided and identify some of the agencies' clients. Use screenshots to illustrate the services offered. If you were a marketing intern for a small chain of clothing stores, which agency would you use? Why? Identify at least three in-store tactics that the agency could provide.

10-40. Point-of-purchase displays should be an important component of a firm's IMC program. Research indicates that effective displays have a positive impact on sales. Access the following firms that produce point-of-purchase displays. Which firm's site is the most attractive? Which firm would be the best from the standpoint of developing displays for a manufacturer? Explain.

   a. Displays2Go (**www.displays2go.com**)
   b. Vulcan Industries (**www.vulcanind.com**)
   c. Display Design & Sales (**www.displays4pop .com**)

Blog Exercises

Access the authors' blog for this textbook at the URLs provided to complete these exercises. Answer the questions that are posed on the blog.

10-41. Coca-Cola: **blogclowbaack.net/2014/05/12/ coca-cola-chapter-10/**

10-42. Harley Davidson: **blogclowbaack.net/2014/05/12/ harley-davidson-chapter-10/**

10-43. Buzz marketing: **blogclowbaack.net/2014/05/12/ buzz-marketing-chapter-10/**

Student Project

CREATIVE CORNER

Ugg is the brand name for an Australian company that sells big, bulky sheepskin boots. The company's marketing team wondered if it would be possible to get fashion-conscious consumers to even consider the boots. Instead of advertising to the fashion-conscious consumer, Ugg's marketing team targeted high-profile fashion influencers. They successfully contacted and convinced Kate Hudson and Sarah Jessica Parker to wear the items. Then Oprah Winfrey praised Uggs on one of her shows. At that point, the boots became fashionable, and retailers couldn't keep them in stock.[48]

Ugg became successful using unique alternative marketing methods. Access Ugg's website at **www.uggaustralia.com** to learn about the company's products and the company itself. Suppose Ugg wanted to initiate a buzz marketing campaign at your university and that the company leaders contacted you for marketing advice. First, they would like to recruit some brand ambassadors as advocates for their brand. Your first task, therefore, is to design a flyer to post around campus announcing that Ugg wants to hire brand ambassadors. Before you can design the flyer, you must decide on the relationship the ambassador will have with Ugg and the type of reward or payment she will receive. After you design the flyer, your second task is to design a buzz marketing program that you believe Ugg and the new brand ambassador should use on your campus.

CASE 1 ▸ MATT AND JERRY'S DISC GOLF COURSE

Matt Jones and Jerry Rogers enjoyed disc or Frisbee® golf for many years. After both graduated from college with degrees in marketing, they decided to build and market a disc golf course on the outskirts of a large metropolitan community. One of the benefits of disc golf for enthusiasts is enjoying an outdoor sport in a serene and scenic setting. With that in mind, Matt and Jerry purchased land in a wooded area that featured several small ponds. They designed a course without dramatic hills so that people of all ages and physical abilities could play.

Disc golf has been in existence since the 1970s. Players throw the discs and move toward the eventual finishing area, often called the Pole Hole®, which is an elevated metal basket. Those involved can keep score (number of tosses until one lands in the basket) or simply play for fun without the burden of numbers.

Matt and Jerry contacted the Professional Disc Golf Association (**www.pdga.com/introduction**) for additional guidance. They discovered that the organization hosts almost 80,000 members. The PDGA encourages people from every walk of life to become involved, stating that the game can be tailored to individuals with special needs or disabilities. Skill levels range from "novice" to "professional."

The PDGA notes that disc golf can be associated with "upper and lower body conditioning," and that it "promotes a combination of physical and mental abilities that allow very little risk of physical injury." Players can build up these physical benefits over time through routine participation. The site suggests that the sport can be enjoyed even in the rain or snow.

To achieve regular attendance, the duo decided to form leagues for players based on skill levels that could be measured over time. The low cost of equipment, often less than $20 for a disc and a low fee for round of play make the prospect of regular involvement more enticing.

The business side of this new venture creates the biggest challenges for Matt and Jerry. They spent most of their start-up fund buying the property and creating the course. At the same time, they recognize the importance of getting the word out and encouraging first time play, which they believe will lead to a loyal set of followers.

One of the tricks to helping this project succeed will be deciding how to reach what is a vast and varied target market.

▲ Disc golf has been in existence since 1970 and has seen a recent resurgence in popularity.

Individuals of both genders, couples on dates, families, and hardcore players all could be the primary group targeted by marketing messages. Matt and Jerry were ready to accept these challenges. It was time to get started.

10-44. Is a buzz marketing program possible for the opening of Matt and Jerry's Disc Golf Course? Why or why not?

10-45. Can you think of a way to use stealth marketing to promote Matt and Jerry's Disc Golf Course? Do you think Matt and Jerry should use stealth marketing? Why or why not?

10-46. How could Matt and Jerry create a guerilla marketing program with a tie-in to a charitable event to promote their business?

10-47. What forms of alternative media offer the best chances to promote Matt and Jerry's Disc Golf Course? Be specific with examples.

10-48. Think about all the forms of alternative marketing presented in this chapter. If you were a marketing intern for Matt and Jerry, which one would you choose? Why? Describe the type of alternative campaign the two could use to build patrons for their disc golf course.

CASE 2 ► AFTER THE RUSH: WHAT'S NEXT FOR RED BULL?

In today's active world, people need help. At least, that would be the position presented by any of the companies that sell energy drinks. Red Bull and other products are designed to jolt a consumer into action.

Red Bull's ingredient list begins with taurine, which occurs naturally in the human body. Red Bull helps to replace the taurine lost during conditions of high stress or physical exertion, which, in turn, helps the person recover more quickly. The carbohydrate glucuronolactone, which also is found naturally in the human body, is added to help with the detoxification processes as well as support the body in eliminating waste substances. The amount of caffeine in a serving of Red Bull is nearly double the amount present in Mountain Dew, a product perceived by many as the highest-energy soft drink. Red Bull also contains acesulfame K, sucrose, glucose, B vitamins, and aspartame, which is well-known as the key ingredient in NutraSweet. The company's marketing materials emphasize that the formula took three years to develop. The 8.3-ounce-can drink was first launched in Australia in 1984. Red Bull tastes sweet and lemony, and, as one fan put it, "like a melted lollypop." The price of a single can is typically higher than a 16-ounce bottle of soda.[49]

When Red Bull was introduced into the United States, the product clearly struck a chord in some markets. Those pulling all-nighters for school, work, or partying, as well as those engaged in extreme sports, quickly gravitated to Red Bull. By 2010, the drink continued to hold a 60 to 70 percent share of the U.S. market for similar drinks and annual sales.

Many marketers view Red Bull's entry into the United States as one of the first and classic uses of alternative and buzz marketing. Red Bull's brand management team began by identifying a target audience—those who would most likely want the buzz created by an energy drink. One key constituent group would be college-age consumers. Consequently, the company provided free samples of the drink to college and university students, who were encouraged to throw big parties where cases of Red Bull would be served.

Red Bull's marketing team created a group of "consumer educators" who traveled to various locations giving out free samples. The brand managers organized and sponsored extreme sporting events, such as skateboarding and cliff diving, for consumer educators to attend. The concept was that the participants and fans of these types of sports had buzz-seeking desires and an interest in products that were positioned as "sleek, sweet, and full-throttle."[50] From the parties and the extreme sports, word-of-mouth communications about the brand spread. The buzz-seeking target audience became Red Bull's first customer base.

The traditional soft-drink companies were slow to react. Eventually, Pepsi created a competing product called Adrenaline Rush; Coca-Cola entered the market with KMX; and Anheuser-Busch developed 180, which is supposed to turn a person's energy level around by 180 degrees. Pepsi may be less concerned with Red Bull due to its ownership of Gatorade. Still, both Coke and Pepsi have concentrated efforts on garnering shelf space in convenience stores and superstores.

▲ Red Bull used alternative marketing to establish a presence in the United States.

More recently, Red Bull's marketing efforts have been expanded to include traditional advertising. At the same time, endorsers tend to be edgier figures, such as famed kayaker Tao Berman, and the commercials themselves remain offbeat. Red Bull creator Dietrich Mateschitz summarized it best, "If we don't create a market, it doesn't exist." And $1.6 billion later, he clearly has a point.

Two challenges have begun to emerge. First, Red Bull has been banned in some countries, including France and Canada. Other nations have examined the product and express fears about its impact on health. The second is keeping Red Bull on the cutting edge. A series of new energy formulas are available, including the heavily advertised 5-Hour Energy drinks. Can Red Bull maintain its edgy marketing presence over a sustained period of time?

10-49. What alternative marketing methods does Red Bull use?

10-50. Visit Red Bull's website (**www.redbull.com**) and identify the alternative media venues used by Red Bull's marketing team.

10-51. What role should traditional media play in Red Bull's future, especially when compared to alternative media?

10-52. Are there ways to build brand communities around Red Bull? What role might Twitter, Digg, or Facebook play in supporting such communities?

10-53. Red Bull's marketing team believes that staying with alternative approaches best fits its image. As you think about all of the alternative marketing methods and alternative media, what suggestions would you make to Red Bull for the future? Describe a campaign for Red Bull using one or more alternative methods.

MyMarketingLab

Go to the Assignments section of your MyLab to complete these writing exercises.

10-54. Describe in your own words each of the forms of alternative marketing listed in Figure 10.1. Suppose your best friend has a band that has been playing at the local nightclubs for the last three years. He has asked you to help market his band. Discuss the pros and cons of each of the alternative marketing methods (see Figure 10.1). Which one would you recommend the band use first? Why? Describe an actual campaign the band could use. Be specific.

10-55. Access Ugg's website at **www.uggaustralia.com**. Evaluate the website in terms of its effectiveness, freshness, and the use of alternative marketing methods. What traditional marketing methods did you see? Do you think Ugg has effectively merged traditional and nontraditional advertising methods? Why or why not?

Buzz Marketing
Communications
Social Media
Advertising
Promotions
Digital
Branding
Mobile Marketing

Part 4

IMC PROMOTIONAL TOOLS

Chapter 11 Database and Direct Response Marketing and Personal Selling

Chapter Objectives

After reading this chapter, you should be able to answer the following questions:

11.1 What role does database marketing, including the data warehouse, data coding and analysis, and data mining, play in creating and enhancing relationships with customers?

11.2 How can database-driven marketing communications programs help personalize interactions with customers?

11.3 How do database-driven marketing programs create sales and build bonds with customers?

11.4 When should direct response marketing programs be used to supplement other methods of delivering messages and products to consumers?

11.5 What are the tasks involved in developing successful personal selling programs for consumers and businesses?

11.6 How should database marketing and personal selling programs be adapted to international settings?

Overview

The fourth section of this textbook examines the promotional tools that help acquire and retain customers, as displayed in Figure 11.1. In this chapter, database programs, direct response marketing, and personal selling are examined. Database marketing provides a vital communication link with customers. This, in turn, helps to produce higher levels of customer acquisition, customer retention, and customer loyalty. New technologies associated with the internet and computer software make it easier to build and develop strong database programs. Sales promotions, both consumer and trade promotions, are presented in Chapter 12, followed by public relations and sponsorship programs in Chapter 13.

Successful businesses continually acquire new customers and work to retain them. Repeat customers purchase more frequently and spend more money. Maintaining repeat business is far less expensive than constantly replacing those who turn to other companies. Personal selling plays a key role in many marketing outcomes.

Many industries and companies offer loyalty programs designed to build solid relationships with customers and encourage repeat business by providing special buys, discounts, and other rewards to preferred customers. Alex McEahern writes that three keys to effective loyalty programs include operating in industries with high levels of repeat product purchases, those with higher price markups or margins, and those with considerable competition.[1] Cosmetics and the more general beauty industry offer a rich environment for creating successful loyalty programs.

One organization that has enjoyed a great deal of success by providing an effective loyalty program is Sephora, which was founded in France by Dominique Mandonnaud in 1970. The company operates in locations worldwide and also in conjunction with JC Penney retail stores in the United States. Sephora sells makeup, skin care products, fragrances, bath and body items, nail accessories, tools and brushes, along with items for men. The company's website highlights the "'Science of Sephora' program, which is designed to ensure Sephora team members have the skill to identify skin types, the knowledge of skin physiology, and how to interact with Sephora's diverse clientele."[2]

One key to the company's success has been the highly sophisticated personalized data program. *Forbes* notes that Sephora delivers great customer experiences at every touch point that are highly personalized and based on relevant data. The end result has been a passionate customer base in a highly competitive marketplace.[3]

Bridget Dolan, Vice President of Interactive Marketing for Sephora, stated that the firm's secret begins with being true to the customer and making that individual the center of every decision. Data collection designed to achieve that purpose includes recording customer information from interactions with in-person salespeople along with computerized records of transactions and other contacts.[4] Then, the right kinds of rewards for repeat purchases can be tailored to the individual customer's desires and preferences. Over time, long term devotion and allegiance to the company have become the result of Sephora's database marketing efforts.

The first part of this chapter examines database marketing, including data warehouses, data coding, and data mining as well as data-driven communications and marketing programs. Three data-driven marketing programs are permission marketing, frequency programs, and customer relationship management systems. Databases are used for direct response marketing techniques, including direct mail, email, television programs, telemarketing, and traditional and alternative media. Databases constitute a key component of personal selling. Finally, international differences in these programs are considered.

Database Marketing

Database marketing involves collecting and utilizing customer data for the purposes of enhancing interactions with customers and developing customer loyalty. Successful database marketing emphasizes identifying customers and building relationships with them. This includes understanding the lifetime values of various customers and the development of customer retention efforts. Database marketing enhances customer loyalty. Although marketers can utilize database programs to sell products and acquire new customers, strengthening retention and relationships should be the primary focus.

objective 11.1

What role does database marketing, including the data warehouse, data coding and analysis, and data mining, play in creating and enhancing relationships with customers?

▶ **FIGURE 11.1**
Overview of Integrated
Marketing Communications

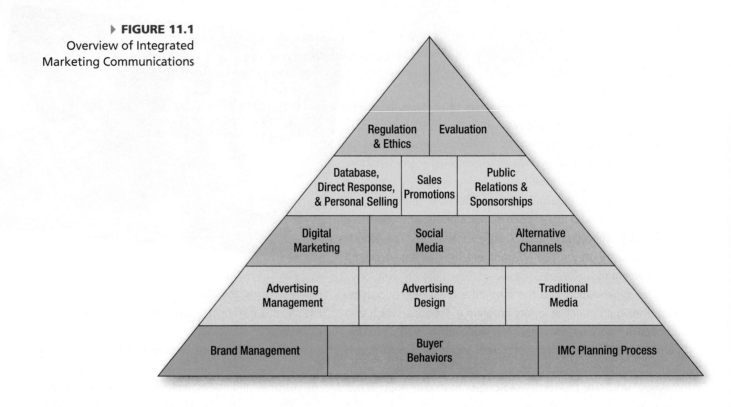

The primary focus of database marketing is customer retention and developing positive relationships.

A number of retail boutiques have captured the power of database marketing. When shoppers visit the store, the sales staff can access data regarding their preferences, sizes, previous purchases, and other information. Purchases are followed up with thank-you notes. Customers receive notices when new shipments of clothes arrive along with invitations to special events. Loyalty to these boutiques grows over time. In some instances, customers who have moved away return to buy merchandise. One vital ingredient stands out: these programs make customers feel special and help build long-term relationships with them. Although selling occurs, it does not drive the database program. Figure 11.2 displays the tasks associated with database marketing.

- Building a data warehouse
- Database coding and analysis
- Data mining
- Data-driven marketing communications
- Data-driven marketing programs

▶ **FIGURE 11.2**
Tasks in Database Marketing

Building a Data Warehouse

Successful database marketing requires a quality **data warehouse** to hold customer data. The IT department and marketing team distinguish between an operational database and the marketing database when building a data warehouse. An *operational database* carries the individual's transactions with the firm and follows accounting principles. The marketing department manages the *marketing database*, which contains information about current customers, former customers, and prospects. Examples of data and analyses found in a marketing data warehouse include:

- Customer names and addresses
- Email addresses and digital records of visits to the company's website
- History of every purchase transaction
- History of customer interactions such as inquiries, complaints, and returns
- Results of any customer surveys
- Preferences and profiles supplied by the customer
- Marketing promotions and response history from marketing campaigns
- Appended demographic and psychographic data from sources such as Knowledge Base Marketing or Claritas
- Database coding such as lifetime value and customer segment clusters

Collecting customer names and addresses is often the easiest part of developing the database. Gathering the other information that turns the data warehouse into a powerful marketing and communication tool can be more challenging.

The marketing team updates addresses on a continual basis, because approximately 20 percent of Americans move each year. When individuals fill out change of address forms with the U.S. Postal Service, the agency sends the information to all of the service bureaus authorized to sell it to businesses. A company that sends database names to one of these bureaus receives address updates for only a few cents per hit, or per individual that moves. Updating mailing addresses takes place at least once each year, but can occur more frequently depending on how often the company uses the database and the regularity of contacts.

▼ Contact information is an important component of building a data warehouse for a business-to-business company such as Scott Powerline & Utility Equipment.

Email, Mobile, and Internet Data

Email addresses are essential elements of a quality database. The internet and email provide cost-effective communication channels to be used in building relationships with customers. Most database programs take advantage of digital tracking to register and store website visits and browsing patterns regardless of the type of digital device (computer, tablet, or mobile phone). This information makes it possible to personalize the firm's website for individual customers. When someone logs on to the site, a greeting such as "Welcome back, Stacy," appears. The tracking technology system recognizes that Stacy, or at least someone using her computer or mobile phone, is accessing the website. If Stacy has purchased products or browsed the catalog, then the content of the pages can be tailored to contain the products she has an interest in buying.

Purchase and Communication Histories

Effective database programs maintain detailed customer purchase histories. Database operators record every interaction between the company and customer. When a customer sends an email to tech

▶ Personal preferences can be an important component of a clothing store's marketing database.

support the information moves to the database. Any person who returns a product or calls customer service has the activity documented. The system identifies items placed in a shopping cart but not purchased. Purchases and interaction histories determine future communications with customers and assist the marketing team in evaluating each customer's lifetime value and other customer value metrics.

Personal Preference Profiles

Purchase and visit histories do not provide complete information. Quality database marketing programs include profiles with specific information about each customer's personal preferences. These profiles are constructed in various ways, including customer surveys and through information provided on an application for a loyalty card.

Every time the company initiates a contact with a customer, the information should be placed in the database, along with the customer's response. This information provides a rich history of what works and what does not. It further supports the customization of communication methods for each customer, which increases the probability of success.

Customer Information Companies

Oftentimes, demographic and psychographic information are not available through internal company records. In these cases, a company obtains the data by working with a marketing research firm specializing in collecting customer data. Knowledge Base Marketing, Donnelly, Dialog, and Claritas are some of the companies that sell this type of information.

Data from website visits can be combined with offline information provided by firms such as Acxiom and Datran Media. Once merged, companies store the information in cookies to assist in future customization and personalization of websites and communications with customers. For instance, based on income level and past purchasing habits, two women in adjoining offices can access the same cosmetics website; one might see a $300 bottle of Missoni perfume and the other might see the $25 house brand.[5]

Geocoding

The process of adding geographic codes to each customer's record so that customer addresses can be plotted on a map, or **geocoding**, helps decision makers finalize placements of retail outlets and directs marketing materials to specific geographic areas. Geocoding often combines demographic information with lifestyle data. This assists the marketing team in selecting the best media for advertisements.

One version of geocoding software, CACI Coder/ Plus, identifies a cluster in which an address belongs. A group such as Enterprising Young Singles in the CACI system contains certain characteristics such as enjoying dining, spending money on DVDs and personal computers, and reading certain magazines. A retailer might then target this group with mailings and special offers.[6]

Database Coding and Analysis

Database coding and analysis provide information for the development of personalized communications. They assist in creating marketing promotional campaigns. Common forms of database coding include lifetime value analysis, customer clusters, and location data tracking.

▲ Geocoding allows a boutique such as Chic Shaque to target customers in specific geographic areas around its stores.

Lifetime Value Analysis

The **lifetime value** figure for a customer or market segment estimates the present value of future profits the individual or segment will generate over a lifetime relationship with a brand or firm.[7] Many marketing experts believe a market segment value provides more accurate information, because it sums costs across multiple customers. Individual lifetime value calculations normally only contain costs for single customers.

The figures needed to calculate the lifetime value of a consumer or set of consumers are revenues, costs, and retention rates. Revenue and costs are normally easy to obtain, because many companies record these numbers for accounting purposes. Retention rates require an accurate marketing database system.

A key figure to be used in a lifetime analysis is the cost of acquiring new customers. It is calculated by dividing the total marketing and advertising expenditures in dollars by the number of new customers obtained. As an example, when a company spends $200,000 and acquires 1,000 new customers as a result, the acquisition cost becomes $200 per customer ($200,000 divided by 1,000).

The cost of maintaining the relationship is another important figure. It measures all costs associated with marketing, communicating, and maintaining the database records. Obtaining these records may be more problematic, because such costs are usually for a campaign, which makes allocating costs to a single customer difficult. Computer and database technology can average or allocate a portion of these costs to individual customer records or to a lifetime value segment.

The lifetime value figure will be the end product for either individual customers or a customer segment. A lifetime value figure for a customer segment of $1,375 represents the amount of revenue, on average, that each customer will generate over his or her lifetime. By communicating with and marketing to the customer segment, the company may be able to increase the lifetime value. A lifetime value analysis informs the company's customer contact and service personnel regarding a customer's potential worth to the company.

▲ Progressive Bank can take advantage of customer clustering to identify the best prospects for its trust and wealth management services.

▲ Location data tracking can be used to locate restaurants individuals patronize around a sports facility before and after games.

Customer Clusters

Marketers use various coding systems to group customers into clusters based on a wide variety of criteria. A bank might group customers based on the number of accounts, types of accounts, and other relationships a customer has with the organization. For example, customers with home mortgages above $100,000 with balances of 30 to 60 percent remaining may be targeted for a home equity loan. A clothing retailer could group customers by the type of clothing each group purchases and then develop marketing programs for the various groups. Teenagers who purchase Western wear would be in a different cluster than teenagers who prefer hip, trendy fashions.

Unified Western Grocers, a wholesale cooperative association serving more than 3,000 grocery stores, used a customer cluster analysis to reduce 19 different advertising campaigns and programs for the various stores it served down to four, based on customer commonalities. The four clusters that emerged from the analysis were affluent urban and suburban households; mid-downscale rural seniors; large, low-income urban households; and non-acculturated Hispanics. The marketing team designed advertisements and created shelf allocations of brands for the four customer clusters. The approach reduced advertising design costs and led to more effective ads.[8]

Location Data Tracking

A new form of data analytics is based on information provided by mobile GPS technology. A cell phone company such as Verizon tracks customer locations and combines it with profile information. The information may be valuable to sports properties as well as restaurants and retailers. For instance, the Phoenix Suns basketball team's marketers took advantage of the technology to better understand fans who attended games. The information helped target specific businesses as potential sponsors.

Verizon and other companies obtain location data to track the movement of individuals inside a sports arena as well as their activities outside the facility. These data are aggregated and then **hashed**—the process of anonymizing the data so that specific individuals cannot be identified. The process provides information regarding the restaurants or businesses patrons visited prior to attending a game as well as after a game. The marketing team then adds profile data from companies such as Experian in order to segment consumers by demographics. The ability to target specific market segments based on their actual patronage behaviors at the game and the businesses around the facility becomes the result.[9]

Data Mining

Data mining involves using computer data analysis software to study data to find meaningful information and help build relationships. Data mining includes two primary activities: building profiles of customer segments and/or preparing models that predict future purchase behaviors based on past purchases.

Data mining assists the marketing team in building profiles of the firm's best customers. These profiles, in turn, identify prospective new customers. Marketers take advantage of them to examine "good" customers to see if they are candidates for sales calls that would move them from "good" to higher values. Companies offering different types of goods and services develop multiple profiles. The profiles help to target sales calls and identify cross-selling possibilities.

▲ Data mining can be used by companies to build profiles of its best customers.

The marketing team at First Horizon National Bank employed data mining tactics to expand the company's wealth management business by studying consumer groups. Data regarding existing customers from the mortgage side of the firm's business made it possible to locate the best prospects for investment services. Linking the data mining program with cross-selling resulted in an increase in company revenues from $26.3 million to $33.8 million in one year.[10]

Marketers for the retailer American Eagle developed a data mining method to analyze consumer responses to price markdowns. The information helped the team determine when to cut prices and by how much in order to optimize sales. Markdown programs were geared to individual stores, because consumers responded differently in each outlet.[11]

The second data mining method involves developing models that predict future sales based on past purchasing activities. Marketing professionals at Staples prepared a modeling program to examine the buying habits of the company's catalog customers. The program identified the names of frequent buyers who were then sent customized mailings.

The specific type of information needed determines the dating mining method. Once the information contained in the data has been analyzed, the team prepares specialized marketing programs. Profiles and models lead to more effective marketing campaigns. A direct-mail program to current customers differs from one designed to attract new customers. The data provide clues regarding the best approach for each customer segment.

Data coding and data mining serve three purposes (see Figure 11.3). First, they assist in developing marketing communications. Marketing employees utilize the information to choose types of promotions, advertising media, and the message to be presented to each customer group. Second, they help when developing marketing programs. Third, company salespeople can use the information to qualify prospects and make in-person sales calls to the individuals or businesses offering the greatest potential.

- Develop marketing communications
- Develop marketing programs
- For personal sales
  - Qualify prospects
  - Information for sales calls

▲ **FIGURE 11.3**
Purposes of Data Coding and Data Mining

Database-Driven Marketing Communications

objective 11.2

How can database-driven marketing communications programs help personalize interactions with customers?

Building a database, coding the information, and performing data mining make it possible to utilize the output with the goal of establishing one-on-one communications with customers. Personalized communications build relationships and lead to repeat business and increased

▶ **FIGURE 11.4**
The Importance of the Internet in Customer Communication

- It is the cheapest form of communication.
- It is available 24/7.
- Metric analysis reveals that the customer read the message, the time it was read, and how much time was spent reading it.
- Customers are able to access additional information whenever they want.
- It can build bonds with customers.

loyalty. They move the company and its products from brand parity to brand equity. A database marketing program contains tools to personalize messages and keep records of the types of effective and ineffective communications. The internet offers the key technology for database-driven communications, especially since many consumers now own smartphones. Figure 11.4 highlights the importance of the internet in customer interactions.

Identification Codes

A database-driven marketing program starts with assigning individual customers IDs and passwords that allow them to access website components that are not available to those who visit the site without logging on. IT professionals tie IDs and passwords to cookies on each customer's computer in order to customize pages and individual offers. When the system works properly, the customer does not have to log in each time. Instead, the cookie automatically completes the task. For example, when a user accesses Barnes & Noble, he receives a personalized greeting, such as "Welcome, Jim." Next, when Jim places an order, he does not have to type in his address or credit card information. The database contains the information and it comes up automatically, which saves Jim time and increases the probability he will buy something.

Companies send special messages after the sale. A series follows the purchase. First, the buyer receives an email confirming the order and thanking her. After the order has been packed and shipped, the email contains a tracking code the buyer can access to locate the order. The message includes an estimated shipping date. Some companies include an email in the interim stating that the order has reached the warehouse. Then, another email will be sent as the order is pulled and ready for shipment. Customers should not be bombarded with too many emails; however most appreciate a series of emails from the time an order is placed until it arrives. It saves them time because they do not have to access the company and check on the order's progress.

At Origin Bank, one size never fits all. We treat you like the unique individual you are, so we can custom-fit a banking solution around your needs.

Community Trust Bank *is evolving into* ⬡ **Origin Bank** *Bank original*

Member FDIC

▲ Identification codes can be used to identify Jim each time he logs into his Origin Bank account.

Personalized Communications

An effective database-driven communication program relies on customer profiles and any other information about their preferences to help individualize messages. Clothing retailers send emails about new fashions that have arrived. These emails do not go to every person in the database. Only those who have indicated a desire to have access to the information or who have indicated they have an interest in fashion news receive the messages. These customers often believe they get special "inside" information.

Customers can be sent birthday greetings based on customer profile data. Recently, a steak and seafood restaurant mailed a card and offered a $10 birthday discount to 215,600 persons who provided their birthdates. The cost of postage and the discount totaled $90,000. Patrons redeemed approximately 40 percent of the cards. Each birthday customer brought an average of two other people, and those individuals paid full price for their meals. The result was $2.9 million in revenues derived from the program.[12]

A recent Fulcrum survey revealed that 74 percent of individuals who received a birthday message from a business thought more positively about the company, and 88 percent of the positive reactions translated into increased brand loyalty. Greetings from brands in the food and beverage industry generated the most positive responses. Birthday wishes with discounts were more effective than birthday greetings sent without incentives. Clearly personalized communications provide an effective means of increasing brand loyalty.[13]

▲ Sending birthday wishes to customers can enhance brand attitude, brand patronage, and brand loyalty.

Customized Content

In addition to personalized communications, marketing teams analyze data in order to customize content. Netflix tracks what movie buffs watch, search for, and rate. Information regarding the time of day, date, the device used (smartphone, tablet, or PC), where individuals browsed, and where they scrolled on a page is recorded. The material aids in suggesting movies to the person and helps stream the suggestions to the individual's most-often checked device at the best time. For instance, if the browsing history indicates that an individual searches for and watches romantic comedies on Friday nights, then a suggestion would be sent to the person's mobile phone or tablet that morning or the day prior. Netflix estimates that 75 percent of viewer selections result from these data-driven recommendations.[14]

In-Bound Telemarketing

Contacts made by telephone work the same way as internet contacts. The service call operator immediately sees the identity of the person calling. Customer data appears on the screen in front of the in-bound telemarketer. The operator treats the caller in a personalized manner. When the company calculates a lifetime value code, the operator knows the customer's value and status. The operator asks about a recent purchase or talks about information provided on the customer's list of preferences or a customer profile. The operator greets and treats each customer as an individual, not as a random person making an in-bound call.

Trawling

Database marketing includes **trawling**, or the process of searching the database for a specific piece of information for marketing purposes. Home Depot's trawling program locates individuals who have recently moved. The company's marketing team knows that when people buy houses or move to a new location, they often need home improvement merchandise. Most of the time, these items include merchandise sold at Home Depot.

Other marketers trawl a database to find anniversary dates of a special purchase, such as a new automobile. Car dealerships send a correspondence on each year's anniversary of a car purchase to inquire about customer satisfaction and interest in trading for a newer

▶ OIB can incorporate trawling to identify individuals who meet specific criteria, such as just moving into a community.

vehicle. A retailer can trawl for individuals who have not made a purchase within the last three months or who purchased a specific item, such as a lawnmower in the last year. Trawling presents a wide variety of ways to communicate with individuals who meet a particular criterion.

Database-Driven Marketing Programs

objective 11.3

How do database-driven marketing programs create sales and build bonds with customers?

Database-driven marketing programs take many forms. They are developed in conjunction with other marketing activities. The more common programs include permission marketing, frequency programs, and customer relationship management efforts.

Permission Marketing

A strong backlash by consumers against spam and junk mail continues. Consequently, many marketing departments turn to **permission marketing**, a program in which companies send promotional information to only those consumers who give the authorization to do so. Firms offer permission marketing programs on the internet, by telephone, or through direct mail. Higher response rates often result from permission programs, because only those customers who give consent receive marketing materials. Results are enhanced when permission marketing programs utilize database technology to segment customers, although not every person who signs up for permission marketing becomes a valuable customer.

Figure 11.5 lists the steps of a permission marketing program. Marketers can obtain permission by providing incentives for sign-ups, such as information, entertainment, a gift, cash, or entries in a sweepstakes. Any information provided should be primarily educational and focus on the company's product or service features.

Reinforcing the relationship requires an additional new incentive beyond the original gift. Marketers can enhance relationships when they acquire more in-depth customer information such as hobbies, interests, attitudes, and opinions. They then tailor information to entice additional purchases by offering special deals.

Keys to Success in Permission Marketing
A permission marketing program succeeds when the marketing team ensures that the recipients agree to participate. Unfortunately, some consumers have been tricked into joining permission marketing programs. One common tactic involves automatically enrolling customers in programs as they complete online surveys or purchase items online. Opting out requires the individual to un-check a box on the site. Although this approach increases the number of individuals enrolled, the technique often leads to bad feelings.

1. Obtain permission from the customer.
2. Offer the consumer an ongoing curriculum that is meaningful.
3. Reinforce the incentive to continue the relationship.
4. Increase the level of permission.
5. Leverage the permission to benefit both parties.

Permission marketing materials should be relevant to consumers. Far too many people who have joined programs encounter situations in which they are bombarded with extraneous messages. This does not create loyalty and runs counter to the purpose of the program.

One recent survey revealed that 80 percent of consumers stopped reading permission emails from companies because they were shoddy or irrelevant. Another 68 percent said the emails came too frequently, and 51 percent reported they lost interest in the goods, services, or topics of the emails. On the whole, consumers delete an average of 43 percent of permission emails without ever reading them.[15]

To overcome these challenges, marketers monitor responses and customize the permission program to meet individual customer needs. Database technology enables customization by tracking responses and browsing behavior. When a customer regularly accesses a website through a link in an email sent by the company to read the latest fashion news, the behavior triggers email offers and incentives on fashions related to the news stories and links the customer followed. An individual who does not access the website and does not appear to be interested in fashion news receives a different type of email offer. By capitalizing on the power of database technology, a firm enhances the permission marketing program and makes it beneficial to the company and the customer.

Permission Marketing Enticements   Figure 11.6 notes the top reasons for opting into email programs. Winning a sweepstakes tops the list. Also, current company customers may be more inclined to examine the company's products.[16] Enticing them into the permission marketing program will be easier than trying to attract new patrons.

Figure 11.7 provides a list of motives that help retain customers in a permission marketing relationship. As shown, consumers remain with such programs for many reasons.[17]

Permission marketing programs hold the potential to build strong, ongoing relationships with customers when they offer something of value. To optimize permission marketing, firms feature empowerment and reciprocity. **Empowerment** means consumers believe they have power throughout the relationship and not just at the beginning when they joined the program. They make decisions and have choices about what to receive.

To maintain positive attitudes, consumers should be given rewards along the way, not just at the beginning. Doing so creates feelings of **reciprocity**, or a sense of obligation toward the company. Only rewarding customers for joining the program will be a mistake. Empowerment and reciprocity lead the customer to believe the company values the relationship, which increases the chances the consumer will continue as an active participant.

▼ Permission marketing can target individuals interested in fashion news.

▶ **FIGURE 11.6**
Reasons Consumers Opt into Email Permission Programs

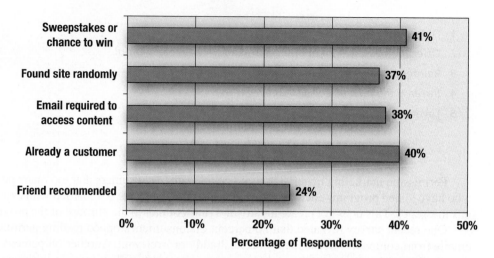

▶ **FIGURE 11.7**
Reasons Consumers Remain in Permission Marketing Programs

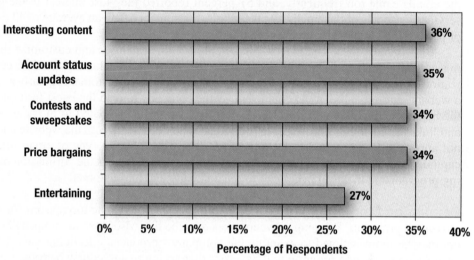

Frequency Programs

A company offers free or discounted merchandise or services for a series of purchases in a **frequency program** or **loyalty program**. These enticements encourage people to make repeat purchases. In the airline industry, frequent-flyer programs offer free flights after a traveler accumulates a given number of miles. Grocery stores grant discounts when purchase totals reach a certain amount within a specified time period.

Chief Marketing Officer (CMO) Council research indicates that about two-thirds of consumers belong to loyalty programs. On average, households are enrolled in 14 programs, but only actively participate in about six. Figure 11.8 provides a list of benefits of such programs mentioned by customers and the percentage that cites each benefit.[18]

Goals Figure 11.9 identifies reasons for developing frequency programs. Originally, many were created to differentiate brands from competitors. Now, however, frequency programs tend to be offered by all companies in an industry (credit card, airline, grocery, hotel, restaurant, etc.). As a result, marketers instead use them to help retain customers, match competitor offers, or gain a larger share of each customer's purchases.

Principles Successful loyalty programs are based on two principles: added value and reciprocity. Participants in a loyalty program should feel value accrues from belonging to the program. When the customer in turn rewards the perceived value by making additional purchases, it creates a sense of reciprocity. When the customer and the company both benefit from the relationship, it continues.

Recent research suggests that the more effort a customer expends to participate in a frequency program, the greater the value of the reward becomes. Many consumers put

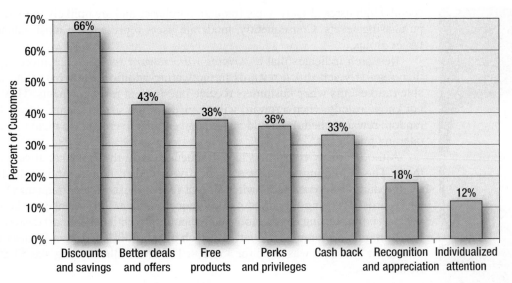

◀ **FIGURE 11.8**
Benefits of Loyalty Programs Cited by Consumers

- Maintain or increase sales, margins, or profits
- Increase loyalty of existing customers
- Preempt or match a competitor's offer

- Encourage cross-selling
- Differentiate the brand
- Discourage entry of a new brand

◀ **FIGURE 11.9**
Goals of Frequency or Loyalty Programs

forth greater energy to obtain luxury rewards as opposed to necessities. Grocery store shoppers are more likely to exert higher levels of effort in order to receive a free overnight stay at a nearby local resort or a free meal at a nice restaurant than they would for a $20 food gift certificate.

Data-Driven Customization Collecting data assists the marketing team in customizing loyalty programs to meet each individual's needs. Mass offers may not be as effective, because customers feel they are being "sold" rather than "rewarded." CVS Pharmacy's marketers understood this principle when they launched the ExtraCare loyalty program. Individuals who belonged to ExtraCare received a tailored version of the weekly print circulars. The data collected from the member's purchases led to suggestions of sale items along with individualized discounts and coupons. These promotional offers were not for competing brands or products that did not interest card members. Instead, they were for brands and products card members regularly purchased. In the words of one customer who likes to drink Coke products rather than Pepsi, "For me to be able to get a coupon to buy more Coke is a lot more relevant. I value more getting coupons for products I like, not for products I don't care for, which is wasting my time."

Maximize Motivation Effective loyalty programs maximize a customer's motivation to make another purchase. Moderate users often become frequency program targets. Light users seldom make purchases and cost more to maintain in the program than they

▲ An advertisement for Karns Quality Foods encouraging consumers to sign up for the store's loyalty program.

spend. High users already make frequent purchases and are unlikely to increase purchasing levels. Consequently, moderate users represent the most valuable target group.

Research indicates that a *variable ratio reward schedule* has more value than regularly scheduled rewards in motivating additional purchases. A variable ratio occurs when customers receive intermittent reinforcements. They do not know exactly when a reward will be given or the size of the incentive. The random reward schedule should be frequent enough to encourage them to make ongoing purchases.[19]

Although many consumers have frequency cards, they may not always use them. The marketing manager of a locally-owned restaurant noticed he had a large number of customers who had not recently used their Frequent Diner Club cards. Trawling identified 4,000 Frequent Diner Club members who did not earn points during the previous three months. To entice these past customers to return, the restaurant sent a letter to each of the 4,000 offering a $5 discount on dinner. The offer was good for 35 days. The cost of the mailing was $1,800. Results were:

- The average number of member visits per day increased from 25 to 42 during the promotion and to 29 per day after the promotion ended.
- Average visits by individual members holding cards increased both during and after the promotion.
- Incremental sales increased by $17,100 during the promotion and by $4,700 after the 35-day promotion.

▲ Restaurants often give loyalty cards to encourage customers to return more often.

By spending $1,800, the promotion led to reactivations by about 600 people who had not dined at the restaurant in 3 months. Of the nearly 600 who were motivated to come back during the promotion, 147 dined at the restaurant after the promotion was over.[20]

Customer Relationship Management

Customer relationship management (CRM) programs provide a method to employ databases that customize products and communications with customers, with the goals of higher sales and profits. Successful CRM programs build long-term loyalty and bonds with customers through a personal touch, facilitated by technology. Effective customer relationship management programs go beyond the development of a database and traditional selling tactics to the mass customization of both communications and products.

Two primary CRM metrics include the lifetime value of the customer and share of customer. The lifetime value concept has already been described in an earlier chapter. As noted, it measures the potential level of purchases to be made by an individual or market segment.

The second metric, share of customer, is based on the concept that some customers are more valuable than others and that, over time, the amount of money a customer spends with a firm can increase. **Share of customer** refers to the percentage of expenditures a customer makes with one particular firm compared to total expenditures in that product's category. Share of customer measures a customer's potential value. The question becomes, "If more is invested by the company in developing a relationship, what will the yield be over time?" When a customer makes only one-fourth of his purchases of a particular product category with a specific brand, increasing the share of the customer would mean increasing that percentage from 25 percent to a higher level, thus generating additional sales revenues. The ultimate achievement would be leading the customer to make 100 percent of his purchases on one brand.[21]

Kellogg's CRM database holds information from 18 million people. Among these, 3.5 million individuals have become part of Kellogg's Family Rewards Program. Each Kellogg product package provides a unique, 16-digit code. Members submit these codes

▲ Centric Federal Credit Union can use a CRM program to enhance relationships with current customers.

online in exchange for points to redeem for discounts or free prizes, such as toys or sports equipment. The code tells Kellogg the type of product, the package size, and the store where the product was purchased. The information creates an individual's Kellogg history for each item purchased, along with when and where it was bought. These data make it possible for the company's marketing group to prepare specific offers designed to match the person's past purchasing behaviors. In addition, the data assist in developing marketing communications that are better aligned with consumer preferences and that facilitate the cross-selling of Kellogg products.[22]

In general, CRM marketing programs should enhance customer loyalty. When a hotel's check-in person knows in advance that a business traveler prefers a nonsmoking room, a queen-size bed, and reads *USA Today*, these items can be made available as the guest arrives. Training hotel clerks and other employees to rely on the database helps them provide better service, thereby increasing loyalty from regular customers. An organization's marketing department can adapt these techniques to fit the needs of its customers and clients.

In addition to permission marketing, frequency programs, and CRM systems, other marketing programs emerge from a database analysis. Internet programs, trade promotions, consumer promotions, and other marketing tactics may be facilitated by using the database.

Direct Response Marketing

One program closely tied to database marketing, **direct response marketing (or direct marketing)**, involves targeting products to customers without the use of other channel members. Figure 11.10 identifies the several forms of direct response marketing and the percentages of companies using them. Notice that direct marketing can be aimed at customers as well as prospects. According to the Direct Marketing Association, about 60 percent of a typical direct marketing budget targets prospecting for new customers; the other 40 percent is spent retaining current customers.[23]

Many pharmaceutical companies employ direct response advertising, especially on television and in magazines. A recent study revealed that this direct response approach works. Ads for prescription medications by pharmaceuticals prompted almost one-third of Americans to ask their doctors about a particular brand of medicine and 82 percent of those who asked doctors received some type of prescription. The prescription was for the

objective 11.4
When should direct response marketing programs be used to supplement other methods of delivering messages and products to consumers?

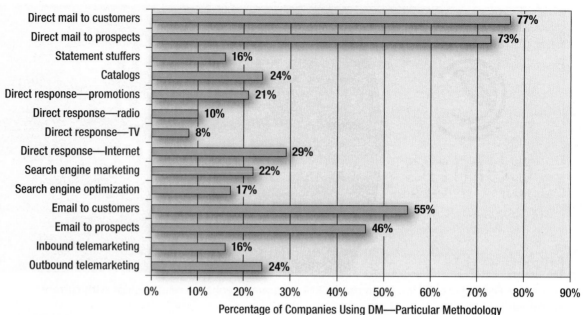

▲ **FIGURE 11.10**
Methods of Direct Response
Marketing

advertised brand 44 percent of the time; for another drug, 56 percent of the time. Sometimes, doctors prescribed the advertised brand as well as another brand.[24]

Individuals and companies respond to direct response marketing in a number of ways, such as by telephone, email, visiting a retail location, or using a PURL (personalized URL). PURLs offer the advantage of preloading all of the individual's personal data to a website, which can then customize the information and any offer. They also assist in tracking the individual's onsite activities and in making real-time changes to offers.[25]

Direct Mail

As shown in Figure 11.10, direct mail remains the most common form of direct response marketing. Direct mail reaches both consumers and business-to-business customers. The quality of the mailing list normally determines the program's success. Companies utilize two sources when compiling a mailing list: the firm's internal database and/or a commercial list.

The company's marketing department parses an internal list and separates active members from inactive members. Prospective new customers receive different direct mail pieces with messages designed to entice repeat purchases. Mailing direct offers to individuals (or businesses) who have not purchased recently but who have purchased in the past often yields a better response rate than cold-call mailing lists from brokers.

Types of Commercial Lists   A company can purchase a commercial list as either a response list or a compiled list. A **response list** consists of customers who have made purchases or who have responded to direct mail offers in the past. Brokers selling these lists provide information about the composition of the list and how much was spent by buyers on the list. In addition, a *hot list* may be requested. It contains the names of individuals who have responded within the past 30 days. Individuals on the hot list are the most likely to make purchases. This type of list costs more: as much as $250 per thousand names. A regular response list may sell for $100 per thousand names.

The second form, a **compiled list**, provides information about consumers who meet a specific demographic profile. The disadvantage of a compiled list is that although someone might fit a demographic category, most American purchasers do not respond to mail offers.

Caterpillar's marketing team wanted to reach potential buyers in the Southwest as part of the "Eat My Dust" campaign. The company purchased 1,700 names of individuals who had purchased industrial loaders during the past five years from Equipment Data Associates, a Charlotte, North Carolina, firm that compiles detailed purchasing histories of more than 870,000 U.S. contractors. Rhea + Kaiser's Nichols agency designed a sweepstakes to win a new Cat 414E. An eye-catching direct mail piece urged contractors to sign up either online, by mail, or at a local Caterpillar dealer. Standard response rates are less than one percent; the response rate for the "Eat My Dust" direct mailer was 18 percent.[26] The highly targeted list made the difference.

▲ First National Bank used these direct mail pieces to target specific financial services customers.

Catalogs

Many consumers enjoy catalogs and view them at their leisure. Catalogs have a longer-term impact because consumers keep and share them. Catalogs feature a low-pressure direct response marketing tactic that gives consumers time to consider goods and prices. Many marketers believe online shopping has replaced catalogs; however, some research suggests that such is not the case. More than half of online shoppers browse a catalog prior to making an online purchase and more than 30 percent have a catalog in hand when placing the online order. More than 85 percent of survey respondents said they had purchased an item online after seeing it in a catalog first.[27]

Successful cataloging requires an enhanced database. Many catalog companies, including L.L.Bean and JCPenney, create specialty catalogs geared to specific market segments. The specialty catalogs have a lower cost and a higher yield, because they reach individual market segments.

Catalogs are essential selling tools for many business-to-business marketing programs. They provide more complete product information to members of the buying center as well as prices for the purchasing agent. When combined with an internet presence, a catalog program facilitates a strong connection with individual customers.

Mass Media

Television, radio, magazines, and newspapers provide additional tools for direct response advertising. Direct response TV commercials are slightly longer (60 seconds), which allows a potential buyer time to find a pen to write down a toll-free number, an address, or a website. Catchy, easy-to-remember contact information is often used, such as "1-800-Go-Green" or "**www.gogreen.com**." Repeating the response format helps customers remember how to respond. Often a "call-now" prompt concludes the commercial.

Television also features infomercials for various types of products, such as exercise equipment and cooking tools. Cable and satellite systems have led to the creation of numerous direct response channels. The Home Shopping Network continues to be one of the most successful. Essentially, the channel runs 24-hour infomercial programs. Other channels feature jewelry, food, and shoes.

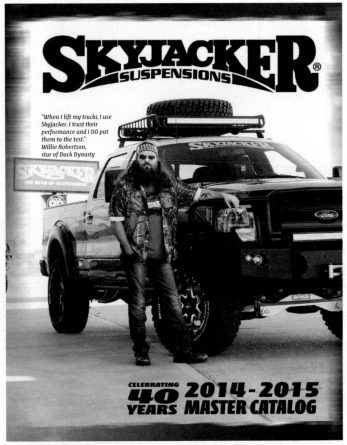

▲ Catalogs are an important component of Skyjacker's integrated marketing communications program.

Direct response techniques are also presented on radio stations and in magazines and newspapers. Radio does not have the reach of television, but it can be designed to match the type of station format. Radio ads repeat the response number or website frequently so that consumers can make contacts.

Print media can be sent to various market segments. Newspaper advertisements feature website information and other quick-response formats. The same holds true for magazines. Both contain website information and toll-free numbers.[28] The more ways provided to respond to an ad, the higher the response rate.

Internet and Email

The internet offers a valuable form of direct marketing. Consumers respond directly to ads placed on a website, and direct response advertisements can be placed on search engines and used in emails.

As Figure 11.10 shows, email is a frequently used form of direct response marketing. Email provides a cost-effective method of reaching prospects. It builds relationships with current customers through personalization of communications and by presenting marketing offers tailored to each consumer's needs, wants, and desires. For business-to-business marketers, email works better than postal mail and other direct marketing forms when the recipient knows the company.[29]

By placing ads on search engines and using search engine optimization, firms make direct response offers directly to individuals and businesses in the market for particular products. A direct response ad for fruit trees that appears when a person types in "apple trees" has the best chance of success.

Direct Sales

In the consumer sector, Amway, Mary Kay, Avon and other companies rely on direct sales. The salesperson contacts friends, relatives, coworkers, and others and provides them with small catalogs or marketing brochures. Alternatively, individuals host parties and invite friends and relatives to see products.

Mark is the Avon flanker brand designed for teenagers and women under 30. In launching a new line of cosmetics, Mark's marketing group brought direct selling into the digital and social media age by hiring 40,000 "Mark Girls" to work in the United States. Mark Girls are primarily women between the ages of 18 and 24 who use grassroots methods to sell Mark cosmetics and fashion accessories in dorms, through sororities, and via Facebook. The brand offers personalized e-boutiques, iPhone apps, and a Facebook e-shop. Kristiauna Mangum, a marketing major at The Ohio State University, serves as a sales manager for Mark. She oversees 155 Mark Girls who earn commissions that range from 20 to 50 percent of the product's price.[30]

Telemarketing

Telemarketing takes place in two ways: inbound or outbound. *Inbound telemarketing* occurs when an individual initiates a call to a company. When a customer places an order, cross-selling can occur by offering other products or services. At times, customers make inbound calls to register complaints or talk about problems. Direct response marketing provides information about how to solve the problem. For example, when a customer calls a mortgage company because of a late fee, the operator encourages the person to sign up for a direct pay program, which

▼ More than 40,000 "Mark Girls" work in the United States for Avon.

means the customer does not have to worry about possible mail delays.

The least popular method for direct marketing is *outbound telemarketing*. New legislation requires prior consent before outbound sales calling or texting to a cell phone. This law has greatly reduced the usage of outbound telemarketing. Successful outbound programs tie into databases that identify the customers or prospects that have had prior relationships with the company. Only those individuals receive contacts. An outbound telemarketing program that contacts customers who have not purchased in a year might bring them back. A company that purchased a copy machine can be called to inquire about interest in paper and toner.

▲ Inbound telemarketing is an important marketing method used by most business-to-business operations.

Personal Selling

Personal selling features a face-to-face opportunity to build relationships with consumers. It takes place in both consumer and business-to-business transactions. Personal selling may result in the acquisition of new customers in addition to influencing current customers to increase levels of purchases. Salespersons provide various services and work to maintain existing relationships. The goal of personal selling should not be limited to making sales. Developing long-term relationships with customers should always be a key objective. **Relationship selling** seeks to create a customer for life, not for a single transaction.

Figure 11.11 identifies the standard steps in the selling process. A quality data warehouse accompanied by effective database technologies provides key tools that assist in personal selling.

objective 11.5

What are the tasks involved in developing successful personal selling programs for consumers and businesses?

Generating Leads

Firms that rely heavily on personal selling to generate sales utilize **referral marketing**, a strategic approach designed to generate leads from both customer and non-customer sources. Figure 11.12 identifies the primary types of referrals.

Experience referrals directly result from a company's work and typically come from current and former customers. Company employees collect leads generated by satisfied customers. The leads are valuable because consumers as well as business buyers have greater confidence in the personal recommendations of others. Experience referrals may be provided by vendors and suppliers. They result from providing attentive service, quality products, and developing positive relationships with other businesses, who then give the company leads in exchange for services or as expressions of gratitude.

In making a sales call, dropping the name of the person who gave the referral helps a salesperson get past gatekeepers. Also, if someone has given a referral, then the potential lead becomes more receptive to the sales call and has a more positive attitude toward the salesperson. These benefits increase the probability that the lead will become a customer.

▲ Personal selling allows a firm to develop long-lasting relationships with customers.

▶ **FIGURE 11.11**
Steps in the Selling Process

- Generating leads
- Qualifying prospect
- Knowledge acquisition
- Sales presentation

- Handling objections
- Sales closing
- Follow-up

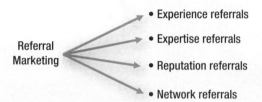

Referral Marketing

- Experience referrals
- Expertise referrals
- Reputation referrals
- Network referrals

▲ **FIGURE 11.12**
Types of Referrals

An *expertise referral* is made by a non-client. It occurs when an individual learns about a company's expertise, quality of work, or a particular specialty through a third person. Although expertise can be shared through word-of-mouth communications, it does not carry the weight of an experience referral because it is not based on a past interaction. A person or company can increase perceptions of his or its expertise in a number of ways. For instance, a contractor that has developed an expertise in home remodeling may host a blog in which he provides information about remodeling and problems homeowners face. He offers advice on his website and writes articles for the local newspaper or magazines. He can be interviewed by the local radio and television stations. Individuals or companies generate expertise referrals by utilizing traditional media as well as digital and social media. The objective is to provide information that creates the image of being an expert, which in turn results in new leads.

Reputation referrals are provided by non-clients. They are based on the reputation that a company holds in a community or industry. They are not based on expertise, but rather on another factor such as fast delivery, empathetic employees, honesty, or connection with particular individuals or companies. For example, a firm may develop a reputation as a reliable supplier of steel or other metals to manufacturers. It could be a firm such as Aramark that is well-known for supplying dining service to universities, hospitals, and other types of businesses. Social media offers an excellent venue for conveying a company's reputation. To generate buzz and reputation referrals, a company can utilize the buzz marketing techniques presented in Chapter 9, such as influencer marketing or content seeding. All of the strategies discussed in Chapter 2 about building strong brands apply to enhancing reputation referrals. The objective is to create the reputation of being a desirable company, which then results in leads and inquiries.

The final method for generating leads is a *network referral*. These referrals are the least attractive because the prospect has limited knowledge of the company. The referral may be generated when a company employee makes contacts during a social gathering, with a business organization, or through social media such as LinkedIn. They may come through an email campaign utilizing a purchased list. While this approach can generate some leads, it typically requires considerable marketing effort to take them from leads to prospects.

WORKERS' COMP IS THE LAST THING
ON MY MIND

LUBA ✦
Workers' Comp
888.884.5822 • LUBAwc.com   Rated A- Excellent by A.M. Best.
Because, it's the biggest thing on ours.

▲ Leads can be generated through business personnel clicking on this digital banner ad for LUBA Workers' Comp.

Qualifying Prospects

Every lead or prospect may not be viable. Also, all prospects do not hold equal value. With this in mind, qualifying prospects means evaluating leads on two dimensions: the potential income the lead can generate and the probability of acquiring the prospect as a customer. Based on the outcomes of these evaluations, marketers make determinations about the best methods of contact and what happens with the lead. The high cost of making personal sales calls means that only the best leads warrant personal visits. Some prospects receive telephone calls or emails from an inside salesperson. Others may be mailed or emailed marketing materials but are not contacted directly by a salesperson.

Once the leads are analyzed using the two categories—sales potential and probability of acquisition—they are then placed into categories, or buckets, with the leads high on both dimensions as the best, or "A" leads. This group normally receives calls from members of the sales staff. The second best group, or "B" leads, often will be contacted by a telemarketer or through email. "C" leads receive marketing materials and are encouraged to make inquiries if interested. Leads that score low on both dimensions may be kept in a database and monitored for future action in case the leads' situation changes.

Knowledge Acquisition

During the knowledge acquisition phase, the company's salespeople or other members of the sales department gather materials about the prospect. Figure 11.13 identifies typical information. The more a salesperson knows about a prospect before making the sales call, the higher the probability of making a sale or gaining permission to demonstrate the company's prospect.

The Sales Presentation

The initial sales call can be designed to gather information, discuss bid specifications, answer questions, or to close the deal with a final pitch or offer.[31] The exact nature of the first sales call depends on the information gathered prior to the call. Also, the stage of the buying process affects the presentation. The types of sales presentations used typically fall into one of these categories: stimulus-response, need-satisfaction, problem-solution, and mission-sharing.[32]

A **stimulus-response** sales approach, or a "canned" sales pitch, involves specific statements (stimuli) designed to elicit specific responses from customers. The salesperson normally memorizes the stimulus statement (the pitch). Telemarketers, retail sales clerks, and new field sales reps often rely on this method.

The **need-satisfaction** sales approach seeks to discover the customer's needs during the first part of the sales presentation and then to provide solutions. The salesperson should skillfully ask the right questions. She should understand the customer's business and customers. Once a need has been identified, the rep then shows how the company's products meet that need.

The **problem-solution** sales approach requires employees from the selling organization to analyze the buyer's business. It usually involves a team of individuals such as engineers, salespeople, and other experts. The team investigates a potential customer's operations and problems, and then offers feasible solutions.

In the **mission-sharing** approach, two organizations develop a common mission. They then share resources to accomplish that mission. This partnership resembles a joint venture as much as a selling relationship.

◀ **FIGURE 11.13**
Knowledge Acquisition Information

- Understand the prospect's business.
- Know and understand the prospect's customers.
- Identify the prospect's needs.
- Evaluate the risk factors and costs in switching vendors.
- Identify the decision makers and influencers.

▲ Understanding customer needs provides the basis for the need-satisfaction sales approach.

- Head-on approach
- Indirect approach
- Compensation method
- "Feel, felt, found"

▲ **FIGURE 11.14**
Methods of Handling Objections

Handling Objections

Companies and individuals seldom make purchases after a sales presentation without raising some objections or concerns. Salespeople anticipate objections and carefully answer them. Figure 11.14 lists the most common methods of handling objections.

With the *head-on approach*, the salesperson answers the objection directly. Doing so, however, suggests that the customer or prospect is wrong. Consequently, the salesperson should use tact. No one likes being told he is in error. The salesperson takes care to not offend the customer.

To avoid a confrontation, some salespeople employ an *indirect approach*. This method allows the salesperson to never really tell the customer he is wrong. Instead, the salesperson sympathizes with the customer's viewpoint and then provides the correct information.

When the customer's objection is partly true, the salesperson may use the *compensation method*. With this approach, the salesperson replies "yes, but . . . " and then explains the product's benefits or features that answer the customer's objection.

Some customers do not have specific objections but are anxious or worried about the consequences of switching to a new vendor. For this situation, a sales rep can apply the *feel, felt, found* method. The salesperson permits the customer to talk about her fears or worries. In response, the salesperson can relate personal experiences or experiences of other customers who had the same fears and worries and how the product resulted in a positive experience.

- Direct close
- Trial close
- Summarization close
- Continuous "yes" close
- Assumptive close

▲ **FIGURE 11.15**
Methods of Closing Sales

Closing the Sale

Often, the most important element of the sales call is the closing; however, it may also be the most difficult part. Salespeople often experience feelings of rejection or failure when prospects or customers say "no." Successful salespeople are masters at making the close. Figure 11.15 identifies some common sales-closing methods. The one to be used depends on the personality of the salesperson, the personality of the prospect, and the situation surrounding the sales call.

With the *direct close*, the salesperson asks for the order outright. The approach may be used when objections have been answered and the salesperson believes the prospect is ready to buy.

When the salesperson cannot be sure if the prospect is ready, he can employ a *trial close*. With this approach, the salesperson solicits feedback that provides information regarding the customer's reaction, without asking directly for the sale. A positive reaction leads the salesperson to ask for the order. If not, then he returns to the sales presentation. The salesperson may also *summarize* the product's benefits and how it meets the customer's needs prior to asking for the order.

Sometimes a salesperson will ask a series of questions along the way, ensuring the customer will *continuously* respond "yes." By answering "yes" to smaller questions about the benefits of a product, when it comes time to ask for the order the customer may be more likely to respond with a "yes."

A salesperson can also *assume* the customer will say "yes." She might ask, "How many cases do you want?" or "How would you like this to be shipped?"

▲ With the summarization close, the salesperson shows how the product meets the customer's needs.

Follow-Up

Keeping customers happy after a purchase can result in repeat business, customer loyalty, and positive referrals. Quality follow-up programs are cost-effective ways to retain customers, which is much cheaper than continually finding new ones. Unfortunately, following up may be neglected by the sales staff, especially if the salesperson receives commission on new sales but not on follow-up activities. In this situation, the company must designate other employees to follow up to ensure that customers are satisfied with their purchases.

International Implications

Database marketing faces the same challenges as other aspects of an IMC program when a firm moves into the international arena. These include differences in technology, which make data collection and analysis difficult due to issues such as language and internet availability. Further, local laws may limit the methods by which information can be collected as well as the types of information a company seeks and/or shares with other companies.

In many parts of the world, customers may only live a few miles apart yet reside in different countries. For example, the European Union consists of many nations in close proximity. Therefore, decisions must be made as to whether data will be country specific.

Permission marketing, frequency, and customer relationship management programs are subject to legal restrictions as well as cultural differences. In some instances, they may be highly accepted. Such is the case for permission marketing in Japan. In many Asian cultures, the giving of gifts takes on added meaning. This may indicate that stronger bonds between customers and companies are important in personal selling.

Direct marketing programs should be adapted to local circumstances. Mail delivery systems may be easier to access in some countries than others. The same holds true for telephone systems, internet access, and other technologies. Infomercials may not be possible in countries with state-run television systems. A company's marketing team considers all local legal, social, cultural, technological, and competitive conditions before embarking on an international database-driven marketing program or direct marketing program.

Some international companies have moved to the forefront of data-based marketing programs. For example, Land, a Russian high-end supermarket chain, has implemented interactive kiosks that create recommendation-styled grocery lists for customers who use the brand's loyalty cards.[33]

objective 11.6
How should database marketing and personal selling programs be adapted to international settings?

Marketers also adapt personal selling tactics to specific countries. Local culture and customs must be carefully observed prior to making a sales call. A cultural assimilator will often be assigned to help the sales team understand the nuances of a specific region or nation such as methods of greeting people, the manner in which gender differences are treated, dining customs, time awareness, personal space in communication, and other factors that affect interpersonal interactions.

Summary

Database marketing constitutes a vital element of a complete IMC program. The two key activities involved at the most general level—identifying customers and building relationships with them—have an impact on numerous other IMC tasks. It is more cost-effective to retain customers than to seek out new ones. Further, the actual message may change when communicating with long-time, loyal customers.

Building a data warehouse begins with collecting data to be used by the marketing department. Beyond basic information, such as a customer's name, address, and email address, other key data include the customer's purchase history and preferences. Geocoding involves adding geographic codes to customer records, which assists in selecting media and creating messages targeted to specific groups.

Database coding and analysis leads to either lifetime value analysis of customers or the clustering of customer groups based on customer spending patterns. Data mining programs involve building profiles of customer segments and/or preparing models that predict future purchase behaviors based on past purchases. The information gathered from data coding and data mining leads to the development of data-driven marketing communications and marketing programs.

Database-driven marketing communications programs are facilitated by effective identification codes that allow for personalization of messages and interactions. An effective database-driven communication program relies on customer profiles combined with other information available regarding specific customers. In-bound telemarketing programs, trawling, advertising, and lifetime value segment programs can be fine-tuned for individual customers.

Database-driven marketing programs include permission marketing, frequency programs, and customer relationship management systems. Permission marketing is a selling approach in which the customer agrees to receive promotional materials in exchange for incentives. Frequency programs are incentives customers receive for repeat business. Both are designed to create customer loyalty over time. CRM is designed to build long-term loyalty and bonds with customers through the use of a personal touch facilitated by technology.

Direct response or direct marketing efforts may be made by mail, catalog, phone, mass media, the internet, or email. Direct mail programs remain popular as outbound telemarketing programs continue to diminish.

The goal of personal selling programs—relationship selling—should be to create a customer for life rather than for a single transaction. The steps involved in personal selling include generating leads, qualifying prospects, knowledge acquisition, designing effective sales presentations, handling objections, closing the sale, and following up. Each of these activities can be made more effective through the use of quality database management programs.

Key Terms

data warehouse The place where customer data are held

geocoding Adding geographic codes to customer records to make it possible to plot customer addresses on a map

lifetime value The present value of future profits a customer generates over his or her life in a relationship with a brand or firm

hashing The process of anonymizing mobile phone data so that specific individuals cannot be identified

data mining The process of using computer data analysis software to mine data for meaningful information and relationships

trawling The process of searching the database for a specific piece of information for marketing purposes

permission marketing A form of database marketing in which the company sends promotional materials to customers who give the company permission to do so

empowerment Consumers believe that they have power throughout the seller–consumer relationship, not just at the beginning when they agreed to join a frequency program

reciprocity A sense of obligation toward a company that results from receiving special deals or incentives such as gifts

frequency (or loyalty) program A marketing program designed to promote loyalty or frequent purchases of the same brand (or company)

customer relationship management (CRM) Programs designed to build long-term loyalty and bonds with customers through the use of a personal touch facilitated by technology

share of customer The percentage of expenditures a customer makes with one particular firm compared to total expenditures in that product's category

direct response (or direct) marketing Vending products to customers without the use of other channel members

response list A list of customers who have made purchases or who have responded to direct mail offers in the past

compiled list A list consisting of information about consumers who meet a specific demographic profile

relationship selling Developing long-term relationships with customers rather than focusing on a single transaction

referral marketing A strategic approach designed to generate leads from both customer and non-customer sources

stimulus-response A sales approach, often called a "canned" sales pitch, that uses specific statements (stimuli) to elicit specific responses from customers

need-satisfaction A sales approach in which the salesperson strives to discover a customer's needs during the first part of the sales presentation and then provides solutions to those needs

problem-solution A sales approach that requires employees from the selling organization to analyze the buyer's operations and offer ways to solve their problems

mission-sharing A sales approach in which two organizations develop a common mission and then share resources to accomplish that mission

MyMarketingLab

To complete the problems with the ★ in your MyLab, go to the end-of-chapter Discussion Questions.

Review Questions

11-1. What two activities are part of a successful database marketing program?

11-2. What is a data warehouse? What is the difference between an operational database and a marketing database?

11-3. List the tasks associated with database marketing.

11-4. Describe geocoding, customer clusters, and location data tracking.

11-5. Define lifetime value. How is it determined?

11-6. What are the two primary functions of data mining?

11-7. Explain how identification codes are used in database-driven marketing communications.

11-8. Explain how consumer profile information is used when sending communications to customers.

11-9. What is trawling?

11-10. Describe a permission marketing program. What are the key benefits of this approach?

11-11. What are the keys to an effective permission marketing program?

11-12. Describe a frequency program.

11-13. What is customer relationship management?

11-14. What is meant by the term share of customer?

11-15. What is direct response marketing?

11-16. Explain how response lists and compiled lists are used in direct mail programs.

11-17. Explain the two ways infomercials are presented as parts of a direct response program.

11-18. Describe relationship marketing and the four types of referral marketing.

11-19. What steps are involved in the personal selling process?

11-20. Identify the four types of sales presentations typically used by sales reps.

11-21. What types of closing methods are available to salespeople?

Critical Thinking Exercises

DISCUSSION QUESTIONS

★**11-22.** Assume you are the account executive at a database marketing agency. A local music retailer with four stores has asked you to develop a database for the company. What information should be in the databases? How would you build a data warehouse and where would you obtain the data? Be specific.

★**11-23.** The Chic Shaque sells contemporary fashions, bedding, bath, gifts, and home décor items in its 14 stores. Explain each of the data coding processes of lifetime value, customer clusters, and location data tracking. For each coding method, describe how the Chic Shaque's marketers could use the data coding process in their database marketing efforts.

11-24. Hickory Outdoor is a retail store that sells fishing, hunting, camping, and other outdoor equipment and supplies, including various items for a number of outdoor sports. The company has built a database of its customers over the last five years. The marketing team can use data mining to improve their marketing efforts. Suggest ways data mining might be used. What type of marketing programs would you suggest based on data mining? What other types of marketing programs can be developed from the database?

11-25. Karen's Formal Dress is a retailer specializing in formal and wedding wear. She has a database with more than 3,000 names of individuals who have purchased or rented formal wear. She would like to develop a permission marketing program. How can the marketing team encourage individuals to give permission to receive marketing materials? Once the company has the customer's permission, how can the relationship be continued to make it beneficial to both the consumer and to Karen's Formal Dress? Describe the methodology Karen should use in her permission marketing program, including the types of materials, methods of distribution, and incentives.

⭐**11-26.** A primary reason for developing a frequency program is to encourage customers to be loyal to a business or brand. For each of the following products, discuss the merits of a frequency program. What types of incentives would individuals need to join the frequency club and then what type of incentives are needed to continue participation in the program?

　　a. Local restaurant
　　b. Auto repair service
　　c. Printing service
　　d. Clothing retailer

⭐**11-27.** Suppose you have been hired as a marketing intern for Centric Federal Credit Union and asked to develop a direct response marketing campaign. For each direct response marketing method, describe how Centric could utilize it. Be specific with the description of the campaign in terms of how and where you would obtain names and type of media outlets used. When you have finished, rank the methods of direct response marketing in terms of their desirability for Centric. Justify your rankings.

11-28. Examine the forms of direct response marketing shown in the graph in Figure 11.10. Which ones have you responded to in the past? Which ones are most likely to influence your purchase decisions? Which ones are the least likely? Explain for each method your personal responses over the last year.

11-29. Examine the direct marketing methods highlighted in Figure 11.10. Think about the following businesses. For each business, identify the best direct response marketing method. Justify your choices. Describe a direct response campaign that you envision for each of the methods chosen.

　　a. Shoe store
　　b. Sporting goods retailer
　　c. Internet calendar and video game retailer (sells only via the internet)
　　d. Accounting and tax services for small businesses and individuals

11-30. Think about a recent personal purchase experience that involved a salesperson. Describe how the salesperson handled you during the sales call. Which sales presentation approach did the salesperson use? Which methods of handling objections were used? Evaluate how well the objection was handled. Which closing did the salesperson use? How well did the salesperson handle the closing?

11-31. In your own words explain the four types of referrals in referral marketing. Suppose you are the marketing intern for a local CPA and corporate tax business. For each type of referral, discuss a viable strategy for obtaining referrals for your business. Of the four strategies you just discussed, which is the most feasible? Why? Which is the second-most feasible? Why?

Integrated Learning Exercises

11-32. Pick a company that sells clothing. Go to the company's website. What evidence do you see of database marketing and of personalization of the website? Use screenshots to illustrate your answer. Identify and describe the best database marketing program the company could use to reach consumers such as yourself.

11-33. Go to the website for Scotts Miracle Gro at **www.scotts.com**. What evidence do you see of database marketing and of personalization? Review the concepts presented in the section "Database-Driven Marketing Communications." What steps could Scotts take to develop data-driven communications with visitors to the website as well as individuals who make purchases?

⭐**11-34.** Describe each of the data-base marketing communications methods identified in the chapter. Go to the website of Weaver Leather at **http://www.weaver-leather.com**. Discuss each of the database-driven marketing communications methods presented in the chapter in relation to Weaver Leather. Explain the importance of each and describe how Weaver Leather could use each to enhance its communications with visitors to its website.

11-35. You have been hired as a marketing intern for a small chain of 17 Chinese food restaurants. Your boss has asked you to locate three database marketing agencies on the Internet. Describe the services of each company and evaluate its feasibility for developing a database marketing program for the Chinese restaurants. Provide the URL for each agency and use screenshots to illustrate your answer. Which company would you recommend? Why?

11-36. *DMNews* is a trade journal for database marketing and CRM programs. Access the website at **www.dmnews.com**. What types of information are available on the site? How could this help companies with database marketing and CRM programs? Access and read one of the articles from the journal. Write a paragraph about what you learned.

11-37. The Direct Marketing Association (DMA) is a global trade association of business and nonprofit organizations that use direct marketing tools and techniques. Access the trade organization's website at **www.the-dma.org**. What services does the DMA provide its members? What value would this be to a business in developing a direct marketing program?

11-38. A primary key in successful direct marketing is the quality of the list used. One company that specializes in compiling lists is U.S. Data Corporation. Access the company's website at **www.usdatacorporation.com**. What types of lists does the company offer?

Access one of the lists and discuss how a company could use U.S. Data Corporation for a direct response marketing campaign. What services does U.S. Data Corporation offer?

11-39. Suppose you are the marketing manager for a chain of 15 beauty salons and have decided to use a direct response marketing campaign. Access the website of US Data Corporation (**www.usdatacorporation.com**). Select five different lists you could purchase from the company and explain why they were chosen. Identify two different services offered by US Data Corporation that would be of interest to you. Explain how that service could be used in your direct response marketing campaign.

11-40. Use the internet to find three companies or organizations that offer advice to salespeople. Write a report about the methods the sites suggest and how those tactics compare to the materials presented in this chapter. Use screenshots to enhance your report and provide the URL of the three companies.

11-41. In your own words describe each of the methods of handling objections and closing sales presented in this chapter. Go to YouTube and locate two videos, one that discusses handling objections and the other that discusses how to close sales. Provide the URLs of the two videos. Describe the methods presented in the videos and how they are similar to or different from the information presented in the textbook.

Blog Exercises

Access the authors' blog for this textbook at the URLs provided to complete these exercises. Answer the questions that are posed on the blog.

11-42. Database marketing: **http://blogclowbaack.net/2014/05/12/database-marketing-chapter-11/**

11-43. Direct response marketing: **http://blogclowbaack.net/2014/05/12direct-response-marketing-chapter-11/**

11-44. Personal selling: **http://blogclowbaack.net/2014/05/12/selling-chapter-11/0/**

Student Project

CREATIVE CORNER

Lilly Fashions sells fashionable, trendy clothes. The company's primary target customer is 20- to 30-year-old females with an average income of $40,000 and some college. Lilly's marketing team wants to capitalize on the concepts of database marketing and direct response marketing. Design a newspaper advertisement that encourages females in the company's target market to visit the retail store and join Lilly's loyalty program. In addition, design a direct mail piece that would go to individuals who are currently in the database but who have not made a purchase within the last three months. Prepare another email that can be sent to members in the database on the person's birthday offering them a free meal at a local restaurant, if they come to the store to pick up the meal voucher. This promotion is a joint promotion with the restaurant, which shares in the cost, which means the restaurant must also be part of the email.

CASE 1   SALON SENSATIONAL

The world of beauty enhancement often changes. Jennifer Swann, owner and manager of Salon Sensational, recognizes that she must constantly adapt to new trends in order to keep her company on top. Jennifer owns four salons, located in Medford and Portland, Oregon. The salons serve both male and female clients. Her current operation offers hair care of all types, manicures, pedicures, and includes space rentals to two popular local massage therapists. The company also sells a line of top quality hair care products including shampoo, conditioner, and coloring rinses.

Salon Sensational has been involved in local community events. Most notably, each year the salon provides low-cost pink hair accents to sponsor Breast Cancer Awareness efforts. Also, twice each year stylists provide free services to low income members of the community as part of a city-wide program for the disadvantaged, held at the local city auditorium.

Jennifer has created a program designed to keep her stylists on the cutting edge. Each receives financial incentives in order to attend training sessions for creating the newest hair styles. She also maintains an incentive system designed to encourage stylists to sell and cross-sell the hair care products that the salon offers.

Five years ago, Jennifer purchased a sophisticated computer software system that allows her to track all customer interactions with the salon, including records of past appointments, purchases of products, methods of payment (cash versus charge), along with notes about past complaints as well as past compliments. The system maintains appointment schedules and also identifies customers who have routinely canceled or not kept their appointments.

Repeat business represents the staple of the salon industry. When customers routinely return, stylists stay busy and the total company benefits. Customer referrals also help to build volume in terms of appointments.

Currently, Jennifer is looking for ways to increase purchase frequencies and facility utilization. She recognizes that care must be given to avoid alienating clientele by appearing to "hard sell" them hair care products or additional visits. At the same time, she knows that part of the frequency displayed by customers is the result of building strong bonds and relationships between individuals and their stylists as well as Jennifer herself.

One approach to building revenues would be to add new services, such as cosmetology. In that way, a person getting ready for a major event, such as a prom or wedding, would be able to have her hair styled, nails polished, and make-up put on, all in the same location. The question is whether sufficient demand for such a

▲ Jennifer styling the hair of one of her customers.

new service exists. She would have to invest in a minor amount of remodeling in order to be able to provide the service.

At the same time, Salon Sensation enjoys a positive reputation in both cities. Many customers report high levels of loyalty. The goal is to build on those aspects in order to continue to succeed.

11-45. Identify the types of data Jennifer should collect from her customers and how she could obtain it.

11-46. Suppose Jennifer wants to start a loyalty card program to build her database. Design a flyer that could be handed to customers of the salons encouraging them to join the loyalty program. What benefits would customers receive? In exchange, what information would Jennifer request from each customer?

11-47. Once the database is built, what database-driven marketing communications should Salon Sensational send out to individuals in its database?

11-48. Which direct response marketing programs would be helpful to Jennifer? How would they be of value? Explain how Jennifer could use each to increase purchase frequencies and visits to her salons.

11-49. What types of personal selling tactics should stylists use? Which should not be used? Why?

11-50. What methods for overcoming objections would best serve Salon Sensational when selling hair care products?

CASE 2   THE TRAVEL AGENCY DILEMMA

Leisure time travel remains a common pursuit across a variety of markets. Numerous forces influence consumers as they seek out restful, adventuresome, romantic, and family-oriented vacations. Factors such as gasoline and airline ticket prices, economic conditions, political unrest, and the changing world of technology factor into personal and family decisions regarding places to go, things to do, people to see, and events to enjoy.

Travel agencies experience the influence of these forces as directly as any other group. When gas prices rise, consumers take shorter trips. When airline tickets are at a premium, travelers look for bargains or seek other alternatives. Unemployment, political turmoil in places such as Mexico and Europe, and other considerations cause people to either stay at home or change travel plans.

The most direct influence on the travel agency business has been the internet and its popular travel sites. Travelocity, Priceline.com, and other airline booking sites allow consumers to shop online for the best air fares and travel times. Hotels.com plus numerous hotel chain-run booking sites, which also offer frequency programs, make it possible to find the most ideal hotel arrangement without the use of a travel agency. Many internet-savvy consumers no longer feel the need to call or drive to a local travel agency. These individuals have become convinced that they are able to match any price or travel arrangement that an agency can find.

To compete in this intense environment, agency managers seek ways to deliver value-added services that entice consumers to continue to utilize their companies. Among the potential methods to maintain customer loyalty are offers of convenience, skill at finding better prices than consumers can obtain online, and the ability to package travel into one-price programs. Many travel agencies create agreements with hotels, cruise lines, and airlines to offer better prices than consumers will receive from other vendors.

Travel agencies can also offer suggestions regarding combinations of activities such as fine dining with an elaborate hotel. Many agency employees visit numerous destinations, seeking to obtain better quality information about local attractions that would go unnoticed by travelers to a specific area.

In the future, the question remains as to whether travel agencies will be able to continue to compete. Only with carefully constructed service programs and quality marketing efforts will it be possible to maintain a set of clientele as the world of internet shopping continues to increase.

11-51. How might database marketing, including the data warehouse, data coding and analysis, and data mining, help a

▲ With access to the internet, many tourists see little value in the services provided by travel agencies.

travel agency create and enhance relationships with customers and potential customers?

11-52. How could data-driven marketing programs, including permission marketing, frequency programs, and customer relationship management systems, be useful to travel agencies?

11-53. Discuss each of the direct response marketing techniques in relation to marketing travel agencies.

11-54. What personal selling tactics are most important to travel agency employees as they work with customers and potential customers?

11-55. Discuss the pros and cons of each of the methods of handling objections in personal selling in relation to a couple who are hesitant to purchase a vacation to one of the Caribbean islands.

11-56. Discuss the pros and cons of each of the closing methods in personal selling in relation to a couple who are hesitant to purchase a vacation to one of the Caribbean islands.

MyMarketingLab

Go to the Assignments section of your MyLab to complete these writing exercises.

11-57. Karen's Formal Dress is a retailer specializing in formal and wedding wear. She has a database with more than 3,000 names of individuals who have purchased or rented formal wear. She would like to develop a permission marketing program. How can the marketing team encourage individuals to give permission to receive marketing materials? Once the company has the customer's permission, how can the relationship be continued to make it beneficial to both the consumer and to Karen's Formal Dress? Describe the methodology Karen should use in her permission marketing program, including the types of materials, methods of distribution, and incentives.

11-58. In your own words describe each of the methods of handling objections and closing sales presented in this chapter. Go to YouTube and locate two videos, one that discusses handling objections and the other that discusses how to close sales. Provide the URLs of the two videos. Describe the methods presented in the videos and how they are similar to or different from the information presented in the textbook.

Buzz Marketing
Communications
Social Media
Advertising
Promotions
Digital
Branding
Mobile Marketing

Chapter 12 Sales Promotions

Chapter Objectives

After reading this chapter, you should be able to answer the following questions:

12.1 What are the differences between consumer promotions and trade promotions?

12.2 How can the various forms of consumer promotions help to pull consumers into stores and push products onto the shelves?

12.3 How do different types of customers respond to consumer promotions?

12.4 What types of trade promotions can help push products onto retailers' shelves and eventually to end users?

12.5 What concerns exist for manufacturers considering trade promotions programs?

12.6 What issues complicate international sales promotions programs?

Overview

Some may think a high-quality advertising program completes the task of promotion. It does not. A fully integrated marketing communications program includes additional key activities. This chapter describes sales promotions programs. **Sales promotions** consist of all of the incentives offered to customers and channel members to encourage product purchases.

Sales promotions take two forms: consumer promotions and trade promotions. Companies offer **consumer promotions** directly to customers and potential customers. Consumer promotions are aimed at those who actually use the product, or end users. They may be individuals or households. Another end user may be a business that consumes the product, when the item is not resold to another business. In other words, companies offer consumer promotions in both consumer markets and business-to-business markets.

Trade promotions are only allotted in the distribution channel. **Trade promotions** consist of the expenditures or incentives used by manufacturers and other members of the marketing channel to purchase goods for eventual resale. Trade promotions provided to other firms help push products through to retailers.

Many parents would likely report that potty training represents one of their least favorite child-raising activities. Huggies (whose parent company is Kimberly-Clark) makes the process more palatable through a series of efforts that include teaching assistance and marketing efforts.

In terms of teaching assistance, the Huggies Big Kid Academy offers resources for parents engaged in potty training. The website includes advice regarding a "readiness quiz," a "prep list," fun activities, and a potty training progress chart. Parents learn to "celebrate the first flush" and have access to musical inspiration through "potty training theme songs" as well as the company's famous Potty Dance program.[2]

In terms of marketing, the company engages in a full spectrum of IMC activities, including sponsorships of ESPN Radio's Major League Baseball coverage as well as Westwood One's Sunday Night Football broadcasts. The company runs traditional advertisements in a variety of media on a regular basis.

Another staple of the marketing efforts for Huggies has been reliance on sales promotions. The company offers coupons in traditional ways through newspaper insert programs, in magazines, as well as online on the organization's website. Additional incentives may be found on the Huggies' Facebook page, YouTube presence, and on other social media.

A contest featuring a tie-in with the Disney Corporation involved customers in the United Kingdom competing by answering the question, "What is the Huggies® Pull-Ups® wetness indicator?" Those with correct responses were placed into a drawing and winners received "1 x iPad 4 + First Years Disney musical potty + Huggies starter pack, 20 x Disney musical potty + Huggies pull-ups bundle."[3]

Huggies engages in trade promotions in order to compete with Pampers and other companies producing similar products. Incentives offered to stores including Target and Costco help ensure the Huggies brand receives prominent attention from retailers. The combination of incentives for individual customers as well as retail stores has kept Huggies at the forefront of potty training and associated parenting events for more than 20 years.

Consumer Promotions vs. Trade Promotions

In the past, some marketing experts believed that any type of sales promotion, whether consumer or trade, eroded brand equity by shifting the focus to price. Now, however, many company leaders recognize that properly managed promotions differentiate a brand from the competition, helping to build brand awareness and improving a brand's image.[1]

The marketing team designs promotional programs to help the company achieve its IMC objectives and to support a brand's position. In the early stages of a product's life cycle, promotions match advertising and other efforts focused on brand awareness, creating opportunities for trial purchases and stimulating additional purchases. Later, the goal shifts to strengthening a brand, increasing consumption, fending off competition, or finding new markets. As just noted, the Huggies brand has taken advantage of sales promotions programs.

This chapter examines consumer promotions first, followed by trade promotions. Although the presentations are separate, the marketing team designs both at the same time. The adjustments made to sales promotions programs in international markets are also described.

objective 12.1
What are the differences between consumer promotions and trade promotions?

Consumer Promotions

objective 12.2

How can the various forms of consumer promotions help to pull consumers into stores and push products onto the shelves?

Enticing a consumer to take the final step and make the purchase constitutes a primary goal for a consumer promotions program. Advertising creates the interest and excitement that brings the consumer to the store. Marketers then deploy other tactics. In addition to leading to the final decision to buy an item, consumer promotions programs help generate store traffic and enhance brand loyalty.

During recent Super Bowls, Denny's offered free breakfast meals to anyone who came into the restaurant from 6:00 a.m. to 2:00 p.m. on the Tuesday following the game. Each year, roughly two million Americans took advantage of the offer. Some waited in line for hours for a breakfast. The goal, according to CEO Nelson Marchioli, was to "re-acquaint America with Denny's." He added, "We've never been thanked this much—and folks are saying they'll come back." The cost of the entire promotion, including food, labor, and the Super Bowl commercial, was about $5 million. In exchange, Denny's earned something money alone cannot buy: a powerful positive public relations blitz. The promotion garnered an estimated $50 million in free, positive media news coverage. The company received 40 million website hits in the week following the Super Bowl, indicating it was a highly successful program.[4] Figure 12.1 identifies the most common consumer promotions.

▲ Free breakfast meals the Tuesday after the Super Bowl was a big winner for Denny's.

- Coupons
- Premiums
- Contests and sweepstakes
- Refunds and rebates
- Sampling
- Bonus packs
- Price-offs

▲ **FIGURE 12.1**
Types of Consumer Promotions

- Print media
  - Freestanding inserts (FSIs)
- Direct mail
- In-or on-package
- In-store
  - Scanner delivered
- Digital
- Employee delivered

▲ **FIGURE 12.2**
Methods of Coupon Distribution

Coupons

A coupon offers a price reduction to the consumer. It may be a percentage off the retail price, such as 25 or 40 percent, or an absolute amount, such as 50 cents or $1. The total value of coupons offered by companies exceeds $500 billion per year. On average consumers redeem about 2.8 billion. The 0.85 redemption rate represents approximately $4.9 billion in savings for consumers, or around $1.94 per coupon. Approximately 72 percent of U.S. households redeem coupons.[5]

Coupon Distribution

Manufacturers issue approximately 80 percent of all coupons. Most coupons are sent through print media, with the vast majority distributed through **freestanding inserts (FSI)**, or sheets of coupons distributed in newspapers, primarily on Sunday. FSI represent almost 90 percent of all coupons distributed, although the percentage has declined as consumers switch to digitally-delivered coupons.[6] Figure 12.2 identifies the various forms of coupon distribution.

FSI and print media remain popular for several reasons. First, the consumer makes a conscious effort to clip or save the coupon. Second, coupons create brand awareness. The consumer sees the brand name on the coupon even when it is not redeemed. Third, FSI encourage consumers to purchase brands on the next trip to the store. Consumers are more likely to purchase a couponed brand and remember the name when they redeem a coupon, which helps move the brand to a consumer's long-term memory.

The popularity of digital coupons continues to grow. About 15 percent of the U.S. population, or 45 million consumers, redeem digital coupons. Digital coupon users tend to be more affluent and better educated. The average household income for a digital coupon user is $97,000. One-third has earned a college degree. Websites make it easy for consumers to find and print coupons, download them onto mobile devices, or transfer them to loyalty cards. Retail stores, including JCPenney, Kroger, and Safeway, feature technologies that permit consumers to redeem coupons from cell phones. CVS Pharmacy customers can scan a loyalty card at a kiosk inside the store entrance to receive instant coupon offers and in-store specials based on their purchase histories. Ease of use spurs the growth of digital coupons.[7]

Types of Coupons

Coupons are distributed in retail stores, offered digitally from the internet or in a store such as CVS, and may be placed on or near packages. In each instance, the consumer is able to use the coupon in the store through an *instant redemption coupon* program. The coupons often lead to trial purchases and purchases of additional packages of a product. Many grocery stores sponsor a company to cook a food product and offer free samples along with coupon giveaways, which is another form of instant redemption couponing.

Some companies place coupons inside packages so that customers cannot redeem them quite as quickly. This encourages repeat purchases. These coupons are called *bounce-back coupons*.

Several retailers issue coupons at the cash register. An item being scanned at a cash register triggers a *scanner-delivered coupon*. The coupon may be for a competing brand, thereby encouraging brand-switching the next time a consumer makes a purchase.

To encourage purchases of additional products, manufactures provide *cross-ruffing coupons*, which means placing a coupon on one product for another product. For example,

▲ Coupons for Wholly Guacamole and Jennie-O Turkey products are part of this advertisement.

▲ Coupon for $1 drinks at SteviB's on Halloween, October 31.

a coupon for French onion dip may be attached to a package of potato chips. Cross-ruff coupons should be for products that logically fit together and that consumers purchase frequently and simultaneously. Occasionally, a manufacturer uses cross-ruffing to encourage consumers to purchase another of its products. Kellogg's may place a coupon on a Rice Krispies box for another cereal, such as Frosted Flakes or an oatmeal product. This tactic encourages consumers to purchase within the same brand or family of products.

Disadvantages of Coupons

Customers with brand preferences redeem approximately 80 percent of all coupons.[8] Some marketers believe that offering price discounts through coupons to those who are willing to pay full price does not make sense. Manufacturers, however, argue that these consumers may be willing to stock up, which means they do not buy from the competition. This might also result in the consumer using more of the product. In essence, manufacturers recognize that brand-preference customer redemptions are a "necessary evil" in mass distribution programs. To avoid sending coupons to current customers, firms may send direct mail coupons to non-loyal customers, thereby targeting nonusers and the competitor's customers. Other disadvantages occur when coupons are counterfeited and when retail stores mistakenly redeem them for the wrong product package size or for similar products offered by a different company.

Premiums

Premiums are prizes, gifts, or other special offers consumers receive when purchasing products. The consumer pays full price for the original good or service with a premium and receives something free. Others offer additional items at a reduced price; such as buy one and get the second at half price.

▲ Coupons for brands sold at Boyer's grocery store.

Types of Premiums

Figure 12.3 identifies four major types of premiums. *Free-in-the-mail premiums* are gifts individuals receive for purchasing products. To receive the gift, the customer mails in a proof of purchase to the manufacturer who then sends the gift to the buyer. More than one purchase may be required to receive some gifts, such as three proofs of purchase.

Credit card companies employ premiums to entice individuals to sign up for various products. Instead of providing a proof of purchase, the consumer activates the card to receive an incentive, which ranges from cash back on a purchase to merchandise and frequent-flier miles.

In- or *on-package premiums* are usually small gifts, such as toys in cereal boxes. The gift may be disguised or packaged so the consumer must buy the product to see the premium, as is the case with Cracker Jack. At other times, the gift will be attached to the package, such as a package of blades with the purchase of a razor.

Store or *manufacturer premiums* are gifts given by either the retail store or the manufacturer when the customer purchases a product. Fast-food restaurants lure children through a toy that accompanies the purchase of a child's meal. Recently, Ulta Beauty offered consumers a 14-piece cosmetic gift with a minimum $19.50 purchase. The free gifts included three shadow palettes, mascara, eye pencil cosmetic brushes, blush, lip gloss, and nail polish. The goal of the premium offer was to attract new customers to the Ulta Beauty brand and to encourage trial purchases of various products.[9]

The fourth type, a *self-liquidating premium*, requires the consumer to pay a small amount of money for the gift or item. The premium may be offered for only $4.99 plus shipping and handling and two proofs of purchase from boxes of Cheerios. The premium is termed self-liquidating because $4.99 covers the premium's cost. The manufacturer may also receive money for shipping and handling so that consumers pay for most or all of the expense of the item.

FREE SMALL TOTS*
with the purchase of any SONIC
Premium Beef Hot Dog**

EXPIRATION DATE:
8/10/2012

* Excludes Sweet Potato Tots.
** At regular price. Limit one with coupon. Not good with combos or other offers. No cash value. Only at participating SONIC® Drive-Ins. No copies. SONIC®'s WHOLLY GUACAMOLE® Dog shown above. ™ & ©2012 America's Drive-In Brand Properties LLC

▲ A premium offer of "free small tots" by Sonic and Wholly Guacamole.

- Free-in-the-mail
- In-or on-package
- Store or manufacturer
- Self-liquidating

▲ **FIGURE 12.3**
Types of Premiums

Keys to Successful Premium Programs

Successful premium programs include several common elements (Figure 12.4). First, the premium should match the target market. A company might target a market consisting of older, high-income individuals through a premium such as china or fine crystal. When young people constitute the primary market, a cartoon figure or a character from Disney or a children's movie becomes more attractive.

The best premiums reinforce the firm's image. They should not be low-cost trinkets. Giving cheap merchandise insults customers and damages the firm's image. Premium programs succeed when they tie in with the firm's products to enhance the image of the company, product or brand.[10]

Premiums should be integrated with the other components of the IMC program. General Mills recently offered collectable Star Wars premiums tied in with the recent Star Wars movie. In-store pallet displays, FSI, and digital efforts on **MyBlogSpark.com**,

- Match the premium to the target market
- Carefully select the premiums (avoid fads, try for exclusivity)
- Pick a premium that reinforces the firm's product and image
- Integrate the premium with other IMC tools (especially advertising and POP displays)
- Don't expect premiums to increase short-term profits

◀ **FIGURE 12.4**
Keys to Successful Premium Programs

▸ An advertisement for Karns Foods featuring both premiums and coupons.

StarWars.com, and Lucasfilm's Twitter supported the program. In addition, to drive awareness of the promotion, General Mills added a 10-second tag to television spots for the cereal brands with the premiums inside the box.[11]

Some marketing experts believe that overusing coupons damages a brand's image. Conversely, premiums might actually enhance an image. Choosing the right type of premium becomes the key. Premiums can be used to boost sales; however, they usually are not as successful as coupons. Nevertheless, premiums provide a valuable consumer promotional tool.

Although premiums add value and enhance the brand, they may not increase profits. Therefore, a clear relationship between the premium's intention and IMC goals should be established. Logically, the goal relates to image rather than profit.

Contests and Sweepstakes

Each year, companies spend approximately $1.9 billion on the various games, contests, and sweepstakes that appear in both consumer and business markets.[12] The prize list largely determines the success or failure of these appeals. Members of the target market for the contest or sweepstakes must desire the prizes in order to entice them to participate.

Contests

The words *contest* and *sweepstakes* tend to be used interchangeably, yet some differences exist, primarily legal. *Contests* normally require the participant to perform an activity. The winner will be selected from the group that performs best or provides the most correct answers. Often, contests require a participant to make a purchase to enter. In some states, however, doing so is illegal. In developing contests, the marketing team first investigates any state and federal laws that apply.

Contests range from the bikini contests at local nightclubs to popular television shows such as *Jeopardy* or *American Idol* in which contestants answer questions or win competitions to earn prizes. Some contests are mostly chance while others require skill. For example, McDonald's Canada ran a unique contest targeted to its employees. Employees were asked to submit their own burger/wrap recipes using McDonald's ingredients. The grand prize winner received $10,000, second place $5,000, third place $2,500, and People's Choice (based on the most online votes) $1,000. The contest spurred interest in McDonald's Canada's employees including their friends and relatives as well others who were encouraged to visit the microsite where the recipes were posted to vote for their favorite.[13]

Sweepstakes

Sweepstake entries do not require a required activity. Consumers enter as many times as they wish, although companies can restrict customers to one entry per visit to the store or location. Probability dictates the chances of winning a sweepstakes. The odds of winning must clearly be stated on all point-of-purchase (POP) displays and advertising materials. In a sweepstakes, the probability of winning each prize must also be published in advance.

Perceived Value

Consumers do not participate in every contest or sweepstakes they encounter. People enter the ones they find to be interesting or challenging. The decision to enter is most often based on the perceived value of the contest or sweepstakes prize combined with the odds of winning. The greater the perceived odds of winning, the more likely it becomes that a person will play.

The perceived value of a contest or sweepstakes has two components: extrinsic value and intrinsic value. The *extrinsic value* is the actual attractiveness of the prize (a car versus a free sandwich). The greater the perceived extrinsic value, the more likely people will become involved. *Intrinsic values* are associated with participating. A contest requiring a skill, such as one for creating recipes or in an essay contest, entices entry by individuals who enjoy demonstrating that ability, and the extrinsic rewards become secondary. Instead, participants enjoy competing and displaying their abilities. This, in part, explains the popularity of fantasy football and baseball leagues and "pick the winner" sports contests such as NCAA basketball tournament bracket-ology events each spring.

American Eagle Outfitters recently launched a sweepstakes that prompted consumers to enter while in one of the store's fitting rooms or while shopping online. In the fitting rooms, posters encouraged shoppers to text JEANS to 32453. Shoppers were invited to upload photos wearing their favorite American Eagle Outfitter's clothes to Twitter using the hashtag #AEOStyle. The sweepstakes offered a $10,000 cash grand prize. Other prizes included a MacBook

▲ A newspaper ad for The Toggery offering a premium "Buy 1 get the 2ⁿᵈ at 50% off".

▼ An advertisement for Wholly Guacamole promoting a contest with high perceived value, a free trip.

▲ American Eagle Outfitters encouraged consumers to enter its sweepstakes from store fitting rooms as well as online.

▼ This advertisement for Skyjacker offers a $35 cash back rebate on purchases of Hydro or Nitro shocks.

Gold laptop computer, Apple Watch, iPhone, or iPad. Entrants received an instant $15-off coupon for in-store shopping or $75 or more for online purchases.[14]

To inspire consumers to continue participation, the extrinsic values of prizes can be increased by allowing small, incremental rewards. A consumer who wins a soft drink or a sandwich in a sweepstakes at Subway may be more likely to continue participating. Scratch-and-win cards tend to be effective because the reward is instant.

The Internet and Social Media

The internet offers a popular location for contests and sweepstakes. It provides opportunities for individuals to see a prize's intrinsic value by creating interactive games to challenge a contestant's ability. The internet features data-capturing capabilities. Internet contests cost less to set up and run than other types of promotions.

The newest trends in contests and sweepstakes include social media. Microsoft, Sephora, NASCAR, Comcast, Chik-fil-A, Wholly Guacamole, and McDonald's have created Twitter sweepstakes or have used Twitter and other social media sites to enlist participants for a contest or sweepstakes. Marketers take advantage of a sweepstakes or contest to ignite a viral buzz about the brand.[15]

Goals of Contests and Sweepstakes

Although contests and sweepstakes can increase customer traffic, the question remains as to whether they boost sales. Some do, others do not. Marketers recognize that intrinsic rewards tend to draw consumers back. This means online games are exciting prospects, because they can be structured to create intrinsic value.

Refunds and Rebates

Refunds and rebates are cash returns given to consumers or businesses following purchases of products. A consumer pays full price for the product but can mail in a proof of purchase. The manufacturer then returns a portion of the purchase price. A *refund* is a cash return on what are called "soft goods," such as food or clothing. *Rebates* are cash returns on "hard goods," which are major ticket items such as automobiles and appliances.

Customers claim only about 30 percent of all rebates. For rebates valued at $50 or more, the percentage rises to about 65 percent. The inconvenience associated with obtaining the rebate is the primary reason for low response rates. Too many steps or the long waiting times associated with "snail mail" are common complaints about rebates. Many consumers wait two to three months to receive a rebate check.[16]

Rebate programs often suffer diminished effectiveness, because consumers have come to expect them. Many customers will wait until the manufacturer or dealer offers a rebate. As a result, no new purchase activity takes place without a rebate program, which delays the purchase process. Further, increasing the amount of a rebate no longer seems to spur additional sales, yet discontinuing or reducing rebate levels tends to have an immediate negative impact.

Refunds and rebates achieve the greatest successes when consumers perceive them as new or original. When they become an entrenched part of doing business, they are expected discounts. To be effective, rebates and refunds should change the buyer's behavior, either by leading to a more immediate purchase or by causing the customer to change brands.

Sampling

Sampling is the actual delivery of a product to consumers for their use or consumption. In business-to-business markets, samples of products may be given to potential clients. Sampling can be featured in the service sector. For example, a tanning salon may offer an initial visit free to encourage new customers to try its facilities. Dentists and lawyers feature sampling when they provide initial consultations free of charge.

In a survey of 1,800 consumers, more than one-third of those who tried a sample purchased the product during the same shopping trip. Fifty-eight percent indicated they would buy the product again. Nearly one-fourth said they bought the product being sampled instead of the brand they intended to purchase.[17] Consequently, sampling can provide an effective method of getting consumers to try and purchase a particular brand.

Sample Distribution

Figure 12.5 lists various methods of sample distribution. The most common consumer method, *in-store distribution*, delivers the sample in the store, such as when an employee cooks a food product and gives it to customers on-site. *Direct sampling* means items are mailed or delivered door-to-door to consumers. In the business-to-business sector, salespeople often deliver direct samples to prospects or to current customers to encourage them to try the company's brand or a newly introduced product.

Response samples are made available to individuals or businesses responding to a media offer on television, on the internet, from a magazine, through social media, or by some other source. *Cross-ruffing* plans provide samples of one product on another, such as a laundry detergent with a free dryer sheet attached to the package.

Media sampling places the sample in a media outlet. Recently, samples for Dr. Scholl's Her Open Shoes insoles were affixed to heavy-stock paper in magazines including *In Style*, *All You*, *Shape*, and *Glamour*. Women could remove the insole and test it on one foot and compare it to the other shoe without an insole. Approximately 3 million were distributed. One month after the run, 11 percent of subscribers had purchased insoles and nearly 60 percent said they planned to make purchases. Approximately 57 percent had peeled the sample insole out of the magazine and 37 percent said they actually tested it.[18]

Salespeople give *professional samples* to professionals, such as doctors who then provide patients with the free drug samples. Companies distribute *selective samples* at sites such as a state fairs, parades, hospitals, restaurants, and sporting events. Procter & Gamble recently distributed 40,000 samples of 25 of its brands in Manhattan. The company opened "pop-up boxes" in five street locations to distribute the sample. Stylists were on hand to deliver beauty tips and some celebrities stopped by the temporary box stands.[19]

- In-store distribution
- Direct sampling
- Response sampling
- Cross-ruffing sampling
- Media sampling
- Professional sampling
- Selective sampling

▲ **FIGURE 12.5**
Methods of Distributing Samples

▼ An individual tasting a sample distributed at a farmer's market.

▲ Maxwell House Coffee's marketing team can use samples to encourage consumers to try various versions of the product.

Benefits of Sampling

Product sampling provides an effective way to introduce a new item, generate interest in it, and collect information about consumers. Internet-based response sampling programs have become popular with both consumers and manufacturers. Bristol-Myers/Squibb was among the first to utilize the internet for product sampling. The company sent a free sample of Excedrin to individuals who requested one. Potential customers had to be willing to provide their names, addresses, and email information. In addition to the 12-pack sample of Excedrin, consumers received coupons for additional purchases, along with the quarterly *Excedrin Headache Relief Update Newsletter*. This form of response has the advantage of sampling only the consumers who requested the product. Companies normally can gather additional information to be added to a database. Seventy percent of those who requested a sample online were willing to complete a survey in order to receive the item.[20]

Successful Sampling Programs

As with the other consumer promotions, sampling will be related to and based on the IMC plan. Sampling encourages a trial use by a consumer or a business. The approach becomes most effective when it introduces a new product or a new version of a product to a market. Samples help to promote a current product to a new target market or to new prospects.

Mass sampling is not as cost-effective as a targeted approach. Successful sampling involves targeting the right audience at the right venue at the right time. For example, Chanel recently sent a sample of its No. 5 fragrance in a package mailer to the 1.2 million subscribers of *Vogue* magazine. With a median income of $63,000, the readership of *Vogue* fits the target audience of the affluent Chanel brand. The sample was placed in the December issue, just in time for making a Christmas gift suggestion. It was coupled with several ads and resulted in an effective targeted sampling campaign.[21]

Bonus Packs

When a company places an additional or extra number of items in a special product package, it is a bonus pack. Examples include offering four bars of soap for the price of three or extra AA batteries in a package that normally holds nine batteries. Typical bonuses range from 20 to 100 percent of the normal number of units in a package. A 30 percent bonus is the most common.

Types of Bonus Packs

Figure 12.6 identifies the major objectives of bonus packs. Increasing the size or quantity of the package might lead to greater product use. When a package that contains eight small candy bars increases by four more bars, consumers may eat more because extras are readily available. This will not be true for products with constant consumption rates. If Colgate offers a bonus pack with an additional tube of toothpaste, consumers do not use more of the product. In effect, this delays the next purchase. Manufacturers offer these types of bonus packs because they preempt the competition. A consumer with a large quantity of the merchandise on hand becomes less likely to switch brands.

- Increase usage of the product
- Match or preempt competitive actions
- Stockpile the product

- Develop customer loyalty
- Attract new users
- Encourage brand switching

Keys to Successful Bonus Packs

Bonus packs reward customer loyalty by presenting, in effect, free merchandise. Bonus packs encourage brand switching when the consumer has used the item previously. Facing purchase decisions, consumers may opt for brands that offer more product at the regular or special price. The packages present an advantage that competitive brands are not offering.

Bonus packs are popular with manufacturers, retailers, and customers. A retailer can build a positive relationship with a manufacturer that features a bonus pack to increase brand switching and stockpiling. Retailers gain an advantage because the bonus pack offers a "bargain" or "value" through the retail outlet. Customers enjoy bonus packs because it feels like they are getting free merchandise. For products with high levels of competition, the bonus pack approach helps maintain brand loyalty and reduces brand switching at a minimal cost.

Bonus packs rarely attract new customers, because they have not previously purchased the brand. Obtaining an extra quantity increases purchase risk rather than reducing it. Most customers do not like to waste a product by throwing it away when they are dissatisfied. Marketing research indicates that a small bonus (20 to 40 percent) leads consumers to conclude the price per unit has not truly changed. Unfortunately, a large bonus, such as doubling the amount, may cause consumers to believe that the price was first increased to compensate for the additional quantity. In that instance, increasing the size of a bonus captures the consumer's attention but does not convey the desired message.[22]

▲ This advertisement for Karns Quality Food includes bonus pack offers.

Price-Offs

A price-off is a temporary reduction in the price of a product to the consumer. A price-off can be physically marked on the product, such as when a bottle of aspirin shows the regular retail price marked out and replaced by a special retail price (for example, $8.99 marked out and replaced by $6.99). Producing a label with the price reduction pre-marked forces the retailer to sell the item at the reduced price. This ensures the price-off incentive will be passed on to consumers. At other times, the price-off will not be printed on the actual item but instead on a point-of-purchase display, sign, or shelf.

Benefits of Price-Offs

Price-offs stimulate sales of existing products. They entice customers to try new products, because the lower price reduces the financial risk of making the purchase. They encourage customers to switch in brand parity situations or when no strong brand loyalty exists. In cases where consumers do have a preference, a price-off on a favorite brand encourages stockpiling of the product and possibly increased consumption of the item.[23] A consumer

▲ A special price of $5.00 for a one-topping pizza to-go at SteviB's.

who purchases additional breakfast bars due to a price-off tends to consume more of them. Again, this will not be true for products such as deodorant or toothpaste. Stockpiling those types of products only delays the next purchase and does not increase consumption. Similar effects occur in the business-to-business arena when price-offs are offered.

Price-offs have proven to be successful consumer promotions for two reasons. First, they create the appeal of monetary savings. Second, they grant immediate rewards. Unlike rebates, refunds, contests, sweepstakes, and other promotional incentives, consumers do not have to wait to receive the incentive.

Problems with Price-Offs

Although price-offs are easy to implement and often increase sales, they can also cause problems. Sales may rise but the program might have a negative impact on a company's profit margin. It normally takes at least a 30 to 60 percent increase in sales to offset each five percent price reduction.

Price-off programs encourage consumers to become more price-sensitive. In the same way that customers respond to rebates, they either wait for a price-off promotion or choose another brand that happens to be on sale. In addition, when used too often, price-offs may lead to a negative impact on a brand's image. David Hale, CEO of Good Eats, noted, "Deep discounting doesn't build loyalty or consistency—it's cheapening your brand."[24] Again, price-off programs should be incorporated into the firm's overall IMC program. Figure 12.7 summarizes the benefits and problems with price-off promotions.

Overlays and Tie-Ins

At times, companies will combine two or more consumer promotions activities into a single campaign, called an *overlay*. To attract Chinese consumers in Canada, Tropicana combined sampling with coupons. Free samples (50,000 cups of orange juice) were given out along with 30,000 coupons at a Chinese New Year's celebration in Vancouver. Asians who live in the United States and Canada are not typically large users of coupons; however, Tropicana Canada's research indicated that the Chinese consider oranges to be harbingers of good luck. A few weeks after the promotion, 40 percent of the coupons were redeemed, and sales of Tropicana orange juice among the Chinese community in Canada increased considerably.[25]

Developing a consumer promotion with another product or company is called a *tie-in*. *Intracompany tie-ins* are the promotion of two different products within one company using one consumer promotion. An *intercompany tie-in* provides an alternative method in

◀ **FIGURE 12.7**
Advantages and Disadvantages of Price-Offs

Advantages	Disadvantages
• Stimulate sales	• Negatively impact profits
• Encourage product trial	• Encourage price-sensitivity
• Encourage brand switching	• Negative impact on brand image
• Stockpiling and increased consumption	

which a firm partners with another company. Fast-food restaurants often use tie-ins with movies and toys to create attractive children's promotions. Stand-alone, overlay, and tie-in programs deserve careful planning to maximize results.

Planning for Consumer Promotions

When planning the consumer promotions component of the IMC, marketers should make sure the program supports the brand's image and the brand positioning strategy. To ensure this occurs, the marketing team considers the target audience. Effective research identifies the core values present in the target audience as well as opinions regarding the firm's products, especially as they relate to the competition. After gathering this information, the marketing team finalizes a consumer promotions plan. In terms of promotions, consumers can be divided into the four categories shown in Figure 12.8.

objective 12.3

How do different types of customers respond to consumer promotions?

- Promotion-prone
- Brand-loyal
- Brand-preferred
- Price-sensitive

◀ **FIGURE 12.8**
Types of Consumers in Relation to Consumer Promotions

▲ Brand-preferred consumers are the ideal group to target.

Promotion-prone consumers regularly respond to various consumer promotions and like to purchase products that are on-deal; that is, during the time the promotion is offered.. They tend to clip coupons on a regular basis, enter contests and sweepstakes, purchase bonus packs, and respond to other promotional offers. In contrast, for **price-sensitive consumers**, price remains the primary, if not the only criterion used in making a purchase decision. Brand names are not important, and these individuals will not pay more for them. They take advantage of any type of promotion that reduces the price.

Brand-loyal consumers purchase only one particular brand and do not substitute, regardless of any deal being offered. They make the necessary effort to purchase their chosen brand. The most common group consists of **brand-preference consumers** who consider a small set of brands for which they have a strong attachment. When a chosen brand offers a promotion, it becomes the one to be purchased. These consumers ignore a promotion for brands not in the brand preferred set, regardless of the size or type of promotion.

Consumers do not fit into one of the four categories for all purchases. They may tend to be one of the four types, but promotion or brand preferences change across product and service categories. A beer drinker may be extremely promotion prone; a wine drinker may be quite brand loyal. The same beer drinker may be extremely loyal to a pizza brand, and the same wine drinker may be price sensitive when it comes to buying potato chips.

In planning promotions, the marketing team knows that promotion-prone consumers look for on-deal brands. Price-sensitive consumers purchase the cheaper brand, regardless of whether it is on-deal or off-deal. Therefore, these two types of consumers are less attractive to pursue with consumer promotions unless the promotional goal is to increase sales, market share, or customer traffic. There will be little or no future allegiance to the brand.

Brand-loyal consumers only redeem promotions for their favorites. Offering a promotion to this group does not make sense, because they will buy the brand anyway. Brand-preferred consumers represent the ideal group to target market, especially when the promotion features a brand in their preference sets. This enhances loyalty toward the brand and prevents them from purchasing from a competitor. It may also move the consumer closer to brand loyalty.

Manufacturers incorporate retailer objectives into promotions programs. It does little good to create a promotion that will be popular with consumers if retailers are not willing to work with the manufacturer to enhance the promotional offer. Retailers prefer promotions that benefit them. The primary reasons retailers support manufacturer consumer promotions programs are to:

- Increase store traffic
- Increase store sales
- Attract new customers
- Increase the basket size[26]

The promotions program revolves around the IMC program's theme while keeping in mind where the promotions will be seen by the consumer. Specific goals associated with the product, the target market, and the retail outlets are first formulated. Building brand loyalty constitutes a long-term goal; generating sales is more short range. Price-based offers normally are designed to attract new customers or to build sales. Marketers feature other consumer promotions, such as high-value premiums to enhance a firm's image over time.

Trade Promotions

Trade promotions are incentives designed by members of the market channel to entice another member to purchase goods for eventual resale. Marketers aim trade promotions at retailers, distributors, wholesalers, brokers, or agents. A manufacturer offers trade promotions to convince another member of the trade channel to carry its goods. Wholesalers, distributors, brokers, and agents use trade promotions to persuade retailers to purchase products for eventual resale.

Twenty years ago, trade promotions totaled only about 25 percent of a manufacturer's marketing budget; today, it reaches nearly 70 percent. Trade promotions often constitute the second largest expense for a manufacturer after the cost-of-goods sold. Trade promotions account for approximately 17 percent of gross sales revenues for manufacturers.[27]

Trade promotions contribute to successful IMC programs. Unfortunately, in other companies, the individual responsible for trade promotions may not be involved in the IMC planning process. Leaders in these firms often view trade promotions as merely a method for placing products onto retail shelves or to satisfy a channel member's request. As a result, little consideration will be given to matching the IMC program when developing trade promotions programs.

Many trade promotions tools are available. Company leaders select trade promotion techniques based on several factors. These include the nature of the business (manufacturer versus distributor), the type of customer to be influenced (for example, retailer versus wholesaler), company preferences, and the objectives of the IMC plan. Figure 12.9 lists the primary types of trade promotions.

▲ When developing promotions, Chic Shaque's marketing team first seeks to understand the type of consumers that shop at its retail stores.

objective 12.4

What types of trade promotions can help push products onto retailers' shelves and eventually to end users?

Trade Allowances

Trade allowances provide financial incentives to channel members to motivate them to make purchases. Trade allowances take a variety of forms, including the ones in Figure 12.10. Each makes it possible for a company to offer discounts or other price-reductions to customers in the channel.

Off-Invoice Allowances Off-invoice allowances are financial discounts given for each item, case, or pallet ordered. They encourage channel members to place orders. Approximately 35 percent of all trade dollars go to off-invoice allowances, making them the largest

◀ **FIGURE 12.9**
Types of Trade Promotions

▶ **FIGURE 12.10**

Types of Trade Allowances

- **Off-invoice allowance:** A per-case rebate paid to retailers for an order.
- **Slotting fees:** Money paid to retailers to stock a new product.
- **Exit fees:** Money paid to retailers to remove an item from their SKU inventory.

- Cost of adding new products to inventory
- Re-allocating shelf space
- Aids decision on choosing new products to stock
- Add to the profit margin

▲ **FIGURE 12.11**

Retailer Justifications for Slotting Fees

expenditure among trade promotions tools.[28] As with refunds, rebates, and price-offs in the consumer sector, many retailers become reluctant to purchase merchandise without some type of trade allowance. In addition, tremendous competitive pressure to offer trade allowances exist as companies selling the same type of products compete for limited shelf space.

Slotting Fees   The most controversial form of trade allowance, **slotting fees**, are funds charged by retailers to stock new products. As shown in Figure 12.11, retailers justify slotting fees in various ways.[29] First, retailers spend money to add new products to inventories and to stock merchandise. An unsuccessful product means the retailer's investment in inventory represents a loss, especially when the retailer has stocked the product in a large number of stores. Slotting fees recover some of the loss.

Second, adding a new product in the retail store means providing shelf space. Shelves are already filled. Adding a new product means either deleting brands or products or reducing the amount of shelf space allocated to them. In both cases, the retailer spends both time and money creating space for a new product.

Third, slotting fees make it easier for retailers to make decisions about new products. A typical supermarket carries 35,000 SKUs (stock-keeping units). The supermarket's managers evaluate 10,000 to 15,000 new products per year. Most fail. Consequently, retailers believe charging slotting fees forces manufacturers to weed out high-risk product introductions. The average total cost in slotting fees for a nationally introduced product ranges from $1.5 to $2 million.[30] Consequently, retailers contend that slotting fees force manufacturers to conduct careful test marketing on products before introducing them. Such testing limits the number of new products offered. This, in turn, drastically reduces the number of new product failures.

▲ Retailers charge slotting fees to place new products on store shelves.

Finally, slotting fees add to the bottom line. Many products have low margins or markups. Slotting fees generate additional monies to support retail operations. Estimates suggest that between 14 and 27 percent of trade promotions monies given to retailers go directly to the retailer's profits.[31]

The other side of the argument comes from manufacturers, who argue that slotting fees are practically a form of extortion. Many believe that slotting fees cost too much and are unfair in the first place. These fees compel manufacturers to pay millions of dollars to retailers that could be dedicated to advertising, sales promotions, or additional marketing efforts. Slotting fees prevent small manufacturers from getting products into stores because they cannot afford the high cost.

Exit Fees   Instead of paying slotting fees, some retailers ask for **exit fees**, or monies paid to remove an item from a retailer's inventory. This approach may be useful when a manufacturer introduces a new size of a product or a new version, such as a 3-liter bottle of Pepsi or Pepsi Diet Vanilla. PepsiCo already has products on the retailer's shelves. Adding a new-sized container or new variety of the product involves lower risk and is not the same as adding a new product. Rather than charging an upfront fee, such as a slotting allowance, retailers request exit fees if the new version of the product fails or if one of the current versions must be removed from the inventory. Few retailers charge exit fees compared to the 82 percent that demand slotting fees.[32]

Trade Allowance Complications When offering trade allowances to retailers, manufacturers assume that some of the price reduction will be passed on to consumers. This occurs only about half of the time. Although consumers receive a portion of the price allowance, retailers often schedule competing brands, so they can have at least one special offer going at all times. Thus, one week Pepsi offers a reduced price and the next week Coke offers a discount. The two products are rarely promoted on-deal at the same time. By offering only one on-deal at a time, the retailer always features a reduced priced brand for the price-sensitive consumer. The retailer charges the brand-loyal consumer full price 50 percent of the time. While accomplishing these goals, the retailer receives special trade allowances from both Pepsi and Coke.

In an effort to increase profit margins, retailers engage in two activities: forward buying and diversion. *Forward buying* occurs when a retailer purchases extra amounts of a product while it is on-deal. The retailer then sells the on-deal merchandise after the deal period ends, saving the cost of purchasing the product at the manufacturer's full price. *Diversion* takes place when a retailer purchases a product on-deal in one location and ships it to another location where it is off-deal. For example, a manufacturer may offer an off-invoice allowance of $5 per case for the product in France. Diversion tactics mean the retailer purchases an excess quantity in France and has it shipped to stores in other European countries. To do so, retailers first examine the potential profits to be earned, less the cost of shipping the product to other locations. Shipping costs tend to be relatively high compared to trade allowances offered. Consequently, retailers do not use diversion nearly as often as forward buying.

▲ Trade promotions offered to retailers may be passed on to customers in terms of lower prices or discounts.

▼ Trade contests were held among travel agents to increase cruise ship bookings.

Trade Contests

To achieve sales targets and other objectives, some channel members provide trade contests. Winners receive prizes or cash, or **spiff money**. Contests are held at every level within the channel. They can be between brokers or agents, wholesalers, or retail stores. To prevent undue influence of contests on buyers, a number of large organizations prohibit employees from participating in vendor contests. Influencing salespeople represents exactly what a contest seeks to accomplish. Many managers in large retail organizations do not want their buyers participating, because the buyers make purchase decisions for as many as 500 to 2,500 stores. Joining in a contest may result in poor decisions.

In recent years, the demand for cruise ship vacations has steadily decreased. As a result, cruise lines combine advertising, consumer promotions, and trade promotions to attract patrons. Royal Caribbean International offered travel agents cooperative advertising programs featuring TV commercials, newspaper ads, as well as an email template to contact potential travelers.

Norwegian Cruise Lines enrolled 5,500 agents in a "Sale of All Sails" promotional contest. Prizes were based on bookings. Each agent that set up a Holland America cruise was enrolled in the trade contest. The prizes offered included a free cruise with five veranda staterooms. The Princess Cruise line offered booking agents the chance to win a West Coast sailing cruise with a mini-suite. One cruise was awarded each week during a 90-day period. Offering travel agents the chance to win prizes and cruises for themselves caused many of them to be motivated to book cruises for the lines holding the contests.[33]

Trade Incentives

Trade incentives are similar to trade allowances. The difference is that **trade incentives** involve the retailer or channel member performing a function in order to receive the funds. The purpose, however, remains the same as for trade allowances: to encourage the channel member either to push the manufacturer's brand or to increase purchases of that brand. Figure 12.12 identifies three major types of trade incentives.

Cooperative Merchandising Agreements The most comprehensive type of trade incentive, a cooperative merchandising agreement (CMA), is a formal agreement between the retailer and manufacturer to undertake a two-way marketing effort. The CMA can be for a wide variety of marketing tasks. A CMA may feature the manufacturer's brand as a price leader in an advertisement. A cooperative agreement can be created in which a retailer will emphasize the manufacturer's brand as part of an in-house offer made by the store or feature the manufacturer's brand on a special shelf display.

Cooperative merchandising agreements remain popular with manufacturers because the retailer performs a function in order to receive the allowance or incentive. The manufacturer retains control of the functions performed. Also, when price allowances are made as part of the CMA, the manufacturer knows that the retailer passes a certain percentage of the entire price discount to the consumer. CMAs allow manufacturers to create annual contracts with retailers. These longer-term commitments reduce the need for last-minute trade incentives or trade allowances.

CMAs also benefit retailers. The primary advantage, from the retailer's perspective, is that the program allows them to develop *calendar promotions*, or promotional campaigns the retailer plans for customers through manufacturer trade incentives. Signing an agreement allows a retailer to schedule the weeks a particular brand will be on sale and offset the other weeks with other brands. Calendar promotions make it possible to always have one brand on sale while the others are off-deal and to rotate the brands on sale. By arranging sales through trade incentives, the margins for the retailer stay approximately the same for all brands, both on-deal and off-deal, because they rotate. As a result, the retailer effectively moves the price reductions given to customers to manufacturers rather than absorbing them. A store may feature Budweiser on-deal one week and Heineken the next. Loyal beer drinkers stay with their preferred brand, while price-sensitive consumers choose the on-deal brand and the store retains a reasonable markup on all beers sold.

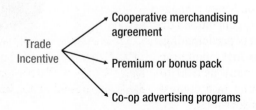

▶ **FIGURE 12.12**
Types of Trade Incentives.

Premiums and Bonus Packs   Instead of providing the retailer with a price discount, a manufacturer might give free merchandise in the form of a premium or bonus pack. For example, a manufacturer would offer a bonus pack of one carton for each 20 purchased within the next 60 days. The bonus packs are free to the retailer and are awarded either for placing the order by a certain date or for agreeing to a minimum-size order. Often, to receive the free merchandise, the retailer must meet both conditions: a specified date and a minimum order size.

Cooperative Advertising   The final trade incentive, a cooperative advertising program, is given when the manufacturer agrees to reimburse the retailer a certain percentage of the advertising costs associated with advertising the manufacturer's products in the retailer's ad. To receive the reimbursement, the retailer follows specific guidelines concerning the placement of the ad and its content. In almost all cases, no competing products can be advertised. Normally, the manufacturer's product must be displayed prominently. There may be other restrictions on how to advertise the product as well as specific photos or copy that must be used.

In most cooperative advertising programs, retailers accrue co-op monies based on purchases, normally a certain percentage of sales. Tire manufacturer B.F. Goodrich offers a 4.5 percent co-op advertising fund on all retailer purchases. The money accrues for one year and then starts over. B.F. Goodrich pays 70 percent of the cost of an approved advertisement. Any medium may be used to present the advertisement, including radio, newspaper, magazines, television, and outdoor.[34]

▲ A co-op advertisement for Bob's Furniture Gallery featuring both the Flexsteel and Thomasville brands.

Co-op advertising programs permit retailers to use the manufacturer's dollars to expand advertising programs. In a co-op ad, the retailer gains additional advertising coverage at a reduced cost. Retailers benefit from the image of a national brand, which attracts new or additional customers to the store. Wal-Mart recently expanded co-op advertising efforts with major manufacturers, who contributed more than $400 million toward Wal-Mart's annual advertising budget. In the Wal-Mart system, manufacturers have considerably more creative input into the ads and are prominently displayed in the ad instead of taking minor roles.[35]

Manufacturers also benefit from co-op ads. By sharing advertising expenditures with retailers, the manufacturer gains additional exposure at a lower cost. More important, almost all co-op advertising programs are tied to sales. The retailer accrues co-op advertising dollars based on a certain percentage of sales. Thus, to obtain the co-op money, the retailer must promote the brand prominently and purchase the product for resale. Consequently, a wide variety of cooperative advertisements appear regularly in every medium for both consumer and business-to-business products.

Trade Shows

Many business-to-business marketing programs include trade show appearances, which benefit manufacturers and retailers. From a manufacturer's standpoint, a trade show provides the opportunity to discover potential customers and sell new products. Relationships with current customers can be strengthened at the show. A trade show often grants the opportunity to investigate the competition. Many times, trade shows establish a situation in which the manufacturer's sales team meets directly with decision makers and buyers from business-to-business clients. A trade show can strengthen the brand name of a product as well as the company's image.

▲ International attendees at trade shows often wish to conduct business during the show, not afterward.

From the retailer's perspective, a trade show helps buyers to compare merchandise and to make contacts with several prospective vendors in a short period of time. In some cases, the retailers negotiate special deals. Trade shows represent an ideal place for buyers and sellers to meet in an informal, low-pressure setting to discuss how to work together effectively.

Thousands of buyers attend some national and international trade shows. A show succeeds when manufacturers seek out key buyers and try to avoid spending too much time with nonbuyers. Figure 12.13 identifies five categories of buyers who attend trade shows. Many marketers try to weed out the education seekers who are not interested in buying. Manufacturers' agents concentrate efforts on three groups: solution seekers, buying teams, and power buyers. Asking the right questions identifies solution seekers and buying teams. The power buyers are more difficult to find because they do not want to be identified. They often do not wear badges at trade shows, which means vendors cannot be sure who they are.

In the United States, few deals are finalized during trade shows. Buyers and sellers meet, discuss, and even negotiate, but seldom complete the sale. Instead, manufacturers collect business cards as leads to be followed up later. This procedure varies for international customers. International attendees tend to be senior executives with the authority to make purchases. They fit into the power buyer category listed in Figure 12.13. U.S. manufacturers know that the international attendee often wishes to conduct business during the show, not afterward. The international attendees spend more time at each manufacturer's booth. They stay longer in order to gather and study information in greater detail. The international guest, who pays more for travel expenses, wants more in-depth information than an American counterpart requires.

The number of international trade show visitors has risen as competition continues to expand globally. The increase in international participants has caused trade show centers to set up more meeting spaces, conference centers, and even places to eat where buyers and sellers meet and transact business.

Trade shows have changed in other ways. Niche and regional shows are replacing large national and international shows. For example, in the 1990s, many megasports trade shows were attended by everybody in the sporting goods business. The National Sporting Goods Association World Sports Expo in Chicago attracted in excess of 90,000 attendees. That number has dwindled to fewer than 40,000. Now, manufacturers and retailers attend specialty trade shows featuring only one sport or regional shows that focus on one section of the country. Smaller shows are less expensive to set up. Many company leaders believe they provide higher-quality prospects and better opportunities to bond with customers and offer more quality one-to-one time with customers and potential customers. In contrast, people can easily get lost in the crowd at a big show.[36]

- **Education seekers** Buyers who want to browse, look, and learn but are not in the buying mode

- **Reinf orcement seekers** Buyers who want reassurance they made the right decision in past purchases

- **Solution seekers** Buyers seeking solutions to specific problems and are in the buying mode

- **Buying teams** A team of buyers seeking vendors for their business; usually are in the buying mode

- **Power buyers** Members of upper management or key purchasing agents with the authority to buy

▶ **FIGURE 12.13**
Five Categories of Buyers Attending Trade Shows

Concerns with Trade Promotions

Successful marketing teams incorporate trade promotions into the overall IMC effort. Unfortunately, in many companies this does not occur, primarily due to employee pay structures. Sales and brand managers face quotas, and when sales fall behind, one quick way to boost them is to offer retailers a trade deal. Further, company leaders often evaluate brand managers based on the sales growth of a brand. Trade deals become the easiest way for a brand manager to ensure continuing growth. The pattern of using trade deals to reach short-term quotas rather than long-term image and theme-building will not change until top management adopts a new approach. The IMC process succeeds when it emphasizes the long-term horizon and the company's compensation structure changes to match.

A strong brand image causes retailers to stock the product even when fewer trade deals are offered, because a strong brand by itself can help pull customers into retail stores. A customer who considers Sony to be a strong brand in the stereo marketplace asks for that brand in an electronics retail store. This makes stocking Sony an advantage, even with limited trade promotions offers.

The cost of trade promotions continues to pose another concern. Manufacturers spend billions of dollars each year on them. These costs are often passed on to consumers in the form of higher prices. Estimates suggest that 11 cents out of every dollar spent for a consumer product goes directly for the cost of trade promotions.[37] The goal should be to keep the cost at a reasonable level. Money should be spent wisely, rather than simply getting into "bidding wars" with competitors. Trade promotions dollars exert the greatest long-term impact when they help build relationships and help achieve other key IMC goals.

An unfortunate situation occurs when merchandise does not move until a trade promotions incentive has been offered. In the grocery industry, the majority of all purchases made by retailers are on-deal with some type of trade incentive. The constant use of deals has trimmed manufacturer margins on products and created competitive pressures to conform. If a manufacturer tries to halt or cut back on trade promotions, retailers replace the manufacturer's products with other brands or reduce shelf space to give more room to manufacturers offering better deals.

One way to correct these problems would be to spend more on advertising focused on building or rebuilding a brand's image. Also, the marketing team should be certain promotions fit the brand's image. "If it doesn't fit," writes Brian Sullivan in *Marketing News*, "don't use it."[38] Unfortunately, to spend more on advertising means cutting trade promotions incentives. The risk becomes that other competitors will move in by giving better trade promotions deals to retailers and gain shelf space as a result. Then, the cycle begins again.

Managing trade promotions programs constitutes a challenging part of the marketing planning process because such a large percentage of the marketing budget goes to trade promotions. Effective IMC programs achieve a balance between all elements of the promotions mix and identify clear goals and targets for trade promotions programs. Only then will the company be able to compete on all levels and not just through a cycle of trade promotions bidding wars.

objective 12.5
What concerns exist for manufacturers considering trade promotions programs?

International Implications

Companies adapt consumer promotions to the countries in which they will be offered. Two complications occur: legal and cultural. Any coupon, premium, contest, sweepstakes, or price change must meet local legal regulations. The marketing team investigates any potential legal problems before launching an international consumer promotions program.

Culturally, citizens in some countries may take a dim view of some promotions. For instance, in some regions, those who redeem coupons may be viewed as being of lower socioeconomic status, which may dissuade some from using them. Participation in contests or sweepstakes may violate religious norms in other nations.

objective 12.6
What issues complicate international sales promotions programs?

The same holds true for trade promotions. Laws vary regarding discounts, spiff money, slotting fees, and exit fees. These issues may also be reflected in cultural values. And, as previously noted, the ways in which managers in companies around the world participate in trade shows varies.

Finally, the emphasis placed on sales promotions will be different, depending on the company involved and the country in which that company operates. Both small companies seeking to do business in foreign countries and large international conglomerates need to adjust to local conditions when employing these marketing tactics. At the same time, the goal remains to be certain that the efforts match the company's image and overall approach to marketing communications.

Summary

An IMC program incorporates all four elements of a promotions mix. Advertising may be considered to be the main "voice" of the IMC message. At the same time, the sales promotion part of the mix, including trade and consumer promotions, plays a crucial role in the success or failure of the overall marketing program.

Attracting customers by using consumer promotions includes the use of coupons, premiums, contests and sweepstakes, refunds, rebates, samples, bonus packs, and price-off deals. These items should be combined with specific promotional goals to have the desired impact on customers. Consumer promotions are often used to boost sales and can be an excellent short-term method to increase sales or a firm's market share. They provide a means of introducing new products. Often, a consumer promotion prompts consumers to at least try the product, where selling it at the regular price will not. Coupons and contests have been successful tactics for gaining new customers. Consumer promotions can boost sales of a particular brand, and evidence suggests that they increase sales of the overall product category rather than just taking sales away from competitors.

Trade promotions complement consumer promotions. The use of trade allowances, trade contests, trade incentives, and participation in trade shows helps the manufacturer or member of the marketing channel maintain positive contact with other organizations and moves products toward the retailer. Trade promotions work best when they are integrated into other IMC efforts rather than being viewed as a necessary evil or simply as a short-term tool to increase sales.

Internationally, sales promotions can be used when they are chosen based on the characteristics, attitudes, laws, regulations, and cultural nuances of a given geographic region. The primary objective of any promotions program must always be to enhance the message sent forth in other aspects of the IMC program in a manner that helps the company reach its long-term marketing objectives in a cost-effective and positive fashion.

Key Terms

sales promotions All of the incentives offered to customers and channel members to encourage product purchases

consumer promotions Incentives directly offered to a firm's customers or potential customers

trade promotions Expenditures or incentives used by manufacturers and other members of the marketing channel to purchase goods for eventual sale

freestanding inserts (FSI) Sheets of coupons distributed in newspapers, primarily on Sunday

promotion-prone consumers Consumers who are not brand loyal and regularly respond to promotions such as coupons, price-off plans, or premiums, only purchasing items that are on-deal

price-sensitive consumers Consumers for whom price is the primary, if not only, criterion used in making a purchase decision

brand-loyal consumers Consumers who purchase only one particular brand and do not substitute, regardless of any deal being offered

brand-preference consumers Consumers who prefer a small set of brands

trade allowances Financial incentives provided to other channel members to motivate them to make purchases

slotting fees A form of trade allowance in which funds are charged by retailers to stock new products

exit fees Monies paid to remove an item from a retailer's inventory

spiff money Rewards given as contest prizes to brokers, retail salespeople, stores, wholesalers, and agents

trade incentives Funds given that require the retailer to perform a function in order to receive the dollars

MyMarketingLab

To complete the problems with the ⭐ in your MyLab, go to the end-of-chapter Discussion Questions.

Review Questions

12-1. Define sales promotion. What are the two main categories of sales promotions?

12-2. Name and describe the types of coupons. Which is the most popular with manufacturers? Which has the highest redemption rate?

12-3. What problems are associated with coupon programs?

12-4. What is a premium? What types of premium programs can companies use?

12-5. What are the keys to successful premium programs?

12-6. What is the difference between a contest and a sweepstakes?

12-7. What are the two main components of prizes rendered in contests and sweepstakes?

12-8. What role does the internet and social media play in offering contests and sweepstakes?

12-9. How is a refund different from a rebate?

12-10. What are the primary types of samples?

12-11. What benefits and problems are associated with sampling?

12-12. What are the benefits of offering bonus packs?

12-13. What benefits and problems are associated with price-off tactics?

12-14. What is an overlay? A tie-in?

12-15. What four categories of consumers can be associated with consumer promotions?

12-16. What are the major types of trade allowances?

12-17. What is a slotting fee? An exit fee?

12-18. What is meant by the term on-deal?

12-19. What complications are associated with trade allowances?

12-20. How does the spiff money relate to trade contests?

12-21. What are the main types of trade incentives?

12-22. Describe a cooperative merchandising agreement.

12-23. How are premiums or bonus packs used as trade incentives?

12-24. How can a cooperative advertising program benefit both a manufacturer and a retailer?

12-25. Describe how to effectively utilize trade promotions.

12-26. What problems must be overcome when developing international sales promotions programs?

Critical Thinking Exercises

DISCUSSION QUESTIONS

12-27. The teen and preteen market segments are important because people that age are developing buying habits that marketers hope will turn into brand loyalty later in life. CVS sells established brands such as Cover Girl and Maybelline, but also younger-oriented brands such as Bonne Bell, Jane, and Naturistics. Drugstores are not typically chosen for the purchase of cosmetics. If you were the marketing manager for CVS, which consumer promotions would be the best to attract teens and preteens to the cosmetics department of CVS? What tie-ins or overlays would you recommend?

⭐12-28. Describe in your own words the basic concept of each of the consumer promotions listed in Figure 12.1. Suppose Sonic hired you as a marketing intern. Discuss each of the consumer promotions in terms of its suitability for Sonic. Give an example of each that you think is appropriate for Sonic to use.

12-29. Refer to the list of consumer promotions in Figure 12.1. Discuss each one in terms of your personal usage. Which ones do you use? How often? Why?

12-30. Design a magazine advertisement with a detachable coupon or premium for one of the following products. Be sure to put an expiration date and other restrictions on the use of the coupon or premium, such as one per customer and one per purchase. You may want to conduct an internet search to see some sample coupons or premiums before you design one.

   a. SunBright Tanning Salon

   b. Dixie Printing

   c. Hamburger Haven

   d. BriarPatch Ice Cream

12-31. The Rawlings Sports Equipment Company plans to increase sales of baseball gloves this season. The company intends to use a coupon program. Discuss the pros and cons of each method of coupon distribution (Figure 12.2) listed in the chapter for Rawlings. Which method or methods should Rawlings use? Why?

12-32. To maintain a strong brand image, Revlon's marketing team decides to use a premium for each of its lipstick products. What type of premium would you suggest for Revlon for each of the target markets listed here? Which premium would you use? Justify your answers.

    a. Females, ages 60 +

    b. Teenagers, ages 14 to 19

    c. College students, ages 18 to 25

    d. Professional females, ages 30 to 50

⭐**12-33.** Explain the difference between a contest and a sweepstakes and the difference between extrinsic and intrinsic rewards. The Toggery, a local upscale clothing boutique, wants to use a contest or sweepstake to generate store traffic. What are the pros and cons of each for The Toggery? Which would you suggest for The Toggery? Why? Briefly describe the contest or sweepstakes you envision.

12-34. How often do you enter contests or sweepstakes? What was the last contest you entered? Why did you enter? Discuss the importance of extrinsic and intrinsic rewards in entering contests and sweepstakes. If you seldom or never enter contests and sweepstakes, why? What type of intrinsic and extrinsic rewards would it take for you to enter?

⭐**12-35.** Video games generate major revenues for many companies. One manufacturer decided to use sampling as a method to reach the primary target market—males between the ages of 15 and 30. The sampling could have been distributed in one of two ways. First, the actual game could be loaded on a computer for targeted individuals. Second, potential customers could be sent an abbreviated version of the game. Which sampling method would be best? Why? Using the list of sampling methods provided in the chapter, discuss the pros and cons of each sampling method in terms of this new video game. Which type and method of sampling would you recommend? Why?

12-36. Consumers can be divided into four broad categories in terms of how they respond to consumer promotions: promotion prone, brand loyal, price sensitive, and brand preference. Identify two services or goods that would fit into each category for you personally. For example, you may be promotion-prone when you buy

soft drinks (your favorite brand is "What's on Sale"), but be very brand-loyal when you buy shoes (Nike, Reebok). What determines which type of category you fit into for the various products you discussed?

⭐**12-37.** Consumers can be divided into four categories based on how they respond to consumer promotions (Figure 12.8). Explain in your own words the characteristics of each group. You are a marketing intern for Chic Shaque, a retailer of contemporary fashions, bedding, bath, gifts and home decor. For each of the consumer promotion groups, identify a consumer promotion that you think is the best. Explain why. Of the four consumer promotions you just identified, which would you recommend for Chic Shaque? Why?

12-38. Interview three people who have lived in another country about the use of consumer promotions in those countries. Make a list of those promotions that are heavily used and those that are not used. Present your findings to the class.

12-39. As with the other consumer promotions, international expansion requires understanding the laws and customs of each country and culture. In Saudi Arabia and other Muslim countries, Clinique had to modify its sampling techniques. In the United States and Western cultures, Clinique provides cosmetics samples in retail outlets for customers to try. In the United States, women normally sell retail cosmetics; in Saudi Arabia, men do. At the same time, Muslim custom prohibits a man from touching a woman if she is not a relative. Female customers must either apply the cosmetics themselves or bring their husbands to the store with them.

Asking a female customer "What color are your eyes?" constitutes a grave offense in Saudi Arabia because the eyes are believed to be the gateway to the soul. Asking her about skin tone does not make sense because women keep their faces covered. Sampling is important for Clinique in Saudi Arabia.[39]

How would you organize a sampling program in light of these cultural factors? What other consumer promotions could be used? If you have someone in your class from a Muslim country, ask your classmate to discuss the use of consumer promotions in her home country.

Integrated Learning Exercises

12-40. Coupons remain a popular form of consumer promotions. Access the following websites. What are the advantages and disadvantages of each to a consumer? How do the websites impact manufacturers? How do they impact retailers?

    a. Coupons.com (**www.coupons.com**)

    b. CoolSavings (**www.coolsavings.com**)

    c. SmartSource (**www.smartsource.com**)

12-41. Sweepstakes and contests provide excellent methods for building customer traffic to a retail outlet and interest in a brand. Certain firms assist in the development of sweepstakes and contests. This is important due to a variety of legal restrictions imposed by different states. Access the following websites. What types of services does each offer? How do the companies assist in developing a contest or sweepstakes?

Which firm would you choose if you were responsible for developing a contest or a sweepstakes program for a new brand of cosmetics?

    a. Promotion Activators, Inc. (**www.promotionactivators.com**)

    b. Compliance Sweepstakes Services (**www.compliancesweeps.com**)

    c. Ventura Marketing & Promotion (**www.sweepspros.com**)

⭐**12-42.** Examine the following websites. Identify all of the promotions offered on the site. Provide a screenshot of each promotion you see. What are the objectives of each consumer promotion? Do the promotions on the websites mesh with the company's advertising and consumer promotions at retail outlets? Explain.

    a. Taco Bell (**www.tacobell.com**)

    b. Hershey's (**www.hersheys.com**)

    c. Huggies (**www.huggies.com**)

    d. Papa John's (**www.papajohns.com**)

12-43. Use a search engine to find and examine the websites for Huggies, Pampers, The Honest Company, and Luvs. What types of promotions are available on each? Provide a screen shot of each promotion. What are the objectives of the various consumer promotions? Which site has the best promotions? Why?

Blog Exercises

Access the authors' blog for this textbook at the URLs provided to complete these exercises. Answer the questions that are posed on the blog.

12-44. Papa John's: **blogclowbaack.net/2014/05/12/papa-johns-chapter-12/**

12-45. Brookshire's: **blogclowbaack.net/2014/05/12/brookshires-chapter-12/**

12-46. Consumer promotions: **blogclowbaack.net/2014/05/12/consumer-promotions-chapter-12/**

Student Project

CREATIVE CORNER

Access the official website of the Springfield Cardinals minor league baseball team. From the following list of special days, pick two and then design an ad for each one you picked. Make sure each advertisement features a consumer promotion that is either mentioned on the website (under "Promotions" or "Promotions Calendar") or that you come up with on your own.

Opening Day	*Cinco de Mayo*
Mother's Day	Father's Day
Fourth of July	Labor Day
Play-off Games	Championship Celebration

CASE 1 SIX FLAGS

One of the staples of summertime fun involves fast-moving rides, live entertainment, dining, shopping, and quality family time. While the Disney Corporation may be the most well-known, one growing and thriving competitor is the Six Flags group. Calling its operations "family entertainment" (rather than "amusement park"), the company's website notes that the company's founder Angus Wynne envisioned "regional parks large in scope but closer to where people lived, making them convenient and affordable."[40]

The Six Flags chain includes 18 theme, water, and zoological parks scattered across the United States and North America. The sites offer a full range of activities for visitors, including thrill rides, children's rides, and numerous activities for families and groups of visitors. The company maintains relationships with D.C. Comics and Warner Brothers Products, which allows the organization to include characters such as Bugs Bunny, Batman, the Green Lantern, and Wonder Woman to play roles in visitor experiences, including meet-and-greets, meals, and photograph sessions.

Park location plays a role in how each operates. Those in warmer climates entice visitors nearly year round. Others, such as the one in St. Louis, re-open in the spring following a winter break.

Each Six Flags location includes discount programs for nearby motels and hotels. Visitors have access to convenient parking and can rest at the shops and restaurants contained in the park. Parades, concerts, and other shows enhance the experience for people of all ages.

The Hollywood Reporter recently noted that, "Theme parks around the world are experiencing a boom. 'It appears it's going to be another strong summer for U.S. theme parks, with the big parks in Southern California and Orlando all trending upward this summer,' says Robert Niles, editor of *Theme Park Insider.* 'These are the most popular in the country, and if they are going up, the industry as a whole is going up.'"[41]

The Six Flags chain enjoyed 26 million visitors in 2014. Economic conditions and other trends continue to influence the ways in which families enjoy vacations. With increasing economic activity, the question becomes whether families will try to make visits to places close to home or travel greater distances to savor a wider variety of experiences. The marketing team for Six Flags and other entertainment venues will undoubtedly seek to use sales promotions to continue the trend of increased theme park patronage.

12-47. What type of "product" does Six Flags offer?

12-48. Which consumer promotions would be most useful for Six Flags? Why?

12-49. Of the four types of consumers, which would be most likely to take advantage of consumer promotions for Six Flags? Why?

12-50. Access the website of Six Flags. Which social media networking sites does Six Flags use? How is each used?

12-51. Design a print advertisement that ties a consumer promotion to Six Flags.

▲ Six Flags has focused its operation on providing "family entertainment."

CASE 2 ▸ MARKETING SPORTS EQUIPMENT

The term "sports" has many meanings, depending on the context and those involved in a conversation. Some may be inclined to think of college and professional athletes playing games at the highest level in front of large crowds. Others view sports as being related to physical fitness. Other groups think in terms of "leisure time" or "children's recreation."

Regardless of the type of sports one considers, Academy Sports + Outdoors offers the equipment, clothing, and support services consumers need to engage in activities as varied as camping, fishing, boating, and barbecues, as well as participating in mainstream sports such as baseball, basketball, soccer, and football, as fans or as participants. Large, brightly lit retail outlets feature a wide variety of merchandise for the majority of sporting and outdoor activities in 130 stores placed in 11 different states in the United States.

Academy Sports + Outdoors competes with numerous vendors, including Dick's Sporting Goods, Modell's, Bass Pro Shop, and big box retailers Wal-Mart, Kmart, and Target. Sports participants can also visit specialty shops, such as golf pro shops and smaller fishing stores and outlets.

Consumer groups range from casual backyard athletes to serious hunters, fishing enthusiasts, Little League sponsors and teams, and families looking for equipment to take on a camping expedition. As a result, discovering which target markets are the most lucrative remains an important challenge for each retail chain in this marketplace.

▲ Families are an important target market for Academy Sports + Outdoors.

Academy Sports + Outdoors' management team has chosen to offer guns and other types of hunting equipment. Retailers offering firearms often encounter controversy, both from those opposed to guns and members of major gun lobbies.

Recently, an additional challenge faced major sports retailers. A declining economy forced many consumers to consider which purchases were absolutely necessary and which product purchases could be put on hold. At the same time, some families chose simpler, less expensive vacations and recreational activities, such as camping and home entertainment through games such as badminton and table tennis.

Academy Sports + Outdoors defines itself as "the destination for active-minded families."? The company's mission defines the goals of providing an "unparalleled shopping experience," creating a trusting relationship with customers, and promoting a high-quality working environment for company associates that includes the opportunity to advance within the company.

It is not surprising that the company receives "an overwhelming volume of requests" for sponsorship activities. Company leaders have established well-defined criteria for examining inquiries. Any organization seeking a sponsorship tie-in must make the request three months in advance and can expect to wait as long as five weeks for a response. A similar backlog exists for its donations and charitable activities.

In the future, Academy Sports + Outdoors will continue to expand. Company policies regarding relationships with suppliers

remain an important priority. In any case, as long as people continue to enjoy a wide variety of recreational activities, the potential for further growth remains possible.

12-52. What are the primary target markets for Academy Sports + Outdoors?

12-53. For each of the target markets identified in the preceding question, what types of consumer promotions should Academy Sports + Outdoors offer? Justify your response.

12-54. Suppose you are the vice president of marketing at Academy Sports + Outdoors. Examine the list of consumer promotions shown in Figure 12.1. Discuss the pros and cons of each promotion if the target market is active-minded families with children under 18 and incomes between $30,000 and $70,000.

12-55. From your answer to the preceding question, pick one of the promotions you feel is the best to reach the designated target market. Design a newspaper ad using that promotion. Be sure to include restrictions such as usage and expiration date.

MyMarketingLab

Go to the Assignments section of your MyLab to complete these writing exercises.

12-56. In your own words describe each of the sampling methods listed in Figure 12.5. Suppose you are a marketing intern for Maxwell House and that Maxwell House has developed three new flavors of coffees. Discuss the pros and cons of each method of sampling for Maxwell House coffee. Keep in mind that in addition to getting consumers to try the product, Maxwell House will also want to convince retailers to stock the coffee on its shelves.

12-57. The Rawlings Sports Equipment Company plans to increase sales of baseball gloves this season. The company intends to use a coupon program. Discuss the pros and cons of each method of coupon distribution listed in the chapter for Rawlings. Which method or methods should Rawlings use? Why?

Chapter 13 | Public Relations and Sponsorship Programs

Chapter Objectives

After reading this chapter, you should be able to answer the following questions:

13.1 What relationships exist between public relations and the marketing activities performed by a company?

13.2 How can the public relations functions build better relationships with all internal and external stakeholders?

13.3 What types of positive, image-building programs can companies feature as parts of a public relations program?

13.4 What steps can companies take to prevent or reduce image damage when negative events occur?

13.5 How can marketers tie sponsorships to public relations efforts to strengthen a customer base?

13.6 What roles can event marketing play in creating customer excitement and brand loyalty?

13.7 How can companies adapt public relations programs, sponsorships, and event marketing to international settings?

Overview

The traditional promotions mix includes advertising, sales promotions, personal selling, and public relations efforts. The first three elements in the mix have been presented. This chapter covers the fourth element: public relations along with the sponsorship and event programs that tie into those activities.

Public relations efforts, sponsorships, and event programs contribute to the overall IMC approach. The same unified message appears in every marketing endeavor, from the appearance of the company's letterhead and stationery to advertisements, promotional items, information in press releases, and in any sponsorship program. Making sure each component of a firm's IMC plan speaks with one voice remains the goal. Extending this objective to public relations and sponsorships constitutes an important task for the marketing team.

WINNING COLORS FOR INTERSTATE BATTERIES

What's in a color? In the world of sprint racing, Interstate Batteries achieved major notoriety using the colors green, red, and white. When combined with effective sponsorships and other marketing activities, brand recognition, brand loyalty, and brand "fans" have become the result. Interstate Batteries is the number one replacement brand battery in North America.

Two decades ago, Interstate Batteries chairman Norm Miller and Joe Gibbs created a partnership that led to racing victories and marketing success. It began following the Interstate Batteries Great American Race sponsorship program, a cross-country driving event. Stops in 44 cities along the way generated contacts with distributors, dealers, consumers, and media. The goal was to build the brand in the consumer marketplace as a real grassroots media program, according to Charlie Brim, Interstate's manager for advertising and sponsorships. As the program wound down, Interstate entered into another arena: NASCAR.

At first, the races were in smaller venues with the objective of reaching the target audience of mechanics and part store dealers, which were mostly male. At that point, Joe Gibbs had achieved the pinnacle of football coaching prizes—two victories in the Super Bowl with the Washington Redskins; however, he always maintained an active interest in racing. The introduction of Miller to Gibbs created a highly successful partnership. The team first moved to the Sprint Cup level or the top level of NASCAR racing. A relationship with championship driver Dale Jarrett resulted in numerous victories on the track.

To stand out on television and at the track, the Interstate Batteries car was wrapped in a bright, fluorescent green color with the bright red number 18 featured prominently. Green had been a primary color on the company's batteries. At the time, the color green was associated with bad luck in racing, so the decision was a bold move. Currently, Kyle Busch is the primary driver for the team. He has become one of the most successful drivers in the sport.

Interstate hosts hospitality events at NASCAR races. Tents near the venue house up to 650 guests. Interstate dealers; wholesale distributors; national account guests including Honda, Toyota, and other automobile manufacturers; retailers including Firestone and Costco; prospective Interstate All Battery Center retail franchisees; the company's employees; and other company partners are invited to enjoy food, drinks, and mingle with Interstate executives and racing officials. Interstate employees and volunteers manage the tent—it is not farmed out to independent vendors. Visitors can take photos and obtain autographs of Joe Gibbs and Kyle Busch at the event. Joe Gibbs Racing partners with Mars, FedEx, Home Depot, and Toyota to tie in with an Interstate promotion at various tracks, including accommodating each other's customers and guests.

A few years ago, Interstate shifted to a white car with a powerful company graphic. The decal displays a battery bursting through the hood, as if the battery is the primary source of the car's energy. The image now appears in a variety of company marketing materials, including route truck back decals, calendars, brochures, retail point-of-purchase signage, business cards, banners at various events, advertising, the company's website, and on a traveling show car.

Interstate eventually decided to cut back on the number of racing events and repurposed sponsorship dollars. The company reached an agreement with Mars, Inc. to divide the number of annual races. The white hot Interstate Batteries wrap appears on the car at some events and the same car is wrapped with an M&M's, Snickers, Doublemint, or other Mars design at others. Interstate diverted some of the funding that it saved by cutting back on races into national advertising on TV, radio, digital, and mobile media to reach non-NASCAR fans and customers. Other sponsorships include a small position in JGRMX's motocross and supercross team (owned by Joe Gibbs's son, Coy Gibbs) to target younger patrons and one in NHRA's Pro Stock division with former champion Mike Edwards. These sponsorships and event marketing programs take advantage of the key strengths of a company and its partners. In the case of Interstate Batteries and NASCAR, the personal connection between Joe Gibbs and Norm Miller has helped the company to grow and achieve success.

This chapter begins with a discussion of the nature of a public relations function within an integrated marketing plan. Second, sponsorship programs and event marketing tactics are outlined to show how the company can make quality contacts with existing customers, new prospects, vendors, and others. Successful positive public relations and sponsorship programs enhance the firm's image, and its brands become better known because they are perceived more favorably. The chapter concludes with an examination of international issues associated with public relations efforts.

Public Relations

objective 13.1

What relationships exist between public relations and the marketing activities performed by a company?

In Hollywood, one well-worn phrase is "There's no such thing as bad publicity." This may be true for a bad-boy actor trying to get his name out to the public; however, in the world of marketing and communications, bad publicity can be far worse than no publicity. Many business organizations spend countless hours fending off negative comments while trying to develop positive and noticeable messages and themes.

The **public relations (PR) department** manages publicity and other communications with every group in contact with the company. Some of the functions performed by the public relations department are similar to those provided by the marketing department. Others are quite different. The two may cooperate with and consult each other, yet each has a unique role. To illustrate, consider a two-pronged approach used by the Mexico Tourism Board to increase tourism. The first component of the campaign featured a branding effort carrying the tagline "The Place You Thought You Knew." Second, public relations employees designed efforts aimed at countering Mexico's drug-and-violence image that has been reported by the U.S. news media. The two programs sought to change Americans' perceptions of Mexico.[1]

Some experts believe public relations should be part of the marketing department, just as advertising, trade promotions, and consumer promotions will be under the direction of the marketing manager. Others suggest that public relations activities differ and cannot operate effectively within a marketing department. Instead, a member of the public relations department should serve as a consultant to the marketing department. Still others contend that a new division, called the "department of communications," should be created to oversee both marketing and public relations activities.

▼ Company leaders decide who should handle public relations activities.

Internal versus External Public Relations

Deciding who will handle various public relations activities will be the first major decision company leaders make. They can be managed by an internal public relations officer or department. Other companies hire public relations firms to complete special projects or manage public relations functions. When a company retains a public relations agency, normally an internal company employee takes charge of internal public relations, because most public relations firms deal only with external publics.

The decision criteria used in selecting advertising agencies can be applied to selecting a public relations firm. Developing a trusting relationship with the public relations agency and clearly spelling out what the firm expects from the agency become high priorities.

Public Relations Tools

Public relations employees utilize a number of tools, including company newsletters, internal messages, public relations releases, correspondences with stockholders, annual reports, and various special events and, increasingly, social media venues. Even the bulletin board in the company's break room conveys messages to internal stakeholders.

Capturing **hits**, or mentions of a company's name in news stories, will be a common goal for a public relations firm. Hits can be positive, negative, or neutral in terms of their impact. Each improves the chance that consumers will see the name of a company in a news-related context, which might increase brand or company awareness; however, the agency should also consider the type of image portrayed. It may be a more prudent strategy to seek fewer hits while making sure that mentions of the company are positive and reinforce the firm's IMC theme.

When hiring a public relations firm, the agency's personnel should be familiar with the client's IMC approach. Then, members of the public relations firm work on ideas that reinforce the theme. The firm develops special events, activities, and news releases designed to strengthen the company's voice.

▲ The marketing department at JD Bank concentrates on building a strong brand that can be reinforced through positive public relations efforts.

Public Relations Functions

Public relations activities are not standard marketing functions. The marketing department concentrates on customers and the channel members on the route to those customers, such as wholesalers and retail outlets. In contrast, the public relations department focuses on internal and external stakeholders, including employees, stockholders, public interest groups, the government, and society. Figure 13.1 displays five key public relations functions. Public relations personnel engage in these tasks, whether they are internal employees or members of a public relations company hired to perform the functions.

objective 13.2

How can the public relations functions build better relationships with all internal and external stakeholders?

- Identify internal and external stakeholders
- Assess the corporate reputation
- Audit corporate social responsibility
- Create positive image-building activities
- Prevent or reduce image damage

◀ **FIGURE 13.1**
Public Relations Functions

Identifying Stakeholders

Each recipient of company communications is important. Any constituent who makes a contact with a company should receive a clear, unified response. A **stakeholder** is a person or group who has a vested interest in the organization's activities. Vested interests may include:

- Profits paid as common stock dividends
- Loan repayments a lending institution seeks to receive
- Sales to the company or purchases made from the company
- Wages paid to employees
- Community well-being
- A special-interest topic

In essence, a wide variety of items can cause people or other companies to believe they hold a stake in the firm's activities. Public relations employees observe stakeholders and, when appropriate, target them with communications. Figure 13.2 identifies the primary internal and external stakeholders that the public relations department monitors.

Communications with each of these stakeholder groups are crucial. To ensure consistency, company leaders develop a communications strategy that fits with the IMC plan and corporate image. The overall message to each stakeholder stays the same. Then, messages can be tailored to meet the different expectations of the various audiences. By customizing the content, style, and channels of communication, each stakeholder group receives a message that best resonates with it, yet it remains consistent with other messages.

In addition to sending communications to individual stakeholders, the public relations department closely studies the actions and opinions of each group. When changes in attitudes, new views, or serious concerns develop, the public relations department remains ready to respond. The department is responsible for making certain all communications to each of these publics consistently present the firm's message and image.

▲ When Community Trust Bank changed its name to Origin Bank, doing so required identifying all of the internal and external stakeholders.

Internal Stakeholders

Effective managers know the value of quality internal communications. Employees provide a powerful channel of communication to people outside the organization. They can either enhance or damage a firm's reputation. What employees say to others has a higher level of credibility than what a company says about itself. Word-of-mouth communications, including informal statements by employees, impact purchasing and investing decisions.[2]

▶ **FIGURE 13.2**
Stakeholders

• Employees	• Media
• Unions	• Local community
• Shareholders	• Financial community
• Channel members	• Government
• Customers	• Special-interest groups

Employees receive a constant stream of company information. Many of these individuals are not in the marketing and public relations departments. They should be made aware of what the company seeks to achieve with the IMC program, even if it means presenting only basic information. Those closest to the marketing department, such as employees serving customers, will be more acutely aware of the nature of the IMC plan, including how the company's message theme should be transmitted to constituents.

To communicate effectively with employees, the public relations department works with the human resource (HR) department. Publications and communications aimed at employees should be consistent with the image and message the firm espouses to customers and others. When a firm advertises that its employees stand ready to assist customers, the public relations team makes sure employees are aware of the message. Employee behaviors should reflect the advertising theme being conveyed to customers. The HR department looks for and hires workers who are attracted to that approach. Performance appraisals and rewards can be structured to favor those who buy into the company's IMC approach. This emphasis on providing quality information about company activities extends to every public relations event and sponsorship program.

▲ Employees are important internal stakeholders.

External Stakeholders

Overseeing external communications continues to be a daunting task, because the company has very little influence over how external publics perceive organizational activities. External stakeholders include groups such as the media, the local community, the financial community, the government, and special interest groups. The company has no control over what these groups say or how they interpret information. The public relations agency continually disseminates positive information and quickly reacts to any negative publicity or complaints.

A totally integrated communications program accounts for every message delivered to internal and external stakeholders. Each contact point provides the opportunity to present a quality message. The marketing department creates contact points with customers and potential customers. To complement these efforts, the public relations department deals with the myriad of contact points that are not created or planned, yet may be just as critical. An unplanned contact point, such as a news story or an individual talking to an employee of the firm at a social gathering, allows the firm to build a positive image or minimize the impact of any negative messages. Dealing with unplanned contact points can be challenging. Continuing investigations of what goes on around the firm will be one key to keeping constituents satisfied while trying to insulate the firm from negative publicity.

▲ Origin Bank ran this advertisement assuring customers that the name change would not change "who we are."

Assessing Corporate Reputation

A corporation's reputation is fragile and valuable. Well-received corporate and brand names enhance businesses during the good times and protect them when a crisis or problem occurs. A company's reputation influences consumer decisions regarding which brands to purchase. Investors select where to place money based on corporate

▲ A strong brand name, such as Kraft, constitutes a valuable asset that should be protected.

reputations. These assessments also affect potential employees as they decide whether to apply for work in a given organization.

Corporate scandals, accounting fraud, and economic and financial downturns have reduced consumer confidence. The Edelman Trust Barometer report indicated that 56 percent of individuals surveyed said they do not trust businesses to do the right thing.[3] Company actions as well as those of individuals within an organization impact a firm's reputation. Figure 13.3 notes activities that can harm an organization's reputation and those that can enhance a firm's reputation.

Assessing and managing a company's reputation will be as important as promoting its products. Yet, with all that is at stake, fewer than half of the companies in the United States have someone assigned to monitor corporate reputation. As a result, many company leaders have little idea what consumers, investors, employees, and the public think or say about the firm. A company cannot effectively pursue a public relations program when company leaders do not know what people believe about it.

Assessment begins when public relations employees conduct surveys and interviews in order to reveal perceptions of the organization. Monitoring online chatter, tweets, and social media produces additional information. These efforts can be completed internally or a public relations firm may lead them. Examining both external and internal views of the corporation's reputation produces a more complete view of the organization.

Corporate Social Responsibility

Corporate social responsibility refers to an organization's obligation to be ethical, accountable, and reactive to the needs of society. It means companies work toward the greater good of society by taking positive actions. Globalization and increased pressures from the public for corporate transparency have led to an increasing emphasis on social responsibility. Bradley K. Googins, director of the Boston College Center for Corporate Citizenship, stated that, "Quality used to be the difference between brands, then it was technology. Now, it really comes back to reputation. It's really the question of who you want to do business with and the relationship between the consumer and the product."[4]

▶ **FIGURE 13.3**
Activities that Affect a Company's Image

Image-Destroying Activities	Image-Building Activities
• Discrimination	• Empowerment of employees
• Harassment	• Charitable contributions
• Pollution	• Sponsoring local events
• Misleading communications	• Selling enviromentally safe products
• Deceptive communications	• Outplacement programs
• Offensive communications	• Supporting community events

A survey of more than 10,000 adults across 28 countries yielded the following information regarding corporate responsibility:[5]

- 78% said transparency is a must, not an option for companies
- 72% want companies to fight injustice
- 71% believe companies have a responsibility to do more than just generate profits
- 67% believe businesses are just as responsible as governments for driving positive social change
- 63% believe that big companies have more power to initiate social change than some countries

Business experts agree that socially responsible firms are more likely to thrive and survive in the long term. Companies engaged in positive activities often generate quality publicity and engender customer loyalty. Firms that work to eliminate unfair practices, pollution, harassment, and other negative activities are more likely to stay out of court. Further, the company receives fewer negative word-of-mouth comments by unhappy employees or consumers. Managing these activities properly leads to a positive corporate image.

A new trend in corporate social responsibility, **purpose marketing**, or **pro-social marketing**, involves advertising that focuses on the values, behaviors, and beliefs of the company. The messages indicate that the company operates in a socially responsible fashion. Outerwear and sports-equipment brand Patagonia, for instance, focuses on social initiatives rather than investing in traditional brand advertising. According to Joy Howard, vice president of marketing at Patagonia, "We have a mission to solve problems in the world." Recently, the company encouraged consumers to embrace sustainability by mending their clothing rather than buying new items. Another Patagonia initiative focused on removing dams across the United States to promote river restoration. Patagonia executives believe it is important to use "business to help solve environmental problems."[6]

An advertisement for Progressive Bank highlighting its involvement in the community.

Creating Positive Image-Building Activities

In an effort to positively influence consumer and other stakeholder views of a company, many firms engage in cause-related marketing and green marketing. These planned events draw positive attention to the organization as a solid corporate citizen, one committed to social responsibility. The public relations department sends out messages in the form of press releases and holds press conferences to highlight these positive, image-building activities.

Cause-Related Marketing

A **cause-related marketing** program ties marketing activities with a charity in order to generate goodwill. U.S. businesses pay more than $1.5 billion each year for the right to feature a nonprofit organization's name or logo in company advertising and marketing programs.[7] This type of partnership agreement between a nonprofit cause and a for-profit business assumes that consumers prefer to purchase from companies that support causes. Marketers engage in cause-related marketing to develop stronger ties and to move consumers, as well as businesses, toward brand loyalty. A Cone Communications and Roper Starch Worldwide survey revealed that:

- 78 percent of consumers are more likely to purchase a brand associated with a cause they care about.
- 54 percent would be willing to pay more for a brand associated with a cause they care about.

objective 13.3

What types of positive, image-building programs can companies feature as parts of a public relations program?

Never underestimate the importance of water safety.

OVER 60 CHILDREN HAVE ALREADY DROWNED IN TEXAS THIS YEAR. Never leave children alone with water, have proper safety equipment on hand, and don't assume children will use caution or good judgement around water. The Emergency staff at Medical Center of Southeast Texas remind you to never let your children out of your sight, especially if playing in or around water. In an crisis situation, immediately call 911.

The Medical Center OF SOUTHEAST TEXAS
CENTERED on SAFETY.
seeandsave.org
medicalcentersetexas.com
(409) 724-7389

▲ This advertisement for the Medical Center of Southeast Texas highlights the importance of water safety.

▼ Fiat Chrysler's Ram truck division partnered with Farmers and Hunters Feeding the Hungry.

These benefits lead companies to get involved. Relationships that do not yield positive benefits to the business sponsor do not last long. In choosing a cause, the marketing and public relations teams concentrate on business-related issues. Supporting such efforts generates greater credibility.

When a fit exists, positive reactions emerge. Fiat Chrysler's Ram truck division partnered with Famers and Hunters Feeding the Hungry (FHFH) where hunters donated some of their quarry to feed the hungry and less fortunate. The Richards Group, Ram's advertising agency, designed four television spots that highlighted the rugged life of hunters and the tie-in with the FHFH. Print ads were designed aimed at outdoor enthusiasts. The ads promoted the Ram truck but also highlighted the company's involvement with feeding the hungry.

Benefits to Nonprofit Organizations

Cause-related marketing assists nonprofit organizations. Competition has increased in both the business world and the nonprofit world. An increasing number of nonprofit organizations compete for contributions and gifts. Strategic relationships with businesses can boost contributions to a nonprofit organization. A General Mills Yoplait campaign raised more than $10 million for the Susan G. Komen Breast Cancer Foundation. Featuring the slogan, "Save Lids to Save Lives," General Mills donated ten cents for each Yoplait lid that was returned by consumers.[8] The relationship resulted in direct increases in revenues for Yoplait and positive publicity for the foundation.

Most of the time, corporate leaders select the nonprofits they wish to support. Occasionally, the reverse occurs. Alice Berkner, founder of the International Bird Rescue Research Center, obtained a small grant to test major dish soaps for cleaning birds harmed by oil spills. Procter & Gamble's Dawn detergent worked the best. When first approached by Berkner about supporting the cause, P&G turned her down. Then, during a major oil spill, volunteers used Dawn on the oil-covered birds to remove the black crude. Extensive media coverage followed. Dawn currently donates about $100,000 annually to the research center. A television commercial created by Kaplan Thaler Group shows a baby duck, penguin, and seal being washed with Dawn detergent. There is no voiceover, just the song "Wash Away" sung by Joe Purdy. The copy on the screen states that Dawn has helped save thousands of animals caught in oil spills.[9]

A complex linkage exists between public relations and cause-related marketing. The company needs publicity to benefit from cause-related marketing. Yet, if the activity is publicized too much, people think the cause is only being used for commercial gain. Further, when the company supports an unrelated cause, consumers may conclude that the business merely seeks to benefit from the nonprofit's reputation. This might lead some to stop buying the company's products or to believe the company wishes to cover up unethical behaviors.

Many consumers are skeptical about the motives behind giving to various charities. In a survey of British consumers, the vast majority said a company should spend funds on communications about cause-related efforts. The same survey indicated that two-thirds also believed the amount should not be significant. The majority of those surveyed said their purchase decisions are influenced by the causes a company supports. This makes informing people about a company's cause-related activities necessary; however, doing so involves walking a thin line between publicizing and what might be viewed as corporate self-aggrandizement.[10] Even though most people understand that a business must benefit from the relationship, they still tend to develop negative views when they conclude that the business exploits a relationship with a nonprofit.

Green Marketing and Pro-Environmental Activities

Green marketing involves the development and promotion of products that are environmentally safe. Most consumers favor green marketing. One recent survey indicated that 58 percent of Americans try to save electricity, 46 percent recycle newspapers, 45 percent return bottles or cans, and 23 percent buy products made from or packaged in recycled materials.[11]

▲ Dawn donates $100,000 annually to the Bird Rescue Research Center.

Although consumers say they support green marketing and environmentally safe products, actual purchases of such products only occur when all things are considered equal. Most consumers often will not sacrifice price, quality, convenience, availability, or performance for the sake of the environment. According to David Donnan, a partner with consulting firm A.T. Kearny, "Every consumer says I want to help the environment. I'm looking for eco-friendly products. But, if it's one or two pennies higher in price, they're not going to buy it. There is a discrepancy between what people say and what they do.[12]

▼ A large percentage of Americans believe in recycling.

To benefit from green marketing, the company's marketing team identifies the segments that are most attracted to environmentally friendly products. In the United States, consumers can be divided into five groups based on their propensity to purchase green products and their attitudes about environmental issues. Only nine percent of American consumers are classified as "True Blue Greens," and another six percent are classified as "Greenback Greens." The True Blue Greens are active environmentalists who support environmentally safe products and shop for green brands. The Greenback Greens purchase environmentally safe products but are not politically active. The other three groups, Sprouts, Grousers, and Basic Browns, are less committed or are not committed to environmental protections.[13]

In making a choice about the degree of emphasis to be placed on green marketing, managers ask three questions. First, what percentage of the company's customer base fits into the green marketing segments? Second, can the brand or company be differentiated from the competition along green lines in such a way that it can become a competitive advantage? Third, will the company's current target market be alienated by adopting a green marketing approach?

Promoting Green Activities   Almost all firms report that they are pro-environment and provide information on company websites about environmental activities. The amount of effort given to publicize these activities varies widely.[14] Coca-Cola tries to protect the environment, but most people are unaware of the company's efforts. Coca-Cola has invested in various recycling programs and recyclable package designs but does not publicize the activities due to concerns that the information might reduce the product's appeal to some of the company's audience.

▲ Only 9 percent of Americans are classified as "True Blue Greens" and only 6 percent are "Greenback Greens".

Promoting the direct, tangible benefits of a product first, with the environmental benefits presented as secondary factors, can be an alternate approach. Toyota launched the Prius model by emphasizing fuel efficiency. Consumers were told they would spend less for gas. Although the Prius is an environmentally advanced, fuel-efficient hybrid vehicle, the feature was mentioned but not stressed. Company marketers concluded that strong environmentalists would want to buy hybrid cars; however, for those who were not strong environmentalists it did not matter, because the car delivered fuel efficiency.

An innovative and new approach involves creating green products within brand lines. Levi Strauss sells designer jeans made from recycled plastic bottles. Nike produces "FlyKnit" shoes with yarn instead of leather uppers. The shoes feature a better fit as well as a reduction in waste. In both instances, the companies sought to reach green-oriented customers.[15]

Some companies integrate environmental activities into an overall business design and marketing approach. This approach achieves the best results when the primary customer base consists of True Blue Greens and the Greenback Greens. The Body Shop, Patagonia, Honest Tea, and Seventh Generation feature this approach. Honest Tea embeds social responsibility into every company activity, from the manufacturing process to the marketing of products. The company features biodegradable tea bags, organic ingredients, and community partnerships. Honest Tea's marketing program emphasizes concern for and support of environmental and social issues.

▶ Companies such as Honest Tea and Seventh Generation have demonstrated concern for the environment.

Seventh Generation has produced natural-ingredient cleaning products for 21 years. Although well known to environmentally conscious shoppers, few people had ever heard about the Seventh Generation brand. To help increase awareness, the company's leaders hired Minneapolis-based Carmichael Lynch to develop print and television commercials about the brand's safety and green ingredients. The campaign's goal was to educate consumers about the products and the importance of protecting the environment.[16]

Greenwashing   Most business leaders believe their companies should be involved in protecting the environment and creating green products; however, the marketing emphasis varies. Companies claiming to make green products have been exposed by bloggers who point out that they do not. Faking green, or **greenwashing**, damages a company's reputation when such information appears on blogs and other social media. Honesty and transparency constitute two important ingredients in an environmentally friendly IMC program.

Preventing or Reducing Image Damage

Another public relations function, **damage control**, involves reacting to negative events caused by a company error, consumer grievances, as well as unjustified or exaggerated negative press. Bad publicity and negative events quickly damage an image. A strong company image that took years to build can be rapidly destroyed. Sales at Target stores plummeted after hackers breached customer credit card data. Recently, Chipotle sales suffered after several pathogen outbreaks sickened more than 300 people. In both cases, some customers were lost forever while others were slow to return.

Bad news travels fast, and it is not always the media that generates negative publicity. Sometimes negative word-of-mouth communications come from customers, employees, or other individuals connected with the company. The internet makes it possible for individuals to report bad experiences and post negative comments for thousands to see in a very short time.

Damage control applies to two situations. The first occurs when the firm has made an error or has caused legitimate consumer or public grievances. The second takes place when unjustified or exaggerated negative press appears. Defending an organization's image and handling damage control takes two forms: proactive prevention strategies and reactive damage-control strategies (see Figure 13.4).

Proactive Prevention Strategies

Proactive prevention means that rather than waiting for harmful publicity to appear and then reacting, many firms charge certain employees with minimizing the effects of any future bad press in advance. Proactive approaches help prevent negative publicity from emerging in the first place. Two techniques are entitlings and enhancements.[17] **Entitlings** are attempts to claim responsibility for positive outcomes of events. **Enhancements** are attempts to increase the impact of the desirable outcome of an event in the eyes of the public.

Entitling takes place when a firm's name is associated with a positive event. For example, an official sponsor of a U.S. Olympic person or team that wins a gold medal ties the company's name to the athletic achievements of people who do not work for the firm, yet advertising may hint that the company helped these individuals achieve success.[18] An advertising campaign by TD Ameritrade featured the stories of seven athletes showing their lifelong journey to make the Olympics along with the fortitude required of long-term investors. The theme of the ads was that Ameritrade can help investors reach long-term goals, one small step at a time, just as these athletes reached the Olympics, one step at a time.[19]

Enhancements occur when the marketing or public relations department suggests that something relatively small is a bigger deal. Any "buy American" program promoted as being patriotic as well as good for the economy (and local workers) seeks to enhance the image of the company that markets the items. Press releases pointing out the "buy American" feature help underscore these advantages to consumers.

objective 13.4

What steps can companies take to prevent or reduce image damage when negative events occur?

- Proactive Strategies
  - Entitlings
  - Enhancements
- Reactive Strategies
  - Internet Interventions
  - Crisis management programs
  - Apology strategy
  - Impression management techniques

▲ **FIGURE 13.4**
Damage-control Strategies

▼ Entitling takes place when a firm associates with an athlete who wins at the Olympics or in other types of competition.

- Internet interventions
- Crisis management programs
- Apology strategies
- Impression management

▲ **FIGURE 13.5**
Reactive Damage-control Strategies

Reactive Damage-Control Strategies

Company leaders often must react to unforeseen events. In these instances, managers work to blunt the effects of unwanted bad publicity. The reactive damage-control strategies companies can use to reduce negative publicity include internet interventions, crisis management programs, apology strategies, and impression management techniques (see Figure 13.5)

Internet Interventions   Firms seek to combat online word-of-mouth with **internet interventions**. Social media and blogs help consumers share negative word-of-mouth and talk about bad experiences. Consumers around the world tell horror stories about companies or products. Individuals can say anything online, even when they unfairly portray various industries, companies, or brands.

Internet outlets allow people to vent emotions, which injure a company's reputation. Ford, Pepsi, Toyota, Southwest Airlines, other companies use software and assign employees to monitor internet postings, social media comments, and tweets. Even with these technological tools, however, monitoring everything said about a company remains a daunting task. It can involve hundreds of posts per day. Employees must quickly decide which to investigate further. Marcus Schmidt, a senior marketing manager for Microsoft, suggests, "If you start seeing a lot of people retweeting it, then you know to pay attention."

Recently, Coke's software identified a Twitter post by a frustrated consumer who was not able to redeem a prize from the MyCoke rewards program. The consumer's profile indicated that he had more than 10,000 followers. Adam Brown, Coke's head of social media, posted an apology on the individual's Twitter profile and offered to help. The consumer received the prize. He later changed his Twitter avatar to a photo of himself holding a bottle of Coke. Brown noted, "We're getting to a point if you're not responding, you're not being seen as an authentic type of brand."[20] Not every activity warrants a formal reaction. Still, social listening keeps the company's leadership informed about what people are saying and thinking.

Crisis Management   A company either accepts the blame for an event, offers an apology, or refutes the charges in a forceful manner in a **crisis management** program. A crisis may be viewed as a problem or an opportunity. Often, a crisis contains the potential to improve the firm's position and image.

Several years ago, PepsiCo encountered claims that hypodermic needles were found in its products. The management team quickly responded with photographs and videos demonstrating that such an occurrence was impossible, because the bottles and cans are turned upside down before being filled. Next, footage of a con artist slipping a needle into a bottle was shown. This fast and powerful answer eliminated the negative publicity, and Pepsi was able to make a strong statement about the safety of its bottling methods.

▼ Social listening allows a company to know what consumers are saying and thinking.

Unfortunately, some company leaders only make matters worse, as was the initial reaction of Toyota to quality problems with its vehicles. Continual denials were not well-received, especially when the problems kept occurring. Many people became angry when it was revealed that Toyota's management team had been aware of the issues without seeking to correct them. Eventually, the president of Toyota Motors, Akio Toyoda, was summoned to Washington to testify before the House Committee on Oversight and Government Reform.

Realizing its image was quickly eroding and the outcry against the company had grown, Toyota launched a full-scale public relations campaign with print, television, and social media networks. Full-page newspaper ads and several television spots reported that Toyota imposed a temporary halt in production followed by an apologetic, but

reassuring, message that Toyota would pull through the crisis. At the same time, the company created a social media response room staffed with individuals who monitored online conversations and responded to consumer concerns.[21]

Apology Strategies   Another reactive damage-control strategy, an **apology strategy**, occurs when an investigation reveals that the firm was at fault. Any sincere apology should be offered quickly. The apology should include the five elements listed in Figure 13.6.[22]

Companies offer apologies in situations for minor violations or at times in which the firm or person cannot deny responsibility. It can be an effective strategy for creating an emotional bond with the public. Consumers are less likely to remain angry with a company that admits a mistake. When customers believe the apology is sincere and heartfelt, they normally forgive the company and at times feel more positively toward the organization afterward.

Chipotle employed an apology strategy after an E-coli outbreak in some company stores. The organization improved its food safety system and contracted with an outside vendor to audit restaurants on a quarterly basis. Company leaders wanted consumers to know they regretted what happened and had made every effort to ensure it did not occur again. Once the U.S. Centers for Disease Control said the E-coli problem had been resolved, the company embarked on an aggressive integrated advertising campaign that included outdoor, radio, television, print, and digital ads to win customers back. Marketing experts believe the best thing a company can do in that type of situation is to admit fault immediately. Failing to respond or to admit fault are what people are more likely to remember.[23]

Impression Management   Trying to project a certain type of image, or **impression management**, includes the conscious or unconscious attempt to control images projected in real or imagined social interactions.[24] In order to maintain or enhance an image, individuals and corporations attempt to influence the identities they display to others. Each can be portrayed in a manner that maximizes positive characteristics while minimizing any negative elements.

Any event that threatens a person's image or a company's identity creates a predicament. When faced with one, public relations officials make concerted efforts to reduce or minimize the negative consequences. When the predicament cannot be avoided or concealed, the individual or company engages in any remedial activity that reduces the potentially harmful consequences, including expressions of innocence, excuses, justifications, and other explanations.

An *expression of innocence* means company leaders provide information designed to convince others (clients, the media, and the government) that the company was not associated with the basis of the event. In other words, they say, "We did not cause this to happen. Someone (or something) else did."

Excuses are explanations designed to convince the public that the firm and its leaders are not responsible for the predicament or that it could not have been foreseen. Thus, they should not be held accountable. They might say, "It was an act of God. It was totally unavoidable. It was the random act of an individual."

Justifications involve using logic designed to reduce the degree of negativity associated with the predicament. Making the event seem minor or trivial is one method. Suggesting

▲ Apology strategies are used in situations in which the violation is minor or cannot be denied.

◀ **FIGURE 13.6**
Elements of an Apology Strategy

1. An expression of guilt, embarrassment, or regret

2. A statement recognizing the inappropriate behavior and acceptance of sanctions for wrong behavior

3. A rejection of the inappropriate behavior

4. Approval of the appropriate behavior and a promise not to engage in inappropriate behavior

5. An offer of compensation or penance to correct the wrong

that the firm had to proceed in the way it did ("We outsource some of the production process because if we don't we'll be out of business, and our other employees will lose their jobs") is another form of justification.

Other explanations may be prepared to persuade individuals that the cause of the predicament does not truly represent what the firm or individual is really like. In other words, the case was the exception rather than the rule, and customers should not judge the firm too harshly. You will hear comments such as "This was a singular incident, and not indicative of the way we do business."[25] Carnival Cruise Lines used this strategy after its ship, the Triumph, caught fire and stranded 3,200 passengers and crew members for five days. In addition to declaring it was an isolated incident, the company also invited ten active participants on Instagram to take a cruise and then post comments and pictures about their experiences.[26]

Each company's management team, marketing department, and public relations specialists should be acutely aware of the speed with which events can cause great damage to a firm's image. Managers may pursue proactive and reactive measures to make sure the firm survives negative publicity with less long-term damage.

Sponsorships

objective 13.5

How can marketers tie sponsorships to public relations efforts to strengthen a customer base?

To build brand loyalty and other positive feelings toward a company, many marketing leaders utilize sponsorships and event marketing. These programs create situations in which prospects, customers, vendors, and others in unique situations gather together. People who attend sponsored activities or special events already have favorable feelings about the activity taking place. These positive attitudes easily transfer to the company that provides funding.[27]

Forms of Sponsorships

Sponsorship marketing occurs when a company pays money to sponsor someone, some group, or something that is part of an activity. A firm can sponsor a long list of groups, individuals, activities, and events. Various businesses sponsor everything from local Little League baseball and soccer teams to national musical tours, NASCAR drivers, and sports stadiums.

North America sponsorship expenditures exceed $21 billion annually; worldwide the amount reaches almost $60 billion.[28] Figure 13.7 provides a breakdown of the spending. Sports account for about 70 percent of all sponsorships. Sporting events are popular and often attract large crowds. In addition to the audience attending the game or competition, many more watch on television. Popular athletes often make effective spokespersons. If possible, the firm should be the exclusive sponsor of the person or team, which makes it easier to remember than when there are multiple sponsors.

Sponsorships became a major part of Ford's integrated advertising and marketing push for the Ford F-Series Super Duty pickup trucks. Although the integrated campaign included television ads, print ads, and online chats, the central component of the campaign was the sponsorship of Toby Keith's concert tour, "America's Toughest Tour." The Ford F-Series trucks were highly visible at the concerts, with truck-themed set pieces on stage and at least one F-Series truck on the stage. In addition to the concert tour, Ford sponsored a Monster Jam truck show and individual professional bull riders. The company sponsors the Future Farmers of America, the American Quarter Horse Association, and the Dallas Cowboys.[29]

▼ Companies often sponsor youth baseball to enhance their images among consumers.

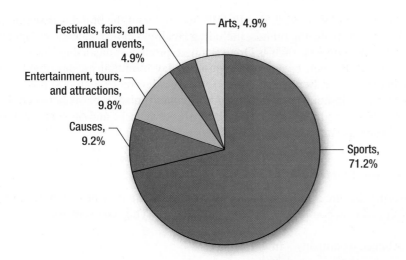

Festivals, fairs, and annual events, 4.9%

Arts, 4.9%

Entertainment, tours, and attractions, 9.8%

Causes, 9.2%

Sports, 71.2%

◀ **FIGURE 13.7**
Marketing Expenditures on Sponsorships

▼ Interstate is a successful sponsor of NASCAR.

Instead of major sports, many brand managers invest in endurance competitions such as Tough Mudder, Spartan Race, and CrossFit Games. Under Armour, Wheaties, and Advil Tough sponsor the 10–12 mile Tough Mudder obstacle course race. The more rigorous Spartan Race includes a time factor. CrossFit Games holds a series of exceedingly difficult workouts from eponymous and cult conditioning programs. Reebok serves as the title sponsor of both the Spartan Race and CrossFit Games. The company chose these unique sports venues because the participants and attendees both tend to be more social-media savvy than the general population. They are also more likely to share involvements through various social media networks.[30]

Some organizations have moved away from sports sponsorships toward cultural events such as classical music groups and jazz bands, visual art exhibits by noted painters, dance troupes, and actors for various theater performances. Cultural sponsorships may not be the best match for every firm. They achieve greater success for items sold to affluent consumers. Consequently, financial institutions often become the primary sponsors of these types of performers and performances. In the past, some institutions provided funds without receiving recognition. Now, marketers leverage philanthropic efforts by having the company's name strongly associated with the cultural activity. This includes printing the name of the firm on programs and regularly mentioning the brand or corporate name as the entity responsible for arranging for the artist to be present at the event. Also, sponsors usually receive choice seats at performances that can be given to key clients.

▼ A new format of sponsorships involves bloggers.

Social Media and Blogs A new format involves sponsoring bloggers. Colleen Padilla, a 33-year-old mother of two and author of the popular website Classy Mommy (**classymommy. com**), has reviewed nearly 1,500 products, including microwave dinners, Nintendo Wii, and baby clothes. Her site attracts 60,000 unique visitors every month. Companies eagerly send her products to test and, if she likes them, to post positive comments on the site. When she does not like an item, nothing will be posted. Padilla tells her readers if the brand was sent to her. She also includes videos featuring brands, including Healthy Choice, labeled as "sponsored posts."

For some bloggers, such as Drew Bennett, product sponsorships have become a lucrative business. Bennett began with a photo-a-day blog that mushroomed into sponsored products at his site **BenSpark.com**. He has written more than 600 posts for firms such as X-Shot, a telescope camera extender. Bennett typically earns between $5.35 and $10 per post. Most product sponsors pay Bennett between 11 and 68 cents each time a reader moves from his site to the brand's site.

Sponsorship Objectives

Measuring the direct impact of a sponsorship program may be difficult. Sponsorships can be designed to accomplish a variety of objectives. They can seek to:

- enhance a company's image
- increase a firm's visibility
- differentiate a company from its competitors
- showcase specific goods and services
- help a firm develop closer relationships with current and prospective customers
- sell excess inventory

◄ The First National Bank is identified as the sponsor of the community wide Easter egg hunt.

The Green Turtle restaurant built visibility and a positive image through a sponsorship program. The company sponsored Amelia's Ace of Hearts Ride to raise money for breast cancer. Approximately 200 of the 400 bike riders registered at the restaurant and 300 people celebrated at an after-party in the restaurant. The event raised $28,000 for the charity. Leho Poldmae, an employee of The Green Turtle, reported, "These events and sponsorships put the human aspect into marketing. They are much more powerful than ads in touching and reaching customers."[31]

Event Marketing

Event marketing and sponsorship marketing are similar. The main difference is that sponsorship marketing involves a person, group, or team. **Event marketing** takes place when a company supports a specific event. Also, event marketing and lifestyle marketing are closely related. Both often include setting up a booth or display and maintaining a physical presence at an event. For instance, in the advertisement shown promoting a community wide Easter egg hunt, First National Bank is identified as the sponsor.

Sponsoring the right event provides a company with brand-name recognition and helps develop closer ties with vendors and customers. Events boost morale for the employees who participate in or attend them. Sponsoring local events such as the Special Olympics often generates free publicity. These events enhance the company's image in the local community.

As is the case with sponsorships, many event marketing programs feature sports. Other events are related to lifestyles. A rodeo sponsored by Lee Jeans, a music concert presented by a local business, or a health fair conducted by a local hospital are all examples of event marketing.

Event marketing has proven to be especially successful with Hispanic consumers. It can be an excellent method of building brand awareness and building brand loyalty. Renata Franco of Cox Communications notes that, "Hispanics are much more community-centered. Events do really well." When Cox Communications sponsors a Hispanic event, the company employs bilingual brand ambassadors who can personally speak to attendees.[32]

objective 13.6
What roles can event marketing play in creating customer excitement and brand loyalty?

Selecting Sponsorships and Events

Several steps are involved in selecting a sponsorship or an event. To ensure the maximum benefit, company employees follow the steps highlighted in Figure 13.8.

Determining Objectives

Company leaders outline communication objectives before becoming involved in a sponsorship or an event. For an objective of rewarding customers, marketers look for sponsorships or events that major customers would enjoy. Some objectives are more internally oriented, especially those designed to increase employee involvement or to boost morale. These can be achieved by finding opportunities internal members will like. Externally oriented objectives include maintaining market share, building a stronger brand presence, enhancing the product or firm's image, and increasing sales.

Matching the Audience to the Company's Target Market

When choosing a sponsorship or an event, the marketing team matches the audience profile with the company's target market. A firm sponsoring a singer at a music show attended mainly by women works best when the company's primary customers are female. Marketing executives also consider how the individual participant or group image relates to the firm's image. A contestant in an upscale event, such as a piano competition, may be sponsored by a tuxedo or formal gown company. The sponsors of the Women's Bassmaster Tour shown in the advertisement in this section are a good match with the participants who attend Tour events.

Promoting the Event

Advertising and public relations releases help promote sponsorships and events. Company officials give extra

▼ Matching the audience profile with the company's target market is important when selecting sponsorships.

- Determine objectives
- Match the audience to company's target market
- Promote the sponsorship or event
- Advertise at the event
- Track results

◄ **FIGURE 13.8**
Steps in Selecting a Sponsorship or Event

▲ Sponsoring an event, such as a rodeo, allows a company to reach consumers in a less-cluttered environment.

effort to contacting interest groups that would benefit from the event. An event such as a local Special Olympics requires commercials, contacts with the press, and finding ways to reach parents and relatives of those who might participate. Sponsorship of NASCAR by Interstate Batteries involves highlighting the partnership in advertising and public relations efforts.

Advertising at the Event

Sponsors insist on placement of the company's name and logo and other product information in every advertisement and brochure for the event. Many attendees of games and events keep programs as souvenirs. Placing the sponsor's name and message on the program generates an advertisement with a longer lifespan. The sponsoring business maximizes brand-name exposure by connecting the firm's name with the event's marketing program. The marketing team works closely with the event management team to make sure the company's name receives prominent attention in all materials associated with the occasion.

Tracking Results

Some events and sponsorships turn out better than others. To find the best opportunities, the marketing team tracks results. In addition to sales, employees can monitor how many pieces of literature were given to attendees, the number of samples distributed, or the number of visitors to the sponsor's display booth. Further, marketing research measures brand awareness or brand image before and after the event to discover whether any new level of awareness or higher image emerged.

When Victoria's Secret launched the brand Pink, it was coupled with a unique event marketing promotion during spring break. Reaching 18- to 24-year-old females was the objective. The event began with a three-story pink box set up on a beach in Miami. Advertisements, internet postings, street teams of employees giving out fliers, aerial signs, posters in nearby hotels, and public relations press releases built excitement during the five-day countdown. Many spring breakers showed up at the pink box. They were treated to a fashion show and a live concert by No Mercy. After the concert, employees distributed Victoria's Secret Pink gift cards and the company hosted nightclub parties. The unique marketing event spurred sales of the new Pink brand and the Victoria's Secret brand. The Victoria's Secret marketing team completed the evaluation stage and discovered a significant increase in Pink brand sales in the Miami area and a dramatic rise in other Victoria's Secret brand sales.[33]

An Advertising Research Foundation study revealed that intentions to purchase increased from 11 to 52 percent among consumers who attended a brand-sponsored event. Further research suggests that purchase intentions translate into sales about half the time.[34]

Cross-Promotions

A cross-promotion with an event sponsor or other companies involved helps boost the impact of the sponsorship. A **cross-promotion** marketing event ties together companies and activities around a specific theme. Recently, eBay partnered with Sony and Baskin-Robbins to create an event called "Camp eBay." During the summer months, consumers typically go outdoors and are less likely to be logged onto the internet. Consequently, eBay's marketing team decided to go to consumers. Camp eBay was the company's first attempt at event marketing. The management team sought to create awareness of eBay and educate people who do not use the site. The program also encouraged existing buyers and sellers to be more active in the summertime.

The Camp eBay program began with the purchase of a refurbished school bus. It went on a mobile marketing tour of six high-traffic areas: the Indy 500, CMA Fan Fest, eBay Live, Taste of Chicago, the Ohio State Fair, and the Minnesota State Fair. The school bus classroom drew 52,000 people who attended 30-minute sessions about how to use eBay. Participants earned badges redeemable for prizes furnished by Sony and Baskin-Robbins. The prizes were worth a total of $85,000. In addition, eBay pitched tents at 20 Clear Channel Entertainment venues that hosted nearly 400 concerts. The impact of this event marketing program was that 45 percent of existing users increased purchases, leading to an overall increase in sales of two percent during the promotion and nine percent following the event.[35]

Sponsorship programs and event marketing have increased in popularity during the past decade due to the potential to interact with consumers on a one-to-one basis. In the future, sponsorships and event marketing tie-ins with other media, especially the internet and specifically social media, will rise. Rock concerts, boat shows, music fairs, and a wide variety of other, more specialized programs are likely to be featured. Many marketing experts believe that making contacts with customers in personalized ways that do not directly involve sales calls are valuable activities. Event marketing and sponsorship programs create those types of contacts.

International Implications

The public relations function has become increasingly valuable in the international arena for several reasons. First, the growing number of international firms creates the need to make sure people view the company positively in every country in which it conducts business.

Second, the impact of terrorism and war has heightened sensitivities between many nations. Any company conducting business in a foreign land will have a public relations officer in charge of monitoring news stories and other events so that the firm can react to negative press.

Third, at times companies suffer from negative publicity when false information is being transmitted. In China, KFC endured rumors and reports that the company was selling chickens vaccinated with unapproved antibiotics and growth hormones and that the ice used in soft drinks sold by the company contained more bacteria than toilet water. Company officials worked diligently to restore the firm's image in the minds of Chinese consumers. Volkswagen and GlaxoSmithKline created similar responses when the companies were criticized by official Chinese media sources.

Many sponsorships now include international events. Some of the more visible ones are found in sports, most notably automobile racing and soccer. Sportswear brand Adidas signed an agreement with the NBA to be the league's official supplier in Europe and worldwide. The sponsorship represents a major effort by Adidas because NBA merchandise is sold in more than 100,000 stores in 100 countries on six continents.[36]

The principles that guide the development of sponsorships domestically apply equally well to any international involvements. To fully prepare an effective sponsorship program in an international setting, the marketing team employs a cultural assimilator to ensure correct usage of a foreign language, the legality of the sponsorship, and that it does not violate any local cultural norms. As the world continues to become smaller, with increasing interactions between countries, companies, and individuals, the growth of multinational sponsorships should continue.

objective 13.7

How can companies adapt public relations programs, sponsorships, and event marketing to international settings?

▼ Basketball has become a popular sponsorship for international brands.

))) INTEGRATED Campaigns in Action

▲ Skyjacker uses an integrated marketing approach to reach both consumers and channel members.

SKYJACKER

Skyjacker was established in 1974 in West Monroe, Louisiana. The company manufactures suspension lift kits and shocks for four-wheel-drive trucks, SUVs, and Jeeps. The kits and shocks are sold to warehouse distributors and distributed internationally. Skyjacker provides retailers and jobbers with point-of-purchase displays and a strong integrated marketing campaign to pull the products through the various channels. Skyjacker engages in both consumer and trade promotions and advertising. Skyjacker uses television and print advertising to sell the products to consumers. The company sponsors drivers and various off-road events. To support the retailers who sell the products, Skyjacker budgets money for trade advertising and trade support.

Include the following blurb with rule around at the end of the Integrated Campaigns in Action. Follow font style of other MML blurbs for MML font.

Summary

The public relations department plays a major role in an integrated marketing communications program, whether the department is separate from marketing or combined as part of a communications division. Public relations efforts are oriented to making sure that every possible contact point delivers a positive and unified message on behalf of the company.

Any person or group with a vested interest in the organization's activities is a stakeholder. Employees and various employee groups are internal stakeholders. External publics include members of the marketing channel, customers, the media, the local community, financial institutions, the government, and special interest groups.

To reach all intended audiences, the public relations department has a series of tools available. These include company newsletters, internal messages, public relations releases, correspondence with stockholders, annual reports, social media posts, and various special events. A bulletin board in the company's break room can be used to convey messages to internal stakeholders.

In the attempt to build a more favorable company image, the public relations department develops special events, such as altruistic activities and cause-related marketing programs. Care must be taken to make certain these acts are not perceived with cynicism and skepticism. This means being certain that any good deed matches with the company's products and other marketing efforts. A natural fit between an altruistic event and the company's brand is more readily accepted by various members of the public.

The public relations team tends to damage control when negative publicity arises. Proactive and reactive tactics help maintain a positive company image. Damage-control tactics include internet interventions, crisis management programs, and impression management techniques.

Sponsorship programs enhance and build the company's image and brand loyalty. A sponsorship of an individual or group involved in an activity—whether a sporting event, a contest, or a performance by an artistic group—can be used to link the company's name with the popularity of the player involved. Sponsorships should match a firm's products and brands.

Event marketing occurs when a firm sponsors an event. A strong physical presence at the event is one of the keys to successfully linking an organization's name with a program. To do so, the firm determines the major objective of the sponsorship, matches it with company customers and publics, and ensures that the firm's name is prominently displayed on all event literature.

Managing public relations, sponsorships, and event marketing programs requires company leaders to assess the goals and the outcomes of individual activities. A cost/benefit approach may not always be feasible, but the marketing team should be able to track some form of change, whether it is increased inquiries, the number of samples passed out at an event, or a shift in the tenor of news articles about the organization. The public relations department serves as the organization's watchdog, making sure those who come in contact with the company believe the firm is working to do things right and to do the right things.

Key Terms

public relations (PR) department A unit in a firm that manages publicity and other communications with all of the groups that make contact with the company

hit The mention of a company's name in a news story

stakeholder A person or group with a vested interest in a firm's activities and well-being

corporate social responsibility An organization's obligation to be ethical, accountable, and reactive to the needs of society

purpose marketing (pro-social marketing) Promoting a brand or company by focusing on values, behavior, and beliefs of the company to sell the company's products

cause-related marketing Matching marketing efforts with some type of charity work or program

green marketing The development and promotion of products that are environmentally safe

greenwashing Activities presented as being green or environmentally friendly that are not

damage control Reacting to negative events caused by a company error, consumer grievances, or unjustified or exaggerated negative press

entitlings Attempts to claim responsibility for positive outcomes of events

enhancements Attempts to increase the impact of a desirable outcome of an event in the eyes of the public

internet interventions Confronting negative publicity on the internet, either in website news releases or by entering chat rooms, blogs, or social networks

crisis management Either accepting the blame for an event and offering an apology or refuting those making the charges in a forceful manner

apology strategy Presenting a full apology when the firm has made an error

impression management The conscious or unconscious attempt to control images projected in real or imagined social situations

sponsorship marketing When the company pays money to sponsor someone or some group that is participating in an activity

event marketing When a company pays money to sponsor an event or program

cross-promotion A marketing event that ties together companies and activities around a specific theme

MyMarketingLab

To complete the problems with the ⭐ in your MyLab, go to the end-of-chapter Discussion Questions.

Review Questions

13-1. Describe the role of the public relations department. How is it related to the marketing department? Should both departments be called the "department of communications?" Why or why not?

13-2. What is a stakeholder?

13-3. Name the major internal stakeholders in organizations.

13-4. Name the major external stakeholders in organizations. Describe each one's major interest in the company.

13-5. What is corporate social responsibility? How is it related to public relations activities?

13-6. What is cause-related marketing? How can company leaders create effective cause-related marketing programs?

13-7. What is green marketing? How do different companies promote environmentally friendly activities?

13-8. What is greenwashing?

13-9. What reactive damage-control techniques are available to the public relations team?

13-10. Describe entitlings and enhancements.

13-11. What five elements are parts of an apology strategy?

13-12. What four forms of impression management are used to combat negative events?

13-13. What is sponsorship marketing?

13-14. Describe an event marketing program. What must accompany the event in order to make it a success?

13-15. What are cross-promotions? How are they related to event marketing programs?

13-16. How are public relations programs and sponsorships adapted to international companies?

Critical Thinking Exercises

DISCUSSION QUESTIONS

13-17. Watch the news on television, read a local news story, or access the internet for a story about a local or national business. Was the report positive or negative? Did the news report or article affect your attitude toward the company? Watch one of the many special investigative shows, such as *60 Minutes*. What companies did it investigate?

13-18. Locate a newscast or news article that presents negative information about a company or brand. Describe the information on the newscast or news article. How should the company respond to the negative story? Justify your response.

13-19. One of the vice presidents of a small but highly respected bank in a local community was charged with sexual harassment by a female employee. What types of communications should be prepared for each of the internal and external stakeholders listed in the chapter? Which stakeholders would be the most important to contact? Why?

13-20. Is the local community important to a manufacturing firm that sells 99 percent of its products outside the area? Does it really matter what the local people say or believe about the manufacturer as long as the firm's customers are happy? Explain your answer.

13-21. Assume you are a marketing intern for a local clothing boutique retail store. List the benefits of cause-related marketing for the retail store. Identify two causes in your community you think the store should

become involved with. Explain why. Should the clothing retailer become involved in green marketing? Why or why not? Identify at least one way the store could become involved in green marketing.

13-22. What causes do you support or are special to you? Do you know which corporations sponsor or support the causes? If not, see if you can find literature or websites that contain that information. Why do you think corporations choose a particular cause to support? What benefits do corporations receive from sponsorships?

13-23. When Starbucks opened its first coffee shop inside a public library, ten percent of all proceeds from coffee sold there went to support the operation of the library. Describe the benefits to Starbucks of this type of sponsorship. What benefits accrue to the library? Some consumers feel this type of sponsorship is inappropriate because it involves a for-profit company selling products in a government entity. Examine the various methods of damage control. Which method or methods should a library use to reduce the criticism and to prevent any negative fallout? Justify your choice.

13-24. In your own words, describe the steps in an apology strategy. Suppose a local retailer's computer system was hacked and a large number of credit card numbers were stolen. Go through each of the steps in the apology strategy explaining the actions or information for this local retailer. Be specific.

13-25. Managers are often the most difficult group for the public relations department to reach. To entice employees to reach departmental goals, managers often communicate using memos or verbal messages. These messages may conflict with the IMC theme. For example, in an effort to trim costs, a manager may send a memo to all employees telling them to only use standard production procedures. Through verbal communications, employees learn that anyone caught violating or even bending the policy to satisfy a customer will be immediately reprimanded. The manager's action suggests that even though he wants employees to provide customer service, in actuality, they had better not do anything that is not authorized. Employees soon get the message that management only cares about costs, not customers. Any advertising message about customer service will be perceived by employees as a big joke. Write a memo to employees that will support the IMC goal of high customer service, yet alert them to the need to follow standard operating procedures. Is there anything else you would do to ensure that this is not a conflicting message being sent to employees?

13-26. The shortage of funds for universities and colleges has led many university leaders to consider using sponsorships to generate revenues. What would you think about your university having stadiums and sports teams sponsored by various corporations? Discuss the pros and cons of your school using corporate sponsors to fund athletics.

Integrated Learning Exercises

13-27. Although some firms handle public relations activities internally, many firms retain public relations firms to work on special projects and to handle unique situations. The Public Relations Society of America (PRSA) is one of the major associations for PR practitioners. In Canada, the primary association is the Canadian Public Relations Society (CPRS). Access the websites of these two organizations at **www.prsa.org** and **www.cprs.ca**. What types of information does each provide? What types of services are offered? How would these organizations be beneficial to various companies?

13-28. Access the online version of *PRWeek* at **www.prweek.com**. What type of information is available? How would this site be valuable to a PR practitioner? How could it be used by a firm seeking a public relations agency? How could it be used by a marketing manager?

13-29. The American Institute of Philanthropy ranks many charities. Access the website at **www.charitywatch.org**. How does the Institute rate the charities? How can this information be used by a company to determine which charities to support?

13-30. Pick two causes that you have been involved with or support. Go to the American Institute of Philanthropy at **www.charitywatch.org**. Write a report on each of the causes you identified providing the charities' ratings, governance and transparency, analysts' notes, salaries, and alerts or articles. Which of the two appears to be the best for your support? Explain why. (If one or both of the causes you support are not listed at **www.charitywatch.org**, then pick two that are listed.)

13-31. A number of companies offer services to help firms plan and develop sponsorships. One company is IEG. Access the website at **www.sponsorship.com**. Review the site. Access each of the menu tabs and describe the information on each page. What types of services does IEG offer? If you were the marketing manager for a company that wanted to develop a sponsorship program, how could IEG help? Be specific.

13-32. A number of companies participate in sponsorship and event marketing. Access the following agencies. What type of services does each offer? What is your evaluation of each of the companies? If you were hosting an event in your community, which company would you hire? Why?
   a. GMR Marketing (**gmrmarketing.com**)
   b. Tandem Partnerships (**tandempartnerships.com**)
   c. EMC Outdoor (**www.emcoutdoor.com**)

13-33. Corporate sponsorships are important to nonprofits. Without the financial assistance provided, many nonprofits would not exist. Look up two organizations from the following list of nonprofits. Who are their corporate sponsors? What benefits do the profit-seeking companies receive from these sponsorships?
   a. American Cancer Society (**www.cancer.org**)
   b. Arthritis Foundation (**www.arthritis.org**)
   c. Multiple Sclerosis Society (**www.mssociety.org.uk**)
   d. United Cerebral Palsy (**www.ucp.org**)
   e. Alliance for the Wild Rockies (**www.wildrockiesalliance.org**)
   f. National Wildlife Federation (**www.nwf.org**)
   g. Trout Unlimited (**www.tu.org**)

Blog Exercises

Access the authors' blog for this textbook at the URLs provided to complete these exercises. Answer the questions that are posed on the blog.

13-34. Interstate Batteries — **blogclowbaack.net/2014/05/05/interstate-batteries-chapter-13/**

13-35. Adidas — **blogclowbaack.net/2014/05/05/adidas-chapter-13/**

13-36. Crisis Management — **blogclowbaack.net/2014/05/05/crisis-management-chapter-13/**

Student Project

CREATIVE CORNER

Circle K Ranch has been selling, training, and boarding horses for almost 20 years. With the recent downturn in the economy, however, Circle K experienced a decline in all facets of its business. In talking with some marketing students at the local university, the owner of Circle K Ranch, Kathy Kroncke, wondered about using cause-related marketing, sponsorships, and even event marketing to boost the awareness and image of her business. She recently added horseback riding to her list of services and developed a 10-mile ride that goes through a local state park. So far, business has not been what she expected, despite research that indicated a high level of interest in riding, especially by 15- to 40-year-old females. Design a cause-related marketing program, a sponsorship program, and an event marketing program for Circle K Ranch. After you have designed each of the programs, choose the one you think would be the best for Circle K Ranch. Design a newspaper ad featuring the program. What other methods would you use, both traditional and nontraditional, to publicize the program you chose?

CASE 1   ADVERTISING ON NBA JERSEYS: IS IT WORTH IT?

In 2016, the National Basketball Association announced that, for the first time, individual teams would be allowed to include advertising on the jerseys of each team. The move corresponds with a switch from jerseys made by Nike that replaced those made by Adidas. The new jerseys would include the Nike Swoosh for every team, except the Charlotte Hornets, which would instead feature the Brand Jordan logo, because the Hornets are owned by Michael Jordan.

NBA commissioner Adam Silver stated that "enormous uncertainty" surrounded the decision, noting that some fans may wish to see jerseys remain commercial free. Merchandising programs would create some jerseys for fans without the advertising and others containing the messages, which would be limited to a 2.5 by 2.5 inch space. Further, the advertising program was limited to a three-year trial period. "There's a reason this is a pilot program," Silver said. "We listen very closely to our fans."

Many professional sports incorporate ads in various ways. NASCAR automobiles are covered with company names and logos. Pro golfers wear caps and shirts promoting various brands. Internationally, many soccer teams carry the names of companies.

At the same time, purists may resist the temptation to sell what amounts to a small amount of revenue for teams and players. Estimates were that ads would generate about $100 million

▲ The NBA will now allow advertising on team jerseys.

annually, a small total when compared to the estimated $7 billion that would be otherwise earned in the inaugural season of the program. Silver noted that the advertising revenues would be shared between teams and players.

Two potential complications immediately appeared. First, a player might endorse a specific brand, such as Reebok, and not wish to wear the logo of competing company like Nike. Second, a specific brand may violate the personal principles of a player.

For example, what if Arby's wished to buy jersey advertising but a player's religious faith or personal preferences prohibits and resists eating meat? Should that player be required to wear the jersey carrying the ad?

Although such questions will require resolution, Silver noted, "The media landscape is changing. People are watching less live television outside of sports. People are watching fewer commercials. This will become an important opportunity for companies for connecting directly with their consumers." Consequently, a new era in sponsorship marketing has begun.[37]

13-37. Describe the stakeholders and the positions of each group involved in this story.

13-38. Which would have been a more valuable approach: To allow for-profit advertising on jerseys or to instead feature cause-related messages, such as for cancer research or anti-drug and -violence messages?

13-39. How should NBA league officials respond to complaints about the program?

13-40. What should happen when a player does not wish to have a particular advertising appear on his jersey?

CASE 2 OLIVE GARDEN: MEET THE GIRLS NEXT DOOR

Public relations challenges come in many forms, some expected and others that could never be imagined. The Olive Garden has developed a strong brand and corporate image focused on family, friends, and fun. The company was launched as a subsidiary of General Mills as an entry into the casual Italian restaurant marketplace. The initial success and growth led to a spin-off, and Darden Restaurants has directed the chain since the early 1990s.

Olive Garden restaurants are distinctive, featuring a casual Italian decor. The menus have been upgraded to move beyond more basic dishes to include items such as Mediterranean Garlic Shrimp and Capellini Pomodoro. Chefs continue to look for ways to treat regular customers to new and exciting dishes to accompany old favorites. All the while, endless bowls of salad and servings of breadsticks, along with tasty servings of soup, are part of the regular fare.

The wholesome family atmosphere projected in the Olive Garden's marketing messages includes the term "Hospitaliano," which suggests the commitment to a warm, comfortable environment for dining. Commercials and advertisements carrying the tagline "When you're here, you're family" have helped Olive Garden establish a strong brand presence in a highly competitive marketplace.

The Girls Next Door recently emerged as a popular television program on E! Entertainment Television. The show featured three beautiful young women who lived in Hugh Hefner's exotic Playboy mansion. In 2008, more than 1.4 million viewers watched the antics of the young women in various stages of dress and settings. One of the three, Kendra Wilkinson, happens to be a genuine fan of the Olive Garden. During one program, she mentioned how much she loved the artichoke dip and breadsticks. She quickly became known as practically a "new spokesperson" for the company.

Without question, Kendra's affection for the Olive Garden was sincere. As she noted, "I love the Olive Garden because I grew up going there. That used to be the place we would go for Mother's Day, for birthdays. My grandpa just died, and right after his funeral, we went to the Olive Garden." She pointed out when asked that

▲ The Olive Garden has communicated an image of being a wholesome family restaurant.

she received no compensation for mentioning the restaurant on *The Girls Next Door*.

Ms. Wilkinson did convince Hefner to create a contest. Women were invited to compete for a chance to become one of the "Sexiest Girls of Olive Garden." The winner was to receive a Playboy photo shoot conducted by Kendra Wilkinson for an upcoming edition of the magazine.

Olive Garden's management and marketing team faced a dilemma. On the one hand, a surprising overlap exists between the types of individuals who dine at the Olive Garden and those who watch *The Girls Next Door*. Many are college-educated, affluent, and enjoy upscale dining. More women watch the television program than men, and more women dine at the Olive Garden than men.

At the other extreme, protests have been lodged against the television show. The Florida Family Association had encouraged advertisers to stop buying spots for the show. Playboy has long been a source of controversy in the United States.

From the Olive Garden's perspective, the publicity generated by the linkage between the two organizations could have been viewed as a blessing or a curse. At first, the company did not make official statements about the contest. Undoubtedly, the marketing and public relations teams believed the company was navigating through some very choppy waters.[38]

13-41. Who are Olive Garden's internal and external stakeholders that have been affected by this turn of events?

13-42. For casual observers of media, would the "Sexiest Girls of Olive Garden" appear to be a sponsorship?

13-43. Is this event an instance in which damage-control programs were in order? If so, which one(s)?

13-44. Kendra Wilkinson said she believed Olive Garden could afford to appear to be a little "edgy" without detracting from its family-friendly brand. Do you agree or disagree? Why?

13-45. If you were the public relations agency for the Olive Garden, how would you handle this situation? What steps would you take and what tactics would you use to ensure Olive Garden's image is not adversely affected?

Sources: Angela Zimm and Justin Blum, "FDA Approves Merck's Cervical Cancer Vaccine," *Boston Globe* and *Bloomberg News* (**www.boston.com/business/healthcare/articles**, accessed January 28, 2008), June 9, 2006; Rob Stein, "Cervical Cancer Vaccine Gets Injected with a Social Issue," *Washington Post* (**www.washingtonpost.com/wp-dyn**, accessed January 28, 2008), October 31, 2005.

MyMarketingLab

Go to the Assignments section of your MyLab to complete these writing exercises.

13-46. When Starbucks opened its first coffee shop inside a public library, ten percent of all proceeds from coffee sold there went to support the operation of the library. Describe the benefits to Starbucks of this type of sponsorship. What benefits accrue to the library? Some consumers feel this type of sponsorship is inappropriate because it involves a for-profit company selling products in a government entity. Examine the various methods of damage control. Which method or methods should a library use to reduce the criticism and to prevent any negative fallout? Justify your choice.

13-47. You are the new marketing intern for a local CPA accounting firm that has both business and consumer customers. List the steps in selecting a sponsorship or event. Identify a sponsorship or event in your community that you believe would be a good fit for the CPA firm. Explain why. For each of the steps you listed, discuss how it would apply to the CPA firm. For instance, for determining objective, what objective do you think is relevant based on the event or sponsorship you picked? Do the same for each of the other steps.

Chapter 14

Regulations and Ethical Concerns

Chapter Objectives

After reading this chapter, you should be able to answer the following questions:

14.1 Which agencies and laws regulate marketing communications?

14.2 What are the relationships between puffery, deception, and substantiation?

14.3 What legal remedies can agencies use to correct deceptive communications practices?

14.4 How do the three major industry regulatory agencies help keep advertising and business practices from injuring customers or other businesses?

14.5 What ethical criticisms have been registered against advertising and marketing practices?

14.6 Which marketing tactics raise ethical concerns?

14.7 How can marketers apply the various ethical frameworks and ethics programs to their activities and actions?

14.8 What international issues influence the discussion of legal and ethical marketing activities?

MyMarketingLab™

⭐ **Improve Your Grade!**

Over 10 million students improved their results using the Pearson MyLabs. Visit **mymktlab.com** for simulations, tutorials, and end-of-chapter problems.

Overview

The final level of an IMC program concentrates on making certain the communications program meets ethical and legal requirements and that effective evaluation of activities takes place. This part of the text will examine these topics. Figure 14.1 displays the completion of an IMC program.

The fields of marketing and marketing communications have long been the subject of scrutiny from the general public, special interest groups, and the government. This may not be surprising. In marketing and sales, people spend money on purchases. Many individuals and organizations express concern about the public trust and the well-being of the community. When companies sell goods and services that can injure people or cause harm in some other way, criticisms and legal actions likely will follow.

REEBOK PAYS $25-MILLION SETTLEMENT

The running shoe and sport shoe industry has dealt with criticism and concern for years. Complaints have been made regarding the high prices of shoes, the foreign labor used to produce them, and the strong amount of social pressure parents and children face to purchase the most fashionable and cutting-edge models.

Recently, Reebok encountered another controversy. The company's EasyTone and RunTone product lines in the toning shoes market feature a rounded or otherwise unstable sole. Companies including Reebok, New Balance, and Skechers make such shoes, claiming they force wearers to use more muscle to maintain balance while working out. Reebok sold more than five million pairs in the United States and 10 million abroad. Toning shoes became a $1.1 billion market in a short period of time.

In ads for the EasyTone and RunTone lines, Reebok made specific claims. A commercial featuring a super-fit woman assured viewers that EasyTone sneakers strengthen hamstrings and calves by up to 11 percent and tone one's butt (gluteus maximus muscles) "up to 28 percent more than regular sneakers, just by walking." One critic wondered how Reebok planned to back up such a claim.

Not long after, the Federal Trade Commission (FTC) ordered Reebok to pay a $25 million settlement, ruling the company made an unsupported advertising claim. David Vladeck, director of the FTC's Bureau of Consumer Protection, said, "The FTC wants national advertisers to understand that they must exercise some responsibility and ensure that their claims for fitness gear are supported by sound science."

Reebok maintained its stance regarding the shoes, stating that "We stand behind our EasyTone technology." A spokesperson suggested it was the first product in the toning category to be inspired by balance-ball training and stated that settling did not mean the company agreed with the FTC's allegations. Citing enthusiastic feedback from EasyTone customers, company leaders said they would remain committed to the further development of the EasyTone line of products.

Reebok was not the only company admonished by the FTC. Skechers agreed to pay $41 million regarding advertising and marketing of a similar product. In both situations, the Federal Trade Commission concluded that the claims companies made were misleading.[1]

This chapter examines two interrelated topics. The first part features a description of the legal environment surrounding marketing and marketing communications. The second part presents views of ethics, morals, and social responsibility as they relate to marketing, advertising, and promotions. Those involved in marketing programs consider both the letter of the law—regulations and other legal limitations—as well as the spirit of the law. Guided by both personal principles and organizational guidelines, marketing professionals work to ensure that their actions are both legal and ethical.

▶ **FIGURE 14.1**
Integrated Marketing
Communications

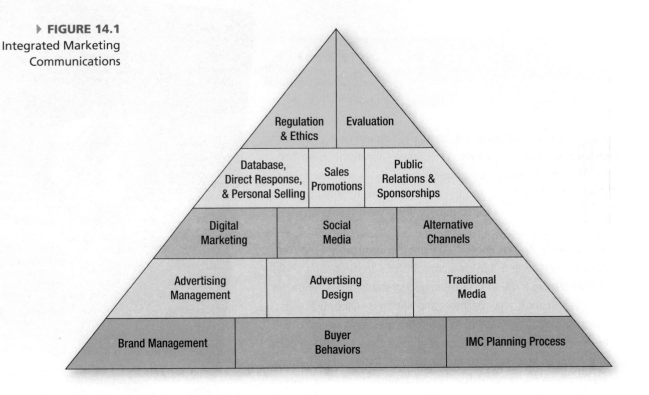

Marketing Communications Regulations

objective **14.1**

Which agencies and laws regulate marketing communications?

The U.S. federal government has enacted considerable legislation designed to prevent companies from taking unfair advantage of consumers and other businesses. Various states regulate for-profit companies and other organizations. Several regulatory agencies enforce many federal and state laws. This section reviews governmental actions in the areas of legislation and regulation of company marketing practices (see Figure 14.2).

Governmental Regulatory Agencies

Governmental agencies serve as watchdogs to monitor for potential violations of the law, some of which are only partially related to marketing. For example, the Food and Drug Administration (FDA) regulates and oversees the packaging and labeling of products. The FDA also monitors advertising on food packages and advertisements for drugs, yet its primary responsibilities involve ensuring food quality and drug safety.

▼ The FCC monitors advertising directed toward children.

The Federal Communications Commission (FCC) regulates television, radio, and the telephone industry. The FCC grants (and revokes) operating licenses for radio and television stations. The FCC also holds jurisdiction over telephone companies. The FCC does not have jurisdiction over the content of advertisements transmitted by mass media. Further, the FCC does not control which products may be advertised; however, the organization does monitor advertising directed toward children. FCC rules limit television stations to 12 minutes per hour of children's advertisements during weekdays and 10 minutes per hour on weekends. Recently, Viacom agreed to pay $1 million for programming on Nickelodeon that violated the time limitation 600 times in the span of one year.[2]

* Food and Drug Administration (FDA)
* Federal Communications Commission (FCC)
* U.S. Postal Service (USPS)
* Bureau of Alcohol, Tobacco and Firearms (ATF)
* Federal Trade Commission (FTC)

◄ **FIGURE 14.2**
Government Regulatory Agencies

The U.S. Postal Service (USPS) holds jurisdiction over mailed marketing materials. The USPS investigates mail fraud schemes and other fraudulent marketing practices. The Bureau of Alcohol, Tobacco, Firearms and Explosives (ATF) rules when the sale, distribution, and advertising of alcohol and tobacco are at issue.

The Federal Trade Commission

Ordinarily, the governmental agency that examines incidents involving any potentially deceptive or misleading marketing tactics is the **Federal Trade Commission, or FTC**, which was created in 1914 by the passage of the Federal Trade Commission Act. The FTC presides over marketing communications. The act's original intent was to create a federal agency to enforce antitrust laws and to protect businesses from one another. It had little authority over advertising and marketing communications except when an advertisement was considered to be unfair to the competition, thereby restricting free trade.

Unfair and Deceptive Marketing Practices

In 1938, Congress passed the Wheeler–Lea Amendment to Section 5 of the Federal Trade Commission Act to increase and expand the authority of the FTC and to prohibit false and misleading advertising. The agency gained the authority to stop unfair or deceptive advertising practices and to levy fines when necessary. The law provided the FTC access to the courts to enforce the law and ensure that violators abide by FTC rulings.

A firm can violate the act even when the company did not expressly intend to deceive. An advertisement or communication is deemed to be deceptive or misleading when:

1. A substantial number of people or the "typical person" is left with a false impression or misrepresentation that relates to the product.
2. The misrepresentation induces people or the "typical person" to make a purchase.

Consumers may be misled by advertisements, mailings, corporate literature, labels, packaging, website materials, and oral or written statements made by salespeople. This gives the government a great deal of latitude in dealing with deceptive practices.

Deception versus Puffery

Puffery can be legally featured in advertisements and marketing messages. **Puffery** exists when a firm makes an exaggerated statement about its goods or services. The difference between puffery and a claim, in terms of the FTC and the courts, is that puffery does not constitute a *factual statement*. In contrast, a *claim* makes a factual statement that can be proven true or false. Firms may make puffery statements without proving them; claims must be substantiated or proven in some manner.

objective 14.2
What are the relationships between puffery, deception, and substantiation?

Terms associated with puffery include words such as *friendliest, best, greatest*, and *finest*. A firm can advertise "our brand is the best" or "our signature dishes use only the finest ingredients." A Gillette ad for the ProGlide razor states it is "The best a man can get." A Smirnoff ad contains the headline "The world's most liked vodka." Starbucks promotes "The best coffee for the best you." Courts and the regulatory agencies view these statements as puffery. They conclude that consumers expect firms to use the terms routinely in advertisements. In this section, the advertisement for Karns Foods calling the company the "Home of Pennsylvania's Best Meat Department" constitutes puffery. Such a statement cannot be proven true or false but rather expresses an opinion.

▶ This Interstate Batteries billboard advertisement provides an example of using puffery by stating its products are "outrageously dependable."

The word *best* will normally be accepted as puffery. The word *better* has been construed to imply a comparison. The term has recently been tested through the FTC, the National Advertising Division of the Better Business Bureau, and the courts. Papa John's Pizza's use of the phrase "Better Ingredients, Better Pizza" was found to be puffery, as was the phrase "Only the best tomatoes grow up to be Hunt's."

In another situation, Progresso stated "Discover the Better Taste of Progresso" in company advertisements. The slogan was challenged by Campbell's Soup Company. Progresso's legal team argued that "better taste" constituted puffery. Representatives for Campbell's contended that taste tests can be used to determine if one food product tastes better than others. The courts agreed and ordered Progresso to either modify the phrase or prove that Progresso soups do taste better.[3]

Many food providers have begun using words such as "wholesome, fresh, natural, and local" to avoid scrutiny by the FTC that was created by ads making health-related claims. Such vague words have no specific marketing-related meaning. In addition, consumers accept them. Darren Tristano, vice president at Technomic, commented, "More-traditional health claims on the menu tend to get adverse reactions by the customer because they associate healthy claims with less taste. The newer descriptors are designed around the idea that the food is better for you."[4]

Substantiation of Marketing Claims

Substantiation means that an advertising claim or promise must be proven with data, facts, or through competent and reliable evidence. Failure to do so can result in a lawsuit or governmental action. The concept of substantiation does not apply to puffery.

An advertisement featuring an endorser must contain truthful statements representing the person's experiences or opinions. When a commercial includes an expert

▼ This advertisement for Karns Foods uses puffery by stating it is the "Best Meat Department."

◀ Southwest General Hospital features puffery in this advertisement by stating its heart care is first and "second to none."

endorsement, the statements must be based on legitimate tests performed by professionals in the field. In the advertisement for Skyjacker shown in this section, reality TV star of *Duck Dynasty* Willie Robertson states, "I've spent my life in the swamps of Louisiana. Skyjacker helps me look at ruts in my rearview mirror."

All marketing claims must reflect the typical experience a customer would expect to encounter from the use of a good or service, unless the advertisement clearly and prominently states otherwise. A few years ago, a Kleenex Cottonelle advertisement claimed that the product was softer. Kleenex provided actual touch tests by consumers as evidence. The company then used engineering and lab tests to show that Kleenex tissue consists of 24 percent more cottony, soft fiber. Thus, Kleenex substantiated the claim. Substantiation may not always be easy. To increase the probability the substantiation will be accepted by the FTC and courts, company leaders use the following principles:[5]

▼ A Skyjacker advertisement featuring Willie Robertson of *Duck Dynasty* as an endorser.

1. The federal government assumes consumers read ads broadly and do not pay much attention to fine print and qualifying language. Thus, hiding a qualifier at the bottom of the ad or using words such as *usually, normally,* or *under typical situations* somewhere in the ad is not normally accepted as substantiation.

2. The evidence has to be for the exact product being tested, not for a similar product, regardless of the similarity.

3. Evidence should come from or be accepted by experts in the relevant area of the product and considered valid and reliable by the experts. Studies conducted by the company or something found on the internet is not acceptable.

4. The FTC and courts consider the totality of the evidence. If the company has one study that supports the claim but there are four studies by other independent organizations that indicate something different, then the evidence will not be accepted as valid substantiation.

Regardless of the type of communication, the FTC prohibits unfair or deceptive marketing communications. Marketers must substantiate claims through competent and reliable evidence. Unfortunately, a great deal of gray area exists between puffery and a claim that must be substantiated. Consequently, lawsuits are filed and governmental agencies are required to address complaints and suspected violations of the law. These agencies and their rulings strongly affect individual marketing practices as well as company actions.

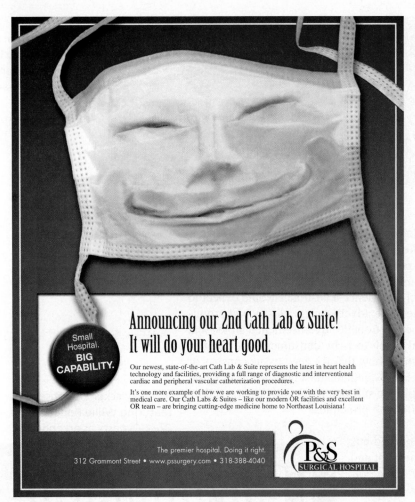

▲ The claim in this advertisement that P & S Surgical Hospital is "the premier hospital" was substantiated through two different patient surveys.

objective 14.3

What legal remedies can agencies use to correct deceptive communications practices?

How Investigations Begin

An investigation into misleading or deceptive advertising can be triggered in a number of ways. Sources of complaints can be registered by:

- Consumers
- Businesses
- Congress
- The media

Each can raise questions about what appears to be an unfair or deceptive practice. Investigations by the FTC remain confidential at first, which protects the agency and the company.

Consent Orders

When the FTC believes a law has been violated, it issues a **consent order**. Company leaders who sign consent orders agree to stop a disputed practice without admitting guilt.

ADT signed consent agreements with the FTC concerning three spokespersons for the company's security system. These spokespersons were conveyed as independent experts and appeared on NBC's *Today Show*, other TV shows, radio news programs, and blogs promoting ADT's Pulse security systems. Although the ads portrayed the spokespersons to be independent experts, each was paid by ADT's public relations department. One received more than $300,000, another more than $200,000, and the endorsers were given security systems with monitoring free of charge. Under the consent agreement, ADT agreed to make it clear ADT paid these experts. ADT had to remove reviews and endorsements from the brand's website and blog that misrepresented the individuals as independent reviewers and disclose any reviews or endorsements when there was any type of material connection with ADT.[6]

FTC Settlements

Occasionally, rather than agreeing to a consent order, company leaders accept a settlement with the FTC. This occurred with retailer Lord & Taylor over a campaign to promote the Design Lab collection. The campaign included a native advertising article in online fashion magazines and posts from 50 social media fashion influencers to various social media platforms. None of the social media influencers indicated they were being compensated by Lord & Taylor and the native article did not state it was a paid advertisement from Lord & Taylor. The settlement with the FTC prohibited Lord & Taylor from misrepresenting its paid native advertising as being from an independent or objective source and that all social media influencers must reveal they are being compensated by Lord & Taylor for endorsing the fashions.[7]

Administrative Complaints

Most FTC investigations end with the signing of a consent order or settlement. When one cannot be reached, the FTC issues an **administrative complaint**. At that point, a formal proceeding similar to a court trial will be held before an administrative law judge. Both sides submit evidence and render testimony. At the end of the administrative hearing, the judge makes a ruling. When the judge concludes a violation of the law has occurred, a *cease and desist order* is issued. The order requires the company to stop the disputed practice immediately and refrain from similar practices in the future. A company that is not satisfied with the decision of the administrative law judge can appeal the case to the full FTC commission.

The *full commission* holds hearings similar to those before administrative law judges. Rulings follow presentations of evidence and testimony. Any company that is dissatisfied with the ruling of the full FTC commission can appeal the case to the U.S. Court of Appeals and further, to the highest level, the U.S. Supreme Court. The danger to a company that appeals a case is that consumer redress can be sought at that point. This means any company found guilty of violating laws might be ordered to pay civil penalties.

▲ Lord & Taylor reached a settlement with the FTC over a campaign promoting its Design Lab collection.

Courts and Legal Channels

Occasionally, the FTC uses the court system to stop unfair and deceptive advertising and marketing communications practices. This takes place when a company violates previous FTC cease and desist orders or when the negative effects of a company's activities are so severe that they require immediate action. The latter occurred in a case involving the National Consumer Council (NCC), a debt reduction and negotiation firm based in Santa Ana, California. The FTC investigation found that the National Consumer Council encouraged consumers to stop paying their debts once they signed up with NCC for debt reduction. At the same time, NCC did not normally start negotiation with debtors for six months. By then, the customer's debtors were irate and not willing to negotiate. In the meantime, the NCC customer had made payments into a fund at NCC. Charges and monthly fees were being withdrawn for payment to NCC. Many customers did not know NCC was making the charges. Eventually, the customers discovered that not only did NCC ruin their credit ratings, but they were also deeper in debt than when they signed on. Almost all of them were forced to declare bankruptcy. Due to the severity of NCC's activities, the FTC obtained a restraining order from a federal court to immediately close NCC's operation. The FTC also obtained a restraining order against the London Financial Group, which provided telemarketing, accounting, and management services to NCC.[8]

The FTC works with other legal entities such as state and federal attorneys general. The FTC, Orange County (CA) district attorney, and the California State Attorney investigated Body Wise International, Inc., for false and deceptive advertising and for violating a consent agreement between Body Wise International and the FTC that had previously been signed. The complaint against Body Wise involved the alleged medical benefits of a product called "AI/E-10." Body Wise International advertised that AI/E-10 could prevent, treat, and cure diseases such as cancer, HIV/AIDS, and asthma. Body Wise supported these claims through the testimony of a physician, Dr. Stoff. The FTC investigation revealed that Stoff received royalties for every bottle sold and that he could not provide medical substantiation for any of the claims. The FTC order banned Body Wise International from making the claims and prohibited Stoff from misrepresenting the tests and studies of AI/E-10. In the final settlement, Body Wise International agreed to pay $2 million to the FTC in civil penalties and $1.5 million in other penalties. The final agreement contained a $358,000 monetary judgment against Dr. Stoff.[9]

1. Investigation
   - Consent order or FTC settlement
2. Administrative complaint
   - Cease and desist order
3. Full commission hearing
4. U.S. Court of Appeals
5. U.S. Supreme Court

▲ **FIGURE 14.3**
FTC Investigation Process.

▼ Occasionally the FTC will use the courts to stop misleading practices, which occurred with National Consumer Council (NCC) and its method of debt reduction.

Corrective Advertising

In the most severe instances of deceptive or misleading advertising, the FTC orders a firm to prepare **corrective advertisements**. These rare situations occur when the members of the FTC believe that discontinuing a false advertisement will not be sufficient. When the FTC concludes that consumers believed the false advertisement, it can require the firm to produce corrective ads to bring consumers back to a neutral state. Consumers should return to the beliefs they held prior to the false or misleading advertising.

The FTC ordered corrective advertising for the Novartis Corporation. The judgment was based on false and deceptive advertisements of a product called Doan's analgesic. During the investigation, members of the FTC concluded that Doan's claim of greater efficiency than competing products was not substantiated. The FTC ordered Novartis to immediately cease comparative advertising and to make this statement in corrective ads: "Although Doan's is an effective pain reliever, there is no evidence that Doan's is more effective than other pain relievers for back pain." Novartis was ordered to spend $8 million on corrective advertising about the statement and include the correction for one year in all advertisements, except for 15-second broadcast ads. Unhappy with the order, leaders at Novartis filed a lawsuit in federal court against the FTC; however, the federal court upheld the FTC order.[10]

▼ The FTC issued a trade regulation ruling that bloggers must reveal if they are being compensated in any way by a company when endorsing a brand.

Trade Regulation Rulings

The final type of action the FTC can take, a **trade regulation ruling**, applies to an entire industry. Normally, the commission will hold a public hearing and accepts both oral and written arguments. The commission then makes a ruling that applies to every firm within an industry. As with other FTC rulings, decisions can be challenged in the U.S. Court of Appeals.

The recent rise in personal blogs led to an explosion of product reviews by bloggers. Often, bloggers are paid or receive free merchandise to post positive comments. Blogger Jessica Smith was given a Ford Flex to use for one month plus a free gas card in exchange for a positive review. Microsoft sent bloggers a free laptop loaded with the newest Microsoft operating system. After investigating the practices, the FTC issued a ruling that bloggers who review products must disclose any connection with the advertiser or product, whether the product provided was free or if they were compensated in any way. The ruling also applies to celebrities who promote products on talk shows or on Twitter.[11]

A similar industry trade ruling occurred with gift cards issued by retailers. Many retailers charged dormancy fees for cards that were not used immediately and many cards had expiration dates. Consumers did not receive this information at the time of purchase. The FTC issued a ruling that any merchant issuing a gift card must "boldly" display any fees or expiration dates on the card.[12]

Industry Oversight of Marketing Practices

objective 14.4

How do the three major industry regulatory agencies help keep advertising and business practices from injuring customers or other businesses?

Federal regulatory agencies cannot handle all industry activity. Although industry regulatory agencies have no legal power, they reduce the load on the FTC and the legal system. The three most common and well-known industry regulatory agencies are all a part of the Council of Better Business Bureaus: the National Advertising Division, the National Advertising Review Board, and the Children's Advertising Review Unit (Figure 14.4).

Council of Better Business Bureaus

The Council of Better Business Bureaus (CBBB) provides resources to both consumers and businesses. Consumers and firms may file complaints with the bureau about unethical business practices or unfair treatment. The bureau compiles a summary of all charges leveled against individual firms. Customers seeking information about the legitimacy of a company or its operations can contact the bureau. The bureau provides a carefully worded report containing any complaints against the company and reveals the general nature of customer concerns. The Better Business Bureau helps individuals and businesses make sure they are dealing with a firm that has a low record of problems.

National Advertising Division Complaints about advertising or some aspect of marketing communications are referred to the National Advertising Division (NAD) of the Council of Better Business Bureaus for review. The NAD reviews the specific claims, and NAD lawyers collect information and evaluate data concerning the complaint to determine whether an advertiser can substantiate a claim. If not, the NAD negotiates with the advertiser to modify or discontinue the advertisement. When the firm's marketing claim can be substantiated, the NAD dismisses the complaint.

- National Advertising Division (NAD)
- National Advertising Review Board (NARB)
- Children's Advertising Review Unit (CARU)

▲ **FIGURE 14.4**
Advertising Industry Self-Regulatory Agencies

Individuals and companies may file complaints about unfair ads. Most complaints are from competing brands and deal with comparative ads. A few do not deal directly with a competitor but are the result of misleading advertising. Such was the case in a print ad for Maybelline Mascara featuring model Freja Beha Erichsen. In the ad, Erichsen's eyelashes looked impressively voluminous and, according to the copy, it was because of Maybelline's "patented supersonic jumbo brush that loads on big, sleek volume instantly" which produces lashes eight times bigger. Fine print at the bottom of the ad indicated Erichsen's eyebrows were also enhanced with lash inserts.

▲ The Better Business Bureau can provide consumers with summary reports about businesses.

After reviewing the advertisement, the NAD ruled the ad was "literally false" because the image of Erichsen was "not an accurate depiction of the volume that can be achieved by applying the mascara alone without the use of lash inserts" and therefore should be discontinued. L'Oreal, owner of the Maybelline brand, argued that at the bottom of the ad, it was disclosed the model's eyebrows were styled with lash inserts. In response, the NAD commented that it is, "axiomatic that disclosures that contradict or substantially change the main message in an advertisement are inadequate to prevent inaccurate consumer takeaways."[13]

The Maybelline decision illustrates the power of the NAD and is typical of NAD recommendations. In 95 percent of the cases in which the NAD recommends an ad be discontinued or modified, the company voluntarily complies with the decision. The NAD is not a legal entity, which means companies do not have to abide by a decision.

National Advertising Review Board When a complaint cannot be resolved by the NAD or the advertiser appeals the NAD's decision, it will be referred to the National Advertising

▼ The NAD investigated a print ad for Maybelline Mascara.

Review Board (NARB), an organization composed of advertising professionals and prominent civic individuals. When the NARB rules that the firm's advertisements cannot be substantiated, it orders the firm to discontinue the advertisements in a manner similar to a consent order by the FTC. The NARB is a private board. When the business or firm being accused refuses to accept the NARB ruling, the matter will be turned over to the FTC or the most appropriate federal regulatory agency.

The NARB also investigated a dispute between Minute Maid and Tropicana. Minute Maid was ordered to modify ads because the copy claimed that consumers preferred Minute Maid orange juice to Tropicana by a 2:1 margin. Tropicana lodged a complaint and won when it was heard by the NAD. Minute Maid disagreed with the NAD ruling and appealed to the NARB. Minute Maid complained that the decision by the NAD placed an unnecessary and unfair burden on comparative advertising, because all claims relative to a competitor must be substantiated. The National Advertising Review Board supported the NAD and issued an order for Minute Maid to comply with the ruling.[14]

Few cases are appealed to the NARB. Over a two-year period, only 19 decisions out of 339 made by the NAD were appealed to the National Advertising Review Board. None were overturned by NARB. Sixteen were upheld and in three cases part of the decision was upheld and other aspects were overturned.[15]

If a company is dissatisfied with the decision of the NARB or refuses to abide by the decision, the next step in the appeal process will be taken by the Federal Trade Commission. The NARB seldom refers a case to the FTC.

▲ The Children's Advertising Review Unit (CARU) monitors all forms of advertising directed toward children.

Children's Advertising Review Unit The Children's Advertising Review Unit (CARU) investigates and monitors all forms of advertising in all media directed toward children younger than 12 years old. It also monitors online privacy practices of websites targeted at children younger than age 13. The CARU operates in a manner similar to the NAD.

In addition to handling complaints about advertising to children, CARU began prescreening ads directed to young people. CARU examines more than 300 ads per year. The prescreening allows CARU to highlight any potential problems with an advertisement before it goes into production. CARU has also issued a series of guidelines to help advertisers prepare ads for children. Figure 14.5 highlights these guidelines.[16]

Children younger than age 12 do not have the same reasoning abilities as adults. Consequently, the CARU stresses the importance of advertisers acting responsibly. Advertisements must show a toy as if a child were playing with it. It must convey the difference between any fantasy used in a commercial and the reality when the child plays with the toy. When accessories are shown, the commercial must clearly state that the accessories do not come

- Ads for toys should not create unreasonable expectations. Toys shown in acts should look and act as they would if a child were playing with it.
- Ads should not blur the line between fantasy and reality.
- Ads should have clear and visible disclosures about what items come with a toy and what items do not.
- Items that require adult supervision must be shown with adults supervising the child.
- Products and ad content should be appropriate for children.

▶ **FIGURE 14.5**
CARU Guidelines for Advertising to Children

◀ FIGURE 14.6
Advantages of Using the CBBB to Regulate Advertising

- Lower cost
- Faster resolution
- Heard by attomeys and business professionlas with experience in advertising

with the original toy so the child will not be disappointed. If an item such as a trampoline is advertised, then adult supervision must also be shown.

Advantages to Self-Regulation   Industry-based actions are designed to control the marketing communications environment and limit legal actions that will be required by the courts or a governmental agency. As highlighted in Figure 14.6, industry regulatory agencies offer several benefits over FTC and legal remedies. Agencies normally hear cases sooner and at a lower cost to the companies involved. Further, attorneys and business professionals with experience in advertising hear the complaints. Although FTC judges may some have familiarity with the advertising industry, they often have less extensive knowledge than the individuals involved in the CBBB's agencies.

Effective management, however, is proactive rather than reactive. Company leaders can work to create an image of a socially responsible firm. This creates a far better approach than reacting to the constant scrutiny of angry consumers and regulatory agencies.

IMC and Ethics

In many instances, an advertising or marketing practice may be legal but be ethically suspect. This section considers various marketing and advertising tactics. Then ethical frameworks and responses involving them are described.

Ethics and morals constitute the key principles used to guide a person's activities in the world of commerce. **Morals** are beliefs or principles that individuals hold concerning what is right and what is wrong. **Ethics** are moral principles that serve as guidelines for both individuals and organizations. Many ethical and moral concerns affect the fields of marketing, advertising, and marketing communication. At the most general level, several major concerns and criticisms have arisen, including the items provided in Figure 14.7.

objective 14.5
What ethical criticisms have been registered against advertising and marketing practices?

Ethics and Advertising

Some critics complain that advertisements cause people to *buy more than they can afford*. This critique is closely connected to the idea that advertising *overemphasizes materialism*. A case can be made that many commercials do indeed stress luxury, social standing, and the prestige of being first to purchase an item. At the same time, the messages are still just commercials. Those who defend advertising point out those consumers should be responsible for spending money wisely.

1. Advertisements cause people to buy more than they can afford.
2. Advertising overemphasizes materialism.
3. Advertising increases the costs of goods and services.
4. Advertising perpetuates stereotyping of males, females, and minority groups.
5. Advertisements often make unsafe products, such as alcohol and tobacco, seem attractive.
6. Advertisements often are offensive.
7. Advertising to children is unethical.

◀ FIGURE 14.7
Ethical Concerns Regarding Advertising

One criticism of advertising is that it causes consumers to buy more than they can afford.

Elderly people are sometimes stereotyped in advertising.

Advertising has been alleged to *increase the costs of goods and services*. This argument has been made for many years. Advertising professionals note that without consumer awareness, products would not be purchased, because consumers would not know of their existence. Further, advertising widens the base of potential customers and may increase repeat business. Additional sales lead to economies of scale and lower prices rather than increasing them.

Perpetuating Stereotypes

Many social commentators suggest that advertising and other forms of media perpetuate stereotyping of men, women, and minority groups. This leads to several questions. For instance, is segmentation the same as stereotyping? In an era in which the term *political correctness* routinely appears, the debate defining "acceptable" continues. In marketing, some of the categories in which market segments are identified include age, race, gender, social status, and income. When marketing to or portraying different individuals from these categories, do advertisers use clichés that are no longer appropriate?

Advertisements may portray a market segment as one-dimensional figures rather than reflecting the complexities of specific gender, racial, or age segments. Teens may be depicted as rebellious, carefree, and sexually starved. Asian Americans may be shown in advertising as technological experts—knowledgeable, savvy, and even mathematically adept or intellectually gifted. They are usually shown in ads for business-oriented or technical products. From a marketing perspective, it may be much easier to group people into smaller subgroups with common interests. Is it unethical, bad business, or simply a practical matter to represent or misrepresent consumers in these ways?

Advertising Unsafe Products

Marketing has been associated with unsafe products such as alcohol, cigarettes, and other potentially harmful items. By the age of 18, the average American teen has viewed more than 100,000 beer commercials. The inclusion of sexuality and social acceptance combined with humor makes the products in commercials appear desirable. Critics of the brewing industry and marketing agree that many beer commercials encourage underage drinking and build brand loyalty or brand switching in a population that should not even use the product. Occasional underage drinking can lead to an addiction in a few months, because underage drinkers are less developed mentally, physically, and emotionally. The question becomes: Do a few public relations advertisements represent a real attempt to reduce underage drinking, or are they designed to placate the government and critics?

The same holds true for tobacco products. After tobacco advertising on television was banned by the government, marketers created a series of tactics to make certain company products are mentioned. Soon after, sponsorships of the Virginia Slims Tennis and Marlboro Cup Racing came under scrutiny, because sports-casters state the names of the products while reporting scores and results.

Offensive Advertisements

Many adult products require tasteful advertising and marketing pro-grams, even when they are allowed to be shown through any medium. Feminine hygiene products, male drugs for erectile dysfunction, condoms, and other personal adult products may be featured in practically any venue. Marketing professionals should select media that are appropriate as well as create ads that will not offend.

In the international arena, the responsibility becomes even greater. In many Islamic countries, citizens find advertisements for personal hygiene or sexually-related products to be offensive. Company lead-ers should explore cultural differences before undertaking any kind of marketing campaign.

Another ethical issue that has arisen concerns the use of nudity and sexuality in advertising. Marketing professionals must carefully consider what the limits should be. Suggesting that sex sells is simply not enough, nor is making a defensive claim about freedom of speech or freedom of expression. Ethics, morals, and a clear conscience should serve as guides when a company pushes the limits of sexuality in advertising.

Advertising to Children

A continuing controversy in the field of marketing is the ethical acceptability of advertising to children. Children represent a tremendous level of spending and buying power, more than $20 billion annually. Critics question the tactics used to reach them.

Mary Pipher, clinical psychologist and author of *The Shelter of Each Other*, suggests that "No one ad is bad, but the combination of 400 ads per day creates in children a combination of narcissism, entitlement, and dissatisfac-tion."[17] Ads targeted to children employ multiple tactics, including building brand awareness through images and logos, featuring toys and collectibles, and developing tie-ins with television programs and movies, including the *Hannah Montana* phenomenon. Characters such as Min-ions, Ronald McDonald, and Angry Birds vend everything from food to toys to clothes.

With so many venues to sell directly to children and to put pressure on their parents, many company leaders believe it is best to "get them while they're young." From a societal perspective, however, the question remains as to whether such impressionable young minds should be sub-jected to so many messages.

▲ Using sex in advertising is seen as offensive to some consumers.

▼ From a social perspective, advertising to children remains a controversial issue.

Marketing and Ethics

Ethical dilemmas arise in places other than advertisements. Many times, a connection exists between a marketing program and what takes place in the marketing communica-tions arena. Figure 14.8 reviews some of these issues.

objective **14.6**
Which marketing tactics raise ethical concerns?

▶ **FIGURE 14.8**
Ethical Issues in Marketing

- Brand infringement
- Professional services marketing
- Gifts and bribery

- Spam and cookies
- Ambush marketing
- Stealth marketing

Brand Infringement

Several ethical challenges have been associated with brand management. A continuing problem, **brand infringement**, occurs when a company creates a brand name that closely resembles a popular or successful brand, such as when the Korrs beer company was formed. In that case, the courts deemed the brand an intentional infringement, and the name was abandoned. Another brand-infringing company ordered by the courts to give up the name was Victor's Secret.

The brand infringement issue becomes more complex when a brand becomes so well-established that it may be considered a generic term, such as a Kleenex tissue or a Xerox copy. Band-Aid encountered the problem in the 1970s, forcing the marketing team to make sure the product was identified as "Band-Aid Brand Strips" rather than simply "band aids," to keep the competition from using the name. The most vulnerable new brand name may be Google, as in "I Googled myself" or "I Googled it."

A newer form of unethical behavior, internet *domain squatting* or *cyber squatting*, is the questionable practice of buying domain names (**barnesandnoble.com**, **kohls.com**, **lebronjames.com**, etc.) that are valuable to specific people or businesses in the hopes of making a profit by reselling the name. At the extreme, **whitehouse.com** was a pornographic website. Any new company trying to build a presence in the marketplace may find itself stifled by domain squatters. Names matter, and cyber squatters are willing to take advantage of these activities to make profits at some else's expense.[18]

Marketing of Professional Services

Is it ethical to advertise a physician's services or new drugs? For many years, attorneys, dentists, and physicians did not advertise for fear of being viewed as "ambulance chasers." Recently, the trend has gone in the opposite direction. For example, a dermatologist will advertise a "skin rejuvenation" practice with only a bare mention that it is part of a medical practice. Critics argue that this takes medicine into the area of merchandising and suggest that doing so is deceptive.

People injured by accidents, poor medical care, or bad medications are encouraged to call a toll-free number for information on how they can obtain compensation. Other ads encourage consumers to get rid of bad debts by filing for bankruptcy. Critics of medical advertising have suggested attorneys are now chasing the same ambulances, hoping for large settlements from which they receive substantial fees.

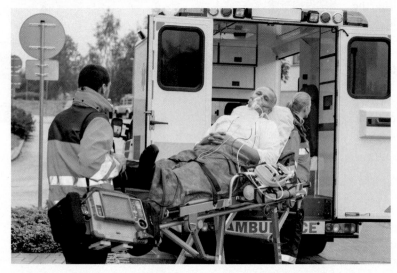

▼ Attorneys and physicians who advertise have been criticized as "ambulance chasers."

Pharmaceutical companies spend millions of dollars advertising new drugs. A great deal of discussion has taken place with regard to sexual dysfunction products. Unfortunately, many young men are buying and using the drugs for recreational purposes. Other drugs have been marketed for "restless leg syndrome" and other uncommon maladies. Marketing critics complain that advertising and promotional tactics can encourage misuse.

The marketing of herbs, supplements, and other untested products also creates concern. Companies make claims regarding a product's contributions to energy level, sexual stamina, and mental acuity. Others items use unsubstantiated reports about weight loss.

Physicians, pharmaceutical companies, and attorneys have the right to market their services. The ethical questions deal with how these services are presented to the public.

Gifts and Bribery in Business-to-Business Marketing Programs

When marketing to other businesses, close personal contacts are often common, both in personal sales calls and in other venues, such as trade shows. Gifts and bribery represent two of the more serious ethical concerns.

To influence sales, purchasing agents and other members of the buying company are often the recipients of gifts, meals, entertainment, and free trips. From a personal ethics standpoint, many concerned leaders question accepting personal gifts designed to influence business decisions. The International Olympics Committee wrestles with this issue when selecting sites for games. Exorbitant gifts, meals, and entertainment have been used by various cities in an effort to sway the selection process.

Closely tied with the issue of receiving gifts is offering or accepting bribes. These can be related to gaining governmental contracts or making business contacts. Without them, permits may not be granted or can be very difficult to obtain. In Germany and France, the government actually allows companies to write off bribes as tax deductions.

Spam and Cookies

Technology creates a double-edged sword for marketers. On the one hand, it leads to ingenious new ways to quickly reach a set of consumers with a key message and to keep in continuous contact with those customers. On the other hand, it can be invasive and intrusive. The use of cookies and other devices presents ethical dilemmas for those working on the web.

Numerous complaints about spamming have been raised. Even with anti-spam legislation, individuals continue to receive unwanted emails. One university in the Midwest receives about 100,000 emails a day, of which approximately 95,000 are spam. Should this be considered an ethical issue or simply a practical matter? Either way, spamming remains a controversial practice.

Cookie technology allows a company's website to track a browser's activities and other websites a consumer has visited. The technology allows a firm to customize and personalize web content to match a consumer's interest. A Harris Interactive survey revealed that 95 percent of consumers believe it is at least somewhat important that companies know "who I am, my buying history, past problems or complaints, preferences, and billing record."[19] At the same time, many consumers express concerns about privacy issues and what firms do with the information collected. Primary questions raised are:

▼ Concerns have been raised about companies that track visitors' browsing activity on the Internet.

- Should an internet company be allowed to gather this information?
- Should the company be allowed to sell the information to other companies?

Answers fall into two categories: legal and moral. Although it may be legal to collect and transfer consumer information in this manner, the ethical issue remains. Marketing professionals continue to need quality information. They try to balance this need with the ethical ramifications of invading privacy rights. Failure to do so may result in long-term implications for both the company and those who use the internet to shop for products.

Ambush Marketing

The rise of dollars spent on sports sponsorships and the use of athletes as endorsers have been accompanied by a rise in **ambush marketing**, which is "a brand's attempt to associate itself with a team or event without buying the rights to do so."[20] Official sponsorships often cost millions. Consequently, some firms have looked at alternative methods of capitalizing on a major sporting event without paying for the rights to be an official sponsor.

To understand the potential impact of ambush marketing, consider Figure 14.8. Chadwick Martin Bailey of Boston surveyed individuals, asking them to recall the official sponsors of the Winter Olympics. In Figure 14.9, the bars in blue represent the $40 million companies paid to become official sponsors. The companies indicated by red were not official sponsors, although many consumers thought they were. Some of this confusion was deliberately created. Figure 14.10 identifies the primary categories of ambush marketing.

Direct ambush marketing occurs when a company intentionally designs an advertising or marketing campaign to capitalize on a major sporting event. The firm seeks to appear to be an official sponsor without stating whether it is or is not a sponsor. VISA was the official credit card sponsor of the Olympics. American Express was not; however, during and after the Olympics, American Express ran television commercials with scenes from the site of the Summer Olympics and a message that said, "You don't need a visa" to visit.

Verizon was also not an official sponsor of the Olympics, but the company ran ads stating that it did sponsor the U.S. speed skating team. The result of the campaign was that seven percent of viewers of the Olympics thought Verizon was a sponsor at a time

▶ **FIGURE 14.9**
Corporations Recalled as Olympic Sponsors

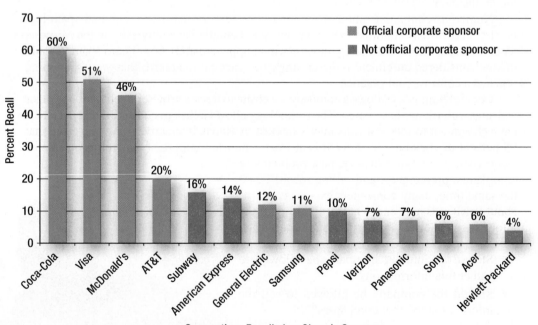

▶ **FIGURE 14.10**
Types of Ambush Marketing

DIRECT AMBUSH ACTIVITIES

INDIRECT AMBUSH ACTIVITIES ——→ Allusion ambushing
Distractive ambushing
Saturation ambushing

INCIDENTAL AMBUSH ACTIVITIES

when other companies paid a $40-million sponsorship fee.[21]

Indirect ambush marketing occurs when a firm suggests or hints an association with a sporting event. The three methods of indirect ambush marketing are allusion ambushing, distractive ambushing, and saturation ambushing.

With **allusion ambushing**, an organization creates an impression that it is a sponsor. During a recent Summer Olympics, Nike ran a series of ads centered on the number 8, which is a symbol of good luck in China, where the games were held. Nothing was said about the Olympics or even the athletes competing in the events.

Distractive ambushing involves a company designing a promotion or event near a major sporting event. At one Winter Olympics, MasterCard, which was not an official sponsor, sent two catering trucks to busy intersections in Vancouver every day to distribute cups of coffee and cocoa. As a result, MasterCard's logo was seen all over downtown Vancouver on cups and napkins.

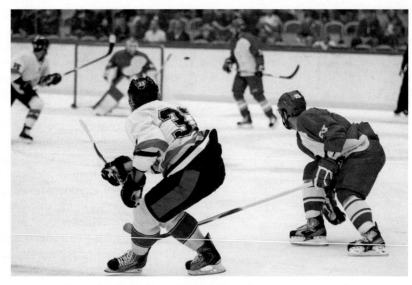

▲ Ambush marketing occurs when a brand is associated with a team or sporting event and is not an official sponsor.

Saturation ambushing happens when a firm increases advertising and marketing during a major event such as the NCAA basketball tournament. No mention is made of the event, but the brand will be seen numerous times by viewers of the event, not only during but also before and after it. This method appears to work best when an event lasts several days, such as the NCAA basketball tournament or the Olympics.[22]

Incidental ambushing takes place when consumers associate a brand with an event without any intentional or indirect effort on the part of the company. At recent collegiate swimming events as well as the Olympics, announcers have mentioned Speedo's LZR Racer swimsuit worn by swimmers. Speedo gained considerable brand exposure, but it was incidental and not planned by Speedo's marketing team.

Ambushing tactics are legal; however, some question whether they are ethical. Clearly, direct and indirect ambush marketing approaches capitalize on the popularity of the event without paying the price to be an official sponsor.

Stealth Marketing

Some companies have engaged in a version of the buzz method known as **stealth marketing**. The approach entices a consumer to examine a product through a personal contact without realizing the person making the pitch is actually paid or compensated in some way.

Jonathan Margolis, CEO of the Michael Alan Group and co-author of the book *Guerilla Marketing for Dummies*, believes the risks of stealth marketing outweigh the benefits. He says, "It's risky to stage something that people think is a natural occurrence."[23] Stealth marketing borders on deception, which can create a negative feeling toward the brand by consumers if they discover it is not genuine.

A recent event illustrates why Margolis says stealth marketing borders on being unethical. An attractive 26-year-old woman was paid by BlackBerry to go to nightclubs and bars and flirt with well-dressed men. She enticed the men to pay attention to her, handed them her BlackBerry, and asked them to put their phone numbers

▲ Stealth marketing involves pitching the benefits of a brand without revealing you are paid to do so.

in the phone, with the promise she would call. She had no intention of calling; rather, she sought to show them the phone, and get them to hold it and use it while she talked about how much she loved it. Many view that level of deception as unethical.

Not all marketers agree. Jason Van Trentlyon, president of Street Guerilla Marketing, argued that "stealth marketing has a greater potential to make a more sincere impact on the public" as opposed to various forms of advertising. People are inundated with a constant barrage of advertising messages, which makes it hard to get their attention and even more difficult to convey a specific brand or product message. As a result, Trentlyon believes stealth marketing provides a legitimate way to create buzz around a brand.[24]

While stealth marketing has not been addressed by the FTC specifically, similar approaches by bloggers and social media influencers have been challenged. The latest FTC ruling requires anyone who endorses a particular brand to reveal that he or she receives compensation for doing so. Some marketers believe this ruling applies to stealth marketing. Others argue it does not because it constitutes a one-on-one conversation which is no different than talking to a friend about a brand the person loves. While stealth marketing may be legal, it constitutes a questionable practice that marketing professionals should carefully consider before engaging in it.

Responding to Ethical Challenges

objective 14.7

How can marketers apply the various ethical frameworks and ethics programs to their activities and actions?

The foundation and frameworks for ethical guidelines are derived from several sources. These include philosophy, law, religion, and common sense.

One *philosophy of life* involves maximizing pleasure and minimizing pain. This idea represents **hedonism**. Critics note that life is often more than the simple pursuit of pleasure and avoidance of pain. **Homeostasis** is the natural craving for balance. People seek to balance a variety of urges throughout life.

The **law** offers guidelines regarding right and wrong as well as what is acceptable and what is not within a geographic area. Legal systems are designed to tell people what they can and cannot do. Remember, however, that not all legal systems are the same.

Many **religions**, or belief systems, profess a version of the philosophy summarized by the *Golden Rule*: Do unto others as you would have them do unto you. Acting in a morally acceptable manner starts with treating others well. Still, specific religious ideologies vary widely. Many disagreements about what is right or wrong exist. Respect, tolerance, discussion, compromise, and accommodation should become ethical guidelines when the religious views of others contradict your own.

In general, one overriding constant may be that ethical actions, moral correctness, and social responsibility all boil down to common sense. Two processes can be used to analyze an ethical concept. The first is logic and reasoning, which leads to common-sense conclusions. One's conscience may become muted over time if it is continually ignored; however, most people know when they are doing something right or wrong. The second element of common sense is gut instinct. Deep down inside, most people think they know when something is appropriate or inappropriate. A person's inner thoughts and gut reaction should never be ignored in an ethical reasoning process.

Ethics Programs

Various individuals and groups have responded to the need for a more ethical environment by creating ethics training programs, codes of ethics, and ethics consulting systems. These attempts are designed to assist individual employees, managers or supervisors, and others within a company facing ethical challenges or dilemmas.

Ethics Training Programs

Ethics training takes place at several points. Moral training begins in many families as part of growing up, both in secular settings and in religious organizations. Those attending college receive further instruction. The Association to Advance Collegiate Schools of Business (AACSB), a major accrediting body for schools of business, has placed a strong emphasis on ethics instruction for more than a decade.

Many corporations now add ethics topics into new-employee training programs as well as manager training systems. Some are self-created; organizational leaders develop others in conjunction with professional organizations and nearby colleges or universities.

Codes of Ethics

Codes of ethics are created in two ways. The first appears within professional organizations. In marketing, two key organizations are the American Marketing Association (AMA) and the American Academy of Advertising (AAA). The AMA code of ethics may be found on the organization's website (**www.marketingpower.com**).

▲ Ethics instructions are given in most business programs at colleges and universities.

The second way ethical codes emerge takes place within business organizations. Many firms have written and revised ethical codes. Figure 14.11 displays common components of codes of ethics.

Ethics Consulting Systems

Numerous individuals and organizations provide counsel regarding ethical dilemmas. Some employ "ethics hotlines" through which a concerned employee can make contact to discuss an ethics problem. The services offered by such organizations vary. Several provide additional instruction, whereas others offer ethical consultations designed o build in-house ethics advisors as well as formulate codes of ethics.

Ethics and social responsibility concerns have the actions and decisions made by individuals and groups as their basis. Any person entering the fields of marketing and advertising should carefully think about what he or she considers to be acceptable and unacceptable acts prior to taking a position as well as while working within any role.

The term *whistle-blower* describes an individual who is willing to go public with charges about an organization doing something that is illegal or unethical. Making the choice to be a whistle-blower is difficult, because it can cause a career setback and make the individual vulnerable to lawsuits and other retaliatory actions. Failure to take action

- The purpose of the code, including (1) regulation of behavior and (2) inspiration to employees.
- A statement of aspirations often included in a preamble that outlines the ideals a company aspires to for its employees. The statement should include the values and principles of the organization.
- A list of principles.
- A list of rules, if needed.
- A statement regarding how the code was created.

- How the code will be implemented.
- How the code will be publicized internally to employees.
- How the code will be publicized externally to constituents and publics.
- How the code will be embraced.
- A statement regarding how and when the code will be revised.
- Most of the time, values, principles, and rules are listed in order of importance.

◀ **FIGURE 14.11**
Components of Codes of Ethics

also represents a choice. One's conscience and belief system provide the ultimate guides as to when and how to respond to moral issues.

International Implications

objective 14.8

What international issues influence the discussion of legal and ethical marketing activities?

Each individual country has its own set of laws regarding what is legal and what is not in the areas of marketing, promotions, and advertising. The marketing department should make sure these laws and regulations are clearly understood and companies try to comply with them. For instance, in China it is important to remember the Communist Party is always in charge. Censorship rules are vague but enforced by the Communist Party. Rules governing the internet are also ambiguous but again can be censored and enforced by the party. Finally, trademarks belong to the first entity that registers it, not the first person or company that uses it. While pro-business, China creates ethical and legal challenges for U.S. companies.

Legal systems vary. In the United States and many Western countries, *common law* is based on local customs, traditions, and precedents. Legal history, previous cases, and national customs serve as guides, and judges typically have more discretion in making legal decisions.

Civil law, which is present in many European countries, is based on a broad set of legal principles, and decisions are made based on legal codes that have been written over time. This gives judges less flexibility.

Theocratic law is based on religious teachings. The foundations of the most common form of theocratic law, Islamic law, are the *Koran* and *Sunna*. Many Islamic countries regulate transactions in different ways. For instance, merchants cannot charge interest in an Islamic system.

Moral reasoning follows a similar pattern in international marketing. One cannot assume that a given system of ethics and morals will be completely acceptable in another country. For example, views of the roles of men and women in society vary widely. Any marketing program with an international outreach should employ a cultural assimilator to help individuals understand ethical principles present in other nations.

Summary

To enforce fair standards in advertising and marketing communications, a number of governmental agencies take action when needed. These include the Federal Trade Commission, the Food and Drug Administration, the Federal Communications Commission, and others. Each tries to keep unfair marketing activities from taking place.

The primary agency regulating marketing communications, the FTC, makes special efforts to stop instances of unfair or deceptive practices. In conjunction with the courts, the FTC and other governmental agencies regulate the majority of companies and industries in the United States. The FTC regulates cases of fraudulent practices targeted at individual consumers as well as conflicts between businesses. Through the use of consent orders, administrative complaints, cease and desist orders, and full commission hearings, the FTC makes its findings and rulings known to the parties concerned. Court actions and corrective advertising programs are utilized in more severe cases. Trade regulation rulings apply when an entire industry has been found guilty of an infraction.

Ethics and morals constitute key principles that can be used to guide a person's activities in the world of commerce.

Morals are beliefs or principles that individuals hold concerning what is right and what is wrong.

Marketing and marketing communications activities are affected by ethical and moral concerns. Some of the more common complaints about advertising include issues of materialism and overconsumption. Also, there are criticisms that advertising perpetuates stereotypes, features unsafe products, sends out offensive messages, is deceptive, and unfairly targets children. Each of these issues requires consideration by anyone entering the profession.

Marketing programs are also subject to ethical concerns. Brand infringement, questionable medical marketing and advertising programs, business-to-business tactics, and internet marketing programs have come under scrutiny. Responses to these criticisms are the responsibility of top management, the marketing department, and those associated with public relations.

A number of ethical frameworks and guidelines are available. Those in the field of marketing may be guided by concepts regarding social responsibility. Also, ethics programs consisting of ethics training, codes of ethics, and ethics consulting systems are accessible to those facing dilemmas or wishing to pose questions.

The issues of legality and morality are present in the international arena as well. Each is complicated by different bodies of law and views of ethics in various nations. Managers in companies seeking to expand internationally should be aware of these differences in order to find ways to respond to them.

Key Terms

Federal Trade Commission (FTC) A federal agency that presides over marketing communications

puffery What takes place when a firm makes an exaggerated claim about its products or services without making an overt attempt to deceive or mislead

substantiation Firms must be able to prove or back up any claims made in their marketing communications

consent order A directive issued when the FTC believes a violation has occurred

administrative complaint A formal proceeding similar to a court trial held before an administrative law judge regarding a charge filed by the FTC

corrective advertisements Ads that bring consumers back to a neutral state, so consumers once again hold beliefs they had prior to being exposed to a false or misleading advertisement

trade regulation ruling Findings that implicate an entire industry in a case of unfair or deceptive practices

morals Beliefs or principles that individuals hold concerning what is right and what is wrong

ethics Moral principles that serve as guidelines for both individuals and organizations

brand infringement Occurs when a company creates a brand name that closely resembles a popular or successful brand

ambush marketing A brand's attempt to associate itself with a team or event without buying the rights to do so

direct ambush marketing When a firm intentionally designs advertising or marketing to capitalize on a major sporting event without becoming a sponsor

indirect ambush marketing When a firm suggests or hints that it is associated with a sporting event when it is not

allusion ambushing When a firm creates an impression that it is a sponsor when it is not

distractive ambushing When a firm designs a promotion or event near a major sporting event without sponsoring the event

saturation ambushing When a firm increases advertising and marketing during a major event without mentioning or sponsoring the event

incidental ambushing When a brand is associated with an event without any intentional or indirect effort on the part of the company

stealth marketing A tactic in which consumers are enticed to look at a product through a personal contact without them realizing that the person making the pitch is paid or compensated

hedonism Maximizing pleasure and minimizing pain

homeostasis The natural craving for balance

law Governmental guidelines for what is right and wrong as well as what is acceptable and what is not within a geographic area

religions Belief systems

MyMarketingLab

To complete the problems with the ⭐ in your MyLab, go to the end-of-chapter Discussion Questions.

Review Questions

14-1. Name the governmental agencies that oversee marketing programs.

14-2. What role did the Wheeler–Lea Amendment play in regulating advertising practices?

14-3. When does an ad or message become false or misleading?

14-4. What is puffery? When is puffery legal?

⭐ **14-5.** What does substantiation mean? How does a company know that the substantiation test has been passed?

14-6. What four groups can trigger an investigation by the FTC?

14-7. What are the steps of the process when the FTC investigates a claim of false or misleading advertising?

14-8. What is a consent order?

14-9. What is an administrative complaint?

14-10. What is the purpose of a corrective advertisement?

14-11. What is a trade regulation ruling? How does it differ from other Federal Trade Commission rulings?

14-12. What is the relationship between the Council of Better Business Bureaus and the National Advertising Division?

14-13. What is the primary function of the National Advertising Review Board?

14-14. How does the Children's Advertising Review Unit operate?

14-15. Define ethics and morals.

14-16. Identify the types of ethical complaints regarding advertising.

14-17. What is brand infringement?

14-18. What types of ethical issues have been raised regarding the marketing of professional services?

14-19. Describe the ethical issues associated with internet marketing.

14-20. Describe all of the forms of ambush marketing.

14-21. What is stealth marketing? How does it create an ethics debate?

14-22. Name the three types of ethics programs that can be used to help marketing professionals cope with moral challenges.

Critical Thinking Exercises

DISCUSSION QUESTIONS

14-23. In labeling food products, marketers walk a fine line between promoting the product and truth in content. Phrases such as "low sodium," "fat free," "no sugar added," and "light" may give the impression that a food is healthy but does not reveal the entire truth. How often do you read package labels and make purchases based on their content? On your next trip to the grocery store, examine various labels that have one of the words identified earlier in this question and compare them to other brands. Do those brands actually contain less than competing brands?

14-24. Reread the section "Deception Versus Puffery." Find three advertisements that are examples of either deception or puffery. How difficult is it to differentiate between the two? When does an ad cease to be puffery and become deceptive?

14-25. One of the industries closely watched by the FTC is the weight-loss industry. Find three advertisements from magazines, newspapers, or television that deal with weight loss. What claims were made? Do you believe the claims are truthful and legitimate? How do you, as a consumer, distinguish between what is truthful and what is deceptive?

14-26. Advertising directed toward children remains a hot topic among parents and educators. Many feel that advertising unfairly targets children and creates materialistic desires. By the time a child is three years old, she already knows many brands of products, such as McDonald's. What is your opinion of advertising to children? Is the current regulation enough, or should it be more stringent?

14-27. One of the criticisms of advertising is that it causes people to buy more than they can afford. Each year, a large number of people in United States declare bankruptcy, often because they have overspent. Do you agree that advertising causes people to buy more than they can afford, or is advertising just responding to the materialistic desire of individuals? Defend your response.

14-28. Advertising does increase the cost of goods and services, but a common defense is that advertising provides people with knowledge about availability of products, which allows consumers to make more intelligent decisions. Do you think this is a valid defense of advertising? Why support the importance of advertising? What other defense could you offer to support the value of advertising?

14-29. Think about advertisements you have seen or heard recently and identify one that you believe is offensive. Why was it offensive? Why do you think the advertiser ran the ad if it is offensive? Do you think offensive ads can be effective? Why or why not?

14-30. What is your opinion of alcohol and tobacco advertising? Should alcohol and tobacco companies have the same freedom to advertise as other product manufacturers? Do you think it is a danger for children to see alcohol or tobacco ads? Does it influence their desire to use these products?

14-31. Using sex to sell products is another area that many consumers find offensive. Locate two print ads or ads on television that are highly sexual in nature, one that you consider offensive and one that you consider to be appropriate. What makes the difference? Are there too many ads that use sexual themes?

14-32. You have seen advertisements by attorneys and medical professionals. Discuss your opinion about these advertisements. Do you think ads by attorneys just increase the number of lawsuits and bankruptcies? Why do medical professionals such as doctors and dentists advertise? Does it affect your opinion of their professionalism? Why or why not?

14-33. What is ambush marketing? Describe each type of ambush marketing that can be used by brands. What are your thoughts about ambush marketing? Is it unethical? Why or why not? Which forms of ambush marketing do you believe are legitimate? Why?

14-34. What is stealth marketing? Do you believe stealth marketing is an ethical marketing practice? Why or why not? Under what circumstances would it be acceptable for a brand to use stealth marketing? Explain.

14-35. Do you believe that ethics can be learned, or is it something an individual has internally? Why or why not? Suppose a company has hired you to teach ethics to its employees. Discuss the concepts of hedonism, homeostasis, law, religion, and common sense as it would relate to teaching a seminar to new employees on ethics. How would ethics training, codes of ethics, and an ethics consulting system be used as part of the training class?

Integrated Learning Exercises

14-36. The Federal Trade Commission (FTC) is the primary federal agency that oversees advertising and other marketing-related communications. Access the website at **www.ftc.gov**. What type of information appears on the website for consumers? For businesses? Pick one of the headlines and write a brief report about the article's contents. Provide the URL of the article.

14-37. The FTC's Bureau of Consumer Protection works for the consumer to prevent fraud, deception, and unfair business practices in the marketplace. Access the FTC's website at **www.ftc.gov** and go to the "For Consumers" section of the site. What information is available? Find an article or recent event from the website and write a short report. Provide a URL for the article in your report.

14-38. Access the FTC's website at **www.ftc.gov**. Access one of the following components of the website. What type of information does each section contain? Why is it important?

   a. About the FTC
   b. News and Events
   c. Enforcement
   d. Policy
   e. Tips and Advice

14-39. One of the primary functions of the FTC is to investigate possible false and deceptive advertising and marketing practices. Access the FTC website at **www.ftc.gov**. Locate the "Commission Actions" section of the site. Read through the list of recent actions. Find two that are interesting. Review the cases and write a brief report on each case. What were the results of the FTC investigations? Provide the URLs of the cases you selected.

14-40. Access the FTC website at **www.ftc.gov**. Locate the "News" section of the website. Read through the list of recent news items. Find two that are interesting to you. Write a brief report about each case and comment on the benefits to either consumers or businesses. Provide the URLs for the two news items in your report.

14-41. The Council of Better Business Bureaus is an important industry organization for businesses as well as consumers. Access the website at **www.bbb.org**. Access the headquarters of the BBB. What information is available on the site? How can this information help consumers? Be specific.

14-42. Access the website of the Council of Better Business Bureaus at **www.bbb.org**. In the "Find a Business" section of the site, type in the name of a local business or a national business that is in your community. Read the report provided by the BBB for that business. Provide a screenshot of the report or save it as a file. Evaluate the business based on the report provided and discuss its usefulness to consumers.

14-43. The National Advertising Division (NAD) of the Council of Better Business Bureaus can be found at **www.asrcreviews.org**. Locate the NAD section of the website. Look through the recent cases the NAD has investigated. Find two of interest to you. Write a report about each case, discussing the issues and the findings of the NAD. Provide the URLs for the two you selected.

14-44. The Children's Advertising Review Unit (CARU) of the Better Business Bureau can be found at **www.asrcreviews.org**. Access the CARU section of the site. Look through the recent cases the CARU has investigated. Find two of interest to you. Write a report about each case discussing the issues and the findings of the CARU. Provide the URLs of the cases you selected.

Blog Exercises

Access the authors' blog for this textbook at the URLs provided to complete these exercises. Answer the questions that are posed on the blog.

14-45. Reebok – **blogclowbaack.net/2014/04/24/reebok-chapter-14**

14-46. Federal Trade Commission – **blogclowbaack.net/2014/04/24/federal-trade-commission-chapter-14**

14-47. Better Business Bureau **blogclowbaack.net/2014/04/28/bbb-chapter-14**

Student Project

CREATIVE CORNER

Solidax ADX was developed in the United States in 2005 and was recently rated by the Weight Loss Institute to be the best weight-loss product on the market. Solidax ADX is based on synephrine, chromium picolinate, and pyrovate and is designed to suppress appetite and increase metabolism and calorie expenditure. Unlike other diet pills, it does not have negative central nervous effects.

The ingredients found in Solidax have been proven to be effective in controlled, laboratory-based human weight-loss studies.[25]

Concerned about recent FTC investigations of false and deceptive advertising of competing brands, the makers of Solidax ADX want a print ad that will be effective but not subject to FTC investigation. Based on the information provided, design a print advertisement for Solidax ADX.

CASE 1 ▸ THE TRUTH ABOUT YOGURT

You don't have to look far to discover that many health professionals believe in the health benefits of yogurt. Elaine Magee, writing for WebMD, notes that "our body needs to have a healthy amount of 'good' bacteria in the digestive tract, and many yogurts are made using active, good bacteria." Yogurt contains probiotics, or the good bacteria that promote healthy digestion. Yogurt also contains protein, which helps prevent osteoporosis, and vitamin D, which provides additional skeletal benefits.[26]

So how does a company get in trouble promoting the health benefits of yogurt? By overstating its advantages over the competition. Dannon, which produces Activia and DanActive, recently paid $45 million in a class action lawsuit to settle complaints regarding its advertising. The company's commercials suggested that the products were "clinically" and "scientifically" proven to regulate digestion and boost immune systems in campaigns featuring actress Jamie Lee Curtis, who called the yogurt "tasty." ABC News noted that "Both yogurts sell at a 30 percent premium over other brands because they claim special bacterial ingredients that the company advertised as clinically proven to help strengthen immune systems and regulate digestion."

"This was a disingenuous advertising campaign that promised something that hasn't been proven," Dr. Roshini Rajapaksa, a gastroenterologist, told ABC News. John Climaco, one of the two attorneys who brought the suit, reported, "The judge agreed that the company was making claims it simply hadn't proven."[27]

Dannon's executive team disputed the court's findings, stating that the company settled to avoid the cost and distraction of litigation. Further, "The lawsuit claims the advertising was not true. Dannon stands by its advertising and denies it did anything wrong."

Still, the terms of the settlement required Dannon to remove the words "clinically" and "scientifically proven" from product labels and advertisements. Instead, the words "clinical studies show," or something similar, could be substituted. The court also required the company to say that Activia and DanActive yogurts are food rather than treatments or cures for medical disorders or diseases. The company was forced to remove the word "immunity"

▲ A female consumer examining various brands of yogurt.

from DanActive labels and ads. Also, the firm was told to include a qualifier to the advertising claim the yogurt "helps strengthen your body's defenses" or "helps support the immune system." Such a statement only pertains, "when (the products are) eaten regularly as part of a balanced diet and healthy lifestyle," according to the judge's order. "This is victory for just about anyone who benefits from accuracy in food labeling," attorney Climaco concluded.[28]

14-48. How do the concepts of deception, puffery, and substantiation apply to this case?

14-49. Could Dannon's executive team have avoided such an expensive outcome? If so, how?

14-50. Do you agree that the term "clinical studies show" is significantly different from "scientifically proven" or "clinically proven"? Should the judge have been more specific about what wording could or could not be used?

14-51. What ethical or moral guidelines, if any, did Dannon violate?

14-52. What role should advertising and marketing communications play in explaining the health benefits of basic products such as yogurt?

CASE 2 › FANDUEL AND DRAFTKINGS

In 2015, advertising budgets exploded for two new entries into the world of sports. FanDuel and DraftKings combined to spend more than $200 million in advertising.[29] Logos and promotions appeared in every imaginable way, including being posted in the warm-up bullpens of major league baseball teams. The companies sponsored brief messages, such as the starting line-ups for games played on television.

Relying on highly sophisticated advertising analytics, marketers from both organizations concluded that potential players of fantasy sports contests were best reached as they watched the very sports programs on which they would later choose fantasy team players.

In general, fantasy sports gaming has become a multibillion dollar industry. Sports and betting enthusiasts can now engage in picking fantasy teams from the comfort of their living rooms, playing online.

The history of gaming and sports has always been a minefield of ethical and legal concerns. Baseball imposes strict regulations on participants, totally banning any betting on baseball games. In perhaps the most widely known case, baseball player Pete Rose received a lifetime suspension from baseball and has been denied access to the Hall of Fame due to his bets on games while serving as a manager of the Cincinnati Reds.

At the same time, it is common practice for local and national newspapers to post "odds" on various sports events, most notably football, where point spreads are published up until the moment a game begins.

Sports fantasy leagues currently are not covered by a great deal of regulation. In late 2015, DraftKings and FanDuel faced charges on what could at least be considered unethical behaviors. Critics argued employees of the two companies had been engaged in what amounted to "insider trading." The employees had access to information about various aspects of games and players, including injury reports that would give them an advantage in selecting fantasy teams for the next game. In one instance, a midlevel manager from DraftKings won $350,000 by choosing a team for the rival FanDuel site[30]

▲ Fantasy sports gaming has become a multibillion dollar industry, but raises some ethical issues and potentially legal issues.

Among the issues raised during the course of the year were the following: Should these sites be considered online gambling? If so, what should be the response of government? What about access to the sites by under-aged players, who would be prevented from gambling onsite in a casino or at a horse track? Third, could gambling in some way "taint" the games themselves? What role should "insider" information play?

In general, the role of gambling in society has received considerable attention. In May, 2016, the state of Texas reached a settlement with FanDuel to cease operations. The current status of fantasy sports sites is in limbo across the United States, as individual governments rule on their legality.[31]

14-53. What role should government play in the oversight of fantasy sports websites?

14-54. Do you consider fantasy sports games to be "gambling," or "entertainment"? Defend your answer.

14-55. Is advertising of fantasy sports websites on television ethical, when under-age fans are likely to be watching?

14-56. As a marketing professional, what issues would you consider if asked to promote a fantasy sports website?

MyMarketingLab

Go to the Assignments section of your MyLab to complete these writing exercises.

14-57. Do you believe that ethics can be learned, or is it something an individual has internally? Why or why not? Suppose a company has hired you to teach ethics to its employees. Discuss the concepts of hedonism, homeostasis, law, religion, and common sense as it would relate to teaching a seminar to new employees on ethics. How would ethics training, codes of ethics, and an ethics consulting system be used as part of the training class?

14-58. Describe the responsibilities and role of each of the advertising industry agencies used to regulate the industry: Better Business Bureau, National Advertising Review Board, and Children's Advertising Review Unit. How do these agencies protect consumers? How do they protect businesses? Overall, do you think the advertising industry can police itself with these agencies? Why or why not?

Buzz Marketing
Communications
Social Media
Advertising
Promotions
Digital
Branding
Mobile Marketing

Chapter 15 Evaluating an Integrated Marketing Program

Chapter Objectives

After reading this chapter, you should be able to answer the following questions:

15.1 What are the three broad categories of evaluation tools used to evaluate IMC systems?

15.2 How do marketing teams match evaluation methods with IMC objectives?

15.3 What forms of message evaluations can be conducted to assess IMC programs?

15.4 Which evaluation criteria are suggested by the positioning advertising copytesting (PACT) system?

15.5 How do online evaluation systems assist advertising managers in assessing the quality of a firm's internet activities?

15.6 What types of behavioral evaluations can be employed to assess IMC programs?

15.7 How are evaluation programs adjusted to match international operations?

Overview

John Wanamaker, a well-known nineteenth-century department store owner, was among the first to use advertising to attract customers to his store. He once remarked, "I know half the money I spend on advertising is wasted, but I can never find out which half." Evaluating the effectiveness of advertising has become increasingly difficult. In today's environment, company executives demand measurable results due to the high costs of advertising campaigns. The challenge for advertising account executives and others who prepare ads continues to be offering evidence regarding the success of campaigns.

To meet the growing insistence for accountability, research and media experts spend time and energy seeking to develop new and accurate measures of success. These measures, known as **metrics**, attempt to accurately portray the effectiveness of a marketing communications plan, which may not be easy.

SANDS RESEARCH, INC.

Neuromarketing on the Cutting Edge

If any single theme emerges from the interviews with members of the various advertising agencies featured in this textbook, it would be that company executives demand clear and convincing evidence that marketing and advertising actually work. Tangible measures such as increases in store traffic, website hits, coupon redemptions, and sales provide behavioral evidence. Many times other factors influence these outcomes, and a lag occurs between the time the advertisement was run and any corresponding behavior resulted.

Advertising agencies continue to look for methods to refine the development and delivery of marketing messages. Finding real-time data suggesting that an advertisement has captured and kept a viewer's attention creates a new level of insight for marketers. Sands Research, Inc., led by its chairman and chief science officer, Dr. Steve Sands, is a leading neuromarketing firm. The company pioneered developments in applications that draw on cognitive neuroscience technology to provide unique insights into consumer responses to television and print advertisements, product packaging, and digital media. By combining its technology with before-and-after questionnaires, Sands Research provides a comprehensive, objective analysis of the viewer's engagement in the marketing material presented by an advertiser.

Recently, Dr. Sands announced a breakthrough in the rapidly growing area of applying neuroscience to market research. Sands Research uses high-density arrays of EEG (electroencephalograph) sensors to capture brainwave activity across the full brain at 10,000 times a second, per sensor. In essence, this means the firm has the ability to study the impact a message has on capturing a person's attention and track times of peak interest as the person stays engaged with that message.

Research suggests that when commercials quickly capture attention, they tend to generate more "peak" moments during the run. Peak moments of attention increase positive feelings toward commercials and potentially influence recall. Peaks are likely to occur when:

- Important news is provided; for example, the announcement of a strong price promotion.
- Inciting incidents appear, typically those involving a moment strongly charged with negative emotion to set up a joke or storyline.
- Surprising moments or turning points in stories take place.
- The delivery of climactic moments or punch lines occurs.

The value of these new techniques may be enhanced through the understanding that three different memory systems may be involved in developing a person's view of a brand: knowledge memories, emotion or episodic memories, and action or procedural memories of bodily experiences and physical sensations. Evidence from these studies suggests that these memories might be stored in different parts of the brain. Consequently, a rational and verbal memory might be reported, but emotional or episodic memories may not. This would explain the underreporting of the impact of musical and visual cues in advertisements.

The full impact of these technologies has yet to be realized. At the least, Sands Research suggests the company can help an advertiser create an advertisement with the greatest potential for capturing attention from storyboard to the run of the commercial. And, an exciting new era in marketing measurement may be well underway.[1]

▶ This advertisement for Scott Equipment could be assessed using message evaluation techniques.

This chapter considers the methods available for evaluating components of an IMC program. Three broad categories of evaluation tools can be used to evaluate IMC systems: message evaluations, online evaluations, and respondent behavior evaluations.

Evaluation Metrics

objective 15.1

What are the three broad categories of evaluation tools used to evaluate IMC systems?

- Message evaluation techniques
- Online evaluation metrics
- Respondent behavior evaluations

▲ **FIGURE 15.1**

Primary Metrics Used to Evaluate Marketing Communications

Three primary metrics help evaluate marketing communications (see Figure 15.1). **Message evaluation techniques** examine the message and the physical design of the advertisement, coupon, or direct marketing piece. Message evaluation procedures include the study of actors in advertisements as well as the individuals who speak in radio ads. A message evaluation program reviews the cognitive components associated with an ad, such as recall and recognition, as well as emotional, attitudinal, and behavioral intention responses.

Online evaluation metrics examine online advertising and social media campaigns. The internet provides a unique set of metrics and techniques that are not available for traditional media. For example, **click-throughs** represent the number of individuals who clicked on a brand message and were taken directly to the brand's website. *Dwell rate* measures the proportion of ad impressions that resulted in a user engaging with the ad, such as clicking on it or just mousing over it. *Dwell time* measures of the amount of time users spend engaged with a particular ad.

In addition, marketers can track other browsing behaviors on a website and buzz activity on social media. The internet provides highly accurate, real-time measures of consumer reactions.

Respondent behavior evaluations count visible customer actions, including store visits, inquiries, or actual purchases. This category contains evaluation technique measures that feature numbers such as the amount of coupons redeemed, hits on a website, and changes in sales.

The importance of providing evidence that advertising works has led to a greater emphasis on respondent behaviors. Higher sales, increases in store traffic, an increase in daily website hits, social media buzz and other numbers-based outcomes appeal to many managers. At the same time, message evaluations, online metrics, and behavioral responses help the marketing manager and advertising team build short-term results and achieve long-term success.

Matching Methods with IMC Objectives

Marketers select methods of evaluation that match the objectives to be measured.[2] An advertising campaign with the objective of increasing customer interest in and recall of a brand will be assessed using the level of customer awareness as the metric. Normally, this means the marketing team measures awareness before, during, and after the ads have run. At other times, objectives focus on customer actions. Redemption rates measure the success of a campaign featuring coupons. Several levels are used to analyze an advertising or IMC program. They include:

- Short-term outcomes (sales, redemption rates)
- Long-term results (brand awareness, brand loyalty, or brand equity)
- Product- and brand-specific awareness
- Affective responses (liking the company and a positive brand image)

The temptation sometimes arises to overemphasize the first factor, short-term outcomes, without considering the longer-term impact of a campaign or marketing program. The company's marketing team endeavors to maintain a voice that carries across campaigns over time.

In light of the overall marketing and advertising goals, the marketing manager considers the various options for evaluating advertising. Selection of evaluation procedures takes place prior to launching a campaign. An advertisement placed in a trade journal can contain a code number, a special telephone number, or a special internet microsite to track responses. For coupons, premiums, and other sales promotions, code numbers are printed on each item to identify the source.

In general, careful planning prior to initiating an IMC program makes the evaluation of the campaign easier and more accurate. At the same time, the evaluation of one advertisement or marketing piece may be complicated, because many factors can affect the outcome being measured. For instance, a retailer may run a series of newspaper and radio ads to boost store traffic. In order to measure the impact of the ads, the retailer keeps records of store traffic before, during, and after the campaign. Unfortunately, the traffic count might be influenced by various factors, even something as simple as the weather. If it rains for two days, the traffic count will be lower. Further, the store's chief competitor might run a special sale during the same time period, which also affects traffic. A TV program, such as the season finale of a major series, or even a special program at the local high school (commencement, school play), could have an impact. In other words, many extraneous factors might affect results. When reviewing an advertising program, marketing professionals consider these factors.

Performing one analysis normally does not adequately assess the impact of a marketing communications piece on a company's image. Even though store traffic was low, the

objective 15.2

How do marketing teams match evaluation methods with IMC objectives?

◀ This banner ad for DuPage Medical Group can be evaluated using various online metrics.

▼ The impact of this ad for SteviB's can be measured by the number of kids buffet meals sold on October 31st.

ad may have been stored in the buyer's long-term memory, which may make a difference later. Conversely, the same ad may have been awkward or offensive in some way. The store owner might believe the weather affected the outcome instead of a poor advertising design. Consequently, company leaders consider short- and long-term implications when assessing an IMC program.

Message Evaluations

objective 15.3

What forms of message evaluations can be conducted to assess IMC programs?

Evaluation or testing of advertising communications occurs at every stage of the development process. This includes the concept stage before an advertisement is produced. Testing at that point often involves soliciting the opinions of a series of experts or from "regular" people. Ads can be tested after completing the design stage but prior to development. Advertising creatives often prepare television commercials using a storyboard such as the one for Interstate Batteries shown in the section. Storyboards are often prepared using artist sketches.

Although ads and marketing pieces may be tested prior to production, most advertising agencies perform a small amount of pretesting, primarily due to the lack of reliable test results. Elena Petukhova from The Richards Group advertising agency indicated that her company does not rely heavily on pretesting because the format can make a difference. Consumers are used to seeing finished ads. Consequently, looking at a sketch or mockup of an ad may result in a lower score. As a result, The Richards Group relies more on after-production ad evaluations.[3]

As shown in Figure 15.2, individual companies and advertising agencies employ three primary methods to evaluate advertising campaign messages: advertising tracking

▶ Storyboards can be used to evaluate broadcast ads.

▶ **FIGURE 15.2**
Evaluating Advertising Messages

research, copytesting, and emotional reaction tests. Each fits differing circumstances, advertising methods, and IMC objectives. A promising new method of advertising evaluation takes advantage of cognitive neuroscience.

Advertising Tracking Research

One common method of evaluation involves tracking an advertisement by one of the major advertising research firms, such as Nielsen IAG or Millward Brown. Tracking research examines ads that have launched. This in-market research method monitors a brand's performance and advertising effectiveness. Marketers perform tests at specific times, intervals, or continuously. Ad tracking provides a general measure of the effect of the media weight (that is, spending level), the effectiveness of the media buys, and the quality of the ad's message and execution. Ad tracking examines the relative impact of a message compared to the competition and over time.

Nielsen IAG provides ad tracking services. The company offers a syndicated database of real-time brand and ad performance tracking based on more than 210,000 television program episodes and 250,000 commercials. In addition to television ads, the service applies to the evaluation of internet ads and in-cinema campaigns. Nielsen conducts thousands of surveys daily measuring viewer engagement with TV programs and the effectiveness of each advertisement on network and cable television channels.[4]

Ad Tracking Methodology With ad tracking, research respondents view a brief portion of an advertisement or a few stills from a TV ad with the brand name removed or not visible. Researchers ask respondents if they recognize the company, which measures brand and ad recognition. They then ask subjects to identify the brand being advertised, which measures unaided brand awareness. Those that cannot correctly identify the sponsor receive a list of brands and are asked to identify the correct brand, which measures aided brand awareness. In addition to recognition and unaided and aided brand awareness, tracking research also measures:

- Memorability
- Likeability
- Unaided and aided message recall
- Unaided and aided campaign recall

Magazine advertisers have access to similar techniques. Mediamark Research & Intelligence's AdMeasure tracks recall and response to advertisements in every issue of 200 magazine titles. Affinity offers a competing service, the American Magazine Study Print Ad Ratings, which contains ad measurements across 125 magazine titles.[5]

When the mcgarrybowen agency created a campaign for Burger King, employees engaged in ad tracking to gauge the brand's impression score. Both Burger King and its primary rival were measured with impression scores. Respondents were asked, "Do you have a general positive feeling about the brand?" Prior to the campaign launch, Burger King's impression score was 24.4 compared to McDonald's score of 48.9. During the campaign, Burger King's score rose to a high of 45.1 then dropped at the end to 38.4. At the same time, McDonald's impression score fell to 34.8. By assessing these results before, during, and after the campaign, marketers from Burger King and mcgarrybowen were able to obtain more accurate measures

▼ Marketers for Maxwell House coffee can use ad tracking to measure the success of the "Stay Grounded" ad campaign.

Lunches, made.

Backpacks, ready.

Hair, braided.

Shoes, tied.

Moment, to savor.

pheel
the joy

KRAFT
PHILADELPHIA
REGULAR

pheel the moment

▲ Ad tracking can help marketers for Philadelphia Cream Cheese detect when wear-out begins to occur.

of the campaign's effectiveness in creating a more positive impression of the restaurant chain.[6]

Report Cards and Benchmarks Dave Snell of The Richards Group notes that the information provided by Nielsen IAG offers a continuous "report card" and a "benchmark." During the second or third week of a new campaign, ad tracking research provides two types of information about a new advertisement's performance. First, it shows how the new ad performs in comparison to the brand's competitors. Second, it indicates how well the advertisement performed in relation to those from previous campaigns.

Nielsen IAG also builds a benchmark for a company as it measures ad performance over months and years. These benchmark data are especially valuable when a new campaign launches. Advertisers compare new messages to previous ones along various dimensions to ensure the commercials perform as expected. The benchmark from previous ads provides a better indicator of performance than comparisons with competitors or ads for similar products.

Tracking services help an advertiser identify when an advertisement begins to wear out. Measuring effectiveness on a biweekly basis and graphing the results indicates when the advertisement has begun to lose impact. At that point, the agency and client can switch to a new campaign, bring back a previous ad, or modify the current commercial.

The Richards Group's Elena Petukhova notes that ad tracking has the disadvantage of failing to provide diagnostics. The data indicate how the ad performs in relation to the competition, against previous ads, and over time. They do not yield information regarding the reasons an advertisement did not perform well. Other types of research explore the reasons an advertisement failed. In essence, ad tracking research indicates when an advertisement has worn out or is not performing, but it does not tell the agency what to do.

Copytesting

The second form of message evaluation, **copytests**, assesses a finished marketing piece or one in the final stages of development. Copytesting elicits responses to the main advertising message as well as the presentation format. Television and print ads have long been evaluated using copytesting procedures. Online print and video ads were seldom copytested, but that trend is changing. According to Jeff Cox, CEO of ARS Group, which performs copytesting, about 75 percent of the firm's clients now test at least some of their digital ads during development.[7]

Common copytesting techniques include portfolio tests, theater tests, and online tests. A **portfolio test** displays a set of print ads containing the one being evaluated. A **theater test** displays a set of television ads, including the one being studied. The people who participate do not know which piece is under scrutiny. Both techniques mimic reality in the sense that consumers normally are exposed to multiple messages, such as when a radio or television station plays a series of commercials in a row or when several newspaper ads appears on a single page. The tests also make it possible for researchers to compare the target piece with other marketing messages. For these approaches to produce the optimal findings, all of the marketing pieces shown must be in the same stage of development, such as preproduction ads or finished ads.

The Ameritest company specializes in copytesting. Recently the firm examined the ad by Carl's Jr. with the model Charlotte McKinney walking what at first appears to be naked through a farmer's market. She is then shown in a bikini and at the end eats the All Natural Burger. Copytests by Ameritest revealed that 27 percent said they would visit Carl Jr. or Hardees after viewing the ad, a considerably lower score than the average 43 percent for other fast food restaurant ads. In addition, copytests revealed that 52 percent found the ad offensive, 51 percent said it was irritating and annoying, and 43 percent felt worse about Carl's Jr. after viewing the ad. The only positive feedback from the copytesting was that 94 percent remembered the ad was for Carl's Jr.[8]

Internet copytesting can replace portfolio and theater tests. Online copytesting costs less and provides immediate results. The Millward Brown advertising firm features online testing procedures, including copytesting. Typically, an agency client performs copytests five to eight times per year. The tests deliver information regarding the in-depth potential of an ad under ideal circumstances. When they are conducted online, consumers pay more attention to the ad than they would for a television show, radio program, or while reading a magazine. Therefore, copytesting results offer a measure of the advertisement's potential when it receives the viewer's complete attention.

Copytesting follows finished ads that have already been launched. Millward Brown typically studies an ad using 150 respondents. Quantitative questions address issues such as:

- Breakthrough ability
- The brand message and image
- The level of ad and brand memory
- Levels of enjoyment
- What the ad communicates
- How well the intended message was communicated
- Potential responses such as the likelihood of making a purchase
- Persuasive power of the advertisement
- Engagement of the viewer with the ad and brand

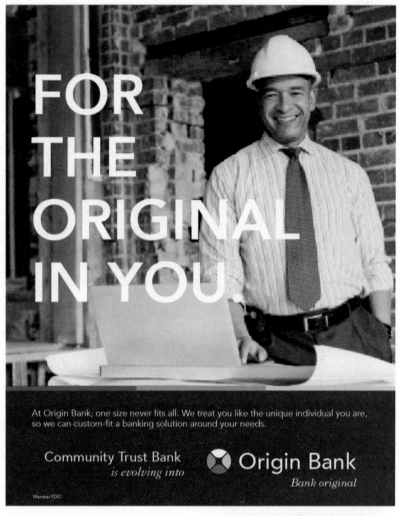

▲ Copytesting can be used to evaluate the visual and message of this print ad for Origin Bank.

Testing Emotional Reactions   In addition to these measures, Millward Brown prepares a second-by-second emotional reaction chart that indicates how viewers feel about an advertisement to be shown on television or the internet. As they watch the commercial on a computer screen, respondents move a computer mouse to indicate their feelings—one direction for positive feelings and the other direction for negative feelings. By superimposing these 150 emotional reaction tests onto one graph, the client sees how the feelings and emotions of the respondents change during the commercial. This information has value because it indicates points at which emotions turn. Although the test does not measure the level of emotion but rather changes in emotion, these data provide sufficient evidence for the agency to develop hypotheses or best practice ideas to assist in making future advertisements.

Verbatim Comments   The final pieces of information provided to clients by Millward Brown and other agencies are the verbatim comments of the respondents. Millward Brown asks a number of open-ended questions to engage respondents and gain

JD Gets Me
an Assist

JD Bank is a proud supporter of
Sulphur High School and the Lady Tors!

Carlyss Branch:
4507 Highway 27 South
Sulphur, LA 70665
337-558-5900

Sulphur Branch:
2905 Maplewood Drive
Sulphur, LA 70663
337-626-2500

JD BANK
jdbank.com

MEMBER FDIC

▲ Emotional reaction tests provide valuable information to advertising agencies and brand managers.

a deeper understanding of their thought processes. Each respondent presents, in his or her own words, thoughts about the advertisement. Verbatim comments tell the agency what people think about the ad, including both positive and negative reactions. Agencies want to know what customers see in ads and the message that comes across. Respondent comments provide this type of information.

As noted previously, ad tracking does not generate evidence regarding the reasons an ad did not perform well or what to do to correct it. Copytesting procedures generate some of this information. Advertising creatives can then determine the next step. By using continuous ad tracking and copytesting, an agency builds a benchmark for a particular client on an advertisement's performance. The agency also gains insights into what works and what does not with regard to a particular product category and brand.

Copytesting Controversies Some controversies regarding copytesting remain. Numerous advertisers and marketers strongly believe the method favors rational approaches over affective and conative (action-inspiring) methods. To correct this potential deficiency, some research firms add emotional tests to copytesting procedures.

Further, several marketers believe copytesting prior to production stifles the creativity needed to produce ads that will stand out in the clutter. Recently, creatives working for Nike, Volkswagen, Budweiser, and Target have been allowed to skip the copytesting phase of advertising design and move straight into production. When the agency Wieden + Kennedy created "the man your man could smell like" campaign for Old Spice cologne, the brand's parent firm Procter & Gamble allowed Wieden to skip the concept testing stage completely. Also, the approval process for the Old Spice campaign was streamlined to just one P&G executive.[9]

Unless the client insists on preproduction copytests, agencies now move directly into production and perform tests after the ad launches. Some advertisers believe copytests tend to lead creatives to design believable and understandable ad messages about the product benefits to show members of a focus group or panel. Many consumers in focus groups know little, if anything, about how to create an effective advertisement. Most creatives believe it does not make sense to have them serve as final judges of an advertisement's quality.

Although a number of marketing professionals do not favor using copytests, the majority believe they are necessary, primarily due to accountability issues. Jeff Cox, CEO of copytesting agency ARS Group, argues that, "Copytesting can squelch creative, but the marketplace and the world's largest advertisers see value in doing this."[10] When the time comes to support a decision for a high-dollar advertising campaign, advertising agency and company executives want evidence that validates the investment. Also, advertising agencies can use the results of copytesting to perfect future ads and campaigns by understanding what will be more likely to succeed in a given marketplace.

Emotional Reaction Tests

Many advertisements seek to elicit emotional responses from consumers. Emotional ads are based on the concept that people remember messages that elicit positive feelings. Also, consumers who have positive attitudes toward ads develop more favorable attitudes regarding the product. This, in turn, should result in increased purchases.[11]

Measuring an advertisement's emotional impact can be challenging. The simplest method involves asking about an individual's feelings and emotions after viewing a marketing communication piece. An alternative method, a **warmth monitor**, relies on the notion that feelings of warmth are positive when they are directed toward an ad or a product. To measure warmth, subjects are asked to manipulate a joystick or the mouse on a computer while watching a commercial, moving one direction for warmer and another for cooler.[12]

Reactions and Opinions can efficiently poll 1,000 or more people using an online-type warmth monitor. As individuals watch the ad on streaming video, the participants use a mouse to move a tab on a sliding scale from 1 to 10. When they like what they see, they slide the tab toward the 10. Those who do not like what they see slide the tab toward the 1. After the data have been collected, a graph will be superimposed over the advertisement to indicate the likable and parts of the message they do not like. The internet offers the advantage of allowing subjects to provide ratings at their convenience. If the agency needs a focus group to discuss the ad, subjects are selected from the participants. The focus group session can be held online.[13]

An innovative approach to measuring emotional reactions, **biometric research**, involves measuring physiological reactions to advertisements and marketing messages. The Innerscope company specializes in biometric research. Carl Marci, CEO and chief science officer, stated that "Innerscope strongly believes that unconscious emotional responses direct attention, enhance learning and memory, and ultimately drive behaviors that our clients care about." Innerscope puts test subjects in a living room setting. A device on the television tracks eye movement to track the subject's attention to stimuli. At the same time, a special belt worn by the subject collects data regarding the person's heartbeat, perspiration levels, respiration, and body movements. By integrating these biological measures, Innerscope measures the level of emotional engagement of viewers during every second of the ad via their emotional, unconscious responses.[14]

Time Warner built a 9,600-square-foot media lab in Manhattan for its own operation but also leases it to clients for biometric research. The company charges about $50,000 for basic focus groups to $120,000 for research featuring biometrics. The lab makes biometric belts available to measure physiological reactions to ads. Cameras measure eye movements and two-way mirrors allow for client observation.[15] Rather than rely on consumers telling researchers how they are reacting via some type of warmth meter, biometrics measure actual emotional reactions. Individuals can lie about how they feel with a warmth meter whereas bodily reactions to ads are more difficult to fake.

▲ Verbatim comments provide SteviB's and its agency, Zehnder Communications, valuable information about this ad.

▼ Companies can conduct emotional reaction tests online using a computer mouse.

Think finances for community projects get in shape on their own?

Think again.

Helping build a better community and a brighter future is something all of us have a stake in.

Meet Michele Thaxton, Senior Vice President, Chief Financial Officer and 10-year member of our ProTeam. She watches over all financial aspects of Progressive Bank to ensure we continue to grow as a strong, vibrant institution, fulfilling our mission every day as a committed and caring community bank.

She also works out in the community as a volunteer on the finance committees and boards of entities like United Way and the Northeast Louisiana Soccer Association. An avid health enthusiast, Michele is equally dedicated to helping keep the financial matters of these key community organizations in shape and running smoothly.

Community service like this does a community good. And you can take that to the bank.

Get to know Michele better – call her at 318-812-5226.

PROGRESSIVE BANK

Banking *reinvented.*

(318) 398-9772 • progressivebank.com

Monroe • West Monroe • Winnsboro • Bossier City • 7 Locations • 31 Convenient ATM Locations

▲ Emotional reaction tests provide valuable information to advertisers, such as Progressive Bank.

Cognitive Neuroscience

In recent years, significant advances have occurred in **cognitive neuroscience**, a brain-image measurement process that tracks brain activity. As noted in the opening vignette for this chapter, it tracks the flow and movement of electrical currents in the brain. One study using cognitive neuroscience (psychophysiology) demonstrated that the currents in a subject's brain indicated a preference for Coke or Pepsi that are the same as for the product a person chooses in a blind taste test. According to neuroscientist Justin Meaux, "Preference has measurable correlates in the brain; you can see it." Richard Silberstein, an Australian neuroscientist, took physiological measurements of the brain to show that successful ads tend to generate higher levels of emotional engagement and long-term memory coding.[16]

Consider a sexually provocative advertisement under development. The members of a focus group may enjoy the ad but cover up these feelings and say it was sexist and inappropriate. Their responses may be due to the desire for social acceptance. In a copytest for the same ad, a respondent may also offer socially acceptable answers even though he is not face-to-face with the researcher. The individual may not move the computer mouse to report his true feelings in a study using an emotional monitor. The negative stigma attached to sex in advertising often affects self-reported reactions. A physiological arousal test, such as cognitive neuroscience, might provide a better indicator of a person's true response. Many advertising researchers believe physiological arousal tests provide more accurate information than emotional reaction tests, because physiological arousal is more genuine.[17]

The most recent research in this area has been undertaken by companies such as EmSense, Neuro-Focus, Sands Research, and OTX Research. These companies experiment with portable devices that measure both brain waves and biologic data. Coca-Cola employed this methodology to select ads to run on the Super Bowl. Coke produced a dozen ads that were evaluated by the EmSense device. The EmSense device measures brain waves and monitors breathing, heart rates, blinking, and skin temperatures as consumers watch ads. Through these physiological measurements, Coca-Cola researchers decided which ads to use. They modified some of the commercials to produce higher levels of emotions.[18]

Frito-Lay engaged in neuroscience to test product packaging. Company marketers discovered that matte beige bags of potato chips picturing potatoes and other healthier ingredients did not trigger anterior cingulated cortex activity (the area of the brain associated with guilt) as much as shiny potato chip bags.

Frito-Lay's chief marketing officer, Ann Mukherjee, said, "Brain-imaging tests can be more accurate than focus groups." After a focus group rejected a Cheetos advertisement, Frito-Lay tested the commercial using neuroscience methods. The ad featured a woman taking revenge on someone in a laundromat by putting the orange snack food in a dryer that was full of white clothes. Members of the

▶ Cognitive neuroscience is likely to produce a more accurate assessment of this billboard ad than a copytest.

focus group said that the prank made Frito-Lay look mean-spirited. The neuroscience test indicated that women loved the commercial.[19]

Cognitive neuroscience reveals physiological reactions to a message. It shows where brain activity occurs and, to some extent, the level of activity. It identifies times when a test subject becomes enthralled with a message. It also indicates when the person merely focuses on the logo or an attractive woman in the commercial. The methodology identifies positive and negative emotions and the intensity of the emotions by the amount of neurons firing. This methodology enables scientists (and marketers) to understand the information being processed, where it is being processed, and how the individual reacted to the ad or marketing piece. Although still in its infancy, cognitive neuroscience offers great potential for evaluating advertising and marketing.

Evaluation Criteria

Each of the evaluation programs mentioned thus far require quality evaluation criteria. One helpful program, **positioning advertising copytesting (PACT)**, was created by 21 leading U.S. advertising agencies to help evaluate television ads.[20] Even though PACT examines the issues involved in copytesting television ads, the principles apply to any type of message evaluation system and all types of media. Figure 15.3 lists the nine main principles to follow when testing a written or verbal marketing communication piece.

Any advertising procedure should be *relevant to the advertising objective being tested*. For a coupon promotion designed to stimulate trial purchases, marketers evaluate the coupon's copy in order to determine its ability to stimulate those purchases. An evaluation of attitudes toward a brand requires a different instrument.

Researchers should agree about how the results are going to be used when selecting test instruments. They should also agree on the design of the test in order to obtain the desired results. This becomes especially important during the preparation stage of an advertisement's development because many tests are used to determine whether the advertisement eventually will be created.

The research team should set a *cutoff score* to be used following the test. This prevents biases from affecting findings about the ad's potential effectiveness. Many advertising agencies use test markets for new advertisements before they are launched in a larger area. A recall method designed to determine if people in the target market remember seeing the ad should contain a prearranged cutoff score. In other words, the acceptable percentage may be established so that 25 percent of the sample should remember the ad in order to move forward with the campaign. An advertisement that does not achieve the percentage has failed the test.

Using multiple measures allows for more precise evaluations of ads and campaigns. A well-designed ad may fail one particular testing procedure yet score higher on others.

objective 15.4
Which evaluation criteria are suggested by the positioning advertising copytesting (PACT) system?

- Testing procedure should be relevant to the advertising objectives.
- In advance of each test, researchers should agree on how the results will be used.
- Multiple measures should be used.
- The test should be based on some theory or model of human response to communication.
- Tha testing procedure should allow for more than one exposure to the advertisement, if necessary.
- In selecting alternate advertisements to include in the test, each should be at the same stage in the process as the test ad.
- The test should provide controls to avoid biases.
- The sample used for the test should be representative of the target sample.
- The testing procedure should demonstrate reliability and valldity.

◀ **FIGURE 15.3**
Copytesting Principles of PACT

The Simple Elegance Of It All

CHIC SHAQUE

"Exquisite Extras"

•Designer Apparel & Denim
•Handbags
•Jewelry •Lingerie
•Bedding •Bath
•Baby & Home Decor

630 Northpark Lane
Joplin, MO 64801
417-623-8887

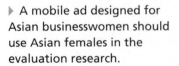
▲ Using multiple measures for this Chic Shaque ad allows for more precise evaluation of the ad and the campaign.

Consumers and business buyers who are targets of marketing communications are complex human beings. Various people perceive individual ads differently. As a result, advertisers usually try to develop more than one measure to be certain greater agreement can be reached about whether the ad or campaign will succeed and reach its desired goals.

The test under consideration should be *based on some theory or model of human response to communication*, which makes it more likely that the test will accurately predict the human response. Enhancing the odds that the communication will produce the desired results (going to the website, visiting the store, or making a purchase) when an ad launches becomes the objective.

Many testing procedures are based on a single exposure. Although many times this may be sufficient for research purposes, sometimes *multiple exposures* are necessary to obtain reliable test results. For complex ads, more than one exposure may be needed. The human mind comprehends only so much information in one viewing. The marketing team should make sure a person can and will comprehend the message to determine whether it achieves the desired effects.

Often ads are tested in combination with other ads to disguise the one being examined. Placing the test marketing piece with others means the test subjects do not know which one is being evaluated. This prevents personal biases from affecting judgments. To ensure valid results, *the alternative ads should be in the same stage of process development*. When ad copy is being tested prior to ad development, the alternative ads should also be in the ad copy development stage.

Next, adequate controls are put in place to *prevent biases and external factors from affecting results*. To help control external factors, researchers often utilize experimental designs. When conducting experiments, researchers hold as many things as constant as possible and manipulate one variable at a time. With a theater test, the temperature, time of day, room lighting, television program, and ads shown should all be the same. Then, the researcher may display the program and ads to an all-male audience followed by an

▶ A mobile ad designed for Asian businesswomen should use Asian females in the evaluation research.

all-female audience. Changing a single variable (gender) makes it possible to see if the ad, in a controlled environment, was perceived differently by men as opposed to women.

As with any research procedure, sampling procedures are important. The *sample being used should be representative of the target population.* A print ad designed for Spanish-speaking Hispanic Americans should be tested using a Spanish questionnaire or interview format.

Finally, researchers continually try to make tests *reliable and valid.* Reliable means "repeatable." In other words, if the same test were given five times to the same person, the individual should respond in the same way each time. If a respondent is "emotional" on one iteration of a warmth test and "neutral" when the ad is shown a second time, the research team will wonder if the test is reliable.

Valid means "generalizable." Valid research findings can be generalized to other groups. For instance, when a focus group of women finds an ad to be funny, and then a group of men reacts in the same way, the finding that the humor was effective becomes more valid. This would be an increasingly valuable outcome if the results were generalizable to people of various ages and races. Many times an ad may be reliable, or repeatable in the same group, but not valid or generalizable to other groups of consumers or business buyers.

The PACT principles provide assistance when agencies design tests of short-term advertising effectiveness. They help when marketers seek to understand larger and more long-term issues such as brand loyalty and identification with the company. Generating data documenting that what a company is doing works should be the objective. When this occurs, the company and its advertising team have access to valuable information.

Online Evaluation Metrics

Current technology enables company leaders to track how individuals got to a website. To determine the effectiveness of social media, marketers track the percentage of visits that came through social media. If contests, coupons, or other promotions are sent via social media, a company's marketing team can tally the click-through rate, which, in turn, reflects the value of the social media advertising or marketing program. Click-throughs, dwell time, and dwell rate remain popular methods for measuring the impact of online advertising.

To evaluate digital marketing communications from the internet, in addition to click-throughs, a number of other metrics provide data that may be used to evaluate digital campaigns. Figure 15.4 identifies methods to measure website traffic and digital marketing campaigns.

Website traffic can be counted in several ways. The number of visits (or hits) offers one common measure. Investigators sum the number of visitors and whether those visitors were new or repeat visitors. While gaining new visitors is important, counting repeat visits provides a gauge regarding the level of interest individuals had in the website. Other metrics include page views, page views per visit, and time on each page as well as the site as a whole.

objective 15.5
How do online evaluation systems assist advertising managers in assessing the quality of a firm's internet activities?

Web Metrics	Conversion and Campaign Metrics
• Number of visits (Hits)	• Click-through rate (CTR)
• Number of visitors	• Cost-per-click (CPC)
• New vs. repeat visitors	• Conversion ratio
• Page views	• Cost-per-conversion (CPC)
• Page views per visit	• Average order value (AOV)
• Time on pages and site	• Revenue-per-visit (RPV)
• Entry and exist pages	• Shopping cart abandonment
• Bounce rates	

◀ **FIGURE 15.4**
Sample of Digital Metrics

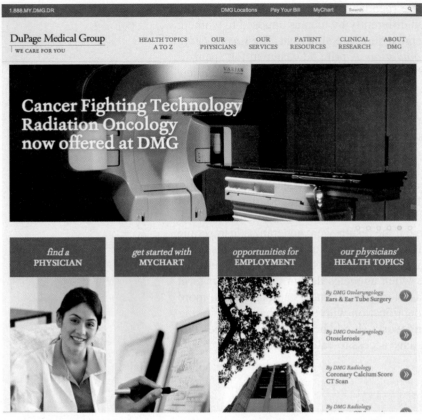

▲ A number of different metrics can be used to evaluate websites, such as this one for DuPage Medical Group.

These metrics indicate a level of engagement. The more time someone spends on a website and the more pages the person views, the more likely it becomes that she will make a purchase.

Entry and exit pages display where individuals come to a site and where they leave. Most traffic to a website does not begin on the main page. Digital campaigns often employ a microsite to bring visitors to a website so that the webpage matches the digital ad. Exit page metrics are critical because they indicate problem pages that might require revision. The bounce rate for each page on the site also deserves consideration. A bounce occurs when a person enters and leaves from the same page. A website page with a 60% bounce rate may create concern because it suggests that people did not find what they wanted and left the page immediately.

Conversion and campaign metrics help marketers quickly evaluate how well a website is doing and whether a particular campaign met expectations. For instance, the click-through rate metric can be further examined to see how many people who saw a digital ad clicked on it and went to the website, but also the cost for each click-through (CPC).

Conversion ratio and cost-per-conversion statistics allow marketers to compare digital campaigns and different webpage and banner ad designs. Marketers also examine average order value (AOV) and revenue-per-visit (RPV) metrics.

Shopping cart abandonment provides a critical metric. It measures the percentage of customers that placed items in a shopping basket but did not complete the order. A higher percentage of abandonment suggests something has gone wrong.

Sales Funnel Efficiency　Another advantage the digital world offers in comparison to traditional media is the measurement of sales funnel efficiency. A sales funnel is an inverted pyramid that draws potential customers through a company's sales process. As the name indicates, it is wide at the top because customers with all levels of engagement enter and eventually the strongest leads are channeled to the bottom to be turned into successful sales. Figure 15.5 illustrates a hypothetical sales funnel.[21]

As an example, Scott Equipment could place a banner ad with one of the digital ad networks. The company could ascertain the number of individuals who saw the banner ad (the number of ad impressions). Assume the banner ad generated 10,000 views, or impressions. Of the 10,000 who saw the banner ad, 2.7% clicked through to the website. Once at the website, 72% browsed more than one page. Other metrics specify which pages were viewed, for how long, and the exact path visitors took around the website. Of

▸ **FIGURE 15.5**
Sales Funnel Efficiency

those who accessed the website, 28% placed items in a shopping cart and of those individuals, 61% completed the purchase process. Most companies want individuals to come back and make additional purchases, so they are encouraged to create an account. While cookies on individual computers can track return visitors, creating accounts results in a more accurate method of examining people's behavior. Sales funnel efficiency allows marketers to compare multiple digital campaigns or ad designs to see which are the most effective.

▲ Sales funnel efficiency can be used by Wholly Guacamole and Sonic to evaluate the success of this banner ad.

Web Chatter A new form of online evaluation measures and monitors web chatter. The WiseWindow company offers software (Mass Opinion Business Intelligence, MOBI) that swiftly analyzes large numbers of opinions posted on the web, blogs, Twitter, and social networking sites such as Facebook. MOBI provides continuous, real-time information concerning consumer sentiment about a brand, business, or advertising campaign from millions of sites virtually instantaneously. Kia, Best Buy, Viacom, Cisco Systems, and Intuit are companies that utilize the software to analyze customer, employee, and investor sentiments.

Gaylord Hotels applied sentiment analysis software called Clarabridge to examine customer feelings about the company's network of upscale resorts. From the sentiment analysis, Gaylord's marketing team concluded that the first 20 minutes of a guest's visit were the most critical and there were five ways the company could increase the likelihood that guests would recommend the hotel to others. The web chat analysis revealed it was important to take a new guest to a location rather than just point out where it was or show them on a map. David C. Kloeppel, chief operating officer for Gaylord Hotels, stated, " . . . if we could perfect the first 20 minutes of the [web visitors] experience, we could drive positive overall guest satisfaction."[22]

Social Media Metrics Figure 15.6 presents the social media metrics organizations use to measure volume of social media traffic, level of engagement, and conversion. While creating a large following is nice, and engaging consumers with the social media site is good, ultimately, conversion levels determine the success of a social media marketing program.

Volume metrics measure the level of traffic to social media sites. Measurement often starts with total views. Counting the number of new followers or visits provides valuable information; however, the number lost will be equally important. When a social media site loses more individuals than it gains, something requires a correction. Volume measures also provide the location of visitors and the time of day and day of the week when the most visits occur.

Other metrics note the level of *engagement* individuals have with the brand's social media platforms. Shares, reposts, re-tweets, likes, and mentions indicate a person liked what he saw and passed it on to other individuals. Social media offers two-way communication. The type and level of comments provides a measure of engagement. A number of social

◀ **FIGURE 15.6**
Social Media Metrics

Volume Metrics	Engagement Metrics	Conversion Metrics
• Views (total audience)	• Mentions	• Click-through rate (CTR)
• New likes/subscribers/ followers	• Shares - Reposts/ re-tweets	• Conversion ratio
• Lost likes/subscribers/ followers	• Likes	• Cost-per-conversion (CPC)
• Location	• Comments	• Average order value (AOV)
• Time/day of visit	• Time on page	• Revenue per visit (RPV)
	• Visits per (day, month)	• Funnel efficiency
	• Bounce rate	

media and digital research firms specialize in providing a **buzz score (or brand buzz)**, which accounts for the number of times a brand receives a mention on social networks within a specific time frame. Although the number of mentions provides an indicator of the popularity of a brand in social media; the sentiment score is more important. *Sentiment* refers to whether the buzz was negative or positive. Marketers recognize that both reactions should be monitored. When positive buzz takes place, employees can join the conversation and thank fans for their support and even reward them in some way. When negative buzz occurs, the marketing team should be prepared to react quickly to prevent the buzz from growing exponentially and going viral.

Social media *conversions* may not necessarily result in sales. Instead, conversion rates offer information about those who accessed a website for more information, downloaded or watched a video, or submitted requests for more information. Regardless of the conversion action desired, the click-through rate and conversion ratio provide insights into the social media's ability to lead individuals to a desired action. Using these metrics, marketers are able to calculate cost and revenue metrics. Marketers examine sales funnel efficiency figures to see which social media channels produced the best conversions and resulted in loyal customers.

objective 15.6

What types of behavioral evaluations can be employed to assess IMC programs?

Behavioral Evaluations

The first part of this chapter regarding message evaluations focuses on insights into what people think and feel. Some marketers contend that sales represent the only valid evaluation criterion. An advertisement may be fun and enjoyable, but if sales do not increase, it

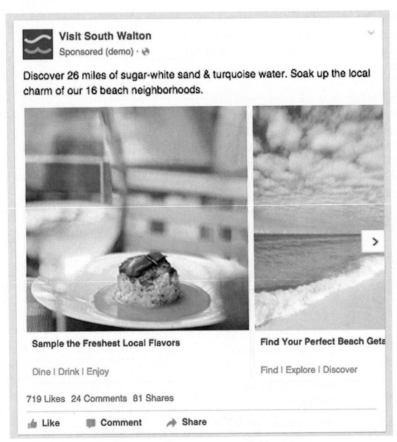

▲ Various social media metrics can be used to evaluate this Facebook post by Visit South Walton.

▲ Sales, coupons redeemed, and free Tater tots given can be used to measure the effectiveness of this advertisement.

was ineffective. The same reasoning applies to other marketing communication tools, such as consumer promotions, trade promotions, and direct marketing tactics.

While it may be true that tangible results should be the bottom line of any marketing program, not all communication objectives should be measured using sales figures. Leaders of companies with low brand awareness may be most interested in the visibility and memorability aspects of a communication plan, even though a marketing program designed to boost brand awareness does not result in immediate sales.

Measuring the results of a consumer promotion campaign featuring coupons using sales figures is easier than measuring the results of a television advertising campaign. Consequently, effective promotions evaluations involve an examination of both message and behavioral elements. This section describes some of the typical behavioral measures used by companies (see Figure 15.7).

Sales Measuring changes in sales in the retail sector following a marketing campaign is relatively simple. Retailers collect information from universal product codes (UPCs) and scanner data. These data are available on a weekly and, in some situations, daily basis for each store. Many retail outlets have access to real-time sales information that can be accessed at any point during a campaign.

Scanner data make it possible for company leaders to monitor sales and assist both the retailer and the manufacturer discover the impact of a marketing program. At the same time, extraneous factors often affect sales. In a multimedia advertising program, it would be difficult to know which advertisement moved the customer to action. A company featuring a fall line of jackets may be affected by a cold snap. If so, what caused the customer to buy—the ad or the weather? Firms utilizing trade and consumer promotion programs should account for the impact of both the promotion and the advertising when studying sales figures. Sales provide one indicator of effectiveness; however, they may be influenced by additional factors.

Evaluating Advertising As highlighted in Figure 15.8, advertisements may be the most difficult component of the IMC program to evaluate, for several reasons. As noted, distinguishing the effects of advertising from other factors may be difficult. Advertisements create short- and long-term effects, and consumers and businesses see them in many different contexts. The direct impact of one advertisement or one campaign on sales will be difficult to decipher.

Advertising often has a delayed impact. Many times, consumers encounter ads and are persuaded to purchase the product but do not make the purchase until later when they actually need the item. A woman may be convinced that she wants to buy a new pair of jeans in response to a sexy and effective advertisement by Calvin Klein. Still, rather than buying them herself, she leaves several well-placed hints for her husband before her next birthday, which could be several months later. The problem could be that her husband purchased another brand or a different gift. So, she either waits for another special occasion for her husband to buy the jeans or she makes the purchase herself at a later time.

Many times consumers decide to make purchases based on an advertisement but change their minds when they arrive at the retail store. A competing brand may be on sale, the store could be out of the desired brand, or the salesperson could persuade the customer

- Sales
- Response rates
- Redemption rates
- Test markets
- Purchase simulation tests

▲ **FIGURE 15.7**
Common Behavioural Measures

We plow. We grow. We harvest. We dig. We dig deep. Because when all is said and done, when we kick the dirt off our boots at night, commitment is what matters. The kind of commitment that gets under your fingernails. Heavy-duty commitment. Call 888.370.7963 or visit SCOTTCOMPANIES.COM.

SCOTT EQUIPMENT HEAVY-DUTY COMMITMENT

CONSTRUCTION & AGRICULTURE EQUIPMENT | CRANES | RENTALS | PARTS & SERVICE

▲ Measuring the sales impact of this Scott Equipment ad is challenging.

- Influence of other factors
- Delayed impact of the ads
- Consumers changing their minds while in the store
- Whether the brand is in the consumer's evoked set
- Level of brand equity

▲ **FIGURE 15.8**
Factors that Make Advertising Difficult to Evaluate

▶ Marketers for O'Nealgas can measure the number of individuals who called the toll-free number in the ad.

▼ Kraft Foods' marketing team can measure how many individuals access the QR code and then use other online metrics to evaluate behavior once at the website.

that another brand is better. In each case, the ad was successful on one level but another factor interfered before the purchase was made.

Further, the brand being advertised may not be part of the consumer's evoked set. Upon hearing or seeing the ad, however, the brand moves into the evoked set. Thus, even when an individual does not consider the brand at first, it will come to mind in the future when the need arises or when the consumer becomes dissatisfied with a current option.

Advertising helps generate brand awareness and brand equity. Although sales may not be the result immediately, the ad may build brand equity, which, in turn, influences future purchases.

Response Rates   Marketers study direct response advertising, direct mail, or other marketing campaign response rates, while still noting that some marketing efforts do not result in immediate sales. Instead, customers make inquiries through toll-free telephone numbers, email, website, or social media platforms. To measure response rates, companies code marketing pieces and use dedicated phone numbers or microsites. Thus, if a visit is made to a particular microsite or to a toll-free number listed on a mailer, the marketer knows which campaign it came from. In the advertisement for O'Nealgas shown in this section, it would be possible to measure how many people called the toll-free number and those who requested a free pressure check.

The Canadian Tourism Commission tested direct response ads placed on television, radio, direct mail, and online. Each ad used a different URL for viewers to access for additional information. To the tourist, there was no perceivable difference, because each URL took the person to the designated Canadian Tourism microsite. The Tourism Commission could track which ad the person viewed and the URL the person used. This made it possible to count the number of visitors from each of the direct-response advertisements.[23]

▲ Wholly Guacamole's marketers evaluated this brand alliance campaign with Disney using the redemption rate for the mail-in rebate.

Many ads now add QR codes for consumers to access through their mobile phones. Some link to a company's website, while others offer special deals or information. The advertisement for Kraft Parmesan Cheese in this section includes a QR code. The marketing department counts how many individuals accessed the code. They also gather information about individuals who used it.

Redemption Rates   Marketers study various kinds of redemption rates to measure behavioral effectiveness. Companies code coupons, premiums, rebates, contests, sweepstakes, and direct-mail pieces. The embedded code allows a marketer to compare the redemption rate of a current campaign with previous campaigns. It measures the various formats of marketing collateral, such as three different versions of direct mail piece or email offer. Even different types of marketing campaigns can be evaluated. For instance, marketers can compare redemption rates from a coupon offer to a price-off or rebate offer.

For trade and consumer promotions and direct-response programs, redemption rates provide a more accurate measure than sales. As stated with measuring the impact of advertising, a change in sales after a coupon promotion may not all be the result of the coupon offer. Extraneous factors may have contributed to the change in sales. Redemption rates provide an accurate measure of how many individuals responded to the marketing offer.

Test Markets

Test markets enable company leaders to examine the effects of a marketing effort on a small scale before launching a national or international campaign. The marketing team can examine several elements of a marketing communication program in one setting. If the test market achieves success, then the likelihood that the national campaign will be effective improves. Test markets measure the effects of a campaign in a new country before launching a full-scale international effort. Test market programs are used to assess:

- Advertisements
- Consumer and trade promotions
- Pricing tactics
- New products

Test markets provide cost-effective methods to analyze and make changes in marketing efforts before millions of dollars are spent on something that might not accomplish its objectives. Advertisements may be modified, promotions revised, and pricing policies revisited before undertaking a more widespread program. For example, McDonald's tested new ads that touted cleaner restaurants and friendlier service. The campaign's goal was to emphasize McDonald's efforts to improve in-store and drive-through services. Two television spots and one radio spot were produced and aired in Tampa and Seattle.

SHAPING THE FUTURE OF TEXAS

Weaver is the firm of choice for companies and individuals with dreams and goals as big as Texas. And bigger.

AUSTIN | DALLAS | FORT WORTH | HOUSTON | MIDLAND | ODESSA | SAN ANTONIO   **weaver**

MORE AT WEAVER.COM

▲ A test market can be used to evaluate various aspects of an advertising campaign for Weaver before it is launched in the seven cities where offices are located.

Reactions from the test markets provided McDonald's marketing team and the advertising agency with information about the impact of the commercials, the parts of the message that should be modified, and whether the campaign should be launched nationally.[24]

Test markets hold the advantage of resembling an actual purchasing situation more than any of the other tests. Making sure the site selected for the test market strongly resembles the target population becomes the key. A product targeted toward senior citizens should be studied in an area with a high concentration of seniors.

A test market campaign should resemble the national or full marketing plan, if possible. A lengthy time lapse may cause a company to experience differing results. Marketers try to make sure the test market provides a mirror image of the actual marketing program.

A test market might be as short as a few days or as long as two to three years. A test that is too short may yield less reliable results. If the test market is too long, the national market situation may change and the test market may no longer be a representative sample. The greater drawback is that the competition can study what takes places, which gives them time to react to the proposed marketing campaign.

Competitive Responses   Competing companies often respond to test market programs in one of two ways. First, some introduce a special promotion in the test market area in order to confound the results. This may reduce sales for the tested product, making the campaign appear to be less attractive than it actually was. The second approach involves not intervening in the test market, but instead using the time to prepare a countermarketing campaign. Firms that use this tactic are ready when the national launch occurs, and the impact may be that the test market results are not as predictive of what will happen.

Scanner Data   Scanner data make it possible for results from test market campaigns to be made quickly available. The figures help determine the acceptability of test market results. A firm can design several versions of a marketing campaign in different test markets. Scanner data assist marketers in comparing the sales from each test market to determine which version works best. For example, in one test market the firm might present an advertising campaign only. In the second test market, coupons are added to the ad program. In the third test market, a premium will be combined with advertising. The results from each area help the marketing team understand which type of marketing campaign fared best.

Test markets present the opportunity to test communication ideas in more true-to-life settings. Test markets examine trade and consumer promotions, direct marketing, and other marketing communication tools. They are not quite as accurate when assessing advertising, because changes in sales take longer and the test market program may not be long enough to measure the full impact. In any case, test markets offer valuable instruments to examine specific marketing features and more general communications campaigns.

Purchase Simulation Tests

Instead of test markets, marketing researchers can employ purchase simulation tests. Simulated purchase tests deliver a cost-effective approach to examine purchase behaviors. Research Systems Corporation (RSC) specializes in purchase simulation studies.

RSC tests the impact of commercials by studying consumer behaviors in a controlled laboratory environment.

In some tests, researchers ask consumers if they would be willing to buy products in a variety of ways, using various methods. Subjects might be questioned about purchase intentions at the end of a laboratory experiment. In those situations, however, intentions are self-reported and may be a less accurate predictor of future purchase behaviors. RSC does not request consumer opinions, ask them to describe their attitudes, or even inquire as to whether they plan to purchase the product. Instead, RSC creates a simulated shopping experience. Subjects choose from a variety of products they would see on a store shelf. After completing a simulated shopping exercise, the subjects are seated and watch a television preview containing various commercials. The participants view the TV program as they would watch any TV show at home. Researchers place the test ad in with others, and the subjects do not know which ad is being tested.

After completing the preview, the subjects participate in a second shopping exercise. Researchers then compare the products chosen in the first shopping trip to those selected in the second. Shifts in brand choices are at least partly due to the effectiveness of the advertisement, because it was the only variable that changed.

This methodology offers the advantage of using test procedures that do not rely on opinions and attitudes. Among other things, this means that RSC's procedure would work in international markets as well as domestic markets.[25] In some cultures, subjects tend to seek to please the interviewer who asks about opinions and attitudes. As a result, they give polite and socially acceptable answers. The same subjects may also seek to provide answers they think the interviewer wants to hear. By studying purchases instead of soliciting opinions, subjects feel free to respond in a more forthright fashion.

In summary, the systems available to examine respondent behaviors are response rates, online metrics, test markets, and purchase simulation tests. Marketers use these programs in conjunction with one another and with the message evaluation techniques described earlier. These approaches are not used in a vacuum. Instead, the data generated and findings revealed are tested across several instruments and with numerous groups of subjects. In that manner, the marketing department manager and the advertising agency heighten the odds that both short- and long-term goals will be reached through the ads, premiums, coupons, and other marketing communications devices sent to consumers.

International Implications

Many of the techniques described in this chapter are available worldwide. IMC programs should be assessed in several ways, including domestic results, results in other countries, and as an overall organization.

objective 15.7
How are evaluation programs adjusted to match international operations?

Individual advertisements and promotional programs are examined in the countries in which they appear. Due to differing standards regarding advertising content, they must be evaluated in light of local cultures and purchasing habits.

Many times, marketers assess advertising and promotional programs across national boundaries. For example, a campaign launched in Europe leads to evaluations in individual countries including France, Spain, and Italy, but also as a collective, such as the European Union. Measures of attitudes may be difficult to collect. Sales are easier to assess due to the use of the euro in all of these nations; however, local conditions influence inflation rates and other statistics.

It is advisable to contract with local advertising agencies to discover the most viable techniques in other countries. In some nations, using coupons may be viewed as a sign of poverty, and users are either secretive or embarrassed about redeeming them. In those situations, it helps to study results in light of cultural norms.

Numerous multinational conglomerates assess advertising and promotional efforts through regional offices. Pacific Rim information will be combined with information from Europe, Africa, and other places. The goal is to make sure an overall image and theme is projected worldwide.

Summary

Assessing an IMC program often involves examining the effects of individual advertisements. These efforts are conducted in three major ways: message evaluations, online evaluation metrics, and evaluating respondent behaviors. Numerous techniques are available. Most of the time, marketing managers and advertisement agencies apply several different methods in order to get the best picture of an ad's potential for success. Advertisements are studied before they are developed, while they are being developed, and after they have been released or launched.

The guiding principles for any marketing tool include agreement on how test results will be used, pre-establishing a cutoff score for a test's results, employing multiple measures, basing studies on models of human behaviors, creating multiple exposures, testing marketing instruments that are in the same stage of development, and preventing as many biases as possible while conducting the test. Many times, certain members of the marketing team may not be objective, especially when they had the idea for the ad or campaign. In these instances, companies retain an outside research agency to study the project.

Message evaluations take place at every stage of the development process. Methods that may be employed include advertising tracking research, copytesting, emotional reaction tests, and cognitive neuroscience.

Positioning advertising copytesting (PACT) is primarily used to evaluate television advertisements. Nine key principles are involved. The principles apply to any type of message evaluation system and all types of media.

Online evaluation metrics include the use of click-throughs, dwell rates, and dwell time. Dwell rates specify the number of impressions that resulted in users clicking on an ad or mousing over it. Dwell time indicates the amount of time a visitor spent engaged with an advertisement. Interactive data are carefully evaluated in light of the company's IMC objectives. The newest form of evaluation is measuring and monitoring web chat.

Behavioral evaluations consist of sales and response rates, toll-free number responses, response cards, internet responses, and redemption rates. Test markets assess advertisements, consumer and trade promotions, pricing tactics, and acceptance of new products. Purchase simulation tests offer cost-effective methods to analyze the impact of advertising and promotion on immediate consumer purchase responses.

When the IMC theme and voice are clear, the company achieves its long-range objectives, the principles stated in this book are applied efficiently and effectively, and the organization is in the best position to succeed at all levels, including in all international operations.

Key Terms

metrics Measures designed to portray the effectiveness of a marketing communications plan

message evaluation techniques Methods used to examine the creative message and the physical design of an advertisement, coupon, or direct marketing piece

online evaluation metrics Methods used to examine online advertising and marketing campaigns

click-throughs the number of individuals who clicked on a brand message and were taken directly to the brand's website

respondent behavior evaluations Methods used to examine visible customer actions, including making store visits, inquiries, or actual purchases

copytests Tests used to evaluate a marketing piece that is finished or in its final stages prior to production

portfolio test A test of an advertisement using a set of print ads, one of which is the ad being evaluated

theater test A test of an advertisement using a set of television ads, including the one being evaluated

warmth monitor A method to measure emotional responses to advertisements

biometric research A method to measure physiological reactions to advertisements and marketing messages

cognitive neuroscience A brain-image measurement process that tracks brain activity

positioning advertising copytesting (PACT) Principles to use when assessing the effectiveness of various messages

buzz score (or brand buzz), A measure of the number of times a brand receives a mention on social networks within a specific time frame.

MyMarketingLab

To complete the problems with the ⭐ in your MyLab, go to the end-of-chapter Discussion Questions.

Review Questions

15-1. What are the three categories of evaluation tools that can be used to evaluate IMC systems?

15-2. What common IMC objectives are matched with methods of evaluation?

15-3. What are message evaluations?

15-4. What is advertising tracking research? What does it help the marketing team assess?

15-5. Describe the use of portfolio tests and theater tests in copytesting programs.

15-6. Describe a warmth monitor and biometric research. What do they measure?

15-7. Describe the advantages and uses of cognitive neuroscience as a method for evaluating advertising and marketing programs.

15-8. What are the positioning advertising copytesting principles that help advertisers prepare quality ads and campaigns?

15-9. What online evaluation metrics can be used to analyze marketing communications?

15-10. What social media metrics can be used to analyze marketing communications?

15-11. Define the terms click-throughs, dwell rate, and dwell time. How are these measures used to evaluate marketing communications?

15-12. What are the primary forms of behavioral evaluations that can be used to test advertisements and other marketing pieces?

15-13. How are behavioral responses to marketing messages measured?

15-14. What items can be evaluated using test markets?

15-15. Describe a purchase simulation test.

15-16. What differences occur when international marketing programs are assessed?

Critical Thinking Exercises

DISCUSSION QUESTIONS

15-17. Explain the differences among message evaluation techniques, online evaluation metrics, and respondent behavior evaluations. Discuss why each is important and explain how Maxwell House coffee could use each for the ad campaign shown in this chapter.

15-18. Describe in your own words each of the message evaluation techniques: advertising tracking research, copytesting, and cognitive neuroscience. If Victoria's Secret's marketing team wanted to evaluate their latest television ad campaign, how could its advertising agency use each of the message evaluation techniques? Which of the three methods would you use? Why?

15-19. Interview five of your friends or relatives. Ask each person to write down two advertisements they enjoyed and their reasons. Ask individuals to write down two advertisements they dislike and their reasons. Finally, ask them to write down an advertisement they believe is offensive and their reasons. Ask other students to read their lists comparing ads that were liked, disliked, or considered offensive. What common elements did you find in each category? What were the differences?

15-20. Review the section of the chapter on cognitive neuroscience. What are your thoughts about using cognitive neuroscience? Besides ads containing sexual content, identify two other situations where cognitive neuroscience would yield superior results to emotional reaction tests or copytests. Explain why.

15-21. Review the digital metrics shown in Figure 15.4 and discussed in the chapter. Imagine you are a marketing intern for Chic Shaque (see the ad in this chapter). Your boss asked you to identify the top three web metrics and the top three conversion and campaign metrics. Which would you choose? Justify your answer.

15-22. Use the following data to calculate the appropriate percentages for a sales funnel efficiency analysis of a banner ad campaign. The average click-through rate for banner ads is 0.5 percent. There were 40,000 visits/impressions and 450 click-throughs. 260 browsed products on the website, 225 placed items in the shopping cart, 196 made a purchase, and 156 created accounts. Which areas would be of most concern to marketers? Why?

15-23. Review the social media metrics shown in Figure 15.6 and discussed in the chapter. You are a marketing intern for Visit South Walton and have been asked to evaluate its social media campaign in Facebook (see the Facebook post shown in the social media section of the chapter). Identify the two most important volume metrics, two most important engagement metrics and two most important conversion metrics. Justify why you selected the metrics you did.

15-24. Are sales figures important when evaluating integrated marketing communications? How should marketers use hard data such as redemption rates, response rates and store traffic in the evaluation of marketing communications? In terms of accountability, how important are behavioral measures of IMC effectiveness?

15-25. A clothing manufacturer spends $6 million on trade promotions and $3 million on consumer promotions. How would you measure the impact of these expenditures? If an agency were hired to manage these expenditures, what type of measures would you insist the company utilize?

⭐**15-26.** In some Asian countries, it is improper to talk about oneself. Therefore, people often are too embarrassed to answer questions about feelings and emotions. Those who do answer the questions would tend to provide superficial answers. Explain the advantages of a simulated purchasing test methodology in this situation. What other methods of evaluating feelings and emotions could an agency use in Asian countries? Justify your choice.

Integrated Learning Exercises

15-27. Decision Analysts, Inc., is a leading provider of advertising and marketing research. Access the company's website at **www.decisionanalyst.com** and investigate the various services the company offers. Examine the advertising research services available. Write a short report about how advertising research services provided by Decision Analysts could be used by companies to evaluate advertising campaigns.

15-28. Ipsos-ASI (**www.ipsos-asi.com**) is an advertising research firm with a high level of expertise in ad testing and measurements. Access the company's products and services. What services are offered? When could the various services be used to evaluate marketing and advertising campaigns? Be specific.

15-29. Adknowledge is a firm that excels at measuring internet and social media traffic. Access the website at **www.adknowledge.com**. What services does the company offer in terms of digital and social media analysis? Describe a research project you believe this company could conduct successfully to assist in advertising or internet research.

15-30. ComScore is a firm that measures mobile, digital, and social media advertising. Access the website at **www.comscore.com**. What services does the company offer to evaluate mobile, digital, and social media campaigns? Be specific. Suppose you wanted to evaluate a digital, social, and mobile campaign for Interstate Batteries. Which comScore services would you use? Why?

15-31. Millward Brown provides marketing and advertising evaluations. Access the company's website at **www.millwardbrown.com**. Describe the various services offered by the company. You have been asked to evaluate an advertising campaign for Forever 21 clothes. Identify and discuss the Millward Brown tools you would use.

15-32. Ameritest provides marketing and advertising evaluations. Access the company's website at **www.ameritest.net**. Describe the various services offered by the company. Suppose you want to evaluate an advertising and digital campaign for Urban Outfitters. Identify four Ameritest tools you could use. Justify your choice of these four evaluation methods.

Student Project

CREATIVE CORNER

After leaders at PepsiCo and Starbucks became concerned about the diminishing supply of fresh, clean water, the companies teamed together to sell Ethos Water. The product's distribution has expanded, and it is now sold in major grocery stores, convenience stores, and drug stores. The goal of Ethos Water is to ensure that children throughout the world have clean water.

Access the Ethos Water website at **www.ethoswater.com**. After reviewing the site, design a print ad for a magazine aimed at college students in your area. If you were responsible for evaluating the advertisement you just created, what evaluation measures would you use? Why? If you were responsible for evaluating the Ethos Water website, which metrics would you use? Why?

THE VASELINE HEALING PROJECT

Recently, Vaseline's management and marketing teams devised a new program. The Vaseline Healing Project was created to place Vaseline and small first aid kits into the hands of people in less-developed countries. One advertisement notes that most people only think of Vaseline when they have chapped lips or some other small malady, but that in some parts of the world a skin problem can result in far more serious health issues.[26]

The program is relatively straightforward. The purchase of one container of Vaseline results in one "healing donation" to the fund. The "relief kits" contain hygiene products as well as Vaseline. Families and first responders are eligible to receive them. The fund also supports "healing stations" in various countries. By the end of 2016, the program had touched more than 1.5 million lives.

An example of the reach of the program took place in Syria. As refugees walked miles to move away from the wars and violence, doctors in aid stations noted many had badly damaged skin, especially on their feet. The refugees were forced to use open fires to cook, which meant many had suffered burns. Vaseline offers relief for these and other skin problems, including worsening eczema and psoriasis that occur due to dry skin.

In addition to television advertisement, a website allows direct contributions to the healing project. The company received a great deal of publicity for the program. To further spread the word, Vaseline produced a film about the program entitled *Not So Ordinary*.

Stories in the *Washington Post* and *Forbes* hailed the program and its champion, Emmy Award winning actress Viola Davis. The company garnered a 100% rating for its efficiency, which means all of the donated dollars turned into aid for people in need. The stories noted that skin ailments prevent children from attending school and adults from being able to work.

The series of advertisements for the healing project shared the common theme that a small effort can lead to a great deal of relief. The advertising tagline summarized the program best: "An ordinary jar can make an extraordinary difference." Many of these ads can still be found on YouTube.

15-33. What message evaluation techniques could be used in evaluating the Vaseline Healing Project advertising campaign? Be specific.

15-34. Describe how advertising tracking research could be used to evaluate the Vaseline Healing Project commercials.

15-35. Describe how cognitive neuroscience could be used in developing and evaluating the healing project campaign.

15-36. Which digital and social media metrics would you use to evaluate the campaign? Explain why.

15-37. Which behavioral evaluations would be most useful for evaluating the healing project campaign?

SPYCH MARKET ANALYTICS

A new age of marketing communication evaluation may be under way. Spych Marketing Analytics provides innovative solutions for companies seeking a better understanding of the future market environments, including the Gen Y and Millennial consumer segments, the advancement of technology, and the quickly evolving world of customer experience. The company tries to delve into the insights and emotions of these groups, providing an innovative portal into the psyches of these markets through its program called Empathic Youth Research and other mixed methodological approaches to consumer insights. CEO Benjamin Smithee argues that it is important to look at the foundations and fundamentals of the advertising industry, and right now we are seeing a dramatic paradigm shift in the ways marketing communications are delivered and consumed. The media include traditional advertising venues and public relations, but also social media and mobile technologies, utilized by an evolving set of consumers.

Company employees work to enhance every aspect of the market research process. On its website, the organization proclaims, " . . . we create natural environments for our respondents, evoking rich insights and opinions that surface only through truly natural and empathic interactions." Further, "The Spych Experience maximizes the return your team obtains from each project overcoming fallacies often associated with traditional youth research."

To achieve these ideals, the company employs innovative concepts regarding marketing metrics and consumer understanding. The concepts are based on the importance of going beyond simply engaging customers to include "re-advertising." CEO Benjamin Smithee notes a new model in which "sharing" becomes a second important outcome from a marketing effort, as shown in Figure 15.9.

Spych seeks to identify levels of engagement in terms of "intensity," in which a message is shared with friends and others.

The concepts of "share-ability" and "virality" take on particular importance in Spych parlance. As a Spych Marketing Analytics employee noted, the company asks a key question: Does this pass the traditional advertising test and then lead to sharing? In previous times, an ad might be shared with one or two other people, such as when a person would tear an advertisement out of a newspaper or magazine and give it to a friend. Now, a message can quickly be re-posted to 200-plus Facebook friends.

In essence, Spych bases its conclusions about a message's success in terms of "engagement" with an advertisement, which is measured by "click commitment." Click commitment indicates the willingness of a person to click on an ad on a medium such as Twitter. Typically the decision is made in three seconds or less. Another measure of success is "socialization," which occurs when a visitor passes the advertisement on to others.

Taking the next step, new technologies allow for tracking of shares and targeted marketing capabilities unlike anything we have ever possessed. Beyond simply counting the number of times a marketing message has been passed along to others, the company can examine the "social profiles" of those receiving re-advertisements and focus on the influences most relevant to a brand, rather than the generic traditional means of targeting. The reasoning behind such tracking goes to the heart of the target market. A new generation of consumer shops in a new manner, communicates through channels that have not been previously available, and responds to companies and marketing messages in ways we have never seen.

The ultimate goals of these measures and concepts remain the same as in any traditional marketing effort. Return visits to various vendors, repeat purchases, word-of-mouth endorsements,

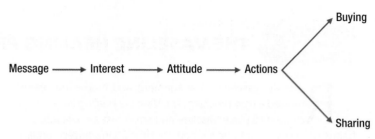

▲ **FIGURE 15.9**
Moving from Message to Buying/Sharing

and feeling a connection (brand loyalty) with a company, all of which lead to increased sales over time suggest that a marketing program has achieved success. Re-advertising and sharing with others enhance the prospects of reaching the right audience, sending the right message, and creating long term relationships with the company. As CEO Smithee summarized, "The more layers you can seamlessly integrate, the better chance of getting something sticky."

15-38. Would the concepts used to measure marketing success match with the message evaluation methods presented in this chapter? Why or why not?

15-39. Compare the concepts used by Spych with the terms "behavioral response" and "attitudinal response."

15-40. What roles do "emotions" and "logic" play in the Spych approach to marketing communications?

15-41. What roles do social media and hand-held technologies such as smart phones play in today's marketing environment? How will they evolve in the future?

MyMarketingLab

Go to the Assignments section of your MyLab to complete these writing exercises.

15-42. Explain the differences between web metrics and conversion and campaign metrics for digital marketing. Explain the differences among volume, engagement, and conversion metrics for social media. Suppose Sonic has launched a digital and social media campaign. Identify the six most important metrics to evaluate both the digital and social media campaign. Justify your choice.

15-43. ComScore is a firm that measures internet traffic and internet advertising. Access the website at **www .comscore.com**. What services does the company offer? Describe a research project you feel this company could do successfully to assist in advertising or internet research.

Endnotes

Chapter 1

1. E. J. Schultz, "Lean Cuisine Makes 'Massive Pivot' Away from Diet Marketing," *Advertising Age,* June 26, 2015, **adage.com/article/cmo-strategy/lean-cuisine-makes-massive-pivot-diet-marketing/299236/**, retrieved December 13, 2015.

2. Donald Baack, "Communication Processes," *Organizational Behavior* (Houston: Dame Publications, Inc., 1998), pp. 313, 37.

3. Brian Morrissey, "Chick-fil-A's Strategy: Give Your Fans Something to Do," *Brandweek* 50, no. 35 (October 5, 2009), p. 40.

4. James G. Hutton, "Integrated Marketing Communications and the Evolution of Marketing Thought," *Journal of Business Research* 37 (November 1996), pp. 155, 62.

5. Diane Brady, "Making Marketing Measure Up," *BusinessWeek* (December 13, 2004), pp. 112, 13; "Top 10: Issues Facing Senior Marketers in 2007," *Advertising Age* 78, no. 17 (April 23, 2007), p. 23.

6. "Campbell Dives Deeper into Digital with Major Spending Hikes," *Advertising Age*, July 23, 2015, **adage.com/article/299631**.

7. Andrew McMains, "Ad Spending Trends Reveal No Surprises," *Adweek* 48, no. 44 (December 3, 2007), p. 9.G14

8. Tim Peterson, "How P&G is Tying Snapchat ads to In-Store Sales," *Adage*, November 18, 2015, **adage.com/article/cmo-strategy/p-g-tying-snapchaat-ads-store-sales/301405**.

9. Katherine Rosman, "In Digital Era, What Does Watching TV Even Mean?" October 8, 2013, **www.wsj.com**.

10. Mark Walsh, "Microsoft Highlights Usage Across Device Pathways," *Online Media Daily*, March 14, 2013, **www.mediapost.com/publications/article/195786**.

11. Lauren Keller Johnson, "Harnessing the Power of the Customer," *Harvard Management Update* 9 (March 2004), pp. 3, 5; Patricia Seybold, *The Customer Revolution* (London: Random House Business Books, 2006).

12. "U.S. Online Retail Sales to Reach $370 Billion by 2017," **www.forrester.com/US+online+retail+sales+to+reach+370+billion+by+2017/-/E-PRE4764**, accessed December 1, 2015.

13. Katy Keim, "Don't Be Fooled: Social-Media Consumers Aren't in a Relationship with You," *Advertising Age*, May 29, 2013, **www.adage.com**.

14. Ibid.

15. "Doritos Launches First Global Campaign," *Advertising Age*, March 6, 2013, **adage.com/print/240173**.

16. M. N. Tripathi, "Customer Engagement & Key to Successful Brand Building," *The XIMB Journal of Management* 6, no. 1 (March 2009), pp. 131, 40.

17. Jean-Noel Kapferer, "The Roots of Brand Loyalty Decline: An International Comparison," *Ivey Business Journal* 69, no. 4 (March & April 2005), pp. 1, 6.

18. Jana Lay-Hwa Bowden, "The Process of Customer Engagement: A Conceptual Framework," *Journal of Marketing Theory & Practice* 17, no. 1 (Winter 2009), pp. 63, 74.

19. "5 Reasons Why Integrated Marketing Works," Zehnder Insights Blog, posted by Beth Swayne, **www.z-comm.com/blog/5-reasons-why-integrated-marketing-works**, accessed December 1, 2015

20. Stephen J. Gould, Dawn B. Lerman, and Andreas F. Grein, "Agency Perceptions and Practices on Global IMC," *Journal of Advertising Research* (January & February 1999), pp. 7, 26.

21. Ibid.

22. Jane L. Levere, "A Campaign from Jaguar to Show its Wild Side," *The New York Times*, February 26, 2012, **www.nytimes.com/2012/02/27/business/media/jaguar-ad-campaign**.

23. Karlene Lukovitz, "Eight O'Clock Coffee Ups Marketing for Brand Refresh," *Marketing Daily,* August 16, 2013, **www.mediapost.com/publications/article/206930/eight-oclock-coffee-ups-marketing-for-brand-refre.html**. Eight O'Clock Coffee, 2013, **www.eightoclock.com/**. *Daily Coffee News,* "Eight O'Clock Coffee Unveils Brand Redesign, Marketing Plans," August 14, 2013, **www.dailycoffeenews.com**.

Chapter 2

1. Katie Kindelan, "Domino's Tells Customers They're Not Always Right, *ABC News, Good Morning America*, April 3, 2012, **www.abcnews.com**, retrieved December 31, 2015.

2. *Advertising Age*, "Domino's Destroys Signs to Remind Us It's Not Just Pizza, June 26, 2015, **adage.com/article/media/watch-newest-ads-tv-june-26/299241/**, retrieved December 31, 2015.

3. Arun Sudhaman, "Brand Quality Still Key to Corporate Reputation: Edelman," *Media Asia* (November 19, 2004), p. 8.

4. Paul Farhi, "Behind Domino's Mea Culpa Ad Campaign, *Washington Post*, January 13, 2010, **www.washingtonpost.com/wp-dyn/content/article/2010/01/12/AR2010011201696.html**, retrieved December 31, 2015/

5. Shelly Banjo, "Wal-Mart Ads Tout American Success Story, *The Wall Street Journal,* May 3, 2013, **www.wsj.com**.

6. Based on "Best Global Brands, 2015 Ranking," *Interbrand,* **interbrand.com/best-brands/best-global-brands/2015/ranking/**, accessed December 4, 2014.

7. Paul McNamara, "The Name Game," *Network World* (April 20, 1998), pp. 77, 78.

8. Max Du Bois, "Making Your Company One in a Million," *Brand Strategy,* no. 153 (November 2001), pp. 10, 11.

9. Michael J. De La Merced, "Kraft, Mondelez and the Art of Corporate Rebranding," *The New York Times,* March 21, 2012, **www.nytimes.com**.

10. Andrew Adam Newman, "Nestle Adds Premium Brand in Still Water Arena," *The New York Times,* **www.nytimes.com**, June 9, 2013.

11. Interview with Tracy Altman, Wholly Guacamole, November 7, 2013.

12. Pamela W. Henderson and Joseph A. Cote, "Guidelines for Selecting or Modifying Logos," *Journal of Marketing* (April 1998), pp. 14, 30.

13. Daniel Andreani, "Go Ahead, Change the Ugly Logo," **www.smartbrief.com/original/2013/06/go-ahead-change-ugly-logo**, June 12, 2013.

14. Robert Klara, "New American Airlines Logo Triggers Ire and a Sense of Déjà vu," *Adweek*, **www.adweek.com/news/advertising-branding/new-american-airlines-logo-triggers-ire-and-sense-d-j-vu-146659**, January 18, 2013

15. David Griner, "IHOP Has a New Logo for the Emoticon Era," *Adweek,* **www.adweek.com/news/advertising-branding/ihop-has-new-logo-emoticon-era-165107**, June 1, 2015.

16. Kristina Monllos, "StubHub's New Logo Signals a Change in Its Mission," *Adweek,* **www.adweek.com/news/advertising-branding/stubhubs-new-logo-signals-change-its-mission-166136**, July 29, 2015.

17. Natalie Zmuda, "What Went into the Updated Pepsi Logo," *Advertising Age,* **adage.com/article/news/pepsi-s-logo-update/132016/**, October 27, 2008.

18. "Nokia Rethinks Global Marketing as a Challenger Brand," *Advertising Age,* **adage.com/print/242956**, July 3, 2013.

19. Brad Dorfman, "Exclusive: Kraft's New Marching Orders: Make Today Delicious," *Reuters,* **uk.reuters.com/article/idUKN15243520090217**, February 17, 2009.

20. Interview with Jami Salter, Scott Equipment, November 25, 2013.

21. Katya Andressen, "4 Ways to Reinvent Your Brand," **www.ragan.com/Main/Articles/46743.aspx**, May 22, 2013; "Comeback Kids: Haggar, Keds Stage Brand Revival," *Advertising Age,* October 30, 2011, **adage.com/article/news/comeback-kids-haggar-keds-stage-brand-revival/230721/**.

22. Stuart Elliott, "L'eggs Returns to TV Advertising," *The New York Times Media Decoder,* April 7, 2011, **mediadecoder.blogs.nytimes.com/2011/04/07/leggs-returns-to-tv-advertising/**.

23. "How PMH Gave Target Its Signature Look," *Advertising Age,* March 18, 2012, **adage.com/article/agency-news/pmh-gave-target-signature/233378**.

24. Branding Isn't Just for Large Companies with Deep Pockets Anymore," *Smart Business* 4, no. 2 (May 2009), pp. 20, 21.

25. Andrew Ehrenberg, Neil Barnard, and John Scriven, "Differentiation or Salience," *Journal of Advertising Research* (November & December 1997), pp. 7, 14.

26. Stuart Elliott, "A Campaign Linking Clean Clothes with Stylish Living," *The New York Times* (**www.nytimes.com/2010/01/08/business/media/08adco.html**), January 8, 2010.

27. "How PMH Gave Target Its Signature Look," *Advertising Age,* March 18, 2012, **adage.com/article/agency-news/pmh-gave-target-signature/233378/**.

28. Based on "Consumers on the Go: Top 10 Models in 2016," Advertising Age's Consumers on the Go Fact Pack, September 28, 2015, p. 20.

29. "Brand Keys 2013 Customer Loyalty Index Finds Seismic Shift I How Consumers Emotionally Engage with Products, Services," Press Release, **brandkeys.com/wp-content/uploads/2013/02/2013-CLEI-Press-Release-FINAL-Overall.pdf**.

30. "Brandz Top 100 Most Valuable Global Brands 2010," Millward Brown Optimor, **www.millwardbrown.com**, accessed March 16, 2012.

31. Kusum L. Ailawaldi, Scott A. Neslin, and Donald R. Lehman, "Revenue Premium as an Outcome Measure of Brand Equity," *Journal of Marketing* 67, no. 4 (October 2003), pp. 1, 18, Don E. Schultz, "Understanding and Measuring Brand Equity," *Marketing Management,* Spring 200, Vol. 9, No. 1, pp. 8, 9; Tanya Irwin, "Apple, Hershey's, Sprite Top Youth Brands," *MediaPost News,* October 26, 2011, **www.mediapost.com/publications/article/161108**.

32. Christopher Heine, "Check Out the Top 100 Beloved Brands," *Adweek,* **www.adweek.com/news/advertising-branding/check-out-top-100-beloved-brands-last-decade-153026**, October 10, 2013.

33. Todd Hale, "How10 Retailers Are Pushing Private Label's Potential," **www.nielsen.com**, March 3, 2014.

34. Stephanie Hilderbrandt, "What's in Store for Private Label," *Beverage Industry,* Vol. 102, No. 9, September 2011, pp. 18, 22.

35. Terri Goldstein, "Battling Brand Malpractice," *BrandWeek* (**www.adweek.com/news/advertising-branding/battling-brand-malpractice-106613**), November 2, 2009; Ellen Byron, "At the Supermarket Checkout, Frugality Trumps Brand Loyalty," *The Wall Street Journal* (**online.wsj.com/article/SB122592835021203025.html**), November 6, 2008.

36. Dongdae Lee, "Image Congruence and Attitude Toward Private Brands," *Advances in Consumer Research* 31 (2004), pp. 435, 41.

37. Rusty Williamson, "Penney's Launching New Line," *Women's Wear Daily (WWD)* 191, no. 83 (April 19, 2006), p. 2.

38. Kelly Nolan, "Apparel & Accessories: A Label for Every Style at JCP," *Retailing Today* 45, no. 14 (August 7, 2006), pp. 27, 36.

39. John Kalkowski, "Private Labels Are Booming."

40. Vanessa L. Facenda, "A Swift Kick to the Privates," *Brandweek* 48, No. 31 (September 3, 2007), pp. 24, 28.

41. Iris Perry, "Do You Help Your Customers Sell or Market?" *Paperboard Packaging* 89, no. 11 (November 2004), p. 8.

42. "Packaging Affects Brand Loyalty," *Supermarket News* 53, no. 45 (November 7, 2005), p. 36.

43. Andrea Zoe Aster, "Good Drinks Come in Smart Packaging," *Marketing Magazine* 109, no. 32 (October 4 & 11, 2004), pp. 13, 15.

44. Stuart Elliott, "A Redesigned Brand Hopes to Avoid Tropicana Storm," *The New York Times,* Media Decoder, August 31, 2011, **www.nytimes.com**.

45. "Banana Republic CMO Talks New Mad Men Collection, Unifying the Brand," *Advertising Age,* **adage.com/print/240484**, March 25, 2013.

46. Andrew McMains, "To Compete Locally, Global Brands Must Adapt," *Adweek.com* (**www.adweek.com/news/advertising-branding/compete-locally-global-brands-must-adapt-97049**), September 25, 2008.

47. Johnny K. Johansson and Ilkka A. Ronkainen, "Consider Implications of Local Brands in a Global Arena."

48. "Datsun's Revival Won't Be a Nostalgia Play," *Adweek.com* (**www.adweek.com/news/advertising-branding/datsuns-revival-wont-be-nostaglia-play-147825**).

Chapter 3

1. *Advertising Age,* Marketing Essentials, Premier Plus, 2016, Case Study: Nescafé.

2. Jeffrey B. Schmidt and Richard A. Spreng, "A Proposed Model of External Consumer Information Search," *Journal of Academy of Marketing Science* 24, no. 3 (Summer 1996), pp. 246–56.

3. Merrie Brucks, "The Effect of Product Class Knowledge on Information Search Behavior," *Journal of Consumer Research* 12 (June 1985), pp. 1–15; Schmidt and Spreng, "A Proposed Model of External Consumer Information Search."

4. Laura M. Buchholz and Robert E. Smith, "The Role of Consumer Involvement in Determining Cognitive Responses to Broadcast Advertising," *Journal of Advertising* 20, no. 1 (1991), pp. 4–17; Schmidt and Spreng, "A Proposed Model of External Consumer Information Search"; Jeffrey J. Inman, Leigh McAllister, and Wayne D. Hoyer, "Promotion Signal: Proxy for a Price Cut," *Journal of Consumer Research* 17 (June 1990), pp. 74–81; Barry J. Babin, William R. Darden, and Mitch

Griffin, "Work and/or Fun: Measuring Hedonic and Utilitarian Shopping Value," *Journal of Consumer Research* 20 (March 1994), pp. 644–56.

5. Schmidt and Spreng, "A Proposed Model of External Consumer Information Search."

6. M. Fishbein and Icek Ajzen, *Belief, Attitude, Intention, and Behavior: An Introduction to Theory and Research* (Reading, MA: Addison-Wesley, 1975).

7. Richard P. Bagozzi, Alice M. Tybout, C. Samuel Craig, and Brian Sternathal, "The Construct Validity of the Tripartite Classification of Attitudes," *Journal of Marketing* 16, no. 1 (February 1979), pp. 88–95.

8. "Jeep Leads List of 25 Most Patriotic Brands," *USA Today*, **www.usatoday.com**, July 1, 2013.

9. Discussion of cognitive mapping based on Anne R. Kearny and Stephan Kaplan, "Toward a Methodology for the Measurement of Knowledge Structures of Ordinary People: The Conceptual Content Cognitive Map (3CM)," *Environment and Behavior* 29, no. 5 (September 1997), pp. 579–617; Stephan Kaplan and R. Kaplan, *Cognition and Environment, Functioning in an Uncertain World* (Ann Arbor, MI: Ulrich's, 1982, 1989).

10. Laura Green, "Esurance Builds it Brand Power to Attract New Customers," *Smart Business*, **www.sbnonline.com/**, May 31, 2013.

11. Discussion of heuristics and multiattribute model based on William L. Wilkie and Edgar A. Pessemier, "Issues in Marketing's Use of Multiattribute Models," *Journal of Marketing Research* 10 (November 1983), pp. 428–41; Peter L. Wright, "Consumer Choice Strategies: Simplifying vs. Optimizing," *Journal of Marketing Research* 11 (February 1975), pp. 60–67; James B. Bettman, *An Information Processing Theory of Consumer Choice* (Reading, MA: Addison-Wesley, 1979).

12. "Truvia Takes Aim at Rival Sugar Substitutes With Wellness Push," *Advertising Age*, **www.adage.com**, October 8, 2013.

13. Mark Sneider, "Create Emotional Ties with Brand for Sales," *Marketing News* 38 (May 15, 2004), pp. 44–45.

14. Peter Leimbach, "Role Reversal: Mr. Mom Goes Shopping," *Adweek.com* (**www.adweek.com**), July 1, 2009.

15. "The Domestication of Man: More Men Taking on Cleaning Chores," *Quirk's Marketing Research Review*, August 2011, Article 20110826-3.

16. Mark Dolliver, "Alas, Free Time Comes at a Price," *Adweek* 45, no. 34 (September 13, 2004), p. 42 Mark Dolliver, "More Money or More Time?" *Adweek* 42, no. 11 (March 12, 2001), p. 44.

17. Discussion of second-chancers based on Richard Halverson, "The Customer Connection: Second-Chancers," *Discount Store News* 37, no. 20 (October 26, 1998), pp. 91–95.

18. "LGBT Consumers Warm to Ads Targeted to Gays," *eMarketer Digital Intelligence*, September 1, 2011, **www.emarketer.com**.

19. Stuart Elliott, "Luxury Hotels Market the Memories They Can Make," *The New York Times*, September 13, 2011, **www.nytimes.com**.

20. "Boomers Bend the Trends," *Private Label Buyer* 21, no. 4 (April 2007), p. 14.

21. Karl Greenberg, "Reebok: Huge New Campaign Touts Healthy Lifestyle," *Marketing Daily*, **www.mediapost.com/publications/article/193657**, February 15, 2013.

22. Discussion based on Frederick E. Webster, Jr., and Yoram Wind, "A General Model for Understanding Organizational Buyer Behavior," *Marketing Management* 4, no. 4 (Winter—Spring 1996), pp. 52–57; Patricia M. Doney and Gary M. Armstrong, "Effects of Accountability on Symbolic Information Search and Information Analysis by Organizational Buyers," *Journal of the Academy of Marketing Science* 24, no. 1 (Winter 1996), pp. 57–66; Rob Smith, "For Best Results, Treat Business Decision Makers as Individuals," *Advertising Age's Business Marketing* 84, no. 3 (1998), p. 39.

23. Patricia M. Doney and Gary M. Armstrong, "Effects of Accountability on Symbolic Information Search and Information Analysis by Organizational Buyers," *Journal of the Academy of Marketing Science* 24, no. 1 (Winter 1996), pp. 57–66.

24. Herbert Simon, *The New Science of Management Decisions,* rev. ed. (Upper Saddle River, NJ: Prentice Hall, 1977).

25. Webster and Wind, "A General Model for Understanding Organizational Buyer Behavior"; Doney and Armstrong, "Effects of Accountability on Symbolic Information Search and Information Analysis by Organizational Buyers"; James A. Eckert and Thomas J. Goldsby, "Using the Elaboration Likelihood Model to Guide Customer Service-Based Segmentation," *International Journal of Physical Distribution—Logistics Management* 27, no. 9–10 (1997), pp. 600–15.

26. Patrick J. Robinson, Charles W. Faris, and Yoram Wind, "Industrial Buying and Creative Marketing," *Marketing Science Institute Series* (Boston: Allyn & Bacon, 1967).

27. Adapted from Webster and Wind, "A General Model for Understanding Organizational Buyer Behavior."

28. Eugene F. Brigham and James L. Pappas, *Managerial Economics,* 2d ed. (Hinsdale, IL: Dryden Press, 1976).

29. Charles A. Weber, John R. Current, and Desai Anand, "Vendor: A Structured Approach to Vendor Selection and Negotiation," *Journal of Business Logistics* 21, no. 1 (2000), pp. 134–69.

30. Discussion of dual channel marketing is based on Wim G. Biemans, "Marketing in the Twilight Zone," *Business Horizons* 41, no. 6 (November—December 1998), pp. 69–76.

31. Ibid.

32. Ibid.

33. Robert Duboff, "True Brand Strategies Do Much More Than Name," *Marketing News* 35, no. 11 (May 21, 2001), p. 16.

Chapter 4

1. Jessica Wohl, "McDonald's US CMO Discusses All-Day Breakfast Effort, *Advertising Age,* October 6, 2015, **adage.com/article/cmo-strategy/mcdonald-s-u-s-cmo-discusses-day-breakfast-effort/300735/**, retrieved January 14, 2016.

2. Melissa Chan, "McDonald's All-Day Breakfast Attracts More Customers: Study, *Time,* December 8, 2015, **time.com/4141795/mcdonalds-breakfast-customers/**, retrieved January 14, 2016.

3. Stuart Elliott, "Playing Up a Scotsman's Lawn Expertise," *The New York Times*, March 12, 2012, **wwwnytimes.com**.

4. Andrew Adam Newman, "Two Sides to a Deodorant Campaign," *The New York Times*, **www.nytimes.com**, March 10, 2013.

5. Nancy Pekala, "Marketing to Today's Women: Focus on Life Stages, Not Ages," *Marketing Matters Newsletter*, American Marketing Association, November 10, 2009.

6. Ibid.

7. Simon Goodall, "How to Connect with the Heart and Mind of the Male Shopper," *Advertising Age*, March 29, 2011, **adage.com/print/149623**.

8. Brian Braiker, "The Next Great American Consumer," *Adweek*, September 26, 2011, **www.adweek.com/print/135207**.

9. Lucia Moses, "Tweens Have a Big Say in Household Spending," *Adweek*, **www.adweek.com/news/advertising-branding/tweens-have-big-say-household-spending-150570**, June 26, 2013.

10. "Status, Fashion, and the Search for Value Driving Teen Spending," *Quirk's Marketing Research Media*, **http://quirksblog.com/**, May 29, 2013.

11. Gary Evans, "This Consumer Has Cash, But She's Tired," *Furniture Today* 31, no. 50 (August 27, 2007), pp. 1, 42.

12. Gavin O'Malley, "Marketers Advised to Target Ethnic Preferences," *Online Media Daily*, November 29, 2011, **www.mediapost.com/publications/article/153175**.

13. Tanya Irwin, "Ram Truck Hispanic Effort Most Comprehensive," *Media Post News Marketing Daily*, September 28, 2011, **www.mediapost.com/publications**.

14. Karlene Lukovitz, "Kraft Mac & Cheese Launches New Hispanic Creative," *Marketing Daily*, **www.mediapost.com**, May 2, 2013; "Brand of Opportunity: Domino's Hispanic Campaign Features Franchisee," *Advertising Age*, **adage.com/print/242873**, June 27, 2013.

15. Rebecca Piirto Heath, "Psychographics," *Marketing Tools* (November–December 1995), pp. 74–81.

16. SRI Consulting Business Intelligence (**www.sric-bi.com**, accessed January 3, 2008); Dana-Nicoleta Lascu and Kenneth E. Clow, *Marketing Principles*, Textbook Media, 2012.

17. Jane L. Levere, "We Have Dinner, Drinks, Swimming . . . Oh, and Gambling, Too," *The New York Times*, April 2, 2012, **www.nytimes.com**.

18. "Infographic: Marketers Are Spending 500% More on Millennials than all Others Combined," *Adweek*, November 7, 2015, **www.adweek.com**.

19. "How To Get Millennials to Love and Share Your Product," *Advertising Age*, **adage.com/print/243624**, August 14, 2013.

20. "Grilling Brands Fire Up New Strategies for Millennials," *Advertising Age*, August 5, 2015, **adage.com/print/299794**.

21. David Feldman, "Segmentation Building Blocks," *Marketing Research* (Summer 2006), pp. 23–29.

22. PRIZM, "My Best Segments" (**www.nielsen.com/us/en.html**, accessed January 3, 2008).

23. Ronald L. Zallocco, "Benefit Segmentation of the Fitness Market," *Journal of Health Care Marketing* 12, no. 4 (December 1992), p. 80.

24. Susan Pechman, "Custom Clusters: Finding Your True Customer Segments," *Bank Marketing* 26, no. 7 (July 1994), pp. 33–35.

25. "Dairy Queen Effort Thinks Beyond the Blizzard to Burgers and Fries," *Advertising Age*, **adage.com/print/241602**, May 21, 2013.

26. Andrew Adam Newman, "Carnival Cruise Campaign Focuses on the First-Timers," *The New York Times*, December 20, 2011, **www.nytimes.com**.

27. Gene Koprowski, "Bovine Inspiration," *Marketing Tools* (October 1996), pp. 10–11.

28. "Lean Cuisine Makes Massive Pivot Away from Diet Marketing," *Advertising Age*, **adage.com/print/299236**, June 26, 2015.

29. Andrew Adam Newman, "Yes, the Diner's Open. How About a Seat at the Counter?" *The New York Times*, February 1, 2011, **www.nytimes.com/2011/02/02/business/media/02adco.html**.

30. Lionell A. Mitchell, "An Examination of Methods of Setting Advertising Budgets: Practice and Literature," *European Journal of Marketing* 27, no. 5 (1993), pp. 5–22.

31. "U.S. Market Leaders by Category: Credit Cards," *Ad Age's Marketing Fact Pack 2016*, December 21, 2015, p. 10.

32. James E. Lynch and Graham J. Hooley, "Increased Sophistication in Advertising Budget Setting," *Journal of Advertising Research* 30, no. 1 (February–March 1990), pp. 67–76.

33. James O. Peckham, "Can We Relate Advertising Dollars to Market Share Objectives?" *How Much to Spend for Advertising*, M. A. McNiver (ed.) (New York: Association of National Advertisers, 1969), p. 30.

34. "Higher Gear," *Promo Industry Trends Report* (**www.promomagazine.com**, accessed January 2, 2008).

35. "2012 Ad-to-Sales Ratios," Schonfield and Associates, July 2012.

36. Ingrid Lunden, "Nielsen: Old School TV Reigns Supreme at 58% of Ad Spend, Internet Display up 27% in Q2," **techcrunch.com/2013/10/22/nielsen-internet-display-ad-spend-up-27-in-q2-but-old-school-tv-reigns-supreme-at-58-of-all-spend**, October 22, 2013.

37. About Benihana, **www.benihana.com/about/corporate-information/**, accessed December 20, 2013.

38. Why is Facebook Blue? The Science Behind Colors in Marketing," *fastcompany.com*, **www.fastcompany.com**, retrieved December 20, 2013.

Chapter 5

1. Jerry Olson and Thomas J. Reynolds, "Understanding Consumers' Cognitive Structures: Implications for Advertising Strategy," *Advertising Consumer Psychology*, L. Percy and A. Woodside, eds. (Lexington, MA: Lexington Books, 1983), pp. 77–90; Thomas J. Reynolds and Alyce Craddock, "The Application of the MECCAS Model to Development and Assessment of Advertising Strategy," *Journal of Advertising Research* 28, no. 2 (1988), pp. 43–54.

2. Laurie A. Babin and Alvin C. Burns, "Effects of Print Ad Pictures and Copy Containing Instructions to Imagine on Mental Imagery That Mediates Attitudes," *Journal of Advertising* 26, no. 3 (Fall 1997), pp. 33–44.

3. Marc Bourgery and George Guimaraes, "Global Ads: Say It with Pictures," *Journal of European Business* 4, no. 5 (May–June 1993), pp. 22–26.

4. Gerard J. Tellis, "Study: Advertising Half as Effective as Previously Believed," *Advertising Age*, June 26, 2011, **adage.com/print/228409**.

5. Margaret Henderson Blair, "An Empirical Investigation of Advertising Wearin and Wearout," *Journal of Advertising Research* 40, no. 6 (November–December 2000), pp. 95–100.

6. Ibid.

7. Gerard J. Tellis, "Study: Advertising Half as Effective as Previously Believed," *Advertising Age*, June 26, 2011, **adage.com/print/228409**.

8. "Leaner Ad Budgets Mean More Marketers Rely on In-House Agencies," *Advertising Age*, **adage.com/print/243976**, September 5, 2013.

9. G+G Advertising (**www.gng.net**, accessed January 16, 2010); "G&G Advertising," *Agency Compile* (**www.agencycompile.com/factsheet/factsheet.aspx?agency_id=7823**, accessed January 16, 2010).

10. Bruce Horovitz, "Amateur Doritos Ad Maker Could Win $1M . . . and a Job," *USA Today, Money*, accessed November 27, 2011, **www.usatoday.com/money/media/story/2011-09-26**.

11. Prashant Malaviya, "Consumer-Generated Ads: Good for Retention, Bad for Growth," *Forbes*, **www.forbes.com**, July 2, 2013.

12. "Uh Oh: SpaghettiOs, Prego, Pace Up For Grabs: Campbell Soup To Consolidate Creative Among 'Simple Meals' Brands," *Advertising Age*, November 12, 2015 (**adage.com/print/301331**).

13. Kate Richards, "How Arby's Broke its Marketing Slump and Became One of Today's Beefiest Brands," *Adweek*, October 16, 2015 (**www.adweek.com**).

14. Heather Jacobs, "How to Make Sure Your Pitch Is Heard," *B&T Weekly* 57, no. 2597 (February 8, 2007), pp. 14–16.

15. Interview with Jane Hilk, Senior Vice President of Marketing, Oscar Mayer, January 28, 2010.

16. Jacobs, "How to Make Sure Your Pitch Is Heard."

17. Steve Miller, "VW Is Going Outdoors, Literally," *Brandweek.com* (**brandweek.com/VW+IS+Going+Outdoor**), June 23, 2008.

18. Jack Neff, "The Newest Ad Agencies: Major Media Companies," *Advertising Age* (**adage.com/print?article_id=140712**), November 3, 2008.

19. "Media Agencies Make Mark as Content Creators," *Advertising Age*, April 24, 2011, **adage.com/print/227163**.

20. Interview with Jane Hilk, Sr. Vice President of Marketing, Oscar Mayer, January 28, 2010.

21. H. Rao Unnava and Deepak Sirdeshmukh, "Reducing Competitive Ad Interference," *Journal of Marketing Research* 31, no. 3 (August 1994), pp. 403–411.

22. Naveen Donthu, "A Cross-Country Investigation of Recall of and Attitudes Toward Comparative Advertising," *Journal of Advertising* 27, no. 2 (Summer 1998), pp. 111–21.

23. "Survey: Clients Must Improve Quality of Briefs to Agencies if They Want Better Work," *Advertising Age*, **adage.com/print/241065**, April 24, 2013.

24. Henry A. Laskey and Richard J. Fox, "The Relationship Between Advertising Message Strategy and Television Commercial Effectiveness," *Journal of Advertising Research* 35, no. 2 (March–April 1995), pp. 31–39.

25. Herbert E. Krugman, "Memory Without Recall, Exposure Without Perception," *Journal of Advertising Research* 40, no. 6 (November–December 2000), pp. 49–55; David Kay, "Left Brain Versus Right Brain," *Marketing Magazine* 108, no. 36 (October 27, 2003), p. 37.

26. "Picking Up the Pace," *Marketing News* 36, no. 7 (April 1, 2002), p. 3.

27. Laurel Wentz and Bradley Johnson, "Top 100 Global Advertisers Heap Their Spending Abroad," *Advertising Age* (**adage.com/print?article_id=140723**), November 30, 2009.

Chapter 6

1. Mark Dolliver, "Assessing the Power of Ads," *Adweek.com* (**www.adweek.com**), June 22, 2009.

2. Henry A. Laskey, Ellen Day, and Melvin R. Crask, "Typology of Main Message Strategies for Television Commercials," *Journal of Advertising* 18, no. 1 (1989), pp. 36–41.

3. David Aaker and Donald Norris, "Characteristics of TV Commercials Perceived as Informative," *Journal of Advertising Research* 22, no. 2 (1982), pp. 61–70.

4. **www.campbellsoupcompany.com** (accessed January 12, 2008).

5. Wolfgang Gruener, "Nintendo Wii Surrenders Market Share in Weak Game Console Market," *TG Daily* (**www.tgdaily.com/trendwatch-features/43289**), July 17, 2009.

6. Tony Smith, "Intel Extends Market Share Gains," *Register Hardware* (**www.reghardware.co.uk/2007/04/20/intel_vs_amd_q1_07/print.html**), April 20, 2007.

7. Shailendra Pratap Jain and Steven S. Posavac, "Valenced Comparisons," *Journal of Marketing Research* 41, no. 1 (February 2004), pp. 46–56.

8. Dhruv Grewal and Sukumar Kavanoor, "Comparative Versus Noncomparative Advertising: A Meta-Analysis," *Journal of Marketing* 61, no. 4 (October 1997), pp. 1–15; Shailendra Pratap Jain and Steven S. Posavac, "Valenced Comparisons," *Journal of Marketing Research* 41, no. 9. (February 2004), pp. 46–56.

9. "Microsoft's Google-Bashing Try Campaign Is Actually Working," *Advertising Age*, **adage.com/print/244691**, October 15, 2013.

10. Aaron Baar, "Subaru Taps Nostalgia for the First Car," *Marketing Daily*, February 26, 2012, **www.mediapost.com/publications/article/168531**.

11. Stuart Elliott, "In New Ads, Stirring Memories of Commercials Past," *The New York Times*, January 12, 2012, **www.nytimes.com**.

12. Joanne Lynch and Leslie de Chernatony, "The Power of Emotion: Brand Communication in Business-to-Business Markets," *Journal of Brand Management* 11, no. 5 (May 2004), pp. 403–420.

13. Based on Rosemary M. Murtaugh, "Designing Effective Health Promotion Messages Using Components of Protection Motivation Theory," *Proceedings of the Atlantic Marketing Association* (1999), pp. 553–57; R. W. Rogers and S. Prentice-Dunn, "Protection Motivation Theory," *Handbook of Health Behavior Research I: Personal and Social Determinants*, D. Gochman, ed. (New York: Plenum Press, 1997), pp. 130–32.

14. Ibid.

15. Michael S. Latour and Robin L. Snipes, "Don't Be Afraid to Use Fear Appeals: An Experimental Study," *Journal of Advertising Research* 36, no. 2 (March–April 1996), pp. 59–68.

16. Martin Eisend, "A Meta-Analysis of Humor Effects in Advertising," *Advances in Consumer Research–North American Conference Proceedings* 34 (2007), pp. 320–23.

17. James J. Kellaris and Thomas W. Cline, "Humor and Ad Memorability," *Psychology & Marketing* 24, no. 6 (June 2007), pp. 497–509.

18. Theresa Howard, "Windex Birds Make Clean Sweep as Most-Liked Ads," *USA Today* (December 18, 2006), p. 7B (Money).

19. Matthew Creamer, "Marketing's Era of Outrage," *Advertising Age* 78, no. 7 (February 12, 2007), pp. 1, 26.

20. "Sex Doesn't Sell," *The Economist* 373, no. 8399 (October 30, 2004), pp. 62–63.

21. Andrew Adam Newman, "Selling a Household Cleaning Product on Its . . . Sex Appeal?" *The New York Times* (**www.nytimes.com/2009/11/13/business/media/13adco.html**), November 13, 2009.

22. Sandra O'Loughlin, "Hanes Shows Some 'Love' in Battle for Intimates," *Brandweek* 48, no. 9 (February 26, 2007), p. 11.

23. Bob Garfield, "Dentyne Spot Makes It Seem That Naysayers Have a Point," *Advertising Age* 76, no. 5 (January 31, 2005), p. 41.

24. Based on G. Smith and R. Engel, "Influence of a Female Model on Perceived Characteristics of an Automobile," *Proceedings of the 76th Annual Convention of the American Psychological*

Association 15, no. 3 (1968), pp. 46–54; Leonard Reid and Lawrence C. Soley, "Decorative Models and the Readership of Magazine Ads," *Journal of Advertising Research* 23 (April–May 1983), pp. 27–32; R. Chestnut, C. LaChance, and A. Lubitz, "The Decorative Female Model: Sexual Stimuli and the Recognition of Advertisements," *Journal of Advertising* 6 (Fall 1977), pp. 11–14.

25. Jessica Severn, George E. Belch, and Michael A. Belch, "The Effects of Sexual and Non-Sexual Advertising Appeals and Information Level on Cognitive Processing and Communication Effectiveness," *Journal of Advertising* 19, no. 1 (1990), pp. 14–22.

26. Tom Reichart, "Sex in Advertising Research: A Review of Content, Effects, and Functions of Sexual Information in Consumer Advertising," *Annual Review of Sex Research* 13 (2002), pp. 242–74; D. C. Bello, R. E. Pitts, and M. J. Etzel, "The Communication Effects of Controversial Sexual Content in Television Programs and Commercials," *Journal of Advertising* 3, no. 12 (1983), pp. 32–42.

27. "Note to Chrysler: Gutter Humor Has No Place in Ads," *Automotive News* 78, no. 6064 (October 27, 2003), p. 12.

28. Tom Reichart, "Sex in Advertising Research: A Review of Content, Effects, and Functions of Sexual Information in Consumer Advertising," *Annual Review of Sex Research* 13 (2002), pp. 242–74; Andrew A. Mitchell, "The Effect of Verbal and Visual Components of Advertisements on Brand Attitude and Attitude Toward the Advertisement," *Journal of Consumer Research* 13 (June 1986), pp. 12–24.

29. Bruce Horovitz, "Risqué May Be Too Risky for Ads," *USA Today* (April 16, 2004), p. 1B.

30. Julie Naughton and Amy Wicks, "Eva's Seduction: Calvin Klein Stirs Controversy with Mendes Ads," *Women's Wear Daily* 196, no. 25 (August 4, 2008), p. 1.

31. Kate Lunau, "Study Finds Real Women Don't Sell," *Maclean's* 121, no. 33 (August 25, 2008), p. 34.

32. Howard Levine, Donna Sweeney, and Stephen H. Wagner, "Depicting Women as Sex Objects in Television Advertising," *Personality and Social Psychology Bulletin* 25, no. 8 (August 1999), pp. 1049–58.

33. Emannuelle Grinberg, "How to create Ads that don't Objectify Women," *CNN Style,* February 18, 2016, **www.cnn.com**, retrieved February 19, 2016.

34. Steve Oakes, "Evaluating Empirical Research into Music in Advertising: A Congruity Perspective," *Journal of Advertising Research* 47, no. 1 (March 2007), pp. 38–50.

35. Andrew Hampp, "A Reprise for Jingles in Madison Avenue," *Advertising Age*, September 6, 2010, **www.adage.com**.

36. Felicity Shea, "Reaching Youth with Music," *B& T Weekly* 54, no. 2491 (October 1, 2004), pp. 16–17.

37. Brian Steinberg, "The Times Are a-Changin' for Musicians and Marketers," *Advertising Age* 78, no. 43 (October 29, 2005) p. 43.

38. Nicole Rivard, "Maximizing Music," *SHOOT* 48, no. 4 (February 23, 2007), pp. 17–21.

39. Douglas Quenqua, "What's That Catchy Tune? A Song for Car Insurance Makes the Charts," *The New York Times* (**www .nytimes.com/2007/12/31/business/media/31allstate.html**), December 31, 2007.

40. Stuart Elliott, "Godiva Rides in a New Direction," *The New York Times* (**www.nytimes.com/2009/11/16/business/ media/16adnewsletter1.html**), November 16, 2009.

41. Joanne Lynch and Leslie de Chernatony, "The Power of Emotion: Brand Communication in Business-to-Business Markets," *Journal of Brand Management* 11, no. 5 (May 2004), pp. 403–20; Karalynn Ott, "B-to-B Marketers Display Their Creative Side," *Advertising Age's Business Marketing* 84, no. 1 (January 1999), pp. 3–4.

42. Stephanie Thompson, "Big Deal," *Mediaweek* 7, no. 44 (November 24, 1997), p. 36 Judann Pollack, "Big G Has Special Cheerios for Big '00," *Advertising Age* (June 14, 1999), pp. 1–2.

43. Jim Hanas, "Rotoscope Redux," *Creativity* 10, no. 1 (February 2002), pp. 40–41.

44. Aaron Baar, "For Stein Mart, It's Love at First Find," *Marketing Daily*, September 10, 2011, **www.mediapost.com/publications**.

45. Matthew Warren, "Do Celebrity Endorsements Still Work?" *Campaign (UK)* 44 (November 2, 2007) p. 13.

46. "Angelina Jolie to be $10m face of Louis Vuitton," *Marketing*, **www.marketingmagazine.co.uk/news/1067170**, accessed May 3, 2011.

47. "Highest Paid Athletes," *Buzzle.com*, **www.buzzle.com/articles/ highest-paid-athletes.html**, accessed April 16, 2012.

48. Craig Giammona, "LeBron Cuts Ties with McDonald's to Promote Small Pizza Company," **www.bloomberg.com/news/ articles/2015-10-08/lebron-cuts-ties-with-mcdonalds-to- promote-small-pizza-company**, October 8, 2015.

49. Laura Petrecca, "Small Companies Seek Publicity from Celebrities," *USA Today*, **www.usatoday.com/ cleanprint/?1296061644796**, accessed January 26, 2011.

50. Claire Murphy, "Stars Brought Down to Earth in TV Ads Research," *Marketing* (January 22, 1998), p. 1.

51. Kamile Junokaite, Sonata Alijosiene, and Rasa Gudonaviciene, "The Solutions of Celebrity Endorsers Selection for Advertising Products," *Economics & Management* 12, no. 3 (2007), pp. 384–90.

52. Stuart Elliott, "La-Z-Boy, Meet Brooke Shields," *The New York Times*, November 29, 2010, **www.nytimes.com**.

53. Suzanne Vranica, "Bill Cosby Falls from #3 to #2,615 in List of Most Trusted Celebrities," *Wall Street Journal* (**blogs.wsj.com/ cmo/2014/11/25/bill-cosby-falls-from-3-to-2615-in-list-of- most-trusted-celebrities**), November 25, 2014.

54. Roobina Ohanian, "Construction and Validation of a Scale to Measure Celebrity Endorsers' Perceived Expertise," *Journal of Advertising* 19, no. 3 (1990), pp. 39–52.

55. Kenneth Hein, "Danica Patrick Talks GoDaddy, Pepsi," *Brandweek* (**www.brandweek.com/bw/content_display/news- and-features/direct/e3i7a35e791d5c**), November 30, 2009.

56. Dipayan Biswas, Abhijit Biswas, and Neel Das, "The Differential Effects of Celebrity and Expert Endorsements on Consumer Risk Perceptions," *Journal of Advertising* 35, no. 2 (Summer 2006), pp. 17–31.

57. David J. Moore and John C. Mowen, "Multiple Sources in Advertising Appeals: When Product Endorsers Are Paid by the Advertising Sponsor," *Journal of Academy of Marketing Science* 22, no. 3 (Summer 1994), pp. 234–43.

58. Raymond R. Burke and Thomas K. Srull, "Competitive Interference and Consumer Memory for Advertising," *Journal of Consumer Research* 15 (June 1988), pp. 55–68.

Chapter 7

1. Sam Thielman, "Ad of the Day: Is Chiddy Bang's Version of Oreo's Wonderfilled Song the Best Yet?, *Adweek*, July 31, 2013, **www.adweek.com/news/advertising-branding/ad-day- oreo-gets-edge-chiddy-bangs-version-wonderfilled-151561**, retrieved January 14, 2014.

2. Creative Blog: Top 35 TV Commercials, Oreos, **www.creativebloq.com/3d/top-tv-commercials-12121024**, retrieved January 14, 2014.

3. Mickey Marks, "Millennial Satiation," *Advertising Age* 14 (February 2000), p. S16; J. Thomas Russell and W. Ronald Lane, *Kleppner's Advertising Procedure,* 15th ed. (Upper Saddle River, NJ: Prentice Hall), 2002, pp. 174–75.

4. Larry Percy, John R. Rossiter, and Richard Elliott, "Media Strategy," *Strategic Advertising Management* (2001), pp. 151–63.

5. Kate Maddox, "Media Planners in High Demand," *BtoB* 89, no. 13 (November 8, 2004), p. 24.

6. Ibid.

7. Arthur A. Andersen, "Clout Only a Part of Media Buyer's Value," *Advertising Age* 70, no. 15 (April 5, 1999), p. 26.

8. Herbert E. Krugman, "Why Three Exposures May Be Enough," *Journal of Advertising Research* 12, no. 6 (1972), pp. 11–14.

9. Erwin Ephron and Colin McDonald, "Media Scheduling and Carry-over Effects: Is Adstock a Useful Planning Tool," *Journal of Advertising Research* 42, no. 4 (July–August 2002), pp. 66–70; Laurie Freeman, "Added Theories Drive Need for Client Solutions," *Advertising Age* 68, no. 31, p. 18.

10. Larry Percy, John R. Rossiter, and Richard Elliott, "Media Strategy," *Strategic Advertising Management* (2001), pp.151–63.

11. Ibid.

12. Cecilia Kang, "The Internet is Slowly but Surely Killing TV," **www.washingtonpost.com/news/the-switch/wp/2015/09/09/the-internet-is-slowly-but-surely-killing-tv**, September 9, 2015.

13. Diane Holloway, "What's On? Ads, Ads, and Maybe a TV Show," *Austin American Statesman* (**www.austin360.com**, accessed January 17, 2008), October 11, 2005.

14. Jack Neff, "Future of Advertising? Print, TV, Online Ads," *Advertising Age* (**www.adage.com/print?article_id=136993**), June 1, 2009; Gregory Solman, "Forward Thought: Ads A-Ok on DVRs," *Hollywood Reporter* (**hollywoodreporter.com**), December 27, 2007.

15. Steve McClellan, "Audit Finds Nielsen's C3 Ratings Hurt Advertisers," *Media Daily News*, September 19, 2011, **www.mediapost.com/publications/article/158818**.

16. Anthony Crupi, "Fox and ABC are Winning the C3 Ratings War," **adage.com/article/media/fox-abc-winning-c3/300877**, October 13, 2015.

17. Wayne Friedman, "Why TV Networks Want to Move From C3 to C7 Ratings," **www.mediapost.com/publications/article/187080/why-tv-networks-want-to-move-from-c3-to-c7-ratings**, November 12, 2012.

18. Adapted from "TV Ad Prices: Football, Walking Dead, Big Bang Theory, Blacklist Top the List," **variety.com/2014/tv/news/tv-ad-prices-football-walking-dead-big-bang-theory-blacklist-top-the-list-1201314484**, September 26, 2014.

19. Karlene Lukovitz, "Regional Gain Uses TV to Take On Big Pizza Brands," *Marketing Daily*, November 15, 2011, **www.mediapost.com/publications/article/162392**.

20. Andy Fixmer, Ian King, and Cliff Edwards, "DirecTV Upends Ad Model with Toyota Spots of Auto Geeks," *Bloomberg Businessweek* **www.businessweek.com**, September 23, 2013.

21. Neal Ungerleider, "This AOL-Owned Product Can Track the Ads You Watch on TV – And Target Your Phone," **www.fastcompany.com/3053820/fast-feed/this-aol-owned-product-can-track-the-ads-you-watch-on-tv-and-target-your-phone**, accessed February 19, 2016.

22. Gavin O'Mally, "Social Media Chatter Ups Live TV Stats," *MediaPost News*, March 22, 2012, **www.mediapost.com/publications/articl/170743**; Jack Loechner, "TV Advertising Most Influential," *Media Post Research Brief*, March 23, 2011, **www.mediapost.com/publications/?fa=articles.printfriendly&artaid=147033**.

23. Anthony Crupi, "Commercial Breaks Aren't Twitter Breaks," *Adweek*, **www.adweek.com**, September 18, 2013.

24. Ki Mae Heussner, "Social Data Uncovers Brand, TV-Show Affinity," *Adweek*, December 22, 2011, **www.adweek.com/print/137243**.

25. Susan Kuchinsakas, "Brands Increase Recall with TV/Digital Mix, Google Says," *ClickZ*, December 6, 2011, **www.clickz.com/print_article/clikz/stats/2130484**.

26. Gabriel Beltrone, "Ads Trump Football in Super Bowl Survey," *Adweek*, **www.adweek.com**, January 24, 2013; Stuart Elliott, "Mainstays Will Reappear in the Big Game Again," *The New York Times*, January 27, 2012, **www.nytimes.com**.

27. Stuart Elliott, "Before the Toss, Super Bowl Ads," *The New York Times*, February 2, 2012, **www.nytimes.com**; Stuart Elliott, "Before Sunday, A Taste of the Bowl," *The New York Times*, February 3, 2012, **www.nytimes.com/2011/02/04/business/media/04adco.html**. G28

28. Doug McPherson, "Into Thin Air," *Response* 18, no. 5 (February 2010), pp. 40–45.

29. Doug McPherson, "Into Thin Air," *Response* 18, no. 5 (February 2010), pp. 40–45.

30. Morianna Morello, "Why Print Media—and Why Now?" *Response* 17, no. 8 (May 2009), p. 77.

31. Edward C. Baig, "DirecTV Takes the Dive with SI's Swimsuit Issue," *USA Today Money*, February 1, 2012, **www.usatoday.com**.

32. Nat Ives, "If You're Rich, You Still Have Time to Read," *Advertising Age* (**www.adage.com/print?articleid=130685**), September 2, 2008.

33. Erik Sass, "Newspaper Ads Still Guide Shopping," *Media Daily News*, April 13, 2011, **www.mediapost.com/publications/?fa=Articles=148632**.

34. Bill Gloede, "Best Use of Newspapers," *Adweek* 48, no. 25 (June 18, 2007), pp. SR22–23.

35. Erik Sass, "Newspaper's Digital Audience Skews Younger, More Affluent," *Media Daily News*, December 13, 2011, **www.mediapost.como/publications/article/164161**.

36. *Marketer Trees 2009* (**adage.com/marketertres09**), December 28, 2009.

37. Lindsay Morris, "Studies Give 'Thumbs Up' to Mags for Ad Awareness," *Advertising Age* 70, no. 32 (August 2, 1999), pp. 16–17; Rachel X. Weissman, "Broadcasters Mine the Gold," *American Demographics* 21, no. 6 (June 1999), pp. 35–37.

38. "ABM Releases Harris Study Data: B2B Advertising Highly Effective," *Min's B2B* 9, no. 26 (June 26, 2006), p. 8.

39. Kate Maddox, "Top 100 B-to-B Advertisers Increased Spending 3% in '06," *BtoB* 92, no. 11 (September 10, 2007), pp. 25–30.

40. Ibid.

41. Eric Pfanner, "TV Still Has a Hold on Teenagers," *The New York Times* (**www.nytimes.com/2009/12/14/business/media/14iht-cache14.html**), December 14, 2009.

42. Joe Mandese, "Power Shift," *Broadcasting & Cable* 135, no. 53 (December 12, 2005), p. 12.

43. Martin Croft, "Media Indies Take on Networks with Consortium," *Marketing Week* 29, no. 28 (July 13, 2006), p. 13.

44. Jack Neff, "Media Buying & Planning." *Advertising Age* 70, no. 32 (August 2, 1999), pp. 1–2.

Chapter 8

1. ycharts.com/indicators/ecommerce_sales_as_percent_retail_sales, accessed February 23, 2016.

2. Michael Stich, Jim Leonard, and Jennifer Rooney, "Ring Up E-Commerce Gains with True Multichannel Strategy," *Advertising Age* 79, no. 10 (March 10, 2008), p. 15.

3. Corey Beale, "2 Ecommerce Image Tips That Increase Sales Conversions," www.hubspot.com, February 17, 2016.

4. Neil Patel, "5 Things to Optimize on Your E-Commerce Site to Gain More Sales," www.searchenginejournal.com/5-things-to-optimize-e-commerce-site-gain-sales/136408, July 22, 2015.

5. "Why Retailers must Optimize Mobile Sites," www.emarketer.com, July 20, 2015.

6. Justin Lafferty, "Mobilegeddon: Is Google Really Ranking Mobile Sites Higher?" www.adweek/com/socialtimes/mobilegeddon-is-google-really-ranking-mobile-sites-higher/622356, June 24, 2015.

7. Amy Cravens, "How New Devices, Networks, and Consumer Habits Will Change the Web Experience," *Giga Omni Media White Paper*, January 22, 2013 (www.pro.gigaom.com).

8. David Sparrow, "Get 'em to Bite," *Catalog Age* 20, no. 4 (April 2003), pp. 35–36.

9. Amanda Gaines, "Leading the Charge," *Retail Merchandiser* 49, no. 6 (November–December 2009), pp. 16–19.

10. Mike Fletcher, "How to Create the Perfect E-Commerce Website," *Revolution* (March 2009), pp. 60–63.

11. Joab Jackson, "E-Consumers Get Smart," *CIO* 23, no. 7 (February 1, 2010), p. 18.

12. Gwen Moran, "Check Out Your Checkout," *Entrepreneur* 38, no. 1 (January 2010), p. 38.

13. Lisa Cervini, "Free Shipping Offers Fueling Online Sales," *This Week in Consumer Electronics* 20, no. 24 (November 21, 2005), p. 16.

14. Jack Loechner, "A Case for More Mobile Advertising," www.mediapost.com/publications/article/266308, January 13, 2016.

15. Andrew Corselli, "A Seamless App Experience or Bust," www.dmenws.com/a-seamless-app-experience-or-bust, July 21, 2015.

16. Roger Matus, "Mobile Action Codes in Magazine Advertising," white paper from Nellymoser, Inc. (www.nellymoser.com), p. 4.

17. Christopher Heine, "Big Brands Like CoverGirl and Coke are Finding the Perfect Moment to Deliver Mobile Ads," www.adweek.com, August 10, 2015.

18. March Cohen, "A Revolutionary Marketing Strategy: Answer Customers' Questions," *The New York Times*, www.nytimes.com, February 27, 2013.

19. William Launder, "Marketers Seek Extra Edge to Go Viral," *Wall Street Journal*, www.wsj.com, August 25, 2013.

20. Rimma Kats, "Applebee's Drives Foot Traffic via Targeted Location-Based Mobile Campaign," www.mobilecommercedaily.com/, May 15, 2013.

21. "Timberland, Kenneth Cole Track Shoppers Who Opt-In for Deals," *Advertising Age*, adage.com/print/243811, August 26, 2013.

22. Mark Walsch, "Location-Based Mobile Ads Deliver Best Engagement, Performance," *Online Media Daily*, www.mediapost.com/publications/article/192780, February 6, 2013.

23. Beth Snyder Bulik, "Does Your Company Need a Chief Blogger?" *Advertising Age* 79, no. 15 (April 14, 2008), p. 24.

24. Sarah Halzack, "Marketing Moves to the Blogosphere," *Washingtonpost.com* (www.washingtonpost.com), August 25, 2008.

25. Ibid.

26. Basil Katz, "Email Newsletters Aim for Inbox and Wallet," *Reuters* (www.reuters.com/articlePrint?articleId=USTRE5894XI20090910), September 10, 2009.

27. Karen J. Bannan, "The Mandate to Integrate," *BtoB* 94, no. 12 (September 28, 2009), p. 23.

28. Greg Sterling, "Only 32 percent of Emails Were Opened On Desktop PCs in 2015," marketingland.com/only-32-percent-of-emails-were-opened-on-desktop-pcs-in-2015-report-164009, February 11, 2016.

29. "Re-Marketing Helps Boost Online Shoppers' Baskets," *Data Strategy* 3, no. 7 (May 2007), p. 9.

30. Ingrid Lunden, "Nielsen: Internet Display Advertising Grew 32% in 2013," www.techcrunch.com, January 27, 2014.

31. "Online Ad Spending Consolidates Among Search, Banners, Video," *eMarketer Digital Intelligence*, February 3, 2012, www.smarketer.com/articles/print.aspx?R=1008815.

32. Brian Morrissey, "Beefing Up Banner Ads," *Adweek* (www.adweek.com), February 15, 2010.

33. Josh Quittner, Jessi Hempel, and Lindsay Blakely, "The Battle for Your Social Circle," *Fortune* 156, no. 10 (November 26, 2007), pp. 11–13.

34. "Is Online Advertising Getting Too Complex?" *Advertising Age*, adage.com/print/245070, November 1, 2013.

35. Suzanne Vranica, "Web Display Ads Often Not Visible," *Wall Street Journal*, www.wsj.com, November 10, 2013.

36. George Slefo, "Google Bolsters Botnet Defenses in Push to Thwart Ad Fraud," adage.com/article/digital/googe-debuts-botnet-protection-push-thwart-ad-fraud/302613, February 9, 2016.

37. Michael Fielding, "We Can All Get Along," *Marketing News*, May 15, 2007, p. 4.

38. Paula Andruss, "Personalized URLS," *Marketing News*, September 1, 2008, p. 10.

39. "Problem Solved," *BtoB* 92, no. 15 (November 12, 2007), p. 21 "Online Ad Spending Consolidates Among Search, Banners, Video," *eMarketer Digital Intelligence*, February 3, 2012, www.smarketer.com/articles/print.aspx?R=1008815.

40. "Problem Solved," *BtoB* 92, no. 15 (November 12, 2007), p. 21.

41. Jack Neff, "Why CPG Brands Better Buy Paid Search," *Advertising Age* (adage.com/print?article_id=130353), August 18, 2008.

42. Josh Quittner, Jessi Hempel, and Lindsay Blakely, "The Battle for Your Social Circle," *Fortune* 156, no. 10 (November 26, 2007), pp. 11–13.

43. "Google Searches for Success in Local Ads," *Advertising Age*, March 1, 2011, adage.com/print/149140.

44. Lynda Radosevich, "Going Global Overnight," *InfoWorld* 21, no. 16 (April 19, 1999), pp. 1–3.

45. "The Worldly Web," *CFO* 19, no. 7 (June 2003), p. 30.

46. "Runza Restaurants," History, www.runza.com/about/history. Runza, www.food.com/recipe/runza-80204, retrieved February 21, 2014.

Chapter 9

1. **eatwholly.com/our-story.html**.

2. Christopher Heine, "Study: Women Love Social Media More Than Men," *Adweek*, **www.adweek.com**, December 30, 2013.

3. "This Year, More Than Half of Americans Will Use Facebook," **www.emarketer.com/Article/1013560**, February 8, 2016.

4. "This Year, More Than Half of Americans Will Use Facebook," **www.emarketer.com/Article/1013560**, February 8, 2016.

5. Brian Womack, "Facebook Boosts Targeting Options for Advertisers," *Bloomberg*, **www.bloomberg.com/**, October 15, 2013.

6. "Facebook Video Ads Go After TV Dollars," **www.fool.com**, December 12, 2015.

7. Reed Albergotti, "Few Facebook Users Share Daily, Survey Says," *Wall Street Journal*, **www.wsj.com**, February 3, 2014; Scott Martin, "Facebook's Teens Plummet as Elders Surge," *USA Today*, **www.usatoday.com**, January 16, 2014.

8. John Koetsier, "Twitter and Social Commerce: Facebook Generates 10X Shares, 20X Traffic, 30X Customers," **www.venturebeat.com**, October 25, 2013.

9. Brian Morrissey, "Brands Seek Fans on Facebook," *Adweek.com* **www.adweek.com**, October 12, 2009.

10. Mark Walsh, "Study: Social Media Pays," *Media Post News, Online Media Daily*, **www.mediapost.com**, July 20, 2009.

11. Vindu Goel, "Is Instagram Another Path to Riches for Facebook?" **www.nytimes.com**, February 18, 2014.

12. Joe McCarthy," Bloomingdale's Balances Selfies with Beauty Tips in Instagram," **www.luxurydaily.com/bloomingdales-balances-selfies-with-beauty-tips-in-instagram**, October 31, 2013; Steve Smith, "Lipton Rides Instagram's Positive Mood," **www.mediapost.com/publications/article/192807**, February 6, 2013.

13. Christina Binley, "More Brands Want You to Model Their Clothes," *The Wall Street Journal*, **www.wsj.com**, May 15, 2013.

14. Lisa Bertagnoli, "How One Small Biz Won on Instagram," **www.chicagobusiness.com/article/20151003/ISSUE01/310039988**, October 3, 2015.

15. Yoree Koh, "Twitter Users' Diversity Becomes an Ad Selling Point," *Wall Street Journal*, **www.wsj.com**, January 20, 2014.

16. Todd Wasserman, "Starbucks 'Tweet-a-Coffee' Campaign Prompted $180,000 in Purchases," **www.mashable.com**, December 5, 2013.

17. Claire Cain Miller, "Marketing Small Businesses with Twitter," *The New York Times* **www.nytimes.com**, July 23, 2009.

18. Chris Heine, "Amazon is Among Pinterest's Best Retailers for the Holidays," *Adweek*, **www.adweek.com**, December 12, 2103; Karlene Lukovitz, "Land 'O Lakes Pinterest Promo Helps Fight Hunger," *Marketing Daily*, **www.mediapost.com/publications/article/195218**, March 7, 2013.

19. Zach James, "Fans Crush Brands When It Comes to YouTube: Branded Content Pales in Comparison to User-Produced Fare," *Adweek*, **www.adweek.com**, June 13, 2013.

20. Tim Nudd, "Meet Devin Graham, Advertising's Daredevil," *Adweek*, **www.adweek.com**, February 11, 2014.

21. "Social Strategies for 2014," *Wildfire by Google Whitepaper, Ad Age Content Strategy Studio*, October 2013; Michael A. Stelzner, "2013 Social Media Marketing Industry Report," *Social Media Examiner*, **www.socialmediaexaminer.com**, 2013.

22. Karlene Lukovitz, "Hooters Dives into Social Media," *Marketing Daily*, **www.mediapost.com/publications/article/206785/hooters-dives-into-social-media**, August 14, 2013.

23. Aaron Baar, "Social Interactions Affect Brand Perceptions," *Marketing Daily*, **www.mediapost.com/publications/article/193609**, February 19, 2013.

24. Bruce Horovitz, "Hate Talk Won't Derail Mixed-Race Cheerios Ad," *USA Today*, **www.usatoday.com**, June 3, 2013.

25. "How Social Data Influenced Hyatt to Pull Part of Campaign Days Before Launch," *Advertising Age*, **adage.com/print/243539**, August 8, 2013.

26. Doug Pruden and Terry Vavra, "How to Find and Activate Your Best Potential Advocates," **www.smartbrief.com/original/2014/01/how-find-and-activate-your-best-potential-advocates**, January 27, 2014.

27. Jack Neff, "Buzzkill: Coca-Cola Finds No Sales Lift from Online Chatter," *Advertising Age*, **www.adage.com/article/cmo-strategy/240409**, March 18, 2013.

28. "McKinsey Finds Social Buzz Can Affect Sales—Negatively Anyway," *Advertising Age*, **adage.com/print/242039**, June 11, 2013.

29. Lara Vogel, "L'Oreal on Social Media: 3 Ideas Worth Stealing." *Hoosh Meaningful Numbers*, September 3, 2013, retrieved March 10, 2014.

30. Amit Bapna and Ravi Balakrishnan, "Brand Using Social Media to Learn About Consumer Preferences," *The Economic Times*, December 4, 2013, **www.indiatimes.com**, retrieved March 10, 2014.

31. "5 Ways to Encourage Customers to Share Your Content," *Marketo White Paper*, **www.marketo.com**, 2013.

32. "Esurance Hands Out That $1.5 Million, Releases Mind-Boggling Stats," *Adweek*, **www.adweek.com**, accessed February 10, 2104.

33. "5 Ways to Encourage Customers to Share Your Content," *Marketo White Paper*, **www.marketo.com**, 2013.

34. Paul Farhi, "Oreo's Tweeted Ad Was Super Bowl Blackout's Big Winner," *Style*, **articles.washingtonpost.com/2013/-02-4/lifestyles/36741262**, February 4, 2013.

35. Christopher Heine, "Starbucks Pushes Snow Day on Facebook, Twitter," *Adweek*, **www.adweek.com**, February 8, 2013.

36. Rick Wion, "McDonald's Finds Quick Social Response Requires Nimble Planning," *eMarketer*, **www.emarketer.com/articles/print/1009716**, March 8, 2013.

37. Lucia Moses, "Online Video Ads Have Higher Impact Than TV Ads," *Adweek*, **www.adweek.com**, May 1, 2013.

38. Zach James, "Forget Amazon. YouTube is Where Shoppers Do Research," *Adweek*, **www.adweek.com**, August 28, 2013.

39. Blaise Lucey, "In a Fragmented Social World, Influencers Rule," **www.adweek.com**, accessed March 8, 2016.

40. David Ensing, "Consumers Take Online Reviews with a Grain of Salt," **www.quirks.com**, October 2013.

41. Andrew Adam Newman, "A Campaign for Clothes by a Guy Not Wearing Any," *The New York Times* **www.nytimes.com/2009/10/29/business/media/29zappos.html**, October 29, 2009.

42. Todd Wasserman, "So Your Ad Went Viral—Big Deal," **mashable.com/2013/12/12/so-your-ad-went-viral-big-deal**, December 12, 2013.

43. Stuart Elliot, "3-M says, 'Go Ahead, Make Something of It," The New York Times, January 28, 2013, **www.nytimes.com**, retrieved March 5, 2014.

Chapter 10

1. Plan your Prairie Fire Experience in Wichita, **www.visitwichita.com/events/annual-events/prairie-fire-marathon/**, retrieved March 23, 2016.
2. Natasha Singer, "On Campus, It's One Big Commercial," *The New York Times*, September 11, 2011, **www.nytimes.com**.
3. Lisa Richwine, "Insight – Disney's Powerful Marketing Force: Social Media Moms," **www.reuters.com/article/2015/06/15**, June 15, 2015.
4. Laurie Burkitt, "Marketers Break Into Homes By Sponsoring Parties," *Forbes.com* (**www.forbes.com/2009/08/19/purina-house-party-cmo-network-houseparty_print.html**), August 19, 2009.
5. Andrew Adam Newman, "Putting Boxed Wine to the Taste Test," *The New York Times*, October 11, 2011, **www.nytimes.com**.
6. Angelo Fernando, "Transparency Under Attack," *Communication World* 24, no. 2 (March–April 2007), pp. 9–11.
7. Ibid.
8. Jim Matorin, "Infectious 'Buzz Marketing' Is a Smart Way to Build Customer Loyalty at Your Operation," *Nation's Restaurant News* 41, no. 18 (April 30, 2007), pp. 18–20.
9. Kate Niederhoffer, Rob Mooth, David Wiesenfeld, and Jonathon Gordon, "The Origin and Impact of CPG New-Product Buzz: Emerging Trends and Implications," *Journal of Advertising Research* 47, no. 4 (December 2007), pp. 420–26.
10. Ibid.
11. Chris Powell, "The Perils of Posing," *Profit* 26, no. 2 (May 2007), pp. 95–96.
12. T. L. Stanley, "Twinkies Relaunch as Dude Food," *Adweek*, **www.adweek.com**, August 7, 2013.
13. Becky Wilkerson, "Bringing Brands to Life," *Marketing,* **www.marketingmagzine.co.uk**, February 18, 2009, pp. 35–38.
14. Karl Greenberg, "Cadillac in the Performance Swim Lane With V-Centric Events," *MediaPost News, Marketing Daily*, April 20, 2011, **www.mediapost.com**.
15. Stuart Elliott, "King Cotton Goes on Tour," *The New York Times*, **www.nytimes.com**, August 24, 2009.
16. Derek Drake, "Prove the Promise of Your Brand," *Adweek* 50, no. 35 (October 5, 2009), pp. S11–S12.
17. Simon Hudson and David Hudson, "Branded Entertainment: A New Advertising Technique or Product Placement in Disguise?" *Journal of Marketing Management* 22, no. 5/6 (July 2006), pp. 489–504.
18. "Product Placement Hits High Gear on American Idol, Broadcast's Top Series for Brand Mentions," *Advertising Age*, April 18, 2011, **adage.com/print/227041**.
19. Linda Moss, "Nielsen: Product Placements Succeed in 'Emotionally Engaging' Shows," *Multichannel News* (**www.multichannel.com/**), December 10, 2007.
20. Stacy Straczynski, "Harley-Davidson Revs Product Placement," *Adweek* (**www.adweek.com**), November 12, 2009.
21. Simon Hudson and David Hudson, "Branded Entertainment: A New Advertising Technique or Product Placement in Disguise?" *Journal of Marketing Management* 22, no. 5/6 (July 2006), pp. 489–504.
22. Andrew Hampp, "How American Airlines Got a Free Ride in 'Up in the Air,'" *Advertising Age* (**adage.com/print?article_id=141059**), December 14, 2009.
23. Marc Graser, "More Ads Set for Videogames," *Variety*, September 13, 2011, **www.variety.com/article/VR1118042795**; Simon Hudson and David Hudson, "Branded Entertainment: A

New Advertising Technique or Product Placement in Disguise?" *Journal of Marketing Management* 22, no. 5/6 (July 2006), pp. 489–504.
24. Raj Persaud, "The Art of Product Placement," *Brand Strategy,* no. 216 (October 2007), pp. 30–31.
25. "Hey, Advertisers: New York Has a Bridge to Sell You," *Advertising Age*, October 26, 2011, **adage.com/print/230643**.
26. Jessica E. Lessin, "Expenses Mount for App Launches," *The Wall Street Journal*, **www.wsj.com**, April 17,2013; Theresa Howard, "As More People Play, Advertisers Devise Game Plans," *USA Today* (July 11, 2006), p. Money, 3b.
27. Ibid.
28. Rita Chang, "Advergames: A Smart Move, If Done Well," *Advertising Age* (**adage.com/print?article_id=131786**), October 16, 2008.
29. Heather Chaplin, "Players Lend a Helping Hand or Thumb," *Adweek*, April 20, 2012, **www.adweek.com/print/139461**; "Brands Friending Social Gaming Amid New Web Craze," *The Wall Street Journal*, August 8, 2010, **online.wsj.com/article/SB10001424052748704657504575411804125832426.html**.
30. Rebecca Borison, "Fall Into Cosi Sweepstakes," **www.mobilecommercedaily.com/**, accessed October 10, 2013.
31. Mike Shields, "IGA: Most Gamers Cool with In-Game Ads," *Mediaweek.com* (**mediaweek.com/mw/content_display/news/digital-downloads/gaming/e3i8d91a7147083886bfb91a8ee5978c1a7**), June 17, 2008.
32. Susan Catto, "Are You Game?" *Marketing Magazine* (November 26, 2007, Supplement), pp. 18–19.
33. Ibid.
34. **WomenGamers.com** (**www.womengamers.com**), May 3, 2010; Yukari Iwatani Kane, "Videogame Firms Make a Play for Women," *The Wall Street Journal* (**online.wsj.com/article/SB10001424052748704882404574463652777885432.html**), October 13, 2009; **CNN.com** (**www.cnn.com/2008/TECH/ptech/02/28/women.gamers/index.html**), May 3, 2010.
35. Katy Bachman, "HP Employs Cinema Experience to Push Printer," *Mediaweek* (**www.mediaweek.com/mw/content_display/news/out-there/place-based/e3i4cb8ab6**), November 29, 2009.
36. Kenneth Hein, "Study: In-Store Marketing Beats Traditional Ads," *Sales & Marketing Management* 161, no. 6 (November 2009), p. 57.
37. Amy Johannes, "Snap Decisions," *Promo* 18, no. 11 (October 2005), p. 16.
38. Tim Dreyer, "In-Store Technology Trends," *Display & Design Ideas* 19, no. 9 (September 2007), p. 92.
39. Ibid.
40. Michael Bellas, "Shopper Marketing's Instant Impact," *Beverage World* 126, no. 11 (November 15, 2007), p. 18.
41. "POP Sharpness in Focus," *Brandweek* 44, no. 24 (June 6, 2003), pp. 31–36; David Tossman, "The Final Push—POP Boom," *New Zealand Marketing Magazine* 18, no. 8 (September 1999), pp. 45–51.
42. Betsy Spethmann, "Retail Details," *Promo SourceBook 2005* 17 (2005), pp. 27–28.
43. RoxAnna Sway, "Four Critical Seconds," *Display & Design Ideas* 17, no. 11 (November 2005), p. 3.
44. Catja Prykop and Mark Heitmann, "Designing Mobile Brand Communities: Concept and Empirical Illustration," *Journal of

Organizational Computing & Electronic Commerce 16, no. 3/4 (2006), pp. 301–23.

45. Sinclair Stewart, "More Marketers Using Word of Mouth to Whip Up Sales," *Seattle PI* **www.seattlepi.com/ business/344656_wordofmouth24.html**, December 23, 2007.

46. James T. Areddy, "Starbucks, PepsiCo Bring 'Subopera' to Shanghai," *The Wall Street Journal Online* (**www.wsj.com**), November 1, 2007, p. B1.

47. Thomas Clouse, "Camp Jeep Comes to China," *Automotive News* 82, no. 6281 (November 12, 2007), p. 48.

48. Jeff Weiss, "Building Brands Without Ads," *Marketing Magazine* 109, no. 32 (October 4–11, 2004), p. 22.

49. "Red Bull's Good Buzz," *Newsweek* (May 14, 2001), p. 83.

50. Jeff Weiss, "Building Brands Without Ads," *Marketing Magazine* 109, no. 32 (October 4–11, 2004), p. 22.

Chapter 11

1. Alex McEachern, "4 Industries Where Loyalty Programs are Super Effective!," SweetToothRewards, **www.sweettoothrewards .com**, August 11, 2015, retrieved April 6, 2016.

2. Sephora, "About Us," **http://www.sephora.com/about-us**, retrieved April 6, 2016.

3. John Ellett, "Sephora's Winning Formula: Highly Relevant Personalized Data," *Forbes,* September 14, 2014, **www.forbes .com**, retrieved April 6, 2016.

4. John Ellett, "Sephora's Winning Formula: Highly Relevant Personalized Data," *Forbes,* September 14, 2014, **www.forbes .com**, retrieved April 6, 2016.

5. Stephanie Clifford, "Ads Follow Web Users, and Get More Personal," *The New York Times* (**www.nytimes.com/2009/07/31/ business/media/31privacy.html**), July 31, 2009.

6. Leo Rabinovitch, "America's 'First' Department Stores Mines Customer Data," *Direct Marketing* 62, no. 8 (December 1999), pp. 42–45.

7. Jason Q. Zhang, Ashutosh Dixit, and Roberto Friedman, "Customer Loyalty and Lifetime Value: An Empirical Investigation of Consumer Packaged Goods," *Journal of Marketing Theory & Practice* 18, no. 2 (February 2010), pp. 127–139.

8. Elliot Zwiebach, "Wholesalers Segment Shoppers Using Lifestyle Clusters," *Supermarket News* 55, no. 7 (February 12, 2007), p. 23.

9. "Verizon Uses Phone Data to Connect Consumer Dots for NBA Teams," *Advertising Age*, **http://adage.com/print/245178**, November 8, 2013.

10. Howard J. Stock, "Connecting the Dots," *Bank Investment Consultant* 13, no. 3 (March 2005), pp. 28–31.

11. Jordan K. Speer, "Digging Deep: Extreme Data Mining," *Apparel Magazine* 45, no. 12 (August 2004), p. 1.

12. Arthur M. Hughes, "The Importance of Customer Communications," *Database Marketing Institute* (**www.dbmarketing.com**), August 23, 2007.

13. "Consumers Appreciate Birthday Wishes from Brands," *Quirk's* **www.quirksblog.com**, December 4, 2013.

14. "Data Mining Boosts Netflix Subscriber Base," *Advertising Age*, **http://adage.com/print/243759**, September 2, 2013.

15. Joseph Gatti, "Poor E-Mail Practices Provoking Considerable Customer Defection," *Direct Marketing* (December 2003), pp. 1–2.

16. Joseph Gatti, "Most Consumers Have Reached Permission E-Mail Threshold," *Direct Marketing* (December 2003), pp. 1–2.

17. Ibid.

18. Mark Dolliver, "Gauging Customer Loyalty," *Adweek* (**www.adweek.com**), February 16, 2010.

19. Mark A. Santillo, "Active Engagement," *Greater Games Industry Catalog* 12 (Spring 2010), p. 14.

20. Arthur M. Hughes, "The Importance of Customer Communications," *Database Marketing Institute* (**www.dbmarketing.com**), August 23, 2007.

21. "CRM Metrics," *Harvard Management Update* 5, no. 3 (March 2000), pp. 3–4.

22. "Kellogg Cracks the Code on Loyalty," *Advertising Age*, **http://adage.com/print/243342**, July 29, 2013.

23. Richard H. Levey, "Prospects Look Good," *Direct* 16, no. 6 (December 1, 2004), pp. 1–5.

24. Julie Appleby, "As Drug Ads Surge, More Rx's Filled," *USA Today* (**www.ustoday.com**), February 29, 2008.

25. Paula Andruss, "Personalized URLs," *Marketing News*, September 1, 2008, p. 10.

26. Jeff Borden, "Eat My Dust," *Marketing News* 42, no. 2, February 1, 2008, pp. 20–22.

27. Kyle Stock, "Why the Analog Catalog Still Drives Digital Sales," *Bloomberg Businessweek*, **www.businessweek.com/ printer/articles/165812**, November 7, 2013.

28. Based on Jay Kiltsch, "Making Your Message Hit Home: Some Basics to Consider When . . . ," *Direct Marketing* 61, no. 2 (June 1998), pp. 32–34.

29. Daniel B. Honigman, "Sweet Science," *Marketing News* 41, no. 16 (October 2, 2007), pp. 16–17.

30. Camille Sweeney, "Avon's Little Sister Is Calling," *The New York Times* (**www.nytimes.com/2010/01/14/fashion/14SKIN .html**), January 14, 2010.

31. Ken Le Meunier-FitsHugh and Nigel F. Piercy, "Does Collaboration Between Sales and Marketing Affect Business Performance," *Journal of Personal Selling & Sales Management* 27, no. 3 (Summer 2007), pp. 207–220.

32. Patricia R. Lysak, "Changing Times Demand Front-End Model," *Marketing News* 28, no. 9 (April 25, 1994), p. 9.

33. Christopher Heine, "Grocery Chain will Pitch Store Patrons with Amazon-Like Recommendations," *Adweek*, December 9, 2013, **www.adweek.com**, retrieved March 21, 2014.

Chapter 12

1. Mariola Palazon-Vidal and Elena Delgado-Ballester, "Sales Promotions Effect on Consumer-Based Brand Equity," *International Journal of Market Research* 47, no. 2 (2005), pp. 179–205.

2. Huggies, Potty Training Activities, **www.pull-ups.com/ activities**, retrieved March 24, 2014.

3. Huggies Contest UK, **contestrage.com/uk/competitions/Win-an-iPad-a-Disney-Musical-Potty-and-a-Huggies-Pull-Ups-bundle-1479.html**, retrieved March 24, 2014.

4. Bruce Horovitz, "2 Million Enjoy Free Breakfast at Denny's," *USA Today* (**www.usatoday.com**), February 10, 2009.

5. "Coupon Statistics," **www.statisticbrain.com/coupon-statistics**, July 8, 2014.

6. Erik Sass, "Is Digital Coupons' Rise Print Inserts' Demise?" *MediaPost News* (**www.mediapost.com**), February 18, 2010;

Patricia Odell, "Now in Vogue." *PROMO* (**www.chiefmarketer .com**), December 1, 2009.

7. Erik Sass, "Is Digital Coupons' Rise Print Inserts' Demise?" *MediaPost News* (**www.chiefmarketer.com**), February 18, 2010; Allen Adamson, "CMOs: Your Brand Is on Digital Time," *Forbes* (**www.forbes.com**), February 2, 2010.

8. Elizabeth Gardener and Minakshi Trivedi, "A Communication Framework to Evaluate Sales Promotion Strategies," *Journal of Advertising Research* 38, no. 3 (May–June 1998), pp. 67–71.

9. Doreen Christensen, "Free 14-Piece Cosmetic Gift with $19.50 Purchase at Ulta Beauty," *Sun Sentinel*, March 3, 2014.

10. Don Jagoda, "The Seven Habits of Highly Successful Promotions," *Incentive* 173, no. 8 (August 1999), pp. 104–05.

11. Karlene Lukovitz, "General Mills Ties Into 3D Star Wars Release," *Marketing Daily*, January 23, 2012, **www.mediapost .com**.

12. Patricia Odell, "Spending Up by a Nose," *PROMO* (**www.chiefmarketer.com**), December 1, 2009.

13. Tim Nudd, "Ad of the Day: McDonald's Seeks Great Recipes in Top-Secret Contest for Employees," *Adweek*, **www.adweek.com**, December 8, 2015.

14. Tanya Gazdik Iriwn, "American Eagle Launches Back-to-School Try-On Sweepstakes," *Mediapost*, **www.mediapost.com/ publications/article/253728**, July 13, 2015.

15. Brian Morrissey, "Brand Sweepstakes Get Twitterized," *Adweek* (**www.adweek.com**), November 22, 2009.

16. Sandra Block, "Rattled About Rebate Hassles? Regulators Starting to Step In," *USA Today* (March 22, 2005), p. 3b.

17. Kenneth Hein, "Study: Sampling Works," **Brandweek .com** (**www.brandweek.com/bw/content_display/ news-and-features/shopper-marketing/ e3i32e9c3e84ea86c79e3ae157688c1ad0a**), September 29, 2008.

18. Andrew Adam Newman, "Dr. Scholl's Widens Its Insole Campaign," *The New York Times* (**www.nytimes .com/2010/04/01/business/media/01adco.html.**), March 31, 2010.

19. Kyle Stock, "The Logic Behind P & G's Old-School Manhattan Giveaway," *Bloomberg Businessweek*, **www.businessweek.com/ print/articles/126706**, June 19, 2013.

20. Betsy Spethman, "Introductory Offer," *PROMO* 16 (2004), p. 27 Jennifer Kulpa, "Bristol-Myers Squibb Breaks Ground with Direct Response Product Sampling Website," *Drug Store News* 19, no. 7 (April 7, 1997), p. 19.

21. Rachel Lamb, "Chanel Taps Vogue Supplement to Spark Holiday Gift-Giving," *Luxury Daily*, November 23, 2011, **www.luxurydaily.com**.

22. Beng Soo Ong and Foo Nin Ho, "Consumer Perceptions of Bonus Packs: An Exploratory Analysis," *Journal of Consumer Marketing* 14, no. 2–3 (1997), pp. 102–12.

23. David R. Bell, Ganesh Iyer, and V. Padmanaghan, "Price Competition Under Stockpiling and Flexible Consumption," *Journal of Marketing Research* 39, no. 3 (August 2002), pp. 292–304.

24. "Papa John's Tries to Hold the Price of Its Pies," *Advertising Age*, March 4, 2012, **adage.com/print/233109**.

25. Showwei Chu, "Welcome to Canada, Please Buy Something," *Canadian Business* 71, no. 9 (May 29, 1998), pp. 72–73.

26. Walter Heller, "Promotion Pullback," *Progressive Grocer* 81, no. 4 (March 1, 2002), p. 19.

27. Miguel Gomez, Vithala Rao, and Edward McLaughlin, "Empirical Analysis of Budget and Allocation of Trade Promotions in the U.S. Supermarket Industry," *Journal of Marketing Research* 44, no. 3 (August 2007), pp. 410–24.

28. Ibid.

29. K. Sudhir and Vithala Rao, "Do Slotting Allowances Enhance Efficiency or Hinder Competition?" *Journal of Marketing Research* 43, no. 2 (May 2006), pp. 137–55.

30. Paula Bone, Karen France, and Richard Riley, "A Multifirm Analysis of Slotting Fees," *Journal of Public Policy & Marketing* 25, no. 2 (Fall 2006), pp. 224–37.

31. "Study: Trade Dollars Up," *Frozen Food Age* 50, no. 2 (September 2001), p. 14.

32. Walter Heller, "Promotion Pullback," *Progressive Grocer* 81, no. 4 (March 1, 2002), p. 19.

33. "Cruise Selling Season Kicks Off with Agent Promotions and Optimism," *Travel Agent* 319 (January 3, 2005), p. 9.

34. Roger A. Slavens, "Getting a Grip on Co-Op," *Modern Tire Dealer* 75, no. 3 (March 1994), pp. 34–37.

35. Jack Neff, "Wal-Mart Ups the Ante with Brand Co-op Ads— in More Ways than One," *Advertising Age* (**adage.com/ article?article_id=140743**), November 30, 2009.

36. Jennifer Gilbert, "The Show Must Go On," *Sales & Marketing Management* 155, no. 5 May 2003), p. 14.

37. Walter Heller, "Promotion Pullback," *Progressive Grocer* 81, no. 4 (March 1, 2002), p. 19.

38. Brian Sullivan, "Make Sure Promotional Items Fit Brand Perfectly," *Marketing News* 35, no. 19 (September 10, 2001), p. 15.

39. Donald Baack, *International Business* (New York: Glencoe McGraw-Hill, 2008), pp. 28–49.

40. Six Flags: A Proud Past, A Thrilling Future, **investors.sixflags .com/phoenix.zhtml?c=61629&p=irol-homeprofile**, retrieved March 24, 2014.

41. The Hollywood Reporter, "Why Disney and Universal Theme Parks Are Breaking Attendance Records This Summer, August 15, 2013, **www.hollywoodreporter.com/news/why-disney- universal-theme-parks-606536**, retrieved March 24, 2014.

Chapter 13

1. "Mexico Leans on PR to Lure Back Tourists," *Advertising Age*, June 26, 2011, **adage.com/print/228385**.

2. Jenny Dawkins, "Corporate Responsibility: The Communication Challenge," *Journal of Communication Management* 9, no. 2 (November 2004), pp. 106–17.

3. Heather Chaplin, "Players Lend a Helping Hand – or, Thumb," *Adweek*, April 10, 2012, **www.adweek.com/print/139461**.

4. Michael Fielding, "Companies that Behave Responsibly Earn Good Rep, Consumers' Attention," *Marketing News* 41, no. 8 (May 1, 2007), pp. 17–18.

5. Larissa Faw, "Havas: Consumers Demand Corporate Social Responsibility," **www.mediapost.com/publications/ article/267428**, January 25, 2016.

6. "Why Advertising is Dead Last Priority at Outerwear Marketer Patagonia," *Advertising Age*, **adage.com/print/245712**, December 17, 2013.

7. Suzanne Vranica, "NBC Universal Tees Up Cause-Related Shows," *The Wall Street Journal* (**online.wsj.com/article/ SB10001424052748704112904574477872926288910.html**), October 19, 2009.

8. Nan Xiaoli and Heo Kwangiun, "Consumer Responses to Corporate Social Responsibility (CSR) Initiatives," *Journal of Advertising* 36, no. 2 (Summer 2007), pp. 63–74.

9. Andrew Adam Newman, "Tough on Crude Oil, Soft on Ducklings," *The New York Times* (**www.nytimes .com/2009/09/25/business/media/25adco.html**), September 25, 2009.

10. Dawkins, "Corporate Responsibility: The Communication Challenge."

11. Jill Meredith Ginsberg and Paul N. Bloom, "Choosing the Right Green Marketing Strategy," *MIT Sloan Management Review* 46, no. 1 (Fall 2004), pp. 79–84.

12. Stephanie Clifford and Andrew Martin, "As Consumers Cut Spending, Green Products Lose Allure," *The New York Times*, April 21, 2011, **www.nytimes.com/2011/04/22/business/ energy-environment/22green.html**.

13. Jill Meredith Ginsberg and Paul N. Bloom, "Choosing the Right Green Marketing Strategy, *MIT Sloan Management Review* 40, no. 1 (Fall 2004) pp. 79–84.

14. Examples based on Ginsberg and Bloom, "Choosing the Right Green Marketing Strategy."

15. Joan Voight, "Green is the New Black," *Adweek*, **www.adweek. com**, October 23, 2013.

16. Tanya Irwin, "Seventh Generation Debuts First National Campaign," *Marketing Daily, MediaPost News* (**www. mediapost.com**), January 14, 2010.

17. Marvin E. Shaw and Philip R. Costanzo, *Theories of Social Psychology,* 2nd ed. (New York: McGraw-Hill, 1982), p. 334.

18. Rich Thomaselli, "New Orleans is a Super Bowl Winner," *Advertising Age* (**adage.com/superbowl10/article?article_ id=141988**), February 8, 2010.

19. Andrew Adam Newman, "TD Ameritrade Commercials Link Olympics and Investing," *The New York Times*, **www.nytimes. com**, December 6, 2013.

20. Sarah E. Needleman, "For Companies, A Tweet in Time Can Avert PR Mess," *The Wall Street Journal* (**www.wsj.com**), August 3, 2009.

21. Michael Bush, "The Cult of Toyota," *Advertising Age* (**adage. com/print?article_id=142335**), March 1, 2010; Rich Thomaselli, "Toyota Sends in Jimi Lentz for Cross-Media Saatchi-Led PR Control," *Advertising Age* (**adage.com/ print?article_id=141856**), February 1, 2010; Laurie Burkitt, "From Trusted to Busted: Brands Have a Credibility Crisis," *Forbes* (**www.forbes.com**), February 25, 2010.

22. Shaw and Costanzo, *Theories of Social Psychology,* 2nd ed., p. 334.

23. "Get Ready to be Blitzed by Chipotle Ads Begging You to Come Back," **www.fastcoexist.com/3056264**, February 2, 2016.

24. Shaw and Costanzo, *Theories of Social Psychology,* 2nd ed., p. 329.

25. Ibid, p. 333.

26. Jane L. Levere, "Spot Shares Moments of Better Cruise Memories," *The New York Times*, **www.nytimes.com**, September 18, 2013.

27. Nigel Pope, Kevin E. Voges, and Mark Brown, "Winning Ways," *Journal of Advertising* 38, no. 2 (Summer 2009), pp. 5–20.

28. *Sponsorship Spending Report: Where the Dollars are Going and Trends for 2015*, IEG, 2015, **www.sponsorship.com**, accessed May 3, 2016.

29. Karl Greenberg, "Ford Intros Integrated Push for F-Series," *Marketing Daily, MediaPost News* (**www.mediapost.com**), April 8, 2010.

30. "Brands Stake Out a Place on Courses of Jaw-Dropping Endurance Competitions," *Advertising Age*, **adage.com/ print/291097**, January 17, 2014.

31. Patricia Cobe, "Working the Neighborhood," *Restaurant Business* 108, no. 11 (November 2009), pp. 20–26.

32. David Tanklefsky, "Events-based Campaigns, Experiential Marketing Prove Successful Among Hispanic Consumers," B&C (**www.broadcastingcable.com/article/print/355270-Hispanic_ TV_Summit_Promotion**), September 24, 2009.

33. Betsy Spethmann, "A Winning Season," *PROMO* 18, no. 1 (December 2004), pp. 32–41.

34. Kenneth Hein, "Study: Purchase Intent Grows with Each Event," *Brandweek* 49, no. 4 (January 28, 2008), p. 4.

35. Diane Anderson, "eBay's Campy Road Tour: One on One, No Mosquitoes," *Brandweek* 46, no. 10 (March 7, 2005), p. R6.

36. Jonathan Clegg, "NBA, Adidas Shoot for Europe," *The Wall Street Journal* (**www.wsj.com**), March 23, 2010.

37. Darren Rovell, "NBA Approves On-Jersey Advertising," ESPN, **espn.go.com/nba/story/_/id/15210151/nba-jerseys-carry- advertisements-beginning-2017-18**, (April 15, 2016).

38. R. Dana, "When You're Here, You're Family—But What About a Playboy Model?; Olive Garden Has Mixed Feelings About Its Biggest Celebrity Fan," *Wall Street Journal* (August 13, 2008). p. A.1; "Playboy.com features 'The Girls of Olive Garden,'" The Bryant Park Project, National Public Radio (**www.npr.org/templates/ story/story.php?storyId=92544599**, accessed May 13, 2010); Korin Miller, "Playboy Dishes up 'Girls of Olive Garden,'" *New York Daily News* (**www.nydailynews.com/ gossip/2008/07/16/2008-07-16_playboy_dishes_up_girls_of_ the_olive_gar.html**, accessed May 13, 2010), July 16, 2008; **www.olivegarden.com** (accessed May 13, 2010).

Chapter 14

1. Sarah Skidmore, "Reebok to Pay $25 Million over Toning Shoe Claims," Business Week, September 28, 2011, **www.businessweek.com**, accessed March 16, 2012.

2. "Broadcasters Breach Kids' Rules," *Marketing Magazine* 109, no. 35 (November 1, 2004), p. 4.

3. "Fast Feeders Serve Up Fresh Buzzwords," *Advertising Age*, March 7, 20Gar11, **adage.com/print/149264**.

4. Bart Lazar, "This Column Is the Best One You'll Ever Read," *Marketing News* 38, no. 13 (August 15, 2004), p. 8.

5. Gary D. Hailey and Jeffrey D. Knowles, "Claiming Sufficient Substantiation is no Easy Task," *Response* 13, no. 4 (January 2005) p. 50.

6. Katy Bachman, "FCT Busts ADT for Failing to Disclose Paid Endorsers," *Adweek*, **www.adweek.com**, March 6, 2014.

7. Robert Hof, "What Facebook's FTC Privacy Settlement Means to Marketers," *Forbes*, November 29, 2011, **www.forbes.com/ sites/orberthof/2011/11/29/what-facebook-ftc-privacy- settlement-means-to-marketers**.

8. Nathalie Tadena, "Lord & Taylor Reaches Settlement with FTC over Native Ad Disclosures," **www.wsj.com**, March 15, 2016.

9. Body Wise International to Pay $3.5 Million to Settle Federal and State Deceptive Advertising Charges," *Federal Trade Commission*, (**www.ftc.gov**, accessed September 20, 2005). "FTC Takes Aim at Another Credit Counseling Firm," *Mortgage Servicing News* 8, no. 7 (August 2004), p. 21.

10. Debbi Mack, "FTC Use of Corrective Advertising Upheld," *Corporate Legal Times* 10, no. 108 (November 2000), p. 80.

11. Tim Arango, "Soon, Bloggers Must Give Full Disclosure," *The New York Times* (**www.nytimes.com/2009/10/06/business/ media/06adco.html**), October 6, 2009; Douglas MacMillan, "Blogola: The FTC Takes on Paid Posts," *BusinessWeek* (**www. businessweek.com**), May 19, 2009.

12. Loraine Dubonis, FTC Sends Issuers a Message: Adequately Disclose Card Fees, *Cards & Payments* 20, no. % (May 2007), pp. 16-17.

13. Andrew Adam Newman, "Mascara Ads: Thick Lashes, Fine Print," *The New York Times*, **www.nytimes.com/fashion/ mascara-ads-thisck-lashes-fine-print**, November 12, 2013.

14. "Minute Maid Complains, But NARB Forces change," *Advertising* Age, 68,, no. 15 (April 14, 1997), p. 51.

15. "NARB Sends Winn-Dixie Complaint to FTC," *Advertising Age* 67, no. 52 (December 23, 1996), p. 2.

16. Wayne Keeley, "Toys and the Truth," *Playthings* 106, no. 2 (February 2008), p. 8.

17. Mary Pipher, *The Shelter of Each Other* (New York: Ballantine Books, 1996).

18. Internet Marketing Register (**www.marketing-register.com**, accessed February 28, 2005).

19. Beth Snyder Bulik, "Consumers to Providers: Do You Know Who I Am" *Advertising Age* 79, no. 10 (March 10, 2008), p. 8.

20. Simon Chadwick and Nicholas Burton, "Ambush" *The Wall Street Journal* (**online.wsj.com/article/SB10001424052970204 7318045743911022699362862.html**), January 25, 2010.

21. Ibid.

22. Aaron Baar, "Olympics Sponsors Benefit, As Do Competitors," *Marketing Daily* (www.mediapost.com/publications/=Articles. printFriendly&art_aid=122665), February 17, 2010.

23. Jacob E. Osterhout, "Stealth Marketing: When You're Being Pitched and You Don't Even Know It," *NY Daily-News* (**www.nydailynews.com**), April 19, 2010.

24. Ibid.

25. **www.weight-loss-institute.com/products/solidax.adx.html**, accessed March 23, 2008,.

26. Elaine McGee, "The Benefits of Yogurt," WebMD, **www .webmd.com/diet/features/benefits-of-yogurt**, retrieved April 19, 2014.

27. Troy McMullen, "Dannon to Pay $45 Million to Settle Yogurt Lawsuit," ABC News, **abcnews.go.com/Business/ dannon-settles-lawsuit/story?id=9950269**, retrieved April 19, 2014.

28. Ibid.

29. Ilan Mochari, "Why DraftKings and FanDuel spent $206 Million on Ads this year," **INC.com, www.inc.com/ilan-mochari/ fantasy-sports-betting-startups-206-million-tv-ads.html**, retrieved May 19, 2016.

30. Joe Drape and Jacqueline Williams, "Scandal Erupts in Unregulated World of Fantasy Sports," New York Times, **www.nytimes.com/2015/10/06/sports/fanduel-draftkings- fantasy-employees-bet-rivals.html?_r=0**, October 5, 2015, retrieved May 19, 2016.

31. Brent Schrotenboer, "Deemed Illegal in Texas, FanDuel to pull out of state," USA Today, **www.usatoday.com/story/ sports/2016/03/04/fanduel-draftkings-daily-fantasy- gambling-texas/81342980**, March 4, 2015, retrieved May 19, 2016.

Chapter 15

1. **www.sandsresearch.com/**, accessed September 14, 2010.

2. Gordon A. Wyner, "Narrowing the Gap," *Marketing Research* 16, no. 1 (Spring 2004), pp. 6–7.

3. Interview with Elena Petukhova, The Richards Group, May 17, 2010, by Kenneth E. Clow.

4. "Nielsen IAG" (**www.nielsen.com**, accessed May 19, 2010).

5. Lucia Moses, "Publishers Offer TV-Like Metrics, But Will Buyers Bite" *Mediaweek*, (**www.mediaweek.com/mw/ content_display/news/magazines-newspapers/e3ieea0d35**), January 17, 2010.

6. "Has Burger King's First mcgarrybowen Ad Helped the Brand" *Advertising Age*, September 19, 2011, **www.adage.com**.

7. "Copy Testing Coming to Digital Marketing," *Advertising Age*, February 27, 2011, **adage.com/print/149100**.

8. "Sex Doesn't Sell, Especially for Carl's Jr., Says Copy-Testing Firm," *Advertising Age*, **www.adage.com**, March 13, 2015.

9. Andrew McMains, "P&G Does Dan Wieden's Bidding," *Adweek*, June 27, 2011, **www.adweek.com/print/132903**.

10. "Copy Testing Coming to Digital Marketing," *Advertising Age*, February 27, 2011, **adage.com/print/149100**.

11. Steven P. Brown and Douglas M. Stayman, "Antecedents and Consequences of Attitude Toward the Ad: A Meta-Analysis," *Journal of Consumer Research* 19 (June 1992), pp. 34–51.

12. Douglas M. Stayman and David A. Aaker, "Continuous Measurement of Self-Report or Emotional Response," *Psychology and Marketing* 10 (May–June 1993), pp. 199–214.

13. Patricia Riedman, "Discover Why Tests TV Commercials Online," *Advertising Age* 71, no. 13 (March 27, 2000), pp. 46–47.

14. Jon Lafayette, "Biometric Study: Broadcast Ads Make Web Work Better," May 9, 2011, **www.broadcastingcable.com/ article/print/467935**.

15. Amy Chozick, "These Lab Specimens Watch 3-D Television," *The New York Times*, January 24, 2012, **www.nytimes.com**.

16. Bruce F. Hall, "On Measuring the Power of Communications," *Journal of Advertising Research* 44, no. 2 (June 2004), pp. 181–88.

17. Hall, "On Measuring the Power of Communications."

18. John Capone, "Microsoft and Initiative Strive for Better Advertising Through Neuroscience," *Online Media Daily* (**www.mediapost.com**), December 9, 2009; Steve McClellan, "Mind Over Matter: New Tools Put Brands in Touch with Feelings," *Adweek* (**www.adweek.com**), February 18, 2008.

19. Laurie Burkitt, "Battle for the Brain," *Forbes* 184, no. 9 (November 16, 2009), pp. 76–78.

20. Based on PACT document published in *Journal of Marketing* 11, no. 4 (1982), pp. 4–29.

21. Sales funnel efficiency definition, **www.google.com**.

22. Rachel King, "Sentiment Analysis Gives Companies Insights into Consumer Opinion," *Bloomberg Business*, March 1, 2011, **www.businessweek.com**.

23. Chris Dillabough, "Web Lets Canadian Tourism Test Media Effectiveness," *New Media Age* (October 31, 2002), p. 12.

24. Kate MacArthur, "McDonald's Tests Ads That Focus on Service," *Advertising Age* 74, no. 1 (January 6, 2003), p. 3.

25. Tim Triplett, "Researchers Probe Ad Effectiveness Globally," *Marketing News* 28, no. 18 (August 29, 1994), pp. 6–7.

26. Vaseline Healing Project, **http://www.vaseline. us/thehealingproject?gclid=Cj0KEQjw94- 6BRDkk568hcyg3-YBEiQAnmuwkmmeyuaJNx0A- k1GPtFXGIxheA8wtH_3R6q72wtW- 2saArh28P8HAQ&gclsrc=aw.ds**, retrieved May 24, 2016.

Name Index

A

ABC (radio networks), 206
ABC India, 86
ABC News, 418
Abercrombie & Fitch, 167
Academy Sports + Outdoors, 364, 365
Acer, 410f
AC Nielsen, 202, 211
Activia, 418
Act Kids, 52
Acxiom, 312
Adams, Karen, 284
AdECN (Microsoft), 243
Adidas, 385, 390
AdKnowledge, 444
AdMeasure, 425
Adrenaline Rush, 306
ADT, 400
Advertising Age, 4, 7, 8, 12, 13, 15, 16,
    25, 34–37, 39, 114, 118, 122, 124,
    127, 132–139, 141, 144, 146, 147,
    149–152, 154, 156, 168, 170, 172,
    179–181, 184, 191, 204, 220, 250,
    251, 279, 286, 298, 303, 369, 374,
    421, 424, 428, 431, 440, 441, 443
Advertising Research Foundation, 384
Advil, 156, 269, 381
Advil Tough, 381
Adware, 197
Adweek, 18, 154, 189, 257
Adweek Media, 154
A&E, 141
AEG Live, 186
Airplay America, 296
Alcoa Rigid Packaging, 45
Alka-Seltzer, 160
Allen, Frances, 107
Allstate Insurance, 23, 24, 64, 169
Allure (magazine), 145, 218
All You (magazine), 347
Altimeter Group, 257
Altman, Tracy, 31
Amazing Race (television
    program), 289
Amazon.com, 94, 269, 271
Ambulatory Health Care Services, 104
AMC, 202
Amelia's Ace of Hearts Ride, 382
American Academy of Advertising
    (AAA), 413

American Airlines, 28, 31, 33, 290
American Business Media, 212
American Eagle, 282, 283, 315,
    345, 346
American Eagle Outfitter, 282, 345, 346
American Express, 82, 110, 141, 179,
    297, 410, 410f
American Family Association, 165
American Idol (television program),
    151, 201, 289, 345
American Magazine Study, 425
American Marketing Association
    (AMA), 413
American Medical Association, 173
American Motors, 300
American Quarter Horse Association, 380
American Society, 263
American Success Story, 25
America's Most Wanted (television
    program), 203
America's Next Top Model (television
    program), 289
America's SuperNanny (television
    program), 203
Amos, Diane, 165
Amway, 326
Anderson Cooper 360, 273
Android, 72, 210
Android phones, 72
Anheuser-Busch, 167, 204, 306
Anthony's Pizza & Pasta, 202
Aoki, Hiroaki Rocky, 118
APCO Worldwide, 42
Apple, 27, 32, 38, 39, 42, 69, 72, 107,
    132, 149, 186, 187, 260, 289, 299,
    326, 346
Applebee's, 40, 53, 62, 63f, 236
Applied Microbiology, 104, 105
Arby's, 137, 292, 391
Arcoroc, 152
Ariel laundry detergent, 31
Arm & Hammer, 106
Arroyave, Mauricio, 98
ARS Group, 426, 428
Artisan, 23
Arvest bank, 35
Association to Advance Collegiate
    Schools of Business (AACSB), 413
A Sunny Day (movie), 300
A.T. Kearny, 375

AT&T, 8, 242, 289, 410
Auchan, 42
Aussie, 31
Avatar (movie), 187, 378
Aveeno, 145
Avis, 106, 141
Avon, 283, 326
Axe, 292

B

Bacardi, 160
Banana Republic, 47
Band-Aid, 46, 408
Bank of America, 23, 24, 110
Barnes & Noble, 195, 316
Barraza, Maria, 179
Baskin-Robbins, 292, 384, 385
Bassmaster, 383
Bass Pro Shop, 364
Bayer, 51, 174
BBDO Worldwide, 8
Beachbody, 205, 206
Bed Bath & Beyond, 25
Benihana restaurant, 118
Ben & Jerry's, 258
Bennett, Drew, 382
BenSpark, 382
Berkner, Alice, 371
Berman, Tao, 306
Bernacchi, Dino, 290
Berry, Amanda, 262
Best Buy, 249, 257, 260, 271, 272, 435
Bethke, Alan, 159
Better Business Bureau, 398, 402, 403,
    403f, 417, 419
Better Homes and Garden (magazine),
    193, 194
Betts, Holly, 241
Betty Crocker Team USA desserts, 171
B.F. Goodrich, 357
Billboard, 198, 202, 206, 218, 269
Bing, 158, 250
BizRate Research, 229
BlackBerry, 187, 411
Black Box, 283
Black Eyed Peas, 186, 187
Blockdot.com, 293
Blogger, 235, 381, 402, 402f
Bloomingdale's, 258
Bluefin Labs, 203

Blum, Justin, 392
BMW, 28, 38, 142, 233
BMW Motorcycles USA, 28
Bob's Furniture Gallery, 357
Body Wise International, Inc., 401
Bojangles, 4, 18
Bongo, 43
Bonick Landscaping, 46, 98
Boost Mobile, 180
Boston College Center for Corporate, 372
Bounce, 31, 433–435
Bounty, 141
Bowden, Don, 255
Bowen, Gordon, 155
Boxcar Creative, 133, 243
Boyer's grocery store, 342f
BP. *see* British Petroleum (BP)
Bradshaw, Terry, 178, 179f
Brand Connections Active
    Outdoor, 141
Brand Keys, 40, 42, 50, 61
Breast Cancer Awareness, 336
Breedlove, Bill, 137
Brees, Drew, 178
Breeze Little System, 52
Brennan, Bob, 216
Bridgestone, 136
Brim, Charlie, 367
Bristol-Myers/Squibb, 348
British Petroleum (BP), 23
Brown, Adam, 378
Bud Light, 156
Budweiser, 172, 173, 218, 356, 428
Buffalo Wild Wings, 293
Buford Hawthorne, 195
Buick, 289
Bureau of Alcohol, Tobacco and
    Firearms (ATF), 397
Burger King, 123, 139, 156, 171, 235,
    252, 425
Burke Marketing Research, 202
Burnett, Bruce, 288
Burnett, Leo, 150, 153, 169, 216, 266
Burroughs, Dianna, 283
Busch, Kyle, 176, 367
Bush, Kyle, 176f, 179, 367
BusinessWeek (magazines), 214, 284
Buzz Lightyear, 52
BzzAgent, 283, 284

C

CACI Coder/Plus (software), 313
Cadillac, 65, 86, 288
Cadillac SRX, 288
Cadillac V-Series, 288
California State Attorney, 401
Calvin Klein, 167, 253, 437

Camerson, James, 187
Campaign for Commercial-Free
    Childhood, 96
Campbell, Eileen, 47
Campbell's, 8, 30, 33, 51, 105, 135,
    157, 398
Campbell's Soup, 33
Camp eBay, 384, 385
Camp Jeep, 299, 300
Canadian Tourism Commission, 438
Canon, 156, 270
Capital One, 110, 141, 142
CareChex, 157
Carl's Jr., 52, 187, 426, 427
Carmichael Lynch, 376
Carnival Cruise Lines, 103, 380
Cartoon Network, 202
Casting Creme Gloss, 265
Cat 414E, 325
Caterpillar, 325
CBBB. *see* Council of Better Business
    Bureaus (CBBB)
CBS (radio networks), 206, 296
CBS Evening News (television
    broadcast), 206
Celebrity Apprentice (television
    program), 289
Celestial Seasonings, 105, 117
Cell Block 6 (television program), 203
Centric Credit Union, 60
Centric Federal Credit Union, 50, 60,
    118, 323, 334
Chadwick Martin Bailey, 410
Chanel, 258, 348
Charm Girls (games), 293
Cheer, 30, 31
Cheerios, 263, 264, 343
Cheetos, 430
Chef Michael's Canine Creations, 283
Chevrolet, 24, 25f, 40, 51, 52, 106, 107,
    204, 289
Chevrolet Camaro, 51, 204
Chevrolet Cruz, 52
Chevrolet Silverado, 40, 107
Chevrolet Silverado 1500, 40
Chevron, 156
Chibe, Paul, 204
Chick-Fil-A, 3–5, 18
Chic Shaque, 313, 333, 353, 362,
    432, 443
Chief Marketing Officer (CMO)
    Council, 8, 23, 47, 91, 107, 170,
    320, 430
Children's Advertising Review Unit
    (CARU), 402–404, 404f, 416,
    417, 419
Chili's, 31

Chipotle Mexican Grill, 86
Chitty Bang, 190
Chocolate Shop, 19
ChristianMingle, 256
Chrysler Group LLC, 97
Church's Chicken, 4, 18
Cincinnati Reds, 419
Cisco Systems, 435
Citibank, 31, 110
Clamato, 300
Clarabridge (software), 435
Claritas, 311, 312
Classy Mommy, 381
Clear Channel Entertainment, 385
Climaco, John, 418
Clinique, 40, 50, 362
Clooney, George, 290
Clorox, 141
CMA Fan Fest, 385
CNN, 141, 206, 273, 286
Coachella music festival, 258
Coca-Cola, 27, 33, 38, 61, 63, 146,
    211, 212, 218, 233, 239, 257,
    264, 265, 276, 289, 297, 306,
    375, 410, 430
Coke, 25, 32, 40, 257, 292, 306, 321,
    355, 378, 430
Colgate, 63, 348
Colgate Comedy Hour (television
    program), 289
Colgate-Palmolive, 146
Colorado Tourism, 170, 251, 252
Combs, Wes, 71
Comcast, 259, 346
Comedy Central, 202
Communist Party, 414
Community Trust Bank, 33, 157f, 178,
    179f, 370f
comScore Inc., 243
ConAgra's Kid's Cafés, 3
Cone Communications, 373
ConocoPhillips, 243
Consumer Reports, 174
Cooper, Frank, 34
Coors, 46, 186
Cornell University, 104
Cosi, 293
Costco, 339, 367
Cotton, Inc., 289
Council of Better Business Bureaus
    (CBBB), 403, 405, 405f
Covergirl, 8, 233, 261, 288
Cox Communications, 383
Cox, Jeff, 426, 428
Cracker Jack, 343
Craftsman, 43, 50
Craig General Hospital, 29, 60, 61

Crest, 38, 52, 157
CrossFit Games, 381
Crowe Horwath, 169
CSI (television program), 151, 192
Cub Cadet, 130
Curebit, 257
CVS Pharmacy, 321, 341

D

Dairy Queen, 19, 103
Dallas (television program), 203, 207, 211, 380
Dallas Cowboys, 203, 380
Dallas Cowboys Cheerleaders (television program), 203
DanActive, 418
Dancing with the Stars (television program), 289
Daniel Taylor Clothier, 92, 116
Dannijo, 259
Dannon, 418
Darden Restaurants, 391
Data, Inc., 240
Datran Media, 312
Datsun brand, 52
David Leadbetter Gold Academy, 288
Davie Brown Entertainment, 290
Dawn, 374, 375f
Dawn detergent, 374
D.C. Comics, 363
Degree deodorant, 94
Del Frisco's Grille, 26f
Dell, 31, 177, 239
Dell, Michael, 177
Deloitte Research, 203
Denny's, 107, 340, 340f
Dentyne, 165
Dentyne Fire, 165
Deschanel, Zooey, 289
Desperate Housewives (television program), 201
DeWalt, 82
DHL Worldwide Express, 246
Dialog, 312
Dick's Sporting Goods, 364
Diesel, 250
Diet Centers, 111
Diet Coke, 32, 40
DiGiorno pizza, 174
Digitas, 190
Direct Marketing Association, 149, 323, 335
DirecTV, 202, 203, 209
Disney, 31, 42, 61, 63, 140, 156, 203, 255, 283, 339, 343, 363, 439f
Doan's, 402
Dodge Dart, 52

Dolan, Bridget, 309
Dolcezza, 239
Domino's, 23, 24, 40, 98
Donnan, David, 375
Donnelly, 312
Dora the Explorer, 171
Doritos, 11, 134, 160
Dos Equis, 175
Double-Click (Google), 243
Doublemint, 367
Dove, 47, 106, 167, 178
Dove Men+Care, 106
Downy, 31, 52
DraftKings, 419
Dreft, 30, 31
Dr. Pepper, 160
Dr. Scholl's, 177, 347
Dr. Scholl's Her Open Shoes, 347
DualBlast, 52
Duboff, Robert, 83
Duck Dynasty (television program), 179, 180f, 299f, 399
Duncan, Robb, 239
DuPage Medical Group, 50, 118, 170, 171, 185, 200, 261, 271f, 423f, 434f
DuPont, 33
Duracell, 219, 269

E

eBay, 384, 385
eBay Live, 385
Edelman, 284, 372
Edmunds, 272
Edouard-Dias, Georges, 265
Edwards, Mike, 368
E! Entertainment Television, 391
Egg McMuffin, 91
Eight O'Clock Coffee's, 20
Emmy awards, 20
EmSense, 430
Energizer, 141
EngageSciences, 264
Equal, 32, 68
Equipment Data Associates, 325
Era, 30, 31
Erichsen, Freja Beha, 403
Ermel, Suzanne, 283
Eskamoe's Frozen Custard & More, 351f
ESPN, 199, 202, 206, 339
ESPN radio, 206, 339
Esurance, 63, 64, 266, 267
E.T., 289
European Union, 331, 441
Everlast, 289
Evian, 31

Excedrin, 348
EZ-pass, 292

F

Facebook, 4, 5, 9, 14, 15, 20, 39, 46, 51, 71, 96, 134, 173, 202, 204, 224, 228, 229f, 230, 231f, 235, 236, 246, 252, 255–259, 258f, 262, 264–268, 274, 276, 293, 306, 326, 339, 435, 436, 443, 446
Facebook Places, 235
Family Guy (television program), 151, 201
Fan Machine, 134
FarmersOnly, 256
Fashion Hunters (television program), 203
Fast and Furious (movies), 52
Febreze Air Fresheners, 31
Federal Communications Commission (FCC), 396, 397, 414
Federal Trade Commission (FTC), 158, 271, 286, 395, 397, 404, 414, 415, 417
FedEx, 28, 246, 367
Feeding America, 260
Female Lockup (television program), 203
Ferguson, Stacy "Fergie," 187
Fiesta Nutrition Center, 107f, 212f
Fiji, 31
Filo, David, 29
Firestone, 52, 367
FirstCarStory.com, 159
First Horizon National Bank, 315
Five Star Fitness Center, 282, 283f, 303
Flamingo Research, 8
Flora, Chris, 3
Florida Family Association, 392
Food and Drug Administration (FDA), 45, 396, 397
Food Network, 202
Ford, 24, 26, 40, 52, 106, 146, 244, 262, 283, 289, 378, 380, 402
Ford Escape, 40
Ford F-150, 40
Ford Flex, 402
Ford F-Series, 380
Forrester Research, 9, 214
Foursquare, 235, 246, 272
Franco, Renata, 363
Free Agents (television program), 203
Freeman, Morgan, 40, 110, 156
Fremont, Carl, 190
French Creative advertising agency, 114
Frequent Diner Club, 322
Friedman, Seth, 187

Frito-Lay, 430, 431
Frosted Flakes, 342
FTC's Bureau of Consumer Protection, 395, 417
Fulcrum, 317
Furniss-Roe, Robert, 160
Future Farmers of America, 380

G

Gaedeke Group, 76
Gain, 30, 31
Gannett, 210
Garza, Martin, 88
Gatorade, 306
Gawker (blog), 273
Gaylord Hotels, 435
GE Café, 210
Geico Insurance, 188, 219
General Electric, 27, 33, 111, 284, 410
General Mills, 3, 50, 171, 263, 343, 344, 374, 391
General Motors (GM), 8, 24, 25, 107, 218
Gerber, 264
G+G Advertising, 133
Gibbs, Coy, 368
Gibbs, Joe, 367, 368
Gibson, Camille, 263
Glade, 52
Glad Odor Shield System, 52
Glamour (magazine), 170, 175, 184, 193, 194, 347
GlaxoSmithKline, 385
Glee (television program), 201
Global Brand Development of Godiva Chocolatier, 170
Gmail, 158
GoDaddy, 107
Godiva Chocolatier, 170
Goldberg, Whoopi, 141
Goldman, Seth, 239
Good Eats, 350
Good Housekeeping (magazine), 193–195
Goodyear, 33
Googins, Bradley K., 372
Google, 27–29, 38, 42, 46, 158, 204, 226, 227, 243, 246, 250, 408
Google+, 229, 235
Gordon, Je, 155
Gowalla, 235
Graham, Devin, 262
Grammys (television broadcast), 187
Great Books for Great Kids, 252
Grey New York, 279
Grey's Anatomy (television program), 201

Gucci, 258
Gulf Coast Seafood, 8, 8f, 10f, 39f, 230, 230f
Gulf Seafood Marketing Coalition, 123

H

Hale, David, 350
Hallmark, 15, 106, 141
Hallmark, Adrian, 15
Hanes, 36, 165
Hanes All-Over Comfort Bra, 165
Hanes Brands, 36
Haney, Megan, 135
Hanks, Tom, 179
Hannah Montana (television program), 407
Hardees', 52
Harley-Davidson, 39, 69, 134, 290, 299, 304
Harris, Ed, 154, 409
Harris Interactive, 154, 409
HARU, 119
Hassan, Tariq, 294
Hawaii 5-0 (television program), 51
Hawkins, Angela, 36
Headless Horseman Hayrides and Haunted, 292
Head & Shoulders, 27, 31
HealthGrades, 157
Healthy Choice, 30, 382
Hefner, Hugh, 391
Heineken, 356
Hendrix, Jimi, 168
Herbal Essences, 31
Hershey's, 19, 61, 63, 283, 363
Hertz, 106
Hewitt, Jennifer Love, 165
Hewlett-Packard (HP), 283, 410f
HGTV'd (television program), 203
Hilton Hotels, 290
Hintz, Greg, 229
Hitler, Adolph, 29
HOG, 299
Holiday Inn, 25, 81, 292
Holland America cruise, 356
HomeAway, 204
Home Depot, 28, 101, 136, 317, 367
Home Shopping Network, 140, 325
Honda, 40, 180, 186, 367
Honda Accord, 40
Honda Civic, 40
Honda CR-V, 40
Honest Tea, 45, 239, 376
Hooper, Inc., 202
Hooters of America, 262
Hostess, 286

Hotels.com, 337
5-Hour Energy drinks, 306
House (television program), 201
House Committee on Oversight and Government, 378
House Party, 283
Houses, 292
Howard, Joy, 373
H&R Block, 256
Huggies, 339, 363
Huggies Big Kid Academy, 339
Hunt's, 398
Hyundai, 184

I

IBM (International Business Machines), 27, 38, 247
IDC Research, 293
IGA Worldwide, 293
IHOP (formerly the International House of Pancakes), 33, 34
i2i Marketing, 288
Imagine (video game), 293
IMC Foundation, 13
Indy 500, 385
Innerscope company, 429
InstaGold Flash System, 174
Instagram, 4, 5, 46, 96, 229, 235, 236, 240, 256–259, 257f, 262, 270, 274, 276, 283, 380
In Style (magazine), 347
Intel, 31, 81, 157
Interbrand, 18, 27
International Bird Rescue Research Center, 374
International Olympics Committee, 409
Interstate All Battery Center, 367
Interstate Batteries, 13f, 21, 28, 176, 200f, 300, 301f, 367, 368, 384, 390, 398, 424, 444
Intuit, 82, 435
iPad, 96, 158, 339, 346
iPhone, 39, 131, 326, 346
iPod, 205
Ipsos, 8, 204, 444
Ireland, Kathy, 177
iTunes, 169, 186
Ivory, 31

J

Jack Morton Worldwide, 289
Jackson, Janet, 167
Jaclyn Smith brand, 43
Jaguar, 15
JaguarUSA.com, 15
James, Lebron, 176

Jarrett, Dale, 367
JC Penney, 195, 325, 341
JD Bank, 4, 4f, 18, 50, 96, 97f, 142f, 143, 149, 150, 191, 191f, 244f, 269f, 369f
J.D. Power and Associates, 263
Jeep, 39, 61, 63, 69, 299, 300, 386
Jeep Jamboree, 299
Jennie-O., 31
Jeopardy (television program), 345
JetBlue, 259
JGRMX's motocross and super-cross team, 368
Joan Ganz Cooney Center, 96
Joe Boxer, 43
John Deere, 33, 141, 150, 269
Johnson & Johnson, 8, 33, 141, 184
Johnson, Magic, 178
Johnson, Paul, 88
Jolie, Angelina, 175
Jovan Musk cologne, 187
Joy, 373
J.P. Morgan, 156
JP Morgan Chase, 40, 110
Jubie, Nancy, 292
Judge, Barry, 249
Just Dance (video game), 293

K

Kaplan Thaler Group, 374
Kapoor, Sonam, 265
Karns Quality Foods, 158f, 321f
Keith, Toby, 380
Kellogg's, 322, 342
Kenmore, 43, 44f, 111
Kenneth Cole, 86, 236
KFC, 3, 18, 385
Kia, 435
Kimball, Curtis, 260
Kimberly-Clark, 141, 339
Kim, Brad, 257
Kindle Fire, 158
Kinko's, 169
Kleenex, 46, 399, 408
Kleenex Cottonelle, 399
Kleenex tissue, 46, 399, 408
Kloeppel, David C., 435
Kmart, 43, 273, 364
Kmart.com, 228
KMX, 306
Knotts, Rose, 88
Knowledge Base Marketing, 311, 312
Kodak, 63, 81
Korrs beer, 46, 408
Kotcher, Laurie Len, 170
Kraft Foods, 8, 438

Kraft Heinz, 23, 34
Kraft Mac & Cheese, 98
Kraft Parmesan Cheese, 297, 439
Kraft Singles, 24, 41f, 56, 57f
Krispy Kreme, 28
Kroger, 341
Krugman, Herbert, 196
Kuester, Joe, 141

L

Lamar Advertising, 219
Lambert, Miranda, 289
Lambert's Café, 119
Land O' Lakes, 260
LandsEnd.com, 228
Lawmakers, 29
La-Z-Boy, 178
Lean Cuisine, 3
Lee Jeans, 383
L'eggs, 36
Lego, 29
Lennon, John, 176
Leo Burnett Agency, 169
Leo Burnett Starcom USA, 216
Lever Brothers, 289
Levinson, Jay Conrad, 286
Levi's, 186
Levi Strauss, 61, 63, 376
Lexicon, Inc., 28
Lifehouse, 169
Lincoln, 81
Lin, Katherine, 258
LinkedIn, 240, 256, 328
Lipman Agency, 170
Lipton, 258
Little League, 151, 364, 380
Littlest Pet Shop (video games), 293
Live with Fire, 72
Liz Claiborne, 243
L.Bean, 325
Logo Company, 33, 119
London Financial Group, 401
L'Oreal, 142, 243, 265, 403
L'Oreal Paris, 142
Louis Vuitton, 175
Lowe's, 42
Lowy, Shuli, 236
LUBA Workers' Comp, 209, 328
Lucasfilm, 344
Lucozade, 142

M

3M, 38
Macy's, 236, 258
Maestro Limpio, 47
Magee, Elaine, 418

Mangum, Kristiauna, 326
Man of Steel (movie), 52
Manoogian, Alex, 309
Marchioli, Nelson, 340
Marci, Carl, 429
Margolis, Jonathan, 411
Mark cosmetics, 326
Marketing News, 359
Mark Girls, 326
Marlboro Cup Racing, 407
Marley, Bob, 176
Marriott, 156, 239
Marriott, Bill, 239
Marriott International, 239
Mars, Inc., 367
Martin Agency, 189
Martin, Brian, 141
Mary Kay, 326
Mass Opinion Business Intelligence (MOBI) (software), 435
MasterCard, 411
Mateschitz, Dietrich, 306
Mattel, 146, 283
Maxwell House, 24, 28, 29, 30f, 37, 37f, 50, 139f, 141, 149, 292, 348f, 365, 425f, 443
Maxwell House Coffee, 28, 30
Maybelline, 361, 403, 403f
Maytag, 131
Mazda, 24
McDonald's, 27, 32, 33, 38, 91, 139, 140, 146, 171, 176, 235, 236, 252, 262, 268, 292, 345, 346, 410f, 425, 439, 440
mcgarrybowen, 37, 133, 137, 142, 150, 154
McKinsey & Co., 265
Meaux, Justin, 430
MediaEDGE, 175
Mediamark Research, Inc., 202
Mediamark Research & Intelligence's, 425
MediaMind, 243
Mel's Diner, 62, 63f
Mendes, Eva, 167
Mexico Tourism Board, 368
Michael Alan Group, 411
Michael Kors, 258
Mickelson, Phil, 180
Microsoft, 27, 38, 158, 168, 239, 243, 257, 266, 267f, 283, 346, 378, 402
Mike's Old-Time Ice Cream, 19
Miller, Norm, 367, 368
Millward Brown, 41, 47, 175, 211, 425, 427, 444
Millward Brown Group, 47

Millward Brown Optimor, 41
Mindshare Entertainment, 141
Minnesota State Fair, 385
Mintel Inspire, 70
Minute Maid, 404
Miracle Whip, 156
Missoni, 37, 312
M&M's, 367
Modell's, 364
Modern Bride (magazine), 209
Mondelez, 29, 267
Monopoly (McDonaldÆs), 140
Monroe, Marilyn, 176
Monster Jam, 380
Motel 6, 118, 136
Mountain Dew, 262, 306
Mr. Clean, 47
Mr. Proper, 47
Mukherjee, Ann, 430
MyBlogSpark.com, 343
MySpace, 224
My Yard Goes Disney (television
    program), 203

N

Nabisco, 29
NASCAR, 176, 283, 346, 347, 367,
    368, 380, 381f, 384, 390
National Advertising Division (NAD),
    398, 402, 403, 417
National Advertising Division of the
    Better, 398
National Advertising Review Board
    (NARB), 402–404, 419
National Consumer Council
    (NCC), 401
National Geographic (magazine),
    193–195
National Sporting Goods Association
    World, 358
Nation's Restaurant News Social 200
    Index, 262
NBA, 385, 390, 391
NBC, 218, 296, 400
NCAA basketball, 345, 411
NCR, 233
Nellymoser, 232
Nescafé, 55
Nestle, 3, 19, 31, 42, 283
Nestlé Purina, 283
Netflix, 42, 260, 317
Neuro-Focus, 430
New Balance, 395
Newcomer, Morris and Young
    advertising agency, 127, 215
New York State Bridge Authority, 292

NFC Championship, 231
NFL, 40, 187
NHRA's Pro Stock division, 368
Nickeldeon, 396
Nicoderm CQ, 162, 163
Nicorette, 290
Nielsen, 42, 197, 202, 203, 211, 236,
    257, 290, 293, 425, 426
Nielsen IAG, 425, 426
Nielsen Media Research, 202
Nielsen SAVE, 197
Nielsen's SocialGuide service, 203
Nielsen survey, 42
Nike, 30, 32, 33, 39, 139, 142, 213, 289,
    362, 376, 390, 411, 428
Nike Swoosh, 32, 33
Niles, Robert, 364
Nintendo, 157
Nintendo Wii, 381
Nissan, 52, 236
NKH&W Advertising Agency, 170
Nokia, 34, 141
NOLA.com/The Times Picayune, 123
No Mercy, 384
Norwegian Cruise Lines, 356
Novak, Tom, 36, 39
Novartis Corporation, 402
NutraSweet, 32, 306

O

Office Depot, 141
Office Furniture Source, 197
Ogilvy and Mather, 47
Ogilvy Public Relations, 55
Ohio State Fair, 385
Ohio State University, 326
OIB Reward Plus, 127
Olay, 31, 94
Old Spice, 27, 31, 52, 428
Olive Garden, 391, 391f, 392
Oliver, Barbara, 246
Olympics, 171, 377, 377f, 382, 384,
    409–411
O'Nealgas, 438, 438f
O'Neal, Shaquille, 178
Open Table, 272
Orange County (CA) district
    attorney, 401
Oreo, 189, 261, 267
Orient-Express Hotels, 72
Origin Bank, 42, 95
Orkin, 136
Oscar Mayer, 24, 137, 142, 156
OTX Research, 430
Ouachita Independent Bank, 109f, 179f,
    198f, 211, 213f, 242

OurTime, 256
Owen, Stewart, 155

P

Paddleford, Clementine, 118
Padilla, Colleen, 381
Paige Premium, 94
Pampers, 339
Panasonic, 410f
Pandora, 207
Pantene, 31
Papa John's, 398
Patagonia, 373, 376
Patrick, Danica, 180
People (magazine), 193
Pepsi, 25, 32, 34, 127, 160, 180, 186,
    236, 300, 306, 321, 354, 355, 378,
    410f, 430
PepsiCo, 354, 378
Pepsi-Cola, 160
Perrier, 31
Perry, Chris, 288
PERT shampoo, 177
Peter Mayer advertising agency, 35
Peterson Milla Hooks, 36, 37, 39
Petukhova, Elena, 424, 426
Pew Research Center, 226
Pfizer, 51, 156
Philadelphia Cream Cheese, 93f, 111f,
    160f, 174, 175f, 193f, 232, 426f
Phillips, Randy, 186
Phoenix Sun basket ball team, 315
Photosmart Premium printer, 294
Pillsbury, 31
Pine-Sol, 165
Ping Mobile, 236
Pink brand, 384
Pink Jacket Creative (advertising
    agency), 137, 191
Pinterest, 46, 101f, 229, 230, 240, 256,
    260, 260f, 274
Pipher, Mary, 407
Pitbull, 267
Pizza Hut, 63f
Placek, David, 28
Planters, 24, 160
Planter's Insurance Company, 88
Platinum Motorcars, 61
Playboy, 391, 392
Playtex, 165
Playtex bra, 165
Plott, Karen, 192, 223
Poggenpohl, 71f
Poise brand, 141
Poldmae, Leho, 382
Pole Hole, 305

Popeye's, 4
Porsche, 24, 145, 150, 151
Post-it notes (3M), 278, 279f
Potty Dance participants, 339
Potty Dance program, 339
PowerBar, 288
Presley, Elvis, 176
Priceline.com, 176, 337
Princess Cruise line, 356
Procter & Gamble (P&G), 8, 27, 30, 31
Progressive Bank, 50, 114, 118, 141, 314f, 373f, 430f
Progressive Insurance, 175
Progresso, 398
Prudential Life Insurance, 33
P&S Surgical Hospital, 157, 157f
Purdy, Joe, 374
Purina, 283
P90X, 205

Q

Quicken software, 82
QVC, 260

R

Radio's All-Dimension Audience Research (RADAR), 205
Raising Cain's Chicken Fingers, 4
Rajapaksa, Roshini, 418
Ralph Lauren, 63
Ram 1500, 40
Ramsey, Charles, 262
RA Sushi, 119
Reactions and Opinions, 429
Reader's Digest (magazine), 193, 194
Rea & Kaiser's Nichols agency, 324
Red Bull, 283, 288, 306, 306f
Red Cross, 11f
Red Lobster, 18, 150, 153
Red Robin Gourmet Burgers, 18
Reebok, 21, 29, 72, 139, 156, 362, 381, 390, 395
Reese's Pieces, 289
Reform, 378
Relationship Optimizer and Prime Response (software), 233
Remington, 235
ReRez, 14, 78f, 127, 127f, 162, 163f, 214
Research Systems Corporation (RSC), 440
Resource, 31
Reuters/Ipsos, 8, 204
Revel, 100
Revlon, 21, 261, 362
Reynolds Protection, 105, 118

Rice Krispies, 342
Richards, Stan, 134
Richer, Mark-Hans, 134
Right Media ad exchange (Yahoo!), 243
Ritz-Carlton, 72
River Pools and Spas, 234, 235
Roberts, Anna, 178
Robertson, Willie, 179, 180f, 399, 399f
Robinson Radio, 205
Rob Stein, 392
Rolling Stones, 168, 187
Ronald McDonald, 407
Roper Starch Worldwide, 373
Rose, Pete, 419
Rossow, Adam, 203
Rotel Tomatoes and Diced Green Chilies, 31
Rothman, Colleen, 381
Royal Caribbean International, 356
Ruby Tuesday, 62, 63f, 64
Rudy's Restaurant Group., 119
Runza Restaurants, 251, 252
Runza Rex, 252
Russian Federation, 215
Ruth's Steak House, 114
Rytila, Tuula, 34

S

Saatchi & Saatchi, 298
Sadler, Catherine, 47
Safeguard, 31
Safeway, 341
Salon Sensational, 336
Salter, Jamie, 34
Salvation Army, 18
Samsung, 27, 29, 187, 410f
Sands Research, Inc., 421
Sands, Steve, 421
San Pellegrino, 31
Sara Lee Corporation, 105
Savvy, 43
Schlotzsky's, 31
Schmidt, Marcus, 234
Scooby-Doo, 52
Scope, 52
Scotch tape, 279
Scott + Cooner, 86, 303
Scott Equipment, 34, 35, 36f, 62f, 80f, 243f, 272f, 422f, 434, 437f
Scotts Miracle-Grow lawn fertilizer, 92
Sears, 44f, 156
Sears.com, 228
Sears2Go, 228
Sears Holdings, 228
Secret, 31, 46, 167, 180, 187, 203, 228, 258, 384

Secret Obsession fragrance, 167
Sega, 181
Senior Living (magazine), 196
Sephora, 309, 346
Seventh Generation, 376, 376f
ShamWow, 140
Shape (magazine), 293, 347
Sharp, 156
Sharpless, Brian, 204
Shedding the Wedding (television program), 289
Shell, 40
Sheridan, Marcus, 234, 235
Sherwin-Williams, 33
Shields, Brook, 178
Shoebox Greetings, 31
Siberstein, Richard, 430
Simmons, Courtney, 293
Simmons Market Research Bureau, 202
Simon, Suzette, 88
Six Flags, 363, 364, 364f
Skechers, 40, 50, 157, 184, 395
Skip Barber Racing School, 288
Skyjacker, 38, 38f, 55, 56f, 133f, 161f, 180f, 228, 264, 299f, 325f, 346f, 386, 399
Skype, 29, 72
Smartwater, 31
Smith, Alexandra, 70
Smithee, Benjamin, 445
Smith, Jessica (blogger), 402
Snapchat, 8, 91, 257
Snapple, 156
Snell, Dave, 426
Snickers, 164, 367
Snoop Dog, 177
Snuggies, 140
Sonic Drive-in, 255
Sony, 42, 117, 172, 267, 293, 359, 384, 385, 401f
Sony Online Entertainment (SOE), 293
Southern Living (magazine), 193, 194
Southwest Airlines, 28, 239, 259, 378
Southwest General Hospital, 399f
Spark 44, 15
Sparks and Honey, 263, 264
Spartan Race, 381
Special Olympics, 382, 384
Spectrum Brands, 235
Speedo, 411
Spicy Jack, 252
Splenda, 68
SpongeBob SquarePants, 52
Sports Active (video game), 293
Sports Expo, 358

Sports Illustrated (magazine), 60, 167, 184, 193, 194, 210
Sprint Cup, 367
Spych Marketing Analytics, 445, 446
Staples, 260, 315
Starbucks, 55, 210, 211, 241, 257, 259, 267, 300, 393, 397, 444
Starch INRA, 202
StarKist, 160
Star Wars, 8, 343
StarWars.com, 344
State Farm Insurance, 23
Stein Mart, 173
SteviB's, 68
St. Francis Community Health Center, 96
St. Francis Medical Center, 50, 73f, 118, 131, 145, 149, 160, 215
Stockwell, Melissa, 269
Stoff, Dr., 401
Straw, Martyn, 8
Street Guerilla Marketing, 412
Stride Sugarless Gum, 285
StubHub, 33, 34
Suave, 292
Subaru, 159, 162, 172
Subway, 23, 40, 252, 292, 294, 300, 310, 346
Sub-Zero, 136
Sullivan, Brian, 359
Sullivan, Jazmine, 289
Summer Olympics, 410, 411
Summize, 259
Sunday Night Football (television broadcast), 200–202, 339
Sunsilk Haircare, 286
Super Bowl, 134, 154, 164, 167, 172, 184, 199, 204, 218, 221, 266, 269, 340, 430
Susan G. Komen Breast Cancer Foundation, 374
Swann, Jennifer, 336
Swann, Mike, 19
Sweeney, Liz, 43
Sweet'N Low, 68
Swiffer, 107, 174, 261
Swift, Jonathan, 29
Swirl app, 236

T

Taco Bell, 233, 292, 363
Talley, Jason, 88
Target, 364
Target's (advertising agency), 36
Taste of Chicago, 385
TD Ameritrade, 377

Technomic, 398
The Biggest Loser (television program), 255
The Body Shop, 376
The Eleventh Hour (television program), 290
The Food Channel, 199
The Girls Next Door (television program), 391, 392
TheGreatIndoors.com, 228
The Green Turtle, 382
The Hollywood Reporter (magazine), 364
The Huffington Post (blog), 273
The Lion King (movie), 140
The Medical Center of Southwest Texas, 374f
The Office (television program), 201
The Oprah Winfrey Show (television program), 187
Therapedic International, 177
The Richards Group, 92, 93, 133, 134, 136, 150, 374, 424, 426
The Salon Channel, 296
The Simpsons (television program), 201
The Snoring Center, 183, 191
The Times-Picayune, 65, 86, 190, 219
The Toggery, 345, 362
The Wall Street Journal, 156, 186
Thielman, Sam, 189
Thompson, Kirk, 34
Thrillist, 239
Tide, 30, 31, 38, 39, 52, 106
Tide Pods, 106
Tide Touch, 52
TidyCat, 52
Timberland, 236
Time, 184, 193
Time Warner, 429
Today Show (television program), 400
Todo Con Todo, 98
Top Secret Recipe (television program), 203
Torbit, 227
TouchSmart Web, 294
Tough Mudder, 381
Toyoda, Akio, 378
Toyota, 8, 23, 24, 27, 40, 106, 177, 203, 238, 367, 376, 378, 379
Toyota Camry, 40
Toyota Corolla, 40
Toyota Sienna, 177
Toy Story series, 52
Travelocity, 249, 337
Trentlyon, Jason Van, 412

TripAdvisor, 272
Tristano, Darren, 398
Tropicana, 350, 404
Truvia, 68
Tumblr, 4, 256
Turbo movie, 52
Tweetscan, 259
Twinkies, 286
Twitter, 4, 5, 28, 33, 46, 51, 71, 72, 91, 96, 177, 203, 225, 228–230, 235, 236, 255–260, 262, 264–268, 274, 276, 306, 344, 346, 378

U

U2, 187
Ubisoft, 293
Under Armour, 381
Unified Western Grocers, 314
Unilever, 47, 190, 269, 286
Union Pacific Railroad, 33
Unistar, 206
United Airlines, 156
United Way, 151
University of North Carolina, 282
7UP, 156
Up (movie), 100, 168, 290
Up in the Air (movie), 290
UPS, 141, 246, 284, 318
UrbanDaddy, 239
Urbanspoon, 272
USA Olympic Crunch cereal, 171
USA Today, 164, 204, 210, 323
U.S. Centers for Disease Control and Prevention (CDC), 379
U.S. Court of Appeals, 401, 402
U.S. Postal Service (USPS), 397
U.S. Supreme Court, 401

V

Velveeta cheese, 31
Vergara, Sofia, 265
Verizon, 29, 141, 156, 186, 314, 410f
Vermont, 3
VF Corporation, 50, 105
Viacom, 396, 435
Viagra, 156
Victoria's Secret, 167, 187, 228, 258, 384
Victor's Secret, 46, 408
Vignelli, Massimo, 33
Virginia Slims Tennis, 407
VISA, 27, 31, 410
Visa, 410
Visit Baton Rouge, 123, 136, 198, 225
Visit South Walton (Florida), 7f, 18, 66f, 72, 99f, 101, 123, 130, 159,

174, 185, 202, 207, 208, 230, 236, 245, 258, 260, 277, 294, 295, 436
V8 juice, 51, 105
Vladeck, David, 395
Vogue (magazine), 36, 37, 239, 348
Volkswagen, 29, 140, 204, 385, 428

W

Wade, Jason, 169
Wahl, Deborah, 91
Wal-Mart, 24, 25, 27, 107, 141, 142, 152, 177, 203, 225, 227, 260, 284, 296, 357, 364
Walt Disney, 63
Wanamaker, John, 420
Warner Brothers, 289, 363
Warner Brothers Products, 363
Water Institute of the Gulf, 34
Wayne, John, 176
Weaver, 77, 334, 440
WebMD, 418
WeighThis, 3
Weight Watchers, 111
Weiner, Russell, 23
Weiss, Rachel, 265
Wendy's, 171, 252

West Coast sailing cruise, 356
Westwood One, 206, 339
WetPaint, 257
Wheaties, 381
Wheel of Fortune (television program), 192
Whirlpool, 111
White, Betty, 179
whitehouse.com, 408
Whole Foods, 42
Wholly Guacamole, 31, 32f, 51, 64f, 140, 171, 229, 254, 255, 257, 341, 343, 345, 346, 435, 436
Wieden + Kennedy, 210, 428
Wife Swap (television program), 203
Wii Fit Plus (video game), 293
Wilkinson, Kendra, 391, 392
will.i.am, 186, 187
Wimpy Kid (movie), 255
Winter Olympics, 410, 411
WiseWindow, 435
Witeck-Combs Communication, 71
Women's Bassmaster Tour, 383
Woods, Dave, 223
Word of Mouth Marketing Association (WOMMA), 284, 286, 303
WPP Group, 215

Wrigley's, 63
Wynne, Angus, 363

X

Xerox, 46, 218, 279, 408
X-Shot, 382

Y

Yahoo!, 29, 42, 229, 243, 250
Yang, Jerry, 29
Yelp, 272
Yoplait, 374
Your Shape (video game), 293
YouTube, 5, 15, 39, 169, 184, 189, 204, 229, 235, 260–265, 267–269, 272–274, 337

Z

Zagat, 272
Zappos, 273
Zehnder Communications, 12, 34, 123, 133, 136, 150, 153, 207, 208, 294, 429
Zehnder, Jeffrey, 123
Zimm, Angela, 392
Zippo, 63

Subject Index

A

Account executives, 138
Account planners, 139
Accountability, in marketing communications, 7–8
Achievers (VALS), 99
Action codes, mobile marketing and, 232
Active lifestyles, 71
Adaptation, 15, 47
Administrative complaints, 400–401
Advergames, 292
Advertisements
  comparative, 158–159
  corrective, 402
  left-brain, 145
  offensive, 407
Advertising
  banner, 242–243
  to children, 404–405, 407
  cooperative, 357
  deceptive, 397
  ethical issues in, 407
  evaluation, 437–438
  at events, 384
  goals for, 139–140
  location-based, 236
  offline, 244
  online, 243–244
  resonance, 159–160
  Super Bowl, 204
  tracking methodology, 425–426
  trends in, 7–8
Advertising agencies. *See also* In-house advertising
  advantages of, 132–133
  agency selection, 138
  budget allocation considerations, 133–134
  creative briefs and, 143–144
  creative pitch, 137
  criteria to select, 135–136
  crowdsourcing, 134
  goal setting to selection, 135
  in-house vs. external, 132–134
  media costs and, 193
  roles within, 138–139
  specialized services of, 133
Advertising appeals
  emotional, 169–171
  explanation of, 161

fear, 162–163
humor, 163–164
music, 168–169
rational, 169
scarcity, 171
sex, 164–168
Advertising campaign management
  advertising expenditures and, 129–132
  advertising personnel roles and, 138–139
  agency choice and, 135–138
  creative brief and, 143–146
  explanation of, 124–129
  in-house vs. external advertising agencies and, 132–134
  international implications and, 146–147
  positioning and, 143
  theoretical approaches to, 124–129
Advertising campaigns
  consistency and, 142–143
  duration of, 143
  goals for, 139–140
  media selection for, 140–141
  positioning and, 143
  taglines and, 142
Advertising design
  advertising appeals and, 161–171
  executional framework and, 171–175
  international implications of, 181
  message strategies and, 156–161
  sources and spokespersons and, 175–181
Advertising expenditures
  carryover effects, 131
  communications goals, 130
  decay effects, 131–132
  diminishing returns, 131
  threshold effects, 130–131
  wear-out effects, 131
Advertising objectives
  brand recall, 198
  brand recognition, 197–198
  effective reach and frequency, 196–197
  explanation of, 195
  recency theory, 196
  three-exposure hypothesis, 196
Advertising research. *See* Research

Advertising terminology
  continuity, 195
  cost, 193
  cost per rating point, 194–195
  frequency, 192
  gross impressions, 195
  gross rating points, 193
  opportunities to see, 192
  ratings, 194–195
  weighted (or demographic) CPM, 194–195
Advertising theory
  hierarchy of effects model, 124–126
  means–end theory, 126–127
  verbal and visual images, 127–129
Advertising tracking research, 425–426
Affect referral, 68–69
Affective component of attitude, 59, 60
Affective message strategy
  emotional, 160
  resonance, 159–160
Age complexity, 69
Age, market segments by, 95–96
Alliance branding. *See* Co-branding
Allusion ambushing, 411
Alternative evaluation
  affect referral, 68–69
  evoked set method, 65–67
  multiattribute approach, 67–68
Alternative marketing
  brand communities and, 298–300
  branded entertainment, 290
  buzz marketing, 282–286
  experiential marketing, 288–289
  explanation of, 281
  guerrilla marketing, 286–287
  in-store marketing, 295–296
  international implications of, 300
  lifestyle marketing, 288
  point-of-purchase marketing, 296–298
  product placements, 289–290
Alternative media venues
  cinema advertising, 294
  miscellaneous, 294–295
  video game advertising, 292–294
Ambush marketing, 410–411
Animation execution framework, 171–172
Anthropological research approach, 92

Apology strategies, 379
Appeals. *See* Advertising appeals
Attitudes, 59–61. *See also* Consumer
    attitudes
    components of, 59, 61
    consumer decision making and, 61
    explanation of, 59
    formation of, 59–61
Attractiveness, of sources, 178
Authoritative executional frameworks,
    173–174

B

Banner advertising, 242–243
Behavior targeting, 238
Behavioral evaluations
    explanation of, 436–437
    purchase simulation tests for,
      440–441
    sales and response rates and, 437–439
    test markets and, 439–440
Behavioral response model, 162
Believers (VALS), 99
Benchmarks, 108, 426
Benefit segmentation, 102
Billboard advertising. *See* Out-of-home
    advertising (OOH)
Biometric research, 429
Block parties, 283–284
Blogs
    company-sponsored, 239
    explanation of, 239
    interactive, 270–271
    sponsorship marketing, 381–382
Bonus packs, 357
    explanation of, 348
    keys to success, 349
    as trade incentives, 357
    types of, 348
Bounce-back coupons, 341
Brand alliance, 27
Brand ambassadors, 282–283
Brand awareness, 139–140
Brand buzz, 282
Brand communities, 298–300
Brand engagement, on e-commerce
    sites, 228
Brand equity, 40–42
Brand extension, 30
Brand image
    company perspective of, 27–28
    components of, 24–25
    consumer perspective of, 25–27
    creating change in, 36–37
    creating the right, 34–35
    identification of desired, 34

    rejuvenations of, 35–36
    social media marketing, 262–263
Brand infringement, 46
Brand Keys Customer Loyalty
    Engagement Index (CLEI),
    40, 42
Brand logos
    creation of, 33–34
    explanation of, 32–33
    stimulus codability of, 32
Brand loyalty, 39–40
    social media marketing, 264–265
Brand management, ethical issues
    related to, 46–47
Brand metrics, 41
Brand names
    categories of, 29
    development of, 29
    function of, 28
    origins of, 28–29
Brand parity, 11, 40–41
Brand recall, 198
Brand recognition
    brand recall vs., 198
    explanation of, 197
    product placement and, 289–290
Brand spiraling, 244
Branded content, 233
Branded entertainment, 290
Branded videos, 262
Brand-loyal consumers, 352
Brand-preference consumers, 352
Brands
    blogs sponsored by, 269
    building strong, 139–140
    co-branding, 31–32
    commitment to, 264
    development of, 37–39
    emotional bonds with, 69
    extension, 30
    family, 30
    flanker, 30–31
    in international markets, 47
    private, 42–44
    recall, 198
    recognition, 197–198
    top ten global, 27
    top-choice, 140
    top-of-mind, 139
    types of, 29–31
Budgets/budgeting
    advertising allocation considerations
      for, 133
    communications schedules, 111–112
    meet the competition, 109–110
    objective and task, 110

    payout planning, 110
    percentage of sales, 109
    quantitative models, 110–111
    "what we can afford," 110
Bureau of Alcohol, Tobacco and
    Firearms (ATF), 397
Business buyers
    categories of purchasing decisions
      made by
    cognitive involvement, 76–77
    motivation, 75
    personal objectives, 77
    personality, 74–75
    power, 75–76
    risk taking and, 76
    roles, 75
Business buying centers
    explanation of, 74
    individual factors and, 74–77
    organizational influences, 74
Business-to-business advertisements
    animation in, 171–172
    media multiplier effect and, 212
    radio for, 206
    recency theory and, 196
    verbal and visual images in, 129
Business-to-business buyer behaviors
    business buying centers and,
      73–77
    overview of, 73
Business-to-business buying process
    establishment of specifications
      in, 79
    evaluation of vendor, 80
    identification of needs in, 79
    identification of vendors, 80
    negotiation of terms, 80
    postpurchase evaluation, 80
    selection of vendor, 80
Business-to-business market
    segmentation, 103–105
Business-to-business markets
    brand image and, 23
    gifts and bribery in, 409
    media selection in, 212–213
    social media and, 10
Business-to-business sales
    modified rebuy, 78
    new tas, 78
    straight rebuy, 77
Buyers. *See* Business buyers
Buyers, in buying centers, 73
Buying centers. *See* Business buying
    centers
Buying environment. *See* Consumer
    buying environment

Buying process. *See* Business-to-business buying process; Consumer buying process
Buying teams, 358
Buzz marketing
  company employees and, 284
  consumers who like a brand and, 282
  explanation of, 282
  preconditions for, 285
  sponsored consumers and, 282–284
  stages in, 284–285
  stealth marketing as form of, 285–286
Buzz score, 436

C

C3 ratings, 200–202
Carryover effects, 131
Catalogs, 325
Cause-related marketing, 373–374
Celebrity spokespersons, 175–177
CEO spokespersons, 177
Channel integration, 228
Channels. *See* Marketing channels
Children, advertising to, 404–405, 407
Children's Advertising Review Unit (CARU)
  Council of Better Business Bureaus, 404–405
Cinema advertising, 294
Civil law, 414
Clarabridge software, 435
Click-throughs, 421, 422
Client retention rates, 136
Clutter
  in business media, 213
  explanation of, 5
  television, 199
Co-branding, 31–32
Codes of ethics, 413
Cognitive ability, of buyers, 76–77
Cognitive component of attitude, 59, 61
Cognitive mapping
  cognitive linkages, 63
  explanation of, 62–63
  information retainion, 64
  marketing messages, 64–65
  new information processing, 63–64
Cognitive message strategy
  comparative advertising, 158–159
  explanation of, 157
  generic, 157
  hyperbole, 158
  preemptive, 157
  unique selling proposition, 157
Cognitive neuroscience, 430–431

Comfort marketing, 159
Commercial lists, 324–325
Common law, 414
Communication. *See also* Integrated marketing communications (IMC); Marketing communications
  explanation of, 3
  global marketing issues and, 246–247
  nature of, 3–5
Communication revolution, 71–72
Companies. *See* Organizations
Comparative advertisements, 158–159
Compensation method, 330
Competitive responses, test markets, 440
Competitors, to establish position, 106
Compiled list, 324
Complementary branding, 31
Conative component of attitude, 59, 61
Conative message strategy, 160–161
Conflicts of interest, 136
Consent orders, 400
Constraints, in creative brief, 145–146
Consumer attitudes. *See also* Attitudes
  information search and, 59–61
  toward brands, 61
Consumer buying environment
  active lifestyles and, 71
  age complexity and, 69
  communication revolution and, 71–72
  diverse lifestyles and, 71
  experience pursuits and, 72
  gender complexity and, 70
  health emphasis and, 72–73
Consumer buying process
  cognitive mapping and, 62–65
  consumer attitudes and, 59–61
  consumer values and, 61–65
  evaluation of alternatives and, 65–69
  information search and, 56–59
Consumer market segmentation. *See* Market segmentation
Consumer promotions
  agencies that handle, 133
  bonus packs as, 348–349
  contests and sweepstakes as, 344–346
  coupons as, 340–342
  explanation of, 338, 340
  overlays and tie-ins as, 350–351
  planning for, 351–353
  premiums as, 342–344
  price-offs as, 349–350
  refunds and rebates as, 346–347
  sampling as, 347–348
Consumer purchasing process, 55–56

Consumer value
  function of, 61
  to measure brand equity, 41–42
Consumer-generated reviews, 271–272
Consumer-oriented research, 92–93
Consumers
  as brand ambassadors, 292–293
  brand-loyal, 352
  brand-preference, 352
  channel power, 10
  empowerment of, 319
  engagement of, 11
  information search and ability of, 57–58
  price-sensitive, 352
  promotion-prone, 352
  reviews by, 271–272
  social media use by, 10
  view of brand image, 25–27
Contact point, 11
Content grazing, 9
Content marketing, 233–235
Content seeding, 266–267
Contests
  explanation of, 344–345
  goals of, 346
  Instagram, 257–259
  Internet, 346
  perceived value of, 345–346
  social media, 346
  trade, 355–356
Continuity, 195
Continuous campaign
  explanation of, 195
  schedule for, 111
Cookies, 409–410
Cooperative advertising, 357
Cooperative branding, 31
Cooperative merchandising agreement (CMA), 356
Copytests
  controversies in, 428
  emotional reactions and, 427
  explanation of, 426–427
  verbatim comments and, 427–428
Corporate image. *See also* Brand image
  company perspective of, 27–28
  components of, 24–25
  consumer perspective of, 25–27
  explanation of, 23–24
Corporate reputation, 371–372
Corporate social responsibility (CSR)
  explanation of, 372–373
  international implications of, 385
Corrective advertising, 402
Cost, 193

Cost per rating point (CPRP), 194–195
Cost per thousand (CPM), 193
Costs vs. benefits, for external search, 58–59
Council of Better Business Bureaus (CBBB)
  Children's Advertising Review Unit, 404–405
  explanation of, 403
  National Advertising Division, 403
  National Advertising Review Board, 403–404
  self-regulation, advantages to, 405
Coupons
  disadvantages of, 342
  distribution of, 340–341
  explanation of, 340
  types of, 341–342
Creative brief
  constraints, 145–146
  explanation of, 143–144
  message theme, 144–145
  objective of, 144
  support, 145
  target audience, 144
Creative pitch, 137
Creatives, 138
Creativity, assessment of
  agency, 136
Credibility, of sources, 178
Crisis management, 379–380
Cross-promotions, 384–385
Cross-ruffing coupons, 341–342
Cross-ruffing plans, 347
Crowdsourcing, 134
Cultural assimilator, 83
Cultural diversity
  advertising design and, 181
  humor and, 164
  purchasing process and, 83
Current situational analysis, 6
Customer clusters, 314
Customer data, for marketing data warehouse, 311
Customer engagement programs, 1, 11
Customer information companies, 312
Customer intelligence, 263
Customer relationship management (CRM), 322–323
Customer value, segmentation based on, 105
Customer-centric design, 226–227
Customers, engagement of, 11
Customized content, 317
Cyber squatting, 46
Cyberbait, 229

D

Damage control, 377
Data mining, 315
Data warehouse, 311
Database coding and analysis
  customer clusters and, 314
  function of, 313
  lifetime value analysis and, 313
  location-data tracking and, 314
Database marketing
  data warehouse building and, 311–313
  explanation of, 309–310
  international implications of, 331–332
Database-driven marketing communications
  customized content and, 317
  explanation of, 315–316
  identification codes and, 316
  in-bound telemarketing and, 317
  personalized communications and, 316–317
  trawling and, 317–318
Database-driven marketing programs
  customer relationship management as, 322–323
  frequency programs as, 320–322
  permission marketing as, 318–320
Data-driven customization, 321
Dead person endorsements, 176
Decay effects, 131–132
Deceptive advertising, 397–398
Deciders, in buying centers, 73
Decoding, 4
Decorative models, 166
Demographic marketing areas (DMAs), 236
Demographics
  explanation of, 94
  market segments based on, 94–99
  social media networks and, 256
Demonstration executional frameworks, 174
Derived demand, 79
Design. *See* Advertising design
Designated marketing areas (DMA), 202
Digital marketing, 223–224. *See also* Smartphones
  behavior targeting and, 238
  blogs and newsletters and, 239
  content marketing and, 233–235
  e-commerce and, 225–230
  email marketing and, 240–242

function of, 8
interactive marketing and, 232–233
international implications of, 246–247
location-based advertising and, 235–236
mobile marketing and, 230–232
native advertising and, 233–235
remarketing and, 237–238
search engine optimization and, 244–246
video tactics and, 268
Web 4.0, 224–225
Web advertising and, 242–244
Digital media, 8
Diminishing returns, 131
Direct ambush marketing, 410
Direct mail, 324–325
Direct response marketing
  catalogs and, 325
  direct mail and, 324–325
  direct sales and, 326
  explanation of, 323–324
  internet and email and, 326
  mass media and, 325–326
  telemarketing and, 326–327
Direct sales, 326
Direct sampling, 347
Direct-marketing agencies, 133
Discontinuous campaigns, 195
Distractive ambushing, 411
Diverse lifestyles, 71
Diversion, 355
Divorce, outlook change and, 71
Domain squatting, 46
Dual channel marketing
  explanation of, 81
  marketing decisions, 82–83
  spin-off sales, 81
Dwell rate, 422
Dwell time, 422
Dynamic advertising, 202–203

E

E-commerce, 225
E-commerce sites
  brand engagement and, 228
  channel integration and, 228
  consistent customer experiences on, 227
  incentives on, 229–230
  shopping cart abandonment and, 229
Effective frequency, 196–197
Effective reach, 196–197
Email, 311
  direct response marketing, 326

Email addresses, for data warehouse, 311
Email marketing, 240–242
Emotional affective approach, 160
Emotional appeals, 169–171
Emotional reaction tests, 428–429
Empowerment, 319
Encoding, 4
Engagement, creation of, 11
Enhancements, 377
Enthusiasm for shopping, 58
Entitlings, 377
Environment. *See* Consumer buying environment
Ethical issues
    advertising to children as, 407
    advertising unsafe products as, 406–407
    ambush marketing as, 410–411
    brand infringement as, 408
    conflicts of interest, 136
    gifts and bribery as, 409
    international implications of, 414
    marketing professional services as, 408–409
    offensive advertisements as, 407
    perpetuating stereotypes as, 406
    responses to, 412
    spam and cookies as, 409–410
    stealth marketing as, 411–412
Ethics
    advertising and, 405–406
    codes of, 413
    explanation of, 405
    marketing and, 407–412
Ethics consulting systems, 413–414
Ethics training programs, 412–413
Ethnicity, 97–99. *See also* Cultural diversity
Evaluation
    behavioral, 436–441
    criteria for, 431–433
    IMC objectives and, 423–424
    international implications for, 441
    message, 424–431
    online metrics, 433–436
Evaluation metrics, 422
Event marketing
    cross-promotions and, 384–385
    explanation of, 382–383
    objectives for, 383–384
Evoked set method, 65–67
Excuses, 378
Executional frameworks
    animation, 171–172
    authoritative, 173–174

demonstration, 174
    explanation of, 171
    fantasy, 174
    informative, 174–175
    slice-of-life, 172
    storytelling, 172–173
    testimonial, 173
Exit fees, 354
Experience pursuits, 72
Experience referrals, 327
Experiencers (VALS), 99
Experiential marketing, 288–289
Expert authority, function of, 173
Expertise, of sources, 179
Expertise referral, 328
Experts sources, 177
External public relations, 368–369
External search
    ability and, 57–58
    cost vs. benefits and, 58–59
    function of, 56–57
    motivation and, 58
External stakeholders, 371
Extrinsic rewards, to fear appeal, 162
Extrinsic value, 345

F

Facebook, 256–257
Family brand, 30
Fantasy executional frameworks, 174
Fear appeals, 162–163
Federal Communications Commission (FCC), 396
Federal Trade Commission (FTC)
    administrative complaints and, 400–401
    consent orders and, 400
    corrective advertising and, 400
    courts and legal challenges and, 401
    deception vs. puffery and, 397–398
    investigations and, 400
    substantiation of claims and, 398–399
    trade regulation rulings and, 402
    unfair and deceptive practices and, 397
Federal Trade Commission Act, 397
Feedback, 5
Feel, felt, found sales approach, 330
Females, video game advertising and, 293–294
Financial value, brand equity based on, 41
Flanker brand, 30–31
Flighting schedule, 111, 195
Focus group, 93

Food and Drug Administration (FDA), 396
Food labels, regulation of, 45
Forward buying, 355
Free-in the-mail premiums, 343
Freestanding inserts (FSIs), 340
Frequency, 192
Frequency programs, 320–322. *See also* Loyalty programs

G

Gatekeepers, in buying centers, 73
Gender complexity, 70
Gender, market segments by, 94–95
General social networking sites, 256. *See also* Social media
Generic message, 157
Geocoding, 312–313
Geodemographic segmentation, 101–102
Geographic location, segmentation by, 104–105
Geo-targeting, 101, 235
Gifts, ethical issues related to, 409
Global integrated marketing communications (GIMC), 47. *See also* International implications
    explanation of, 15
    international implications, 112–114
Global marketing. *See also* International implications
    humor appeals and, 164
    trends in, 10–11
Government regulation
    agencies involved in, 396–397
    consent orders and, 400
    deception vs. puffery and, 397–398
    Federal Trade Commission and, 397, 400–402
    investigations and, 400
    marketing claims substantiation and, 398–399
Green marketing
    activities for, 375–376
    explanation of, 375
    greenwashing and, 377
Greenwashing, 377
Gross impressions, 195
Gross rating points (GRPs), 193
Guerrilla marketing, 286–287

H

Head-on approach, 330
Health, consumer interest in, 72–73
Hedonism, 412
Heuristics, 74

Hierarchy of effects model
explanation of, 124–126
message strategy and, 169
Homeostasis, 412
Humor appeals, 163–164
Hyperbole, 158

I

Identification codes, 316
IMC. *See* Integrated marketing
communications (IMC)
Impression management, 379–380
Inbound telemarketing, 317,
326–327
Incidental ambushing, 411
Income, market segments by, 96–97
Indirect ambush marketing, 411
Industry segmentation, 104
Inept set, 66
Inert set, 66
Influencer marketing, 269–270
Influencers, in buying centers, 73
Information processing, cognitive
mapping and, 62–65
Information, retentionn of, 168
Information search
cognitive mapping, 62–65
consumer attitudes, 59–61
consumer values, 61
external search, 56–59
internal search, 56
Information technology, global
marketing and, 10–11
Informative executional frameworks,
174–175
Ingredient branding, 31
In-house advertising. *See also*
Advertising agencies
advantages of, 132–133
budget allocation considerations and,
133–134
crowdsourcing, 134
Innovators (VALS), 99
In-/on-package premiums, 343
Instagram, 257–259
Instant redemption coupons, 341
In-store distribution, 347
In-store marketing, 295–296
explanation of, 295
social media and, 296
tactics, 295–296
In-stream, 204
Integrated marketing
communications (IMC)
components, 12–15, 112
explanation of, 5–6

international implications, 15,
112–114
overview, 224
role of, 12
social media and, 4–5
Integrated marketing communications
planning process
budgets and, 109–112
business-to-business market
segmentation and, 103–105
communications research, 92–93
consumer market segmentation and,
93–103
elements of, 6–7
objectives and, 108–109
product positioning and, 105–108
Interactive blogs, 270–271
Interactive marketing, 232–233
Interactive websites, 133
Intercompany tie-ins, 350–351
Internal public relations, 368–369
Internal search, consumer
information, 56
Internal stakeholders, 370–371
International implications, 274. *See
also* Global integrated marketing
communications (GIMC); Global
marketing
in advertising design, 181
in advertising management,
146–147
alternative marketing, 300
in brand management, 47–48
in buyer behaviors, 83
database marketing, 331–332
digital marketing, 246–247
in digital marketing, 274
ethical issues, 414
evaluation, 441
GIMC, 112–114
in integrated marketing
communications, 15
in media strategy, 214–215
overview of, 15
public relations, 385
sales promotions, 359–360
sponsorship marketing, 385
Internet. *See also* Digital marketing
channel power and, 9
contests, 346
damage-control strategies on, 378
direct response marketing, 326
interaction between television
viewing and, 203
interactive marketing and, 233
sweepstakes, 346

Internet data, 311
Internet interventions, 378
Intracompany tie-ins, 350
Intrinsic rewards, to fear appeal, 162
Intrinsic value, 345
Intrusion value, 196
Investigative spider-webbing, 9
Involvement, 58

J

Justification, 379–380

L

Labels/labeling
functions of, 45–46
in global firms, 47–48
with QR codes, 46
Law, 412
Left-brain advertisements, 145
Lesbian, gay, bisexual, and transgender
(LGBT) individuals, buying
environment and, 71
Lifestyle
active, 71
diverse, 71
marketing, 288
Lifetime value analysis, 313
Likeability, of sources, 178
Location-based advertising, 235–236
Location-data tracking, 314
Logos. *See* Brand logos
Loyalty, brand. *See* Brand loyalty
Loyalty programs, 320

M

Magazine advertising
advantages, 209–210
by business-to-business
advertisers, 212
disadvantages, 210
Makers (VALS), 99
Managers, 138–139
Manufacturers, private brands and, 44
Market segment, 93
Market segmentation
by age, 95–96
benefit, 102
business-to-business, 103–105
by consumer groups, 93–103
by customer value, 105
by demographics, 94–99
by ethnicity, 97–99
explanation of, 93
by gender, 94–95
by generations, 100–101

by geodemographic, 101–102
by geographic area, 101
by geographic location, 104–105
by income, 96–97
by industry, 104
by product usage, 105
by psychographics, 99–100
by size, 104
by usage, 102–103
Market share, 109–110
Marketing. *See also* Alternative
  marketing; Digital marketing;
  Social media marketing
ambush, 410–411
buzz, 282–286
comfort, 159
content, 233–235
database, 331–332
developing strategies for, 6–7
dual channel, 81–83
email, 240–242
establishing objectives for, 6–7
event, 384–385
experiential, 288–289
green, 375–376
guerrilla, 286–287
in-store, 295–296
interactive, 232–233
lifestyle, 288
point-of-purchase, 296–298
pro-social, 373
real-time, 267–268
sponsorship, 380–381
stealth, 411–412
viral, 272–273
Marketing channels
  explanation of, 9
  shifts in power of, 9–10
Marketing communications
  accountability and measurable results
    and, 7–8
  brand parity and, 11
  channel power and, 9–10
  customer engagement and, 11
  digital media and, 8
  global competition and, 10–11
  media platform integration and, 8–9
Marketing communications budget. *See*
  Budgets/budgeting
Marketing communications regulations,
    396–402
  administrative complaints and,
    400–401
  consent orders and, 400
  corrective advertising and, 402
  courts and legal challenges and, 401

deception vs. puffery and, 397–398
federal regulatory agencies and,
    396–397 (*See also* Federal Trade
    Commission (FTC))
FTC settlements and, 400
substantiation of claims and,
    398–399
trade regulation rulings and, 402
unfair and deceptive practices and,
    397
Marketing database, 311
Marketing mix, 5
Marketing tactics, 6–7
Mass media, 325–326
Mass Opinion Business Intelligence
  (MOBI) software, 435
Means–end chain, 126
Means–end conceptualization of
  components for advertising
  strategy (MECCAS), 126–127
Media buyers, 191
Media buys, 133
Media mix, 211–212
Media multiplier effect, 211–212
Media planners, 190–191
Media planning, 190–192
Media purchasing services, assessment
  of, 136
Media sampling, 347
Media selection. *See also specific media*
  business-to-business markets, 141
  in business-to-business markets,
    212–214
  magazines, 208–210
  media mix, 211–212
  newspapers, 210–211
  out-of-home, 206–207
  print media, 208
  radio, 205–206
  television, 198–204
Media service companies, 133
Media strategy
  advertising analysis and, 189
  explanation of, 189
  for international markets, 214–215
  marketing analysis and, 189
Meet-the-competition budget, 109–110
Message evaluation
  advertising tracking research as,
    425–426
  cognitive neuroscience as, 430–431
  copytesting as, 426–428
  emotional reaction tests as, 428–429
  explanation of, 422, 424–425
Message evaluation techniques, 422
Message strategies

affective, 159–160
cognitive, 157–159
conative, 160–161
explanation of, 156
Message theme, 144–145
Metrics
  brand, 41
  evaluation, 422
  social media, 435–436
Millennials, 100
Mission-sharing approach, 329
Mobile data, 311
Mobile marketing, 230–232. *See also*
  Digital marketing
Mobile phones. *See also* Smartphones
  location-based advertising and,
    235–236
  videos and, 257
Mobile-optimized design, 227
Modified rebuy, 78
Motivation
  of buyer center member, 75
  external search and, 58
  loyalty programs and, 321–322
Multiattribute approach, 67–68
Music appeals, 168–169

N

National Advertising Division (NAD)
  Council of Better Business Bureaus,
    403
National Advertising Review Board
  (NARB)
  Council of Better Business Bureaus,
    403–404
Native advertising, 233–235
Natural/organic emergence, 245
Need for cognition, 58
Needs, identification of business, 79
Need-satisfaction sales approach, 329
Negative comparative advertisements,
    158
Network referrals, 328
Neuromarketing, 421
New task, 78
Newsletters, 239
Newspaper advertising
  advantages, 210–211
  disadvantages, 211
Niche social networking site, 256,
  Social media
Noise, 5
Nonprofit organizations, 374–375
North American Industry Classification
  System (NAICS), 104
Nudity, in advertisements, 165

O

Objective-and-task budget, 110
Offensive advertising, 407
Off-invoice allowances, 353
Offline advertising, 244
Offline marketing integration, 230
Online advertising
  banner, 242–243
  impact of, 243–244
  offline branding integrated with, 244
  widgets, 243
Online evaluation metrics
  explanation of, 422, 433–434
  sales funnel efficiency, 434–435
  social media metrics, 435–436
  web chatter, 435
On-package premiums, 343
Operational database, 311
Opportunities to see (OTS), 192
Organizations
  assessing reputation of, 371–372
  blogs owned by, 371
  corporate social responsibility of, 372–373
  damage control for, 377–380
  image-building activities for, 373–377
  nonprofit, 374–375
  segmentation based on size of, 104
  sponsorships by, 380–382
  view of brand image, 23–28
Outbound telemarketing, 327
Out-of-home (OOH) advertising
  advantages, 207
  disadvantages, 207
  expenditures of, 207
  explanation of, 206
  technology advances and, 206
Overlays, 350–351
Overt sexuality, 165

P

Packaging
  changes in, 45
  function of, 44–45
  in global firms, 47–48
Paid search ads, 245–246
Paid search insertion, 245
Payout-planning budget, 110
Percentage-of-sales budget, 109
Permission marketing
  enticements in, 319–320
  explanation of, 318
  strategies for, 318–319

Personal objectives, of buying center members, 77
Personal preference profiles, 312
Personal selling
  after purchase follow-up in, 331
  closing the sale in, 330–331
  explanation of, 327
  generating leads for, 327–328
  handling objections in, 330
  knowledge acquisition for, 329
  qualifying prospects for, 328–329
  sales presentation in, 329, 330
Personality, of buyer center member, 74–75
Personalized communications, 316–317
Personalized URLs (PURLs), 244
Pinterest, 260
Point-of-purchase (POP) displays
  design of, 297–298
  effectiveness of, 297–298
  explanation of, 296–297
  statistics related to, 298
Portfolio test, 426
Positioning. *See* Product positioning
Positioning advertising copytesting (PACT), 431–433
Power, of buyer center member, 75–76
Preemptive message, 157
Premiums, 357
  explanation of, 342
  strategies for success with, 343–344
  types of, 343
Pre-roll, 204
Price-offs
  benefits of, 349–350
  explanation of, 349
  problems with, 350
Price-quality relationship, positioning and, 106–107
Price-sensitive consumers, 352
Print media, 208. *See* also Magazine advertising; Newspaper advertising
Private brands
  advantages to retailers, 43–44
  explanation of, 42
  manufacturers respond, 44
Private labels. *See* Private brands
Proactive prevention strategies, 377
Problem-solution sales approach, 329
Product placements
  explanation of, 289–290
  strategies for success in, 291
  video games and, 292–294
Product positioning
  approaches, 106–107
  consistency in, 142–143

  explanation of, 105–106
  international, 107
Product usage, segmentation by, 105
Product user strategy, 107
Products
  advertising unsafe, 406–407
  attributes, 106
  as cultural symbols, 107
Product-specific research, 92
Professional samples, 347
Professional services, marketing of, 408–409
Promotion-prone consumers, 352
Promotions. *See* Consumer promotions; Sales promotions; Trade promotions
Pro-social marketing, 373
Psychographics, 99–100
Psychological motives, 92
Public relations (PR)
  explanation of, 368
  firms specializing in, 132
  internal vs. external, 368–369
  international implications of, 385
  tools for, 369
Public relations functions
  assessing corporate risk as, 371–372
  auditing corporate social responsibility as, 372–373
  creating positive image-building activities as, 373–377
  explanation of, 369
  identifying stakeholders as, 370–371
  preventing or reducing image damage as, 377–380
Pulsating schedule, 111, 195
Purchase simulation tests, 440–441
PURL (personalized URL), 244
Purpose marketing, 373

Q

QR codes, 46
Quantitative models, budgeting and, 110–111
Quantum journey, 9

R

Radio advertising
  advantages, 205–206
  for business-to-business advertising, 206
  disadvantages, 206
  explanation of, 205
  humor appeals in, 164
  reach of, 205

Ratings, 194–195
  C3, 200–202
  explanation, 199–200
  formula for, 199–200
Ratings providers, 202
Rational appeals, 169
Reach
  effective, 196–197
  social media, 265
Reactive damage-control strategies, 378–380
Real-time marketing, 267–268
Rebates, 346–347
Receivers, 4
Recency theory, 196
Reciprocity, 319
Redemption rates, 423, 439
Referral marketing, 327
Refunds, 346–347
Regulations. *See* Marketing communications regulations
Relationship selling, 327
Religions, 412
Remarketing, 237–238
Report cards, 426
Reputation referrals, 328
Research Systems Corporation (RSC) tests, 440–441
Resonance advertising, 159–160
Respondent behavior evaluations, 422
Response efficacy, 162–163
Response list, 324
Response rates, 438–439
Response samples, 347
Restaurant industry, advertising perceptions and, 9
Retailers
  advantage of private brands to, 43–44
  channel power and, 9
Retargeting, 203
Revenue premium, as brand equity measurement, 41
Reviews, consumer-generated, 266
Risk taking, in buyer center member, 76
Role, of buyer center member, 75
Rotoscoping, 171

S

Sales
  and response rates, 437–439
  social media marketing, 264–265
Sales funnel efficiency, 434–435
Sales presentation, 329
Sales promotions

consumer promotions as, 340–352 (*See also* Consumer promotions)
  explanation of, 338
  international implications for, 359–360
  trade promotions, 353–359 (*See also* Trade promotions)
Salient, 38
Sampling
  benefits, 347
  distribution, 347
  explanation of, 347
  successful programs, 348
Saturation ambushing, 411
Scanner data, 440
Scanner-delivered coupons, 341
Scarcity appeals, 171
Schedules, types of, 111
Screen time, statistics related to, 8
Search engine
  behavioral targeting and, 244–246
  social media and rankings, 263
Search engine optimization (SEO), 244–246
Search engine results page (SERP), 226
Search rankings, social media marketing and, 263
Search-optimized design, 226
Second chancers, 71
Seeding. *See* Content seeding
Segmentation. *See* Market segmentation
Selective samples, 347
Self-efficacy, 163
Self-liquidating premiums, 343
Senders, 3–4
Sensuality, 165
SEO. *See* Search engine optimization (SEO)
75–15–10 breakdown rule, 133
Severity, focus on, 162
Sex appeals
  criticisms, 167–168
  decorative models, 166
  effectiveness of, 166
  nudity, 165
  overt sexuality, 165
  overview, 164–165
  sensuality, 165
  sexual suggestiveness, 165
  societal trends, 167
  subliminal approach, 165
Sexual suggestiveness, 165
Share of customer, 322
Shootout, 137
Shopping cart abandonment, 229
Similarity, of sources, 178

Slice-of-life executional frameworks, 172
Slotting fees, 354
Smartphones
  consumer buying environment and, 71
  location-based advertising and, 235–236
  marketing and, 230–232
  statistics on, 231
Social listening, 263–264
Social media
  agencies that handle, 133
  in communications strategy, 4–5
  consumers and, 10
  contests, 346
  endorsements in, 177
  explanation of, 255
  marketing communications and, 8, 11
  sponsorship marketing, 381–382
  sweepstakes, 346
  television advertising and, 203–204
Social media marketing
  brand image and, 262–263
  brand loyalty and, 264–265
  explanation of, 255
  sales and, 264–265
  search rankings and, 263
  social listening and, 263–264
Social media marketing strategies
  consumer-generated reviews as, 271–272
  content seeding as, 266–267
  following brands as, 273–274
  influencer marketing as, 269–270
  interactive blogs as, 270–271
  real-time marketing as, 267–268
  video marketing as, 268–269
  viral marketing as, 272–273
Social media metrics, 435–436
Social media sites. *See also specific social media sites*
  bookmarking, 256
  demographic makeup, 256
  Facebook, 256–257
  general, 256
  Instagram, 257–259
  niche, 256
  Pinterest, 260
  Twitter, 259–260
  YouTube, 260–262
Social responsibility, 372–373. *See also* Corporate social responsibility (CSR)
Social spider-webbing, 9
Sociological analysis, 92

Software
data analysis, 315
geocoding, 313
new globalization, 246–247
for online evaluation, 435
Sources
celebrity, 175–177
CEO, 177
characteristics of, 177–179
experts, 177
explanation, 175
selection of, 180–181
typical persons, 177
Spam, 409
Specifications, establishment of, 79
Spiff money, 355
Spin-off sales, 81
Spokespersons
celebrity, 175–177
CEO, 177
characteristics of, 177–179
experts, 177
explanation, 175
selection of, 180–181
typical persons, 177
Sponsored content, 233
Sponsorship marketing
explanation of, 380–381
forms of, 380–381
international implications of, 385
objectives of, 382–385
tracking results of, 384
Spontaneous trait transference, 158
Stakeholders, 370–371
Standardization, 15, 47
Stealth marketing, 285–286
Stereotypes, 406
Stimulus codability, 32
Stimulus-response sales approach, 329
Stock market value, brand equity based
on, 41
Store/manufacturer premiums, 343
Storytelling executional frameworks,
172–173
Straight rebuy, 77
Strategic marketing plans, function of, 6
Strivers (VALS), 99
Subliminal approach, 165
Substantiation, 398–399
Super Bowl advertising
explanation of, 204
social media and, 266, 267
Support, for creative strategy, 145
Survivors (VALS), 99
Sweepstakes

explanation of, 344–345
goals of, 346
internet, 346
perceived value of, 345–346
social media, 346
SWOT analysis, 6

T

Taglines, 142
Target audience
examination of, 144
interactive marketing and, 232–233
Targeting
behavioral, 238
by demographic marketing
areas, 236
Target-market research, 93
Technological advances. *See also*
Internet; Social media
consumer buying environment and,
71–72
cookies and spam and, 409
video game advertising and,
292–294
Telemarketing, 326–327
Television advertising
advantages, 199
cost of, 199
disadvantages, 199
dynamic, 202–203
humor appeals in, 164
local and regional, 202
ratings, 199–202
ratings providers, 202
social media and, 203–204
Super Bowl, 204
viewership, 202
YouTube and, 204
Terrorism, 385
Test markets, 439–440
Testimonial executional
frameworks, 173
Theater test, 426
Theocratic law, 414
Theory. *See* Advertising theory
Thinkers (VALS), 99
Three-exposure hypothesis, 196
Threshold effects, 130–131
Tie-ins, 350–351
Toll-free numbers, 438
Top-choice brands, 140
Top-of-mind brands, 139
Trade allowances
complications related to, 355
exit fees, 354

off-invoice allowance, 353–354
slotting fees, 354
Trade contests, 355–356
Trade incentives
explanation of, 356
types of, 356–357
Trade promotions
agencies that handle, 133
concerns related to, 359
explanation of, 338, 353
trade allowances as, 353–355
trade contests as, 355–356
trade incentives as, 356–357
trade shows as, 357–358
Trade regulation rulings, 402
Trade shows, 357–358
Traffic managers, 138–139
Transmission devices, 4
Trawling, 317–318
Trial close, 331
Trust, in brands, 38
Trustworthiness, of sources, 179
Twitter, 259–260
2D barcodes, 232
Typical persons, as sources, 177

U

Unique selling proposition (USP), 157
Universal product codes (UPCs), 437
U.S. Postal Service (USPS), 397
Usage segmentation, 102–103
Users, in buying centers, 73

V

VALS typology, 99
Value-added incentives, 229, 230
Values, 61
Variability theory, 142
Verbal images
in business-to-business
advertising, 129
explanation of, 127
finding appropriate, 127
power of, 127
Verbatim comments, 427–428
Video game advertising
benefits of, 293
explanation of, 292–293
females and, 293–294
technological advances and, 293
Video marketing, 268–269
Videos. *See also* YouTube
advertising on, 268–269
mobile marketing and, 231
Viral marketing, 272–273

Visual esperanto, 127–128, 181
Visual images
   in business-to-business advertising, 129
   explanation of, 127
   finding appropriate, 127
   power of, 127
Vloggers, 269
Voiceovers, celebrity, 176
Vulnerability, focus on, 162

W

Wear-out effects, 131
Web 3.0, 224
Web 4.0, 224–225
Web advertising, 242–244. *See also*
   Online advertising
Web chatter, 435
Website design, interactive, 133

Website traffic marketing, 433–434
Weighted (or demographic) CPM,
   194–195
Word-of-mouth marketing. *See* Buzz
   marketing

Y

YouTube, 204, 260–262

Credits

Chapter 1

p. 3, photo: jolopes/Fotolia
p. 4, ad: JD Bank/Zehnder Communications
p. 5, photo: Donald E. Baack
p. 7 ad: Visit South Walton/Zehnder Communications
p. 8, ad: Gulf Coast Seafood
p. 9: Figure 1.6: Source: Based on Mark Walsh, "Microsoft Highlights Usage Across Device Pathways," Online Media Daily, March 14, 2013, www.mediapost.com/publications/article/195786
p. 10, ad: Gulf Coast Seafood
p. 11, photo (top): Ariwasabi/Fotolia
p. 11, photo (bottom): Jsnewtonian/Fotolia
p. 13, ad: Interstate Batteries
p. 14, ad: ReRez
p. 15, photo: Photocreo Bednarek/Fotolia
p. 19, photo: rh2010/Fotolia
p. 20, photo: Michaeljung/Fotolia

Chapter 2

p. 23, photo: william87/Fotolia
p. 24, ad: Kraft Foods, Inc.
p. 25, photo: Tyler Olson/Fotolia
p. 26, ad: JR Media Services
p. 27, photo: Monkey Business/Fotolia
p. 27, Figure 2.3: Source: Based on "Best Global Brands, 2015 Rankings," *Interbrand*, http://interbrand.com/best-brands/best-global-brands/2015/ranking/ accessed December 4, 2015.
p. 28, ad: Interstate Batteries
p. 29, ad: Choice Marketing, Joplin, MO
p. 30, ad: Kraft Foods, Inc.
p. 32, ad: Fresherized Foods
p. 33, photo: ad: Origin Bank
p. 33, Figure 2.11: Source: Based on Samuel Weigley, Alexander Hess, and Paul Ausick, "The Oldest Company Logos in America," http://247wallst.com/special-report/2013/06/18/the-oldest-company-logos-in-america, June 18, 2013.
p. 34, ad: Water Institute of the Gulf
p. 35, ad: Choice Marketing, Joplin, MO
p. 36, photo: Olesiabilkei/Fotolia
p. 36, ad: Scott Equipment
p. 37, ads: Kraft Foods, Inc.
p. 38, ad: Advertisements furnished by Skyjacker Suspensions
p. 39, ad: Gulf Coast Seafood
p. 40, Figure 2.15: Source: Based on "Consumers on the Go: Top 10 Models in 2016," *Advertising Age's Consumers on the Go Fact Pack*, September 28, 2015, page 20.
p. 40, Figure 2.16: Source: Based on "Brand Keys 2013 Customer Loyalty Index Finds Seismic Shift I How Consumers Emotionally Engage with Products, Services," Press Release, http://brandkeys.com/wpcontent/ uploads/2013/02/2013-CLEIPress-Release-FINAL-Overall.pdf
p. 41, ad: Kraft Foods, Inc.
p. 42, ad: Choice Marketing, Joplin, MO
p. 42, Figure 2.18: Source: Based on Christopher Heine, "Check Out the Top 100 Beloved Brands," http://www.adweek.com/news/advertising-branding/check-out-top-100-beloved-brands-last-decade-153026, October 10, 2013.
p. 43, photo: bst2012/Fotolia
p. 44, photo: Art Allianz/Fotolia
p. 45, photo: Monkey Business/Fotolia
p. 46, ad: Bonick Landscaping
p. 47, photo: OutdoorPhoto/Fotolia
p. 51, photo: Anna Lurye/Fotolia
p. 52, photo: Pavel Losevsky/Fotolia

Chapter 3

p. 55, photo: Jenner/Fotolia
p. 56, ad: Advertisements furnished by Skyjacker Suspensions
p. 57, ad: Kraft Foods, Inc.
p. 58, ad: Kenneth E. Clow
p. 59, photo: iofoto/Fotolia
p. 60, ad (top right): Emogen Marketing
p. 60, ad (bottom left): Choice Marketing, Joplin, MO
p. 62, ad: Scott Equipment
p. 63, Figure 3.4: Source: Based on "Jeep Leads List of 25 Most Patriotic Brands," *USA Today*, http://www.usatoday.com/story/driveon/2013/07/01/most-patriotic-brands-jeep/2481337/, July 1, 2013.
p. 64, ad: Fresherized Foods
p. 65, ad: NOLA Media Group
p. 66, ad: Visit South Walton/Zehnder Communications
p. 67, ad: zhu difeng/Fotolia
p. 68, ad: SteviB's and PepsiCo. Inc./Zehnder Communications
p. 69, photo: JackF/Fotolia
p. 70, ad: Kraft Foods, Inc.
p. 71, ad: Poggenpohl
p. 72, ad: Visit South Walton/Zehnder Communications
p. 73, ad: Newcomer, Morris, and Young
p. 76, ad (top right): Gaedeki Group
p. 76, photo (bottom left): pressmaster/Fotolia

Ad Age Content Strategy Studio, October 2013; Michael A. Stelzner, "2013 Social Media Marketing Industry Report," Social Media Examiner, www.socialmediaexaminer.com, 2013.

p. 263, ad: Gulf Coast SeaFood

p. 264, photo (top left) Eurobanks/Fotolia

p. 264, ad (bottom left) Advertisements furnished by Skyjacker Suspensions

p. 265, photo: Foxy_A/Fotolia

p. 266, ad: Sazarec Chila'Orchata/Zehnder Communications

p. 267, photo: Diego Cervo/Fotollia

p. 268, photo: goodluz/Fotolia

p. 269, ad: JD Bank/Zehnder Communications

p. 270, photo: imanol2014/Fotolia

p. 271, ad: DuPage Medical Group/Zehnder Communications

p. 272, ad (top right): Visit Baton Rouge

p. 272, ad (middle left): Scott Equipment

p. 273, Figure 9.13: Source: Based on Lenna Garibian, "Digital Influence: Blogs Beat Social Networks for Driving Purchases," MarketingProfs, http://www .marketingprofs.com/charts/2013/10336/digital -influence-blogs-beat-social-networks-for-driving -purchases, March 18, 2013.

p. 274, ad: Kraft Foods, Inc.

p. 278, photo: Creative Images/Fotolia

p. 279, photo: Photorack/Fotolia

Chapter 10

p. 281, photo: Fotolia

p. 282, ad: Scott+Cooner

p. 283, ad (top right): Photographer Steven Palowsky Photography LLC, Instagram@stevenpalowsky

p. 283, photo (bottom right): Andrews Rodriguez/ Shutterstock

p. 284, photo (top left): Vgstudio/Fotolia

p. 284, photo (bottom left): Fotolia

p. 286, photo: AntonioDiaz/Fotolia

p. 287, photo: nenetus/Fotolia

p. 287, Figure 10.6: Source: Adapted from Lin Zuo and Shari Veil, "Guerilla Marketing and the Aqua Teen Hunger Force Fiasco," Public Relations Quarterly, Vol. 51, No. 4 (Winter 2006/.2007), pp. 8-11.

p. 288, photo (top left): Monkey Business/Fotolia

p. 288, photo (bottom left): JackF/Fotolia

p. 289, Figure 10.7: Source: Based on "Product Placement Hits High Gear on American Idol, Broadcast's Top Series for Brand Mentions," Advertising Age, April 18, 2011, http://adage.com/article/media/product -placement-hits-high-gear-american-idol/227041/

p. 290, photo: M. Camerin/Fotolia

p. 291, Figure 10.8: Source: Adapted from Simon Hudson and David Hudson, "Branded Entertainment: A New Advertising Technique or Product Placement in Disguise?" Journal of Marketing Management, Vol. 22, No. 5/6 (July 2006), pp. 489-504.

p. 291, photo: Gstockstudio/Fotolia

p. 293, photo (top right): AlexandreNunes/Fotolia

p. 293, photo (bottom right): Eléonore H/Fotolia

p. 294, photo (top left): Fotolia

p. 294, ad (bottom left): Choice Marketing, Joplin, MO

p. 295, ad (top): Visit South Walton/Zehnder Communications

p. 295, ad (middle right): Visit South Walton/Zehnder Communications

p. 296, Figure 10.11: Source: Adapted from Amy Johannes, "Snap Decisions," Promo, Vol. 18, No. 11 (October 2005), p. 16.

p. 296, photo: pressmaster/Fotolia

p. 297, photo (top right): Tyler Olson/Fotolia

p. 297, ad (bottom right): Kraft Foods, Inc.

p. 299, ad: Advertisements furnished by Skyjacker Suspensions

p. 305, photo: sianc/Fotolia

p. 306, photo: Jeffrey Blackler/Alamy Stock Photo

Chapter 11

p. 309, photo: berc/Fotolia

p. 310, photo: Michaeljung/Fotolia

p. 311, ad: Scott Equipment

p. 312, photo: Antonio Diaz/Fotolia

p. 313, ad: Joplin Globe

p. 314, ad (top left): French Creative

p. 314, photo (bottom left): Monkey Business/Fotolia

p. 315, ad: V&P Photo Studio/Fotolia

p. 316, ad: Origin Bank

p. 317, photo: WavebreakMediaMicro/Fotolia

p. 318, ad: Newcomer, Morris and Young

p. 319, photo: Shock/Fotolia

p. 320, Figures 11.6 and 11.7: Source: Based on Joseph Gatt, "Most Consumers Have Reached Permission E-mail Threshold," Direct Marketing (December 2003), pp. 1-2.

p. 321, ad: Karns Quality Foods

p. 322, photo: Monkey Business/Fotolia

p. 323, ad: Emogen Marketing

p. 324, Figure 11.10: Source: Based on Richard H. Levy, "Prospects Look Good," Direct, Vol. 16 (December 1, 2004), pp. 1-5.

p. 325, ad (top right): Choice Marketing, Joplin, MO

p. 325, ad (bottom right): Advertisements furnished by Skyjacker Suspensions

p. 326, photo: Sergey Novikov/Fotolia

p. 327, photo(top right): Jenner/Fotolia

p. 327, photo (bottom right): twinsterphoto/Fotolia

p. 328, ad: LUBA Workers' Comp

p. 330, photo: shock/Fotolia

p. 331, photo: Creativa/Fotolia

p. 336, photo: JackF/Fotolia

p. 337, photo: 1000words/Fotolia

Chapter 12

p. 339, photo: Aseph/Fotolia

p. 340, photo: Igor Mojzes/Fotolia

p. 341, photo (bottom left): Fresherized Foods

p. 341, photo (bottom right): SteviB's and PepsiCo. Inc./ Zehnder Communications

p. 342, photo: Boyers Food Markets, Inc. Orwigsburg, PA

p. 343, ad: Fresherized Foods

p. 344, ad: Karns Quality Foods

p. 345, ads: Fresherized Foods

p. 346, photo (top left): Monkey Business/Fotolia

p. 346, ad (bottom left): Advertisements furnished by Skyjacker Suspensions

p. 347, photo: Berc/Fotolia

p. 348, ad: Mcgarrybowen/Maxwell House

p. 349, ad: Karns Quality Foods

p. 350, ad: SteviB's and PepsiCo. Inc./Zehnder Communications

p. 351, ad: Alliance One Advertising

p. 352, photo: michael jung/Fotolia

p. 353, ad: Joplin Globe

p. 354, photo: Art Allianz/Fotolia

p. 355, ad (top right): Karns Quality Foods

p. 355, photo (bottom right): bst2012/Fotolia

p. 357, ad: Joplin Globe

p. 358, photo: Imtmphoto/Fotolia

p. 364, photo (top right): Roman Milert/Fotolia

p. 364, photo (bottom right): Elenathewise/Fotolia

Chapter 13

p. 367, ads: Interstate Batteries

p. 368, photo: micro10x/Fotolia

p. 369, ad: JD Bank/Zehnder Communications

p. 370, ad: Origin Bank

p. 371, photo (top right): UBER IMAGES/Fotolia

p. 371, ad (middle right): Origin Bank

p. 372, ad: Kraft Foods, Inc.

p. 373, ad: French Creative

p. 374, ad (top left): Alliance One Advertising

p. 374, photo (bottom left): Steve Oehlenschlager/Fotolia

p. 375, photo (top right): Riverwalker/Fotolia

p. 375, photo (bottom Fight): Fotolia

p. 376, photo (top left): Rido/Fotolia

p. 376, photo (bottom right): Fotofreundin/Fotolia

p. 377, photo: Berc/Fotolia

p. 378, photo: Monkey Business/Fotolia

p. 380, photo: Tammykayphoto/Fotolia

p. 381, Figure 13.7: Source: "Events & Sponsorships," *Marketing News*, Vol. 38, No. 2 (July 15, 2004), p. 18.

p. 381, ad (middle right): Interstate Batteries

p. 381, photo (bottom right): antgor/Fotolia

p. 382, ad: Choice Marketing, Joplin, MO

p. 383, ad: Newcomer, Morris and Young

p. 384, photo: Tyler Olsen/Fotolia

p. 385, photo: Cristovao31/Fotolia

p. 386, ad: Advertisements furnished by Skyjacker Suspensions

p. 390, photo: shock/Fotolia

p. 391, photo: Noam/Fotolia

Chapter 14

p. 395, photo: Piotr Marcinski/Fotolia

p. 396, photo: Petro Feketa/Fotolia

p. 398, ad (top): Interstate Batteries

p. 398, ad (bottom left): Karns Quality Foods

p. 399, ad (top): Alliance One Advertising

p. 399, ad (bottom right): Advertisements furnished by Skyjacker Suspensions

p. 400, ad: French Creative

p. 401, photo (top right): sezer66/Fotolia

p. 401, photo (bottom right): Fotos 593/Fotolia

p. 402, photo: Tagstock2/Fotolia

p. 403, photo (middle right): Greg Pickens/Fotolia

p. 403, photo (botton right): Antonioguillem/Fotolia

p. 404, photo: karelnoppe/Fotolia

p. 404, Figure 14.5: Source: Adapted from Wayne Keeley, "Toys and the Truth," *Playthings*, Vol. 106, No. 2 (February 2008), p. 8.

p. 406, photos: iofoto/Fotolia

p. 407, photo (top right): Ivan Montero/Fotolia

p. 407, photo (bottom right): Anatoliy Samara/Fotolia

p. 408, photo: CandyBox Images/Fotolia

p.409, photo: Monkey Business/Fotolia

p. 410, Figure 14.9: Source: Adapted from Aaron Baar, "Olympics Sponsors Benefit, As Do Competitors," *Marketing Daily*, http://www.mediapost.com/ publications/article/122665/olympics-sponsors-benefit -as-do-competitors.html?edition, February 17, 2010.

p. 411, photo (top right): Mdestil/Fotolia

p. 411, photo (bottom right): micromonkey/Fotolia

p. 413, photo: Monkey Business/Fotolia

p. 418, photo: Art Allianz/Fotolia

p. 419, photo: Jason Stitt/Fotolia

Chapter 15

p. 421, photo: psdesign1/Fotolia

p. 422, ad: Scott Equipment

p. 423, ad (top right): DuPage Medical Group/Zehnder Communications

p. 423, ad (bottom right): SteviB's and PepsiCo. Inc./ Zehnder Communications

p. 424, ad: Interstate Batteries

p. 425, ad: Kraft Foods, Inc.

p. 426, ad: Kraft Foods, Inc.

p. 427, ad: Origin Bank

p. 428, ad: JD Bank/Zehnder Communications

p. 429, ad (top right): SteviB's and PepsiCo. Inc./Zehnder Communications

p. 429, photo (bottom right): ruigsantos/Fotolia

p. 430, ad (bottom right): Kenneth E. Clow